# 21st-CENTURY OX

GENERAL

# SEAMUS

This volume in the 21st-Century Oxford Authors series offers students and readers a comprehensive selection of the work of Algernon Charles Swinburne (1837–1909). This authoritative edition presents students with a new, more complete, more challenging, but also more credible Swinburne than ever before.

This edition presents the first rigorous scholarly edition of a substantial selection of Swinburne's work ever produced. Swinburne was one of the most brilliant and controversial poets of the nineteenth century: a republican; a scorner of established Christianity; a writer of sexual daring; a poet of loss and of love. Yet he is also the most misunderstood poet of the Victorian period. This new edition, with substantial editorial material, presents a new and convincing portrait of a man sharply different from what is usually said of him. Beginning with his unpublished 'Ode to Mazzini' (1857) and ending with his last major critical work on *The Age of Shakespeare* (1908), this edition offers Swinburne in the round—a man of astonishing consistency whose formal innovations and critical penetration remain persistently engaging as well as provocative. A major introduction explores Swinburne's complicated reaction to the scandal of his first major collection, *Poems and Ballads* (1866); his life-long commitment to radical voices (Blake, Hugo, Landor, Shelley); his permanent hostility to tyranny; his sense of literature as a living form and of the heroic personality of the artist; his dazzling art criticism and adroit analysis of Renaissance and modern literature; his exceptional elegies for dead friends; his burlesques and richly atmospheric fiction and drama. The edition draws on rich contemporary sources, manuscripts, and the diverse print culture of Swinburne's day, as well as moving through ancient and modern languages that Swinburne wrote with fluency.

Explanatory notes and commentary are included to enhance the study, understanding, and enjoyment of these works, and the edition includes an Introduction to the life of Swinburne.

**Francis O'Gorman** was educated as C.S. Deneke Organ Scholar of Lady Margaret Hall, Oxford, where he read English. He is now Saintsbury Professor of English Literature at the University of Edinburgh. He has written widely, mostly on English and Irish literature from 1780–1920, and has authored or edited 23 books. His most recent include *Forgetfulness: Making the Modern Culture of Amnesia* (Bloomsbury, 2017), volume 5 of the *Oxford Selected Prose of Edward Thomas* (OUP, 2017), and an edition of Wilkie Collins's *The Moonstone* (OUP, 2019). He is currently writing, separately, about Yeats, Emily Brontë, and the literature of London.

**Seamus Perry** is the General Editor of the 21st-Century Oxford Authors series. He is Massey Fellow in English Literature, Balliol College, and a Lecturer in the English Faculty, University of Oxford. His publications include *Coleridge and the Uses of Division*, *Coleridge's Notebooks: A Selection*, and, co-edited with Robert Douglas-Fairhurst, *Tennyson Among the Poets* (all OUP).

21st-CENTURY OXFORD AUTHORS

# Algernon Charles Swinburne

EDITED BY

FRANCIS O'GORMAN

UNIVERSITY PRESS

OXFORD
UNIVERSITY PRESS

Great Clarendon Street, Oxford, OX2 6DP,
United Kingdom

Oxford University Press is a department of the University of Oxford.
It furthers the University's objective of excellence in research, scholarship,
and education by publishing worldwide. Oxford is a registered trade mark of
Oxford University Press in the UK and in certain other countries



First published 2016
First published in paperback 2020

Impression: 1



Published in the United States of America by Oxford University Press
198 Madison Avenue, New York, NY 10016, United States of America

British Library Cataloguing in Publication Data
Data available

Library of Congress Cataloging in Publication Data
Data available

ISBN 978–0–19–967224–0 (Hbk.)
ISBN 978–0–19–885877–5 (Pbk.)

Printed and bound by
CPI Group (UK) Ltd, Croydon, CR0 4YY

# ACKNOWLEDGEMENTS

I am grateful to many scholars, archivists, curators, friends, and occasional strangers who have supported this edition. I thank, in particular, Nicholas Shrimpton not least for my first introduction to Swinburne and inspiration thereafter, but for many years of conversations about the nineteenth century. I am grateful to the General Editor, Seamus Perry for much constructive advice, and to Timothy Beck, Caroline Hawley, and Rachel Platt for steering this volume through the Press. Thanks to Jacqueline Baker at OUP for initial helpful conversations and to Ela Kotkowska.

I am grateful to the President and Fellows of St John's College Oxford for a Visiting Scholarship in the summer of 2013; to staff in the Bodleian Library and Worcester College Oxford archives; in the British Library at St Pancras particularly in Rare Books and Manuscripts; and in Special Collections of the Brotherton Library, University of Leeds. I have profited from studies in Carlyle's House, 24 Cheyne Row, Chelsea; the Galleria degli Uffizi, Florence; the Palazzo Medici Riccardi, Florence; the National Gallery London and Tate Britain; Birmingham Museum and Art Gallery; the Laing Art Gallery, Newcastle-upon-Tyne; the Musée du Louvre, Paris; the Maison de Victor Hugo, Place des Vosges, Paris; the Galeria Sztuki Polskiej XIX wieku w Sukiennicach, Kraków; the Altes Museum, Berlin; the *Εθνό Αρχαιολογικό Μουσείο*, Athens; the National Museum of Ireland, Dublin; the Ulster Museum, Belfast; the Kunsthalle, Hamburg; and both the Magyar Nemzeti Múzeum and Magyar Nemzeti Galéria, Budapest. British exhibitions including 'The Cult of Beauty' (V&A, 2 April–17 July 2011) and Tate Britain's 'Pre-Raphaelites: Victorian Avant-Garde', 12 September 2012–13 January 2013, have been valuable as has a long connection with Wightwick Manor, Wolverhampton.

For discussion of facts or ideas about Swinburne, I am grateful to the editors and external readers of *The Cambridge Quarterly* and *The Review of English Studies*; to Dinah Birch, Michael G. Brennan, Martin Butler, Matthew Campbell, Simon Dentith†, Heather Glen, Hugh Haughton, Graham Huggan, Cathy Hume, Scott Lewis, Sara Lyons, Catherine Maxwell, Chris and Michelle O'Gorman, John and Joyce O'Gorman, Clare Pettitt, Stephen Platten, Richard Salmon, Caroline Shenton, Helen Small, David R. Sorensen, E.G. Stanley, and Francis Sypher. I am particularly grateful to Laura Kilbride, Michael O'Neill, and, most of all, Jane Wright for comments on a draft of the Introduction and discussions thereafter. The work of previous Swinburne editors—particularly Timothy A.J. Burnett, Kenneth Haynes, Clyde K. Hyder†, Cecil Y. Lang†, Jerome McGann, Terry L. Meyers, and Charles

L. Sligh—is thankfully acknowledged even where I have significantly deviated from it. I thank all the institutions and their curatorial staff who have helped with or provided me with the images listed on xiii. All errors remaining are mine.

I dedicate the editorial part of this collection to Kate Williams, with my love.

The Grange, Edinburgh
14 November 2016

# CONTENTS

List of Illustrations xiii
Introduction xv
Note on the Texts xlix
Note on the Translations and Abbreviations lv

'ODE TO MAZZINI' 1

OF THE BIRTH OF SIR TRISTRAM, AND HOW HE VOYAGED INTO IRELAND (*QUEEN YSEULT*) 12

TO THE EDITOR OF *THE SPECTATOR*, 7 JUNE 1862 (pp. 632–3) 23

'CHARLES BAUDELAIRE: *LES FLEURS DU MAL*', *THE SPECTATOR,* 1784 (6 SEPTEMBER 1862), pp. 998–1000 26

'DEAD LOVE', *ONCE-A-WEEK*, IV (OCTOBER 1862), pp. 432–4 33

*ATALANTA IN CALYDON: A TRAGEDY* (1865) 39

FROM 'PREFACE' TO *A SELECTION FROM THE WORKS OF LORD BYRON* (1866) 110

FROM *POEMS AND BALLADS* (1866) 115
Laus Veneris 116
The Triumph of Time 129
Les Noyades 139
Itylus 142
Anactoria 144
Hymn to Proserpine 152
Hermaphroditus 156
The Leper 158

Before the Mirror 163

Dolores 165

The Garden of Proserpine 177

Dedication, 1865 180

FROM 'MR ARNOLD'S *NEW POEMS*' (1867) 183

FROM *WILLIAM BLAKE: A CRITICAL ESSAY* (1868), II.—'LYRICAL POEMS' 197

FROM 'NOTES ON DESIGNS OF THE OLD MASTERS AT FLORENCE' (1868) 219

FROM *NOTES ON THE ROYAL ACADEMY EXHIBITION, 1868* (1868) 225

FROM 'THE POEMS OF DANTE GABRIEL ROSSETTI' (1870) 231

FROM *SONGS BEFORE SUNRISE* (1871) 237

Super Flumina Babylonis 238

Mentana: First Anniversary 242

The Litany of Nations 245

Hertha 250

Before a Crucifix 256

Tenebræ 262

Cor Cordium 266

In San Lorenzo 267

On the Downs 268

An Appeal 273

FROM 'SIMEON SOLOMON: NOTES ON HIS "VISION OF LOVE AND OTHER STUDIES"' (1871) 276

'TRISTRAM AND ISEULT: PRELUDE OF AN UNFINISHED POEM' (1871) 281

FROM 'VICTOR HUGO'S *L'ANNÉE TERRIBLE*' (1872) 288

FROM *BOTHWELL: A TRAGEDY*, Act 5, sc. 13 293

FROM *SONGS OF TWO NATIONS* (1875) 299

*From* Diræ 300

VII. Celæno 300
VIII. A Choice 300
IX. The Augurs 300
X. A Counsel 301

FROM 'REPORT OF THE FIRST ANNIVERSARY MEETING OF THE NEWEST SHAKESPEARE SOCIETY: 1 APRIL 1876' (1876/1880) 302

FROM *NOTE OF AN ENGLISH REPUBLICAN ON THE MUSCOVITE CRUSADE* (1876) 308

'THE SAILING OF THE SWALLOW' (1877) 313

FROM *POEMS AND BALLADS, SECOND SERIES* (1878) 333

The Last Oracle (A.D. 361) 334

A Forsaken Garden 338

Relics 340

*Ave Atque Vale*: In Memory of Charles Baudelaire 342

Memorial Verses, On the Death of Théophile Gautier 347

Sonnet (with a copy of *Mademoiselle de Maupin*) 353

In Memory of Barry Cornwall (October 4, 1874) 354

Inferiae 355

Cyril Tourneur 356

A Ballad of François Villon, Prince of All Ballad-Makers 357

A Vision of Spring in Winter 358

The Epitaph in Form of a Ballad Which Villon made for Himself and his Comrades, Expecting to be Hanged along with them 361

FROM *A STUDY OF SHAKESPEARE* (1880) 362

FROM *SONGS OF THE SPRINGTIDES* (1880) 368

Thalassius 368

On the Cliffs 381

FROM *SPECIMENS OF MODERN POETS: THE HEPTALOGIA OR THE SEVEN AGAINST SENSE: A CAP WITH SEVEN BELLS* (1880) 393

The Higher Pantheism in a Nutshell 394

Nephelidia 395

Poeta Loquitur (c.1880?) 396

FROM *STUDIES IN SONG* (1880) 399

After Nine Years: To Joseph Mazzini 400

Evening on the Broads 402

By the North Sea 407

'EMILY BRONTË' (1883) 421

FROM *A CENTURY OF ROUNDELS* (1883) 427

In Harbour 428

Plus Ultra 429

The Death of Richard Wagner 430

Plus Intra 432

The Roundel 433

Wasted Love 434

Before Sunset 435

A Flower-piece by Fantin 436

To Catullus 437

'Insularum Ocelle' 438

FROM *A MIDSUMMER HOLIDAY AND OTHER POEMS* (1884) 439
IX. On the Verge 440
Lines on the Monument of Giuseppe Mazzini 442
Les Casquets 444
In Sepulcretis 450
On the Death of Richard Doyle 452
A Solitude 453
Clear the Way! 454

FROM *POEMS AND BALLADS, THIRD SERIES* (1889) 455
March: An Ode, 1887 456
To a Seamew 459
Neap-Tide 463
The Interpreters 465
In Time of Mourning 467
To Sir Richard F. Burton (On his Translation of the Arabian Nights) 468
A Reiver's Neck-Verse 469
The Tyneside Widow 470

'RECOLLECTIONS OF PROFESSOR JOWETT' (1893) 473

FROM *ASTROPHEL AND OTHER POEMS* (1894) 485
A Nympholept 486
Loch Torridon: To E.H. 493
Elegy, 1869–1891 498
Threnody, October 6, 1892 502
A Reminiscence 504
Hawthorn Dyke 505

'THE BALLADS OF THE ENGLISH BORDER' 506

FROM *A CHANNEL PASSAGE AND OTHER POEMS* (1904) 509
The Lake of Gaube 510
In a Rosary 513
Trafalgar Day 515
Cromwell's Statue 516
Russia: An Ode, 1890 517
On the Death of Mrs Lynn Linton 520
Carnot 522
The Transvaal 523
DEDICATION OF SWINBURNE'S *POEMS* (1904) 524
FROM *THE AGE OF SHAKESPEARE* (1908) 537
Christopher Marlowe (1883/1908) 538

Notes 545
Index of First Lines of Poems 671
Index of All Titles 673

# LIST OF ILLUSTRATIONS


1. Title page of *Atalanta in Calydon* (London: Moxon, 1865), a copy from the Brotherton Library, Special Collections, University of Leeds, reproduced with permission. 38
2. Algernon Charles Swinburne, London Stereoscopic & Photographic Company, *carte de visite*, *c.*1865 © National Portrait Gallery, London, reproduced with permission. 109
3. Title page of *Poems and Ballads* (London: Hotten, 1866), a copy reproduced by kind permission of the Master and Fellows of Balliol College Oxford. 114
4. First page of MS of 'The Triumph of Time', reproduced by kind permission of the Master and Fellows of Balliol College Oxford. 128
5. Title page of *William Blake: A Critical Essay* (London: Hotten, 1868), a copy from the Brotherton Library, Special Collections, University of Leeds, reproduced with permission. 196
6. Dante Gabriel Rossetti, *Venus Verticordia*. Photograph reproduced with the kind permission of the Russell-Cotes Art Gallery & Museum, Bournemouth. 228
7. Title page of *Poems and Ballads, Second Series* (London: Chatto & Windus, 1878), a copy from the Brotherton Library, Special Collections, University of Leeds, reproduced with permission. 332
8. Stanza 6 of the MS of 'By the North Sea', reproduced by kind permission of the Master and Fellows of Balliol College Oxford. 406
9. Title page of *Astrophel and Other Poems* (London: Chatto & Windus, 1894), a copy from the Brotherton Library, Special Collections, University of Leeds, reproduced with permission. 484

# INTRODUCTION

'"I am that I am"; it is the only solid and durable reply to any impertinence of praise or blame'

Swinburne on Coleridge, 1869[1]

Thomas Hardy, the journalist Frank Harris remembered, 'astonished me one evening by continuing some verses of Swinburne's *Atalanta in Calydon* [1865] that I had quoted and by confessing that he loved and admired Swinburne's genius almost beyond limit'.[2] It was an apt compliment. Swinburne had long been associated with going beyond limits. The scandal of *Poems and Ballads* (1866), certainly, was difficult to forget (it will be described presently). Hardy remembered the commotion in *The Life of Thomas Hardy* (1928–30), his autobiography (though he didn't like that term), which was posthumously published under his second wife Florence's name. He mulled over, there, what he called the 'onslaught' on his novel, *Jude the Obscure* (1895), as darkly as he could. That book's reception, Hardy observed in *The Life*, was 'unequalled in violence since the publication of Swinburne's *Poems and Ballads* thirty years before'. Swinburne's volume was seemingly a benchmark in the history of censorship; of the work of the 'vituperative section of the press'.[3] Swinburne's reputation has returned over and again to these matters—rightly or wrongly, but certainly frequently. Thomas Hardy, the author of the peculiar elegy for Swinburne, 'A Singer Asleep' (1910), was not alone in thinking that Swinburne's popular reputation was dominated by a quarrel over *Poems and Ballads*. That was a volume that supposedly woke what T. Earle Welby called in 1926 the 'rather agreeably tedious Victorian tea-party'.[4] If that tells us more about Welby and his post-Victorian moment than about 1866, it is true that the intoxicating power of Swinburne's early verse, its rhythmic music and extraordinary verbal dexterity, was conjoined with a remarkable capacity to offend.

Swinburne's work—of which there is a substantial amount—has often been regarded as uneven in quality. There is, said the poet and dramatist John

For an explanation of the abbreviations used in the notes to this Introduction, see lv–lviii.

[1] *'Christabel' and the Lyrical and Imaginative Poems of S. T. Coleridge*, introduced and arranged by Algernon Charles Swinburne (London: Samson Low, Son, and Marston, 1869), vi. 'I am that I am' are God's words said to Moses in Exodus 3:14.

[2] Frank Harris, '*Ephemeridae*, We Men!' in *Thomas Hardy Remembered*, ed. Martin Ray (Aldershot: Ashgate, 2007), 77.

[3] Florence Hardy, *The Life of Thomas Hardy* (London: Studio, 1994), ii.39. On Hardy's exaggerations about the fate of *Jude*, see Francis O'Gorman, 'Thomas Hardy and the Bishop of Wakefield', *N&Q*, 61 (2014), 86–9.

[4] T. Earle Welby, *A Study of Swinburne* (London: Faber and Gwyer, 1926), 14. The best survey of Swinburne criticism is Rikky Rooksby's 'A Century of Swinburne' in *WMP*, 1–21.

Drinkwater in 1913, 'no great poet whose bad work bears superficially so marked a resemblance to his good'.[5] The later poetry, seeming superficially so like the early, suffered in particular for many years after Swinburne's death. 'To the ordinary reader', remarked Harold Nicolson, Vita Sackville-West's husband, in 1926 in a psychologically experimental biography, 'the vast bulk and uniformity of Swinburne's later verse is apt, unless care is taken, to destroy all zest for what is really important in his work, since the whole business, in appearance at least, is so very much the same'.[6] Swinburne, as I go on to explain, has been blamed for (allegedly) changing his political views from his early days—and for (allegedly) not changing his poetics. Sometimes opinions of the supposedly leaden decline of Swinburne's career in poetry have reached absurdity. Robert Nye's opening two sentences from his Faber edition, *A Choice of Swinburne's Verse* (1973), are noteworthy. 'Swinburne's reputation as an empty vessel', Nye said, making 'a lot of meaningless if musical noise relates to only about nine-tenths of his poetic production. The other tenth is worth salvaging.'[7] That was hardly an enticing way to begin an anthology. As it happens, Nye's edition consisted of a group of twenty-eight pieces, almost all of which were from *Poems and Ballads* of 1866: 'in my opinion that book represents Swinburne at the height of his powers.'[8] Swinburne was, apparently, a comet not a poet. He burned once in a lifetime.

As for the politics—a major portion of Swinburne's writing and a profound part of how he saw himself—the usual story is falling-off too. William Michael Rossetti, who knew Swinburne through much of his life, believed the poet began as a radical and ended a jingoistic imperialist. '"'Tis true 'tis pity, and pity 'tis 'tis true": so, at least, I think',[9] Rossetti regretted. That was a regular claim: Swinburne was another lost leader. '[Swinburne] was never stupid exactly', said George Bernard Shaw with a mixture of loftiness and mischief,

> but he often produced an impression of disloyalty by the transition from the splendour and vigour of his echoes of revolutionary writers to the conventionality of his own views, which were made in Putney. It is quite staggering to pass from his inspired exposition of Blake's meaning to his suburban disapprobation of it.[10]

Of course Swinburne, like other major poets, could write bad verse. He held views the contemporary world no longer finds appropriate, though he is hardly unique in that. In some respects, he was capable of contradiction and

[5] John Drinkwater, *Swinburne: An Estimate* (London: Dent, 1913), 11.

[6] Harold Nicolson, *Swinburne* (London: Macmillan, 1926), 166.

[7] *A Choice of Swinburne's Verse*, selected by Robert Nye (London: Faber, 1973), 13.

[8] Ibid., 9.

[9] WMR, 'The Genius and Influence of Swinburne', *The Bookman*, 36 (June 1909), 126–31 (127).

[10] Ibid., 129.

occasionally of change. But he was also bracingly, defiantly consistent. As we know from the mini-family saga of Virginia Woolf's *The Years* (1937), though, what was radical in one generation can sound out-of-date in another. The familiar opinions of Swinburne are misleading. He remains the most misunderstood poet of the Victorian period.

* * *

From where did Algernon Charles Swinburne, poet, come?

On first thought, the influences that helped make him are disorientatingly mongrel. It is as if a wildly talented boy had somehow been let loose in aristocratic and ancient school libraries to read with a prodigious memory and no sense of boundaries except his own aesthetic judgment. On second thought, this is true, but the very concept of 'influence' is not helpful. Many readers have been persuaded, temporarily or otherwise, by Harold Bloom's Protestant argument that poets are anxious about their predecessors; that progress comes through rejecting the past; that a new generation of (male) writers fears literary castration by previous generations.[11] Swinburne suggests little of that iconoclasm. What Swinburne wrote of Coleridge in 1869 is in part true of himself: the Romantic was '[receptive] at once and communicative of many influences, [but] he has received from none and to none did he communicate any of those which mark him as a man memorable to all students of men'.[12] Like Athena, Swinburne springs into (poetic) life more or less fully formed.

There is not much that is nervous in any Bloomian sense in Swinburne's public writing as there was little of unconfidence in his public persona (insofar as he went into public at all). True to his aristocratic upbringing, Swinburne—grandson of George, third Earl of Ashburnham (1760–1830)—breathed the air of a man who owned the literary past. As a schoolboy at Eton, Swinburne wrote plays in the manner of Elizabethan and Jacobean dramatists and in December 1857 he published an informed review on 'The Early English Dramatists' in the journal of the Old Mortality Society.[13] He discovered Sappho in his Greek reader at school and never forgot her. He came to find in Aeschylus—mainly the *Oresteia*—one of the two greatest voices in European letters (the other was Shakespeare). In *Atalanta in Calydon* and *Erechtheus* (1876), he considered he was offering his nineteenth-century readership 'fresh' ancient Greek tragedies: 'New words, in classic guise',[14] said Hardy,

[11] See Harold Bloom, *The Anxiety of Influence: A Theory of Poetry* (New York: Oxford University Press, 1973).

[12] *'Christabel' and the Lyrical and Imaginative Poems of S.T. Coleridge*, v.

[13] See *NWS*, 31–9.

[14] 'A Singer Asleep (Algernon Charles Swinburne, 1837–1909)', previously titled 'A South Coast Nocturne', dated from Bonchurch, Isle of Wight, 1910: *The Complete Poems of Thomas Hardy* (London: Macmillan, 1976), 323.

appositely. The intense, luxurious, and almost static lyricism of these texts, particularly *Atalanta*, means that they are not really like Athenian drama. But they were bewitchingly original in the middle of the nineteenth century. All historical writing that Swinburne admired was breathing in the sense that it was not merely confined to its historical moment. And he liked, in turn, to think of his own words as conjuring life, which is no doubt one reason why he chose so frequently to read (sometimes flamboyantly) his poetry and drama aloud to friends.[15] His literary mind inhabited a persistent historical present where he did not struggle with 'influence' but looked around, like E.M. Forster in *Aspects of the Novel* (1927), at a reading room full of writers, alive, well, and simultaneous.

It is possible, forgetting Bloomian methods, to speak of Swinburne's literary allies and of literary practices to which he laid imaginative claim. He thought, for instance, that the folk-voice of his family county of Northumberland was partly his own. To write Northumbrian ballads—'A Reiver's Neck-Verse' (469), 'The Tyneside Widow' (470)—was to be loyal to a cultural area that Swinburne believed different from both England and the Borders of Scotland, which had too long, he considered, been regarded as the centre of British balladry. Composing such poems, Swinburne felt a connection with François Villon (*c.*1431–63?) too, the vagabond balladeer: he became an imaginary literary comrade from fifteenth-century France. Similarly, Swinburne discerned in modern French literature a writer engaged on a political crusade like his own: Victor Hugo, scourge of Napoleon III. Hugo was an ally and a hero, not a castrator. Among the English Romantics, Swinburne placed himself in the same line as Percy Bysshe Shelley: radical, controversialist, a champion of an instinctive kind of 'liberty', a scorner of established religion. Swinburne admired his own version of William Blake, too. Yet, again, this revealed no Bloomian anxiety but sureness of cultural location. The supporter of Giuseppe Mazzini, Swinburne regarded Walter Savage Landor a cantankerous ally not a father who loomed intimidatingly. Swinburne was poetically closest to Alfred Tennyson in his own day in the music of his verse. Swinburne is a 'reed', the Laureate is supposed to have said, according to his son, 'through which all things blow into music'.[16] Here was a bond. Tennyson, the man whom W.H. Auden thought 'had the finest ear, perhaps, of any English poet',[17] celebrated the fineness of Swinburne's. But this congruence did not mean Swinburne was anxious. He challenged the Laureate, certainly: in *Tristram of Lyonesse* (1882), he resisted Tennyson's representations of adultery in *Idylls of the King* (1859–85). Swinburne considered Tennyson had 'degraded

[15] For a lively account of Swinburne reading his own and others' poetry, see W.H. Mallock, *Memoirs of Life and Literature*, 2nd edn (London: Chapman and Hall, 1920), 54–5.

[16] As reported in Hallam Tennyson, *Alfred Lord Tennyson: A Memoir*, 2 vols (London: Macmillan, 1897), ii.285. Quoted in *SL*, i.xix.

[17] W.H. Auden, *Forewords and Afterwords* (London: Faber, 1973), 222.

and debased' the story of Tristram: 'as usual',[18] he added waspishly. And he spectacularly deplored Tennyson's acceptance of a peerage in September 1883.[19] Yet he was not cowed. His knew his mind and his own poetic place.

Swinburne made his most significant entry into the public world of print with *Atalanta in Calydon*, the 'Greek' tragic poem that plays out a dismal sense of curse—of a life doomed to be destroyed by a decision of the gods. Thematically, it is not surprising that Hardy admired it. *Atalanta*'s language, the rhythms of the famous choruses, the 'beautiful cadences of his Calydonian fatalism',[20] as *The Fortnightly Review* said, brought a new voice to English poetry. The poem, in what Lord Houghton called its 'majestic wail',[21] revealed a mind free from the pensive troubles of Tennyson's ruminative mourning or Matthew Arnold's speculative fretfulness. Here was an idiom quite different from the earnest polemic of Elizabeth Barrett Browning or the psychological probing of Robert Browning. Here, too, was a distinctive harmonizing of Greek dramatic form—parados, episode, stasimon, exodus, kommos—with, mostly, the rhythms of English qualitative metres. The undergraduate Swinburne imitated William Morris (see 'Of the Birth of Sir Tristram', 12–22). Yet *Atalanta* was no Pre-Raphaelite poem—assuming for a moment that there is such a thing. The poetic drama, musing on the cruel dispensation of gods, is characteristically fatalistic: Swinburne's mind returned later to other stories heavy with calamity even as, in different ways, he was optimistic. He was absorbed by tragedy and persuaded by forms of hope. Alongside his faith in an orderly world, in the sense that natural laws made, in the τέλος [*telos*] of the world, Swinburne existed in a decidedly modern shadow, thinking of how human lives could be blighted by cruel circumstances, of how suffering and death attended what men and women did and made. He was lured, like Hardy, by human histories where the punishment did not fit the crime.

But it was the gods, and in particular the Judaeo-Christian God, against which (and whom) Swinburne wrote most boldly in *Poems and Ballads* in 1866. He was the opposite, here, of Pindar who, in the Olympian 'Ode to Hieron of Syracuse', thought it wise to avoid the public censure that came after criticizing deities.[22] *Poems and Ballads*, following quickly on from *Atalanta*, included verse written several years before.[23] It is one of the many occasions when thinking only of the volume publication date misleads readers about the shape of Swinburne's creativity.[24] The title of *Poems and Ballads*

[18] *SL*, iv.260 (letter of 13 April 1882).

[19] See Francis O'Gorman, 'Swinburne and Tennyson's Peerage', *English Studies*, 96 (2015): 277–92.

[20] J. Leicester Warren, 'Atalanta in Calydon', *FR*, 1 (15 May 1865), 75–80 (75).

[21] Lord Houghton, *Monographs: Personal and Social* (London: Murray, 1873), 80.

[22] Pindar, 'Olympian Ode 1', l. 35.

[23] See xlix.

[24] See 'Note on the Texts', xlix–liv.

echoes the subtitle of George Meredith's controversial *Modern Love and Poems of the English Roadside, with Poems and Ballads*, a collection Swinburne defended in a letter to *The Spectator* in June 1862 (23–5). *Poems and Ballads* was not to be a book from which Swinburne, in a number of senses, easily moved on—and he was divided about how far he wanted to. With its anti-Christian verses and daring poems about sex, *Poems and Ballads* grew from Swinburne's irritable private sense—and he would often frame his work in terms of masculine bravery, of standing his corner, of not deserting his post—that he should be free from restraint in publishing on subjects that interested him so long as aesthetic form was the first priority.[25] Here was a personal interpretation of an Oxford liberal commitment in the 1850s and '60s, amid which Swinburne had grown up, to J.S. Mill's *On Liberty* (1859).

*On Liberty* seems to have been one of the few political books Swinburne had in his library.[26] Mill memorably argued for 'free and daring speculation on the highest subjects'.[27] Without such freedom, mental life perished; the development of human communities, Mill thought, was stopped. Swinburne took Mill's encouragement to freedom in intellectual thought as freedom to talk about religion, certainly. That was within the brave, inquiring spirit of *On Liberty*. But the poet also interpreted 'free thought' to mean permission to speak about private desires and fantasies: sado-masochism, torture, eroticized executions of innocent men and women, loveless sex, perpetual damnation. And Swinburne did not only think or talk about these but printed what he imagined. He modified and controversially extended the spirit of *On Liberty*, and in a further sense he plainly challenged it. The poet approved of the freedom of opinion. But he was not very interested, as the history of the first *Poems and Ballads* made clear, in freedom of discussion. When confronted with objections to his poems, Swinburne was often inclined to resist rather than explain. A liberal in intellectual terms, he had a fractious relationship with the liberal ideal of open conversation through which truths could supposedly be advanced or revived. He did not like being challenged and was usually more irritated than discursive. Later, where politics and Shakespeare scholarship were concerned, he could be bracingly, rudely intolerant.[28] Agreeing to change his mind could sometimes appear to him a form of cowardice.

*Poems and Ballads*, published in the summer of 1866, was admired and it sold exceptionally well (though Hotten, when he took over the contract, seems to have kept back money that should have been given to the author).[29] But *Poems and Ballads*—or rather some specific poems in it—was also

[25] See Francis O'Gorman, 'Swinburne and Cowardice: Running Away and Poems and Ballads (1866)', *The Journal of Pre-Raphaelite Studies*, 26 (2017): 61–80.

[26] See *The Catalogue of the Library of Algernon Charles Swinburne sold 19–21 June 1916 at Sotherby's, London* (unpaginated). This is not a complete catalogue of his library.

[27] *The Collected Works of John Stuart Mill*, ed. J.M. Robson, 33 vols (Toronto: University of Toronto Press, 1963–91), xviii.242.

[28] See 302–7.

[29] See l.

deplored. The collection revealed many things about this new flame-haired, physically tremulous writer who seemed to glide more than walk. The volume made clear Swinburne's eclectic learning—Old French, the chthonic deities of ancient Classical religions, the Marquis de Sade, the Risorgimento, Baudelaire, the Christian liturgy. For those in the know, there might well have been some private revelation too, since the volume muses on his break with, probably, his cousin Mary Gordon.[30] Swinburne, it seems, had once believed that Mary and he had a future together. The story of their separation, consequent on Mary's acceptance of another man, may well have been refracted in, among other poems, 'The Triumph of Time' (129–38).

In aesthetic terms, *Poems and Ballads* confirmed Swinburne, after the craftsmanship of *Atalanta*, as a poet of formal and verbal dexterity: roundel, ballad, sonnet, hymn, litany, a dexterous re-invention of the dramatic monologue;[31] hexameter, tetrameter, trimeter, rhyming decasyllables; interlocking rhyme schemes sometimes of considerable complexity; patterning of sounds in internal rhymes and resonances; a dazzling and persistently inventive control of, usually, iambic, anapaestic, and trochaic feet (Swinburne was suspicious of spondees and dactyls). He had, apparently, a poor ear for actual music and he seems to have had little interest in attending concerts. He wrote no private letters revealing any significant knowledge of the art (except a fondness for the Prelude to Wagner's *Tristan und Isolde*: see 547). But he was, in *Poems and Ballads* of 1866 as always, absorbed by the 'musical' possibilities of words. Formal invention and control, the orchestration of language, remained for him the first thing needful in any writing that could be defined as art.[32]

But the discord of *Poems and Ballads* was real. The volume's audacity made Swinburne's name short-hand among detractors for dangerous, disturbed writing. The collection was 'full of a mad and miserable indecency', said *The Pall Mall Gazette* in August: 'Otway raving fine verses in Bedlam is not a more pitiable spectacle.'[33] In the same month, John Morley in *The Saturday Review* remarked witheringly that Swinburne was 'either the vindictive and scornful apostle of a crushing iron-shod despair, or else he is the libidinous laureate of a pack of satyrs'.[34] It is easy to forget the first part of this sentence: one of the complaints was about Swinburne's gloom, his morbidity. But it is even easier to

[30] See 566–7.

[31] For a significant account of Swinburne's handling of this form, see Nicholas Shrimpton, 'Swinburne and the Dramatic Monologue', *WMP*, 52–72.

[32] On Swinburne and music generally, see Francis O'Gorman, 'On Not Hearing: Victorian Poetry and Music' in *The Oxford Handbook to Victorian Poetry*, ed. Matthew Bevis (Oxford: Oxford University Press, 2013), 745–61.

[33] 'Swinburne's Folly', *PMG*, 20 August 1866, 9. Indicatively, it is worth remembering the more celebratory review in *The Examiner*, 22 September 1866, 567. Swinburne was told by WMR on 8 October 1866 that there were only, in fact, six critical attacks: see *UL*, i.75–7.

[34] 'Mr Swinburne's New Poems', *SRev*, 22 (4 August 1866), 145–7 (147).

forget that Morley, future statesman and Liberal Lord President of the Council, repented. He said to Swinburne on 25 August 1872 that he had 'regretted both my tone and the jist [*sic*] of [that] criticism ever since'.[35] Morley published Swinburne's later work and occasionally, after *Poems and Ballads*, encouraged him to accept editorial pruning of inflammatory lines.[36] But, in the summer of 1866, Swinburne hardly had the reputation he wanted even if he said he was proud of causing such a fuss. That fuss made the young poet dig his heals in. Objections prompted Moxon, Swinburne's publisher, to withdraw *Poems and Ballads* from sale (the publisher had clearly not seen anything worrying when looking through the manuscript on submission). There were apparently rumours of a law case on the grounds of blasphemy—a link with Shelley that Moxon was clearly not keen to pursue.[37] Swinburne was determined. He renegotiated, arranging for a re-issue of the volume from John Camden Hotten (1832–73), a publisher whom Simon Eliot rightly calls 'a natural risk taker'.[38] Hotten may have run a side-line in pornography and flagellation literature (did Swinburne know this?). But he had a long and interesting list of titles in serious literature, history, and antiquarianism. When *Poems and Ballads* was re-issued, not a significant word was changed.[39]

Friends—inconsistently—had urged Swinburne to omit passages to save his reputation among publishers, libraries, and readers. He was only just starting out, after all. 'I hope [Swinburne] may be induced not to brave and defy that storm [of criticism],' said Lord Lytton on 20 August after Moxon's retreat, 'but to purgate his volume of certain pruriences into which it amazes me any poet could fall.'[40] Swinburne would not 'purgate' his poetry for friends as he would not for critics. Persuaded eventually by Hotten into saying something

[35] *UL*, i.235.

[36] See, for instance, *UL*, ii.221–2 (23 May 1880) and *UL*, ii.236 (21 November 1880), where Morley asks for 'some gentler phrase than "stercorous feculence"' (and on this occasion did not succeed). See Swinburne's 'Short Notes on English Poetry', *FR*, 28 (December 1880), 708–21 (719) (this page also includes 'autocoprophagous animalcules').

[37] Moxon had been charged under common law with blasphemic libel over his publication of Shelley's *Queen Mab* (1839) and was tried on 23 June 1841 (the company lost and printed *Queen Mab* thereafter with the offensive passages omitted). It should be noted that Edward Moxon, the founder of Moxon publishers, had died in 1858. Business with Swinburne was conducted by Moxon's manager, James Bertrand Payne. On the final bankruptcy of the company and Payne's conviction for fraud, see Jim Cheshire, '*The Fall of the House of Moxon: James Bertrand Payne and the Illustrated Idylls of the King*', *VP*, 50 (2012), 67–90.

[38] *ODNB*.

[39] There are a small number of errors—see the Note on the Texts, xlix–l. Swinburne wrote to correct misprints in the Greek and Old French on 14 November 1866: *UL*, i.85. Chatto & Windus's printers defended themselves in 1875 pointing out that Swinburne's handwriting was hard to read; he did not use conventional proof marks; he did not notice errors in proof and only pointed them out in print; and did not return proofs in proper time (see *UL*, ii.49–50n).

[40] *SL*, i.174n.

about why he had published *Poems and Ballads* in the first place, he wrote a provocative defence in *Notes on Poems and Reviews* (1866) in which he argued—if 'argued' is quite the word—against what he described as the hypocrisy of his reviewers. Swinburne thought hostile readers were scurrilous and foul, though he offered no evidence and named no names: 'Where free speech and fair play are interdicted,' he asserted fiercely, 'foul hints and evil suggestions are hatched into fetid life.'[41] This, perhaps, was his private, peculiar, and contradictory version of Mill: Swinburne, in his own way, was defending uninhibited speech while deploring the freedom of others to criticize what he had said.

The poet did not consistently meet head-on his critics' objections that his own writing involved 'foul hints' and 'fetid life'. He blamed the pressmen for being low forms of existence ('animalcules and infusoria'[42]) then denied that his poems were on risky topics anyway. He claimed, for instance, that 'Anactoria' (144–51)—the lesbian sado-masochism poem that prompted particular discomfort—presented the 'violence of affection between one and another which hardens into rage and deepens into despair'.[43] That 'Anactoria' was a poem envisaging a woman's pleasure in torturing her girlfriend to death was not mentioned. Edith Sitwell—not adverse to controversy—as late as 1960 could only bring herself to publish extracts from this poem, parts of which she still thought 'extremely unwholesome'.[44] Swinburne's tactic in *Notes on Poems and Reviews* was, in part, to defend free speech. Yet also he denied that he had said anything contentious. 'But *now* to alter my course or mutilate my published work', he told Lytton after Moxon withdrew, 'seems to me somewhat like deserting one's colours. One may or may not repent having enlisted, but to lay down one's arms except under compulsion, remains intolerable.'[45] It might be that, somewhere in the back of his mind, Swinburne did repent of having enlisted. But he was always a devoted admirer of heroes, especially military ones, and a loather of spinelessness.[46] As a child Swinburne had, he claimed, literally risked his life to prove he was not afraid.[47] He did the same for his professional career in the summer of 1866. The delicate, fragile,

[41] *NPR*, 21. [42] Ibid., 6. [43] Ibid., 8.

[44] 'Introduction' to *Swinburne: A Selection*, compiled with an Introduction by Edith Sitwell (London: Weidenfeld and Nicolson, 1960), 31.

[45] *SL*, i.173 (letter of 13 August 1866). Hotten had hoped that Swinburne would omit 'a very few lines' from *Poems and Ballads* and thus significantly improve sales (see *UL*, i.71–2, letter of 29 August 1866). If Swinburne would not change the poems, it is noteworthy that he was willing to change *Notes on Poems and Reviews* to avoid additional controversy: see *SR*, 3–4. Swinburne was also prepared to remove anything disrespectful in *William Blake* (1868)—see *UL*, i.29—and he accepted an intervention from John Morley to reduce a potential 'scandal' in 'Note on the Text of Shelley', *FR*, 5 (May 1869), 539–61: see *UL*, i.154–5.

[46] For a revision of the view that Swinburne's father was an angry domestic tyrant, see F.A.C. Wilson, 'Fabrication and Fact in Swinburne's "The Sisters"', *VP*, 9 (1971), 237–48.

[47] He claimed that he had climbed Culver Cliff on the Isle of Wight as a teenager in response to his father's refusal to allow him to join the army. See his account, *SL*, vi.251–3.

haughty poet took the complaints over *Poems and Ballads*, wisely or otherwise, as a challenge to his masculinity.[48]

*Poems and Ballads* did not come from nowhere though it is easy to misunderstand its context, not least in the sometimes disingenuous, performatively ironic, and mercurial turns of *Notes on Poems and Reviews*. Some of Swinburne's intrepid accounts of sexuality had been tried out in his early fiction, including 'Dead Love' (33–8), the only story to be published in his lifetime from the projected collection, *The Triameron*. As a prose critic, Swinburne had been exploring attitudes that were not irrelevant for the 1866 collection either. He had defended Charles Baudelaire's prosecuted *Les Fleurs du mal* (1857) in a letter to *The Spectator* on 6 September 1862 (26–32), arguing against morality as the *first* aim of poetry. He had defended Meredith's *Modern Love* (23–5) with its bleak Darwinian drama of adultery, emotional destruction, and suicide. The 'business of verse-writing', Swinburne said about that volume, 'is hardly to express convictions'.[49] That is no doubt the kind of statement that backed-up William Empson's recognition that 'People are oddly determined to regard Swinburne as an exponent of Pure Sound with no intellectual content.'[50] Yet such an assertion about Meredith should not mislead readers into believing that Swinburne, in the 1860s or at any point, simply did not care what a poem said. As with other intellectual matters, he could shift his emphasis in different circumstances but leave the overall consistency of this argument intact. A single line in a specific context cannot sum up his whole understanding.

Shortly after Swinburne celebrated Baudelaire and doubted whether poetry expressed convictions, he observed, when writing in the mid-1860s about Blake, that the starting-point of his own criticism was the view 'that the artist has something to say or do worth doing or saying in an artistic form'.[51] It was rather Carlylean. Form was not everything. Walter Pater would later, surprisingly, be plainer: 'the distinction between great art and good art', Pater observed in 1888, '[depends] immediately, as regards literature at all events, not on its form, but on the matter.'[52] Reviewing Victor Hugo's *L'Année terrible* (1872, 288–92), Swinburne developed his point from the study of Blake, stressing, more mildly, that the priority of form was not to the exclusion of something worth saying. The poet's political meanings, Swinburne declared, for instance, of Hugo's writing on the Franco-Prussian War, were obviously to

[48] Terry L. Meyers in 'Swinburne's Speech to the Royal Literary Fund, May 2, 1866', *Modern Philology*, 86 (1988), 195–201, finds *Notes on Poems and Reviews* in the same idiom of burlesque as the Literary Fund speech. But it is helpful to think about it as something less single-minded—part burlesque, part defiance, part *post hoc* defensiveness, part performative, part an expression of outrage at being challenged in the first place.

[49] See 23.

[50] William Empson, *Seven Types of Ambiguity* (London: Chatto & Windus, 1949), 165.

[51] See 198.

[52] Walter Pater, 'Style', *FR*, 44 (December 1888), 728–43 (743).

be taken into account. 'There never was', he confirmed that same year in *Under the Microscope* (1872), 'and will never be a poet who had verbal harmony and nothing else; if there was in him no inner depth or strength or truth, then that which men took for music in his mere speech was no such thing as music.'[53] But, even so, Swinburne could always return to an apparently exclusive embrace of form when faced with a peculiarly problematic poet. When he thought a writer unable to understand what poetry actually was, Swinburne's language even as late as 1887 could appear to offer a narrower view. 'There is no more important, no more radical and fundamental truth of criticism than this', Swinburne announced in his essay on 'Whitmania' (1887): 'that, in poetry perhaps above all other arts, the method or treatment, the manner of touch, the tone of expression, is the first and last thing to be considered.'[54] First *and last*? Swinburne could readily overlook what a poem said on any occasion when he thought the way of saying it meant there was no poetry.

Swinburne had other important things to observe about poetry in the 1860s. In the work of Matthew Arnold, whom he had heard lecture at Oxford, Swinburne found lyrical gifts but also off-putting mournfulness (see 183–95). 'This alone I find profitless and painful in Arnold's work', Swinburne observed, 'this occasional habit of harking back and loitering in mind among the sepulchres.'[55] The poetry of minor doubts, of the 'small troubles of spirits that nibble and quibble about beliefs long living or dead',[56] was not for Swinburne either. He was a poet of the emphatic, of the committed. In the first two volumes of *Poems and Ballads* (1866 and 1878), he ruminated on the fault-lines of national faiths. But fretting about loss of faith was merely dispiriting. 'Nothing which leaves us depressed is a true work of art', Swinburne said generally, sounding like Arnold in the redactory 1853 'Preface', then adding: 'We must have light though it be lightning, and air though it be storm' (195).

It was certainly not to words of doubt that Swinburne turned at the beginning of the 1870s. Poems on radical political themes had been included in *Poems and Ballads* ('A Song in Time of Order, 1852', 'A Song in Time of Revolution, 1860'); *A Song of Italy* had been published by Hotten in 1867 with a dedication to Giuseppe Mazzini. And the 'Ode to Mazzini' (1–11) belonged to Swinburne's undergraduate career.[57] But now, as the 1860s

[53] *SR*, 65.

[54] Algernon Charles Swinburne, 'Whitmania', *FR*, 42 (August 1887), 170–6 (175).

[55] See 195. [56] See ibid.

[57] It was sometimes thought, for instance by Edward Thomas in *Algernon Charles Swinburne: A Critical Study* (London: Secker, 1912), that poems published in *Fraser's Magazine* 1848–51 with the initials 'A.C.S.' were very early works. *LS* gave authority to this view (12). But this is a different 'A.C.S.' as the date, the quality, the association of one poem with the Carlton Club, the subject matter including politics, and the lack of acknowledgement all confirm. Some of the *Fraser's* poems—but by no means all—were gathered into *Metrical Miscellanies by A.C.S.* (London: p.p., 1854), which has been associated with Sir Anthony Coningham Sterling (1805–71, see *ODNB*). There is a copy in the BL.

became the 1870s, and partly in response to the public image created by 1866, Swinburne absorbed himself more fully in a bloody public world (though he tended not to notice the blood). He wrote to support violent campaigns for a (superficially) less intellectually troublesome conception of liberty than the freedom to write about dissenting sexuality and theology. Poetry, he underlined, was a modern nation's political conscience; the gift of its unacknowledged but unsilenceable legislators.

What concerned Swinburne most prominently was Italy. He believed deeply in Mazzini, the intellectual leader of the republican side of the Risorgimento, part of the campaign to free Italy from occupying forces in the first half of the nineteenth century. (Acts of belief are significant in Swinburne's politics: he was, as a thinker, a man of faith.) Swinburne and Mazzini shared defining political concepts. Most importantly, Swinburne accepted, from Mazzini, that the Romantic category of 'nationhood' was critical for the future shape of Europe. A 'true' nation, one worthy of being a nation-state, was a pre-given entity in Mazzini's political thought, a geo-political category justified by long histories, shared customs, cultures, and language. 'To reconstruct the map of Europe', Mazzini remarked, 'in accordance with the special mission assigned to each people by their geographical, ethnographical, and historical conditions, was the first step necessary for all.'[58] Such language Swinburne found indispensable for what he believed ought to be liberated—and what not. He rarely articulated, or made explicit, the intellectual assumptions of his political writing. But that does not mean he was without them. Extrapolation, hypothesizing, and a willingness to make some leaps of thought are needed from his readers to re-construct what really, in terms of political ideas, were at the heart of his polemic. Swinburne's political poetry of liberty was permanently grounded in this Mazzinian conception of what was rightfully a nation (and thus could legitimately be a nation-state), much to the confusion of readers then and now. Italy was a nation in Mazzinian terms because it had a long history, its own language, traditions, and customs, and a distinctive cultural identity. Italy had, in turn, every right to become an independent political whole; every right to throw off its Hapsburg, Bourbon, and Papal occupiers in order to liberate the special mission of its coherent, unifiable people. Italy, 'Strong with old strength of great things fallen and fled',[59] was *worthy* of being free.

With Mazzini, and against the royalist side of the Risorgimento represented by Count Cavour, Swinburne accepted that only in a republic were human beings able to express their innate identities.[60] His youthful friendship

[58] 'Notes on the Organisation of Young Italy' (1861) in *Life and Writings of Joseph Mazzini*, new edition, 6 vols (London: Smith, Elder, 1890), i.175–6.

[59] Algernon Charles Swinburne, *A Song of Italy* (London: Hotten, 1867), 66.

[60] He faced an important challenge to this idea when faced with the 'tyranny' of the Boer republics at the end of the century: see 663.

with John Nichol was important in developing this faith in the enabling nature of a republic, a 'bloodless and a bondless world', too.[61] It is important to stress that the poet's conception of human liberty here, like that of a true nation and an authentic work of art, was based in an idea of natural law, of innate organization and inherited purpose. When, in 1904, Swinburne remarked of poetry that 'Law, not lawlessness, is the natural condition of poetic life' (529), he could have been talking about anything that, in his conception, should be legitimately permitted to express its own nature. Liberty, for a human being as much as for a poem or for Italy, was not licence. All rightful things, Swinburne assumed, have inborn laws that direct their being. To these his writing returns as he writes fantasias to the free in the most controlled of literary forms, bringing together exultation with regulation in a controlled expression of what he hoped as much from politics as from verse. The purpose of governments was to enable the uninhibited articulation of natural identities, to liberate the pulses of individual beings as well as individual nations so they could be themselves. In Swinburne's optimistic mind what would follow would not be chaos, not the conflict of individuals or nation-states seeking incompatible things, but harmony. Swinburne was compelled by natural elements and wild creatures, especially the birds that soar and sing through his verse, living out the inherited laws of their natures. Such creatures, free under law, peculiarly emblematize what he thought poetry should be and what the foundation of political liberty was.

Swinburne hated impediments to rightful self-development. In particular, he was sickened by what he saw, sometimes without looking into the matter too carefully, as the work of tyranny. In Italy, for instance, foreign oppressors had inhibited the natural laws of a true Mazzinian nation. Elsewhere, tyrants cut off ordinary men and women's life-blood. They imprisoned those with whom they disagreed, those who did not conform. Swinburne, like Landor, could be ruthless in his treatment of those he thought ruthless. Indeed, he willingly accepted that violence, what would seem to some 'terrorism', was a legitimate tool in any attempt to obtain freedom for those worthy of it. In London, the poet lived on the remote edge of the revolutionaries themselves, the men whom opponents might describe as the agents of terror. Mazzini, as a member of Young Italy, had once been thought such by the British press.[62] Later, the London-based German revolutionary Karl Blind, who had introduced Swinburne to Mazzini and remained an ally, acknowledged violence as

[61] Swinburne, *A Song of Italy*, 65. On Nichol, see 545.

[62] Cf. the account of Mazzini and Great Britain in Michael J. Hughes, 'British Opinion and Russian Terrorism in the 1880s', *European History Quarterly*, 41 (2011), 255–77. See also Marjorie Stone, 'Joseph Mazzini, English Writers, and the Post Office Espionage Scandal: British and Italian Politics, Privacy, and Twenty-First-Century Parallels', <http://www.branchcollective.org/?ps_articles=marjorie-stone-on-the-post-office-espionage-scandal-1844> (last accessed 6 August 2013).

a regrettable necessity. Assassinating tyrants sometimes simply had to be done.[63] In Swinburne's 'Russia: An Ode, 1890' (517–19), the poet, in another daring salute to Landor, publicly risked supporting what, to the legitimate rulers, was undoubtedly terrorism. He publicly risked, as I have described elsewhere, being criminally liable under the Offences Against the Person Act 1861.[64] Swinburne—whom Lord Houghton had once called 'a Nihilist'[65]—defiantly expressed himself in favour of the assassination of Tsar Alexander III. He was the son of Tsar Alexander II who actually had been blown apart on a St Petersburg street on 13 March 1881. The 'Ode', regarded by one Irish MP as evidence of the hypocrisy of the Westminster government where incentives to violence were concerned, was argued over in the House of Commons and in the press.[66] Swinburne's friend and biographer Edmund Gosse thought the 'Ode' and its relish for nitro-glycerin might have cost Swinburne the Laureateship after Tennyson's death.[67] But Swinburne was an antagonist of rulers and regimes he believed despotic. And if he thought a bomb had to be hurled, he declared that it had to be hurled.

Swinburne was ready to play down the significance of human pain where a good cause was served.[68] His 'Ode to Mazzini' (1–11), written in the spring of 1857 while he was at Balliol College, Oxford, contains much that the poet would not alter. It is the foundational text of his work as a political poet. Swinburne overlooked Mazzini's theology, forgivingly, and was still musing on his disagreement with Mazzini's faith as late as 1904.[69] (He overlooked Victor Hugo's theology, too: Swinburne's heroes were not wholly heroic.) But Swinburne would not significantly deviate from Mazzini in other ways. With his devotion to human freedom and self-realization, Swinburne conceived political imprisonment as the most telling emblem of unjust rule, the most poignant embodiment of the constraining of natural laws by the iron bonds of cruelty. The incarcerated Risorgimento lawyer, Carlo Poerio, whose treatment was memorably recorded by Gladstone,[70] is a central figure in the 'Ode'. And he would never be forgotten. Peculiar lover of pain in some respects,

[63] See, for instance, Blind's 'Conspiracies in Russia', *The Contemporary Review*, 35 (June 1879), 422–57.

[64] See O'Gorman, 'Swinburne and Cowardice'.

[65] See letter of 29 January 1881, *UL*, ii.244.

[66] The MP Patrick O'Brien (*c.*1847–1917), the Member then for Monaghan North. He endeavoured to draw attention, using Swinburne's poem, to the difference between the Westminster government's obsessive vetting of Irish nationalist newspapers for anything that looked like an incitement to violence and the apparent indifference of the same government to Swinburne's explicit encouragement to blow up a head of state.

[67] See Coulson Kernahan, *Swinburne as I Knew Him, With Some Unpublished Letters from the Poet to His Cousin the Hon. Lady Henniker Heaton* (London: Bodley Head, 1919), 55–6.

[68] It is true that he equivocated over this in places: for instance, in *Erechtheus*, where the reader is invited to feel the anguish of Chthonia as she gives her life for her country.

[69] See 'Dedication', 180–2.

[70] See headnote on 545.

Swinburne found intolerable the thought of principled men chained up in gaol. Their condition was for him the most horribly personal example of what was wrong with kings.

Swinburne, as I have said, is often thought to have mellowed or betrayed himself into conservatism. Theodore Watts-Dunton,[71] who rescued the poet from alcoholism in the late 1870s, has been blamed for this.[72] The 'evidence' of conservatism (usually axiomatically ruled as a form of mental impairment) is most often alleged in relation to Swinburne's rejection of Irish nationalism (see, for instance, in this collection, the note on 'An Appeal', 599–600 and 'Cromwell's Statue', 516); his celebration in his later years of British national events including the Queen's jubilees, the fourth centenary of the Spanish Armada, and, in this collection, the anniversary of the Battle of Trafalgar (515); and his violent hostility to the Boers and support of British imperial forces fighting against them in the Second Anglo-Boer War (1899–1902) (523). But what is more important about Swinburne here, despite appearances, is not change but consistency.[73]

In keeping with his Mazzinian conception of nationhood, the poet deplored, as did Mazzini, the idea of Irish separatism.[74] Like Mazzini, Swinburne could not accept that Ireland was a 'nation' and so, in turn, Ireland could not be a nation-state. He thought the Irish had no shared, long, and independent history; no native culture and traditions; no real linguistic identity. And so Ireland had no right, in his view, to political autonomy. The Union was not necessarily good for England in Swinburne's conception but it was, for him, necessary for Ireland. Where the Second Anglo-Boer War was concerned, Swinburne was certain that he was acting on other life-long values. It is easy to misread his support of Great Britain's armies as merely an imperialist gesture. But that was not Swinburne's intention (though he was pleased to find Great Britain acting well, as he saw it, unlike in 'An Appeal'). In 1882, Swinburne had admired Landor's 'constancy to the same principles [. . .] the same love, the same loyalty, the same wrath, scorn, and hatred, for the same several objects respectively'.[75] He was partly talking of himself. Swinburne followed *The Daily Telegraph* and *The Daily Graphic*. He followed *The Times*, too, and shared the paper's view in deploring Boer treatment of native black South Africans and *uitlanders* (foreign settlers and labourers). With many others, he accepted this unjust treatment as an honourable reason

[71] Walter Theodore Watts (1832–1914) added his mother's surname to his own in 1896. But for convenience he is referred to as Theodore Watts-Dunton (TWD) throughout this edition.

[72] See, for instance, Max Beerbohm, 'No. 2 The Pines' in *And Even Now* (London: Heinemann, 1920), 60–1.

[73] Cf. the statements in the 'Dedication' of *Poems* (1904) on 525–6.

[74] See Francis O'Gorman, 'Swinburne and Ireland', *RES*, 64 (2013), 654–74. On the misperceptions of 'An Appeal', see the note in the present edition on 599–600. Note Karl Blind's affirmation to Swinburne on 6 May 1887 that Mazzini did not support Irish nationalism (*UL*, ii.428–9).

[75] Algernon Charles Swinburne, 'Landor', *Miscellanies* (London: Chatto & Windus, 1886), 201. The essay was first published in *Encylopaedia Britainnica*, vol. xiv (1882).

for declaring war, a struggle against those he called on 12 November 1901 'the cruellest and most faithless tyrants and slavedrivers of our time—the Boers of Transvaal'.[76] Within Great Britain, such views were on the liberal side (as distinct from the Parliamentary Liberal side) even if modern literary scholars dislike them.[77] Swinburne found allies in purely House of Commons terms among the non-Home Rule Liberals (the Liberal Unionists) and also among the usually hated Tories. The Conservative MP for the City of London thought in 1884, for instance, that the Boers 'consider a black man as a beast of burden to be treated with the consideration due to an ox, as long as he is able to work, but to be ruthlessly slaughtered if he asserts the rights of a man'.[78] From the 1880s, Swinburne found himself aligned with unexpected parliamentary groups because liberal views were not confined to the Liberals or, he came to think, espoused by many Liberals at all. He continued to deplore the parliamentary Liberals, after what he thought the Home Rule betrayal, as insufficiently principled, insufficiently committed to liberty. Not least, he was dismayed by the Liberal leader during the Anglo-Boer War, Sir Henry Campbell-Bannerman, who strongly disapproved of the conflict and came to think of British involvement, in a memorable word, as 'barbarous'.[79] That disapproval, implicitly, caused the final break of Swinburne's misplaced (and, in the challenging world of real politics, misconceived) hopes for the future of Gladstone's version of Liberalism as a principled antagonist of tyranny.

The turn to Risorgimento politics and the coruscating opinions of *Note of an English Republican* were sincere. But they also helped deflect, or distract from, the lingering after-effects of *Poems and Ballads*. More personally, they helped draw attention from Swinburne's dissolute life-style. There was order in his verse in the 1870s. But not in his life. As a champion of the free expression of a man's inner nature, Swinburne was literally shortening his days by an uninhibited pursuit of the freedom to drink himself to death. According to one story told by Edmund Gosse, Mazzini was called in to help.[80] The Italian nationalist wrote to Swinburne on 10 March 1867 telling him: 'Don't lull us to sleep with pages of egotistical love and idolatry of physical beauty: shake us, reproach, encourage, insult, brand the cowards, hail the martyrs, tell us all that we have a great Duty to fulfill.'[81] Swinburne's friends, assuming they really had encouraged this intervention, had sensibly realized that if the poet

[76] *SL*, vi.154.

[77] See, for instance, Julia F. Saville, 'Swinburne's Swimmers: From Insular Peace to the Anglo-Boer War', in *Algernon Charles Swinburne: Unofficial Laureate*, ed. Catherine Maxwell and Stefano Evangelista (Manchester: Manchester University Press, 2013), 33–51.

[78] R.N. Fowler, 'The Boers', *The National Review*, 2 (February 1884), 851–8 (853).

[79] See Hansard Commons Debates, 17 June 1901, vol. 95 c.620.

[80] See Edmund Gosse, *The Life of Swinburne* (London, privately printed at the Chiswick Press, 1912), 26–7.

[81] *UL*, i.97.

were to take advice from anyone, it would be from Mazzini. *Poems and Ballads* of 1866 and drink had become the two defining features of Swinburne's early career. And where alcohol was concerned, the poet had to give it up (however little he *actually* drank[82]) or, so it seemed to his friends, die.

Looking back on this turbulent period in 'Thalassius' (368–80), one of the most important of Swinburne's autobiographical poems, the poet dramatized himself in the autumn of 1879 as a kind of political prophet who had returned to who he was. It is an important piece of self-fashioning, of self-refashioning. Swinburne, now, projected his own recent past as the history of a champion of liberty who had been temporarily seduced. 'Thalassius' tries to change doubtful readers' minds about what Swinburne's true calling was. The poem marks, though it does not make explicit, the successful intervention at the end of the 1870s of Watts-Dunton in rescuing Swinburne from what Thomas Woolner had politely described as early as July 1867 as his 'sadly wild and unwholesome life'.[83] 'Thalassius' is a 'saved-by-Putney' poem. And it is also a deft piece of, so to speak, market repositioning: a proposal that the public, principled, divinely-gifted poet of human liberty was, beneath everything, the person Swinburne had been all along.

The poet, however, never gave up risky topics. Swinburne's verse was always disinclined merely to be safe, however much he was subsequently caricatured as reforming himself to accommodate those mysterious things, 'the accepted moral standards of the Victorian middle class'.[84] Swinburne had long been interested in the doomed erotic history of Tristan and Isolde (or, as he and his circle preferred, Tristram and Iseult). Their story, the poet said, was 'always in my eyes the loveliest of mediaeval legends'.[85] 'Of the birth of Sir Tristram, and how he voyaged into Ireland', first canto, published in December 1857 (12–22), was the only portion of a long poem probably to be called *Queen Yseult* that reached print. It was born of Morrisian Oxford. In 1871, Swinburne was still thinking about the same subject, as he would for a further decade. 'Tristram and Iseult: Prelude of an Unfinished Poem' (281–7), published in 1871, began with Swinburne's effort to describe what he thought the distinctive power of his verse to persuade a reader of the vitality of passion (and it is worth devoting some thought to Gerard Manley Hopkins's observation to Robert Bridges on 22 April 1879 that Swinburne was a poet of

[82] It might be the case, it seems to me, that Swinburne's frail constitution was disproportionately affected by relatively little alcohol. For evidence that Swinburne 'could not stand much "booze"' and was badly drunk on 'a little champagne & sherry', see *UL*, i, 316n.

[83] Quoted in *SL*, i.250n.

[84] The words of Humphrey Hare in *Swinburne: A Biographical Approach* (London: Witherby, 1949), 187, talking of Swinburne's life after 1879. For the earlier controversy with Robert Buchanan, the Rossettis, and the role of Swinburne's 'Under the Microscope' (1872), see the 'Fleshly School Controversy' documents assembled on <http://www.robertbuchanan.co.uk/> (last accessed 5 January 2016).

[85] *SL*, iv.260.

passion not of feeling[86]). Swinburne borrowed Robert Browning's figure from *The Ring and the Book* (1868–9) for the miraculous work of the poet as a life-breather.[87] Poetry was resurrection. It re-animated history and re-energized myth. Tristram and Iseult are swept by desire into a tormented drama that ends in their deaths. About illegitimate love, the Arthurian legend was supposedly protected from moral disapprobation because the cause of the lovers' transgression was enchantment not will—they accidentally not deliberately drink a magic potion. But the poet's defensive strategy, if that is what it was, did not entirely work. Here was a 'topic so out of nature that it can hardly be redeemed by art', said the now unfriendly *Saturday Review*. There is 'no story', it added, 'of the Arthurian cycle in which so much is made of the animal passion of love'.[88] 1866 was heard again.

Swinburne's poetry did not elsewhere enter so fully into the lives of others as in *Tristram* (the first canto, 'The Sailing of the Swallow', was separately published in addition to the 'Prelude' and is included here, 313–31). The major scenes of this text, as it imagines the ardour of two lovers and the reeling calamity of their infatuation, are substantial monologues with moods of bitterness, suffering, solitude, rapture, and grief. This is a text, taken as a whole, of sailing and swimming, of light and vivid colours, and, as the opening declares, of the love that is the first and last of all things made. Nowhere else did Swinburne better catch imaginatively the motion of the sea as in the tidal movements of these words. The rhyming pairs are the controlling shapes, bringing rhythmic and acoustic structure at the level of the individual lines. But through them is heard not constraint but the *Unendliche Melodie* of the poet's fatalism. Nowhere else did Swinburne's language work so effectively within a narrative and nowhere did the individual moment stand out so meaningfully against the orchestrated sounds of the whole. Take, as just one instance in 'The Sailing of the Swallow', the emotional clarity of the few seconds before the cup is drunk. There, for a moment, Swinburne envisages a man and woman's delight that is uniquely precious because they do not realize it is about to end:

> The last hour of their hurtless hearts at rest,
> The last that peace should touch them breast to breast,
> The last that sorrow far from them should sit,
> This last was with them, and they knew not it.[89]

For all his polysyllabic sumptuousness, Swinburne could make shattering use of monosyllables and the plainness of an iambic line. He could, too, exquisitely retard a line ('they knew not it') as he approached his climax.

[86] Claude Colleer Abbott, ed., *The Letters of Gerard Manley Hopkins to Robert Bridges* (London: Oxford University Press, 1935), 79. Hopkins continues that Swinburne's 'genius is astonishing, but it will, I think, only do one thing'.

[87] See note on 603.

[88] 'Tristram of Lyonesse', *SRev*, 54 (29 July 1882), 156–7 (157).

[89] See 330.

Swinburne declined significantly to moderate his views about the place of the Christian religion in oppressing human beings, in preventing men and women from being themselves. He was as blunt in the 1870s as he had been in the 1860s. In *Songs Before Sunrise*, he included a fresh version of a pagan creation myth in 'Hertha' (250–5), imagining the half-human and half-divine spirit of Man that lay behind or above humanity. It was a counter-Christian myth, a celebration of man-as-god, which defied orthodox Christian teachers. And in 'Before a Crucifix' (256–61), Swinburne envisaged the complicity of the Christian (implicitly Catholic) church in human suffering, recognizing Jesus the man's pain on the cross but deploring Christ the supposed Messiah's manipulation by the clergy. With its weary sense of impoverished workers carrying a burden created by priests, the poem shocked one reviewer as much as the 'lascivious' poems of 1866: 'Kept out from one muddy pool, [Swinburne] has gone into another almost as muddy', *The Saturday Review* regretted (it was not for the most part a journal on good terms with the poet after 1866).[90] The admiring novelist Marie Corelli, in her best-selling Faustian romance *The Sorrows of Satan* (1895), was still remembering the shock of 'Before a Crucifix' a quarter of a century later. In Sibyl's confession in that novel—she is the apparently ice-cold society lady with whom the hero falls in love—we read that 'I drank in Swinburne's own fiendish contempt of God, and I read over and over again his verses "Before a Crucifix" till I knew them by heart.'[91] Here was a draught of rebellious independence. Swinburne's poem, Sibyl continues, taught her to call Christ 'carrion crucified' (see l.192 of the poem) and 'helped me to live mentally, if not physically, through such a phase of vice as had poisoned my thoughts for ever'.[92] Swinburne was both a new Prometheus and a new Mephistopheles.

Yet Swinburne could not easily relinquish an intellectual and emotional bond with the language of religion. His poetry required spirit-like forces. And it needed forms of hope in the endurance of human beings beyond death. Swinburne could not imaginatively manage without figures of divinity. Thinking over the natural laws of the organic world, the sea, sun, stars, and air, he turned to (often Classical) nature gods to emblematize, to give physical visibility to, those governing principles. The Norse-derived Hertha is a figure of Man re-imagined as a spirit. But it is the Greek Aphrodite and Apollo who recur in Swinburne's poetry partly because they capture the living vitality of elements as supreme figures of natural law. They give to free natures human shapes that elevate nature to divinity. That is a peculiarly Swinburnean movement of thought. Aphrodite is born of the ocean ('flushed from the full-flushed

[90] 'Swinburne's "Songs Before Sunrise"', *SRev*, 31 (14 January 1871), 54–5 (54).

[91] Marie Corelli, *The Sorrows of Satan or The Strange Experience of One Godfrey Tempest, Millionaire* (New York: American News, 1900), 394.

[92] Ibid., 395. Corelli wrote a flattering letter to ACS in the third person on 31 May 1883: *UL*, ii.338–9.

wave, and imperial, her foot on the sea'[93]) and Apollo is the god of the sun (as well, of course, of poetry). The indispensability of theological ideas in Swinburne's mind, recast but recognizable, was evident elsewhere. That indispensability was clearest in his other masterpiece: *Poems and Ballads, Second Series* (1878). Here, in that title, was apparently a characteristically roguish decision to revive the memory of his earlier volume and all its commotion. He was still stubbornly declaring, it seemed, that he was standing by his choices of 1866.

In fact, this was *grand*standing. The title was misleading.[94] The 1878 volume had little directly in common with what was now re-branded as the 'first series' of *Poems and Ballads*. 'The Last Oracle' (334–7), the opening text of the new collection, took the reader back to 1866 for a moment, to the end of paganism and the old gods. But much else was retrospective in different ways. Swinburne's principal subject in 1878 was death. *Poems and Ballads, Second Series* is a volume of elegies. And it is an imagined, literary friendship group, a circle of those whom Swinburne admired, who were gathered posthumously together to be praised by this new laureate not of the libidinous but of the lost. Yet not the entirely lost. Addressing these dead men, Swinburne invented a fresh nineteenth-century language for mourning that was not Christian but which at the same time recast Christian hopes into the synaesthetic vocabularies of fame, of perpetuation among the stars, of music that would not fade.

*Poems and Ballads, Second Series* searched out versions of perpetuation that were rooted in the optimism of antiquity, recast in ambivalent language that avoided mere clarity in favour of promise and possibility. Where had Baudelaire's personality—unconventional, defiant, profane—gone after his death? Swinburne's '*Ave Atque Vale*' (342–6) ruminates on that question, posing possibilities without reductive certainty. The result is a pledge that exists in the assurance that inquiry can itself be a form of consolation:

Hast thou found any likeness for thy vision?
  O gardener of strange flowers, what bud, what bloom,
  Hast thou found sown, what gathered in the gloom?
What of despair, of rapture, of derision,
  What of life is there, what of ill or good?
  Are the fruits grey like dust or bright like blood?
Does the dim ground grow any seed of ours,
  The faint fields quicken any terrene root,
  In low lands where the sun and moon are mute

[93] See 154.

[94] Swinburne later told Chatto & Windus on 1 December 1899: 'There is no consecutive or necessary connection between the three series or volumes, which bear the same serial name because I could not think of a better'; *UL*, iii.170. On the title, cf. Hugo's *Odes et ballades* (1822).

And all the stars keep silence? Are there flowers
  At all, or any fruit?[95]

Swinburne was sorrowful, respectful, serious. He incorporated Baudelaire's poems from *Les Fleurs du mal* into his tribute as if Swinburne's poetry were perpetuation itself. He did the same with Catullus, the only Latin poet whose work he said he extensively admired. Writing on the death of his friend 'Barry Cornwall' (Bryan Procter), Swinburne teased his reader with a vision of re-uniting, of the dead welcoming the dead beyond the earth, as if he were more certain that personality continued than Tennyson in *In Memoriam* (1850). Yet the sound of 'In Memory of Barry Cornwall' (354), the draw of what feels like a pattern of anapaests, was hard to hear through to the sense beneath or within.[96] The real promise, the persuasive power, was partly *in* that rhythm; the order that reached the ear before verbal meaning reached the mind:

Time takes them home that we loved, fair names and famous,
  To the soft long sleep, to the broad sweet bosom of death;
But the flower of their souls he shall take not away to shame us,
  Nor the lips lack song for ever that now lack breath.
For with us shall the music and perfume that die not dwell,
Though the dead to our dead bid welcome, and we farewell.[97]

'A poem is that species of composition', said Samuel Taylor Coleridge in *Biographia Literaria* (1817), 'which is opposed to works of science, by proposing for its *immediate* object pleasure, not truth; and from all other species—(having *this* object in common with it)—it is discriminated by proposing to itself such delight from the *whole*, as is compatible with a distinct gratification from each component *part*.'[98] Swinburne's rhythms and the internal chiming of sounds of *Poems and Ballads, Second Series*, offered acoustic appeal, framing in musical language the proposition that what might last of poets was, metaphorically, their music. One should not search 'each component' too forensically, looking out the mere 'ideas' of Swinburne's poetry here. A reader may pause to reflect on the work of that final comma in 'In Memory of Barry Cornwall'; he or she might recognize the secret promise of greeting in those re-iterated words ('the dead to our dead bid welcome') where verbal recurrence half-tempts the ear with an acoustic fulfilment of a miraculous hope of

[95] See 343–4.

[96] I do not mean these *are* anapaestic lines but the ear hears how a few real anapaests are joined with apparent anapaests produced from other feet ('takes them home... that we loved... To the soft... to the broad... But the flower of their souls'). This impression is not uncommon in Swinburne's verse.

[97] See 354.

[98] S.T. Coleridge, *Biographia Literaria, Or, Biographical Sketches of My Literary Life and Opinions* ([1817] London: Dent, 1906), 164.

re-union. These are effects—Coleridgean pleasures—the significance of which cannot adequately be summarized. Swinburne's lyric gift made verbal music that creates 'meaning' in and through sound and shape; sound and shape which, at their most alluring, entice beyond what can simply be told.

Sometimes he tricks us. Swinburne was a convincing imitator and he could manage, so to speak, a persuasive imitation of sincerity. He put this gift to impish uses. About his life there still hang improbable and uncertain tales—not least the ones Guy de Maupassant told concerning Swinburne's residence in Étretât with George Powell and a monkey (was he called Nip?) in the autumn of 1868.[99] Yet Swinburne could test the limits of veracity himself. Once in 1862, he tried to persuade R.H. Hutton, the editor of *The Spectator*, to take two reviews of contemporary French poetry. These were 'Les Amours étiques. Par Félicien Cossu' and 'Les Abîmes. Par Ernest Clouët'. He nearly succeeded. But they were hoaxes.[100] Swinburne would hardly have burnished his reputation had these half-obscene, made-up pieces reached print. It is odd—incredible—that he thought they would have helped. Yet the most surprising imitations that Swinburne created were of—himself. It is tempting to think that Swinburne quietly parodied his own voice in serious 'non-parodic' poems: the opening of 'On the Cliffs' (381), for instance,[101] or 'Evening on the Broads' (402). We cannot always be sure where the 'real' Swinburne begins and ends. His manner, too, tempted others to parody him—the 'Ballad of Blunders' by 'Chatouillard'; Andrew Lang's 'Ode of Jubilee by A.C.S.'; Amy Levy's 'Felo de Se: With Apologies to Mr Swinburne'.[102] But in the *Heptalogia* (1880), Swinburne smiled at himself, caricaturing his rhythmic trademarks, aural patterning, ambitious line lengths: 'From the depth of the dreamy decline of the dawn through a notable nimbus of nebulous noonshine . . . '. There was egotism in this self-parody (see 395). But there was self-knowledge and playfulness too.

Swinburne was successfully removed from physical danger, from the perils of alcoholism, in 1879 when Watts-Dunton took him to live in Putney. Serious matters attended the decade that followed. Tyranny, parliamentary reform, and the post–Home Rule crisis of the Liberal Party occupied his political thoughts. 'Clear the Way!' (1884, 454), for instance, was hopeful about dramatic reform of the House of Lords—a misplaced hope, it proved. Mazzini

[99] See *SPP*, 144–9. 'Nip' may be the monkey in question, according to Terry Meyers's comments on Powell's letter to Swinburne, 12 December 1868: *UL*, i.139–40n. But we are lacking hard evidence as to what really happened in Étretât. See *UL*, ii.312–14 for a useful assessment. On Maupassant and Swinburne, see also *Poèmes et ballades de A.C. Swinburne* [traduit par] Gabriel Mourey; notes sur Swinburne par Guy de Maupassant (Paris: Savine, 1891).

[100] The texts are included in *NWS*, 88–96, 97–102 respectively.

[101] I'm grateful to Dr Sara Lyons for this observation.

[102] See 'Chatouillard' [George du Maurier], 'Ballad of Blunders', *Punch*, 1 December 1866, 227; Andrew Lang, *Poetical Works*, 4 vols (London: Longmans, Green, 1923), iii.123–5; Amy Levy, *A London Plane-Tree and Other Verse* (London: Fisher Unwin, 1889), 68–70.

was still to be admired. Writing 'Lines on the Monument of Giuseppe Mazzini' (442–443), included in *A Midsummer Holiday and Other Poems* (1884), Swinburne was back in 1857, hailing the now dead hero of Italy as he always had. The poet looked to his own past in other ways and more intimately. He remembered holidays. He meditated on the ruined Suffolk town of Dunwich, first seen in 1875. The slow decline into the sea of this once-major medieval port struck Swinburne as another version of the West Undercliff garden of his childhood. Imaginatively transformed, that had been 'A Forsaken Garden' (338–9). Dunwich, desolate and once important, was not to Swinburne one of Robert Macfarlane's natural and restorative 'wild places'.[103] Its charm was that it had once not been wild at all. Dunwich had the peculiar attraction of abandonment, like the old pagan religions, the last oracle of Delphi, perhaps even like Tannhäuser unforgiven by the Pope.[104] And Swinburne's attraction to the abandoned or remote is discerned in many places. The marine setting of 'Les Casquets' (444–9), a reply to Matthew Arnold's 'Forsaken Merman', was more obviously isolated, more lonely 'than the heart of grief' (446). Yet this sea-bound space was not wholly abandoned, because it was also home. Hardly ever imagining contented domestic life in his published work (except perhaps in the enthusiastic baby poems he wrote through much of his life in praise of feet and hands, smiles and curls), Swinburne narrated in 'Les Casquets' a strange hospitality. Here was, despite the remoteness of the rocks, an answer to a human need for companionship in a landscape encircled by the sublime forces of the ocean. Together, these are some of the poems that bring us closest to the sympathies, the deepest emotional connections, of Swinburne's later life. He loved things best that did not love back.

In 1883 came a volume of roundels. Swinburne took on this test of form, then varied what he could within it—particularly the line lengths. Form was delight and the reader could become intimate with a poem's most subtle ways of being by recognizing—feeling and seeing—poetry as shape. *Poems and Ballads, Third Series*, was published in 1889. That expressed some more of Swinburne's rage at Gladstone and his betrayals, which had also been audible in his angry play about weak, unprincipled leadership that required an act of treachery in defence of loyalty: *Marino Faliero* (1885). Short poems in the *Third Series* mourned more dead friends. 'To a Seamew' (459–62) was among the most emotionally sensitive of Swinburne's late poems, quietly written to a friend in distress, the blind poet Philip Bourke Marston.[105] Substantial elegies were included in *Astrophel and Other Poems* (1894) as Swinburne

[103] See Robert Macfarlane, *The Wild Places* (London: Granta, 2007). For a different, catastrophist, perspective on Swinburne, Watts-Dunton, and the fall at Dunwich, see W.G. Sebald, *Die Ringe des Saturn: Ein englische Wallfahrt* (Frankfurt: Eichborn Verlag, 1995), 200–7.

[104] See 'Laus Veneris', 116–27.

[105] See Francis O'Gorman, 'Swinburne and the "unutterable sadness" of Philip Bourke Marston', *Literary Imagination*, 15 (2013), 165–80.

extended both his gift for commemoration and his construction of a literary circle through memorial. 'Elegy 1869–1891' (498–501) remembered Sir Richard Burton, linguist, explorer, translator, and friend, whose sexual freedoms were only one element of Swinburne's admiration for him. The poem—its opening line an exemplary concentration of matching sounds—recalled another holiday, in the summer of 1869, which Swinburne had taken with Burton, a name that he characteristically said would last till fame be dead. Like the painter J.M.W. Turner, Swinburne brought recollections of places, scenes, climates, and events, back with a luminous clarity. '[Your] memory', said the poet-painter Simeon Solomon aptly, 'is so tremendous that you always seem to me to retain everything you have once seen or heard.'[106] Thinking of the poet's resurrectionary power over ancient legend in the 'Prelude to an Unfinished Poem', Swinburne declared he could make Tristram and Iseult's story 'real' again, imparting his own poetic breath 'to make their dead life live'.[107] And he lived with the vital presence of his own past, including his life-long reading, too.

Swinburne's last book of poetry was not the work of twilight. *A Channel Passage and Other Poems* (1904) recalled in its title poem a channel storm as long ago as 1855. That was 'full of incessant sound and fire,' Swinburne said elsewhere, 'lightening and darkening so rapidly that it seemed to have life, and a delight in its life'.[108] The volume was a thunderous collection of protest too. *A Channel Passage* included writing against the Boers and their treatment of black South Africans and *uitlanders*; against the prisons of Tsarist Russia; against the Tories and the Irish MPs for objecting to a publicly funded statue of Cromwell, whom Swinburne admired as a republican (though not uncritically). He celebrated moments, too, when, as he perceived it, Great Britain had been on the side of justice, not least when defeating the despot Bonaparte's navy at Trafalgar (515). There was much Swinburne deplored about his country. Yet he relished opportunities to commend public actions when the nation had, as he saw it, supported freedom against oppression (including against Catholic powers) and when it had seen the redoubtable victories of British or imperial heroes against the agents of, as Swinburne saw

[106] *UL*, i.214, letter of [late May 1871]. Among the liveliest records of Swinburne at large (in 1862) is that in *The Education of Henry Adams* (Washington: p.p., 1907), where Adams remembers a dinner party with Richard Monckton Milnes. There, guests 'could not believe [Swinburne's] incredible memory and knowledge of literature, classic, medieval, and modern; his faculty of reciting a play of Sophocles or a play of Shakespeare, forward or backward, from end to beginning; or Dante, or Villon, or Victor Hugo. They knew not what to make of his rhetorical recitation of his own unpublished ballads Faustine; the Four Boards of the Coffin Lid; the Ballad of Burdens which he declaimed as though they were books of the Iliad' (121).

[107] See 287.

[108] Algernon Charles Swinburne, 'Victor Hugo: "L'Homme qui rit"', *FR*, 6 (July 1869), 73–81 (73). Swinburne uses the storm in this article as 'the best possible definition I can give of Victor Hugo's genius' (ibid.).

them, tyranny. 'On the Death of Mrs Lynn Linton' (520–21) and 'The Lake of Gaube' (510–12)—which was Swinburne's last distinguished poem on the natural world—were elegiac. And they were far from 'modern'; far from contemplative only of unconsoled vacancy. Remembering the poet and controversial journalist Eliza Lynn Linton, Swinburne probed what promise there was, if not in God, then at least in the subjunctive:

> If life there be that flies not, fair
>   The life must be
> That thrills her sovereign spirit there
>   And sets it free.[109]

The thought of what might be true, to speak in terms of Swinburne's Classical Greek, almost transforms the optative into the optimistic.

Swinburne's career has been variously represented in anthologies. Indeed, he is known to most readers through them. There is poetic material that does not read well now: the baby poems; some of the occasional political pieces; the flagellation writing with which Stevie Smith had such mischievous fun.[110] These I have omitted, though they are part of who Swinburne was. The ballads are briefly represented and he was a notable writer and collector of such forms (see 655–6). Swinburne's letters—a substantial source of information about his opinions and friendships—are used extensively in the Explanatory Notes rather than included separately as texts as in other volumes of the *21st-Century Oxford Authors*. Swinburne's explorations of fiction, including the stories for the projected *Triameron*, the long piece now known as *Lucretia Borgia, or, The Chronicle of Tebaldeo Tebaldei* (published in 1942), and the two novels—*A Year's Letters* and the unfinished *Lesbia Brandon*—were serious matters. *A Year's Letters*, published in part in 1877, is, aside from anything else, a valuable source of autobiography; a confirmation of how Swinburne thought autobiography could be written obliquely. Some pieces of fiction, including *La Fille du policeman* (1861), were deliberately not serious. That burlesque was the 'funniest rampingest satire on French novelists dealing with English themes that you can imagine', said George Meredith.[111] Swinburne's fiction is briefly represented here in 'Dead Love' (33–6).

Where *Tristram* is concerned, I have chosen to give a portion of a masterpiece in order to create space to reveal that Swinburne's achievement was

[109] See 521.

[110] See 'Seymour and Chantelle or Un peu de vice: *In Memory of A. Swinburne and Mary Gordon*', in Stevie Smith, *Collected Poems* (New York: New Directions, 1976), 514.

[111] *Letters of George Meredith Collected and Edited by His Son*, 2 vols (London: Scribners, 1912), i.55. This is the passage in which Meredith notes that 'he is not subtle; and I don't see any internal centre from which springs anything that he does' (ibid.). This view has sometimes been thrown back at Swinburne and it is worth noting its early context and that it related to a piece of youthful satire. *La Fille du policeman* was printed in *NWS*, 119–74.

wider, more varied, than his masterpieces. Any Swinburne anthology also has, now, to be properly annotated. Swinburne was a learned poet, a quirky one, and a man who wrote out of particular occasions with distinctive people, ideas, books, places, and issues on his mind. His exceptional memory meant that allusion was almost impossible to avoid. This all needs to be recovered. Swinburne, moreover, did not like to spell things out. 'The pure artist never asserts; he suggests',[112] the poet observed in a note to *William Blake*. It was typically playful of Swinburne that he should have lodged such an important comment about not asserting in the unassertive shade of a footnote. This conception of how a 'pure artist' should 'mean' is true of many of his own poems, not least where political assumptions are concerned. (Swinburne could be witty in not making things clear even in mourning. Consider the exact point when the reader discovers the name of the subject of 'Elegy, 1869–1891'.) When he gathered occasional pieces into volumes, Swinburne rarely made any effort to indicate what the original occasions had been, to what this poem or that had been a response, beyond sometimes retaining a date at the end. He has been accused of living too much in words: 'Wondrous pattern leading nowhere', said Ezra Pound archly.[113] But actually, from an editor, he now needs more words.

There has been, as I said, a long argument about the later poetry. Edith Sitwell in 1960, who did not arrange her material chronologically, had included almost nothing after 1866: merely '*Ave Atque Vale*' and a song from *Locrine* (1887). Only a year after Sitwell, Bonamy Dobrée in 1961 had taken a brave direction in his Penguin edition, representing work from all the major collections from *Atalanta* to *A Channel Passage*. But Robert Nye turned the clock back and cast the late work out entirely. L.M. Findlay's Carcanet *Selected Poems* in 1982 was more generous to the middle and late period, including even a few brief extracts from plays: *Rosamond* (1860), *Chastelard* (1865), and *Bothwell* (1874). Catherine Maxwell's compact Everyman edition in 1997 concentrated on *Poems and Ballads* of 1866 but included a small number of poems from the later volumes too, though none of the great elegies. The renewed status of the late work was most obviously suggested in Jerome McGann and Charles L. Sligh's edition of *Major Poems and Selected Prose: Algernon Charles Swinburne* (2004), a collection that presents Swinburne richly, including as a prose writer, though with very few notes. I have assumed that interested readers of Swinburne will wish to be readers of the late as well as the early work and my selection reflects that.[114]

[112] See 207.

[113] Ezra Pound, 'Swinburne: A Critique', *Collected Early Poems* (New York: New Directions, 1976), 261.

[114] The assumption is beginning to generate critical analysis of the later writing. See, for instance, the essays collected in *A.C. Swinburne and the Singing Word: New Perspectives on the Mature Work*, ed. Yisrael Levin (Farnham: Ashgate, 2010).

Swinburne, in the selected edition in which *he* was involved, tried another attempt at turning away from the first *Poems and Ballads*. In the 1887 *Selections* organized by Watts-Dunton in which the poet presumably played a role, Swinburne's poems were presented in a way hardly possible today. They were cut up into pieces and re-titled. Chronology was avoided. Lighter material was included and major works from across his life omitted. The most significant casualty was the first *Poems and Ballads*. Only the more or less uncontroversial 'Itylus' (142–3) was included. Poets can make surprising choices about how to anthologize their work and re-present their careers.[115] But *Selections*, mostly comprising verse published between 1880 and 1884, was an unusually drastic act of re-writing even for a poet who had a divided relationship with his own beginnings. Here in *Selections*, observes Rikky Rooksby, was 'one of the most audacious attempts in the history of English poetry to re-position a poet in the mind of the reading public by blatant suppression of parts of his work'.[116] In fact, it was not blatant. The reader new to Swinburne would never know what had happened. There are no dates; there is no time-line; no indication of which volumes Swinburne had published; no clue to what was unrepresented. The re-positioning involved in *Selections* was as silent as it was thorough. Managed by Watts-Dunton, Swinburne had almost succeeded in suggesting that he had not enlisted in 1866 (see xxiii) after all.

Writing for those he knew, Swinburne also wrote about them. So doing, he created a living, as distinct from a memorial, literary circle through words.[117] His friendship groups—registered in or created by his poetry and prose—are the community in which to read him. Swinburne did not know William Blake, of course. But his 1868 study came out of a private circle nevertheless: that of Dante Gabriel and William Michael Rossetti, who shared his enthusiasm for, and scholarly interest in, the radical visionary.[118] Swinburne knew Barry Cornwall's widow, Ann Benson Skepper (1799–1888), and she really had met Blake. Swinburne corresponded with the strange antiquarian Seymour Kirkup (1788–80) who had known Blake as well. Swinburne was acquainted with Baudelaire and with Victor Hugo ('Victor Hugo's *L'Année terrible*', 288–92) and Matthew Arnold ('Mr Arnold's *New Poems*', 183–95). For a while he was friends with the painter-poet Simeon Solomon ('Simeon Solomon: Notes on his "Vision of Love and Other Studies"', 276–9) until Swinburne broke

[115] See, for instance, the discussions of 'collected works' in Michael Millgate, *Testamentary Acts: Browning, Tennyson, James, Hardy* (Oxford: Clarendon, 1992) and Samantha Matthews, *Poetical Remains: Poets' Graves, Bodies, and Books in the Nineteenth Century* (Oxford: Oxford University Press, 2004).

[116] Rikky Rooksby, 'Anthologizing Algernon: The Problem of Swinburne's Later Poetry', *English Literature in Transition, 1880–1920*, 40 (1997), 299–309 (300).

[117] Note that Swinburne's habit of reading work aloud to intimate circles might have first been established with the Old Mortality Society at Oxford: see Gerald C. Monsman, 'Old Mortality at Oxford', *Studies in Philology*, 67 (1970), 359–89.

[118] For other Blake readers in Swinburne's circle, see 581.

relations, shocked by the artist's public demonstration of homosexuality and his transformation into a 'thing unmentionable alike by men and women'.[119] Swinburne's sexual freedoms had plain, unbreakable limits.

About D.G. Rossetti, with whom Swinburne had unsatisfactorily shared a house, there were essays on both visual and poetic achievement (*Notes on the Royal Academy Exhibition, 1868*, 225–30; 'The Poems of Dante Gabriel Rossetti', 231–5). Prose, Swinburne said in 1872, was 'a strange soil instead of my natural ground', but he had 'a great ambition to write prose well'.[120] Certainly, writing critical essays on literary and visual topics enabled Swinburne to reveal the more analytical side of his mind, his ability to think rigorously and to study the significance of empirical knowledge and the ideas of others. The first Rossetti essay, with its ironic title (see 588), comprised Swinburne's reflections on Rossetti's pictures that were *not* in the Academy. Exclusion, as well as complaint, fired Swinburne's prose. Much of his critical writing included in this selection is in defence of something or of someone, even if Swinburne's mode of defence is usually attack. His writing on visual art was brief but penetrating. Hotten wanted him to carry on, to write more—and it is easy to see why. Walter Pater's *The Renaissance* (1873) might have owed (it certainly *seems* as if it did) more than a little to Swinburne's habits in analyzing pictures: his evocative *ekphrasis*; his personal judgment; his ability to enter into the spirit of an artist's conception without a flattening historical contextualization or anything like Ruskin's sense of an over-arching ethical narrative. But Swinburne—whose apparent influence on Pater might be mere coincidence[121]—made no significant contributions to art criticism after 1871.

Part of the problem, I think, was that Swinburne could not deal with the new uncertainty about painters' identities, let alone with collaboration and the challenge of artist's workshops. Art criticism was changing. The re-attributions of paintings in the second half of the nineteenth century—in Italian art led by Joseph Archer Crowe and Giovanni Battista Cavalcaselle's *A History of Painting* (1871)—disturbed accepted views of who had painted what. However unconvincing it may initially sound, the significance for Swinburne of a name, a personality, a presiding genius, behind pictures as well as books is hard to over-estimate. He made of authors and painters heroes too. Pater did not know exactly what that historical but mysterious personality called 'Giorgione' had really produced. In response, he constructed the notion of a '*school* of Giorgione' that was different from a single, knowable, nameable personality. A 'school' permitted Pater to speak of a spirit-like presence visible in art that relieved the Aesthetic critic of any scholarly need to be certain about who,

[119] *SL*, iv.107 (letter of 15 October 1879). See headnote on 601. Note that Swinburne was—so the surviving evidence indicates—unsympathetic to John Addington Symonds' homosexuality, referring to him on 1 September 1894 as 'the late Mr Soddington Symonds' (*SL*, vi.74).

[120] *UL*, i.237, letter of 1 September 1872 to Morley.

[121] See 585–7.

exactly, had painted canvasses supposedly by a man called 'Giorgione'.[122] Swinburne, disciple and admirer of the gallant personalities of authors and artists, of great art as the inevitable manifestation of the natural inner laws of individual creators, could hardly countenance such a thing. So, for this and other reasons, he gave art criticism up.

The integrity of a name mattered as, in fact, it did elsewhere for Pater, who in 1888 explained the quality of literary style as the true expression of a unique man's unique experience.[123] In praising *Wuthering Heights* (1847) in 'Emily Brontë' (421–6), Swinburne dwelt on the wholeness of a true work of word art—this is what he thought Brontë's novel was—and the sense of artistic inevitability behind it. *Wuthering Heights* was perfectly in accord with the natural genius of its author, he asserted; an expression of Emily's inner artistic being. 'The book is what it is because the author was what she was', Swinburne said with one of those statements that was meant to close off discussion: 'this is the main and central fact to be remembered.'[124] The unifying presence of a noble and nameable artist, whose unrestricted personality ensured the unity and quality of true works of art, was not clearer for Swinburne than in his noisy argument with the new Shakespeare scholarship of the middle of the Victorian period. His conflict with F.J. Furnivall's New Shakspere (*sic*) Society was particularly bad-tempered.[125] The disagreement reveals the rootedness of Swinburne's conception of word art in heroic personality and his faith in the alert reader's ability to see the wholeness of genius behind language, to sense the inner laws of an individual personality. Swinburne in 1880 castigated those 'men and scholars' who claimed Shakespeare's work was misattributed or collaborative: 'Englishmen and editors, who have detected the alien voice of a pretender'.[126] They were worse than cloth-eared. They were traitors to the noble conception of the solitary genius that lay behind, and guaranteed, the integrity of real literary writing. Such editors, in Swinburne's intellectual world, were the equivalent of the Hapsburgs, the Bourbons, and the Papal States in holding back the freedom of a re-unified, newly complete Italy. They were deadly impediments to what was meant to be whole or self-evidently *was* whole. There can be a quite astonishing coherence in the shape of Swinburne's thinking across aesthetics and politics.

That coherence also concerns, as I have implied, the place of heroes in Swinburne's life. He mistrusted—even deplored—the windy, pseudo-philosophical, peevishly Scottish (as he saw it), pro-Russian Thomas Carlyle, the 'Arch-Quack of Cheyne Row, Chelsea'.[127] But he had a similar faith in the heroic as the author of *On Heroes, Hero-Worship, and the Heroic in History* (1841). Swinburne's pol-

[122] See Walter Pater, 'The School of Giorgione', *FR*, 22 (October 1877), 526–38.

[123] See Pater, 'Style'. [124] See 423. [125] See headnote on 608–11.

[126] Algernon Charles Swinburne, *A Study of Shakespeare* (London: Chatto & Windus, 1880), 19 (these words relate to Macbeth's last rallying cry).

[127] *SL*, iv.224.

itical ideas were ignited by a small cadre of men. He followed, and in a way loved, those to whom he gave exceptional moral authority in his peculiarly militaristic imagining of men as commanders of minds. He recognized this feature of himself and smiled at it in *The Sisters* (1892), an autobiographical play. There he has Sir Arthur say of Redgie, the Swinburne character, that

> You're just a hothead still—
> The very schoolboy that I knew you first—
> On fire with admiration and with love
> Of some one or of something, always.[128]

In turn, Swinburne was always inclined to see the figure of the artist, the compelling personality, behind language. Such personalities gave to the best of aesthetic artefacts—whatever they were—the unavoidable coherence born from human presence. Swinburne is rarely autobiographical in any plain way (assuming for a moment that anyone *can* be autobiographical in a 'plain way'). Many readers have felt the strange absence of an inner life in his poetry, the peculiar vanishing point of Swinburne's personality in the seemingly missing personal heart of his writing. Yet Swinburne, for all that, was a critic who usually felt that works of art were incomprehensible except as convincing manifestations of single, brave, creative minds who could not act otherwise.[129]

Swinburne came to dislike the theatre. 'I never go', he told Gosse bluntly in 1893.[130] It was partly because, in his late years, he was deaf. But Swinburne, I speculate, also may have wanted to *read* drama without the mediating, distracting presence of a producer or actor between him and the words. Earlier, he had been only mildly interested in allowing others to think about staging *Bothwell*, the second play in Swinburne's substantial Mary Queen of Scots trilogy (see 293–7).[131] In 1926, T. Earle Welby thought that that intimidating figure, the 'really capable anthologist',[132] should produce a selection of Swinburne's poetry *and plays*. But, if that is desirable, it is not so easy to divide Swinburne's plays sensibly into separable sections. The dramas have their wholeness too. An exception, perhaps, is the last scene from the (ultimately unstaged) *Bothwell* where Mary leaves Scotland after her defeat at the Battle

[128] Algernon Charles Swinburne, *The Sisters: A Tragedy* (London: Chatto & Windus, 1892), 31. 'Redgie' was Swinburne's familiar autobiographical pseudonym: sometimes in correspondence (*SL*, i.62), in *A Year's Letters*, and in this play.

[129] On Swinburne's collaborative authorship, see liv. Note his confidence in handling confirmed dual authorship—as a fresh expression of artistic unity and inevitability—in his discussion of Thomas Middleton, in *Thomas Middleton*, with an Introduction by Algernon Charles Swinburne, Mermaid Series (London: Fisher Unwin, [1887]), xxi–xxxviii.

[130] *SL*, vi.59.

[131] *Locrine* was experimentally staged by the Elizabethan Stage Company in 1899: see *The Times*, 27 December 1899, 6. Clara Watts-Dunton asserts that *Atalanta* was staged in 1907 (*HLS*, 138) and it certainly was in 1911 (see 553).

[132] Welby, *A Study of Swinburne*, 226.

of Langside on 13 May 1568. It is included here—as, happily, it was in *Selections*. Heavy with brooding, the episode returns to the emotional spaces of *Atalanta*. But the presiding deities, the Erinyes, are not Classical divinities but English politicians and a fair and fatal English queen.

Swinburne's writing of drama began at school. We know of his Elizabethan/Jacobean imitations; we know now of his flogging play, *First Fault for the Hundredth Time*, written at, and apparently performed in, Eton.[133] The early published work includes *The Queen Mother* (1860), about Catherine de' Medici and the St Bartholomew's Day Massacre in August 1572. History—particularly the history of the rebellious—remained Swinburne's principal inspiration as a dramatist. *Marino Faliero* challenged Byron's version of the same story, *Marino Faliero, Doge of Venice* (1821), by making the treacherous fourteenth-century Venetian a man of principle, a kind of forerunner of Mazzini.[134] *Locrine* was set in ancient pre-Christian Britain. It interrogated Tennyson's *Idylls* in its depiction of a king's rather than a queen's adultery and ruminated yet again on the unforgotten treachery of Gladstone over Russia, General Gordon, and the perceived calamity of Home Rule. *The Sisters* was personal, reflecting Swinburne's childhood, his early military ambitions (he had once apparently seriously wanted to be a cavalryman[135]), his love for (presumably) Mary Gordon, his admiration of heroes. As a blank-verse society drama, *The Sisters* was one of the ways in which Swinburne—poet, scholar of Renaissance drama, literary critic, student of myth—occupied rather similar ground to T.S. Eliot. But Eliot was the Modernist who, ironically enough, and with some largely second-hand opinions, would later do him famous and lasting damage in *The Sacred Wood* (1920).

A lofty, emphatic, remarkably delicate writer, Swinburne can be fierce and tender, shocking and enticing, rough and refined. Readers come swiftly to recognize the characteristic turns and patterns of his verse as the writing of no other.[136] The exploration of form—the peculiar challenges Swinburne set himself in rhythm and in rhyme—tests the readily available vocabulary of English criticism for describing how poems are formed, what poetry as 'form' is.[137] Swinburne peculiarly makes readers aware, for example, of the difference

[133] See Peter Leggatt, 'He's catching it! Isn't it nuts!: Algernon Charles Swinburne's Eton Swishing Play', *Times Literary Supplement*, 10 January 2014, 14–15.

[134] For John Nichol's negative assessment of Byron's version, see his *Byron* (London: Macmillan, 1880), 143.

[135] See *SL*, vi.251.

[136] Some of the early poems do not establish the characteristic voice (e.g. 'Of the birth of Sir Tristram', 12–22) even if they establish enduring themes and interests. 'By the sea-side', first published in *WMP*, 177–80, and probably dated from 1859 or 1860, is a striking example. Its conversational, Arnoldian opening ('It is near evening; wait a little yet. | See, the salt water-mark | High on the crumbling sandslope is not wet [. . .]', 177) is hardly familiar as ACS's voice but the sea-side setting is.

[137] For a recent re-assessment what 'form' means in relation to literature, see Angela Leighton, *On Form: Poetry, Aestheticism and the Legacy of a Word* (Oxford: Oxford University Press, 2007).

between how a line can be scanned and what rhythmic patterns are heard beyond or outside the official 'feet'.[138] He invites his audience in a concentrated way to feel how the ideas of 'heavy stresses' and 'light stresses' are inadequate descriptors of rhythm: how two 'heavy stresses', for instance, are not simply equal but capable of gradation that can be heard but not easily mapped (Swinburne's poetry blooms when it is read aloud, as he well knew). Is there really such a thing as a 'spondee' (however much Swinburne didn't like the foot)? What shadings of stress, for instance, can there be in that cluster from 'The Interpreters', caught somewhere between the iambic, trochaic, and spondaic: 'Dead air, dead fire, dead shapes…' (465)? Verbal and rhythmic patterns constitute the immediately recognizable sound of his voice. They include, particularly, the anapaest ('In a coign of the cliff', 338); the grouping of words in threes ('marriage and death and division', 169); the double adjective ('low last edge of the long lone land', 338); the ubiquitous modulated conversation of alliteration and assonance ('Upon the flowery forefront of the year, | One wandering by the grey-green April sea', 368); the repetition of a single term so that the reader can come back and perceive it from a different angle ('Only the sleep eternal | In an eternal night', 179); the rhythmic tipping over of a hypercatalectic line ('For the wind's is their doom and their blessing', 416); the synaesthetic sentence that feels as if it is reaching for the ineffable ('The music that puts light into the spheres', 380);[139] the deployment of monosyllables or short lines or both in the midst of richer textures ('Now lie dead', 338); and the accretion of long syntactic structures as they move towards a climactic, sometimes enormously delayed, main verb (like the opening of 'The Sailing of the Swallow').

Swinburne's voice is not faked, though it can be mocked. And it is not heard again, however much his role among a new generation, including Rupert Brooke (a serious Swinburne reader), Edward Thomas (who published *Swinburne: A Critical Study* in 1912), and John Drinkwater (whose book on Swinburne has already been mentioned), is worth thinking about.[140] A writer who had cast a spell over words, Swinburne turned his art at times to causes that were violent and subjects that, to some readers, were vile. As a poet of ideas, he was bracingly independent and sometimes hazardously loyal. He defended and celebrated *Poems and Ballads* of 1866 as much as he struggled with its legacy. He was changeful and conflicted; he was sometimes contradictory (not least over what 1866 had really meant) but he was in other ways profoundly,

[138] See, for instance, note 96 above. I am grateful to Dr Laura Kilbride for an invaluable conversation about Swinburne's metre, reflected here.

[139] Cf. Empson's argument in *Seven Types* that synaethesia in Swinburne's verse is only appearance and really the result of a 'diffused use of grammar', 13.

[140] See my Introduction to vol. 5 of *Edward Thomas Prose Writings: A Selected Edition*, ed. Francis O'Gorman (General Editors Guy Cuthbertson and Lucy Newlyn) (Oxford: Oxford University Press, 2017).

uniquely, almost suspiciously consistent. His poetry reached out of time to enduring myths and permanent human experiences. But, as a thinker, he was remarkably confined by a small cluster of ideas and a small group of men that belonged to his youth. Something of the late 1850s and early '60s remained alive and well for him across his life. Swinburne's mind—with both its high sense of poetry and its private fondness for the ludicrous and juvenile—could be both daringly open and oddly closed. That is, perhaps, not the worst that one can say of a man.

He had no very intimate relationships in his life, so far as we know. He might, indeed, have been the chastest of all poets to write so much about sex. But Swinburne's poems are, at their best, movingly intimate and sometimes erotically entangled with their subjects—wild abandoned places, the edges of lands where they meet the sea, long-past troubles, the exultation of free things, European legends of love and loss, the memory of gifted friends. The most opinionated and sometimes dogmatic of writers, Swinburne could work with heart-stopping sensitivity. He is an unforgettable elegist, conjuring nearly unspoken hopes of survival alongside the finality of death. Yet he is also an unblushing enthusiast for blowing up tyrants and cutting down their forces with sword and shot. Swinburne, who almost never spoke in public, could write like an orator punching the air. Yet he could also create the most nuanced of rhythmic effects, exploiting with grace the forms of words, the forms made by words. Swinburne in 1862 was, said Henry Adams in 1907, 'quite original, wildly eccentric, astonishingly gifted and convulsingly droll'. And then he added, 'but what more he was, even [Richard Monckton Milnes, Swinburne's friend] hardly dared say.'[141] It is a revealing lack of revelation. Swinburne has never been an author, or a person, easy to sum up without qualification, hesitation, or confusion—or, as Milnes knew here, tactful omission. His poetry has not convinced every reader and it never will. Perhaps, as Swinburne says somewhat inaccurately of *Wuthering Heights*, 'It may be true that not many will ever take it to their hearts'.[142] But it is certainly true, and without qualification, that Algernon Charles Swinburne is a writer about whom it is impossible to remain without an opinion.

[141] Adams, 121. [142] See 426.

# NOTE ON THE TEXTS

This collection follows chronological order but not exactly. In keeping with the principles of the *21st-Century Oxford Authors*, the poetry is arranged by order of volume publication. The obvious exceptions are texts unpublished during Swinburne's lifetime, which are inserted either where they are known to have been written or where, in the absence of hard evidence, they might have been. The ordering of poetry by volume can, however, obscure in an important way the development of Swinburne's creativity. We do not know exactly, for instance, when many poems in *Poems and Ballads* (1866) were written except that it was before 1866.[1] Eight had been published in 1862. We do know that many poems that were later included in other volumes had been written earlier—sometimes considerably earlier—because they too had been previously published in periodicals.

A distinctive example, because of the time-gap, is the celebrated elegy on the supposed death of Charles Baudelaire, '*Ave Atque Vale*' (342–6). This was written in the late spring of 1866, on the basis of a mistaken report of the French poet's death in April (see headnote, 621). The elegy was then published first in the January 1868 edition of *The Fortnightly Review*, by which time Baudelaire really had died. When the poem was reprinted in a volume, that is, in *Poems and Ballads, Second Series* (1878), it was more than a decade old. On first publication, William Harrison Ainsworth's *The New Monthly Magazine* had ranked '*Ave Atque Vale*' with Milton's 'Lycidas' and Shelley's 'Adonais'.[2] By 1874, Swinburne was looking back to say: 'I cannot believe it worthy to tie the shoes (so to speak) of the least, whoever be the least, of the great English triad or Trinity of elegies, Milton's, Shelley's and Arnold's.'[3] And his opinion would continue to deteriorate (see headnote, 621). Readers will want to consult my Explanatory Notes to see when and where all the pieces in this collection were originally issued. Where possible, I have given documentary evidence that confirms or implies a date of composition though we still lack full publication, in hard copy or electronically, of the diverse manuscript material distributed across the world that reveals the full surviving history of Swinburne's writing life.

In accordance with the Oxford series' principles, the first editions of the poetry volumes have been used (and any subsequent amendments noted). There is one complication and that is with *Poems and Ballads* of 1866. That, as mentioned, was first published by Moxon and then, after Moxon withdrew,

[1] What exactly, for instance, were in the 'MSS' on which Ruskin commented on 5 July 1863? See *UL*, i.26.

[2] See 'New Elegies', *The New Monthly Magazine*, 145 (October 1869), 403–10.

[3] *SL*, ii.282, letter of 23 February 1874 to E.C. Stedman.

by J.C. Hotten. Hotten's edition—T.J. Wise accuses Hotten of some fraud in not indicating fresh printings of the volume so as to avoid paying additional sums to Swinburne (*Bibliography*, i.129–31)—was the text through which Swinburne's controversial collection was principally known. Or, at least, known before Chatto & Windus took over Hotten's business (Andrew Chatto had worked for Hotten). The first version of Moxon's volume, submitted to the author for his consideration, contained a number of errors that Swinburne had to correct before it was more widely introduced to the public. What happened subsequently was that a few unbound Moxon sheets, with those errors uncorrected, were included under Hotten's covers when Hotten took over the contract for *Poems and Ballads*. It is more strangely the case that Hotten set up his own type from Moxon's uncorrected sheets and so previously corrected errors re-appeared. The text presented here includes, where necessary, ACS's corrections both to Moxon and, in effect, to Hotten together with those that were overlooked in both (and noted in Wise's *Bibliography*, i.118). All this is documented in the Explanatory Notes.

Swinburne, in general, was not a significant reviser of his published work. He is at the other end of the scale from, say, W.H. Auden or, in music, Pierre Boulez. '[It] is odd', Swinburne said on 27 March 1876, 'how a book once published goes out of my head—drops as it were out of one's life or thought [...] Till it is in print, it is still part one's self, and concerns one's thoughts, and one takes a personal interest in it which vanishes on publication.'[4] He cared, to be sure, about the publication process including the correction of page proofs (though sometimes could be surprisingly indifferent even to a poem's or a volume's title). Looking at Chatto & Windus's proofs, he was not always pleased with what he found (see xxii, for instance). Disputes concerned both the texts and the commercial value of them. Swinburne periodically wrangled over money. Income from writing was, after all, necessary.[5] I provide information about the financial transactions of Swinburne's work in the Explanatory Notes. But, as Swinburne remarked, once material was in the public domain, his eye was on the future—unless he found more mistakes as he did, for example, in the first printing of *Bothwell*.[6] Of course, Swinburne disliked errors. He struggled with Chatto's team, frequently listing the alleged faults of their compositors, and once the printers hit back with complaints about how difficult Swinburne was to work with.[7] The complete story of Swinburne's dealings with Chatto has yet to be told though a helpful first step is Clive Simmonds' University of Reading PhD thesis, 'Publishing

[4] *SL*, iii.160 (letter to J.C. Collins).

[5] Though note Clara Watts-Dunton's description of Swinburne's indifference to cheques for large amounts of money in Ch. 11, 'The Bard as a Man of Business', *HLS*.

[6] See the notes for letter to Andrew Chatto, early July 1874, *UL*, i.320, and to Watts-Dunton, *SL*, ii.309.

[7] See n. 39 on xxii.

Swinburne: The Poet, His Publishers and Critics' (2013). If this maintains unchallenged the conventional story of Swinburne's supposed rejection of liberalism, it also valuably explores what lies behind the fact that, as Simmonds says, Swinburne's sales 'totalled perhaps no more than 150,000 volumes across fifty titles (of which about forty were poetry or verse drama)'.[8] Simmonds persuasively suggests that Chatto was, in commercial terms, canny despite this relatively small figure.

Chatto's publication standards—like those of his former employer, Hotten—are not, for a contemporary reader, high. His large fonts and widely spaced lines did not always produce pleasing visual effects. (The original volumes can now be studied for free on the <http://www.archive.org> website.) Yet Swinburne, as much as he was vexed by errors, does not seem to have been too bothered about this. He certainly did care about how his lines were laid out. He cared, in particular, for the implementation of indentations which, when used, had to follow rhyme schemes.[9] This, naturally, is reproduced in the present edition (though I need to note that some editorial judgment has been required to decide exactly how the indentations should be graded in the 'Ode to Mazzini' and 'By the North Sea' as the published texts are not unambiguous and, in the case of the former, the MS as well).

There are other issues with the original publishers. In many of Swinburne's collections, verse with long lines often *looks* different from how, properly, it should be displayed. His publishers—and most notably Chatto—break Swinburne's sometimes very long lines, sometimes twice, in order to leave an (often small) margin. What is poetry of long, sweeping lines can, thus, look almost like tiered patterns of lines of decreasing length, ending sometimes with a few words like the *rentrement* of one of Swinburne's roundels. The placing of capitalization proves the real line structure, of course, but the initial perception of shape is different from the true form. In *Tristram of Lyonesse*, Swinburne's decasyllabic rhyming couplets ought to leave a perfect left justification except where there is an indentation for a new verse section. But Chatto & Windus regularly break the lines (twice on p.4 of the first edition, for instance), disturbing the visual appearance of the poem's crafted regularity that is importantly in tension with its emotional drama. There is some evidence that Swinburne was annoyed about these kinds of problems. The 'arrangement of lines and stanzas', he said, in a vexed letter to Andrew Chatto on 10 April 1889 about proofs for *Poems and Ballads, Third Series*, 'is repeatedly neglected—thrown into utter confusion'.[10] That confusion might, perhaps, include the effect of splitting long lines.[11] But on other matters

[8] Clive Simmonds, 'Publishing Swinburne: The Poet, His Publishers and Critics', 2 vols (University of Reading PhD thesis, 2013), i.274.

[9] See, for instance, *SL*, iv.291.

[10] *SL*, v.263.

[11] Certainly the 1889 volume includes many examples of re-disposed lines, e.g. 'The Armada', 'The Ballad of Bath', 'A Word with the Wind'.

Swinburne in the public world of the published artefact seems to have been oddly easy to satisfy. The *l'art pour l'art* idea of the book as a beautiful object was not a priority even though, early in Swinburne's career, Rossetti had provided characterful binding designs for *Atalanta* in 1865 and *Songs Before Sunrise* in 1871.[12]

Significant textual changes between first publication and volume edition are observed in my Explanatory Notes. It is usually the case with Swinburne's prose that the differences are conspicuous—but not often very conspicuous. Perhaps the most significant issue in terms of re-printing is where Swinburne decided not to reprint at all. It is worth reflecting, for instance, that the often-quoted 1862 piece on Baudelaire's *Les Fleurs du mal* (26–32) was not reissued. Neither was the letter on George Meredith's *Modern Love* (23–5) nor the essay on Simeon Solomon (276–9). Much else of greater length was. Prose essays on a range of literary critical subjects were usually (though not always) gathered into collections: *Essays and Studies* (1875), *Miscellanies* (1886), *Studies in Prose and Poetry* (1894). Making a distinction from the copy-texts for the poetry, I have not always employed the volume version in the edition that follows for the prose texts, for reasons individually explained in the Explanatory Notes. On two occasions—the 'Ode to Mazzini' and 'The Ballads of the English Border'—the copy-text is the MS.

The question of my editorial intervention into Swinburne's texts can be described as follows. There are a few misprints which, despite Swinburne's efforts, survived into modern times and they have been corrected (and noted). OUP's house style has been adopted in the case of converting double inverted commas to single; removing points from familiar contractions ('Mr.' to 'Mr'); and not setting titles or the first word or words of poetry in small capitals. No spelling has been altered without a note. Swinburne was insistent, by the way, that the spelling of 'today' and 'tomorrow' was 'to-day' and 'to-morrow'.[13] Stanza numbers have been removed for greater page clarity but numbers have been retained where they mark out sections or verse paragraphs of irregular length. I have used modern continental practice throughout in rendering foreign language titles instead of Swinburne's British practice (*Les Fleurs du mal* for Swinburne's *Les Fleurs du Mal*). No punctuation has been altered from copy-texts except where there was clearly a mistake: such alterations are noted. For one text (Swinburne's essay on Simeon Solomon), I have taken the liberty of introducing an editorial break (noted) to divide one of Swinburne's very long paragraphs. I have not done this for the Blake essay because the torrent of enormously long paragraphs seemed worth preserving as Swinburne catches something of Blake's own defiance of conventions and restraints.

[12] These can be seen on <http://www.rossettiarchive.org/>.

[13] See *SL*, vi.27–8.

An important source for bibliographical and biographical history is the poet's own correspondence, now gathered into nine volumes together with online supplementary material.[14] I have usually chosen to reproduce all of interest in the letters as they relate to individual pieces. Allusions in the poetry and prose have been glossed; significant critical responses have been discussed and, where appropriate, Swinburne's defence of his poems described (there is self-dramatization in some of his post-1866 accounts of alleged quarrels for which I have found little or no evidence). I have endeavoured, in glossing allusions, to draw on versions of texts that Swinburne did or could have known rather than modern editions. On a few occasions, however, I have failed to establish a likely or at least a plausible edition for Swinburne's original source and have turned to more recent versions of texts to indicate material to which he refers. I have used Lemprière's celebrated *Classical Dictionary* (first published in 1788) as one source of information about Classical proper names because Swinburne, like every nineteenth-century public schoolboy, knew it well. The context of each text is established in as much detail as publicly available evidence, to the best of my knowledge, permits.

Swinburne lived with close intellectual friendships or, rather, his friendships were mostly defined by intellectual sympathies (and in a few cases by flagellation interests). As mentioned, literary circles help define who he was, and to whom and how he wrote. Accordingly, I point out significant similarities and disagreements with members of close circles in the Notes (e.g. with Mary Gordon, Lord Houghton, Edward Burne-Jones, Dante Gabriel and William Michael Rossetti, John Nichol, Watts-Dunton). Realizing how Swinburne's texts belong within 'conversations', or at least within shared intellectual or emotional environments, can help clarify the way in which his writing might be read as personal expressions of collective perspectives (note the single reader to whom the 1904 'Dedication' is written, 524–35). Moreover, grasping the role of these groups in Swinburne's life assists a contemporary reader in comprehending with some exactness the tiered nature of the poet's implied audiences: a particular individual or small group first; then a hazier wider public (sometimes contaminated by the low-life of the journal critics). Swinburne could deliberately provoke this hazily grasped wider audience (and his publishers) and I do not mean simply in the terms in which he defended *Poems and Ballads* of 1866. Consider, for instance, a letter on 6 August 1882 when the poet asked Chatto to include the following words, and only the following words, from a recent *Saturday Review* article on *Tristram of Lyonesse and Other Poems* in advertising the volume: 'We have some difficulty in taking this kind of thing seriously. Any man who abandoned his mind

[14] See *SM*.

to it "could reel it off for hours together." '[15] That was quite some puff with which an author intended to entice his unknown readers.

Swinburne's composition process could involve his literary circles practically. From surviving MSS, it is clear that writing involved trial for Swinburne: extensive revision, rethinking, crossings-out, and starting anew with a fresh copy (see Figure 8). A good single example of this is discussed by Timothy A.J. Burnett in his 1993 essay, 'Swinburne at Work: The First Page of "Anactoria" ',[16] which considers three MS versions—in the Harry Ransom Humanities Research Center; the Fitzwilliam Museum Cambridge; and the Bibliotheca Bodmeriana at Geneva. Burnett's conclusions are worthy of attention not least when he reminds us that Swinburne simply did not start at the beginning and work logically through to the end of a poem, and neither did he edit precision into vagueness. The present edition, in keeping with the principles of the Oxford series, does not draw in a sustained way on the internationally distributed MS sources. But it does return to the MSS at particularly significant moments (as described in the Notes). Two important facets of Swinburne's composition process are visible in the Notes that relate to my broader point about the role of Swinburne's circles. First, I include, as an example, earlier drafts of the sonnet 'Cor Cordium' (1871, 596–8) that indicatively reveal the extent of Swinburne's collaborative authorship. The correspondence with William Michael Rossetti over 'Cor Cordium' might be compared to—one further example—the poet seeking Watts-Dunton's approval for a portion of 'Les Casquets', 641. Texts literally arise from discussion here (though to what extent the faithful Watts-Dunton was really being invited to propose changes is a relevant question). Second, the discussion over 'Cor Cordium' is an example of Swinburne's readiness to take the advice of those he trusted in order to avoid controversy (in this case, religious controversy over what he and Shelley called the Galilean serpent).

Finally, on this topic of more personal circles, I end with a speculation. I have drawn attention in the Explanatory Notes to the many points of intellectual and aesthetic correspondence between Swinburne's work and the painter-poet with whom he shared Tudor House, Cheyne Walk, Chelsea, London in the mid-1860s. The significance of Dante Gabriel Rossetti's friendship with Swinburne, though much evidence has gone, seems to me likely to have been of signal importance in the early and subsequent direction of Swinburne's creative energies. He, if anyone did, helped make Swinburne Swinburne.

[15] *SL*, v.292. Swinburne is quoting from a review in *SRev*, 54 (29 July 1882), 156–7 (157) and in fact the journal's sentence continues: 'nevertheless, it is of evil example to weak brethren.'

[16] *WMP*, 148–58.

# NOTE ON THE TRANSLATIONS AND ABBREVIATIONS

## TRANSLATIONS

Translations from modern French and Italian are mine. Translations from Swinburne's Old French are mine with the generous help of Ros Brown-Grant, University of Leeds. Translations from Classical Greek are as indicated and I am very grateful to Kenneth Haynes, Brown University, for permission to re-print his translations of ACS's Greek poems about Walter Savage Landor in *AiC*. Where no translator is given, Classical Greek translations are mine. Translators of ACS's Latin are indicated in notes and where none is given, translations are mine.

## ABBREVIATIONS

All references to Shakespeare are to *The Oxford Shakespeare: The Complete Works*, 2nd edn, ed. Stanley Wells and Gary Taylor (Oxford: Oxford University Press, 2005). Note that this contains both Quarto and Folio versions of *King Lear*, signified as appropriate below. All references to the Bible are to *The King James Version* in the 1769 Oxford 'Authorized' edition. All references to the Anglican liturgy, unless stated otherwise, are to *The Book of Common Prayer* (1662 version). Cranmer's *BCP* draws on prior (Catholic) texts but I have not indicated, here or elsewhere, sources for sources unless they are relevant for ACS. Note that, where allusions to other texts are concerned, I use 'cf.' to indicate that the allusion is a paraphrase or that ACS's text simply closely relates to another text. I use 'see…' where the 'allusion' is an exact quotation.

| | |
|---|---|
| *AiC* | *Atalanta in Calydon* (London: Moxon, 1865) |
| *AiC*GL | *Swinburne's Atalanta in Calydon: A Facsimile of the First Edition*, with a Preface by Georges Lafourcade (London: Oxford University Press, 1930) |
| *ACP* | *A Channel Passage and Other Poems* (London: Chatto & Windus, 1904) |
| ACS | Algernon Charles Swinburne |
| *AOP* | *Astrophel and Other Poems* (London: Chatto & Windus, 1894) |
| *APL* | Rikky Rooksby, *Algernon Charles Swinburne: A Poet's Life* (Aldershot: Scolar, 1997) |
| *BACS* | Mrs Disney Leith [formerly Mary Gordon], *The Boyhood of Algernon Charles Swinburne* (London: Chatto & Windus, 1917) |
| *BCP* | *The Book of Common Prayer* (1662) |
| BL | British Library, St Pancras, London |
| Bonchurch | Edmund Gosse and T.J. Wise, eds, *Bonchurch Edition of the Complete Works of Algernon Charles Swinburne*, 20 vols (London: Heinemann and Wells, 1925–7) |

| | |
|---|---|
| *CH* | Clyde K. Hyder, ed., *Swinburne: The Critical Heritage* (London: Routledge & Kegan Paul, 1970) |
| Collins | John Collins, *The Two Forgers: A Biography of Harry Buxton Forman and Thomas James Wise* (Aldershot: Scolar, 1992) |
| Conington | *The Satires, Epistles and Art of Poetry of Horace*, translated by John Conington (London: Bell & Daldy, 1870) |
| DGR | Dante Gabriel Rossetti (1828–82) |
| *DGRFL* | William Michael Rossetti, *Dante Gabriel Rossetti: His Family Letters with a Memoir*, 2 vols (London: Ellis and Elvey, 1895) |
| EBJ | Edward Burne-Jones (1833–98) |
| *ELN* | *English Language Notes* |
| *ES* | *Essays and Studies* (London: Chatto & Windus, 1875) |
| EWG | Edmund Gosse (1849–1928) |
| *FR* | *The Fortnightly Review* |
| G | John S. Mayfield Papers: Algernon Charles Swinburne Series, Georgetown University Manuscripts, Georgetown University Special Collections Research Center |
| *GL* | *Greek Lyric: Sappho and Alcaeus*, ed. David A. Campbell, Loeb Classical Library 142 (Cambridge MA: Harvard University Press, 1982) |
| Haynes | *Poems and Ballads & Atalanta in Calydon*, ed. Kenneth Haynes (London: Penguin, 2000) |
| *HEP* | George Saintsbury, *A History of English Prosody from the Twelfth Century to the Present Day*, 3 vols (London: Macmillan, 1910) |
| *HLS* | Clara Watts-Dunton, *The Home Life of Swinburne* (London: Philpot, 1922) |
| JM | John Morley (1838–1923), editor of *FR* (1867–82) |
| *JWMS* | *Journal of the William Morris Society* |
| *LACS* | Edmund Gosse, *The Life of Algernon Charles Swinburne* (New York: Macmillan, 1917) |
| Lemprière | J. Lemprière, *Classical Dictionary Containing a Full Account of All the Proper Names Mentioned in Ancient Authors,* 4th edn, corrected (London: Cadell and Davies, 1801) |
| *Library* | *The Catalogue of the Library of Algernon Charles Swinburne* sold 19–21 June 1916 at Sotherby's, London |
| *LS* | Edmund Gosse, *The Life of Swinburne with a Letter on Swinburne at Eton by Lord Redesdale* (London: Chiswick, 1912) |
| *LWB* | Alexander Gilchrist [with Anne Gilchrist, W.J. Linton, DGR, and WMR], *Life of William Blake, 'Pictor Ignotus'*, 2 vols (London: Macmillan, 1863) |
| Malory | *Le Morte Darthur: Sir Thomas Malory's Book of King Arthur and of his Noble Knights of the Round Table*, the text of Caxton ed. Sir Edward Strachey (London: Macmillan, 1897) |
| Maxwell | *Swinburne*, Everyman's Poetry Library Series, ed. Catherine Maxwell (London: Everyman, 1997) |

*Meleager* *Euripides, Fragments: Aegeus–Meleager*, ed. and trans. Christopher Collard and Martin Cropp, Loeb Classical Library 504 (Cambridge, MA: Harvard University Press, 2008)

*Miscellanies* *Miscellanies* (London: Chatto & Windus, 1886)

*MLR* *Modern Language Review*

*MP* *The Morning Post*

*MS* *The Morning Star*

*MPSP* *Algernon Charles Swinburne: Major Poems and Selected Prose*, ed. Jerome McGann and Charles L. Sligh (New Haven: Yale University Press, 2004)

*MHOP* *A Midsummer Holiday and Other Poems* (London: Chatto & Windus, 1884)

*NACS* *The Novels of A.C. Swinburne* with an Introduction by Edmund Wilson (New York: Farrar, Straus, and Cudahy, 1962)

*NC* *The Nineteenth Century*

*NER* *Note of an English Republican on the Muscovite Crusade* (London: Chatto & Windus, 1876)

Nott *The Poems of Caius Valerius Catullus, in English Verse*, trans. John Nott (London: Johnson, 1795)

*NPR* *Notes on Poems and Reviews* (London: Hotten, 1866)

*N&Q* *Notes & Queries*

*NWS* *New Writings by Swinburne*, ed. Cecil Y. Lang (New York: Syracuse University Press, 1964)

*OED* *Oxford English Dictionary*, <http://www.oed.com>

*ODNB* *Oxford Dictionary of National Biography*, <http://www.oxforddnb.com>

*PMG* *Pall Mall Gazette*

*PMLA* *Publications of the Modern Language Association of America* (journal)

p.p. privately printed

*PP* *Posthumous Poems by Algernon Charles Swinburne*, ed. Edmund Gosse and Thomas James Wise (London: Heinemann, 1917)

*RES* *Review of English Studies*

*SBS* *Songs Before Sunrise* (London: Ellis, 1871)

*Selections* *Selections from the Poetical Works of Algernon Charles Swinburne* [ed. TWD] (London: Chatto & Windus, 1887)

*SEML* Harold Nicolson, *Swinburne*, English Men of Letters (London: Macmillan, 1926)

*SL* *The Swinburne Letters*, ed. Cecil Y. Lang, 6 volumes (New Haven: Yale University Press, 1959–62)

*SLWMR* *Selected Letters of William Michael Rossetti*, ed. Roger W. Peattie (University Park, PA: Pennsylvania State University Press, 1990)

*SM* Supplementary Material to the *Uncollected Letters of Algernon Charles Swinburne* accessed at <http://swinburnearchive.indiana.edu/>

*SPP* Philip Henderson, *Swinburne: The Portrait of a Poet* (London: Routledge & Kegan Paul, 1974)

| | |
|---|---|
| *SR* | *Swinburne Replies: 'Notes on Poems and Reviews', 'Under the Microscope', 'Dedicatory Epistle'*, ed. Clyde Kenneth Hyder (New York: Syracuse University Press, 1966) |
| *SRev* | *Saturday Review* |
| *SS* | *Songs of the Springtides* (London: Chatto & Windus, 1880) |
| *STN* | *Songs of Two Nations* (London: Chatto & Windus, 1875) |
| *SVH* | *A Study of Victor Hugo* (London: Chatto & Windus, 1886) |
| *SW* | T.S. Eliot, *The Sacred Wood: Essays on Poetry and Criticism* (London: Faber, 1960) |
| *TL* | *Tristram of Lyonesse* in *TLOP* |
| *TLOP* | *Tristram of Lyonesse and Other Poems* (London: Chatto & Windus, 1882) |
| TWD | Walter Theodore Watts, from 1896 Watts-Dunton (1832–1914), always referred to here by his hyphenated name |
| *UL* | *Uncollected Letters of Algernon Charles Swinburne*, ed. Terry L. Myers, 3 vols (London: Pickering & Chatto, 2005) |
| *UTM* | *Under the Microscope* (1872) in *SR* |
| *VLC* | *Victorian Literature and Culture* |
| *VP* | *Victorian Poetry* |
| *VS* | *Victorian Studies* |
| Wharton | Henry Thornton Wharton, *Sappho: Memoir, Text, Selected Renderings and a Literal Translation*, 2nd edn (London: Stott, 1887) |
| WM | William Morris (1834–96) |
| WMs | Western Manuscripts |
| *WMP* | Rikky Rooksby and Nicholas Shrimpton, eds, *The Whole Music of Passion: New Essays on Swinburne* (Aldershot: Scolar, 1993) |
| WMR | William Michael Rossetti (1829–1919) |

# 'ODE TO MAZZINI'

I

A voice comes from the far unsleeping years,
An echo from the rayless verge of time,
Harsh, laden with the weight of kingly crime,
Whose soul is stained with blood and bloodlike tears;
And hearts made hard and blind with endless pain,
And eyes too dim to bear
The light of the free air,
And hands no longer restless in the wonted chain,
And valiant lives worn out
By silence and the doubt
That comes with hope found weaponless and vain;
All these cry out to thee,
As thou to Liberty,
All, looking up to thee, take heart and life again.

II

Too long the world has waited. Year on year
Has died in voiceless fear
Since tyranny began the silent ill,
And Slaughter satiates yet her ravenous will.
Surely the time is near—
The dawn grows wide and clear;
And fiercer beams than pave the steps of day
Pierce all the brightening air,
And in some nightly lair
The keen white lightning hungers for his prey,
Against his chain the growing thunder yearns,
With hot swift pulses all the silence burns,
And the earth hears, and maddens with delay.

III

Dost thou not hear thro' the hushed heart of night,
The voices wailing for thy help, thy sight,

The souls that call their lord?
'We want the voice, the sword,
We want the hand to strike, the love to share
The weight we cannot bear;
The soul to point our way, the heart to do and dare.
We want the unblinded eye,
The spirit pure and high,
And consecrated by enduring care:
For now we dare not meet
The memories of the past;
They wound us with their glories bright and fleet,
The fame that would not last,
The hopes that were too sweet;
A voice of lamentation
Shakes the high places of the thronèd nation,
The crownless nation sitting wan and bare
Upon the royal seat.'

IV

Too long the world has waited. Day by day
The noiseless feet of murder pass and stain
Palace and prison, street and loveliest plain,
And the slow life of freedom bleeds away.
Still bleached in sun and rain,
Lie the forgotten slain
On bleak slopes of the dismal mountain-range.
Still the wide eagle-wings°
Brood o'er the sleep of kings,
Whose purples shake not in the wind of change.
Still our lost land is beautiful in vain,
Where priests and kings defile with blood and lies
The glory of the inviolable skies;
Still from that loathsome lair
Where crawls the sickening air,
Heavy with poison, stagnant as despair,
Where soul and body moulder in one chain
Of inward-living pain:
From wasted lives, and hopes proved unavailing;
In utterance harsh and strange,
With many a fitful change,
In laughter and in tears,

In triumph and in fears,
The voice of earth goes heavenward for revenge:
And all the children of her dying years
Fill up the unbroken strain
From priestly tongues that scathe with lies and railing°
The Bourbons' murderous dotard,° sick of blood,
To the 'How long?' of stricken spirits, wailing
Before the throne of God.

V

Austria! The voice is deepening in thine ears
And art thou still asleep,
Drunken with blood and tears?
A murderer's rest should hardly be so deep
Till comes the calm unbroken by the years,
And those, whose life crawls on thro' dying shame,
A thing made up of lies and fears, more vile
That aught that lives and bears a hateful name
—For the crowned serpent, skilled in many a wile,
Charmed with the venomous honey of its guile
The guards until they slept,
And only fawned and crept
Till Fortune gave it leave to sting and smile!
Have not the winds of Heaven and the free waves
A voice to bear the curses of thy slaves
And the loud hatred of the world? O thou
Upon whose shameless brow
The crown is as a brand,
The sceptre trembles in thy trothless hand,
Shrinks not thy soul before the shame it braves,
The gathered anger of a patient land,
The loathing scorn that hardly bears to name thee?
By all the lies that cannot shame thee,
By all the memories thou must bear
In hushed unspeakable despair;
By the Past that follows thee,
By the Future that shall be
We curse thee by the freedom living still,
We curse thee by the hopes thou canst not kill,
We curse thee in the name of the wronged earth
That gave thy treasons birth!

## VI

Out of a court alive with creeping things
 A stench has risen to thicken and pollute
The inviolate air of heaven that clad of yore
Our Italy with light, because these Kings
Gather like wasps about the tainted fruit,
And eat their venomous way into its core
And soil with hateful hands its golden hue;
 Till on the dead branch clings
A festering horror blown with poison-dew;
Then laugh 'So Freedom loses her last name
And Italy is shamèd with our shame!'
  For blindness holds them still
  And lust of craving will:
A mist is on their souls who cannot see
 The ominous light, nor hear the fateful sounds;
Who know not of the freedom that shall be,
 And was, ere Austria loosed her wingèd hounds—
These double beak'd and bloody-plumaged things,
Whose shadow is the hiding-place of kings.

## VII

Behold, even they whose shade is black around,
 Whose names make dumb the nations in their hate,
  Tremble to other tyrants; Naples[o] bows
Aghast, and Austria cowers like a scourged hound[o]
 Before the priestly hunters: 'tis their fate,
  Whose fear is as a brand-mark on men's brows,
Themselves to shrink beneath a fiercer dread;
  The might of ancient error
 Round royal spirits folds its shroud of terror,
And at a name the imperial soul is dead.
 Rome! as from thee the primal curse came forth
  So comes the retribution:
 As the flushed murderers of the ravening north
  Crouch for thine absolution.
 Exalt thyself, that love or fear of thee
 Hath shamed thine Austrian bondsmen, and their shame
Avenges the vext spirits of the free,
 Repays the trustless lips, the bloody hands,
 And all the sin that makes the Austrian name

A by-word among liars—fit to lie[o]
Thy herald, Rome, among the wasted lands!

## VIII

For wheresoe'er thou lookest death is there
And a slow curse that stains the sacred air:
Such as must hound Italia till she learn
Whereon to lean the weight of reverent trust;
Learn to see God within her, and not bare
Her glories to the ravenous eyes of lust;
Vain of this honour that proclaims her fair.
Such insolence of listless pride must earn
The scourge of Austria—till mischance in turn
Defile her eagles with fresh blood and dust.
For tho' the faint heart burn
In silence: yet a sullen flame is there
Which yet may leap into the sunless air
And gather in the embrace of its wide wings
The shining spoil of kings.

## IX

But now the curse lies heavy. Where art thou,
Our Italy, among all these laid low?
Too powerless or too desperate to speak—
Thou, robed in purple for a priestly show,
Thou, buffeted and stricken, blind and weak!
Doth not remembrance light thine utter woe?
Thine eyes beyond this Calvary look, altho'
Brute-handed Austria smite thee on the cheek
And her thorns pierce thy forehead, white and meek;
In lurid mist half-strangled sunbeams pine,
Yet purer than the flame of tainted altars;
And tho' thy weak hope falters,
It clings not to the desecrated shrine.
Tho' thy blank eyes look wanly thro' dull tears,
And thy weak soul is heavy with blind fears,
Yet art thou greater than thy sorrow is,
Yet is thy spirit nobler than of yore,
Knowing the keys thy reverence used to kiss
Were forged for emperors to bow down before,
Not for free men to worship: So that Faith,

Blind portress of the gate that opens death,
  Shall never prate of Freedom any more;
For on a priest's tongue such a word is strange,
  And when they laud who did but now revile,
  Shall we believe? Rome's lying lips defile
The graves of heroes, giving us in change
  Enough of Saints and Bourbons. Dare ye now
Receive her who speaks pleasant words and bland
And stretches out the blessing of her hand
  While the pure blood of freemen stains her brow?
O dream not of such reconcilement! Be
  At least in spirit free
When the great sunrise floods your glorious land.

## X

For yet the dawn is lingering white and far,
  And dim its guiding star;
There is a sorrow in the speechless air,
And in the sunlight a dull painful glare;
  The winds that fold around
  Her° soft enchanted ground
Their wings of music, sadden into song:
  The holy stars await
  Some dawn of glimmering fate
In silence—but the time of pain is long,
  But here no comfort stills
This sorrow that o'erclouds the purple hills.

## XI

The sun is bright, and fair the foamless sea;
The winds are loud with light and liberty:
  But when shall these be free?
These hearts that beat thro' stifled pain, these eyes
Strained thro' dim prison air toward the free skies:
  When shall their light arise?

## XII

  Thou! whose best name on earth
  Is love—whose fairest birth
The freedom of the fair world thou hast made;

Whose light in heaven is life,
Whose rest above our strife—
Whose bright sky overvaults earth's barren shade;
Who hearest all ere this weak prayer can rise—
Before whose viewless eyes
Unrolled and far the starry future lies;
Behold what men have done,
What is beneath thy sun—
What stains the sceptred hand sin lifts to thee
In prayer-like mockery;
What binds the heart Thou madest to be free.
Since we are blind, give light—
Since we are feeble, smite—
How long shall man be scornful in thy sight,
'Fear not—He cares not, or He does not see'?

## XIII

We keep our trust tho' all things fail us—
Tho' Time nor baffled Hope avail us,
We keep our faith—God liveth and is love.
Not one groan rises there
Tho' choked in dungeon air
But He has heard it, though no thunders move—
And though no help is here,
No royal oath, no Austrian lie,
But echoes in the listening sky;
We know not, yet perchance His wide reply is near.
Ah, let no sloth delay
No discord mar its way,
Keep wide the entrance for that Hope divine;
Truth never wanted swords,
Since with his swordlike words
Savonarola° smote the Florentine.
Even here she is not weaponless, but waits
Silent at the palace gates,
Her wide eyes kindling eastward to the far sunshine.
When out of Naples came a tortured voice:
Whereat the whole earth shuddered, and forbade
The murderous smile on lying lips to fade,
The murderous heart in silence to rejoice;
She also smiled—no royal smile—as knowing
Some stains of sloth washed by the blood then flowing;

Their lives went out in darkness, not in vain;
Earth cannot hear, and sink to bloodless rest again.
And if indeed her waking strength shall prove
Worthy the dreams that passing lit her sleep,
Who then shall lift such eyes of triumph, who
Respond with echoes of a louder love
Than Cromwell's England?° Let fresh praise renew
The wan brow's wither'd laurels with its dew,
And one triumphal peace the crownèd earth shall keep.

## XIV

As one who dreaming on some cloud-white peak
Hears the loud wind sail past him far and free
And the faint music of the misty sea,
Listening till all his life reels blind and weak;
So discrownèd Italy,
With the world's hope in her hands
Ever yearning to get free,
Silent between the past and future stands.
Dim grows the past, and dull,
All that was beautiful,
As scattered stars drawn down the moonless night:
And the blind eyes of Scorn
Are smitten by strange morn,
And many-throned treason wastes before its might:
And every sunless cave
And time-forgotten grave,
Is pierced with one intolerable light;
Not one can falsehood save
Of all the crowns she gave,
But the dead years renew their old delight,
The worshipped evil wanes
Thro' all its godless fanes
And falters from its long imperial height,
As the last altar flame
Dies with a glorious nation's dying shame.

## XV

And when that final triumph-time shall be
Whose memory shall be kept

First of the souls that slept
In death ere light was on their Italy?
Or which of men more dear than thee
To equal-thoughted liberty,
Whom here on earth such reverence greets.
Such love from Heaven's free spirit meets°
As few dare win among the free!
Such honour ever follows thee
In peril, banishment, and blame.
And all the loud blind world calls shame,
Lives, and shall live, thy glorious name
Tho' death, that scorns the robèd slave,
Embrace thee, and a chainless grave.
While thou livest, there is one
Free in soul beneath the sun:
And thine outlaboured heart shall be
In death more honoured—not more free.

## XVI

And men despond around thee; and thy name
The tyrant smiles at, and his priests look pale;
And weariness of empty-throated fame,
And men who live and fear all things but shame,
Comes on thee, and the weight of aimless years
Whose light is dim with tears
And hope dies out, like a forgotten tale.
O brother, crownèd among men—O chief
In glory as in grief
O throned by sorrow over time and fate
And the blind strength of hate!
From soul to answering soul
The thunder-echoes roll,
And truth grows out of suffering still and great.
To have done well is victory,—to be true
Is truest guerdon, tho' blind hands undo
The work begun too late.
God gives to each man power by toil to earn
An undishonoured grave:
The praise that lives on every name in turn
He leaves the laurell'd slave.
We die, but freedom dies not like the power

That changes with the many-sided hour.
Though trampled under the brute hoofs of crime,
    She sees thro' tears and blood,
Above the stars and in the night of time,
    The sleepless watch of God;
Past fear and pain and errors wide and strange
The veiled years leading wingless-footed Change;
    Endure, and they shall give
Truth and the law whereby men work and live.

## XVII

From Ischia° to the loneliest Apennine
    Time's° awful voice is blown;
    And from her clouded throne
Freedom looks out and knows herself divine.
    From walls that keep in shame
    Poerio's martyr-name,
From wild rocks foul with children's blood, it rings;
    Their murderers gaze aghast
    Through all the hideous past,
And fate is heavy on the souls of kings.
    No more their hateful sway
    Pollutes the equal day,
Nor stricken truth pales under its wide wings,
Even when the awakened people speaks in wrath,
  Wrong shall not answer wrong in blinding patience;
The bloody slime upon that royal path
  Makes slippery standing for the feet of nations.
Our freedom's bridal robe no wrong shall stain
  No lie shall taint her speech;
But equal knowledge shall be born of pain,
  And wisdom shaping each.
True leaders shall be with us, nobler laws
Shall guide us calmly to the final Cause:
  And thou, earth's crownless queen,
  No more shalt wail unseen,
But front the weary ages without pain:
  Time shall bring back for thee
  The hopes that lead the free,
And thy name fill the charmèd world again.
  The shame that stains thy brow

Shall not for ever mark thee to fresh fears:
For in the far light of the buried years
Shines the undarkened future that shall be
A dawn o'er sunless ages.° Hearest thou,
Italia? though deaf sloth hath sealed thine ears,
The world has heard thy children—and God hears.

# OF THE BIRTH OF SIR TRISTRAM, AND HOW HE VOYAGED INTO IRELAND (*QUEEN YSEULT*)

## Canto 1

### Of the birth of Sir Tristram, and how he voyaged into Ireland

In the noble days were shown
Deeds of good knights many one,
Many worthy wars were done.

It was time of scath and scorn
When at breaking of the morn
Tristram the good knight was born.

He was fair and well to see
As his mother's child might be:
Many happy wars had he;

Slew Moronde the knight alone,
Whence was all the ill begun
That on Blancheflour was done.

For long since Queen Blancheflour
Took a knight to paramour,
Who had served her well of yore.

And across the waters dim
And by many a river's rim
Went Queen Blancheflour with him.

Many a bitter path she went,
Many a stone her feet had rent,
But her heart was well content.

'Lo!' she said, 'I lady free
Took this man for lord of me
Where the crowned saints might see.

'And I will not bid him go,
Not for joyance nor for woe,
Till my very love he know.'

When he kissed her as they went,
All her heart was well content,
For the love that she him meant.

Now this knight was called Roland,
And he had within his hand
Ermonie° the happy land.

So five months in Ermonie
Dwelt they in their pleasure free;
For they knew not what should be.

Then came Moronde with his men,
Warring with her lord again.
All her heart was bitter then.

But she said: 'If this be so,
Tho' I die, he shall not know.'
And she kissed and bade him go;

And he wept and went from her.
Then was all the land astir
With a trouble in the air.

When Roland the knight was gone,
Praise of men his warriors won
Warring well before the sun.

But Moronde the evil knight
Smote him falsely in the fight,
Slew him basely out of sight.

Then was weeping long and sore:
For the great love they him bore
All men wept but Blancheflour.

But she took her golden ring
And a fair sword of the king
Wrought with many a carven thing.

With no crown about her head,
Thinking wild thoughts of the dead,
Evermore she fled and fled.

Far within the forest fair,
A great anguish came on her
Till a strong manchild she bare.

And she fain had suckled him,
There beneath the lindens dim,
Round a fountain's weedy brim.

But too soon came death to take
All her beauty for his sake;
And ere death she moaned and spake.

'Ah, fair child,' the lady said,
'For this anguish that it had
All thy mother's heart is dead.

'Sweet, I would not live to see
Any sorrow rest on thee,
Better thou hadst died with me.

'Only thou art still too fair
For that smile I cannot bear
In such eyes as Roland's were.

'Now, fair child, mine own wert thou
(And she kissed the small soft brow)
But for death that takes me now.

'And a bitter birth is thine;
But no man can stain thy line
With a shame that was not mine.

'Thou art pure and princely born;
Fairer name was never worn,
Past the touch of any scorn.

'Now thy grief has come on me,
As I prayed that it might be
Lest some woe should rest on thee.'

Wept the low voice musical;
'Now that mine has given thee all,
Better love thy love befall.

'Purer prayers be round thy sleep,
Truer tears than these that drip
On thy tender cheek and lip.

'Now, dear child, of all on earth
Thou art yet the fairest birth
For the pain thy life was worth.

'Sweetest name and sweetest heart,
Now I see thee as thou art
I have had the better part.

'For the grief my love has had,
May the sweet saints keep thee glad
Tho' thy birth were strange and sad.

'Now, dear child' (her thin voice strove
Thro' the drawn dry sobs to move),
'Leave I thee to Christ's own love.'

So she died in that dark place,
With the anguish in her face;
Mary took her into grace.

On the robe was sown her name,
Where a fine thread white as flame
Thro' the coloured samite came.

For on skirt and hem between
Wrought she letters white and green
'This is Blancheflour the Queen.'

There men found her as they sped,
Very beautiful and dead,
In the lilies white and red.

And beside her lying there,
Found a manchild strong and fair
Lain among the lilies bare.

And they thought it were ill fate,
If the child, for fear or hate,
They should leave in evil state.

So they took him lying there,
Playing with the lady's hair,
For his face was very fair.

And so tenderly he played,
Half asmile and half afraid,
With her lips and hair, I said,

That the strong men for his sake
Could have wept for dear heartache
At the murmurs he did make.

And the strongest lightly stept
Forth to where the mother slept;
Stooping over her, he wept.

Lightly bowed above the child
The large face whose might was mild
With black-bearded lips that smiled.

Then he took it of his grace,
Bowed him where she lay in place,
Put to hers the little face.

Then they softly buried her
Where the greenest leaves did stir,
With some white flowers in her hair.

And for the sweet look he had,
Weeping not but very sad,
Tristram by his name they bade.

'For he looks upon her so,
Pity where he should not grow
All the piteous thing to know.'

And they took the sword and ring
That were of Roland the king,
Wrought with many a carven thing.

So they bred him as they knew;
And a noble child he grew,
Like a tree in sun and dew.

Ere he was ten summers old
All the sorrow they him told,
Showed the sword and ring of gold.

Kissed the boy both sword and ring;
'As my father was a king,
I will wreak this bitter thing.'

Kissed the boy both ring and sword;
'As my mother to her lord,
Fast I cling to this my word.'

So he grew in might and grace,
With her look about his face:
All men saw his royal race.

But when twenty years were done
At the rising of the sun
Tristram from his place was gone.

Forth with warriors is he bound
Over many a change of ground,
To have wreak of Sir Moronde.

When he came to Ermonie,
Bare upon the earth bowed he,
Kissed the earth with kisses three.

To the city men him bring,
Where the herald stood to sing
'Largesse of Moronde the king!'

To the king came Tristram then,
To Moronde the evil man,
Treading softly as he can.

Spake he loftily in place:
A great light was on his face:
'Listen, king, of thy free grace.

'I am Tristram, Roland's son;
By thy might my lands were won,
All my lovers were undone.

'Died by thee Queen Blancheflour,
Mother mine in bitter hour,
That was white as any flower.

'Tho' they died not well aright,
Yet, for thou art belted knight,
King Moronde, I bid thee fight.'

A great laughter laughed they all,
Drinking wine about the hall,
Standing by the outer wall.

But the pale king leapt apace,
Caught his staff that lay in place
And smote Tristram on the face.

Tristram stood back paces two,
All his face was reddened so
Round the deep mark of the blow.

Large and bright the king's eyes grew:
As knight Roland's sword he drew,
Fiercely like a pard he flew.

And above the staring eyes
Smote Moronde the king flatwise,
That men saw the dear blood rise.

At the second time he smote,
All the carven blade, I wot,
With the blood was blurred and hot.

At the third stroke that he gave,
Deep the carven steel he drave,
Thro' King Moronde's heart it clave.

Well I ween his wound was great
As he sank across the seat,
Slain for Blancheflour the sweet.

Then spake Tristram, praising God;
In his father's place he stood
Wiping clean the smears of blood,

That the sword, while he did pray,
At the throne's foot he might lay;
Christ save all good knights, I say.

Then spake all men in his praise,
Speaking words of the old days,
Sweeter words than sweetest lays.

Said one, 'Lo the dead queen's hair
And her brows so straight and fair;
So the lips of Roland were.'

For all praised him as he stood,
That such things none other could
Than the son of kingly blood.

Round he looked with quiet eyes;
'When ye saw King Moronde rise,
None beheld me on this wise.'

At such words as he did say,
Bare an old man knelt to pray;
'Christ be with us all to-day.

'This is Tristram the good lord;
Knightly hath he held his word,
Warring with his father's sword.'

Then one brought the diadem,
Clear and golden like pure flame;
And his thanks did grace to them.

Next in courteous wise he bade
That fair honour should be had
Of the dear queen that was dead.

So in her great sorrow's praise
A fair tomb he bade them raise
For a wonder to the days.

And between its roof and floor
Wrote he two words and no more,
Wrote *Roland* and *Blancheflour*.

That was carven sharp in gold,
For a great praise to behold,
Where the queen lay straight and cold,

All was graven deep and fine,
In and out, and line with line,
That all men might see it shine.

So far off it sprang and shone,
Ere ten paces one had gone,
Showing all the sorrow done.

And the pillars, that upbore
The large roof for evermore,
In wrought flowers her sweet name wore:

Points of stone carved gently all,
Wrought in cusp and capital,
Climbing still to creep and fall.

And in many a tender nook,
Traced soft as running brook,
Shone her face's quiet look.

And above they wrought to lie
King Roland all white on high,
With the lady carven by.

Very patient was her face,
Stooping from its maiden place
Into strange new mother-grace.

Parted lips and closing eyes,
All the quiet of the skies
Fills her beauty where she lies.

On her hair the forest crown
Lets the sliding tresses down,
Touched ere dark with golden brown;

Both with carven hands uplift,
Praying softly as at shrift,
So it stood a kingly gift.

And when all was graven fair
Tristram came, and standing there
Kissed his mother's tender hair.

Then he bade them take for King
His true father in each thing,
Him who saved the sword and ring.

So they hearkened to his word,
And they took to be their lord
Him who kept the ring and sword.

Then by many painful ways,
With a noble thought in chase,
Tristram journeyed many days.

Towards the Cornwall king he bore,
Since an oath of love he swore
For the name of Blancheflour,

That King Mark, her brother true,
He would honour as he knew;
This was he I tell to you.

When he stood in Cornwall there,
Mark beheld him standing bare,
And he knew his sister's hair.

All these things to Mark he told,
To the king so lean and cold,
And he showed her ring of gold.

Then wept all the valiant men,
Wept King Mark upon him then,
Thinking what a grief had been.

Then was Tristram belted knight,
For his happy hand in fight.
Then spake Mark in all men's sight:

'For the love my sister won,
I will honour as I can
This her son, the loved man.

'And this praise I give him here:
He shall go to bring anear
My new bride with noble cheer.

'For strange things are said in place
Of the wonder of her face
And her tender woman's grace.'

Spake the king so lean and cold:
'She hath name of honour old,
Yseult queen, the hair of gold.

'All her limbs are fair and strong,
And her face is straight and long,
And her talk is as a song.

'And faint lines of colour stripe
(As spilt wine that one should wipe)
All her golden hair corn-ripe;

'Drawn like red gold ears that stand
In the yellow summer land;
Arrow-straight her perfect hand,

'And her eyes like river-lakes
Where a gloomy glory shakes
Which the happy sunset makes.

'Her shall Tristram go to bring,
With a gift of some rich thing
Fit to free a prisoned king.'

As Sir Mark said, it was done;
And ere set the morrow's sun,
Tristram the good knight was gone.

Forth to Ireland bade he come,
Forth across the grey sea-foam,
All to bring Queen Yseult home.

# TO THE EDITOR OF *THE SPECTATOR*, 7 JUNE 1862 (pp. 632–3)

Sir,—I cannot resist asking the favour of admission for my protest against the article on Mr Meredith's last volume of poems in the *Spectator* of May 24th. That I personally have for the writings, whether verse or prose of Mr Meredith, a most sincere and deep admiration is no doubt a matter of infinitely small moment. I wish only, in default of a better, to appeal seriously on general grounds against this sort of criticism as applied to one of the leaders of English literature. To any fair attack Mr Meredith's books of course lie as much open as another man's; indeed, standing where he does, the very eminence of his post makes him perhaps more liable than a man of less well-earned fame to the periodical slings and arrows[o] of publicity. Against such criticism no one would have a right to appeal, whether for his own work or for another's. But the writer of the article in question blinks at stating the fact that he is dealing with no unfledged pretender. Any work of a man who has won his spurs and fought his way to a foremost place among the men of his time, must claim at least a grave consideration of respect. It would hardly be less absurd, in remarking on a poem by Mr Meredith, to omit all reference to his previous work, and treat the present book as if its author had never tried his hand at such writing before, than to criticise the *Légende des Siècles*, or (coming to a nearer instance) the *Idyls of the King*,[o] without taking into account the relative position of the great English or the greater French poet. On such a tone of criticism as this any one who may chance to see or hear of it has a right to comment.

But even if the case were different, and the author were now at his starting-point, such a review of such a book is surely out of date. Praise or blame should be thoughtful, serious, careful, when applied to a work of such subtle strength, such depth of delicate power, such passionate and various beauty, as the leading poem of Mr Meredith's volume: in some points, as it seems to me (and in this opinion I know that I have weightier judgments than my own to back me) a poem above the aim and beyond the reach of any but its author. Mr Meredith is one of the three or four poets now alive whose work, perfect or imperfect, is always as noble in design, as it is often faultless in result. The present critic falls foul of him for dealing with 'a deep and painful subject on which he has no conviction to express.'[o] There are pulpits enough for all preachers in prose; the business of verse-writing is hardly to express convictions; and if some poetry, not without merit of its kind, has at times dealt in dogmatic morality, it is all the worse and all the weaker for that. As to subject, it is too much to expect that all schools of poetry are to be for ever subordinate to the one just now so much in request with us, whose scope of sight is bounded by the nursery walls; that all Muses are to bow down before her who babbles, with lips yet warm from their pristine pap, after the dangling delights of a child's coral; and jingles with flaccid fingers one knows not whether a jester or a baby's bells. We have not too many writers capable of duly handling a subject worth the serious interest of men. As to execution, take almost any sonnet at random out of this series, and let any man qualified to judge for himself of metre, choice of expression, and splendid language, decide on its claims. And, after all, the test will be unfair, except as regards metrical or pictorial merit; every section of this great progressive poem being connected with the other by links of the finest and most studied workmanship. Take, for example, that noble sonnet, beginning

> 'We saw the swallows gathering in the skies,'°

a more perfect piece of writing no man alive has ever turned out; witness these three lines, the grandest perhaps in all the book:

> 'And in the largeness of the evening earth,
> Our spirit grew as we walked side by side;
> *The hour became her husband, and my bride;*'°

but in transcription it must lose the colour and effect given it by its place in the series; the grave and tender beauty, which makes it at once a bridge and a resting-place between the admirable poems of passion it falls among. As specimens of pure power, and depth of imagination at once intricate and vigorous, take the two sonnets on a false passing reunion of wife and husband; the sonnet on the rose;° that other beginning:

> 'I am not of those miserable males
> Who snip at vice, and daring not to snap
> Do therefore hope for Heaven.'°

And, again, that earlier one:

> 'All other joys of life he strove to warm.'°

Of the shorter poems which give character to the book I have not space to speak here; and as the critic has omitted noticing the most valuable and important (such as the 'Beggar's Soliloquy,' and the 'Old Chartist,' equal to Béranger° for completeness of effect and exquisite justice of style, but noticeable for a thorough dramatic insight, which Béranger missed through his personal passions and partialities), there is no present need to go into the matter. I ask you to admit this protest simply out of justice to the book in hand, believing as I do that it expresses the deliberate unbiased opinion of a sufficient number of readers to warrant the insertion of it, and leaving to your consideration rather their claims to a fair hearing than those of the book's author to a revised judgment. A poet of Mr Meredith's rank can no more be profited by the advocacy of his admirers than injured by the rash or partial attack of his critics.

A.C. Swinburne

# ‘CHARLES BAUDELAIRE: *LES FLEURS DU MAL*’, *THE SPECTATOR*, 1784 (6 SEPTEMBER 1862), pp. 998–1000

---

It is now some time since France has turned out any new poet of very high note or importance; the graceful, slight, somewhat thin-spun classical work of M. Théodore de Banville hardly carries weight enough to tell across the Channel; indeed, the best of this writer’s books, in spite of exquisite humorous character and a most flexible and brilliant style, is too thoroughly Parisian to bear transplanting at all. French poetry of the present date, taken at its highest, is not less effectually hampered by tradition and the taste of the greater number of readers than our own is. A French poet is expected to believe in philanthropy, and break off on occasion in the middle of his proper work to lend a shove forward to some theory of progress. The critical students there, as well as here, judging by the books they praise and the advice they proffer, seem to have pretty well forgotten that a poet’s business is presumably to write good verses, and by no means to redeem the age and remould society. No other form of art is so pestered with this impotent appetite for meddling in quite extraneous matters; but the mass of readers seem actually to think that a poem is the better for containing a moral lesson or assisting in a tangible and material good work. The courage and sense of a man who at such a time ventures to profess and act on the conviction that the art of poetry has absolutely nothing to do with didactic matter at all, are proof enough of the wise and serious manner in which he is likely to handle the materials of his art. From a critic who has put forward the just and sane view of this matter with a consistent eloquence, one may well expect to get as perfect and careful poetry as he can give.

To some English readers the name of M. Baudelaire may be known rather through his admirable translations, and the criticisms on American and English writers appended to these, and framing them in fit and sufficient commentary, than by his volume of poems, which, perhaps, has hardly yet had time to make its way among us. That it will in the long run fail of its meed of admiration, whether here or in France, we do not believe. Impeded at starting by a foolish and shameless prosecution, the first edition was, it appears, withdrawn before anything like a fair hearing had been obtained for it. The book now comes before us with a few of the original poems cancelled, but with important additions. Such as it now is, to sum up the merit and meaning of it is not easy to do in a few sentences. Like all good books, and all work of any original savour and strength, it will be long a debated point of argument, vehemently impugned and eagerly upheld.

We believe that M. Baudelaire's first publications were his essays on the contemporary art of France,° written now many years since. In these early writings there is already such admirable judgment, vigour of thought and style, and appreciative devotion to the subject, that the worth of his own future work in art might have been foretold even then. He has more delicate power of verse than almost any man living, after Victor Hugo, Browning, and (in his lyrics) Tennyson. The sound of his metres suggests colour and perfume. His perfect workmanship makes every subject admirable and respectable. Throughout the chief part of this book, he has chosen to dwell mainly upon sad and strange things—the weariness of pain and the bitterness of pleasure—the perverse happiness and wayward sorrows of exceptional people. It has the languid, lurid beauty of close and threatening weather—a heavy heated temperature, with dangerous hothouse scents° in it; thick shadow of cloud about it, and fire of molten light. It is quite clear of all whining and windy lamentation; there is nothing of the blubbering and shrieking style long since exploded. The writer delights in problems, and has a natural leaning to obscure and sorrowful things. Failure and sorrow, next to physical beauty and perfection of sound or scent, seem to have an infinite attraction for him. In some points he resembles Keats, or still more his chosen favourite among modern poets, Edgar Poe; at times, too, his manner of thought has a relish of Marlowe, and even the sincerer side of Byron. From Théophile Gautier, to whom the book is dedicated, he has caught the habit of a faultless and studious simplicity; but, indeed, it seems merely natural to him always to use the right word and the right rhyme. How supremely musical and flexible a perfect artist in writing can make the French language, any chance page of the book is enough to prove; every description, the slightest and shortest even, has a special mark on it of the writer's keen and peculiar power. The style is sensuous and weighty; the sights seen are steeped most often in sad light and sullen colour. As instances of M. Baudelaire's strength and beauty of manner, one might take especially the poems headed *Le Masque, Parfum Exotique, La Chevelure, Les Sept Vieillards, Les Petites Vieilles, Brumes et Pluies*; of his perfect mastery in description, and sharp individual drawing of character and form, the following stray verses plucked out at random may stand for a specimen:—

'Sur ta chevelure profonde
Aux âcres parfums,
Mer odorante et vagabonde
Aux flots bleus et bruns,

Comme un navire qui s'éveille
Au vent du matin,
Mon âme réveuse appareille
Pour un ciel lointain.

Tes yeux où rien ne se révèle
De doux ni d'amer
Sont deux bijoux froids où se mèle
L'or avec le fer.

———

Et ton corps se penche et s'allonge
Comme un fin vaisseau
Qui roule bord sur bord et plonge
Ses vergues dans l'eau.'

The whole poem is worth study for its vigorous beauty and the careful facility of its expression. Perhaps, though, the sonnet headed *Causerie* is a still completer specimen of the author's power. The way in which the sound and sense are suddenly broken off and shifted, four lines from the end, is wonderful for effect and success. M. Baudelaire's mastery of the sonnet form is worth remarking as a test of his natural bias towards such forms of verse as are most nearly capable of perfection. In a book of this sort, such a leaning of the writer's mind is almost necessary. The matters treated of will bear no rough or hasty handling. Only supreme excellence of words will suffice to grapple with and fitly render the effects of such material. Not the luxuries of pleasure in their simple first form, but the sharp and cruel enjoyments of pain, the acrid relish of suffering felt or inflicted, the sides on which nature looks unnatural, go to make up the stuff and substance of this poetry. Very good material they make, too; but evidently such things are unfit for rapid or careless treatment. The main charm of the book is, upon the whole, that nothing is wrongly given, nothing capable of being re-written or improved on its own ground. Concede the starting point, and you cannot have a better runner.

Thus, even of the loathsomest bodily putrescence and decay he can make some noble use; pluck out its meaning and secret, even its beauty, in a certain way, from actual carrion; as here,° of the flies bred in a carcase.

'Tout cela descendait, montait comme une vague;
  Ou s'élançait en pétillant.
On eût dit que le corps, enflé d'un souffle vague,
  Vivait en se multipliant.

Et ce monde rendait une étrange musique,
  Comme l'eau courante et le vent,
Ou le grain qu'un vanneur d'un mouvement rhythmique
  Agite et tourne dans son van.'

Another of this poet's noblest sonnets is that *A une Passante*, comparable with a similar one of Keats, 'Time's sea hath been five years at its slow ebb,'° but superior for directness of point and forcible reality. Here for once the beauty of a poem is rather passionate than sensuous. Compare the delicate emblematic manner in which Keats winds up his sonnet to this sharp perfect finale:—

> 'Fugitive beauté
> Dont le regard m'a fait soudainement renaître,
> Ne te verrai-je plus que dans l'éternité?
> Ailleurs, bien loin d'ici, trop tard! jamais peut-être!
> Car j'ignore où tu fuis, tu ne sais où je vais,
> O toi que j'eusse aimée, ô toi qui le savais!'

There is noticeable also in M. Baudelaire's work a quality of *drawing* which recalls the exquisite power in the same way of great French artists now living. His studies are admirable for truth and grace; his figure-painting has the ease and strength, the trained skill, and beautiful gentle justice of manner, which come out in such pictures as the *Source* of Ingres,° or that other splendid study by Flandrin, of a curled-up naked figure under full soft hot light, now exhibiting here.° These verses° of Baudelaire's are as perfect and good as either.

> '[Quoique tes] sourcils méchants
> Te donnent un air étrange,
> Qui n'est pas celui d'un ange,
> Sorcière aux yeux alléchants
>
> ———
>
> 'Sur ta chair le parfum rôde
> Comme autour d'un encensoir;
> Tu charmes comme le soir,
> Nymphe ténébreuse et chaude.
>
> ———
>
> 'Le désert et la forêt
> Embaument tes tresses rudes;
> Ta tête a les attitudes
> De l'énigme et du secret.
>
> '*Tes hanches sont amoureuses*
> *De ton dos et de tes seins*,
> Et tu ravis les coussins
> Par tes poses langoureuses.'

Nothing can beat that as a piece of beautiful drawing.

It may be worth while to say something of the moral and meaning of many among these poems. Certain critics, who will insist on going into this matter, each man as deep as his small leaden plummet will reach, have discovered what they call a paganism on the spiritual side of the author's tone of thought.

Stripped of its coating of jargon, this may mean that the poet spoken of endeavours to look at most things with the eye of an old-world poet; that he aims at regaining the clear and simple view of writers content to believe in the beauty of material subjects. To us, if this were the meaning of these people, we must say it seems a foolish one; for there is not one of these poems that could have been written in a time when it was not the fashion to dig for moral motives and conscious reasons. Poe, for example, has written poems without any moral meaning at all; there is not one poem of the *Fleurs du mal* which has not a distinct and vivid background of morality to it. Only this moral side of the book is not thrust forward in the foolish and repulsive manner of a half-taught artist; the background, as we called it, is not out of drawing. If any reader could extract from any poem a positive spiritual medicine—if he could swallow a sonnet like a moral prescription—then clearly the poet supplying these intellectual drugs would be a bad artist; indeed, no real artist, but a huckster and vendor of miscellaneous wares. But those who will look for them may find moralities in plenty behind every poem of M. Baudelaire's; such poems especially as *Une Martyre*. Like a mediæval preacher, when he has drawn the heathen love, he puts sin on its right hand, and death on its left. It is not his or any artist's business to warn against evil; but certainly he does not exhort to it, knowing well enough that the one fault is as great as the other.

But into all this we do not advise any one to enter who can possibly keep out of it. When a book has been so violently debated over, so hauled this way and that by contentious critics, the one intent on finding that it means something mischievous, and the other intent on finding that it means something useful, those who are in search neither of a poisonous compound nor of a cathartic drug had better leave the disputants alone, or take only such notice of them as he absolutely must take. Allegory is the dullest game and the most profitless taskwork imaginable; but if so minded a reader might extract most elaborate meanings from this poem of *Une Martyre*; he might discover a likeness between the Muse of the writer and that strange figure of a beautiful body with the head severed, laid apart

> 'Sur la table de nuit comme une renoncule.'°

The heavy 'mass of dark mane and heap of precious jewels'° might mean the glorious style and decorative language clothing this poetry of strange disease and sin; the hideous violence wrought by a shameless and senseless love might stand as an emblem of that analysis of things monstrous and sorrowful, which stamps the whole book with its special character. Then again, the divorce between all aspiration and its results might be here once more given in type; the old question re-handled:—

> 'What hand and brain went ever paired?
> What heart alike conceived and dared?'°

and the sorrowful final divorce of will from deed accomplished at last by force; and the whole thing summed up in that noble last stanza:—

'Ton époux court le monde: et ta forme immortelle
   Veille près de lui quand il dort;
Autant que toi sans doute il te sera fidèle,
   Et constant jusques à la mort.'°

All this and more might be worked out if the reader cared to try; but we hope he would not. The poem is quite beautiful and valuable enough as merely the 'design of an unknown master.'° In the same way one might use up half the poems in the book; for instance, those three beautiful studies of cats° (fitly placed in a book that has altogether a feline style of beauty—subtle, luxurious, with sheathed claws); or such carefully tender sketches as *Le Beau Navire*; or that Latin hymn 'Franciscæ meæ:'°—

'Novis te cantabo chordis,
O novelletum quod ludis
In solitudine cordis.
Esto sertis implicata,
O fœmina delicata
Per quam solvuntur peccata!'

Some few indeed, as that *ex-voto* poem *A une Madone*,° appeal at once to the reader as to an interpreter; they are distinctly of a mystical moral turn, and in that rich symbolic manner almost unsurpassable for beauty.

'Avec mes Vers polis, treillis d'un pur métal
Savamment constellé de rimes de cristal,
Je ferai pour ta tête une énorme Couronne;
Et dans ma Jalousie, ô mortelle Madone,
Je saurai te tailler un Manteau, de façon
Barbare, roide et lourd, et doublé de soupçon,
Qui comme une guérite enfermera tes charmes;
Non de Perles brodé, mais de toutes mes Larmes!
Ta Robe, ce sera mon Désir, frémissant,
Onduleux, mon Désir qui monte et qui descend,
Aux pointes se balance, aux vallons se repose,
Et revêt d'un baiser tout ton corps blanc et rose.'

Before passing on to the last poem we wish to indicate for especial remark, we may note a few others in which this singular strength of finished writing is most evident. Such are, for instance, *Le Cygne, Le Poison, Tristesses de la Lune, Remords Postume, Le Flacon, Ciel Brouillé, Une Mendiante Rousse* (a simpler study than usual, of great beauty in all ways, noticeable for its revival of the old fashion of unmixed masculine rhymes), *Le Balcon, Allégorie, L'Amour et le Crâne*, and the two splendid sonnets marked xxvii. and xlii. We cite these headings in no sort of order, merely as they catch one's eye in revising the list of contents and recall the poems classed there. Each of them we regard as worth a separate study, but the *Litanies de Satan*, as in a way the keynote to this whole complicated tune of poems, we had set aside for the last, much as (to judge by its place in the book) the author himself seems to have done.

Here it seems as if all failure and sorrow on earth, and all the cast-out things of the world—ruined bodies and souls diseased—made their appeal, in default of help, to Him in whom all sorrow and all failure were incarnate. As a poem, it is one of the noblest lyrics ever written; the sound of it between wailing and triumph, as it were the blast blown by the trumpets of a brave army in irretrievable defeat.

'O toi qui de la Mort, ta vieille et forte amante,
Engendras l'Espérance—une folle charmante!
  O Satan, prends pitié de ma longue misère!
Toi qui fais au proscrit ce regard calme et haut
Qui damne tout un peuple autour d'un échafaud,
  O Satan, prends pitié de ma longue misère!

———

Toi qui, magiquement, assouplis les vieux os
De l'ivrogne attardé foulé par les chevaux,
  O Satan, prends pitié de ma longue misère!
Toi qui, pour consoler l'homme frêle qui souffre,
Nous appris à mêler le salpêtre et le soufre,
  O Satan, prends pitié de ma longue misère!'

These lines are not given as more finished than the rest; every verse has the vibration in it of naturally sound and pure metal. It is a study of metrical cadence throughout, of wonderful force and variety. Perhaps it may be best, without further attempts to praise or to explain the book, here to leave off, with its stately and passionate music fresh in our ears. We know that in time it must make its way; and to know when or how concerns us as little as it probably concerns the author, who can very well afford to wait without much impatience.

# 'DEAD LOVE', *ONCE-A-WEEK*, IV (OCTOBER 1862), pp. 432–4

About the time of the great troubles in France, that fell out between the parties of Armagnac and of Burgundy, there was slain in a fight in Paris a follower of the Duke John, who was a good knight called Messire Jacques d'Aspremont. This Jacques was a very fair and strong man, hardy of his hands, and before he was slain he did many things wonderful and of great courage, and forty of the folk of the other party he slew, and many of these were great captains, of whom the chief and the worthiest was Messire Olivier de Bois-Percé; but at last he was shot in the neck with an arrow, so that between the nape and the apple the flesh was cleanly cloven in twain. And when he was dead his men drew forth his body of the fierce battle, and covered it with a fair woven cloak. Then the people of Armagnac, taking good heart because of his death, fell the more heavily upon his followers, and slew very many of them. And a certain soldier, named Amaury de Jacqueville, whom they called Courtebarbe, did best of all that party; for, crying out with a great noise, 'Sus, sus!'° he brought up the men after him, and threw them forward into the hot part of the fighting, where there was a sharp clamour; and this Amaury, laughing and crying out as a man that took a great delight in such matters of war, made of himself more noise with smiting and with shouting than any ten, and they of Burgundy were astonished and beaten down. And when he was weary, and his men had got the upper hand of those of Burgundy, he left off slaying, and beheld where Messire d'Aspremont was covered up with his cloak; and he lay just across the door of Messire Olivier, whom the said Jacques had slain, who was also a cousin of Amaury's. Then said Amaury:

'Take up now the body of this dead fellow, and carry it into the house; for my cousin Madame Yolande shall have great delight to behold the face of the fellow dead by whom her husband has got his end, and it shall make the tiding sweeter to her.'

So they took up this dead knight Messire Jacques, and carried him into a fair chamber lighted with broad windows, and herein sat the wife of Olivier, who was called Yolande de Craon, and she was akin far off to Pierre de Craon, who would have slain the Constable. And Amaury said to her:

'Fair and dear cousin, and my good lady, we give you for your husband slain the body of him that slew my cousin; make the best cheer that you may, and comfort yourself that he has found a good death and a good friend to do justice on his slayer; for this man was a good knight, and I that have revenged him account myself none of the worst.'

And with this Amaury and his people took leave of her. Then Yolande, being left alone, began at first to weep grievously, and so much that she was heavy and weary; and afterward she looked upon the face of Jacques d'Aspremont, and held one of his hands with hers, and said:

'Ah, false thief and coward! it is great pity thou wert not hung on a gallows, who hast slain by treachery the most noble knight of the world, and to me the most loving and the faithfulest man alive, and that never did any discourtesy to any man, and was the most single and pure lover that ever a married lady had to be her knight, and never said any word to me but sweet words. Ah, false coward! there was never such a knight of thy kin.'

Then, considering his face earnestly, she saw that it was a fair face enough, and by seeming the face of a good knight; and she repented of her bitter words, saying with herself:

'Certainly this one, too, was a good man and valiant,' and was sorry for his death.

And she pulled out the arrow-head that was broken, and closed up the wound of his neck with ointments. And then beholding his dead open eyes, she fell into a great torrent of weeping, so that her tears fell all over his face and throat. And all the time of this bitter sorrow she thought how goodly a man this Jacques must have been in his life, who being dead had such power upon her pity. And for compassion of his great beauty she wept so exceedingly and long that she fell down upon his body in a swoon, embracing him, and so lay the space of two hours with her face against his; and being awaked she had no other desire but only to behold him again, and so all that day neither ate nor slept at all, but for the most part lay and wept. And afterward, out of her love, she caused the body of this knight to be preserved with spice, and made him a golden coffin open at the top, and clothed him with the fairest clothes she could get, and had this coffin always by her bed in her chamber. And when this was done she sat down over against him and held his arms about her neck, weeping, and she said:

'Ah, Jacques! although alive I was not worthy, so that I never saw the beauty and goodness of your living body with my sorrowful eyes, yet now being dead, I thank God that I have this grace to behold you. Alas, Jacques! you have no sight now to discern what things are beautiful, therefore you may now love me as well as another, for with dead men there is no difference of women. But, truly, although I were the fairest of all Christian women that now is, I were in nowise worthy to love you; nevertheless, have compassion upon me that for your sake have forgotten the most noble husband of the world.'

And this Yolande, that made such complaining of love to a dead man, was one of the fairest ladies of all that time, and of great reputation; and there were many good men that loved her greatly, and would fain have had some favour at her hands; of whom she made no account, saying always, that her dead lover was better than many lovers living. Then certain people said that she was bewitched; and one of these was Amaury. And they would have taken the body to burn it, that the charm might be brought to an end; for they said that a demon had entered in and taken it in possession; which she hearing fell into extreme rage, and said that if her lover were alive, there was not so good a knight among them, that he should undertake the charge of that saying; at which speech of hers there was great laughter. And upon a night there came into her house Amaury and certain others, that were minded to see this matter for themselves. And no man kept the doors; for all her people had gone away, saving only a damsel that remained with her; and the doors stood open, as in a house where there is no man. And they stood in the doorway of her chamber, and heard her say this that ensues:—

'O most fair and perfect knight, the best that ever was in any time of battle, or in any company of ladies, and the most courteous man, have pity upon me, most sorrowful woman and handmaid. For in your life you had some other lady to love you, and were to her a most true and good lover; but now you have none other but me only, and I am not worthy that you should so much as kiss me on my sad lips, wherein is all this lamentation. And though your own lady were the fairer and the more worthy, yet consider, for God's pity and mine, how she has forgotten the love of your body and the kindness of your espousals, and lives easily with some other man, and is wedded to him with all honour; but I have neither ease nor honour, and yet I am your true maiden and servant.' And then she embraced and kissed him many times. And Amaury was very wroth, but he refrained himself: and his friends were troubled and full of wonder. Then they beheld how she held his body between her arms, and kissed him in the neck with all her strength; and after a certain time it seemed to them that the body of Jacques moved and sat up; and she was no whit amazed, but rose up with him, embracing him. And Jacques said to her:

'I beseech you, now that you would make a covenant with me, to love me always.'

And she bowed her head suddenly, and said nothing.

Then said Jacques:

'Seeing you have done so much for love of me, we twain shall never go in sunder: and for this reason has God given back to me the life of my mortal body.'

And after this they had the greatest joy together, and the most perfect solace that may be imagined: and she sat and beheld him, and many times fell into a little quick laughter for her great pleasure and delight.

Then came Amaury suddenly into the chamber, and caught his sword into his hand, and said to her:

'Ah, wicked leman, now at length is come the end of thy horrible love and of thy life at once;' and smote her through the two sides with his sword, so that she fell down, and with a great sigh full unwillingly delivered up her spirit, which was no sooner fled out of her perishing body, but immediately the soul departed also out of the body of her lover, and he became as one that had been all those days dead. And the next day the people caused their two bodies to be burned openly in the place where witches were used to be burned: and it is reported by some that an evil spirit was seen to come out of the mouth of Jacques d'Aspremont, with a most pitiful cry, like the cry of a hurt beast. By which thing all men knew that the soul of this woman, for the folly of her sinful and most strange affection, was thus evidently given over to the delusion of the evil one and the pains of condemnation.

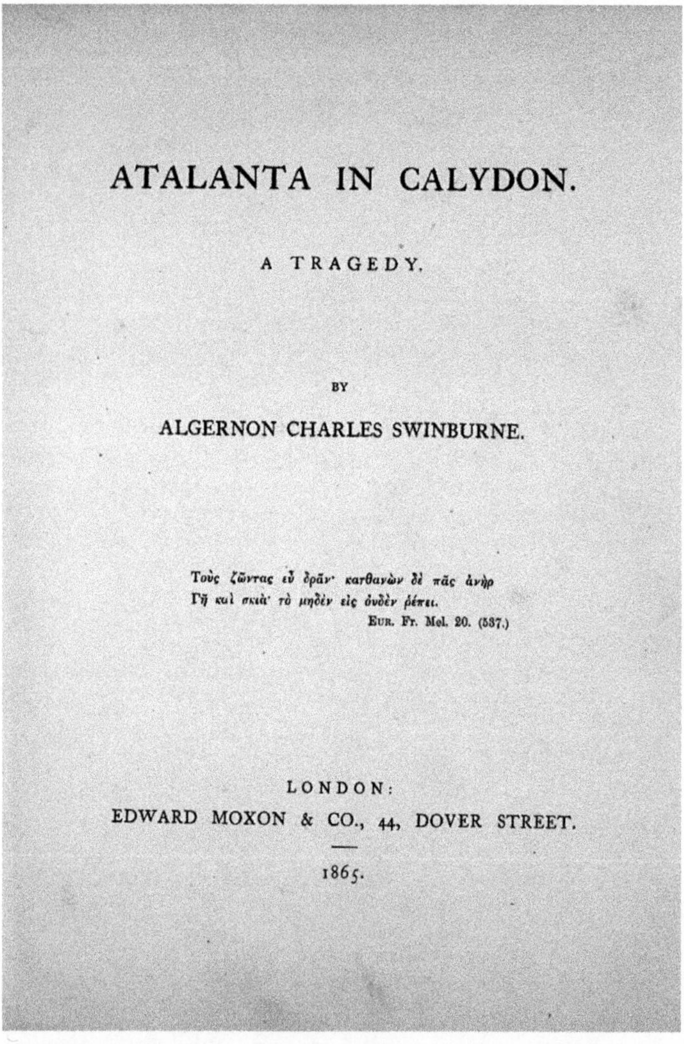

ATALANTA IN CALYDON.

A TRAGEDY.

BY

ALGERNON CHARLES SWINBURNE.

Τοὺς ζῶντας εὖ δρᾶν· κατθανὼν δὲ πᾶς ἀνὴρ
Γῆ καὶ σκιά· τὸ μηδὲν εἰς οὐδὲν ῥέπει.
EUR. FR. MEL. 20. (537.)

LONDON:
EDWARD MOXON & CO., 44, DOVER STREET.

1865.

FIG. 1. Title page of *Atalanta in Calydon* (London: Moxon, 1865), a copy from the Brotherton Library, Special Collections, University of Leeds, reproduced with permission.

# *ATALANTA IN CALYDON: A TRAGEDY* (1865)

*Τοὺς ζῶντας εὖ δρᾶν· κατθανὼν δὲ πᾶς ἀνὴρ*
*Γῆ καὶ σκιά· τὸ μηδὲν εἰς οὐδὲν ῥέπει.*°

EUR. FR. MEL. 20. (537)

To the memory of Walter Savage Landor°

I NOW DEDICATE, WITH EQUAL AFFECTION, REVERENCE, AND REGRET, A POEM INSCRIBED TO HIM WHILE YET ALIVE IN WORDS WHICH ARE NOW RETAINED BECAUSE THEY WERE LAID BEFORE HIM; AND TO WHICH, RATHER THAN CANCEL THEM, I HAVE ADDED SUCH OTHERS AS WERE EVOKED BY THE NEWS OF HIS DEATH; THAT THOUGH LOSING THE PLEASURE I MAY NOT LOSE THE HONOUR OF INSCRIBING IN FRONT OF MY WORK THE HIGHEST OF CONTEMPORARY NAMES.

*ᾤχεο δὴ Βορέηθεν ἀπότροπος· ἀλλά σε Νύμφαι*
*ἤγαγον ἀσπασίαν ἡδύπνοοι καθ' ἅλα,*
*πληροῦσαι μέλιτος θεόθεν στόμα, μή τι Ποσειδῶν*
*βλάψῃ, ἐν ὠσὶν ἔχων σὴν μελίγηρυν ὄπα,*
*τοῖος ἀοιδὸς ἔφυς· ἡμεῖς δ' ἔτι κλαίομεν, οἵ σου*
*δευόμεθ' οἰχομένου, καί σε ποθοῦμεν ἀεί.*
*εἶπε δὲ Πιερίδων τις ἀναστρεφθεῖσα πρὸς ἄλλην·*
*ἦλθεν, ἰδού, πάντων φίλτατος ἦλθε βροτῶν·*
*στέμματα δρεψάμενος νεοθηλέα χερσὶ γεραιαῖς,*
*καὶ πολιὸν δάφναις ἀμφεκάλυψε κάρα*
*ἡδύ τι Σικελικαῖς ἐπὶ πηκτίσιν, ἡδύ τι χόρδαις,*
*ᾀσόμενος· πολλὴν γὰρ μετέβαλλε λύραν,*
*πολλάκι δ' ἐν βήσσαισι καθήμενον εὗρεν Ἀπόλλων,*
*ἄνθεσι δ' ἔστεψεν, τερπνὰ δ' ἔδωκε λέγειν,*
*Πᾶνα τ' ἀείμνηστόν τε Πίτυν Κόρυθόν τε δύσεδρον,*
*ἥν τ' ἐφίλησε θεὰν θνητὸς Ἁμαδρύαδα·*
*πόντου δ' ἐν μεγάροισιν ἐκοίμισε Κυμοδάμειαν,*
*τήν τ' Ἀγαμεμνονίαν παῖδ' ἀπέδωκε πατρὶ,*
*πρὸς δ' ἱεροὺς Δελφοὺς θεόπληκτον ἔπεμψεν Ὀρέστην*
*τειρόμενον στυγεραῖς ἔνθα καὶ ἔνθα θεαῖς.°*

*ᾤχεο δὴ καὶ ἄνευθε φίλων καὶ ἄνευθεν ἀοιδῆς,*
*δρεψόμενος μαλακῆς ἄνθεα Περσεφόνης.*
*ᾤχεο· κοὐκ ἔτ' ἔσει, κοὐκ αὖ ποτέ σοι παρεδοῦμαι*
*ἁζόμενος, χειρῶν χερσὶ θιγὼν ὁσίαις·*
*νῦν δ' αὖ μνησάμενον γλυκύπικρος ὑπήλυθεν αἰδὼς,*
*οἷα τυχὼν οἵου πρὸς σέθεν οἷος ἔχω·*
*οὔποτε σοῖς, γέρον, ὄμμα φίλοις φίλον ὄμμασι τέρψω,*
*σῆς, γέρον, ἁψάμενος, φίλτατε, δεξιτερᾶς·*
*ἦ ψαφαρὰ κόνις, ἦ ψαφαρὸς βιός ἐστι· τὶ τούτων*
*μεῖον ἐφημερίων; οὐ κόνις ἀλλὰ βίος.*
*ἀλλά μοι ἡδύτερός γε πέλεις πολὺ τῶν ἔτ' ἐόντων,*
*ἔπλεο γάρ· σοὶ μὴν ταῦτα θανόντι φέρω,*
*παῦρα μὲν, ἀλλ' ἀπὸ κῆρος ἐτήτυμα· μηδ' ἀποτρεφθῇς,*
*πρὸς δὲ βαλὼν ἔτι νῦν ἥσυχον ὄμμα δέχου.*
*οὐ γὰρ ἔχω, μέγα δή τι θέλων, σέθεν ἄξια δοῦναι*
*θαπτομένου περ ἀπών· οὐ γὰρ ἔνεστιν ἔμοι·*
*οὐδὲ μελικρήτου παρέχειν γάνος· εἰ γὰρ ἐνείη*
*καί σε χεροῖν ψαύσαι καί σέ ποτ' αὖθις ἰδεῖν,*
*δάκρυσί τε σπονδαῖς τε κάρα φίλον ἀμφιπολεύειν*
*ὀφθαλμούς θ' ἱεροὺς σοὺς ἱερόν τε δέμας.*
*εἴθ' ὄφελον· μάλα γὰρ τάδ' ἂν ἀμπαύσειε μερίμνης·*
*νῦν δὲ πρόσωθεν ἄνευ σήματος οἶκτον ἄγω·*
*οὐδ' ἐπιτυμβίδιον θρηνῶ μέλος, ἀλλ' ἀπαμυνθεὶς,*

*ἀλλ᾽ ἀπάνευθεν ἔχων ἀμφιδακρυτὰ πάθη.*
*ἀλλὰ σὺ χαῖρε θανών, καὶ ἔχων γέρας ἴσθι πρὸς ἀνδρῶν*
*πρός τε θεῶν, ἐνέροις εἴ τις ἔπεστι θεός.*
*χαῖρε γέρον, φίλε χαῖρε πατέρ, πολὺ φέρτατ᾽ ἀοιδῶν*
*ὧν ἴδομεν, πολὺ δὴ φέρτατ᾽ ἀεισομένων·*
*χαῖρε, καὶ ὄλβον ἔχοις, οἷόν γε θανόντες ἔχουσιν,*
*ἡσυχίαν ἔχθρας καὶ φιλότητος ἄτερ.*°

*σήματος οἰχομένου σοι μνήματ᾽ ἐς ὕστερον ἔσται,*
*σοί τε φιλὴ μνήμη μνήματος οἰχομένου·*
*ὃν Χάριτες κλαίουσι θεαί, κλαίει δ᾽ Ἀφροδίτη*
*καλλιχόροις Μουσῶν τερψαμένη στεφάνοις·*
*οὐ γὰρ ἅπαξ ἱερούς ποτε γῆρας ἔτριψεν ἀοιδούς·*
*τήνδε τὸ σὸν φαίνει μνῆμα τόδ᾽ ἀγλαΐαν,*
*ἦ φίλος ἦς μακάρεσσι βροτὸς, σοὶ δ᾽ εἴ τινι Νύμφαι*
*δῶρα ποθεινὰ νέμειν, ὕστατα δῶρ᾽, ἔδοσαν.*
*τὰς νῦν χάλκεος ὕπνος ἔβη καὶ ἀνήνεμος αἰών,*
*καὶ συνθαπτομέναι μοῖραν ἔχουσι μίαν.*
*εὕδεις καὶ σύ, καλὸν καὶ ἀγάκλυτον ἐν χθονὶ κοίλῃ*
*ὕπνον ἐφικόμενος, σῆς ἀπόνοσφι πάτρας,*
*τῆλε παρὰ ξανθοῦ Τυρσηνικὸν οἶδμα καθεύδεις*
*νάματος, ἡ δ᾽ ἔτι σὴ μαῖά σε γαῖα ποθεῖ,*
*ἀλλ᾽ ἀπέχεις, καὶ πρόσθε φιλόπτολις ὢν περ ἀπεῖπας·*
*εὗδε· μάκαρ δ᾽ ἡμῖν οὐδ᾽ ἀμέγαρτος ἔσει.*
*βαιὸς ἐπιχθονίων γε χρόνος καὶ μοῖρα κρατήσει,*
*τοὺς δέ ποτ᾽ εὐφροσύνη τοὺς δέ ποτ᾽ ἄλγος ἔχει·*
*πολλάκι δ᾽ ἢ βλάπτει φάος ἢ σκότος ἀμφικαλύπτει*
*μυρομένους, δάκνει δ᾽ ὕπνος ἐγρηγορότας·*
*οὐδ᾽ ἔθ᾽ ὅτ᾽ ἐν τύμβοισι κατέδραθεν ὄμμα θανόντων*
*ἢ σκότος ἤ τι φάος δήξεται ἠελίου·*
*οὐδ᾽ ὄναρ ἐννύχιον καὶ ἐνύπνιον οὐδ᾽ ὕπαρ ἔσται*
*ἤ ποτε τερπομένοις ἤ ποτ᾽ ὀδυρομένοις·*
*ἀλλ᾽ ἕνα πάντες ἀεὶ θᾶκον συνέχουσι καὶ ἕδραν*
*ἀντὶ βροτῆς ἄβροτον, κάλλιμον ἄντι κακῆς.*°

## *The Argument*°

Althæa, daughter of Thestius and Eurythemis, queen of Calydon, being with child of Meleager her first-born son, dreamed that she brought forth a brand burning; and upon his birth came the three Fates and prophesied of him three things, namely these; that he should have great strength of his hands, and good fortune in this life, and that he should live no longer when the brand then in the fire were consumed: wherefore his mother plucked it forth and kept it by her. And the child being a man grown sailed with Jason after the fleece of gold, and won himself great praise of all men living; and when the tribes of the north and west made war upon Ætolia, he fought against their army and scattered it. But Artemis, having at the first stirred up these tribes to war against Œneus king of Calydon, because he had offered sacrifice to all the gods saving her alone, but her he had forgotten to honour, was yet more wroth because of the destruction of this army, and sent upon the land of Calydon a wild boar which slew many and wasted all their increase, but him could none slay, and many went against him and perished. Then were all the chief men of Greece gathered together, and among them Atalanta daughter of Iasius the Arcadian, a virgin; for whose sake Artemis let slay the boar, seeing she favoured the maiden greatly; and Meleager having despatched it gave the spoil thereof to Atalanta, as one beyond measure enamoured of her; but the brethren of Althæa his mother, Toxeus and Plexippus, with such others as misliked that she only should bear off the praise whereas many had borne the labour, laid wait for her to take away her spoil; but Meleager fought against them and slew them: whom when Althæa their sister beheld and knew to be slain of her son, she waxed for wrath and sorrow like as one mad, and taking the brand whereby the measure of her son's life was meted to him, she cast it upon a fire; and with the wasting thereof his life likewise wasted away, that being brought back to his father's house he died in a brief space; and his mother also endured not long after for very sorrow; and this was his end, and the end of that hunting.

## THE PERSONS

CHIEF HUNTSMAN
CHORUS
ALTHÆA
MELEAGER
ŒNEUS
ATALANTA
TOXEUS
PLEXIPPUS
HERALD
MESSENGER
SECOND MESSENGER

*ἴστω δ' ὅστις οὐχ ὑπόπτερος*
*φροντίσιν δαεὶς*
*τὰν ἁ παιδολύμας τἄλαινα θεστιὰς μήσατο*
*πυρδαῆ τινα πρόνοιαν,*
*καταίθουσα παιδὸς δαφοινὸν*
*δαλὸν ἥλικ' ἐπεὶ μολὼν ματρόθεν κελάδησε*
*σύμμετρόν τε διαὶ βίου μοιρόκραντον ἐς ἆμαρ.*°

ÆSCH. Cho. 602–12.

CHIEF HUNTSMAN

Maiden, and mistress of the months and stars
Now folded in the flowerless fields of heaven,
Goddess whom all gods love with threefold heart,
Being treble in thy divided deity,°
A light for dead men and dark hours, a foot
Swift on the hills as morning, and a hand
To all things fierce° and fleet that roar and range
Mortal, with gentler shafts than snow or sleep;
Hear now and help and lift no violent hand,
But favourable and fair as thine eye's beam
Hidden and shown in heaven; for I all night
Amid the king's hounds and the hunting men
Have wrought and worshipped toward thee; nor shall man
See goodlier hounds or deadlier edge of spears;
But for the end, that lies unreached at yet
Between the hands and on the knees of gods.
O fair-faced sun killing the stars and dews
And dreams and desolation of the night!
Rise up, shine, stretch thine hand out, with thy bow
Touch the most dimmest height of trembling heaven,
And burn and break the dark about thy ways,
Shot through and through with arrows; let thine hair
Lighten as flame above that flameless shell
Which was the moon, and thine eyes fill the world
And thy lips kindle with swift beams; let earth
Laugh, and the long sea fiery from thy feet
Through all the roar and ripple of streaming springs
And foam in reddening flakes and flying flowers
Shaken from hands and blown from lips of nymphs
Whose hair or breast divides the wandering wave
With salt close tresses cleaving lock to lock,
All gold, or shuddering and unfurrowed snow;
And all the winds about thee with their wings,
And fountain-heads of all the watered world;
Each horn of Acheloüs,° and the green
Euenus,° wedded with the straitening sea.
For in fair time thou° comest; come also thou,
Twin-born with him, and virgin, Artemis,
And give our spears their spoil, the wild boar's hide,
Sent in thine anger against us for sin done
And bloodless altars without wine or fire.
Him now consume thou; for thy sacrifice

With sanguine-shining steam divides the dawn,
And one, the maiden rose of all thy maids,
Arcadian Atalanta, snowy-souled,
Fair as the snow and footed as the wind,
From Ladon and well-wooded Mænalus°
Over the firm hills and the fleeting sea
Hast thou drawn hither, and many an armèd king,
Heroes, the crown of men, like gods in fight.
Moreover out of all the Ætolian land,
From the full-flowered Lelantian pasturage°
To what of fruitful field the son of Zeus
Won from the roaring river and labouring sea
When the wild god shrank in his horn and fled
And foamed and lessened through his wrathful fords,
Leaving clear lands that steamed with sudden sun,
These virgins with the lightening of the day
Bring thee fresh wreaths and their own sweeter hair,
Luxurious locks and flower-like mixed with flowers,
Clean offering, and chaste hymns; but me the time
Divides from these things; whom do thou not less
Help and give honour, and to mine hounds good speed,
And edge to spears, and luck to each man's hand.

CHORUS

When the hounds° of spring are on winter's traces,
  The mother of months° in meadow or plain
Fills the shadows and windy places
  With lisp of leaves and ripple of rain;
And the brown bright nightingale amorous
Is half assuaged for Itylus,°
For the Thracian ships and the foreign faces,
  The tongueless vigil, and all the pain.

Come with bows bent and with emptying of quivers,
  Maiden most perfect, lady of light,
With a noise of winds and many rivers,
  With a clamour of waters, and with might;
Bind on thy sandals, O thou most fleet,
Over the splendour and speed of thy feet;
For the faint east quickens, the wan west shivers,
  Round the feet of the day and the feet of the night.

Where shall we find her, how shall we sing to her,
  Fold our hands round her knees, and cling?

O that man's heart were as fire and could spring to her,
  Fire, or the strength of the streams that spring!
For the stars and the winds are unto her
As raiment, as songs of the harp-player;
For the risen stars and the fallen cling to her,
  And the southwest-wind and the west-wind sing.

For winter's rains and ruins are over,
  And all the season of snows and sins;
The days dividing lover and lover,
  The light that loses, the night that wins;
And time remembered is grief forgotten,
And frosts are slain and flowers begotten,
And in green underwood and cover
  Blossom by blossom the spring begins.

The full streams feed on flower of rushes,
  Ripe grasses trammel a travelling foot,
The faint fresh flame of the young year flushes
  From leaf to flower and flower to fruit;
And fruit and leaf are as gold and fire,
And the oat is heard above the lyre,
And the hoofèd heel of a satyr crushes
  The chestnut-husk at the chestnut-root.

And Pan by noon and Bacchus° by night,
  Fleeter of foot than the fleet-foot kid,°
Follows with dancing and fills with delight
  The Mænad and the Bassarid;°
And soft as lips that laugh and hide
The laughing leaves of the trees divide,
And screen from seeing and leave in sight
  The god pursuing, the maiden hid.

The ivy falls with the Bacchanal's hair
  Over her eyebrows hiding her eyes;
The wild vine slipping down leaves bare
  Her bright breast shortening into sighs;
The wild vine slips with the weight of its leaves,
But the berried ivy catches and cleaves
To the limbs that glitter, the feet that scare
  The wolf that follows, the fawn that flies.

ALTHÆA

What do ye singing?° what is this ye sing?

CHORUS

Flowers bring we, and pure lips that please the gods,
And raiment meet for service: lest the day
Turn sharp with all its honey in our lips.

ALTHÆA

Night, a black hound, follows the white fawn day,
Swifter than dreams the white flown feet of sleep;
Will ye pray back the night with any prayers?
And though the spring put back a little while
Winter, and snows that plague all men for sin,
And the iron time of cursing, yet I know
Spring shall be ruined with the rain, and storm
Eat up like fire the ashen autumn days.
I marvel what men do with prayers awake
Who dream and die with dreaming; any god,
Yea the least god of all things called divine,
Is more than sleep and waking; yet we say,
Perchance by praying a man shall match his god.
For if sleep have no mercy, and man's dreams
Bite to the blood and burn into the bone,
What shall this man do waking? By the gods,
He shall not pray to dream sweet things to-night,
Having dreamt once more bitter things than death.

CHORUS

Queen, but what is it that hath burnt thine heart?
For thy speech flickers like a blown-out flame.

ALTHÆA

Look, ye say well, and know not what ye say;
For all my sleep is turned into a fire,
And all my dreams to stuff that kindles it.

CHORUS

Yet one doth well being patient of the gods.°

ALTHÆA

Yea, lest they smite us with some four-foot plague.

CHORUS

But when time spreads find out some herb for it.

ALTHÆA

And with their healing herbs infect our blood.

CHORUS

What ails thee to be jealous of their ways?

ALTHÆA

What if they give us poisonous drinks for wine?

CHORUS

They have their will; much talking mends it not.

ALTHÆA

And gall for milk, and cursing for a prayer?

CHORUS

Have they not given life, and the end of life?

ALTHÆA

Lo, where they heal, they help not;° thus they do,
They mock us with a little piteousness,
And we say prayers and weep; but at the last,
Sparing awhile, they smite and spare no whit.

CHORUS

Small praise man gets dispraising the high gods:
What have they done that thou dishonourest them?

ALTHÆA

First Artemis for all this harried land
I praise not, and for wasting of the boar
That mars with tooth and tusk and fiery feet
Green pasturage and the grace of standing corn
And meadow and marsh with springs and unblown leaves,
Flocks and swift herds and all that bite sweet grass,
I praise her not; what things are these to praise?

CHORUS

But when the king did sacrifice, and gave
Each god fair dues of wheat and blood and wine,
Her not with bloodshed nor burnt-offering
Revered he, nor with salt or cloven cake;
Wherefore being wroth she plagued the land; but now
Takes off from us fate and her heavy things.
Which deed of these twain were not good to praise?
For a just deed looks always either way
With blameless eyes, and mercy is no fault.

ALTHÆA

Yea, but a curse she hath sent above all these

To hurt us where she healed us; and hath lit
Fire where the old fire went out, and where the wind
Slackened, hath blown on us with deadlier air.

CHORUS

What storm is this that tightens all our sail?

ALTHÆA

Love, a thwart sea-wind full of rain and foam.

CHORUS

Whence blown, and born under what stormier star?

ALTHÆA

Southward across Euenus from the sea.

CHORUS

Thy speech turns toward Arcadia like blown wind.

ALTHÆA

Sharp as the north sets when the snows are out.

CHORUS

Nay, for this maiden hath no touch of love.

ALTHÆA

I would she had sought in some cold gulf of sea
Love, or in dens where strange beasts lurk, or fire,
Or snows on the extreme hills, or iron land
Where no spring is; I would she had sought therein
And found, or ever love had found her here.

CHORUS

She is holier than all holy days or things,
The sprinkled water or fume of perfect fire;
Chaste, dedicated to pure prayers, and filled
With higher thoughts than heaven; a maiden clean,
Pure iron, fashioned for a sword; and man
She loves not; what should one such do with love?

ALTHÆA

Look you, I speak not as one light of wit,
But as a queen speaks, being heart-vexed; for oft
I hear my brothers wrangling in mid hall,
And am not moved; and my son chiding them,
And these things nowise move me, but I know
Foolish and wise men must be to the end,

And feed myself with patience; but this most,
This moves me, that for wise men as for fools
Love is one thing, an evil thing, and turns
Choice words and wisdom into fire and air.
And in the end shall no joy come, but grief,
Sharp words and soul's division and fresh tears
Flower-wise upon the old root of tears brought forth,
Fruit-wise upon the old flower of tears sprung up,
Pitiful sighs, and much regrafted pain.
These things are in my presage, and myself
Am part of them and know not; but in dreams
The gods are heavy on me, and all the fates
Shed fire across my eyelids mixed with night,
And burn me blind, and disilluminate
My sense of seeing, and my perspicuous soul
Darken with vision; seeing I see not, hear
And hearing am not holpen, but mine eyes
Stain many tender broideries in the bed
Drawn up about my face that I may weep
And the king wake not; and my brows and lips
Tremble and sob in sleeping, like swift flames
That tremble, or water when it sobs with heat
Kindled from under; and my tears fill my breast
And speck the fair dyed pillows round the king
With barren showers and salter than the sea,
Such dreams divide me dreaming; for long since
I dreamed that out of this my womb had sprung
Fire and a firebrand; this was ere my son,
Meleager, a goodly flower in fields of fight,
Felt the light touch him coming forth, and wailed
Childlike; but yet he was not; and in time
I bare him, and my heart was great; for yet
So royally was never strong man born,
Nor queen so nobly bore as noble a thing
As this my son was: such a birth God sent
And such a grace to bear it. Then came in
Three weaving women,° and span each a thread,
Saying This for strength and That for luck, and one
Saying Till the brand upon the hearth burn down,
So long shall this man see good days and live.
And I with gathered raiment from the bed
Sprang, and drew forth the brand, and cast on it
Water, and trod the flame bare-foot, and crushed

With naked hand spark beaten out of spark
And blew against and quenched it; for I said,
These are the most high Fates that dwell with us,
And we find favour a little in their sight,
A little, and more we miss of, and much time
Foils us; howbeit they have pitied me, O son,
And thee most piteous, thee a tenderer thing
Than any flower of fleshly seed alive.
Wherefore I kissed and hid him with my hands,
And covered under arms and hair, and wept,
And feared to touch him with my tears, and laughed;
So light a thing was this man, grown so great
Men cast their heads back, seeing against the sun
Blaze the armed man carven on his shield, and hear
The laughter of little bells along the brace
Ring, as birds singing or flutes blown, and watch,
High up, the cloven shadow of either plume
Divide the bright light of the brass, and make
His helmet as a windy and wintering moon
Seen through blown cloud and plume-like drift, when ships
Drive, and men strive with all the sea, and oars
Break, and the beaks dip under, drinking death;
Yet was he then but a span long, and moaned
With inarticulate mouth inseparate words,
And with blind lips and fingers wrung my breast
Hard, and thrust out with foolish hands and feet,
Murmuring; but those grey women with bound hair
Who fright the gods frighted not him; he laughed
Seeing them, and pushed out hands to feel and haul
Distaff and thread, intangible; but they
Passed, and I hid the brand, and in my heart
Laughed likewise, having all my will of heaven.
But now I know not if to left or right
The gods have drawn us hither; for again
I dreamt, and saw the black brand burst on fire
As a branch bursts in flower, and saw the flame
Fade flower-wise, and Death came and with dry lips
Blew the charred ash into my breast; and Love
Trampled the ember and crushed it with swift feet.
This I have also at heart; that not for me,
Not for me only or son of mine, O girls,
The gods have wrought life, and desire of life,
Heart's love and heart's division; but for all

There shines one sun and one wind blows till night.
And when night comes the wind sinks and the sun,
And there is no light after, and no storm,
But sleep and much forgetfulness of things.
In such wise I gat knowledge of the gods
Years hence, and heard high sayings of one most wise,
Eurythemis° my mother, who beheld
With eyes alive and spake with lips of these
As one on earth disfleshed and disallied
From breath or blood corruptible; such gifts
Time gave her, and an equal soul to these
And equal face to all things; thus she said.
But whatsoever intolerable or glad
The swift hours weave and unweave, I go hence
Full of mine own soul, perfect of myself,
Toward mine and me sufficient; and what chance
The gods cast lots for and shake out on us,
That shall we take, and that much bear withal.
And now, before these gather to the hunt,
I will go arm my son and bring him forth,
Lest love or some man's anger work him harm.

CHORUS

Before the beginning of years°
  There came to the making of man
Time, with a gift of tears;
  Grief, with a glass that ran;
Pleasure, with pain for leaven;
  Summer, with flowers that fell;
Remembrance fallen from heaven,
  And madness risen from hell;
Strength without hands to smite;
  Love that endures for a breath;
Night, the shadow of light,
  And life, the shadow of death.

And the high gods took in hand
  Fire, and the falling of tears,
And a measure of sliding sand
  From under the feet of the years;
And froth and drift of the sea;
  And dust of the labouring earth;
And bodies of things to be
  In the houses of death and of birth;

And wrought with weeping and laughter,
  And fashioned with loathing and love;
With life before and after
  And death beneath and above,
For a day and a night and a morrow,
  That his strength might endure for a span
With travail and heavy sorrow,
  The holy spirit of man.

From the winds of the north and the south
  They gathered as unto strife;
They breathed upon his mouth,
  They filled his body with life;
Eyesight and speech they wrought
  For the veils of the soul therein,
A time for labour and thought,
  A time to serve and to sin;
They gave him light in his ways,
  And love, and a space for delight,
And beauty and length of days,
  And night, and sleep in the night.
His speech is a burning fire;
  With his lips he travaileth;
In his heart is a blind desire,
  In his eyes foreknowledge of death;
He weaves, and is clothed with derision;
  Sows, and he shall not reap;[o]
His life is a watch or a vision
  Between a sleep and a sleep.

MELEAGER

O sweet new heaven[o] and air without a star,
Fair day, be fair and welcome, as to men
With deeds to do and praise to pluck from thee.
Come forth a child, born with clear sound and light,
With laughter and swift limbs and prosperous looks;
That this great hunt with heroes for the hounds
May leave thee memorable and us well sped.

ALTHÆA

Son, first I praise thy prayer, then bid thee speed;
But the gods hear men's hands before their lips,
And heed beyond all crying and sacrifice
Light of things done and noise of labouring men.

But thou, being armed and perfect for the deed,
Abide; for like rain-flakes in a wind they grow,
The men thy fellows, and the choice of the world,
Bound to root out the tuskèd plague, and leave
Thanks and safe days and peace in Calydon.

MELEAGER

For the whole city and all the low-lying land
Flames, and the soft air sounds with them that come;
The gods give all these fruit of all their works.

ALTHÆA

Set thine eye thither and fix thy spirit and say
Whom there thou knowest; for sharp mixed shadow and wind
Blown up between the morning and the mist,
With steam of steeds and flash of bridle or wheel,
And fire, and parcels of the broken dawn,
And dust divided by hard light, and spears
That shine and shift as the edge of wild beasts' eyes,
Smite upon mine; so fiery their blind edge
Burns, and bright points break up and baffle day.

MELEAGER

The first, for many I know not, being far off,
Peleus the Larissæan,[o] couched with whom
Sleeps the white sea-bred wife and silver-shod,
Fair as fled foam, a goddess; and their son
Most swift[o] and splendid of men's children born,
Most like a god, full of the future fame.

ALTHÆA

Who are these shining like one sundered star?

MELEAGER

Thy sister's sons,[o] a double flower of men.

ALTHÆA

O sweetest kin to me in all the world,
O twin-born blood of Leda, gracious heads
Like kindled lights in untempestuous heaven,
Fair flower-like stars on the iron foam of fight,
With what glad heart and kindliness of soul,
Even to the staining of both eyes with tears
And kindling of warm eyelids with desire,
A great way off I greet you, and rejoice

Seeing you so fair, and moulded like as gods.
Far off ye come, and least in years of these,
But lordliest, but worth love to look upon.

MELEAGER

Even such (for sailing hither I saw far hence,
And where Eurotas° hollows his moist rock
Nigh Sparta with a strenuous-hearted stream)
Even such I saw their sisters; one swan-white,
The little Helen, and less fair than she
Fair Clytæmnestra, grave as pasturing fawns
Who feed and fear some arrow; but at whiles,
As one smitten with love or wrung with joy,
She laughs and lightens with her eyes, and then
Weeps; whereat Helen, having laughed, weeps too,
And the other chides her, and she being chid speaks nought,
But cheeks and lips and eyelids kisses her,
Laughing; so fare they, as in their bloomless bud
And full of unblown life, the blood of gods.

ALTHÆA

Sweet days befall them and good loves and lords,
And tender and temperate honours of the hearth,
Peace, and a perfect life and blameless bed.
But who shows next an eagle wrought in gold,
That flames and beats broad wings against the sun
And with void mouth gapes after emptier prey?

MELEAGER

Know by that sign the reign of Telamon°
Between the fierce mouths of the encountering brine
On the strait reefs of twice-washed Salamis.

ALTHÆA

For like one great of hand he bears himself,
Vine-chapleted, with savours of the sea,
Glittering as wine and moving as a wave.
But who girt round there roughly follows him?

MELEAGER

Ancæus, great of hand, an iron bulk,
Two-edged for fight as the axe against his arm,
Who drives against the surge of stormy spears
Full-sailed; him Cepheus° follows, his twin-born,
Chief name next his of all Arcadian men.

ALTHÆA

Praise be with men abroad; chaste lives with us,
Home-keeping days and household reverences.

MELEAGER

Next by the left unsandalled foot know thou
The sail and oar of this Ætolian land,
Thy brethren, Toxeus and the violent-souled
Plexippus,° over-swift with hand and tongue;
For hands are fruitful, but the ignorant mouth
Blows and corrupts their work with barren breath.

ALTHÆA

Speech too bears fruit, being worthy; and air blows down
Things poisonous, and high-seated violences,
And with charmed words and songs have men put out
Wild evil, and the fire of tyrannies.

MELEAGER

Yea, all things have they, save the gods and love.

ALTHÆA

Love thou the law and cleave to things ordained.

MELEAGER

Law lives upon their lips whom these applaud.

ALTHÆA

How sayest thou these? what god applauds new things?

MELEAGER

Zeus, who hath fear and custom under foot.

ALTHÆA

But loves not laws thrown down and lives awry.

MELEAGER

Yet is not less himself than his own law.

ALTHÆA

Nor shifts and shuffles old things up and down.

MELEAGER

But what he will remoulds and discreates.

ALTHÆA

Much, but not this, that each thing live its life.

MELEAGER

Nor only live, but lighten and lift up higher.

ALTHÆA

Pride breaks itself, and too much gained is gone.

MELEAGER

Things gained are gone, but great things done endure.

ALTHÆA

Child, if a man serve law through all his life
And with his whole heart worship, him all gods
Praise; but who loves it only with his lips,
And not in heart and deed desiring it
Hides a perverse will with obsequious words,
Him heaven infatuates and his twin-born fate°
Tracks, and gains on him, scenting sins far off,
And the swift hounds of violent death devour.
Be man at one with equal-minded gods,
So shall he prosper; not through laws torn up,
Violated rule and a new face of things.
A woman armed makes war upon herself,
Unwomanlike, and treads down use and wont
And the sweet common honour that she hath,
Love, and the cry of children, and the hand
Troth plight and mutual mouth of marriages.
This doth she, being unloved; whom if one love,
Not fire nor iron and the wide-mouthed wars
Are deadlier than her lips or braided hair.
For of the one comes poison, and a curse
Falls from the other and burns the lives of men.
But thou, son, be not filled with evil dreams,
Nor with desire of these things; for with time
Blind love burns out; but if one feed it full
Till some discolouring stain dyes all his life,
He shall keep nothing praiseworthy, nor die
The sweet wise death of old men honourable,°
Who have lived out all the length of all their years
Blameless, and seen well-pleased the face of gods,
And without shame and without fear have wrought
Things memorable, and while their days held out
In sight of all men and the sun's great light
Have gat them glory and given of their own praise
To the earth that bare them and the day that bred,

Home friends and far-off hospitalities,
And filled with gracious and memorial fame
Lands loved of summer or washed by violent seas,
Towns populous and many unfooted ways,
And alien lips and native with their own.
But when white age and venerable death
Mow down the strength and life within their limbs,
Drain out the blood and darken their clear eyes,
Immortal honour is on them, having past
Through splendid life and death desirable
To the clear seat and remote throne of souls,
Lands indiscoverable in the unheard-of west,
Round which the strong stream of a sacred sea
Rolls without wind for ever, and the snow
There shows not her white wings and windy feet,
Nor thunder nor swift rain saith anything,
Nor the sun burns, but all things rest and thrive;
And these, filled full of days, divine and dead,
Sages and singers fiery from the god,
And such as loved their land and all things good
And, best beloved of best men, liberty,
Free lives and lips, free hands of men free-born,
And whatsoever on earth was honourable
And whosoever of all the ephemeral seed,
Live there a life no liker to the gods
But nearer than their life of terrene days.
Love thou such life and look for such a death.
But from the light and fiery dreams of love
Spring heavy sorrows and a sleepless life,
Visions not dreams, whose lids no charm shall close
Nor song assuage them waking; and swift death
Crushes with sterile feet the unripening ear,
Treads out the timeless vintage; whom do thou
Eschewing embrace the luck of this thy life,
Not without honour; and it shall bear to thee
Such fruit as men reap from spent hours and wear,
Few men, but happy; of whom be thou, O son,
Happiest, if thou submit thy soul to fate,
And set thine eyes and heart on hopes high-born
And divine deeds and abstinence divine.
So shalt thou be toward all men all thy days
As light and might communicable, and burn
From heaven among the stars above the hours,

And break not as a man breaks nor burn down:
For to whom other of all heroic names
Have the gods given his life in hand as thine?
And gloriously hast thou lived, and made thy life
To me that bare thee and to all men born
Thankworthy, a praise for ever; and hast won fame
When wild wars° broke all round thy father's house,
And the mad people of windy mountain ways
Laid spears against us like a sea, and all
Ætolia thundered with Thessalian hoofs;
Yet these, as wind baffles the foam, and beats
Straight back the relaxed ripple, didst thou break
And loosen all their lances, till undone
And man from man they fell; for ye twain stood
God against god, Ares and Artemis,
And thou the mightier; wherefore she unleashed
A sharp-toothed curse thou too shalt overcome;
For in the greener blossom of thy life
Ere the full blade caught flower, and when time gave
Respite, thou didst not slacken soul nor sleep,
But with great hand and heart seek praise of men
Out of sharp straits and many a grievous thing,
Seeing the strange foam of undivided seas°
On channels never sailed in, and by shores
Where the old winds cease not blowing, and all the night
Thunders, and day is no delight to men.

CHORUS

Meleager, a noble wisdom and fair words
The gods have given this woman; hear thou these.

MELEAGER

O mother, I am not fain to strive in speech
Nor set my mouth against thee, who art wise
Even as they say and full of sacred words.
But one thing I know surely, and cleave to this;
That though I be not subtle of wit as thou
Nor womanlike to weave sweet words, and melt
Mutable minds of wise men as with fire,
I too, doing justly and reverencing the gods,
Shall not want wit to see what things be right.
For whom they love and whom reject, being gods,
There is no man but seeth, and in good time
Submits himself, refraining all his heart.

And I too as thou sayest have seen great things;
Seen otherwhere, but chiefly when the sail°
First caught between stretched ropes the roaring west,
And all our oars smote eastward, and the wind
First flung round faces of seafaring men
White splendid snow-flakes of the sundering foam,
And the first furrow in virginal green sea
Followed the plunging ploughshare of hewn pine,
And closed, as when deep sleep subdues man's breath
Lips close and heart subsides; and closing, shone
Sunlike with many a Nereid's hair, and moved
Round many a trembling mouth of doubtful gods,
Risen out of sunless and sonorous gulfs
Through waning water and into shallow light,
That watched us; and when flying the dove was snared
As with men's hands, but we shot after and sped
Clear through the irremeable Symplegades;°
And chiefliest when hoar beach and herbless cliff
Stood out ahead from Colchis, and we heard
Clefts hoarse with wind, and saw through narrowing reefs
The lightning of the intolerable wave
Flash, and the white wet flame of breakers burn
Far under a kindling south-wind, as a lamp
Burns and bends all its blowing flame one way;
Wild heights untravelled of the wind, and vales
Cloven seaward by their violent streams, and white
With bitter flowers and bright salt scurf of brine;
Heard sweep their sharp swift gales, and bowing birdwise
Shriek with birds' voices, and with furious feet
Tread loose the long skirts of a storm; and saw
The whole white Euxine° clash together and fall
Full-mouthed, and thunderous from a thousand throats:
Yet we drew thither and won the fleece and won
Medea, deadlier than the sea; but there
Seeing many a wonder and fearful things to men
I saw not one thing like this one seen here,
Most fair and fearful, feminine, a god,
Faultless; whom I that love not, being unlike,
Fear, and give honour, and choose from all the gods.

ŒNEUS

Lady, the daughter of Thestius, and thou, son,
Not ignorant of your strife nor light of wit,

Scared with vain dreams and fluttering like spent fire,
I come to judge between you, but a king
Full of past days and wise from years endured.
Nor thee I praise, who art fain to undo things done;
Nor thee, who art swift to esteem them overmuch.
For what the hours have given is given, and this
Changeless; howbeit these change, and in good time
Devise new things and good, not one thing still.
Us have they sent now at our need for help
Among men armed a woman, foreign born,
Virgin, not like the natural flower of things
That grows and bears and brings forth fruit and dies;
Unlovable, no light for a husband's house,
Espoused; a glory among unwedded girls,
And chosen of gods who reverence maidenhood.
These too we honour in honouring her; but thou,
Abstain thy feet from following, and thine eyes
From amorous touch; nor set toward hers thine heart,
Son, lest hate bear no deadlier fruit than love.

ALTHÆA

O king, thou art wise, but wisdom halts; and just,
But the gods love not justice more than fate,°
And smite the righteous and the violent mouth,
And mix with insolent blood the reverent man's,
And bruise the holier as the lying lips.
Enough; for wise words fail me, and my heart
Takes fire and trembles flamewise, O my son,
O child, for thine head's sake; mine eyes wax thick,
Turning toward thee, so goodly a weaponed man,
So glorious; and for love of thine own eyes
They are darkened, and tears burn them, fierce as fire,
And my lips pause and my soul sinks with love.
But by thine hand, by thy sweet life and eyes,
By thy great heart and these clasped knees, O son,
I pray thee that thou slay me not with thee.
For there was never a mother woman-born
Loved her sons better; and never a queen of men
More perfect in her heart toward whom she loved.
For what lies light on many and they forget,
Small things and transitory as a wind o' the sea,
I forget never; I have seen thee all thine years
A man in arms, strong and a joy to men

Seeing thine head glitter and thine hand burn its way
Through a heavy and iron furrow of sundering spears;
But always also a flower of three suns old,[o]
The small one thing that lying drew down my life
To lie with thee and feed thee; a child and weak,
Mine, a delight to no man, sweet to me.
Who then sought to thee? who gat help? who knew
If thou wert goodly? nay, no man at all.
Or what sea saw thee, or sounded with thine oar,
Child? or what strange land shone with war through thee?
But fair for me thou wert, O little life,
Fruitless, the fruit of mine own flesh, and blind,
More than much gold, ungrown, a foolish flower.
For silver nor bright snow nor feather of foam
Was whiter, and no gold yellower than thine hair,
O child, my child; and now thou art lordlier grown,
Not lovelier, nor a new thing in mine eyes,
I charge thee by thy soul and this my breast,
Fear thou the gods and me and thine own heart,
Lest all these turn against thee; for who knows
What wind upon what wave of altering time
Shall speak a storm and blow calamity?
And there is nothing stabile in the world
But the gods break it; yet not less, fair son,
If but one thing be stronger, if one endure,
Surely the bitter and the rooted love
That burns between us, going from me to thee,
Shall more endure than all things. What dost thou,
Following strange loves? why wilt thou kill mine heart?
Lo, I talk wild and windy words, and fall
From my clear wits, and seem of mine own self
Dethroned, dispraised, disseated; and my mind,
That was my crown, breaks, and mine heart is gone,
And I am naked of my soul, and stand
Ashamed, as a mean woman; take thou thought:
Live if thou wilt, and if thou wilt not, look,
The gods have given thee life to lose or keep,
Thou shalt not die as men die, but thine end
Fallen upon thee shall break me unaware.

MELEAGER

Queen, my whole heart is molten with thy tears,
And my limbs yearn with pity of thee, and love

Compels with grief mine eyes and labouring breath:
For what thou art I know thee, and this thy breast
And thy fair eyes I worship, and am bound
Toward thee in spirit and love thee in all my soul.
For there is nothing terribler to men
Than the sweet face of mothers, and the might.
But what shall be let be; for us the day
Once only lives a little, and is not found.
Time and the fruitful hour are more than we,
And these lay hold upon us; but thou, God,
Zeus, the sole steersman of the helm of things,
Father, be swift to see us, and as thou wilt
Help: or if adverse, as thou wilt, refrain.

CHORUS

We have seen thee,[o] O Love, thou art fair; thou art goodly, O Love;
Thy wings make light in the air as the wings of a dove.[o]
Thy feet are as winds that divide the stream of the sea;
Earth is thy covering to hide thee, the garment of thee.
Thou art swift and subtle and blind as a flame of fire;
Before thee the laughter, behind thee the tears of desire;
And twain go forth beside thee, a man with a maid;
Her eyes are the eyes of a bride whom delight makes afraid;
As the breath in the buds that stir is her bridal breath:
But Fate is the name of her; and his name is Death.

For an evil blossom was born
  Of sea-foam[o] and the frothing of blood,
    Blood-red and bitter of fruit,
      And the seed of it laughter and tears,
And the leaves of it madness and scorn;
  A bitter flower from the bud,
    Sprung of the sea without root,
      Sprung without graft from the years.

The weft of the world was untorn
  That is woven of the day on the night,
  The hair of the hours was not white
Nor the raiment of time overworn,
  When a wonder, a world's delight,
A perilous goddess was born;
  And the waves of the sea as she came
Clove, and the foam at her feet,
    Fawning, rejoiced to bring forth

A fleshly blossom, a flame
Filling the heavens with heat
To the cold white ends of the north.
And in air the clamorous birds,
And men upon earth that hear
Sweet articulate words
Sweetly divided apart,
And in shallow and channel and mere
The rapid and footless herds,
Rejoiced, being foolish of heart.

For all they said upon earth,
She is fair, she is white like a dove,
And the life of the world in her breath
Breathes, and is born at her birth;
For they knew thee for mother of love,
And knew thee not mother of death.
What hadst thou to do being born,
Mother, when winds were at ease,
As a flower of the springtime of corn,
A flower of the foam of the seas?
For bitter thou wast from thy birth,
Aphrodite, a mother of strife;
For before thee some rest was on earth,
A little respite from tears,
A little pleasure of life;
For life was not then as thou art,
But as one that waxeth in years
Sweet-spoken, a fruitful wife;
Earth had no thorn, and desire
No sting, neither death any dart;
What hadst thou to do among these,
Thou, clothed with a burning fire,
Thou, girt with sorrow of heart,
Thou, sprung of the seed of the seas
As an ear from a seed of corn,
As a brand plucked forth of a pyre,
As a ray shed forth of the morn,
For division of soul and disease,
For a dart and a sting and a thorn?
What ailed thee then to be born?
Was there not evil enough,
Mother, and anguish on earth

Born with a man at his birth,
Wastes underfoot, and above
Storm out of heaven, and dearth
Shaken down from the shining thereof,
Wrecks from afar overseas
And peril of shallow and firth,
And tears that spring and increase
In the barren places of mirth,
That thou, having wings as a dove,
Being girt with desire for a girth,
That thou must come after these,
That thou must lay on him love?

Thou shouldst not so have been born:
But death should have risen with thee,
Mother, and visible fear,
Grief, and the wringing of hands,
And noise of many that mourn;
The smitten bosom, the knee
Bowed, and in each man's ear
A cry as of perishing lands,
A moan as of people in prison,
A tumult of infinite griefs;
And thunder of storm on the sands,
And wailing of wives on the shore;
And under thee newly arisen
Loud shoals and shipwrecking reefs,
Fierce air and violent light;
Sail rent and sundering oar,
Darkness, and noises of night;
Clashing of streams in the sea,
Wave against wave as a sword,
Clamour of currents, and foam;
Rains making ruin on earth,
Winds that wax ravenous and roam
As wolves in a wolfish horde;
Fruits growing faint in the tree,
And blind things dead in their birth;
Famine, and blighting of corn,
When thy time was come to be born.

All these we know of; but thee
Who shall discern or declare?

In the uttermost ends of the sea°
The light of thine eyelids and hair,
The light of thy bosom as fire
Between the wheel of the sun
And the flying flames of the air?
Wilt thou turn thee not yet nor have pity,
But abide with despair and desire
And the crying of armies undone,
Lamentation of one with another,
And breaking of city by city;
The dividing of friend against friend,
The severing of brother and brother;
Wilt thou utterly bring to an end?
Have mercy, mother!

For against all men from of old
Thou hast set thine hand as a curse,
And cast out gods from their places.
These things are spoken of thee.
Strong kings and goodly with gold
Thou hast found out arrows to pierce,
And made their kingdoms and races
As dust and surf of the sea.
All these, overburdened with woes
And with length of their days waxen weak,
Thou slewest; and sentest moreover
Upon Tyro° an evil thing,
Rent hair and a fetter and blows
Making bloody the flower of the cheek,
Though she lay by a god as a lover,
Though fair, and the seed of a king.
For of old, being full of thy fire,
She endured not longer to wear
On her bosom a saffron vest,
On her shoulder an ashwood quiver;
Being mixed and made one through desire
With Enipeus, and all her hair
Made moist with his mouth, and her breast
Filled full of the foam of the river.

ATALANTA

Sun, and clear light° among green hills, and day
Late risen and long sought after, and you just gods
Whose hands divide anguish and recompense,

But first the sun's white sister,° a maid in heaven,
On earth of all maids worshipped—hail, and hear,
And witness with me if not without sign sent,
Not without rule and reverence, I a maid
Hallowed, and huntress holy as whom I serve,
Here in your sight and eyeshot of these men
Stand, girt as they toward hunting, and my shafts
Drawn; wherefore all ye stand up on my side,
If I be pure and all ye righteous gods,
Lest one revile me, a woman, yet no wife,
That bear a spear for spindle, and this bow strung
For a web woven; and with pure lips salute
Heaven, and the face of all the gods, and dawn
Filling with maiden flames and maiden flowers
The starless fold o' the stars, and making sweet
The warm wan heights of the air, moon-trodden ways
And breathless gates and extreme hills of heaven.
Whom, having offered water and bloodless gifts,
Flowers, and a golden circlet of pure hair,
Next Artemis I bid be favourable
And make this day all golden, hers and ours,
Gracious and good and white to the unblamed end.
But thou, O well-beloved, of all my days
Bid it be fruitful, and a crown for all,
To bring forth leaves and bind round all my hair
With perfect chaplets woven for thine of thee.
For not without the word of thy chaste mouth,
For not without law given and clean command,
Across the white straits of the running sea
From Elis even to the Acheloïan horn,°
I with clear winds came hither and gentle gods,
Far off my father's house, and left uncheered
Iasius, and uncheered the Arcadian hills
And all their green-haired waters, and all woods
Disconsolate, to hear no horn of mine
Blown, and behold no flash of swift white feet.

MELEAGER

For thy name's sake and awe toward thy chaste head,
O holiest Atalanta, no man dares
Praise thee, though fairer than whom all men praise,
And godlike for thy grace of hallowed hair
And holy habit of thine eyes, and feet
That make the blown foam neither swift nor white

Though the wind winnow and whirl it; yet we praise
Gods, found because of thee adorable
And for thy sake praiseworthiest from all men:
Thee therefore we praise also, thee as these,
Pure, and a light lit at the hands of gods.

TOXEUS

How long will ye whet spears with eloquence,
Fight, and kill beasts dry-handed with sweet words?
Cease, or talk still and slay thy boars at home.

PLEXIPPUS

Why, if she ride among us for a man,
Sit thou for her and spin; a man grown girl
Is worth a woman weaponed; sit thou here.°

MELEAGER

Peace, and be wise; no gods love idle speech.

PLEXIPPUS

Nor any man a man's mouth woman-tongued.

MELEAGER

For my lips bite not sharper than mine hands.

PLEXIPPUS

Nay, both bite soft, but no whit softly mine.

MELEAGER

Keep thine hands clean; they have time enough to stain.

PLEXIPPUS

For thine shall rest and wax not red to-day.

MELEAGER

Have all thy will of words; talk out thine heart.

ALTHÆA

Refrain your lips, O brethren, and my son,
Lest words turn snakes and bite you uttering them.

TOXEUS

Except she give her blood before the gods,
What profit shall a maid be among men?

PLEXIPPU

Let her come crowned and stretch her throat for a knife,
Bleat out her spirit and die, and so shall men

Through her too prosper and through prosperous gods;
But nowise through her living; shall she live
A flower-bud of the flower-bed, or sweet fruit
For kisses and the honey-making mouth,
And play the shield for strong men and the spear?
Then shall the heifer and her mate lock horns,
And the bride overbear the groom, and men
Gods; for no less division sunders these;
Since all things made are seasonable in time,
But if one alter unseasonable are all.
But thou, O Zeus, hear me that I may slay
This beast before thee and no man halve with me
Nor woman, lest these mock thee, though a god,
Who hast made men strong, and thou being wise be held
Foolish; for wise is that thing which endures.°

ATALANTA

Men, and the chosen of all this people, and thou,
King, I beseech you a little bear with me.
For if my life be shameful that I live,
Let the gods witness and their wrath; but these
Cast no such word against me. Thou, O mine,
O holy, O happy goddess, if I sin
Changing the words of women and the works
For spears and strange men's faces, hast not thou
One shaft of all thy sudden seven that pierced
Seven through the bosom or shining throat or side,
All couched about one mother's loosening knees,
All holy born, engraffed of Tantalus?°
But if toward any of you I am overbold
That take thus much upon me, let him think
How I, for all my forest holiness,
Fame, and this armed and iron maidenhood,
Pay thus much also; I shall have no man's love°
For ever, and no face of children born
Or feeding lips upon me or fastening eyes
For ever, nor being dead shall kings my sons
Mourn me and bury, and tears on daughters' cheeks
Burn; but a cold and sacred life, but strange,
But far from dances and the back-blowing torch,
Far off from flowers or any bed of man,
Shall my life be for ever: me the snows
That face the first o' the morning, and cold hills

Full of the land-wind and sea-travelling storms
And many a wandering wing of noisy nights
That know the thunder and hear the thickening wolves—
Me the utmost pine and footless frost of woods
That talk with many winds and gods, the hours
Re-risen, and white divisions of the dawn,
Springs thousand-tongued with the intermitting reed
And streams that murmur of the mother snow—
Me these allure, and know me; but no man
Knows, and my goddess only. Lo now, see
If one of all you these things vex at all.
Would God that any of you had all the praise
And I no manner of memory when I die,
So might I shew before her perfect eyes
Pure, whom I follow, a maiden to my death.
But for the rest let all have all they will;
For is it a grief to you that I have part,
Being woman merely, in your male might and deeds
Done by main strength? yet in my body is throned
As great a heart, and in my spirit, O men,
I have not less of godlike. Evil it were
That one a coward should mix with you, one hand
Fearful, one eye abase itself; and these
Well might ye hate and well revile, not me.
For not the difference of the several flesh
Being vile or noble or beautiful or base
Makes praiseworthy, but purer spirit and heart
Higher than these meaner mouths and limbs, that feed,
Rise, rest, and are and are not; and for me,
What should I say? but by the gods of the world
And this my maiden body, by all oaths
That bind the tongue of men and the evil will,
I am not mighty-minded, nor desire
Crowns, nor the spoil of slain things nor the fame;
Feed ye on these, eat and wax fat; cry out,
Laugh, having eaten, and leap without a lyre,
Sing, mix the wind with clamour, smite and shake
Sonorous timbrels and tumultuous hair,
And fill the dance up with tempestuous feet,
For I will none; but having prayed my prayers
And made thank-offering for prosperities,
I shall go hence and no man see me more.°
What thing is this for you to shout me down,

What, for a man to grudge me this my life
As it were envious of all yours, and I
A thief of reputations? nay, for now,
If there be any highest in heaven, a god
Above all thrones and thunders of the gods
Throned, and the wheel of the world roll under him,
Judge he between me and all of you, and see
If I transgress at all: but ye, refrain
Transgressing hands and reinless mouths, and keep
Silence, lest by much foam of violent words
And proper poison of your lips ye die.

ŒNEUS

O flower of Tegea,° maiden, fleetest foot
And holiest head of women, have good cheer
Of thy good words: but ye, depart with her
In peace and reverence, each with blameless eye
Following his fate; exalt your hands and hearts,
Strike, cease not, arrow on arrow and wound on wound,
And go with gods and with the gods return.

CHORUS

Who hath given° man speech? or who hath set therein
A thorn for peril and a snare for sin?
For in the word his life is and his breath,
  And in the word his death,
That madness and the infatuate heart may breed
  From the word's womb the deed
And life bring one thing forth ere all pass by,
Even one thing which is ours yet cannot die—
Death. Hast thou seen him ever anywhere,
Time's twin-born brother, imperishable as he
Is perishable and plaintive, clothed with care
  And mutable as sand,
But death is strong and full of blood and fair
And perdurable and like a lord of land?
Nay, time thou seest not, death thou wilt not see
Till life's right hand be loosened from thine hand
  And thy life-days from thee.
For the gods very subtly fashion
  Madness with sadness upon earth:
Not knowing in any wise compassion,
  Nor holding pity of any worth;
And many things they have given and taken,

And wrought and ruined many things;
The firm land have they loosed and shaken,
And sealed the sea with all her springs;
They have wearied time with heavy burdens
And vexed the lips of life with breath:
Set men to labour and given them guerdons,
Death, and great darkness after death:
Put moans into the bridal measure
And on the bridal wools a stain;
And circled pain about with pleasure,
And girdled pleasure about with pain;
And strewed one marriage-bed with tears and fire
For extreme loathing and supreme desire.

What shall be done with all these tears of ours?
Shall they make watersprings in the fair heaven
To bathe the brows of morning? or like flowers
Be shed and shine before the starriest hours,
Or made the raiment of the weeping Seven?°
Or rather, O our masters, shall they be
Food for the famine of the grievous sea,
A great well-head of lamentation°
Satiating the sad gods? or fall and flow
Among the years and seasons to and fro,
And wash their feet with tribulation°
And fill them full with grieving ere they go?
Alas, our lords, and yet alas again,
Seeing all your iron heaven° is gilt as gold
But all we smite thereat in vain;
Smite the gates barred with groanings manifold,
But all the floors are paven with our pain.
Yea, and with weariness of lips and eyes,
With breaking of the bosom, and with sighs,
We labour, and are clad and fed with grief
And filled with days we would not fain behold
And nights we would not hear of; we wax old,
All we wax old and wither like a leaf.
We are outcast, strayed between bright sun and moon;
Our light and darkness are as leaves of flowers,
Black flowers and white, that perish; and the noon
As midnight, and the night as daylight hours.
A little fruit a little while is ours,
And the worm finds it soon.

But up in heaven the high gods one by one
  Lay hands upon the draught that quickeneth,
Fulfilled with all tears shed and all things done,
  And stir with soft imperishable breath
  The bubbling bitterness of life and death,
And hold it to our lips and laugh; but they
Preserve their lips from tasting night or day,
  Lest they too change and sleep, the fates that spun,
The lips that made us and the hands that slay;
  Lest all these change, and heaven bow down to none,
Change and be subject to the secular sway
  And terrene revolution of the sun.
Therefore they thrust it from them, putting time away.

I would the wine of time, made sharp and sweet
  With multitudinous days and nights and tears
  And many mixing savours of strange years,
Were no more trodden of them under feet,
  Cast out and spilt about their holy places:
That life were given them as a fruit to eat
And death to drink as water; that the light
Might ebb, drawn backward from their eyes, and night
  Hide for one hour the imperishable faces.
That they might rise up sad in heaven, and know
Sorrow and sleep, one paler than young snow,
  One cold as blight of dew and ruinous rain;
Rise up and rest and suffer a little, and be
Awhile as all things born with us and we,
  And grieve as men, and like slain men be slain.

For now we know not of them; but one saith
  The gods are gracious, praising God; and one,
When hast thou seen? or hast thou felt his breath
  Touch, nor consume thine eyelids as the sun,
Nor fill thee to the lips with fiery death?
  None hath beheld him, none
Seen above other gods and shapes of things,
Swift without feet and flying without wings,
Intolerable, not clad with death or life,
  Insatiable, not known of night or day,
The lord of love and loathing and of strife
  Who gives a star and takes a sun away;
Who shapes the soul, and makes her a barren wife

To the earthly body and grievous growth of clay;
Who turns the large limbs to a little flame
And binds the great sea with a little sand;
Who makes desire, and slays desire with shame;
Who shakes the heaven as ashes in his hand;
Who, seeing the light and shadow for the same,
Bids day waste night as fire devours a brand,
Smites without sword, and scourges without rod;
The supreme evil, God.

Yea, with thine hate, O God, thou hast covered us,
One saith, and hidden our eyes away from sight,
And made us transitory and hazardous,
Light things and slight;
Yet have men praised thee, saying, He hath made man thus,
And he doeth right.
Thou hast kissed us, and hast smitten; thou hast laid
Upon us with thy left hand life, and said,
Live: and again thou hast said, Yield up your breath,
And with thy right hand laid upon us death.
Thou hast sent us sleep, and stricken sleep with dreams,
Saying, Joy is not, but love of joy shall be;
Thou hast made sweet springs for all the pleasant streams,
In the end thou hast made them bitter with the sea.
Thou hast fed one rose with dust of many men;
Thou hast marred one face with fire of many tears;
Thou hast taken love, and given us sorrow again;
With pain thou hast filled us full to the eyes and ears.
Therefore because thou art strong, our father, and we
Feeble; and thou art against us, and thine hand
Constrains us in the shallows of the sea
And breaks us at the limits of the land;
Because thou hast bent thy lightnings as a bow,
And loosed the hours like arrows; and let fall
Sins and wild words and many a wingèd woe
And wars among us, and one end of all;
Because thou hast made the thunder, and thy feet
Are as a rushing water when the skies
Break, but thy face as an exceeding heat
And flames of fire the eyelids of thine eyes;
Because thou art over all who are over us:
Because thy name is life and our name death;
Because thou art cruel and men are piteous,

And our hands labour and thine hand scattereth;
Lo, with hearts rent and knees made tremulous,
Lo, with ephemeral lips and casual breath,
At least we witness of thee ere we die
That these things are not otherwise, but thus;
That each man in his heart sigheth, and saith,
That all men even as I,
All we are against thee, against thee, O God most high.

But ye, keep ye on earth
Your lips from over-speech,
Loud words and longing are so little worth;
And the end is hard to reach.
For silence after grievous things is good,
And reverence, and the fear that makes men whole,
And shame, and righteous governance of blood,
And lordship of the soul.
But from sharp words and wits men pluck no fruit,
And gathering thorns they shake the tree at root;[o]
For words divide and rend;
But silence is most noble till the end.

ALTHÆA

I heard within[o] the house a cry of news
And came forth eastward hither, where the dawn
Cheers first these warder gods[o] that face the sun
And next our eyes unrisen; for unaware
Came clashes of swift hoofs and trampling feet
And through the windy pillared corridor
Light sharper than the frequent flames of day
That daily fill it from the fiery dawn;
Gleams, and a thunder of people that cried out,
And dust and hurrying horsemen; lo their chief,
That rode with Œneus rein by rein, returned.
What cheer, O herald of my lord the king?

HERALD

Lady, good cheer and great; the boar is slain.

CHORUS

Praised be all gods that look toward Calydon.

ALTHÆA

Good news and brief; but by whose happier hand?

HERALD

A maiden's and a prophet's and thy son's.

ALTHÆA

Well fare the spear that severed him and life.

HERALD

Thine own, and not an alien, hast thou blest.

ALTHÆA

Twice be thou too for my sake blest and his.

HERALD

At the king's word I rode afoam for thine.

ALTHÆ

Thou sayest he tarrieth till they bring the spoil?

HERALD

Hard by the quarry, where they breathe, O queen.

ALTHÆA

Speak thou their chance; but some bring flowers and crown
These gods and all the lintel, and shed wine,
Fetch sacrifice and slay; for heaven is good.

HERALD

Some furlongs northward where the brakes begin
West of that narrowing range of warrior hills
Whose brooks have bled with battle when thy son
Smote Acarnania, there all they made halt,
And with keen eye took note of spear and hound,
Royally ranked; Laertes island-born,
The young Gerenian Nestor, Panopeus,
And Cepheus and Ancæus, mightiest thewed,
Arcadians; next, and evil-eyed of these,
Arcadian Atalanta, with twain hounds
Lengthening the leash, and under nose and brow
Glittering with lipless tooth and fire-swift eye;
But from her white braced shoulder the plumed shafts
Rang, and the bow shone from her side; next her
Meleager, like a sun in spring that strikes
Branch into leaf and bloom into the world,
A glory among men meaner; Iphicles,
And following him that slew the biform bull
Pirithous, and divine Eurytion,

And, bride-bound to the gods, Æacides.
Then Telamon his brother, and Argive-born
The seer and sayer of visions and of truth,
Amphiaraus; and a four-fold strength,
Thine, even thy mother's and thy sister's sons.
And recent from the roar of foreign foam
Jason, and Dryas twin-begot with war,
A blossom of bright battle, sword and man
Shining; and Idas, and the keenest eye
Of Lynceus, and Admetus twice-espoused,
And Hippasus and Hyleus, great in heart.°
These having halted bade blow horns, and rode
Through woods and waste lands cleft by stormy streams,
Past yew-trees and the heavy hair of pines,
And where the dew is thickest under oaks,
This way and that; but questing up and down
They saw no trail nor scented; and one said,
Plexippus, Help, or help not, Artemis,
And we will flay thy boarskin with male hands;
But saying, he ceased and said not that he would,
Seeing where the green ooze of a sun-struck marsh
Shook with a thousand reeds untunable,
And in their moist and multitudinous flower
Slept no soft sleep, with violent visions fed,
The blind bulk of the immeasurable beast.
And seeing, he shuddered with sharp lust of praise
Through all his limbs, and launched a double dart,
And missed; for much desire divided him,
Too hot of spirit and feebler than his will,
That his hand failed, though fervent; and the shaft,
Sundering the rushes, in a tamarisk stem
Shook, and stuck fast; then all abode save one,
The Arcadian Atalanta; from her side
Sprang her hounds, labouring at the leash, and slipped,
And plashed ear-deep with plunging feet; but she
Saying, Speed it as I send it for thy sake,
Goddess,° drew bow and loosed; the sudden string
Rang, and sprang inward, and the waterish air
Hissed, and the moist plumes of the songless reeds
Moved as a wave which the wind moves no more.
But the boar heaved half out of ooze and slime
His tense flank trembling round the barbèd wound,
Hateful; and fiery with invasive eyes

And bristling with intolerable hair
Plunged, and the hounds clung, and green flowers and white
Reddened and broke all round them where they came.
And charging with sheer tusk he drove, and smote
Hyleus; and sharp death caught his sudden soul,
And violent sleep shed night upon his eyes.
Then Peleus, with strong strain of hand and heart,
Shot; but the sidelong arrow slid, and slew
His comrade born and loving countryman,
Under the left arm smitten, as he no less
Poised a like arrow; and bright blood brake afoam,
And falling, and weighed back by clamorous arms,
Sharp rang the dead limbs of Eurytion.
Then one shot happier, the Cadmean seer,
Amphiaraus; for his sacred shaft
Pierced the red circlet of one ravening eye
Beneath the brute brows of the sanguine boar,
Now bloodier from one slain; but he so galled
Sprang straight, and rearing cried no lesser cry
Than thunder and the roar of wintering streams
That mix their own foam with the yellower sea;
And as a tower that falls by fire in fight
With ruin of walls and all its archery,
And breaks the iron flower of war beneath,
Crushing charred limbs and molten arms of men;
So through crushed branches and the reddening brake
Clamoured and crashed the fervour of his feet,
And trampled, springing sideways from the tusk,
Too tardy a moving mould of heavy strength,
Ancæus;[°] and as flakes of weak-winged snow
Break, all the hard thews of his heaving limbs
Broke, and rent flesh fell every way, and blood
Flew, and fierce fragments of no more a man.
Then all the heroes drew sharp breath, and gazed,
And smote not; but Meleager, but thy son,
Right in the wild way of the coming curse
Rock-rooted, fair with fierce and fastened lips,
Clear eyes, and springing muscle and shortening limb—
With chin aslant indrawn to a tightening throat,
Grave, and with gathered sinews, like a god,—
Aimed on the left side his well-handled spear
Grasped where the ash was knottiest hewn, and smote,
And with no missile wound, the monstrous boar

Right in the hairiest hollow of his hide
Under the last rib, sheer through bulk and bone,
Deep in; and deeply smitten, and to death,
The heavy horror with his hanging shafts
Leapt, and fell furiously, and from raging lips
Foamed out the latest wrath of all his life.
And all they praised the gods with mightier heart,
Zeus and all gods, but chiefliest Artemis,
Seeing; but Meleager bade whet knives and flay,
Strip and stretch out the splendour of the spoil;
And hot and horrid from the work all these
Sat, and drew breath and drank and made great cheer
And washed the hard sweat off their calmer brows.
For much sweet grass grew higher than grew the reed,
And good for slumber, and every holier herb,
Narcissus, and the low-lying melilote,
And all of goodliest blade and bloom that springs
Where, hid by heavier hyacinth, violet buds
Blossom and burn; and fire of yellower flowers
And light of crescent lilies, and such leaves
As fear the Faun's and know the Dryad's foot;
Olive and ivy and poplar dedicate,
And many a wellspring overwatched of these.
There now they rest; but me the king bade bear
Good tidings to rejoice this town and thee.
Wherefore be glad, and all ye give much thanks,
For fallen is all the trouble of Calydon.

ALTHÆA

Laud ye the gods;° for this they have given is good,
And what shall be they hide until their time.
Much good and somewhat grievous hast thou said,
And either well; but let all sad things be,
Till all have made before the prosperous gods
Burnt-offering, and poured out the floral wine.
Look fair, O gods, and favourable; for we
Praise you with no false heart or flattering mouth,
Being merciful, but with pure souls and prayer.

HERALD

Thou hast prayed well; for whoso fears not these,
But once being prosperous waxes huge of heart,
Him shall some new thing unaware destroy.

CHORUS

O that I now,° I too were
By deep wells and water-floods,
Streams of ancient hills, and where
All the wan green places bear
Blossoms cleaving to the sod,
Fruitless fruit, and grasses fair,
Or such darkest ivy-buds
As divide thy yellow hair,
Bacchus, and their leaves that nod
Round thy fawnskin brush the bare
Snow-soft shoulders of a god;
There the year is sweet, and there
Earth is full of secret springs,
And the fervent rose-cheeked hours,
Those that marry dawn and noon,
There are sunless, there look pale
In dim leaves and hidden air,
Pale as grass or latter flowers
Or the wild vine's wan wet rings
Full of dew beneath the moon,
And all day the nightingale
Sleeps, and all night sings;
There in cold remote recesses
That nor alien eyes assail,
Feet, nor imminence of wings,
Nor a wind nor any tune,
Thou, O queen and holiest,
Flower the whitest of all things,
With reluctant lengthening tresses
And with sudden splendid breast
Save of maidens unbeholden,
There art wont to enter, there
Thy divine swift limbs and golden
Maiden growth of unbound hair,
Bathed in waters white,
Shine, and many a maid's by thee
In moist woodland or the hilly
Flowerless brakes where wells abound
Out of all men's sight;
Or in lower pools that see
All their marges clothed all round
With the innumerable lily,

Whence the golden-girdled bee
Flits through flowering rush to fret
White or duskier violet,
Fair as those that in far years
With their buds left luminous
And their little leaves made wet
From the warmer dew of tears,
Mother's tears in extreme need,
Hid the limbs of Iamus,°
Of thy brother's seed;
For his heart was piteous
Toward him, even as thine heart now
Pitiful toward us;
Thine, O goddess, turning hither
A benignant blameless brow;
Seeing enough of evil done
And lives withered as leaves wither
In the blasting of the sun;
Seeing enough of hunters dead,
Ruin enough of all our year,
Herds and harvests slain and shed,
Herdsmen stricken many an one,
Fruits and flocks consumed together,
And great length of deadly days.
Yet with reverent lips and fear
Turn we toward thee, turn and praise
For this lightening of clear weather
And prosperities begun.
For not seldom, when all air
As bright water without breath
Shines, and when men fear not, fate
Without thunder unaware
Breaks, and brings down death.
Joy with grief ye great gods give,
Good with bad, and overbear
All the pride of us that live,
All the high estate,
As ye long since overbore,
As in old time long before,
Many a strong man and a great,
All that were.
But do thou, sweet, otherwise,

Having heed of all our prayer,
Taking note of all our sighs;
We beseech thee by thy light,
By thy bow, and thy sweet eyes,
And the kingdom of the night,°
Be thou favourable and fair;
By thine arrows and thy might
And Orion overthrown;°
By the maiden thy delight,
By the indissoluble zone
And the sacred hair.

MESSENGER

Maidens,° if ye will sing now, shift your song,
Bow down, cry, wail for pity; is this a time
For singing? nay, for strewing of dust and ash,
Rent raiment, and for bruising of the breast.

CHORUS

What new thing wolf-like lurks behind thy words?
What snake's tongue in thy lips? what fire in the eyes?

MESSENGER

Bring me before the queen and I will speak.

CHORUS

Lo, she comes forth as from thank-offering made.

MESSENGER

A barren offering for a bitter gift.

ALTHÆA

What are these borne on branches, and the face
Covered? no mean men living, but now slain
Such honour have they, if any dwell with death.

MESSENGER

Queen, thy twain brethren and thy mother's sons.

ALTHÆA

Lay down your dead till I behold their blood
If it be mine indeed, and I will weep.

MESSENGER

Weep if thou wilt, for these men shall no more.

ALTHÆA

O brethren, O my father's sons, of me
Well loved and well reputed, I should weep
Tears dearer than the dear blood drawn from you
But that I know you not uncomforted,
Sleeping no shameful sleep, however slain,
For my son surely hath avenged you dead.

MESSENGER

Nay, should thine own seed slay himself, O queen?

ALTHÆA

Thy double word brings forth a double death.

MESSENGER

Know this then singly, by one hand they fell.

ALTHÆA

What mutterest thou with thine ambiguous mouth?

MESSENGER

Slain by thy son's hand; is that saying so hard?

ALTHÆA

Our time is come upon us: it is here.°

CHORUS

O miserable, and spoiled at thine own hand.

ALTHÆA

Wert thou not called Meleager from this womb?

CHORUS

A grievous huntsman° hath it bred to thee.

ALTHÆA

Wert thou born fire, and shalt thou not devour?

CHORUS

The fire thou madest, will it consume even thee?

ALTHÆA

My dreams are fallen upon me; burn thou too.

CHORUS

Not without God are visions born and die.

ALTHÆA

The gods are many about me; I am one.

CHORUS

She groans as men wrestling with heavier gods.

ALTHÆA

They rend me, they divide me, they destroy.

CHORUS

Or one labouring in travail of strange births.[o]

ALTHÆA

They are strong, they are strong; I am broken, and these prevail.

CHORUS

The god is great against her; she will die.

ALTHÆA

Yea, but not now; for my heart too is great.
I would I were not here in sight of the sun.[o]
But thou, speak all thou sawest, and I will die.

MESSENGER

O queen, for queenlike hast thou borne thyself,
A little word may hold so great mischance.
For in division of the sanguine spoil
These men thy brethren wrangling bade yield up
The boar's head and the horror of the hide
That this might stand a wonder in Calydon,
Hallowed; and some drew toward them; but thy son
With great hands grasping all that weight of hair
Cast down the dead heap clanging and collapsed
At female feet, saying This thy spoil not mine,
Maiden, thine own hand for thyself hath reaped,
And all this praise God gives thee: she thereat
Laughed, as when dawn touches the sacred night
The sky sees laugh and redden and divide
Dim lips and eyelids virgin of the sun,
Hers, and the warm slow breasts of morning heave,
Fruitful, and flushed with flame from lamp-lit hours,
And maiden undulation of clear hair
Colour the clouds; so laughed she from pure heart
Lit with a low blush to the braided hair,
And rose-coloured and cold like very dawn,
Golden and godlike, chastely with chaste lips,
A faint grave laugh; and all they held their peace,
And she passed by them. Then one cried Lo now,

Shall not the Arcadian shoot out lips° at us,
Saying all we were despoiled by this one girl?
And all they rode against her violently
And cast the fresh crown from her hair, and now
They had rent her spoil away, dishonouring her,
Save that Meleager, as a tame lion chafed,°
Bore on them, broke them, and as fire cleaves wood
So clove and drove them, smitten in twain; but she
Smote not nor heaved up hand; and this man first,
Plexippus, crying out This for love's sake, sweet,
Drove at Meleager, who with spear straightening
Pierced his cheek through; then Toxeus made for him,
Dumb, but his spear spake; vain and violent words,
Fruitless; for him too stricken through both sides
The earth felt falling, and his horse's foam
Blanched thy son's face, his slayer; and these being slain,
None moved nor spake; but Œneus bade bear hence
These made of heaven infatuate in their deaths,
Foolish; for these would baffle fate, and fell.
And they passed on, and all men honoured her,
Being honourable, as one revered of heaven.

ALTHÆA

What say you, women? is all this not well done?

CHORUS

No man doth well but God hath part in him.

ALTHÆA

But no part here; for these my brethren born
Ye have no part in, these ye know not of
As I that was their sister, a sacrifice
Slain in their slaying. I would I had died for these;°
For this man dead walked with me, child by child,
And made a weak staff for my feebler feet
With his own tender wrist and hand, and held
And led me softly and shewed me gold and steel
And shining shapes of mirror and bright crown
And all things fair; and threw light spears, and brought
Young hounds to huddle at my feet and thrust
Tame heads against my little maiden breasts
And please me with great eyes; and those days went
And these are bitter and I a barren queen
And sister miserable, a grievous thing

And mother of many curses; and she too,
My sister Leda, sitting overseas
With fair fruits round her, and her faultless lord,
Shall curse me, saying A sorrow and not a son,
Sister, thou barest, even a burning fire,
A brand consuming thine own soul and me.
But ye now, sons of Thestius, make good cheer,
For ye shall have such wood to funeral fire
As no king hath; and flame that once burnt down
Oil shall not quicken or breath relume or wine
Refresh again; much costlier than fine gold,
And more than many lives of wandering men.

CHORUS

O queen, thou hast yet with thee love-worthy things,
Thine husband, and the great strength of thy son.

ALTHÆA

Who shall get brothers° for me while I live?
Who bear them? who bring forth in lieu of these?
Are not our fathers and our brethren one,
And no man like them? are not mine here slain?
Have we not hung together, he and I,
Flowerwise feeding as the feeding bees,
With mother-milk for honey? and this man too,
Dead, with my son's spear thrust between his sides,
Hath he not seen us, later born than he,
Laugh with lips filled, and laughed again for love?
There were no sons then in the world, nor spears,
Nor deadly births of women; but the gods
Allowed us, and our days were clear of these.
I would I had died unwedded, and brought forth
No swords to vex the world; for these that spake
Sweet words long since and loved me will not speak
Nor love nor look upon me; and all my life
I shall not hear nor see them living men.
But I too living, how shall I now live?
What life shall this be with my son, to know
What hath been and desire what will not be,
Look for dead eyes and listen for dead lips,
And kill mine own heart with remembering them,
And with those eyes that see their slayer alive
Weep, and wring hands that clasp him by the hand?
How shall I bear my dreams of them, to hear

False voices, feel the kisses of false mouths
And footless sound of perished feet, and then
Wake and hear only it may be their own hounds
Whine masterless[o] in miserable sleep,
And see their boar-spears and their beds and seats
And all the gear and housings of their lives
And not the men? shall hounds and horses mourn,
Pine with strange eyes, and prick up hungry ears,
Famish and fail at heart for their dear lords,
And I not heed at all?[o] and those blind things
Fall off from life for love's sake, and I live?
Surely some death is better than some life,
Better one death for him and these and me.
For if the gods had slain them it may be
I had endured it; if they had fallen by war
Or by the nets and knives[o] of privy death
And by hired hands while sleeping, this thing too
I had set my soul to suffer; or this hunt,
Had this despatched them, under tusk or tooth
Torn, sanguine, trodden, broken; for all deaths
Or honourable or with facile feet avenged
And hands of swift gods following, all save this,
Are bearable; but not for their sweet land
Fighting, but not a sacrifice, lo these
Dead; for I had not then shed all mine heart
Out at mine eyes: then either with good speed,
Being just, I had slain their slayer atoningly,
Or strewn with flowers their fire and on their tombs
Hung crowns, and over them a song, and seen
Their praise outflame their ashes: for all men,
All maidens, had come thither, and from pure lips
Shed songs upon them, from heroic eyes
Tears; and their death had been a deathless life;
But now, by no man hired nor alien sword,
By their own kindred are they fallen, in peace,
After much peril, friendless among friends,
By hateful hands they loved; and how shall mine
Touch these returning red and not from war,
These fatal from the vintage of men's veins,
Dead men my brethren? how shall these wash off
No festal stains of undelightful wine,
How mix the blood, my blood on them, with me,
Holding mine hand? or how shall I say, son,

That am no sister? but by night and day
Shall we not sit and hate each other, and think
Things hate-worthy? not live with shamefast eyes,
Brow-beaten, treading soft with fearful feet,
Each unupbraided, each without rebuke
Convicted, and without a word reviled
Each of another? and I shall let thee live
And see thee strong and hear men for thy sake
Praise me, but these thou wouldest not let live
No man shall praise for ever? these shall lie
Dead, unbeloved, unholpen, all through thee?
Sweet were they toward me living, and mine heart
Desired them, but was then well satisfied,
That now is as men hungered; and these dead
I shall want always to the day I die.
For all things else and all men may renew;
Yea, son for son the gods may give and take,
But never a brother or sister any more.°

CHORUS

Nay, for the son lies close about thine heart,
Full of thy milk, warm from thy womb, and drains
Life and the blood of life and all thy fruit,
Eats thee and drinks thee as who breaks bread and eats,°
Treads wine and drinks, thyself, a sect° of thee;
And if he feed not, shall not thy flesh faint?
Or drink not, are not thy lips dead for thirst?
This thing moves more than all things, even thy son,
That thou cleave to him; and he shall honour thee,
Thy womb that bare him and the breasts he knew,
Reverencing most for thy sake all his gods.

ALTHÆA

But these the gods too gave me, and these my son,
Not reverencing his gods nor mine own heart
Nor the old sweet years nor all venerable things,
But cruel, and in his ravin like a beast,
Hath taken away to slay them: yea, and she,
She the strange woman, she the flower, the sword,
Red from spilt blood, a mortal flower to men,
Adorable, detestable—even she
Saw with strange eyes and with strange lips rejoiced,
Seeing these mine own slain of mine own, and me
Made miserable above all miseries made,

A grief among all women in the world,
A name to be washed out with all men's tears.

CHORUS

Strengthen thy spirit; is this not also a god,
Chance, and the wheel of all necessities?
Hard things have fallen upon us from harsh gods,
Whom lest worse hap rebuke we not for these.

ALTHÆA

My spirit is strong against itself, and I
For these things' sake cry out on mine own soul
That it endures outrage, and dolorous days,
And life, and this inexpiable impotence.
Weak am I, weak and shameful; my breath drawn
Shames me, and monstrous things and violent gods.
What shall atone? what heal me? what bring back
Strength to the foot, light to the face? what herb
Assuage me? what restore me? what release?
What strange thing eaten or drunken, O great gods,
Make me as you or as the beasts that feed,
Slay and divide and cherish their own hearts?
For these ye show us; and we less than these
Have not wherewith to live as all these things
Which all their lives fare after their own kind
As who doth well rejoicing; but we ill,
Weeping or laughing, we whom eyesight fails,
Knowledge and light of face and perfect heart,
And hands we lack, and wit; and all our days
Sin, and have hunger, and die infatuated.
For madness have ye given us and not health,
And sins whereof we know not; and for these
Death, and sudden destruction unaware.
What shall we say now? what thing comes of us?

CHORUS

Alas, for all this all men undergo.

ALTHÆA

Wherefore I will not that these twain, O gods,
Die as a dog dies, eaten of creeping things,
Abominable, a loathing; but though dead
Shall they have honour and such funereal flame
As strews men's ashes in their enemies' face
And blinds their eyes who hate them: lest men say,

'Lo how they lie, and living had great kin,
And none of these hath pity of them, and none
Regards them lying, and none is wrung at heart,
None moved in spirit for them, naked and slain,
Abhorred, abased, and no tears comfort them:'
And in the dark this grieve Eurythemis,
Hearing how these her sons come down to her
Unburied, unavenged, as kinless men,
And had a queen their sister.° That were shame
Worse than this grief. Yet how to atone at all
I know not; seeing the love of my born son,
A new-made mother's new-born love, that grows
From the soft child to the strong man, now soft
Now strong as either, and still one sole same love,°
Strives with me, no light thing to strive withal;
This love is deep, and natural to man's blood,
And ineffaceable with many tears.
Yet shall not these rebuke me though I die,
Nor she in that waste world with all her dead,
My mother, among the pale flocks fallen as leaves,
Folds of dead people, and alien from the sun;
Nor lack some bitter comfort, some poor praise,
Being queen, to have borne her daughter like a queen,
Righteous; and though mine own fire burn me too,
She shall have honour and these her sons, though dead.
But all the gods will, all they do, and we
Not all we would, yet somewhat; and one choice
We have, to live and do just deeds and die.

CHORUS

Terrible words she communes with, and turns
Swift fiery eyes in doubt against herself,
And murmurs as who talks in dreams with death.

ALTHÆA

For the unjust also dieth, and him all men
Hate, and himself abhors the unrighteousness,
And seeth his own dishonour intolerable.
But I being just, doing right upon myself,
Slay mine own soul, and no man born shames me.
For none constrains nor shall rebuke, being done,
What none compelled me doing; thus these things fare.
Ah, ah, that such things should so fare; ah me,

That I am found to do them and endure,
Chosen and constrained to choose, and bear myself
Mine own wound through mine own flesh to the heart
Violently stricken, a spoiler and a spoil,
A ruin ruinous, fallen on mine own son.
Ah, ah, for me too as for these; alas,
For that is done that shall be, and mine hand
Full of the deed, and full of blood mine eyes,
That shall see never nor touch anything
Save blood unstanched and fire unquenchable.°

CHORUS

What wilt thou do? what ails thee? for the house
Shakes ruinously; wilt thou bring fire for it?

ALTHÆA

Fire in the roofs, and on the lintels fire.
Lo ye, who stand and weave, between the doors,
There; and blood drips from hand and thread, and stains
Threshold and raiment and me passing in
Flecked with the sudden sanguine drops of death.

CHORUS

Alas that time is stronger than strong men,
Fate than all gods: and these are fallen on us.

ALTHÆA

A little since and I was glad; and now
I never shall be glad or sad again.

CHORUS

Between two joys a grief grows unaware.

ALTHÆA

A little while and I shall laugh; and then
I shall weep never and laugh not any more.

CHORUS

What shall be said? for words are thorns to grief.
Withhold thyself a little and fear the gods.

ALTHÆA

Fear died when these were slain; and I am as dead,
And fear is of the living; these fear none.

CHORUS

Have pity upon all people for their sake.

ALTHÆA

It is done now; shall I put back my day?

CHORUS

An end is come, an end; this is of God.

ALTHÆA

I am fire, and burn myself; keep clear of fire.

CHORUS

The house is broken, is broken; it shall not stand.°

ALTHÆA

Woe, woe for him that breaketh; and a rod
Smote it of old, and now the axe is here.

CHORUS

Not as with sundering° of the earth
  Nor as with cleaving of the sea
Nor fierce foreshadowings of a birth
  Nor flying dreams of death to be
Nor loosening of the large world's girth
And quickening of the body of night,
  And sound of thunder in men's ears
And fire of lightning in men's sight,
  Fate, mother of desires and fears,
  Bore unto men the law of tears;
But sudden, an unfathered flame,
  And broken out of night, she shone,
She, without body, without name,
  In days forgotten and foregone;
And heaven rang round her as she came°
Like smitten cymbals, and lay bare;
  Clouds and great stars, thunders and snows,
The blue sad fields and folds of air,
  The life that breathes, the life that grows,
  All wind, all fire, that burns or blows,
Even all these knew her: for she is great;
  The daughter of doom, the mother of death,
The sister of sorrow; a lifelong weight
  That no man's finger lighteneth,
Nor any god can lighten fate;
A landmark seen across the way
  Where one race treads as the other trod;
An evil sceptre, an evil stay,

Wrought for a staff, wrought for a rod,
The bitter jealousy of God.

For death is deep as the sea,
And fate as the waves thereof.
Shall the waves take pity on thee
Or the southwind offer thee love?
Wilt thou take the night for thy day
Or the darkness for light on thy way
Till thou say in thine heart Enough?
Behold, thou art over fair, thou art over wise;
The sweetness of spring in thine hair, and the light in thine eyes.
The light of the spring in thine eyes, and the sound in thine ears;
Yet thine heart shall wax heavy with sighs and thine eyelids with tears.
Wilt thou cover thine hair with gold, and with silver thy feet?
Hast thou taken the purple to fold thee, and made thy mouth sweet?
Behold, when thy face is made bare, he that loved thee shall hate;
Thy face shall be no more fair at the fall of thy fate.
For thy life shall fall as a leaf and be shed as the rain;
And the veil of thine head shall be grief; and the crown shall be pain.

ALTHÆA

Ho, ye that wail,° and ye that sing, make way
Till I be come among you. Hide your tears,
Ye little weepers, and your laughing lips,
Ye laughers for a little; lo mine eyes
That outweep heaven at rainiest, and my mouth
That laughs as gods laugh at us. Fate's are we,
Yet fate is ours a breathing-space; yea, mine,
Fate is made mine for ever; he is my son,
My bedfellow, my brother. You strong gods,
Give place unto me; I am as any of you,
To give life and to take life. Thou, old earth,
That hast made man and unmade; thou whose mouth
Looks red from the eaten fruits of thine own womb;
Behold me with what lips upon what food
I feed and fill my body; even with flesh
Made of my body. Lo, the fire I lit
I burn with fire to quench it; yea, with flame
I burn up even the dust and ash thereof.

CHORUS

Woman, what fire is this thou burnest with?

ALTHÆA

Yea to the bone, yea to the blood and all.

CHORUS

For this thy face and hair are as one fire.

ALTHÆA

A tongue that licks and beats upon the dust.

CHORUS

And in thine eyes are hollow light and heat.

ALTHÆA

Of flame not fed with hand or frankincense.

CHORUS

I fear thee for the trembling of thine eyes.

ALTHÆA

Neither with love they tremble nor for fear.

CHORUS

And thy mouth shuddering like a shot bird.

ALTHÆA

Not as the bride's mouth when man kisses it.

CHORUS

Nay, but what thing is this thing thou hast done?

ALTHÆA

Look, I am silent, speak your eyes for me.

CHORUS

I see a faint fire lightening from the hall.

ALTHÆA

Gaze, stretch your eyes, strain till the lids drop off.

CHORUS

Flushed pillars down the flickering vestibule.

ALTHÆA

Stretch with your necks like birds: cry, chirp as they.

CHORUS

And a long brand that blackens: and white dust.

ALTHÆA

O children, what is this ye see? your eyes
Are blinder than night's face at fall of moon.

That is my son, my flesh, my fruit of life,
My travail, and the year's weight of my womb,
Meleager, a fire enkindled of mine hands
And of mine hands extinguished; this is he.

CHORUS

O gods, what word has flown out at thy mouth?

ALTHÆA

I did this and I say this and I die.

CHORUS

Death stands upon the doorway of thy lips,°
And in thy mouth has death set up his house.

ALTHÆA

O death, a little, a little while, sweet death,
Until I see the brand burnt down and die.

CHORUS

She reels as any reed under the wind,
And cleaves unto the ground with staggering feet.

ALTHÆA

Girls, one thing will I say and hold my peace.
I that did this will weep not nor cry out,
Cry ye and weep: I will not call on gods,
Call ye on them; I will not pity man,
Shew ye your pity. I know not if I live;
Save that I feel the fire upon my face
And on my cheek the burning of a brand.
Yea the smoke bites me, yea I drink the steam
With nostril and with eyelid and with lip
Insatiate and intolerant; and mine hands
Burn, and fire feeds upon mine eyes; I reel
As one made drunk with living, whence he draws
Drunken delight; yet I, though mad for joy,
Loathe my long living and am waxen red
As with the shadow of shed blood; behold,
I am kindled with the flames that fade in him,
I am swollen with subsiding of his veins,
I am flooded with his ebbing; my lit eyes
Flame with the falling fire that leaves his lids
Bloodless; my cheek is luminous with blood
Because his face is ashen. Yet, O child,

Son, first-born, fairest—O sweet mouth, sweet eyes,
That drew my life out through my suckling breast,
That shone and clove mine heart through—O soft knees
Clinging, O tender treadings of soft feet,
Cheeks warm with little kissings—O child, child,
What have we made each other? Lo, I felt
Thy weight cleave to me, a burden of beauty, O son,
Thy cradled brows and loveliest loving lips,
The floral hair, the little lightening eyes,
And all thy goodly glory; with mine hands
Delicately I fed thee, with my tongue
Tenderly spake, saying, Verily in God's time,
For all the little likeness of thy limbs,
Son, I shall make thee a kingly man to fight,
A lordly leader; and hear before I die,
'She bore the goodliest sword of all the world.'
Oh! oh! For all my life turns round on me;
I am severed from myself, my name is gone,
My name that was a healing,° it is changed,
My name is a consuming. From this time,
Though mine eyes reach to the end of all these things,
My lips shall not unfasten till I die.°

SEMICHORUS

She has filled° with sighing the city,
    And the ways thereof with tears;
  She arose, she girdled her sides,
  She set her face as a bride's;
  She wept, and she had no pity;
    Trembled, and felt no fears.

SEMICHORUS

Her eyes were clear as the sun,
    Her brows were fresh as the day;
  She girdled herself with gold,
  Her robes were manifold;
  But the days of her worship are done,
    Her praise is taken away.

SEMICHORUS

For she set her hand to the fire,
    With her mouth she kindled the same;
  As the mouth of a flute-player,
  So was the mouth of her;

With the might of her strong desire
She blew the breath of the flame.

SEMICHORUS

She set her hand to the wood,
She took the fire in her hand;
As one who is nigh to death,
She panted with strange breath;
She opened her lips unto blood,
She breathed and kindled the brand.

SEMICHORUS

As a wood-dove newly shot,
She sobbed and lifted her breast;
She sighed and covered her eyes,
Filling her lips with sighs;
She sighed, she withdrew herself not,
She refrained not, taking not rest;

SEMICHORUS

But as the wind which is drouth,
And as the air which is death,
As storm that severeth ships,
Her breath severing her lips,
The breath came forth of her mouth
And the fire came forth of her breath.

SECOND MESSENGER

Queen, and you maidens, there is come on us
A thing more deadly than the face of death;
Meleager the good lord is as one slain.

SEMICHORUS

Without sword, without sword is he stricken;
Slain, and slain without hand.

SECOND MESSENGER

For as keen ice divided of the sun
His limbs divide, and as thawed snow the flesh
Thaws from off all his body to the hair.

SEMICHORUS

He wastes as the embers quicken;
With the brand he fades as a brand.

SECOND MESSENGER

Even while they sang and all drew hither and he
Lifted both hands to crown the Arcadian's hair
And fix the looser leaves, both hands fell down.

SEMICHORUS

With rending of cheek and of hair
Lament ye, mourn for him, weep.

SECOND MESSENGER

Straightway the crown slid off and smote on earth,
First fallen; and he, grasping his own hair, groaned
And cast his raiment round his face and fell.

SEMICHORUS

Alas for visions that were,
And soothsayings spoken in sleep.

SECOND MESSENGER

But the king twitched his reins in and leapt down
And caught him, crying out twice 'O child' and thrice,
So that men's eyelids thickened with their tears.

SEMICHORUS

Lament with a long lamentation,
Cry, for an end is at hand.°

SECOND MESSENGER

O son, he said, son, lift thine eyes, draw breath,
Pity me; but Meleager with sharp lips
Gasped, and his face waxed like as sunburnt grass.

SEMICHORUS

Cry aloud, O thou kingdom, O nation,
O stricken, a ruinous land.

SECOND MESSENGER

Whereat king Œneus, straightening feeble knees,
With feeble hands heaved up a lessening weight,
And laid him sadly in strange hands, and wept.

SEMICHORUS

Thou art smitten, her lord, her desire,
Thy dear blood wasted as rain.

SECOND MESSENGER

And they with tears and rendings of the beard

Bear hither a breathing body, wept upon
And lightening at each footfall, sick to death.

SEMICHORUS

Thou madest thy sword as a fire,
With fire for a sword thou art slain.

SECOND MESSENGER

And lo, the feast turned funeral, and the crowns
Fallen; and the huntress and the hunter trapped;
And weeping and changed faces and veiled hair.

MELEAGER

Let your hands meet
Round the weight of my head;
Lift ye my feet
As the feet of the dead;
For the flesh of my body is molten, the limbs of it molten as lead.

CHORUS

O thy luminous face,
Thine imperious eyes!
O the grief, O the grace,
As of day when it dies!
Who is this bending over thee, lord, with tears and suppression
of sighs?

MELEAGER

Is a bride so fair?
Is a maid so meek?
With unchapleted hair,
With unfilleted cheek,
Atalanta, the pure among women, whose name is as blessing
to speak.

ATALANTA

I would that with feet
Unsandalled, unshod,
Overbold, overfleet,
I had swum not nor trod
From Arcadia to Calydon northward, a blast of the envy
of God.

MELEAGER

Unto each man his fate;
Unto each as he saith

In whose fingers the weight
Of the world is as breath;
Yet I would that in clamour of battle mine hands had laid hold upon death.

CHORUS

Not with cleaving of shields
And their clash in thine ear,
When the lord of fought fields
Breaketh spearshaft from spear,
Thou art broken, our lord, thou art broken, with travail and labour and fear.

MELEAGER

Would God he had found me
Beneath fresh boughs!
Would God he had bound me
Unawares in mine house,
With light in mine eyes, and songs in my lips, and a crown on my brows!

CHORUS

Whence art thou sent from us?
Whither thy goal?
How art thou rent from us,
Thou that wert whole,
As with severing of eyelids and eyes, as with sundering of body and soul!

MELEAGER

My heart is within me
As an ash in the fire;
Whosoever hath seen me,
Without lute, without lyre,
Shall sing of me grievous things, even things that were ill to desire.

CHORUS

Who shall raise thee
From the house of the dead?
Or what man praise thee
That thy praise may be said?
Alas thy beauty! alas thy body! alas thine head!

MELEAGER

But thou, O mother,

The dreamer of dreams,
Wilt thou bring forth another
To feel the sun's beams
When I move among shadows a shadow, and wail by impassable streams?

ŒNEUS

What thing wilt thou leave me
Now this thing is done?
A man wilt thou give me,
A son for my son,
For the light of mine eyes, the desire of my life, the desirable one?

CHORUS

Thou wert glad above others,
Yea, fair beyond word;
Thou wert glad among mothers;
For each man that heard
Of thee, praise there was added unto thee, as wings to the feet of a bird.

ŒNEUS

Who shall give back
Thy face of old years,
With travail made black,
Grown grey among fears,
Mother of sorrow, mother of cursing, mother of tears?

MELEAGER

Though thou art as fire
Fed with fuel in vain,
My delight, my desire,
Is more chaste than the rain,
More pure than the dewfall, more holy than stars are that live without stain.

ATALANTA

I would that as water
My life's blood had thawn,
Or as winter's wan daughter
Leaves lowland and lawn
Spring-stricken, or ever mine eyes had beheld thee made dark in thy dawn.

CHORUS

When thou dravest the men

Of the chosen of Thrace,
None turned him again
Nor endured he thy face
Clothed round with the blush of the battle, with light from a terrible place.

ŒNEUS

Thou shouldst die as he dies
For whom none sheddeth tears;
Filling thine eyes
And fulfilling thine ears
With the brilliance of battle, the bloom and the beauty, the splendour of spears.°

CHORUS

In the ears of the world
It is sung, it is told,
And the light thereof hurled
And the noise thereof rolled
From the Acroceraunian° snow to the ford of the fleece of gold.

MELEAGER

Would God ye could carry me
Forth of all these;
Heap sand and bury me
By the Chersonese°
Where the thundering Bosphorus answers the thunder of Pontic seas.

ŒNEUS

Dost thou mock at our praise
And the singing begun
And the men of strange days
Praising my son
In the folds of the hills of home, high places of Calydon?

MELEAGER

For the dead man no home is;
Ah, better to be
What the flower of the foam is
In fields of the sea,
That the sea-waves might be as my raiment, the gulf-stream a garment for me.

CHORUS

Who shall seek thee and bring

And restore thee thy day,
When the dove dipt her wing
And the oars won their way,
Where the narrowing Symplegades whitened the straits of
Propontis with spray?

MELEAGER

Will ye crown me my tomb
Or exalt me my name,
Now my spirits consume,
Now my flesh is a flame?
Let the sea slake it once, and men speak of me sleeping to
praise me or shame.

CHORUS

Turn back now, turn thee,
As who turns him to wake;
Though the life in thee burn thee,
Couldst thou bathe it and slake
Where the sea-ridge of Helle° hangs heavier, and east upon
west waters break?

MELEAGER

Would the winds blow me back
Or the waves hurl me home?
Ah, to touch in the track
Where the pine learnt to roam
Cold girdles and crowns of the sea-gods, cool blossoms of water
and foam!

CHORUS

The gods may release
That they made fast;
Thy soul shall have ease
In thy limbs at the last;
But what shall they give thee for life, sweet life that is overpast?

MELEAGER

Not the life of men's veins,
Not of flesh that conceives;
But the grace that remains,
The fair beauty that cleaves
To the life of the rains in the grasses, the life of the dews on
the leaves.

CHORUS

Thou wert helmsman and chief;
Wilt thou turn in an hour,
Thy limbs to the leaf,
Thy face to the flower,
Thy blood to the water, thy soul to the gods who divide
and devour?

MELEAGER

The years are hungry,
They wail all their days;
The gods wax angry
And weary of praise;
And who shall bridle their lips? and who shall straiten their ways?

CHORUS

The gods guard over us
With sword and with rod;
Weaving shadow to cover us,
Heaping the sod,
That law may fulfil herself wholly, to darken man's face before God.

MELEAGER

O holy head of Œneus, lo thy son
Guiltless, yet red from alien guilt, yet foul
With kinship of contaminated lives,
Lo for their blood I die; and mine own blood
For bloodshedding of mine is mixed therewith,
That death may not discern me from my kin.
Yet with clean heart I die and faultless hand,
Not shamefully; thou therefore of thy love
Salute me, and bid fare among the dead
Well, as the dead fare; for the best man dead
Fares sadly; nathless I now faring well
Pass without fear where nothing is to fear
Having thy love about me and thy goodwill,
O father, among dark places and men dead.

ŒNEUS

Child, I salute thee with sad heart and tears,
And bid thee comfort, being a perfect man
In fight, and honourable in the house of peace.
The gods give thee fair wage and dues of death,
And me brief days and ways to come at thee.

MELEAGER

Pray thou thy days be long before thy death,
And full of ease and kingdom; seeing in death
There is no comfort and none aftergrowth,
Nor shall one thence look up and see day's dawn
Nor light upon the land whither I go.
Live thou and take thy fill of days and die
When thy day comes; and make not much of death
Lest ere thy day thou reap an evil thing.
Thou too, the bitter mother and mother-plague
Of this my weary body—thou too, queen,
The source and end, the sower and the scythe,
The rain that ripens and the drought that slays,
The sand that swallows and the spring that feeds,
To make me and unmake me—thou, I say,
Althæa, since my father's ploughshare, drawn
Through fatal seedland of a female field,
Furrowed thy body, whence a wheaten ear
Strong from the sun and fragrant from the rains
I sprang and cleft the closure of thy womb,
Mother, I dying with unforgetful tongue
Hail thee as holy and worship thee as just
Who art unjust and unholy; and with my knees
Would worship, but thy fire and subtlety,
Dissundering them, devour me; for these limbs
Are as light dust and crumblings from mine urn
Before the fire has touched them; and my face
As a dead leaf or dead foot's mark on snow,
And all this body a broken barren tree
That was so strong, and all this flower of life
Disbranched and desecrated miserably,
And minished all that god-like muscle and might
And lesser than a man's: for all my veins
Fail me, and all mine ashen life burns down.
I would thou hadst let me live; but gods averse,
But fortune, and the fiery feet of change,
And time, these would not, these tread out my life,
These and not thou; me too thou hast loved, and I
Thee; but this death was mixed with all my life,
Mine end with my beginning; and this law,
This only, slays me, and not my mother at all.
And let no brother or sister grieve too sore,
Nor melt their hearts out on me with their tears,

Since extreme love and sorrowing overmuch
Vex the great gods, and overloving men
Slay and are slain for love's sake; and this house
Shall bear much better children; why should these
Weep? but in patience let them live their lives
And mine pass by forgotten: thou alone,
Mother, thou sole and only, thou not these,
Keep me in mind a little when I die
Because I was thy first-born; let thy soul
Pity me, pity even me gone hence and dead,
Though thou wert wroth, and though thou bear again
Much happier sons, and all men later born
Exceedingly excel me; yet do thou
Forget not, nor think shame; I was thy son.
Time was I did not shame thee; and time was
I thought to live and make thee honourable
With deeds as great as these men's; but they live,
These, and I die; and what thing should have been
Surely I know not; yet I charge thee, seeing
I am dead already, love me not the less,
Me, O my mother; I charge thee by these gods,
My father's, and that holier breast of thine,
By these that see me dying, and that which nursed,
Love me not less, thy first-born: though grief come,
Grief only, of me, and of all these great joy,
And shall come always to thee; for thou knowest,
O mother, O breasts that bare me, for ye know,
O sweet head of my mother, sacred eyes,
Ye know my soul albeit I sinned, ye know
Albeit I kneel not neither touch thy knees,
But with my lips I kneel, and with my heart
I fall about thy feet and worship thee.
And ye farewell now, all my friends; and ye,
Kinsmen, much younger and glorious more than I,
Sons of my mother's sister; and all farewell
That were in Colchis with me, and bare down
The waves and wars that met us: and though times
Change, and though now I be not anything,
Forget not me among you, what I did
In my good time; for even by all those days,
Those days and this, and your own living souls,
And by the light and luck of you that live,
And by this miserable spoil, and me

Dying, I beseech you, let my name not die.
But thou, dear, touch me with thy rose-like hands,
And fasten up mine eyelids with thy mouth,
A bitter kiss; and grasp me with thine arms,
Printing with heavy lips my light waste flesh,
Made light and thin by heavy-handed fate,
And with thine holy maiden eyes drop dew,
Drop tears for dew upon me who am dead,
Me who have loved thee; seeing without sin done
I am gone down to the empty weary house
Where no flesh is nor beauty nor swift eyes
Nor sound of mouth nor might of hands and feet.
But thou, dear, hide my body with thy veil,
And with thy raiment cover foot and head,
And stretch thyself upon me and touch hands
With hands and lips with lips: be pitiful
As thou art maiden perfect; let no man
Defile me to despise me, saying, This man
Died woman-wise, a woman's offering, slain
Through female fingers in his woof of life,
Dishonourable; for thou hast honoured me.
And now for God's sake kiss me once and twice
And let me go; for the night gathers me,
And in the night shall no man gather fruit.°

ATALANTA

Hail thou: but I with heavy face and feet
Turn homeward and am gone out of thine eyes.

CHORUS

Who shall contend with his lords
  Or cross them or do them wrong?
Who shall bind them as with cords?
  Who shall tame them as with song?°
Who shall smite them as with swords?
  For the hands of their kingdom are strong.

FIG. 2. Algernon Charles Swinburne, London Stereoscopic & Photographic Company, *carte de visite*, *c.*1865 © National Portrait Gallery, London, reproduced with permission.

# FROM 'PREFACE' TO *A SELECTION FROM THE WORKS OF LORD BYRON* (1866)

The most delicate and thoughtful of English critics° has charged the present generation of Englishmen with forgetfulness of Byron. It is not a light charge: and it is not ungrounded. Men born when this century was getting into its forties were baptized into another church than his with the rites of another creed. Upon their ears, first after the cadences of elder poets, fell the faultless and fervent melodies of Tennyson. To them, chief among the past heroes of the younger century, three men appeared as pre-dominant in poetry; Coleridge, Keats, and Shelley. Behind these were effaced, on either hand, the two great opposing figures of Byron and Wordsworth. No man under twenty can just now be expected to appreciate these. The time was when all boys and girls who paddled in rhyme and dabbled in sentiment were wont to adore the presence or the memory of Byron with foolish faces of praise. It is of little moment to him or to us that they have long since ceased to cackle and begun to hiss. They have become used to better verse and carefuller workmen; and must be forgiven if after such training they cannot at once appreciate the splendid and imperishable excellence which covers all his offences and outweighs all his defects: the excellence of sincerity and strength. Without these no poet can live; but few have ever had so much of them as Byron. His sincerity indeed is difficult to discover and define; but it does in effect lie at the root of all his good works: deformed by pretension and defaced by assumption, masked by folly and veiled by affectation; but perceptible after all, and priceless.°

It is no part of my present office to rewrite the history of a life in which every date and event that could be given would now seem trite and stale to all possible readers. If, after so many promises and hints, something at once new and true shall at length be unearthed or extricated, which may affect for the better or the worse our judgment of the man, it will be possible and necessary to rewrite it. Meantime this among other chances 'lies on the lap of the gods;' and especially on the lap of a goddess who still treads our earth.° Until she speaks, we cannot guess what she may have to say; and can only pass by with reverent or with sceptical reticence.

Thus much however we may safely assert: that no man's work was ever more influenced by his character; and that no man's character was ever more influenced by his circumstances. Rather from things without than from things within him did the spirit of Byron assume colour and shape. His noblest verse leapt on a sudden into life after the heaviest evils had fallen upon him which even he ever underwent. From the beginning indeed he had much to fight against: and three impediments hung about him at starting, the least of which would have weighed down a less strong man: youth, and genius, and an ancient name. In spite of all three he made his way; and suffered for it. At the first chance given or taken, every obscure and obscene thing that lurks for pay or prey among the fouler shallows and thickets of literature flew against him; every hound and every hireling lavished upon him the loathsome tribute of their abuse; all nameless creatures that nibble and prowl, upon whom the serpent's curse has fallen, to go upon his belly and eat dust all the days of his life,° assailed him with their foulest venom and their keenest fangs. And the promise given of old to their kind was now at least fulfilled; they did bruise his heel. But the heads of such creatures are so small that it is hard to bruise them in return; it would first be necessary to discern them.

That Byron was able to disregard and to outlive the bark and the bite of such curs as these is small praise enough: the man who cannot do as much is destructible, and therefore contemptible. He did far more than this; he withstood the weight of circumstances to the end; not always without complaint, but always without misgiving. His glorious courage, his excellent contempt for things contemptible, and hatred of hateful men, are enough of themselves to embalm and endear his memory in the eyes of all who are worthy to pass judgment upon him. And these qualities gave much of their own value to verse not otherwise or not always praiseworthy. Even at its best, the serious poetry of Byron is often so rough and loose, so weak in the screws and joints which hold together the framework of verse, that it is not easy to praise it enough without seeming to condone or to extenuate such faults as should not be over-looked or forgiven. No poet is so badly represented by a book of selections. It must show something of his weakness; it cannot show all of his strength. Often, after a noble overture, the last note struck is either dissonant or ineffectual. His magnificent masterpiece, which must endure for ever among the precious relics of the world, will not bear dissection or extraction. The merit of 'Don Juan' does not lie in any part, but in the whole. There is in that great poem an especial and exquisite balance and sustenance of alternate tones which cannot be expressed or explained by the utmost ingenuity of selection. Haidée is supplanted by Dudu, the shipwreck by the siege, the Russian court by the English household;° and this perpetual change, this tidal variety of experience and emotion, gives to the poem something of the breadth and freshness of the sea. Much of the poet's earlier work is or seems unconsciously dishonest; this, if not always or wholly unaffected, is as honest as the sunlight, as frank as the sea-wind. Here, and here alone, the student of his work may recognize and enjoy the ebb and flow of actual life. Here the pulse of vital blood may be felt in tangible flesh. Here for the first time the style of Byron is beyond all praise or blame: a style at once swift and supple, light and strong, various and radiant. Between 'Childe Harold' and 'Don Juan' the same difference exists which a swimmer feels between lake-water and sea-water;° the one is fluent, yielding, invariable; the other has in it a life and pulse, a sting and a swell, which touch and excite the nerves like fire or like music. Across the stanzas of 'Don Juan' we swim forward as over 'the broad backs of the sea';° they break and glitter, hiss and laugh, murmur and move, like waves that sound or that subside. There is in them a delicious resistance, an elastic motion, which salt water has and fresh water has not. There is about them a wide wholesome air, full of vivid light and constant wind, which is only felt at sea. Life undulates and death palpitates in the splendid verse which resumes the evidence of a brave and clear-sighted man concerning life and death. Here, as at sea, there is enough and too much of fluctuation and intermission; the ripple flags and falls in loose and lazy lines: the foam flies wide of any mark, and the breakers collapse here and there in sudden ruin and violent failure. But the violence and weakness of the sea are preferable to the smooth sound and equable security of a lake: its buoyant and progressive impulse sustains and propels those who would sink through weariness in the flat and placid shallows. There are others whom it sickens, and others whom it chills; these will do well to steer inshore. [...]

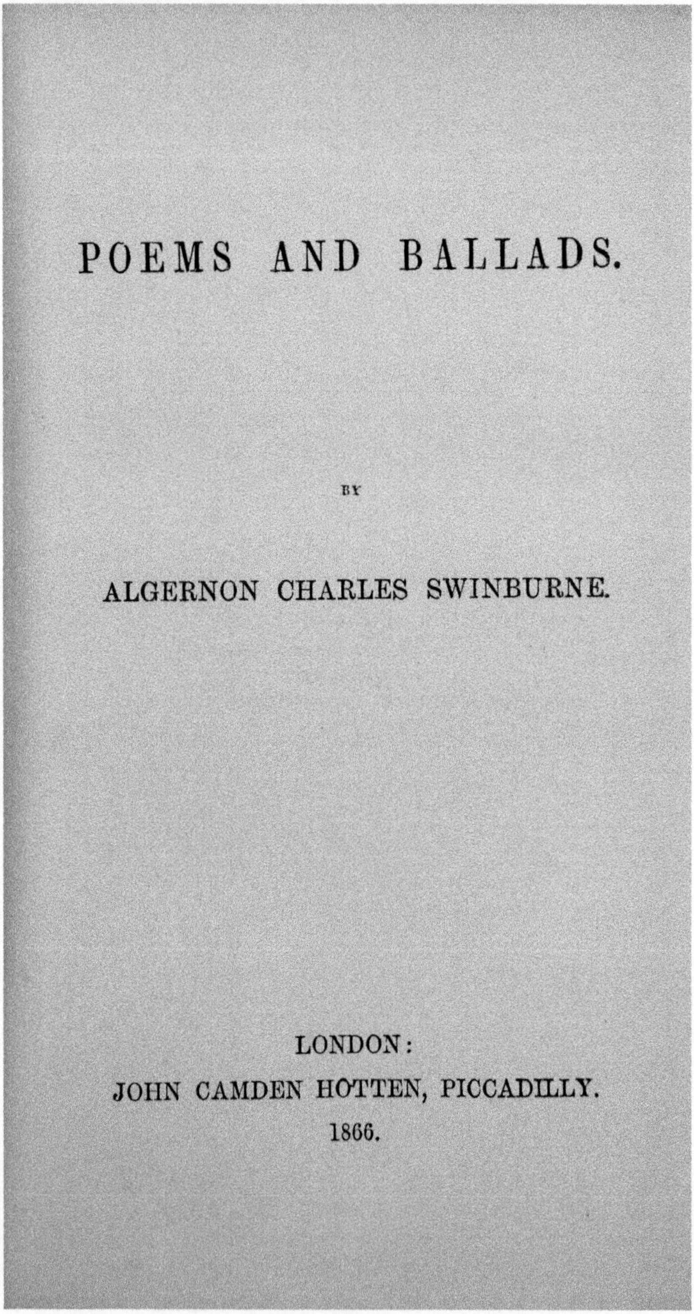

POEMS AND BALLADS.

BY

ALGERNON CHARLES SWINBURNE.

LONDON:

JOHN CAMDEN HOTTEN, PICCADILLY.

1866.

Fig. 3. Title page of *Poems and Ballads* (London: Hotten, 1866), a copy reproduced by kind permission of the Master and Fellows of Balliol College Oxford.

# FROM *POEMS AND BALLADS* (1866)

# Laus Veneris

Lors dit en plourant; Hélas trop malheureux homme et mauldict pescheur, oncques ne verrai-je clémence et miséricorde de Dieu. Ores m'en irai-je d'icy et me cacherai dedans le mont Horsel, en requérant de faveur et d'amoureuse merci ma doulce dame Vénus, car pour son amour serai-je bien à tout jamais damné en enfer. Voicy la fin de tous mes faicts d'armes et de toutes mes belles chansons. Hélas, trop belle estoyt la face de ma dame et ses yeulx, et en mauvais jour je vis ces chouses-là. Lors s'en alla tout en gémissant et se retourna chez elle, et là vescut tristement en grand amour près de sa dame. Puis après advint que le pape vit un jour esclater sur son baston force belles fleurs rouges et blanches et maints boutons de feuilles, et ainsi vit-il reverdir toute l'escorce. Ce dont il eut grande crainte et moult s'en esmut, et grande pitié lui prit de ce chevalier qui s'en estoyt départi sans espoir comme un homme misérable et damné. Doncques envoya force messaigers devers luy pour le ramener, disant qu'il aurait de Dieu grace et bonne absolution de son grand pesché d'amour. Mais oncques plus ne le virent; car toujours demeura ce pauvre chevalier auprès de Vénus la haulte et forte déesse ès flancs de la montagne amoureuse.

*Livre des grandes merveilles d'amour, escript en latin et en françо[y]s par Maistre Antoine Gaget.* 1530.°

Asleep or waking is it?° for her neck,
Kissed over close, wears yet a purple speck
  Wherein the pained blood falters and goes out;
Soft, and stung softly—fairer for a fleck.

But though my lips shut sucking on the place,
There is no vein at work upon her face;
  Her eyelids are so peaceable, no doubt
Deep sleep has warmed her blood through all its ways.

Lo, this is she that was the world's delight;
The old grey years were parcels of her might;
  The strewings of the ways wherein she trod
Were the twain seasons of the day and night.

Lo, she was thus when her clear limbs enticed
All lips that now grow sad with kissing Christ,
  Stained with blood fallen from the feet of God,
The feet and hands whereat our souls were priced.

Alas, Lord, surely thou art great and fair.
But lo her wonderfully woven hair!

And thou didst heal us with thy piteous kiss;
But see now, Lord; her mouth is lovelier.

She is right fair; what hath she done to thee?
Nay, fair Lord Christ, lift up thine eyes and see;
Had now thy mother such a lip—like this?
Thou knowest how sweet a thing it is to me.

Inside the Horsel here the air is hot;
Right little peace one hath for it, God wot;
The scented dusty daylight burns the air,
And my heart chokes me till I hear it not.

Behold, my Venus, my soul's body, lies
With my love laid upon her garment-wise,
Feeling my love in all her limbs and hair
And shed between her eyelids through her eyes.

She holds my heart in her sweet open hands
Hanging asleep; hard by her head there stands,
Crowned with gilt thorns and clothed with flesh like fire,
Love, wan as foam blown up the salt burnt sands—

Hot as the brackish waifs of yellow spume
That shift and steam—loose clots of arid fume
From the sea's panting mouth of dry desire;
There stands he, like one labouring at a loom.

The warp holds fast across; and every thread
That makes the woof up has dry specks of red;
Always the shuttle cleaves clean through, and he
Weaves with the hair of many a ruined head.

Love is not glad nor sorry, as I deem;
Labouring he dreams, and labours in the dream,
Till when the spool is finished, lo I see
His web, reeled off, curls and goes out like steam.

Night falls like fire; the heavy lights run low,
And as they drop, my blood and body so
Shake as the flame shakes, full of days and hours
That sleep not neither weep they as they go.

Ah yet would God this flesh of mine might be
Where air might wash and long leaves cover me,
Where tides of grass break into foam of flowers,
Or where the wind's feet shine along the sea.

Ah yet would God that stems and roots were bred
Out of my weary body and my head,
  That sleep were sealed upon me with a seal,
And I were as the least of all his dead.

Would God my blood were dew to feed the grass,
Mine ears made deaf and mine eyes blind as glass,
  My body broken as a turning wheel,
And my mouth stricken ere it saith Alas!

Ah God, that love were as a flower or flame,
That life were as the naming of a name,
  That death were not more pitiful than desire,
That these things were not one thing and the same!

Behold now, surely somewhere there is death:
For each man hath some space of years, he saith,
  A little space of time ere time expire,
A little day, a little way of breath.

And lo, between the sundawn and the sun,
His day's work and his night's work are undone;
  And lo, between the nightfall and the light,
He is not, and none knoweth of such an one.

Ah God, that I were as all souls that be,
As any herb or leaf of any tree,
  As men that toil through hours of labouring night,
As bones of men under the deep sharp sea.

Outside it must be winter among men;
For at the gold bars of the gates again
  I heard all night and all the hours of it,
The wind's wet wings and fingers drip with rain.

Knights gather, riding sharp for cold; I know
The ways and woods are strangled with the snow;
  And with short song the maidens spin and sit
Until Christ's birthnight, lily-like, arow.

The scent and shadow shed about me make
The very soul in all my senses ache;°
  The hot hard night is fed upon my breath,
And sleep beholds me from afar awake.

Alas, but surely where the hills grow deep,
Or where the wild ways of the sea are steep,

Or in strange places somewhere there is death,
And on death's face the scattered hair of sleep.

There lover-like with lips and limbs that meet
They lie, they pluck sweet fruit of life and eat;
But me the hot and hungry days devour,
And in my mouth no fruit of theirs is sweet.

No fruit of theirs, but fruit of my desire,
For her love's sake whose lips through mine respire;
Her eyelids on her eyes like flower on flower,
Mine eyelids on mine eyes like fire on fire.

So lie we, not as sleep that lies by death,
With heavy kisses and with happy breath;
Not as man lies by woman, when the bride
Laughs low for love's sake and the words he saith.

For she lies, laughing low with love; she lies,
And turns his kisses on her lips to sighs,
To sighing sound of lips unsatisfied,
And the sweet tears are tender with her eyes.

Ah, not as they, but as the souls that were
Slain in the old time, having found her fair;
Who, sleeping with her lips upon their eyes,
Heard sudden serpents hiss across her hair.

Their blood runs round the roots of time like rain:
She casts them forth and gathers them again;
With nerve and bone she weaves and multiplies
Exceeding pleasure out of extreme pain.

Her little chambers drip with flower-like red,
Her girdles, and the chaplets of her head,
Her armlets and her anklets; with her feet
She tramples all that winepress of the dead.

Her gateways smoke with fume of flowers and fires,
With loves burnt out and unassuaged desires;
Between her lips the steam of them is sweet,
The languor in her ears of many lyres.

Her beds are full of perfume and sad sound,
Her doors are made with music, and barred round
With sighing and with laughter and with tears,
With tears whereby strong souls of men are bound.

There is the knight Adonis° that was slain;
With flesh and blood she chains him for a chain;
  The body and the spirit in her ears
Cry, for her lips divide him vein by vein.

Yea, all she slayeth; yea, every man save me;
Me, love, thy lover that must cleave to thee
  Till the ending of the days and ways of earth,
The shaking of the sources of the sea.

Me, most forsaken of all souls that fell;
Me, satiated with things insatiable;
  Me, for whose sake the extreme hell makes mirth,
Yea, laughter kindles at the heart of hell.

Alas thy beauty! for thy mouth's sweet sake
My soul is bitter to me, my limbs quake
  As water, as the flesh of men that weep,
As their heart's vein whose heart goes nigh to break.

Ah God, that sleep with flower-sweet finger-tips
Would crush the fruit of death upon my lips;
  Ah God, that death would tread the grapes of sleep
And wring their juice upon me as it drips.

There is no change of cheer for many days,
But change of chimes high up in the air, that sways
  Rung by the running fingers of the wind;
And singing sorrows heard on hidden ways.

Day smiteth day in twain, night sundereth night,
And on mine eyes the dark sits as the light;
  Yea, Lord, thou knowest I know not, having sinned,
If heaven be clean or unclean in thy sight.

Yea, as if earth were sprinkled over me,
Such chafed harsh earth as chokes a sandy sea,
  Each pore doth yearn, and the dried blood thereof
Gasps by sick fits, my heart swims heavily,

There is a feverish famine in my veins;
Below her bosom, where a crushed grape stains
  The white and blue, there my lips caught and clove
An hour since, and what mark of me remains?

I dare not always touch her, lest the kiss
Leave my lips charred. Yea, Lord, a little bliss,

Brief bitter bliss, one hath for a great sin;
Nathless thou knowest how sweet a thing it is.

Sin, is it sin whereby men's souls are thrust
Into the pit? yet had I a good trust
To save my soul before it slipped therein,
Trod under by the fire-shod feet of lust.

For if mine eyes fail and my soul takes breath,
I look between the iron sides of death
Into sad hell where all sweet love hath end,
All but the pain that never finisheth.

There are the naked faces of great kings,
The singing folk with all their lute-playings;
There when one cometh he shall have to friend
The grave that covets and the worm that clings.

There sit the knights that were so great of hand,
The ladies that were queens of fair green land,
Grown grey and black now, brought unto the dust,
Soiled without raiment, clad about with sand.

There is one end for all of them; they sit
Naked and sad, they drink the dregs of it,
Trodden as grapes in the wine-press of lust,
Trampled and trodden by the fiery feet.

I see the marvellous mouth[o] whereby there fell
Cities and people whom the gods loved well,
Yet for her sake on them the fire gat hold,
And for their sakes on her the fire of hell.

And softer than the Egyptian lote-leaf is,
The queen[o] whose face was worth the world to kiss,
Wearing at breast a suckling snake of gold;
And large pale lips of strong Semiramis,[o]

Curled like a tiger's that curl back to feed;
Red only where the last kiss made them bleed;
Her hair most thick with many a carven gem,
Deep in the mane, great-chested, like a steed.

Yea, with red sin the faces of them shine;
But in all these there was no sin like mine;
No, not in all the strange great sins of them
That made the wine-press froth and foam with wine.

For I was of Christ's choosing, I God's knight,
No blinkard heathen stumbling for scant light;
 I can well see, for all the dusty days
Gone past, the clean great time of goodly fight.

I smell the breathing battle sharp with blows,
With shriek of shafts and snapping short of bows;
 The fair pure sword smites out in subtle ways,
Sounds and long lights are shed between the rows

Of beautiful mailed men; the edged light slips,
Most like a snake that takes short breath and dips
 Sharp from the beautifully bending head,
With all its gracious body lithe as lips

That curl in touching you; right in this wise
My sword doth, seeming fire in mine own eyes,
 Leaving all colours in them brown and red
And flecked with death; then the keen breaths like sighs,

The caught-up choked dry laughters following them,
When all the fighting face is grown a flame
 For pleasure, and the pulse that stuns the ears,
And the heart's gladness of the goodly game.

Let me think yet a little; I do know
These things were sweet, but sweet such years ago,
 Their savour is all turned now into tears;
Yea, ten years since, where the blue ripples blow,

The blue curled eddies of the blowing Rhine,
I felt the sharp wind shaking grass and vine
 Touch my blood too, and sting me with delight
Through all this waste and weary body of mine

That never feels clear air; right gladly then
I rode alone, a great way off my men,
 And heard the chiming bridle smite and smite,
And gave each rhyme thereof some rhyme again,

Till my song shifted to that iron one;
Seeing there rode up between me and the sun
 Some certain of my foe's men, for his three
White wolves across their painted coats did run.

The first red-bearded, with square cheeks—alack,
I made my knave's blood turn his beard to black;

The slaying of him was a joy to see:
Perchance too, when at night he came not back,

Some woman fell a-weeping, whom this thief
Would beat when he had drunken; yet small grief
Hath any for the ridding of such knaves;
Yea, if one wept, I doubt her teen was brief.

This bitter love is sorrow in all lands,
Draining of eyelids, wringing of drenched hands,
Sighing of hearts and filling up of graves;
A sign across the head of the world he stands,

As one that hath a plague-mark on his brows;
Dust and spilt blood do track him to his house
Down under earth; sweet smells of lip and cheek,
Like a sweet snake's breath made more poisonous

With chewing of some perfumed deadly grass,
Are shed all round his passage if he pass,
And their quenched savour leaves the whole soul weak,
Sick with keen guessing whence the perfume was.

As one who hidden in deep sedge and reeds
Smells the rare scent made where a panther feeds,
And tracking ever slotwise° the warm smell
Is snapped upon by the sweet mouth and bleeds,

His head far down the hot sweet throat of her—
So one tracks love, whose breath is deadlier,
And lo, one springe and you are fast in hell,
Fast as the gin's grip of a wayfarer.

I think now, as the heavy hours decease
One after one, and bitter thoughts increase
One upon one, of all sweet finished things;
The breaking of the battle; the long peace

Wherein we sat clothed softly, each man's hair
Crowned with green leaves beneath white hoods of vair:
The sound of sharp spears at great tourneyings,
And noise of singing in the late sweet air.

I sang of love, too, knowing nought thereof;
'Sweeter,' I said, 'the little laugh of love
Than tears out of the eyes of Magdalen,
Or any fallen feather of the Dove.°

'The broken little laugh that spoils a kiss,
The ache of purple pulses, and the bliss
  Of blinded eyelids that expand again—
Love draws them open with those lips of his,

'Lips that cling hard till the kissed face has grown
Of one same fire and colour with their own;
  Then ere one sleep, appeased with sacrifice,
Where his lips wounded, there his lips atone.'

I sang these things long since and knew them not;
'Lo, here is love, or there is love, God wot,
  This man and that finds favour in his eyes,'
I said, 'but I, what guerdon have I got?

'The dust of praise that is blown everywhere
In all men's faces with the common air;
  The bay-leaf that wants chafing to be sweet
Before they wind it in a singer's hair.'

So that one dawn I rode forth sorrowing;
I had no hope but of some evil thing,
  And so rode slowly past the windy wheat,
And past the vineyard and the water-spring,

Up to the Horsel. A great elder-tree
Held back its heaps of flowers to let me see
  The ripe tall grass, and one that walked therein,
Naked, with hair shed over to the knee.

She walked between the blossom and the grass;
I knew the beauty of her, what she was,
  The beauty of her body and her sin,
And in my flesh the sin of hers, alas!

Alas! for sorrow is all the end of this.
O sad kissed mouth,° how sorrowful it is!
  O breast whereat some suckling sorrow clings,
Red with the bitter blossom of a kiss!

Ah, with blind lips I felt for you, and found
About my neck your hands and hair enwound,
  The hands that stifle and the hair that stings,
I felt them fasten sharply without sound.

Yea, for my sin I had great store of bliss:
Rise up,° make answer for me, let thy kiss

Seal my lips hard from speaking of my sin,
Lest one go mad to hear how sweet it is.

Yet I waxed faint with fume of barren bowers,
And murmuring of the heavy-headed hours;
And let the dove's beak fret and peck within
My lips in vain,° and Love shed fruitless flowers.

So that God looked upon me when your hands
Were hot about me; yea, God brake my bands
To save my soul alive, and I came forth
Like a man blind and naked in strange lands°

That hears men laugh and weep, and knows not whence
Nor wherefore, but is broken in his sense;
Howbeit I met folk riding from the north
Towards Rome, to purge them of their souls' offence,

And rode with them, and spake to none; the day
Stunned me like lights upon some wizard way,
And ate like fire mine eyes and mine eyesight;
So rode I, hearing all these chant and pray,

And marvelled; till before us rose and fell
White cursed hills, like outer skirts of hell
Seen where men's eyes look through the day to night,
Like a jagged shell's lips, harsh, untunable,

Blown in between by devils' wrangling breath;
Nathless we won well past that hell and death,
Down to the sweet land where all airs are good,
Even unto Rome where God's grace tarrieth.

Then came each man and worshipped at his knees
Who in the Lord God's likeness bears the keys
To bind or loose,° and called on Christ's shed blood,
And so the sweet-souled father gave him ease.

But when I came I fell down at his feet,
Saying, 'Father, though the Lord's blood be right sweet,
The spot it takes not off the panther's skin,
Nor shall an Ethiop's stain° be bleached with it.

'Lo, I have sinned and have spat out at God,
Wherefore his hand is heavier and his rod
More sharp because of mine exceeding sin,
And all his raiment redder than bright blood

'Before mine eyes; yea, for my sake I wot
The heat of hell is waxen seven times hot
  Through my great sin.' Then spake he some sweet word,
Giving me cheer; which thing availed me not;

Yea, scarce I wist if such indeed were said;
For when I ceased—lo, as one newly dead
  Who hears a great cry out of hell, I heard
The crying of his voice across my head.

'Until this dry shred staff, that hath no whit
Of leaf nor bark, bear blossom and smell sweet,
  Seek thou not any mercy in God's sight,
For so long shalt thou be cast out from it.'

Yea, what if dried-up stems wax red and green,
Shall that thing be which is not nor has been?
  Yea, what if sapless bark wax green and white,
Shall any good fruit grow upon my sin?

Nay, though sweet fruit were plucked of a dry tree,
And though men drew sweet waters of the sea,
  There should not grow sweet leaves on this dead stem,
This waste wan body and shaken soul of me.

Yea, though God search it warily enough,
There is not one sound thing in all thereof;
  Though he search all my veins through, searching them
He shall find nothing whole therein but love.

For I came home right heavy, with small cheer,
And lo my love, mine own soul's heart, more dear
  Than mine own soul, more beautiful than God,
Who hath my being between the hands of her—

Fair still, but fair for no man saving me,
As when she came out of the naked sea
  Making the foam as fire whereon she trod,°
And as the inner flower of fire was she.

Yea, she laid hold upon me, and her mouth
Clove unto mine as soul to body doth,
  And, laughing, made her lips luxurious;
Her hair had smells of all the sunburnt south,

Strange spice and flower, strange savour of crushed fruit,
And perfume the swart kings tread underfoot

For pleasure when their minds wax amorous,
Charred frankincense and grated sandal-root.°

And I forgot fear and all weary things,
All ended prayers and perished thanksgivings,
Feeling her face with all her eager hair
Cleave to me, clinging as a fire that clings

To the body and to the raiment, burning them;
As after death I know that such-like flame
Shall cleave to me for ever; yea, what care,
Albeit I burn then, having felt the same?

Ah love, there is no better life than this;
To have known love, how bitter a thing it is,
And afterward be cast out of God's sight;
Yea, these that know not, shall they have such bliss

High up in barren heaven before his face
As we twain in the heavy-hearted place,
Remembering love and all the dead delight,
And all that time was sweet with for a space?°

For till the thunder in the trumpet be,
Soul may divide from body, but not we
One from another; I hold thee with my hand,
I let mine eyes have all their will of thee,

I seal myself upon thee with my might,
Abiding alway out of all men's sight
Until God loosen over sea and land
The thunder of the trumpets of the night.

EXPLICIT LAUS VENERIS.°

The Triumph of Time

1

Before our lives divide for ever,
While time is with us & hands are free,
(Time, swift to fasten & swift to sever
Hand from hand, as we stand by the sea)
I will say no word that a man might say
Whose whole life's love goes down in a day;
For this could never have been; & never,
Though the gods & the years relent, shall be.

2

Is it worth a tear, is it worth an hour,
To think of things that are well outworn?
Of fruitless husk & fugitive flower,
The dream foregone & the deed forborne?
Though joy be done with & grief be vain,
Time shall not sever us wholly in twain;
Earth is not spoilt for a single shower;
But the rain has ruined the ungrown corn.

3

It will grow not again, this fruit of my heart,
Smitten with sunbeams, ruined with rain.
The singing seasons divide & depart,
Winter & summer depart in twain.
It will grow not again, it is ruined at root,
The bloodlike blossom, the dull red fruit;
Though the heart yet sickens, the lips yet smart,
With sullen savour of poisonous pain.

4

I have given no man of my fruit to eat;
I trod the grapes, I have drunken the wine.
Had you eaten & drunken & found it sweet,
This wild new growth of the corn & vine,
This wine & bread without lees or leaven,
We had grown as gods, as the gods in heaven,
Souls fair to look upon, goodly to greet,
One splendid spirit, your soul & mine.

FIG. 4. First page of MS of 'The Triumph of Time', reproduced by kind permission of the Master and Fellows of Balliol College Oxford.

# The Triumph of Time

Before our lives divide for ever,
While time is with us and hands are free,
(Time, swift to fasten and swift to sever
Hand from hand, as we stand by the sea)
I will say no word that a man might say
Whose whole life's love goes down in a day;
For this could never have been; and never,
Though the gods and the years relent, shall be.

Is it worth a tear, is it worth an hour,
To think of things that are well outworn?
Of fruitless husk and fugitive flower,
The dream foregone and the deed forborne?
Though joy be done with and grief be vain,
Time shall not sever us wholly in twain;
Earth is not spoilt for a single shower;
But the rain has ruined the ungrown corn.

It will grow not again, this fruit of my heart,
Smitten with sunbeams, ruined with rain.
The singing seasons divide and depart,
Winter and summer depart in twain.
It will grow not again, it is ruined at root,
The bloodlike blossom, the dull red fruit;
Though the heart yet sickens, the lips yet smart,
With sullen savour of poisonous pain.

I have given no man of my fruit to eat;
I trod the grapes, I have drunken the wine.
Had you eaten and drunken and found it sweet,
This wild new growth of the corn and vine,
This wine and bread without lees or leaven,
We had grown as gods, as the gods in heaven,
Souls fair to look upon, goodly to greet,
One splendid spirit, your soul and mine.

In the change of years, in the coil of things,
In the clamour and rumour of life to be,
We, drinking love at the furthest springs,
Covered with love as a covering tree,
We had grown as gods, as the gods above,
Filled from the heart to the lips with love,

Held fast in his hands, clothed warm with his wings,
  O love, my love, had you loved but me!

We had stood as the sure stars stand, and moved
  As the moon moves, loving the world;° and seen
Grief collapse as a thing disproved,
  Death consume as a thing unclean.
Twain halves of a perfect heart, made fast
Soul to soul while the years fell past;
Had you loved me once, as you have not loved;
  Had the chance been with us that has not been.

I have put my days and dreams out of mind,
  Days that are over, dreams that are done.
Though we seek life through, we shall surely find
  There is none of them clear to us now, not one.
But clear are these things; the grass and the sand,
Where, sure as the eyes reach, ever at hand,
With lips wide open and face burnt blind,
  The strong sea-daisies feast on the sun.

The low downs lean to the sea; the stream,
  One loose thin pulseless tremulous vein,
Rapid and vivid and dumb as a dream,
  Works downward, sick of the sun and the rain;
No wind is rough with the rank rare flowers;
The sweet sea, mother of loves and hours,
Shudders and shines as the grey winds gleam,
  Turning her smile to a fugitive pain.

Mother of loves that are swift to fade,
  Mother of mutable winds and hours.
A barren mother, a mother-maid,
  Cold and clean as her faint salt flowers.
I would we twain were even as she,
Lost in the night and the light of the sea,
Where faint sounds falter and wan beams wade,
  Break, and are broken, and shed into showers.

The loves and hours of the life of a man,
  They are swift and sad, being born of the sea.
Hours that rejoice and regret for a span,
  Born with a man's breath, mortal as he;
Loves that are lost ere they come to birth,
Weeds of the wave, without fruit upon earth.

I lose what I long for, save what I can,
My love, my love, and no love for me!

It is not much that a man can save
On the sands of life, in the straits of time,
Who swims in sight of the great third wave°
That never a swimmer shall cross or climb.
Some waif washed up with the strays and spars
That ebb-tide shows to the shore and the stars;
Weed from the water, grass from a grave,
A broken blossom, a ruined rhyme.

There will no man do for your sake, I think,
What I would have done for the least word said.
I had wrung life dry for your lips to drink,
Broken it up for your daily bread;
Body for body and blood for blood,°
As the flow of the full sea risen to flood
That yearns and trembles before it sink,
I had given, and lain down for you, glad and dead.

Yea, hope at highest and all her fruit,
And time at fullest and all his dower,
I had given you surely, and life to boot,
Were we once made one for a single hour.
But now, you are twain, you are cloven apart,
Flesh of his flesh, but heart of my heart;
And deep in one is the bitter root,
And sweet for one is the lifelong flower.

To have died if you cared I should die for you, clung
To my life if you bade me, played my part
As it pleased you—these were the thoughts that stung,
The dreams that smote with a keener dart
Than shafts of love or arrows of death;
These were but as fire is, dust, or breath,
Or poisonous foam on the tender tongue
Of the little snakes that eat my heart.

I wish we were dead together to-day,
Lost sight of, hidden away out of sight,
Clasped and clothed in the cloven clay,
Out of the world's way, out of the light,
Out of the ages of worldly weather,
Forgotten of all men altogether,

As the world's first dead, taken wholly away,
  Made one with death, filled full of the night.

How we should slumber, how we should sleep,
  Far in the dark with the dreams and the dews!
And dreaming, grow to each other, and weep,
  Laugh low, live softly, murmur and muse;
Yea, and it may be, struck through by the dream,
Feel the dust quicken and quiver, and seem
Alive as of old to the lips, and leap
  Spirit to spirit as lovers use.

Sick dreams and sad of a dull delight;
  For what shall it profit when men are dead
To have dreamed, to have loved with the whole soul's might,°
  To have looked for day when the day was fled?
Let come what will, there is one thing worth,
To have had fair love in the life upon earth:
To have held love safe till the day grew night,
  While skies had colour and lips were red.

Would I lose you now? would I take you then,
  If I lose you now that my heart has need?
And come what may after death to men,
  What thing worth this will the dead years breed?
Lose life, lose all; but at least I know,
O sweet life's love, having loved you so,
Had I reached you on earth, I should lose not again,
  In death nor life, nor in dream or deed.

Yea, I know this well: were you once sealed mine,
  Mine in the blood's beat, mine in the breath,
Mixed into me as honey in wine,
  Not time that sayeth and gainsayeth,
Nor all strong things had severed us then;
Not wrath of gods, nor wisdom of men,
Nor all things earthly, nor all divine,
  Nor joy nor sorrow, nor life nor death.

I had grown pure as the dawn and the dew,
  You had grown strong as the sun or the sea.
But none shall triumph a whole life through:
  For death is one, and the fates are three.°
At the door of life, by the gate of breath,
There are worse things waiting for men than death;

Death could not sever my soul and you,
  As these have severed your soul from me.

You have chosen and clung to the chance they sent you,
  Life sweet as perfume and pure as prayer.
But will it not one day in heaven repent you?
  Will they solace you wholly, the days that were?
Will you lift up your eyes between sadness and bliss,
Meet mine, and see where the great love is,
And tremble and turn and be changed? Content you;
  The gate is strait;° I shall not be there.

But you, had you chosen, had you stretched hand,
  Had you seen good such a thing were done,
I too might have stood with the souls that stand
  In the sun's sight, clothed with the light of the sun;
But who now on earth need care how I live?
Have the high gods anything left to give,
Save dust and laurels and gold and sand?
  Which gifts are goodly; but I will none.

O all fair lovers about the world,
  There is none of you, none, that shall comfort me.
My thoughts are as dead things, wrecked and whirled
  Round and round in a gulf of the sea;
And still, through the sound and the straining stream,
Through the coil and chafe, they gleam in a dream,
The bright fine lips so cruelly curled,
  And strange swift eyes where the soul sits free.

Free, without pity, withheld from woe,
  Ignorant; fair as the eyes are fair.
Would I have you change now, change at a blow,
  Startled and stricken, awake and aware?
Yea, if I could, would I have you see
My very love of you filling me,
And know my soul to the quick, as I know
  The likeness and look of your throat and hair?

I shall not change you. Nay, though I might,
  Would I change my sweet one love with a word?
I had rather your hair should change in a night,
  Clear now as the plume of a black bright bird;
Your face fail suddenly, cease, turn grey,
Die as a leaf that dies in a day.

I will keep my soul in a place out of sight,
   Far off, where the pulse of it is not heard.

Far off it walks, in a bleak blown space,
   Full of the sound of the sorrow of years.
I have woven a veil for the weeping face,
   Whose lips have drunken the wine of tears;
I have found a way for the failing feet,
A place for slumber and sorrow to meet;
There is no rumour about the place,
   Nor light, nor any that sees or hears.

I have hidden my soul out of sight, and said
   'Let none take pity upon thee, none
Comfort thy crying: for lo, thou art dead,
   Lie still now, safe out of sight of the sun.
Have I not built thee a grave, and wrought
Thy grave-clothes on thee of grievous thought,
With soft spun verses and tears unshed,
   And sweet light visions of things undone?

'I have given thee garments and balm and myrrh,
   And gold, and beautiful burial things.
But thou, be at peace now, make no stir;
   Is not thy grave as a royal king's?°
Fret not thyself though the end were sore;
Sleep, be patient, vex me no more.
Sleep; what hast thou to do with her?
   The eyes that weep, with the mouth that sings?'

Where the dead red leaves of the years lie rotten,
   The cold old crimes and the deeds thrown by,
The misconceived and the misbegotten,
   I would find a sin to do ere I die,
Sure to dissolve and destroy me all through,
That would set you higher in heaven, serve you
And leave you happy, when clean forgotten,
   As a dead man out of mind, am I.

Your lithe hands draw me, your face burns through me,
   I am swift to follow you, keen to see;
But love lacks might to redeem or undo me,
   As I have been, I know I shall surely be;
'What should such fellows as I do?'° Nay,
My part were worse if I chose to play;

For the worst is this after all;° if they knew me,
   Not a soul upon earth would pity me.

And I play not for pity of these; but you,
   If you saw with your soul what man am I,
You would praise me at least that my soul all through
   Clove to you, loathing the lives that lie;
The souls and lips that are bought and sold,
The smiles of silver and kisses of gold,
The lapdog loves that whine as they chew,
   The little lovers that curse and cry.

There are fairer women, I hear; that may be;
   But I, that I love you and find you fair,
Who are more than fair in my eyes if they be,
   Do the high gods know or the great gods care?
Though the swords in my heart for one were seven,
Should° the iron hollow of doubtful heaven,
That knows not itself whether night-time or day be,
   Reverberate words and a foolish prayer?

I will go back to the great sweet mother,
   Mother and lover of men, the sea.
I will go down to her, I and none other,
   Close with her, kiss her and mix her with me;°
Cling to her, strive with her, hold her fast;
O fair white mother, in days long past
Born without sister, born without brother,
   Set free my soul as thy soul is free.

O fair green-girdled mother of mine,
   Sea, that art clothed with the sun and the rain,
Thy sweet hard kisses are strong like wine,
   Thy large embraces are keen like pain.
Save me and hide me with all thy waves,
Find me one grave of thy thousand graves,
Those pure cold populous graves of thine,
   Wrought without hand in a world without stain.

I shall sleep, and move with the moving ships,
   Change as the winds change, veer in the tide;
My lips will feast on the foam of thy lips,
   I shall rise with thy rising, with thee subside;
Sleep, and not know if she be, if she were,
Filled full with life to the eyes and hair,

As a rose is fulfilled to the roseleaf tips
  With splendid summer and perfume and pride.

This woven raiment of nights and days,
  Were it once cast off and unwound from me,
Naked and glad would I walk in thy ways,
  Alive and aware of thy ways and thee;
Clear of the whole world, hidden at home,
Clothed with the green and crowned with the foam,
A pulse of the life of thy straits and bays,
  A vein in the heart of the streams of the sea.

Fair mother, fed with the lives of men,
  Thou art subtle and cruel of heart, men say
Thou hast taken, and shalt not render again;
  Thou art full of thy dead, and cold as they.
But death is the worst that comes of thee;
Thou art fed with our dead, O mother, O sea,
But when hast thou fed on our hearts? or when,
  Having given us love, hast thou taken away?

O tender-hearted, O perfect lover,
  Thy lips are bitter, and sweet thine heart.
The hopes that hurt and the dreams that hover,
  Shall they not vanish away and apart?
But thou, thou art sure, thou art older than earth;
Thou art strong for death and fruitful of birth;
Thy depths conceal and thy gulfs discover;
  From the first thou wert; in the end thou art.

And grief shall endure not for ever, I know.
  As things that are not shall these things be;
'We shall live through seasons of sun and of snow,
  And none be grievous as this to me.
We shall hear, as one in a trance that hears,
The sound of time, the rhyme of the years;
Wrecked hope and passionate pain will grow
  As tender things of a spring-tide sea.

Sea-fruit that swings in the waves that hiss,
  Drowned gold and purple and royal rings.
And all time past, was it all for this?
  Times unforgotten, and treasures of things?
Swift years of liking and sweet long laughter,
That wist not well of the years thereafter

Till love woke, smitten at heart by a kiss,
With lips that trembled and trailing wings?

There lived a singer in France° of old
By the tideless dolorous midland sea.
In a land of sand and ruin and gold
There shone one woman, and none but she.
And finding life for her love's sake fail,
Being fain to see her, he bade set sail,
Touched land, and saw her as life grew cold,
And praised God, seeing; and so died he.

Died, praising God for his gift and grace:
For she bowed down to him weeping, and said
'Live;' and her tears were shed on his face
Or ever the life in his face was shed.
The sharp tears fell through her hair, and stung
Once, and her close lips touched him and clung
Once, and grew one with his lips for a space;
And so drew back, and the man was dead.

O brother, the gods were good to you.
Sleep, and be glad while the world endures.
Be well content as the years wear through;
Give thanks for life, and the loves and lures;
Give thanks for life, O brother, and death,
For the sweet last sound of her feet, her breath,
For gifts she gave you, gracious and few,
Tears and kisses, that lady of yours.

Rest, and be glad of the gods; but I,
How shall I praise them, or how take rest?
There is not room under all the sky
For me that know not of worst or best,
Dream or desire of the days before,
Sweet things or bitterness, any more.
Love will not come to me now though I die,
As love came close to you, breast to breast.

I shall never be friends again with roses;
I shall loathe sweet tunes, where a note grown strong
Relents and recoils, and climbs and closes,
As a wave of the sea turned back by song.
There are sounds where the soul's delight takes fire,
Face to face with its own desire;

A delight that rebels, a desire that reposes;
  I shall hate sweet music my whole life long.

The pulse of war and passion of wonder,
  The heavens that murmur, the sounds that shine,
The stars that sing and the loves that thunder,
  The music burning at heart like wine,
An armed archangel whose hands raise up
All senses mixed in the spirit's cup
Till flesh and spirit are molten in sunder—
  These things are over, and no more mine.

These were a part of the playing I heard
  Once, ere my love and my heart were at strife;
Love that sings and hath wings as a bird,
  Balm, of the wound and heft of the knife.
Fairer than earth is the sea, and sleep
Than overwatching of eyes that weep,
Now time has done with his one sweet word,
  The wine and leaven of lovely life.

I shall go my ways, tread out my measure,
  Fill the days of my daily breath
With fugitive things not good to treasure,
  Do as the world doth, say as it saith;
But if we had loved each other—O sweet,
Had you felt, lying under the palms of your feet,
The heart of my heart, beating harder with pleasure
  To feel you tread it to dust and death—

Ah, had I not taken my life up and given
  All that life gives and the years let go,
The wine and honey, the balm and leaven,
  The dreams reared high and the hopes brought low?
Come life, come death, not a word be said;
Should I lose you living, and vex you dead?
I never shall tell you on earth; and in heaven,
  If I cry to you then, will you hear or know?

# Les Noyades

Whatever a man of the sons of men
  Shall say to his heart of the lords above,
They have shown man verily, once and again,
  Marvellous mercies and infinite love.

In the wild fifth year of the change of things,
  When France was glorious and blood-red, fair
With dust of battle and deaths of kings,
  A queen of men, with helmeted hair,

Carrier came down to the Loire and slew,
  Till all the ways and the waves waxed red:
Bound and drowned, slaying two by two,
  Maidens and young men, naked and wed.

They brought on a day to his judgment-place
  One rough with labour and red with fight,
And a lady noble by name and face,
  Faultless, a maiden, wonderful, white.

She knew not, being for shame's sake blind,
  If his eyes were hot on her face hard by.
And the judge bade strip and ship them, and bind
  Bosom to bosom, to drown and die.

The white girl winced and whitened; but he
  Caught fire, waxed bright as a great bright flame
Seen with thunder far out on the sea,
  Laughed hard as the glad blood went and came.

Twice his lips quailed with delight, then said,
  'I have but a word to you all, one word;
Bear with me; surely I am but dead;'
  And all they laughed and mocked him and heard.

'Judge, when they open the judgment-roll,
  I will stand upright before God and pray:
"Lord God, have mercy on one man's soul,
  For his mercy was great upon earth, I say.

'"Lord, if I loved thee—Lord, if I served—
  If these who darkened thy fair Son's face
I fought with, sparing not one, nor swerved
  A hand's-breadth, Lord, in the perilous place—

'"I pray thee say to this man, O Lord,
  *Sit thou for him at my feet on a throne.*
I will face thy wrath, though it bite as a sword,
  And my soul shall burn for his soul, and atone.

'"For Lord, thou knowest, God most wise,
  How gracious on earth were his deeds toward me.
Shall this be a small thing in thine eyes,
  That is greater in mine than the whole great sea?"

'I have loved this woman my whole life long,
  And even for love's sake when have I said
"I love you"? when have I done you wrong,
  Living? but now I shall have you dead.

'Yea, now, do I bid you love me, love?
  Love me or loathe, we are one not twain.
But God be praised in his heaven above
  For this my pleasure and that my pain!

'For never a man, being mean like me,
  Shall die like me till the whole world dies.
I shall drown with her, laughing for love; and she
  Mix with me, touching me, lips and eyes.

'Shall she not know me and see me all through,
  Me, on whose heart as a worm she trod?
You have given me, God requite it you,
  What man yet never was given of God.'

O sweet one love, my life's delight,
  Dear, though the days have divided us,
Lost beyond hope, taken far out of sight,
  Not twice in the world shall the gods do thus.

Had it been so hard for my love? but I,
  Though the gods gave all that a god can give,
I had chosen rather the gift to die,
  Cease, and be glad above all that live.

For the Loire would have driven us down to the sea,
  And the sea would have pitched us from shoal to shoal;
And I should have held you, and you held me,
  As flesh holds flesh, and the soul the soul.

Could I change you, help you to love me, sweet,
  Could I give you the love that would sweeten death,

We should yield, go down, locked hands and feet,
  Die, drown together, and breath catch breath;

But you would have felt my soul in a kiss,
  And known that once if I loved you well;
And I would have given my soul for this
  To burn for ever in burning hell.

# Itylus

Swallow, my sister, O sister swallow,
  How can thine heart be full of the spring?
    A thousand summers are over and dead.
What hast thou found in the spring to follow?
  What hast thou found in thine heart to sing?
    What wilt thou do when the summer is shed?

O swallow, sister, O fair swift swallow,
  Why wilt thou fly after spring to the south,
    The soft south whither thine heart is set?
Shall not the grief of the old time follow?
  Shall not the song thereof cleave to thy mouth?
    Hast thou forgotten ere I forget?

Sister, my sister, O fleet sweet swallow,
  Thy way is long to the sun and the south;
    But I, fulfilled of my heart's desire,
Shedding my song upon height, upon hollow,
  From tawny body and sweet small mouth
    Feed the heart of the night with fire.

I the nightingale all spring through,
  O swallow, sister, changing swallow,
    All spring through till the spring be done,
Clothed with the light of the night on the dew,
  Sing, while the hours and the wild birds follow,
    Take flight and follow and find the sun.

Sister, my sister, O soft light swallow,
  Though all things feast in the spring's guest-chamber,
    How hast thou heart to be glad thereof yet?
For where thou fliest I shall not follow,
  Till life forget and death remember,
    Till thou remember and I forget.

Swallow, my sister, O singing swallow,
  I know not how thou hast heart to sing.
    Hast thou the heart? is it all past over?
Thy lord the summer is good to follow,
  And fair the feet of thy lover the spring:
    But what wilt thou say to the spring thy lover?

O swallow, sister, O fleeting swallow,
  My heart in me is a molten ember
    And over my head the waves have met.
But thou wouldst tarry or I would follow,
  Could I forget or thou remember,
    Couldst thou remember and I forget.

O sweet stray sister, O shifting swallow,
  The heart's division divideth us.
    Thy heart is light as a leaf of a tree;
But mine goes forth among sea-gulfs hollow
  To the place of the slaying of Itylus,
    The feast of Daulis, the Thracian sea.

O swallow, sister, O rapid swallow,
  I pray thee sing not a little space.
    Are not the roofs and the lintels wet?
The woven web that was plain to follow,
  The small slain body, the flower-like face,
    Can I remember if thou forget?

O sister, sister, thy first-begotten!
  The hands that cling and the feet that follow,
    The voice of the child's blood crying yet
*Who hath remembered me? who hath forgotten?*
  Thou hast forgotten, O summer swallow,
    But the world shall end when I forget.

# Anactoria

*τίνος αὖ τὺ πειθοῖ*
*μὰψ σαγηνεύσας φιλότατα;°*
Sappho

My life is bitter with thy love; thine eyes
Blind me, thy tresses burn me, thy sharp sighs
Divide my flesh and spirit with soft sound,
And my blood strengthens, and my veins abound.
I pray thee sigh not, speak not, draw not breath;
Let life burn down, and dream it is not death.
I would the sea had hidden us, the fire
(Wilt thou fear that, and fear not my desire?)
Severed the bones that bleach, the flesh that cleaves,
And let our sifted ashes drop like leaves.
I feel thy blood against my blood: my pain
Pains thee, and lips bruise lips, and vein stings vein.
Let fruit be crushed on fruit, let flower on flower,
Breast kindle breast, and either burn one hour.
Why wilt thou follow lesser loves? are thine
Too weak to bear these hands and lips of mine?
I charge thee for my life's sake, O too sweet
To crush love with thy cruel faultless feet,
I charge thee keep thy lips from hers or his,
Sweetest, till theirs be sweeter than my kiss:
Lest I too lure, a swallow for a dove,
Erotion or Erinna to my love.
I would my love could kill thee; I am satiated
With seeing thee live, and fain would have thee dead.
I would earth had thy body as fruit to eat,
And no mouth but some serpent's found thee sweet.
I would find grievous ways to have thee slain,
Intense device, and superflux of pain;
Vex thee with amorous agonies, and shake
Life at thy lips, and leave it there to ache;
Strain out thy soul with pangs too soft to kill,
Intolerable interludes, and infinite ill;
Relapse and reluctation of the breath,
Dumb tunes and shuddering semitones of death.
I am weary of all thy words and soft strange ways,
Of all love's fiery nights and all his days,

And all the broken kisses salt as brine
That shuddering lips make moist with waterish wine,
And eyes the bluer for all those hidden hours
That pleasure fills with tears and feeds from flowers,
Fierce at the heart with fire that half comes through,
But all the flower-like white stained round with blue;
The fervent underlid, and that above
Lifted with laughter or abashed with love;
Thine amorous girdle, full of thee and fair,
And leavings of the lilies in thine hair.
Yea, all sweet words of thine and all thy ways,
And all the fruit of nights and flower of days,
And stinging lips wherein the hot sweet brine
That Love was born of burns and foams like wine,
And eyes insatiable of amorous hours,
Fervent as fire and delicate as flowers,
Coloured like night at heart, but cloven through
Like night with flame, dyed round like night with blue,
Clothed with deep eyelids under and above—
Yea, all thy beauty sickens me with love;
Thy girdle empty of thee and now not fair,
And ruinous lilies in thy languid hair.
Ah, take no thought for Love's sake; shall this be,
And she who loves thy lover not love thee?
Sweet soul, sweet mouth of all that laughs and lives,
Mine is she, very mine; and she forgives.
For I beheld in sleep the light that is
In her high place in Paphos,° heard the kiss
Of body and soul that mix with eager tears
And laughter stinging through the eyes and ears;
Saw Love, as burning flame from crown to feet,
Imperishable, upon her storied seat;
Clear eyelids lifted toward the north and south,
A mind of many colours, and a mouth
Of many tunes and kisses; and she bowed,
With all her subtle face laughing aloud,
Bowed down upon me, saying, 'Who doth thee wrong,
Sappho?'° but thou—thy body is the song,
Thy mouth the music; thou art more than I,
Though my voice die not till the whole world die;
Though men that hear it madden; though love weep,
Though nature change, though shame be charmed to sleep.
Ah, wilt thou slay me lest I kiss thee dead?

Yet the queen laughed from her sweet heart and said:
'Even she that flies shall follow for thy sake,
And she shall give thee gifts that would not take,
Shall kiss that would not kiss thee' (yea, kiss me)
'When thou wouldst not'—when I would not kiss thee!
Ah, more to me than all men as thou art,
Shall not my songs assuage her at the heart?
Ah, sweet to me as life seems sweet to death,
Why should her wrath fill thee with fearful breath?
Nay, sweet, for is she God alone? hath she
Made earth and all the centuries of the sea,
Taught the sun ways to travel, woven most fine
The moonbeams, shed the starbeams forth as wine,
Bound with her myrtles, beaten with her rods,
The young men and the maidens and the gods?
Have we not lips to love with, eyes for tears,
And summer and flower of women and of years?
Stars for the foot of morning, and for noon
Sunlight, and exaltation of the moon;
Waters that answer waters, fields that wear
Lilies, and languor of the Lesbian air?
Beyond those flying feet of fluttered doves,
Are there not other gods for other loves?
Yea, though she scourge thee, sweetest, for my sake,
Blossom not thorns, and flowers not blood should break.
Ah that my lips were tuneless lips, but pressed
To the bruised blossom of thy scourged white breast!
Ah that my mouth for Muses' milk were fed
On the sweet blood thy sweet small wounds had bled!
That with my tongue I felt them, and could taste
The faint flakes from thy bosom to the waist!
That I could drink thy veins as wine, and eat
Thy breasts like honey! that from face to feet
Thy body were abolished and consumed,
And in my flesh thy very flesh entombed!
Ah, ah, thy beauty! like a beast it bites,
Stings like an adder, like an arrow smites.
Ah sweet, and sweet again, and seven times sweet,
The paces and the pauses of thy feet!
Ah sweeter than all sleep or summer air
The fallen fillets fragrant from thine hair!
Yea, though their alien kisses do me wrong,
Sweeter thy lips than mine with all their song;

Thy shoulders whiter than a fleece of white,
And flower-sweet fingers, good to bruise or bite
As honeycomb of the inmost honey-cells,
With almond-shaped and roseleaf-coloured shells,
And blood like purple blossom at the tips
Quivering; and pain made perfect in thy lips
For my sake when I hurt thee; O that I
Durst crush thee out of life with love, and die,
Die of thy pain and my delight, and be
Mixed with thy blood and molten into thee!
Would I not plague thee dying overmuch?
Would I not hurt thee perfectly? not touch
Thy pores of sense with torture, and make bright
Thine eyes with bloodlike tears and grievous light!
Strike pang from pang as note is struck from note,
Catch the sob's middle music in thy throat,
Take thy limbs living, and new-mould with these
A lyre of many faultless agonies?
Feed thee with fever and famine and fine drouth,
With perfect pangs convulse thy perfect mouth,
Make thy life shudder in thee and burn afresh,
And wring thy very spirit through the flesh?
Cruel? but love makes all that love him well
As wise as heaven and crueller than hell.
Me hath love made more bitter toward thee
Than death toward man; but were I made as he
Who hath made all things to break them one by one,
If my feet trod upon the stars and sun
And souls of men as his have alway trod,
God knows I might be crueller than God.
For who shall change with prayers or thanksgivings
The mystery of the cruelty of things?
Or say what God above all gods and years,
With offering and blood-sacrifice of tears,
With lamentation from strange lands, from graves
Where the snake pastures, from scarred mouth of slaves,
From prison, and from plunging prows of ships
Through flamelike foam of the sea's closing lips—
With thwartings of strange signs, and wind-blown hair
Of comets, desolating the dim air,
When darkness is made fast with seals and bars,
And fierce reluctance of disastrous stars,
Eclipse, and sound of shaken hills, and wings

Darkening, and blind inexpiable things—
With sorrow of labouring moons, and altering light
And travail of the planets of the night,
And weeping of the weary Pleiads seven,°
Feeds the mute melancholy lust of heaven?
Is not this incense bitterness, his meat
Murder? his hidden face and iron feet
Hath not man known, and felt them on their way
Threaten and trample all things and every day?
Hath he not sent us hunger? who hath cursed
Spirit and flesh with longing? filled with thirst
Their lips who cried unto him? who bade exceed
The fervid will, fall short the feeble deed,
Bade sink the spirit and the flesh aspire,
Pain animate the dust of dead desire,
And life yield up her flower to violent fate?
Him would I reach, him smite, him desecrate,
Pierce the cold lips of God with human breath,
And mix his immortality with death.
Why hath he made us? what had all we done
That we should live and loathe the sterile sun,
And with the moon wax paler as she wanes,
And pulse by pulse feel time grow through our veins?
Thee too the years shall cover; thou shalt be
As the rose born of one same blood with thee,
As a song sung, as a word said, and fall
Flower-wise, and be not any more at all,
Nor any memory of thee anywhere;
For never Muse has bound above thine hair
The high Pierian° flowers whose graft outgrows
All summer kinship of the mortal rose
And colour of deciduous days, nor shed
Reflex and flush of heaven about thine head,
Nor reddened brows made pale by floral grief
With splendid shadow from that lordlier leaf.
Yea, thou shalt be forgotten like spilt wine,
Except these kisses of my lips on thine
Brand them with immortality; but me—
Men shall not see bright fire nor hear the sea,
Nor mix their hearts with music, nor behold
Cast forth of heaven with feet of awful gold
And plumeless wings that make the bright air blind,
Lightning, with thunder for a hound behind

Hunting through fields unfurrowed and unsown—
But in the light and laughter, in the moan
And music, and in grasp of lip and hand
And shudder of water that makes felt on land
The immeasurable tremor of all the sea,
Memories shall mix and metaphors of me.
Like me shall be the shuddering calm of night,
When all the winds of the world for pure delight
Close lips that quiver and fold up wings that ache;
When nightingales are louder for love's sake,
And leaves tremble like lute-strings or like fire;
Like me the one star swooning with desire
Even at the cold lips of the sleepless moon,
As I at thine; like me the waste white noon,
Burnt through with barren sunlight; and like me
The land-stream and the tide-stream in the sea.
I am sick with time as these with ebb and flow,
And by the yearning in my veins I know
The yearning sound of waters; and mine eyes
Burn as that beamless fire which fills the skies
With troubled stars and travailing things of flame;
And in my heart the grief consuming them
Labours, and in my veins the thirst of these,
And all the summer travail of the trees
And all the winter sickness; and the earth,
Filled full with deadly works of death and birth,
Sore spent with hungry lusts of birth and death,
Has pain like mine in her divided breath;
Her spring of leaves is barren, and her fruit
Ashes; her boughs are burdened, and her root
Fibrous and gnarled with poison; underneath
Serpents have gnawn it through with tortuous teeth
Made sharp upon the bones of all the dead,
And wild birds rend her branches overhead.
These, woven as raiment for his word and thought,
These hath God made, and me as these, and wrought
Song, and hath lit it at my lips; and me
Earth shall not gather though she feed on thee.
As a shed tear shalt thou be shed; but I—
Lo, earth may labour, men live long and die,
Years change and stars, and the high God devise
New things, and old things wane before his eyes
Who wields and wrecks them, being more strong than they—

But, having made me, me he shall not slay.
Nor slay nor satiate, like those herds of his
Who laugh and live a little, and their kiss
Contents them, and their loves are swift and sweet,
And sure death grasps and gains them with slow feet,
Love they or hate they, strive or bow their knees—
And all these end; he hath his will of these.
Yea, but albeit he slay me, hating me—
Albeit he hide me in the deep dear sea
And cover me with cool wan foam, and ease
This soul of mine as any soul of these,
And give me water and great sweet waves, and make
The very sea's name lordlier for my sake,
The whole sea sweeter—albeit I die indeed
And hide myself and sleep and no man heed,
Of me the high God hath not all his will.
Blossom of branches, and on each high hill
Clear air and wind, and under in clamorous vales
Fierce noises of the fiery nightingales,
Buds burning in the sudden spring like fire,
The wan washed sand and the waves' vain desire,
Sails seen like blown white flowers at sea, and words
That bring tears swiftest, and long notes of birds
Violently singing till the whole world sings—
I Sappho shall be one with all these things,
With all high things for ever; and my face
Seen once, my songs once heard in a strange place,
Cleave to men's lives, and waste the days thereof
With gladness and much sadness and long love.
Yea, they shall say, earth's womb has borne in vain
New things, and never this best thing again;
Borne days and men, borne fruits and wars and wine,
Seasons and songs, but no song more like mine.
And they shall know me as ye who have known me here,
Last year when I loved Atthis, and this year
When I love thee; and they shall praise me, and say
'She hath all time as all we have our day,
Shall she not live and have her will'—even I?
Yea, though thou diest, I say I shall not die.
For these shall give me of their souls, shall give
Life, and the days and loves wherewith I live,
Shall quicken me with loving, fill with breath,
Save me and serve me, strive for me with death.

Alas, that neither moon nor snow nor dew
Nor all cold things can purge me wholly through,
Assuage me nor allay me nor appease,
Till supreme sleep shall bring me bloodless ease;
Till time wax faint in all his periods;
Till fate undo the bondage of the gods,
And lay, to slake and satiate me all through,
Lotus and Lethe on my lips like dew,
And shed around and over and under me
Thick darkness and the insuperable sea.

# Hymn to Proserpine

## (After the Proclamation in Rome of the Christian Faith)

*Vicisti, Galilæe.*

I have lived long enough, having seen one thing, that love hath an end;
Goddess and maiden and queen, be near me now and befriend.
Thou art more than the day or the morrow, the seasons that laugh
or that weep;
For these give joy and sorrow; but thou, Proserpina, sleep.
Sweet is the treading of wine, and sweet the feet of the dove;
But a goodlier gift is thine than foam of the grapes or love.
Yea, is not even Apollo, with hair and harpstring of gold,
A bitter God to follow, a beautiful God to behold?
I am sick of singing: the bays burn deep and chafe: I am fain
To rest a little from praise and grievous pleasure and pain.
For the Gods we know not of, who give us our daily breath,°
We know they are cruel as love or life, and lovely as death.
O Gods dethroned and deceased, cast forth, wiped out in a day!
From your wrath is the world released, redeemed from your
chains, men say.
New Gods° are crowned in the city; their flowers have broken
your rods;
They are merciful, clothed with pity, the young compassionate Gods.
But for me their new device is barren, the days are bare;
Things long past over suffice, and men forgotten that were.
Time and the Gods are at strife; ye dwell in the midst thereof,
Draining a little life from the barren breasts of love.
I say to you, cease, take rest; yea, I say to you all, be at peace,°
Till the bitter milk of her breast and the barren bosom shall cease.
Wilt thou yet take all, Galilean? but these thou shalt not take,
The laurel, the palms and the paean, the breast of the nymphs in
the brake;
Breasts more soft than a dove's, that tremble with tenderer breath;
And all the wings of the Loves, and all the joy before death;
All the feet of the hours that sound as a single lyre,
Dropped and deep in the flowers, with strings that flicker like fire.
More than these wilt thou give, things fairer than all these things?
Nay, for a little we live, and life hath mutable wings.
A little while and we die; shall life not thrive as it may?

For no man under the sky lives twice, outliving his day.
And grief is a grievous thing, and a man hath enough of his tears:
Why should he labour, and bring fresh grief to blacken his years?
Thou hast conquered, O pale Galilean; the world has grown grey
from thy breath;
We have drunken of things Lethean, and fed on the fulness of death.
Laurel is green for a season, and love is sweet for a day;
But love grows bitter with treason, and laurel outlives not May.°
Sleep, shall we sleep after all? for the world is not sweet in the end;
For the old faiths loosen and fall, the new years ruin and rend.
Fate is a sea without shore, and the soul is a rock that abides;
But her ears are vexed with the roar and her face with the foam of
the tides.
O lips that the live blood faints in, the leavings of racks and rods!
O ghastly glories of saints, dead limbs of gibbeted Gods!
Though all men abase them before you in spirit, and all knees bend,°
I kneel not neither adore you, but standing, look to the end.°
All delicate days and pleasant, all spirits and sorrows are cast
Far out with the foam of the present that sweeps to the surf of
the past:
Where beyond the extreme sea-wall, and between the remote sea-gates,
Waste water washes, and tall ships founder, and deep death waits:
Where, mighty with deepening sides, clad about with the seas as
with wings,
And impelled of invisible tides, and fulfilled of unspeakable things,
White-eyed and poisonous-finned, shark-toothed and serpentine-curled,
Rolls, under the whitening wind of the future, the wave of the world.
The depths stand naked in sunder behind it, the storms flee away;
In the hollow before it the thunder is taken and snared as a prey;
In its sides is the north-wind bound; and its salt is of all men's tears;
With light of ruin, and sound of changes, and pulse of years:
With travail of day after day, and with trouble of hour upon hour;
And bitter as blood is the spray; and the crests are as fangs that devour:
And its vapour and storm of its steam as the sighing of spirits to be;
And its noise as the noise in a dream; and its depth as the roots of the sea:
And the height of its heads as the height of the utmost stars of the air:
And the ends of the earth at the might thereof tremble, and time is
made bare.
Will ye bridle the deep sea with reins, will ye chasten the high sea
with rods?
Will ye take her to chain her with chains, who is older than all ye Gods?
All ye as a wind shall go by, as a fire shall ye pass and be past;
Ye are Gods, and behold, ye shall die, and the waves be upon you at last.

In the darkness of time, in the deeps of the years, in the changes of things,
Ye shall sleep as a slain man sleeps, and the world shall forget you for kings.
Though the feet of thine high priests tread where thy lords and our forefathers trod,
Though these that were Gods are dead, and thou being dead art a God,
Though before thee the throned Cythereanº be fallen, and hidden her head,
Yet thy kingdom shall pass, Galilean, thy dead shall go down to thee dead.
Of the maiden thy motherº men sing as a goddess with grace clad around;
Thou art throned where another was king; where another was queen she is crowned.
Yea, once we had sight of another: but now she is queen, say these.
Not as thine, not as thine was our mother, a blossom of flowering seas,
Clothed round with the world's desire as with raiment, and fair as the foam,
And fleeter than kindled fire, and a goddess, and mother of Rome.º
For thine came pale and a maiden, and sister to sorrow; but ours,
Her deep hair heavily laden with odour and colour of flowers,
White rose of the rose-white water, a silver splendour, aflame,
Bent down unto us that besought her, and earth grew sweet with her name.
For thine came weeping, a slave among slaves, and rejected;º but she
Came flushed from the full-flushed wave, and imperial, her foot on the sea.
And the wonderful waters knew her, the winds and the viewless ways,
And the roses grew rosier, and bluer the sea-blue stream of the bays.
Ye are fallen, our lords, by what token? we wist that ye should not fall.
Ye were all so fair that are broken; and one more fair than ye all.
But I turn to her still, having seen she shall surely abide in the end;
Goddess and maiden and queen, be near me now and befriend.
O daughter of earth, of my mother, her crown and blossom of birth,
I am also, I also, thy brother; I go as I came unto earth.
In the night where thine eyes are as moons are in heaven, the night where thou art,
Where the silence is more than all tunes, where sleep overflows from the heart,
Where the poppies are sweet as the rose in our world, and the red rose is white,

And the wind falls faint as it blows with the fume of the flowers of the night,
And the murmur of spirits that sleep in the shadow of Gods from afar
Grows dim in thine ears and deep as the deep dim soul of a star,
In the sweet low light of thy face, under heavens untrod by the sun,
Let my soul with their souls find place, and forget what is done and undone.
Thou art more than the Gods who number the days of our temporal breath;
For these give labour and slumber; but thou, Proserpina, death.
Therefore now at thy feet I abide for a season in silence. I know
I shall die as my fathers died, and sleep as they sleep; even so.
For the glass of the years is brittle wherein we gaze for a span;
A little soul for a little bears up this corpse which is man.[1]
So long I endure, no longer; and laugh not again, neither weep.
For there is no God found stronger than death; and death is a sleep.

[1] *ψυχάριον εἶ βαστάζον νεκρόν*, Epictetus.°

# Hermaphroditus

Lift up thy lips, turn round, look back for love,
Blind love that comes by night and casts out rest;
Of all things tired thy lips look weariest,
Save the long smile that they are wearied of.
Ah sweet, albeit no love be sweet enough,
Choose of two loves and cleave unto the best;
Two loves at either blossom of thy breast
Strive until one be under and one above.
Their breath is fire upon the amorous air,
Fire in thine eyes and where thy lips suspire:
And whosoever hath seen thee, being so fair,
Two things turn all his life and blood to fire;
A strong desire begot on great despair,
A great despair cast out by strong desire.

Where between sleep and life some brief space is,
With love like gold bound round about the head,
Sex to sweet sex with lips and limbs is wed,
Turning the fruitful feud of hers and his
To the waste wedlock of a sterile kiss;
Yet from them something like as fire is shed
That shall not be assuaged till death be dead
Though neither life nor sleep can find out this
Love made himself of flesh that perisheth
A pleasure-house for all the loves his kin;
But on the one side sat a man like death,
And on the other a woman sat like sin.
So with veiled eyes and sobs between his breath
Love turned himself and would not enter in.

Love, is it love or sleep or shadow or light
That lies between thine eyelids and thine eyes?
Like a flower laid upon a flower it lies,
Or like the night's dew laid upon the night.
Love stands upon thy left hand and thy right,
Yet by no sunset and by no moonrise
Shall make thee man and ease a woman's sighs,
Or make thee woman for a man's delight.
To what strange end hath some strange god made fair
The double blossom of two fruitless flowers?

Hid love in all the folds of all thy hair,
  Fed thee on summers, watered thee with showers,
Given all the gold that all the seasons wear
  To thee that art a thing of barren hours?

Yea, love, I see; it is not love but fear.
  Nay, sweet, it is not fear but love, I know;
  Or wherefore should thy body's blossom blow
So sweetly, or thine eyelids leave so clear
Thy gracious eyes that never made a tear—
  Though for their love our tears like blood should flow,
  Though love and life and death should come and go,
So dreadful, so desirable, so dear?
Yea, sweet, I know; I saw in what swift wise
  Beneath the woman's and the water's kiss
  Thy moist limbs melted into Salmacis,°
And the large light turned tender in thine eyes,
And all thy boy's breath softened into sighs;
  But Love being blind, how should he know of this?

*Au Musée du Louvre, Mars 1863.*

# The Leper

Nothing is better, I well think,
Than love; the hidden well-water
Is not so delicate to drink:
This was well seen of me and her.

I served her in a royal house;
I served her wine and curious meat.
For will to kiss between her brows
I had no heart to sleep or eat.

Mere scorn God knows she had of me;
A poor scribe, nowise great or fair,
Who plucked his clerk's hood back to see
Her curled-up lips and amorous hair.

I vex my head with thinking this.
Yea, though God always hated me,
And hates me now that I can kiss
Her eyes, plait up her hair to see

How she then wore it on the brows,
Yet am I glad to have her dead
Here in this wretched wattled house
Where I can kiss her eyes and head.

Nothing is better, I well know,
Than love; no amber in cold sea
Or gathered berries under snow:
That is well seen of her and me.

Three thoughts I make my pleasure of:
First I take heart and think of this:
That knight's gold hair she chose to love,
His mouth she had such will to kiss.

Then I remember that sundawn
I brought him by a privy way
Out at her lattice, and thereon
What gracious words she found to say.

(Cold rushes for such little feet—
Both feet could lie into my hand.
A marvel was it of my sweet
Her upright body could so stand.)

'Sweet friend, God give you thank and grace:
  Now am I clean and whole of shame,
Nor shall men burn me in the face
  For my sweet fault that scandals them.'

I tell you over word by word.
  She, sitting edgewise on her bed,
Holding her feet, said thus. The third,
  A sweeter thing than these, I said.

God, that makes time and ruins it,
  And alters not, abiding God,
Changed with disease her body sweet,
  The body of love wherein she abode.

Love is more sweet and comelier
  Than a dove's throat strained out to sing.
All they spat out and cursed at her
  And cast her forth for a base thing.

They cursed her, seeing how God had wrought
  This curse to plague her, a curse of his.
Fools were they surely, seeing not
  How sweeter than all sweet she is.

He that had held her by the hair,
  With kissing lips blinding her eyes,
Felt her bright bosom, strained and bare,
  Sigh under him, with short mad cries

Out of her throat and sobbing mouth
  And body broken up with love,
With sweet hot tears his lips were loth
  Her own should taste the savour of,

Yea, he inside whose grasp all night
  Her fervent body leapt or lay,
Stained with sharp kisses red and white,
  Found her a plague to spurn away.

I hid her in this wattled house,
  I served her water and poor bread.
For joy to kiss between her brows
  Time upon time I was nigh dead.

Bread failed; we got but well-water
  And gathered grass with dropping seed.

I had such joy of kissing her,
  I had small care to sleep or feed.

Sometimes when service made me glad
  The sharp tears leapt between my lids,
Falling on her, such joy I had
  To do the service God forbids.

'I pray you let me be at peace,
  Get hence, make room for me to die.'
She said that: her poor lip would cease,
  Put up to mine, and turn to cry.

I said, 'Bethink yourself how love
  Fared in us twain, what either did;
Shall I unclothe my soul thereof?
  That I should do this, God forbid.'

Yea, though God hateth us, he knows
  That hardly in a little thing
Love faileth of the work it does
  Till it grow ripe for gathering.

Six months, and now my sweet is dead
  A trouble takes me; I know not
If all were done well, all well said,
  No word or tender deed forgot.

Too sweet, for the least part in her,
  To have shed life out by fragments; yet,
Could the close mouth catch breath and stir,
  I might see something I forget.

Six months, and I sit still and hold
  In two cold palms her cold two feet.
Her hair, half grey half ruined gold,
  Thrills me and burns me in kissing it.

Love bites and stings me through, to see
  Her keen face made of sunken bones.
Her worn-off eyelids madden me,
  That were shot through with purple once.

She said, 'Be good with me; I grow
  So tired for shame's sake, I shall die
If you say nothing:' even so.
  And she is dead now, and shame put by.

Yea, and the scorn she had of me
  In the old time, doubtless vexed her then.
I never should have kissed her. See
  What fools God's anger makes of men!

She might have loved me a little too,
  Had I been humbler for her sake.
But that new shame could make love new
  She saw not—yet her shame did make.

I took too much upon my love,
  Having for such mean service done
Her beauty and all the ways thereof,
  Her face and all the sweet thereon.

Yea, all this while I tended her,
  I know the old love held fast his part:
I know the old scorn waxed heavier,
  Mixed with sad wonder, in her heart.

It may be all my love went wrong—
  A scribe's work writ awry and blurred,
Scrawled after the blind evensong—
  Spoilt music with no perfect word.

But surely I would fain have done
  All things the best I could. Perchance
Because I failed, came short of one,
  She kept at heart that other man's.

I am grown blind with all these things:
  It may be now she hath in sight
Some better knowledge; still there clings
  The old question. Will not God do right?[o, 1]

[1] En ce temps-là estoyt dans ce pays grand nombre de ladres et de meseaulx, ce dont le roy eut grand desplaisir, veu que Dieu dut en estre moult griefvement courroucé. Ores il advint qu'une noble damoyselle appelée Yolande de Sallières estant atteincte et touste guastée de ce vilain mal, tous ses amys et ses parens ayant devant leurs yeux la paour de Dieu la firent issir fors de leurs maisons et oncques ne voulurent recepvoir ni reconforter chose mauldicte de Dieu et à tous les homines puante et abhominable. Ceste dame avoyt esté moult belle et gracieuse de formes, et de son corps elle estoyt large et de vie lascive. Pourtant nul des amans qui l'avoyent souventesfois accollée et baisée moult tendrement ne voulut plus héberger si laide femme et si détestable pescheresse. Ung seul clerc qui feut premièrement son lacquays et son entremetteur en matière d'amour la reçut chez luy et la récéla dans une petite cabane. Là mourut la meschinette

de grande misère et de male mort: et après elle décéda ledist clerc qui pour grand amour l'avoyt six mois durant soignée, lavée, habillée et deshabillé tous les jours de ses mains propres. Mesme dist-on que ce meschant homme et mauldict clerc se remémourant de la grande beauté passée et guastée de ceste femme se délectoyt maintesfois à la baiser sur sa bouche orde et lépreuse et l'accoller doulcement de ses mains amoureuses. Aussy est-il mort de ceste mesme maladie abhominable. Cecy advint près Fontainebellant en Gastinois. Et quand ouyt le roy Philippe ceste adventure moult en estoyt esmerveillé.

*Grandes chroniques de France,* 1505.

# Before the Mirror

## (Verses written under a picture)

Inscribed to J.A. Whistler

### I.

White rose in red rose-garden
 Is not so white;
Snowdrops that plead for pardon
 And pine for fright
Because the hard East blows
Over their maiden rows
 Grow not as this face grows from pale to bright.

Behind the veil, forbidden,
 Shut up from sight,
Love, is there sorrow hidden,
 Is there delight?
Is joy thy dower or grief,
White rose of weary leaf,
 Late rose whose life is brief, whose loves are light?

Soft snows that hard winds harden
 Till each flake bite
Fill all the flowerless garden
 Whose flowers took flight
Long since when summer ceased,
And men rose up from feast,
 And warm west wind grew east, and warm day night.

### II

'Come snow, come wind or thunder
  High up in air,
I watch my face, and wonder
  At my bright hair;
Nought else exalts or grieves
The rose at heart, that heaves
  With love of her own leaves and lips that pair.

'She knows not loves that kissed her
 She knows not where,
Art thou the ghost, my sister,

White sister there,
Am I the ghost, who knows?
My hand, a fallen rose,
Lies snow-white on white snows, and takes no care.

'I cannot see what pleasures
Or what pains were;
What pale new loves and treasures
New years will bear;
What beam will fall, what shower,
What grief or joy for dower;
But one thing knows the flower; the flower is fair.'

III

Glad, but not flushed with gladness,
Since joys go by;
Sad, but not bent with sadness,
Since sorrows die;
Deep in the gleaming glass
She sees all past things pass,
And all sweet life that was lie down and lie.

There glowing ghosts of flowers
Draw down, draw nigh;
And wings of swift spent hours
Take flight and fly;
She sees by formless gleams,
She hears across cold streams,
Dead mouths of many dreams that sing and sigh.

Face fallen and white throat lifted,
With sleepless eye
She sees old loves that drifted,
She knew not why,
Old loves and faded fears
Float down a stream that hears
The flowing of all men's tears beneath the sky.

# Dolores

## (Notre-Dame des sept douleurs.)

Cold eyelids that hide like a jewel
   Hard eyes that grow soft for an hour;
The heavy white limbs, and the cruel
   Red mouth like a venomous flower;
When these are gone by with their glories,
   What shall rest of thee then, what remain,
O mystic and sombre Dolores,
   Our Lady of Pain?

Seven sorrows the priests give their Virgin;
   But thy sins, which are seventy times seven,[o]
Seven ages would fail thee to purge in,
   And then they would haunt thee in heaven:
Fierce midnights and famishing morrows,
   And the loves that complete and control
All the joys of the flesh, all the sorrows
   That wear out the soul.

O garment not golden but gilded;
   O garden where all men may dwell,
O tower not of ivory,[o] but builded
   By hands that reach heaven from hell;
O mystical rose of the mire,
   O house not of gold but of gain,
O house of unquenchable fire,
   Our Lady of Pain!

O lips full of lust and of laughter,
   Curled snakes that are fed from my breast,
Bite hard, lest remembrance come after
   And press with new lips where you pressed.
For my heart too springs up at the pressure,
   Mine eyelids too moisten and burn;
Ah, feed me and fill me with pleasure,
   Ere pain come in turn.

In yesterday's reach and to-morrow's,
   Out of sight though they lie of to-day,
There have been and there yet shall be sorrows,
   That smite not and bite not in play.

The life and the love thou despisest,
  These hurt us indeed and in vain,
O wise among women, and wisest,
  Our Lady of Pain.

Who gave thee thy wisdom? what stories
  That stung thee, what visions that smote?
Wert thou pure and a maiden, Dolores,
  When desire took thee first by the throat?
What bud was the shell of a blossom
  That all men may smell to and pluck?
What milk fed thee first at what bosom?
  What sins gave thee suck?

We shift and bedeck and bedrape us,
  Thou art noble and nude and antique;
Libitina thy mother, Priapus
  Thy father, a Tuscan and Greek.°
We play with light loves in the portal,
  And wince and relent and refrain;
Loves die, and we know thee immortal,
  Our Lady of Pain.

Fruits fail and love dies and time ranges;
  Thou art fed with perpetual breath,
And alive after infinite changes,
  And fresh from the kisses of death;
Of languors rekindled and rallied,
  Of barren delights and unclean,
Things monstrous and fruitless, a pallid
  And poisonous queen.

Could you hurt me, sweet lips, though I hurt you?
  Men touch them, and change in a trice
The lilies and languors of virtue
  For the raptures and roses of vice;
Those lie where thy foot on the floor is,
  These crown and caress thee and chain,
O splendid and sterile Dolores,
  Our Lady of Pain.

There are sins it may be to discover,
  There are deeds it may be to delight.
What new work wilt thou find for thy lover,
  What new passions for daytime or night?

What spells that they know not a word of
  Whose lives are as leaves overblown?
What tortures undreamt of, unheard of,
  Unwritten, unknown?

Ah beautiful passionate body
  That never has ached with a heart!
On thy mouth though the kisses are bloody,
  Though they sting till it shudder and smart,
More kind than the love we adore is,
  They hurt not the heart or the brain,
O bitter and tender Dolores,
  Our Lady of Pain.

As our kisses relax and redouble,
  From the lips and the foam and the fangs
Shall no new sin be born for men's trouble,
  No dream of impossible pangs?
With the sweet of the sins of old ages
  Wilt thou satiate thy soul as of yore?
Too sweet is the rind, say the sages,
  Too bitter the core.

Hast thou told all thy secrets the last time,
  And bared all thy beauties to one?
Ah, where shall we go then for pastime,
  If the worst that can be has been done?
But sweet as the rind was the core is;
  We are fain of thee still, we are fain,
O sanguine and subtle Dolores,
  Our Lady of Pain.

By the hunger of change and emotion,
  By the thirst of unbearable things,
By despair, the twin-born of devotion,
  By the pleasure that winces and stings,
The delight that consumes the desire,
  The desire that outruns the delight,
By the cruelty deaf as a fire
  And blind as the night,

By the ravenous teeth that have smitten
  Through the kisses that blossom and bud,
By the lips intertwisted and bitten
  Till the foam has a savour of blood,

By the pulse as it rises and falters,
  By the hands as they slacken and strain,
I adjure thee, respond from thine altars,
  Our Lady of Pain.

Wilt thou smile as a woman disdaining
  The light fire in the veins of a boy?
But he comes to thee sad, without feigning,
  Who has wearied of sorrow and joy;
Less careful of labour and glory
  Than the elders whose hair has uncurled;
And young, but with fancies as hoary
  And grey as the world.

I have passed from the outermost portal
  To the shrine where a sin is a prayer;
What care though the service be mortal?
  O our Lady of Torture, what care?
All thine the last wine that I pour is,
  The last in the chalice we drain,
O fierce and luxurious Dolores,
  Our Lady of Pain.

All thine the new wine of desire,
  The fruit of four lips as they clung
Till the hair and the eyelids took fire,
  The foam of a serpentine tongue,
The froth of the serpents of pleasure,
  More salt than the foam of the sea,
Now felt as a flame, now at leisure
  As wine shed for me.°

Ah thy people, thy children, thy chosen,
  Marked cross from the womb and perverse!
They have found out the secret to cozen
  The gods that constrain us and curse;
They alone, they are wise, and none other;
  Give me place, even me, in their train,
O my sister, my spouse, and my mother,
  Our Lady of Pain.

For the crown of our life as it closes
  Is darkness, the fruit thereof dust;
No thorns go as deep as a rose's,
  And love is more cruel than lust.

Time turns the old days to derision,
  Our loves into corpses or wives;°
And marriage and death and division
  Make barren our lives.

And pale from the past we draw nigh thee,
  And satiate with comfortless hours;
And we know thee, how all men belie thee,
  And we gather the fruit of thy flowers;
The passion that slays and recovers,
  The pangs and the kisses that rain
On the lips and the limbs of thy lovers,
  Our Lady of Pain.

The desire of thy furious embraces
  Is more than the wisdom of years,
On the blossom though blood lie in traces,
  Though the foliage be sodden with tears.
For the lords in whose keeping the door is
  That opens on all who draw breath
Gave the cypress to love, my Dolores,
  The myrtle to death.

And they laughed, changing hands in the measure,
  And they mixed and made peace after strife;
Pain melted in tears, and was pleasure;
  Death tingled with blood, and was life.
Like lovers they melted and tingled,
  In the dusk of thine innermost fane;
In the darkness they murmured and mingled,
  Our Lady of Pain.

In a twilight where virtues are vices,
  In thy chapels, unknown of the sun,
To a tune that enthralls and entices,
  They were wed, and the twain were as one.
For the tune from thine altar hath sounded
  Since God bade the world's work begin,
And the fume of thine incense abounded,
  To sweeten the sin.

Love listens, and paler than ashes,
  Through his curls as the crown on them slips.
Lifts languid wet eyelids and lashes,
  And laughs with insatiable lips.

Thou shalt hush him with heavy caresses,
  With music that scares the profane;
Thou shalt darken his eyes with thy tresses,
  Our Lady of Pain.

Thou shalt blind his bright eyes though he wrestle,
  Thou shalt chain his light limbs though he strive;
In his lips all thy serpents shall nestle,
  In his hands all thy cruelties thrive.
In the daytime thy voice shall go through him,
  In his dreams he shall feel thee and ache;
Thou shalt kindle by night and subdue him
  Asleep and awake.

Thou shalt touch and make redder his roses
  With juice not of fruit nor of bud;
When the sense in the spirit reposes,
  Thou shalt quicken the soul through the blood.
Thine, thine the one grace we implore is,
  Who would live and not languish or feign,
O sleepless and deadly Dolores,
  Our Lady of Pain.

Dost thou dream, in a respite of slumber,
  In a lull of the fires of thy life,
Of the days without name, without number,
  When thy will stung the world into strife;
When, a goddess, the pulse of thy passion
  Smote kings as they revelled in Rome;
And they hailed thee re-risen, O Thalassian,°
  Foam-white, from the foam?

When thy lips had such lovers to flatter;
  When the city lay red from thy rods,
And thine hands were as arrows to scatter
  The children of change and their gods;
When the blood of thy foemen made fervent
  A sand never moist from the main,
As one smote them, their lord and thy servant,
  Our Lady of Pain.

On sands by the storm never shaken,
  Nor wet from the washing of tides;
Nor by foam of the waves overtaken,
  Nor winds that the thunder bestrides;

But red from the print of thy paces,
  Made smooth for the world and its lords,
Ringed round with a name of fair faces,
  And splendid with swords.

There the gladiator, pale for thy pleasure,
  Drew bitter and perilous breath;
There torments laid hold on the treasure
  Of limbs too delicious for death;
When thy gardens were lit with live torches;°
  When the world was a steed for thy rein;
When the nations lay prone in thy porches,
  Our Lady of Pain.

When, with flame all around him aspirant,
  Stood flushed, as a harp-player stands,
The implacable beautiful tyrant,°
  Rose-crowned, having death in his hands;
And a sound as the sound of loud water
  Smote far through the flight of the fires,
And mixed with the lightning of slaughter
  A thunder of lyres.

Dost thou dream of what was and no more is,
  The old kingdoms of earth and the kings?
Dost thou hunger for these things, Dolores,
  For these, in a world of new things?
But thy bosom no fasts could emaciate,
  No hunger compel to complain
Those lips that no bloodshed could satiate,
  Our Lady of Pain.

As of old when the world's heart was lighter,
  Through thy garments the grace of thee glows,
The white wealth of thy body made whiter
  By the blushes of amorous blows,
And seamed with sharp lips and fierce fingers,
  And branded by kisses that bruise;
When all shall be gone that now lingers,
  Ah, what shall we lose?

Thou wert fair in the fearless old fashion,
  And thy limbs are as melodies yet,
And move to the music of passion
  With lithe and lascivious regret.

What ailed us, O gods, to desert you
  For creeds that refuse and restrain?
Come down and redeem us from virtue,
  Our Lady of Pain.

All shrines that were Vestal° are flameless;
  But the flame has not fallen from this;
Though obscure be the god, and though nameless
  The eyes and the hair that we kiss;
Low fires that love sits by and forges
  Fresh heads for his arrows and thine;
Hair loosened and soiled in mid orgies
  With kisses and wine.

Thy skin changes country and colour,
  And shrivels or swells to a snake's.
Let it brighten and bloat and grow duller,
  We know it, the flames and the flakes,
Red brands on it smitten and bitten,
  Round skies where a star is a stain,
And the leaves with thy litanies written,
  Our Lady of Pain.

On thy bosom though many a kiss be,
  There are none such as knew it of old.
Was it Alciphron once or Arisbe,°
  Male ringlets or feminine gold,
That thy lips met with under the statue,
  Whence a look shot out sharp after thieves
From the eyes of the garden-god at you
  Across the fig-leaves?°

Then still, through dry seasons and moister,
  One god had a wreath to his shrine;
Then love was the pearl of his oyster,[1]
  And Venus rose red out of wine.
We have all done amiss, choosing rather
  Such loves as the wise gods disdain;
Intercede for us thou with thy father,
  Our Lady of Pain.

In spring he had crowns of his garden,
  Red corn in the heat of the year,

[1] 'Nam te præcipuè in suis urbibus colit ora
Hellespontia, cæteris ostreosior oris.'
CATULL. *Carm.* xviii.°

Then hoary green olives that harden
  When the grape-blossom freezes with fear;
And milk-budded myrtles with Venus°
  And vine-leaves with Bacchus he trod;
And ye said, 'We have seen, he hath seen us,
  A visible God.'

What broke off the garlands that girt you?
  What sundered you spirit and clay?
Weak sins yet alive are as virtue
  To the strength of the sins of that day.
For dried is the blood of thy lover,
  Ipsithilla,° contracted the vein;
Cry aloud, 'Will he rise and recover,
  Our Lady of Pain?'

Cry aloud; for the old world is broken:
  Cry out; for the Phrygian is priest,
And rears not the bountiful token
  And spreads not the fatherly feast.
From the midmost of Ida, from shady
  Recesses that murmur at morn,
They have brought and baptized her, Our Lady,
  A goddess new-born.

And the chaplets of old are above us,
  And the oyster-bed teems out of reach;
Old poets out sing and outlove us,
  And Catullus makes mouths at our speech.
Who shall kiss, in thy father's own city,
  With such lips as he sang with, again?
Intercede for us all of thy pity,
  Our Lady of Pain.

Out of Dindymus° heavily laden
  Her lions draw bound and unfed
A mother, a mortal, a maiden,
  A queen over death and the dead.
She is cold, and her habit is lowly,
  Her temple of branches and sods;
Most fruitful and virginal, holy,
  A mother of gods.

She hath wasted with fire thine high places,
  She hath hidden and marred and made sad

The fair limbs of the Loves, the fair faces
  Of gods that were goodly and glad.
She slays, and her hands are not bloody;
  She moves as a moon in the wane,
White-robed, and thy raiment is ruddy,
  Our Lady of Pain.

They shall pass and their places be taken,
  The gods and the priests that are pure.
They shall pass, and shalt thou not be shaken?°
  They shall perish, and shalt thou endure?°
Death laughs, breathing close and relentless
  In the nostrils and eyelids of lust,
With a pinch in his fingers of scentless
  And delicate dust.

But the worm shall revive thee with kisses;
  Thou shalt change and transmute as a god,
As the rod to a serpent that hisses,°
  As the serpent again to a rod.
Thy life shall not cease though thou doff it;
  Thou shalt live until evil be slain,
And good shall die first, said thy prophet,
  Our Lady of Pain.

Did he lie? did he laugh? does he know it,
  Now he lies out of reach, out of breath,
Thy prophet, thy preacher, thy poet,
  Sin's child by incestuous Death?
Did he find out in fire at his waking,
  Or discern as his eyelids lost light,
When the bands of the body were breaking
  And all came in sight?

Who has known all the evil before us,
  Or the tyrannous secrets of time?
Though we match not the dead men that bore us
  At a song, at a kiss, at a crime—
Though the heathen outface and outlive us,
  And our lives and our longings are twain—
Ah, forgive us our virtues, forgive us,
  Our Lady of Pain.

Who are we that embalm and embrace thee
  With spices and savours of song?

What is time, that his children should face thee?
  What am I, that my lips do thee wrong?
I could hurt thee—but pain would delight thee;
  Or caress thee—but love would repel;
And the lovers whose lips would excite thee
  Are serpents in hell.

Who now shall content thee as they did,
  Thy lovers, when temples were built
And the hair of the sacrifice braided
  And the blood of the sacrifice spilt,
In Lampsacus fervent with faces,
  In Aphaca° red from thy reign,
Who embraced thee with awful embraces,
  Our Lady of Pain?

Where are they, Cotytto or Venus,
  Astarte or Ashtaroth,° where?
Do their hands as we touch come between us?
  Is the breath of them hot in thy hair?
From their lips have thy lips taken fever,
  With the blood of their bodies grown red?
Hast thou left upon earth a believer
  If these men are dead?

They were purple of raiment and golden,
  Filled full of thee, fiery with wine,
Thy lovers, in haunts unbeholden,
  In marvellous chambers of thine.
They are fled, and their footprints escape us,
  Who appraise thee, adore, and abstain,
O daughter of Death and Priapus,
  Our Lady of Pain.

What ails us to fear overmeasure,
  To praise thee with timorous breath,
O mistress and mother of pleasure,
  The one thing as certain as death?
We shall change as the things that we cherish,
  Shall fade as they faded before,
As foam upon water shall perish,
  As sand upon shore.

We shall know what the darkness discovers,
  If the grave-pit be shallow or deep;

And our fathers of old, and our lovers,
  We shall know if they sleep not or sleep.
We shall see whether hell be not heaven,
  Find out whether tares be not grain,°
And the joys of thee seventy times seven,
  Our Lady of Pain.

# The Garden of Proserpine

Here, where the world is quiet;
 Here, where all trouble seems
Dead winds' and spent waves' riot
 In doubtful dreams of dreams;
I watch the green field growing
For reaping folk and sowing,
For harvest-time and mowing
 A sleepy world of streams.

I am tired of tears and laughter,
 And men that laugh and weep;
Of what may come hereafter
 For men that sow to reap:
I am weary of days and hours,
Blown buds of barren flowers,
Desires and dreams and powers
 And everything but sleep.

Here life has death for neighbour,
 And far from eye or ear
Wan waves and wet winds labour,
 Weak ships and spirits steer;
They drive adrift, and whither
They wot not who make thither;
But no such winds blow hither,
 And no such things grow here.

No growth of moor or coppice,
 No heather-flower or vine,
But bloomless buds of poppies,
 Green grapes of Proserpine,
Pale beds of blowing rushes
Where no leaf blooms or blushes
Save this whereout she crushes
 For dead men deadly wine.

Pale, without name or number,
 In fruitless fields of corn,
They bow themselves and slumber
 All night till light is born;
And like a soul belated,

In hell and heaven unmated,
By cloud and mist abated
 Comes out of darkness morn.

Though one were strong as seven,
 He too with death shall dwell,
Nor wake with wings in heaven,
 Nor weep for pains in hell;
Though one were fair as roses,
His beauty clouds and closes;
And well though love reposes,
 In the end it is not well.

Pale, beyond porch and portal,
 Crowned with calm leaves, she stands
Who gathers all things mortal
 With cold immortal hands;
Her languid lips are sweeter
Than love's who fears to greet her
To men that mix and meet her
 From many times and lands.

She waits for each and other,
 She waits for all men born;
Forgets the earth her mother,°
 The life of fruits and corn;
And spring and seed and swallow
Take wing for her and follow
Where summer song rings hollow
 And flowers are put to scorn.

There go the loves that wither,
 The old loves with wearier wings;
And all dead years draw thither,
 And all disastrous things;
Dead dreams of days forsaken,
Blind buds that snows have shaken,
Wild leaves that winds have taken,
 Red strays of ruined springs.

We are not sure of sorrow,
 And joy was never sure;
To-day will die to-morrow;
 Time stoops to no man's lure;
And love, grown faint and fretful,

With lips but half regretful
Sighs, and with eyes forgetful
   Weeps that no loves endure.

From too much love of living,
   From hope and fear set free,
We thank with brief thanksgiving
   Whatever gods may be
That no life lives for ever;
That dead men rise up never;
That even the weariest river
   Winds somewhere safe to sea.

Then star nor sun shall waken,
   Nor any change of light:
Nor sound of waters shaken,
   Nor any sound or sight:
Nor wintry leaves nor vernal,
Nor days nor things diurnal;
Only the sleep eternal
   In an eternal night.

# Dedication

## 1865

The sea gives her shells to the shingle,
  The earth gives her streams to the sea;
They are many, but my gift is single,
  My verses, the firstfruits of me,
Let the wind take the green and the grey leaf,
  Cast forth without fruit upon air;
Take rose-leaf and vine-leaf and bay-leaf
  Blown loose from the hair.

The night shakes them round me in legions,
  Dawn drives them before her like dreams;
Time sheds them like snows on strange regions,
  Swept shoreward on infinite streams;
Leaves pallid and sombre and ruddy,
  Dead fruits of the fugitive years;
Some stained as with wine and made bloody,
  And some as with tears.

Some scattered in seven years' traces,
  As they fell from the boy that was then;
Long left among idle green places,
  Or gathered but now among men;
On seas full of wonder and peril,
  Blown white round the capes of the north;
Or in islands where myrtles are sterile°
  And loves bring not forth.

O daughters of dreams and of stories
  That life is not wearied of yet,
Faustine, Fragoletta, Dolores,
  Félise and Yolande and Juliette,
Shall I find you not still, shall I miss you,
  When sleep, that is true or that seems,
Comes back to me hopeless to kiss you,
  O daughters of dreams?

They are past as a slumber that passes,
  As the dew of a dawn of old time;
More frail than the shadows on glasses,
  More fleet than a wave or a rhyme.

As the waves after ebb drawing seaward,
  When their hollows are full of the night,
So the birds that flew singing to me-ward
  Recede out of sight.

The songs of dead seasons, that wander
  On wings of articulate words;
Lost leaves that the shore-wind may squander,
  Light flocks of untameable birds;
Some sang to me dreaming in class-time
  And truant in hand as in tongue;
For the youngest were born of boy's pastime,
  The eldest are young.

Is there shelter while life in them lingers,
  Is there hearing for songs that recede,
Tunes touched from a harp with man's fingers
  Or blown with boy's mouth in a reed?
Is there place in the land of your labour,
  Is there room in your world of delight,
Where change has not sorrow for neighbour
  And day has not night?

In their wings though the sea-wind yet quivers,
  Will you spare not a space for them there
Made green with the running of rivers
  And gracious with temperate air;
In the fields and the turreted cities,
  That cover from sunshine and rain
Fair passions and bountiful pities
  And loves without stain?

In a land of clear colours and stories,
  In a region of shadowless hours,
Where earth has a garment of glories
  And a murmur of musical flowers;
In woods where the spring half uncovers
  The flush of her amorous face,
By the waters that listen for lovers,
  For these is there place?

For the song-birds of sorrow, that muffle
  Their music as clouds do their fire:
For the storm-birds of passion, that ruffle
  Wild wings in a wind of desire;

In the stream of the storm as it settles
  Blown seaward, borne far from the sun,
Shaken loose on the darkness like petals
  Dropt one after one?

Though the world of your hands be more gracious
  And lovelier in lordship of things
Clothed round by sweet art with the spacious
  Warm heaven of her imminent wings,
Let them enter, unfledged and nigh fainting,
  For the love of old loves and lost times;
And receive in your palace of painting
  This revel of rhymes.

Though the seasons of man full of losses
  Make empty the years full of youth,
If but one thing be constant in crosses,
  Change lays not her hand upon truth;
Hopes die, and their tombs are for token
  That the grief as the joy of them ends
Ere time that breaks all men has broken
  The faith between friends.

Though the many lights dwindle to one light,
  There is help if the heaven has one;
Though the skies be discrowned of the sunlight
  And the earth dispossessed of the sun,
They have moonlight and sleep for repayment,
  When, refreshed as a bride and set free,
With stars and sea-winds in her raiment,
  Night sinks on the sea.

# FROM 'MR ARNOLD'S *NEW POEMS*' (1867)

There are two things which most men begin by hating until they have won their way, and which when combined are more than doubly hateful to all in whose eyes they are not doubly admirable: perfection of work, and personality in the workman.° As to perfection, it must be seen to be loved, and few have eyes to see it. To none but these few can it be acceptable at first; and only because these few are the final legislators of opinion, the tacit and patient lawgivers of time, does it ever win acceptance. A strong personal tone of character stamped and ingrained into a man's work, if more offensive at first to the mass, is likelier to find favour before long in the sight of some small body or sect of students. If not repulsive, it must be attractive and impressive; and there are always mental cripples in plenty to catch at a strong man's staff and cut it down into a crutch for themselves. But the more love a man has for perfection, the more faith in form, the more instinct for art, the fewer will these early believers be, and the better worth having; the process of winning their suffrages° will be slower, and surer the hold of them when won.

For some years the immediate fame of Mr Matthew Arnold has been almost exclusively the fame of a prose writer. Those students could hardly find hearing—they have nowhere of late found expression that I know of—who, with all esteem and enjoyment of his essays, of their clearness, candour, beauty of sentiment and style, retained the opinion that, if justly judged, he must be judged by his verse, and not by his prose; certainly not by this alone; that future students would cleave to that with more of care and of love; that the most memorable quality about him was the quality of a poet. Not that they liked the prose less, but that they liked the verse more.° His best essays ought to live longer than most, his best poems cannot but live as long as any, of their time. So it seemed to some who were accordingly more eager to receive and more careful to study a new book of his poems than most books they could have looked for; and since criticism of the rapid and limited kind possible to contemporaries can be no more than the sincere exposition of the writer's belief and of his reasons for it, I, as one of these, desire, with all deference but with all decision, to say what I think of this book, and why. For the honour of criticism, if it is to win or to retain honour at all, it must be well for the critic to explain clearly his personal point of view, instead of fighting behind the broad and crestless shield of a nameless friend or foe. The obscurest name and blazon are at least recognisable; but a mere voice is mere wind, though it affect to speak with the tongues and the authority of men and of angels.[o]

First on this new stage is the figure of an old friend and teacher. Mr Arnold says that the poem of 'Empedocles on Etna' was withdrawn before fifty copies of the first edition were sold.[o] I must suppose then that one of these was the copy I had when a schoolboy—how snatched betimes from the wreck and washed across my way, I know not; but I remember well enough how then, as now, the songs of Callicles clove to my ear and memory. Early as this was, it was not my first knowledge of the poet; the 'Reveller,' the 'Merman,' the 'New Sirens,' I had mainly by heart in a time of childhood just ignorant of teens. I do not say I understood the latter poem in a literal or logical fashion, but I had enjoyment enough of its music and colour and bright sadness as of a rainy sunset or sundawn. A child with any ear or eye for the attraction of verse or art can dispense with analysis, and rest content to apprehend it without comprehension; it were to be wished that adults equally incapable would rest equally content. Here I must ask, as between brackets, if this beautiful poem is never to be reissued after the example of its younger? No poet could afford to drop or destroy it; I might at need call into court older and better judges to back my judgment in this; meantime 'I hope here be proofs'[o] that, however inadequate may be my estimate of the poet on whom I am now to discourse, it is not inadequate through want of intimacy with his work. At the risk of egotism, I record it in sign of gratitude; I cannot count the hours of pure and high pleasure, I cannot reckon the help and guidance in thought and work, which I owe to him as to all other real and noble artists, whose influence it was my fortune to feel when most susceptible of influence, and least conscious of it, and most in want. In one of his books, where he presses rather hard upon our school as upon one devoid of spiritual or imaginative culture, he speaks of his poems as known to no large circle—implies this at least, if I remember: he will not care to be assured that to some boys at Eton Sohrab and Rustum, Tristram and Iseult, have been close and common friends, their stream of Oxus and bays of Brittany familiar almost as the well-loved Thames weirs and reaches. However, of this poem of 'Empedocles' the world it seems was untimely robbed, though I remember on searching to have found a notice of it here and there. Certain fragments were then given back by way of dole, chiefly in the second series of the author's revised poems. But one, the largest, if not the brightest jewel, was withheld; the one long and lofty chant of Empedocles. The reasons assigned by Mr Arnold in a former preface[o] for cancelling the complete poem had some weight: the subject-matter is oppressive, the scheme naked and monotonous; the blank verse is not sonorous, not vital and various enough; in spite of some noble interludes, it fails on the whole to do the work and carry the weight wanted; its simplicity is stony and grey, with dry flats and rough whinstones.

To the lyrics which serve as water-springs and pastures I shall have to pay tribute of thanks in their turn; but first I would say something of that strain of choral philosophy which falls here 'as the shadow of a great rock in a weary land.'° It is a model of grave, clear, solemn verse; the style plain and bare, but sufficient and strong; the thought deep, lucid, direct. We may say of it what the author has himself said of the wise and sublime verses of Epictetus, that 'the fortitude of that is for the strong, yet the few; even for them, the spiritual atmosphere with which it surrounds them is bleak and grey;'° but the air is higher and purer, the ground firmer, the view clearer; we have a surer foothold on these cold hills of thought than in the moist fragrance of warmer air which steeps the meadows and marshes of sentiment and tradition.

> 'Thin, thin the pleasant human noises grow,
>   And faint the city gleams;
> Rare the lone pastoral huts; marvel not thou!
> The solemn peaks but to the stars are known,
> But to the stars, and the cold lunar beams;
> Alone the sun arises, and alone
>   Spring the great streams.'

These noble verses of another poem clipped from Mr Arnold's first book, and left hanging in fragments about one's memory—I here make my protest against its excision—may serve as types of the later, the more immediate and elaborate discourse of thought here embodied and attired in words of stately and simple harmony. It is no small or common comfort, after all the delicate and ingenious shuffling of other English poets about the edge of deep things, to come upon one who speaks with so large and clear and calm an utterance; who begins at the taproot and wellspring of the matter, leaving others to wade ankle-deep in still waters and weave river-flags or lake-lilies in lieu of stemming the stream. Nothing in verse or out of verse is more wearisome than the delivery of reluctant doubt, of half-hearted hope and half-incredulous faith. A man who suffers from the strong desire either to believe or disbelieve something he cannot, may be worthy of sympathy, is certainly worthy of pity, until he begins to speak; and if he tries to speak in verse, he misuses the implement of an artist. We have had evidences of religion, aspirations and suspirations of all kinds, melodious regrets and tortuous returns in favour or disfavour of this creed or that—all by way of poetic work; and all within the compass and shot-range of a single faith; all, at the widest, bounded north, south, east, and west by material rivers or hills, by an age or two since, by a tradition or two; all leaving the spirit cramped and thirsty. We have had Christian sceptics, handcuffed fighters, tongue-tied orators, plume-plucked eagles; believers whose belief was a sentiment, and free-thinkers who saw nothing before Christ or beyond Judæa. To get at the bare rock is a relief after acres of such quaking ground.

[...]

Elsewhere, in minor poems, Mr Arnold also has now and then given signs of an inclination for that sad task of sweeping up dead leaves fallen from the dying tree of belief; but has not wasted much time or strength on such sterile and stupid work. Here, at all events, he has wasted none; here is no melodious whine of retrospective and regretful scepticism; here are no cobwebs of plea and counterplea, no jungles of argument and brakes of analysis. 'Ask what most helps when known;'° let be the oracular and the miraculous, and vex not the soul about their truth or falsehood; the soul, which oracles and miracles can neither make nor mar, can neither slay nor save.

'Once read thy own breast right,
And thou hast done with fears!
Man gets no other light,
Search he a thousand years.
Sink in thyself! there ask what ails thee, at that shrine!'

This is the gospel of *αὐτάρκεια*, the creed of self-sufficience,[1] which sees for man no clearer or deeper duty than that of intellectual self-reliance, self-dependence, self-respect; an evangel not to be cancelled or supplanted by any revelation of mystic or prophet or saint. Out of this counsel grows the exposition of obscure and afflictive things. Man's welfare—his highest sphere and state of spiritual well-doing and well-being—this indeed is his true aim; but not this is the aim of nature: the world has other work than this to do; and we, not it, must submit; submit, not by ceasing to attempt and achieve the best we can, but by ceasing to expect subservience to our own ends from all forces and influences of existing things; it is no reason or excuse for living basely instead of nobly, that we must live as the sons, not as the lords of nature. 'To tunes we did not call our being must keep chime;'° but this bare truth we will not accept. Philosophy, as forcibly and clearly as religion, indicates the impediments of sin and self-will; 'we do not what we ought, what we ought not we do;'° but there religion stops, as far as regards this world, and passes upward into a new world and life; philosophy has further to go without leaving her hold upon earth. Even were man pure, just, wise, instead of unwise, unjust, and impure, this would not affect the 'other existences that clash with ours.'

'Like us, the lightning fires
Love to have scope and play;
The stream, like us, desires
An unimpeded way;
Like us, the Libyan wind delights to roam at large.

[1] I take leave to forge this word, because 'self-sufficingness' is a compound of too barbaric sound, and 'self-sufficiency' has fallen into a form of reproach. Archbishop Trench° has pointed out how and why a word which to the ancient Greek signified a noble virtue came to signify to the modern Christian the base vice of presumption. I do not see that human language has gained by this change of meaning, or that the later mood of mind which dictated this debasement of the word is at all in advance of the older, or indicative of any spiritual improvement; rather the alteration seems to me a loss and discredit, and the tone of thought which made the quality venerable more sound and wise than that which declares it vile.

'Streams will not curb their pride
The just man not to entomb,
Nor lightnings go aside
To leave his virtues room;
Nor is that wind less rough which blows a good man's barge.

'Nature, with equal mind,
Sees all her sons at play;
Sees man control the wind,
The wind sweep man away:
Allows the proudly-riding and the founder'd bark.'

Again, there are 'the ill-deeds of other men' to fill up the account against us of painful and perilous things. And we, instead of doing and bearing all we can under our conditions of life, must needs 'cheat our pains' like children after a fall who 'rate the senseless ground:'

'So, loath to suffer mute,
We, peopling the void air,
Make gods to whom to impute
The ills we ought to bear;
With God and Fate to rail at, suffering easily.

'Yet grant—as sense long miss'd
Things that are now perceiv'd,
And much may still exist
Which is not yet believ'd—
Grant that the world were full of Gods we cannot see;

'All things the world which fill
Of but one stuff are spun,
That we who rail are still,
With what we rail at, one;
One with the o'er-labour'd Power that through the breadth and length

'Of earth, and air, and sea,
In men, and plants, and stones,
Hath toil perpetually,
And struggles, pants, and moans;
Fain would do all things well, but sometimes fails in strength.

'And patiently exact,
This universal God
Alike to any act
Proceeds at any nod,
And quietly declaims the cursings of himself.

'This is not what man hates,
  Yet he can curse but this.
Harsh Gods and hostile Fates
  Are dreams! this only *is*;
Is everywhere; sustains the wise, the foolish elf.'

Again, we must have comfortable Gods to bless, as well as these discomfortable to curse; 'kind Gods who perfect what man vainly tries;' we console ourselves for long labour and research and failure by trust in their sole and final and sufficient knowledge. Then comes the majestic stroke of reply, to rebuke and confute the feeble follies of inventive hope, the futile forgeries of unprofitable comfort; scornful and solemn as the forces themselves of nature.

'Fools! that in man's brief term
  He cannot all things view,
Affords no ground to affirm
  That there are Gods who do!
Nor does being weary prove that he has where to rest!'

In like manner, when pleasure-seekers fail of pleasure in this world, they turn their hearts Godward, and thence in the end expect that joy which the world could not give; making sure to find happiness where the foiled student makes sure to find knowledge. Again the response from natural things unseen, or from the lips of their own wisest, confronts their fancies as before.

'Fools! that so often here
  Happiness mocked our prayer,
I think, might make us fear
  A like event elsewhere!
Make us, not fly to dreams, but moderate desire!'

Nor, finally, when all is said, need the wise despair or repine because debarred from dreams of a distant and dubious happiness in a world outside of ours.

'Is it so small a thing
  To have enjoyed the sun,
To have lived light in the spring,
  To have loved, to have thought, to have done?'

The poorest villager feels that it is not so small a thing that he should not be loth to lose the little that life can yield him. Let the wiser man, like him, trust without fear the joys that are; life has room for effort and enjoyment, though at sight of the evil and sorrow it includes, one may have abjured false faith and foolish hope and fruitless fear.

[...]

This elegy and the poem headed 'Resignation' are, in my eyes, the final flower of Mr Arnold's poems after Wordsworth—as I take leave to qualify a certain division of his work. The second of these is an unspotted and unbroken model of high calm thought, couched in pure and faultless words; the words more equal and the vision more clear than his old teacher's, more just in view and more sure in grasp of nature and life. Imbued with the old faith at once in the necessity of things and in the endurance of man, it excels in beauty and in charm the kindred song of Empedocles; from first to last there rests upon it a serene spell, a sad supremacy of still music that softens and raises into wisdom the passionless and gentle pain of patience; the charm of earth and sorrowful magic of things everlasting; the spell that is upon the patient hills and immutable rocks, awake and asleep in 'the life of plants and stones and rain';° the life to which we too may subdue our souls and be wise. At times he writes simply as the elder poet might have written, without sensible imitation, but with absolute identity of style and sentiment; at times his larger tone of thought, his clearer accent of speech, attest the difference of the men. So perfect and sweet in speech, so sound and lucid in thought as the pupil is at his best, the master perhaps never was; and at his best the pupil is no more seen, and in his stead is a new master. He has nothing of Wordsworth's spirit of compromise with the nature of things, nothing of his moral fallacies and religious reservations; he can see the face of facts and read them with the large and frank insight of ancient poets; none of these ever had a more profound and serene sense of fate. But he has not grasped, and no man, I suppose, will ever grasp, the special and imperial sceptre of his elder. The incommunicable, the immitigable might of Wordsworth, when the god has indeed fallen upon him, cannot but be felt by all, and can but be felt by any; none can partake or catch it up. There are many men greater than he; there are men much greater; but what he has of greatness is his only. His concentration, his majesty, his pathos have no parallel; some have gone higher, many lower, none have touched precisely the same point as he; some poets have had more of all these qualities, and better; none have had exactly his gift. His pathos, for instance, cannot be matched against any other man's; it is trenchant, and not tender; it is an iron pathos. Take for example the most passionate of his poems, the 'Affliction of Margaret;' it is hard and fiery, dry and persistent as the agony of a lonely and a common soul which endures through life, a suffering which runs always in one groove without relief or shift. Because he is dull and dry and hard, when set by the side of a great lyrist or dramatist; because of these faults and defects, he is so intense and irresistible when his iron hand has hold of some chord which it knows how to play upon. How utterly unlike his is the pathos of Homer or Æschylus, Chaucer or Dante, Shakespeare or Hugo; all these greater poets feel the moisture and flame of the fever and the tears they paint; their pathos when sharpest is full of sensitive life, of subtle tenderness, of playing pulses and melting colours; his has but the downright and trenchant weight of swinging steel; he strikes like the German headsman, one stroke of a loaded sword. This could not be done even by the poets who could do more and better than this. His metre too is sublime, his choice or chance of language casual or chosen has miraculous effects in it, when he feels his foot firm on ground fit for him; otherwise his verse is often hard as wood and dry as dust and weak as water. In this as in other ways his influence has been now good and now bad. The grave cadence of such a poem as the 'Resignation,' in this point also one of Mr Arnold's most noble and effective, bears with it a memory and a resonance of the master's music, such as we find again in the lovely single couplets and lines which now and then lift up the mind or lull it in the midst of less excellent verse; such for instance as these, which close a scale of lower melodies, in a poem not wholly or equally pleasurable: but these are faultless verses, and full of the comfort of music, which tell us how, wafted at times from the far-off verge of the soul,

> 'As from an infinitely distant land,
> Come airs, and floating echoes, and convey
> A melancholy into all our day.'

These have a subtle likeness to Wordsworth's purer notes, a likeness undefined and unborrowed; the use of words usually kept back for prose (such as 'convey') is a trick of Wordsworth's which either makes or mars a passage; here the touch, it may be by accident, strikes the exact chord wanted, elicits the exact tone.

But indeed, as with all poets of his rank, so with Mr Arnold, the technical beauty of his work is one with the spiritual; art, a poet's art above all others, cannot succeed in this and fail in that. Success or achievement of an exalted kind on the spiritual side ensures and enforces a like executive achievement or success; if the handiwork be flawed, there must also have been some distortion or defect of spirit, a shortcoming or a misdirection of spiritual supply. There is no such thing as a dumb poet or a handless painter. The essence of an artist is that he should be articulate. It is the mere impudence of weakness to arrogate the name of poet or painter with no other claim than a susceptible and impressible sense of outward or inward beauty, producing an impotent desire to paint or sing. The poets that are made by nature are not many; and whatever 'vision' an aspirant may possess, he has not the 'divine faculty' if he cannot use his vision to any poetic purpose. There is no cant more pernicious to such as these, more wearisome to all other men, than that which asserts the reverse. It is a drug which weakens the feeble and intoxicates the drunken; which makes those swagger who have not learnt to walk, and teach who have not been taught to learn. Such talk as this of Wordsworth's is the poison of poor souls like David Gray. Men listen, and depart with the belief that they have this faculty or this vision which alone, they are told, makes the poet; and once imbued with that belief, soon pass or slide from the inarticulate to the articulate stage of debility and disease. Inspiration foiled and impotent is a piteous thing enough, but friends and teachers of this sort make it ridiculous as well. A man can no more win a place among poets by dreaming of it or lusting after it than he can win by dream or desire a woman's beauty or a king's command; and those encourage him to fill his belly with the east wind who feign to accept the will for the deed, and treat inarticulate or inadequate pretenders as actual associates in art. The Muses can bear children and Apollo can give crowns to those only who are able to win the crown and beget the child; but in the school of theoretic sentiment it is apparently believed that this can be done by wishing.

Small things suffice to give immediate proof or disproof of the requisite power. In music or in painting all men admit this for a truth; it is not less certain in poetry. There is nothing in either of the poets I speak of more distinctive and significant than the excellence of their best sonnets. These are almost equally noble in style, though the few highest of Wordsworth's remain out of reach of emulation, not out of sight of worship. Less adorable and sublime, not less admirable and durable, Mr Arnold's hold their own in the same world of poetry with these. All in this new volume are full of beauty, sound and sweet fruits of thought and speech that have ripened and brought forth together; the poetry of religious thought when most pure and most large has borne no fairer than that one on the drawing in the Catacombs of the Good Shepherd° bearing the young, not of a sheep, but of a goat; or that other on the survival of grace and spirit when the body of belief lies dead, headed (not happily) 'Anti-Desperation;' but all, I repeat, have a singular charm and clearness. I have used this word already more than once or twice; it comes nearest of all I can find to the thing I desire to express; that natural light of mind, that power of reception and reflection of things or thoughts, which I most admire in so much of Mr Arnold's work. I mean by it much more than mere facility or transparency, more than brilliance, more than ease or excellence of style. It is a quality begotten by instinct upon culture; one which all artists of equal rank possess in equal measure.

There are in the English language three elegiac poems so great that they eclipse and efface all the elegiac poetry we know; all of Italian, all of Greek. It is only because the latest born is yet new to us that it can seem strange or rash to say so. The 'Thyrsis' of Mr Arnold makes a third, with 'Lycidas' and 'Adonais.' It is not so easy as those may think who think by rote and praise by prescription, to strike the balance between them. The first however remains first, and must remain; its five opening lines are to me the most musical in all known realms of verse; there is nothing like them; and it is more various, more simple, more large and sublime than the others; lovelier and fuller it cannot be.

'The leader is fairest,
But all are divine.'°

The least pathetic of the three is 'Adonais,' which indeed is hardly pathetic at all; it is passionate, subtle, splendid; but 'Thyrsis,' like 'Lycidas,' has a quiet and tender undertone which gives it something of sacred. Shelley brings fire from heaven, but these bring also 'the meed of some melodious tear.'° There is a grace ineffable, a sweet sound and sweet savour of things past, in the old beautiful use of the language of shepherds, of flocks and pipes; the spirit is none the less sad and sincere because the body of the poem has put on this dear familiar raiment of romance; because the crude and naked sorrow is veiled and chastened with soft shadows and sounds of a 'land that is very far off;'° because the verse remembers and retains a perfume and an echo of Grecian flutes and flowers,

> 'Renews the golden world, and holds through all
> The holy laws of homely pastoral,
> Where flowers and founts, and nymphs and semi-gods,
> And all the Graces find their old abodes.'

Here, as in the 'Scholar Gipsy,' the beauty, the delicacy and affluence of colour, the fragrance and the freedom as of wide wings of winds in summer over meadow and moor, the freshness and expansion of the light and the lucid air, the spring and the stream as of flowing and welling water, enlarge and exalt the pleasure and power of the whole poem. Such English-coloured verse no poet has written since Shakespeare, who chooses his field-flowers and hedgerow blossoms with the same sure and loving hand, binds them in as simple and sweet an order. All others, from Milton downward to Shelley and onward from him, have gathered them singly or have mixed them with foreign buds and alien bloom. No poem in any language can be more perfect as a model of style, unsurpassable certainly, it may be unattainable. Any couplet, any line proves it. No countryman of ours since Keats died has made or has found words fall into such faultless folds and forms of harmonious line. He is the most efficient, the surest-footed poet of our time, the most to be relied on; what he does he is the safest to do well; more than any other he unites personality and perfection; others are personal and imperfect, perfect and impersonal; with them you must sometimes choose between inharmonious freedom and harmonious bondage. Above all, he knows what as a poet he should do, and simply does that; the manner of his good work is never more or less than right. His verse comes clean and full out of the mould, cast at a single jet; placed beside much other verse of the time, it shows like a sculptor's work by an enameller's. With all their wealth and warmth of flowers and lights, these two twin poems are solid and pure as granite or as gold. Their sweet sufficiency of music, so full and calm, buoys and bears up throughout the imperial vessel of thought. Their sadness is not chill or sterile, but as the sorrow of summer pausing with laden hands on the middle height of the year, the watershed that divides the feeding fountains of autumn and of spring; a grave and fruitful sadness, the triumphant melancholy of full-blown flowers and souls full-grown. The stanzas from the sixth to the fourteenth of 'Thyrsis,' and again from the sixteenth to the twentieth, are, if possible, the most lovely in either poem; the deepest in tone and amplest in colour; the choiceness and sweetness of single lines and phrases most exquisite and frequent.

> 'O easy access to the hearer's grace,
> When Dorian shepherds sang to Proserpine!
> For she herself had trod Sicilian fields,
> She knew the Dorian water's gush divine,
> She knew each lily white which Enna yields,
> Each rose with blushing face;
> She loved the Dorian pipe, the Dorian strain.
> But, ah! of our poor Thames she never heard!
> Her foot the Cumnor cowslips never stirred;
> And we should tease her with our plaint in vain.'

She has learnt to know them now, the river and the river-meadows, and access is as easy for an English as a Dorian prayer to the most gentle of all worshipped gods. It is a triumphal and memorial poem, a landmark in the high places of verse to which future travellers, studious of the fruits and features of the land, may turn and look up and see what English hands could rear.

This is probably the highest point of Mr Arnold's poetry, though for myself I cannot wholly resign the old preference of things before familiar; of one poem in especial, good alike for children and men, the 'Forsaken Merman,' which has in it the pathos of natural things, the tune of the passion we fancy in the note of crying birds or winds weeping, shrill and sweet and estranged from us; the swift and winged wail of something lost midway between man's life and the life of things soulless, the wail overheard and caught up by the fitful northern fancy, filling with glad and sad spirits the untravelled ways of nature; the clear cry of a creature astray in the world, wild and gentle and mournful, heard in the sighing of weary waters before dawn under a low wind, in the rustle and whistle and whisper of leaves or grasses, in the long light breaths of twilight air heaving all the heather on the hills, in the coming and going of the sorrowful strong seas that bring delight and death, in the tender touch and recoil of the ripple from the sand; all the fanciful pitiful beauty of dreams and legends born in grey windy lands on shores and hillsides whose life is quiet and wild. No man's hand has pressed from the bells and buds of the moors and downs, by cape or channel of the north, a sweeter honey than this. The song is a piece of the sea-wind, a stray breath of the air and bloom of the bays and hills; its mixture of mortal sorrow with the strange wild sense of a life that is not after mortal law—the childlike moan after lost love mingling with the pure outer note of a song not human—the look in it as of bright bewildered eyes with tears not theirs and alien wonder in the watch of them—the tender, marvellous, simple beauty of the poem, its charm as of a sound or a flower of the sea—set it and save it apart from all others in a niche of the memory. This has all the inexplicable inevitable sweetness of a child's or a bird's in its note; 'Thyrsis' has all the accomplished and adult beauty of a male poem. In the volume which it crowns there is certainly no new jewel of equal water. 'Palladium' is a fresh sample of the noble purity and clearness which we find always and always praise in his reflective poetry; its cool aerial colour, like that of a quiet sky between full sunset and full moonrise, made ready for the muster of the stars, swept clean of cloud and flame, and laved with limpid unruffled air from western green to eastern grey; a sky the cenotaph of unburied sunlight, the mould of moonlight unborn. 'A Southern Night' is steeped in later air, as gentle and more shining; the stanzas on the Grande Chartreuse are stamped with the impression of a solemn charm, and so the new verses on Obermann,[2] the new verses on Marguerite, strange to read for those who remember reading the first at the time when all the loves we read of assume a form and ascend a throne in our thoughts, the old and the new side by side, so that now this poem comes under our eyes like a new love-song of Petrarca to Laura, or Coleridge to Geneviève.° It is fine and high in tone, but not such as the famous verses, cited and admired even by critics sparing of their priceless praise, beginning—

'Yes, in this sea of life enisled—.'

These in their profound and passionate calm strike deeper and sound fuller than any other of the plaintive dejected songs of Switzerland. 'Dover Beach' marks another high point in the volume; it has a grand choral cadence as of steady surges, regular in resonance, not fitful or gusty, but antiphonal and reverberate. But nothing of new verse here clings closer to the mind than the overture of that majestic fragment from the chorus of a *Dejaneira*.°

'O frivolous mind of man,
Light ignorance, and hurrying unsure thoughts,
Though man bewails you not,
How I bewail you!'

We must hope to have more of the tragedy in time; that must be a noble statue which could match this massive fragment. The story of Merope, though dramatic enough in detail, is upon the whole more of a narrative romance than a

[2] Among these the stanzas on the advent of Christianity, of 'the Mother with the Child,' and their enduring life while only faith in them endured, recall the like passage, more thoughtful and fruitful still, in that wise and noble poem, Mr W.B. Scott's 'Year of the World;'° a poem to whose great qualities and affluent beauties of letter and of spirit, the requisite and certain justice of time remains hitherto a debt unpaid. Its author must divide with Mr Arnold the palm of intellectual or philosophic poetry, the highest achieved in England since Wordsworth, and in many things of moment higher than his.

tragic subject; and in Mr Arnold's poem the deepest note is that struck by the tyrant Polyphontes, whose austere and patient figure is carved with Sophoclean skill of hand. It is a poem which Milton might have praised, an august work, of steady aim and severe success; but this of Dejaneira has in it a loftier promise and a larger chance. Higher matter of tragedy there can be none; none more intense and impressive, none fuller of keen and profound interest, none simpler or statelier; none where the weight and gravity, the sweetness and shapeliness of pure thought, could be better or closelier allied with the warmth and width of common tenderness and passion. We must all hope that the poet will keep to this clear air of the ancient heights, more natural and wholesome for the spirit than the lowlands of depression and dubiety where he has set before now a too frequent foot. This alone I find profitless and painful in his work; this occasional habit of harking back and loitering in mind among the sepulchres. Nothing is to be made by an artist out of scepticism, half-hearted or double-hearted doubts or creeds; nothing out of mere dejection and misty mental weather. Tempest or calm you may put to use, but hardly a flat fog. In not a few of his former poems, in some reprinted here, there is a sensible and stagnant influence of moist vapour from those marshes of the mind where weaker souls paddle and plunge and disappear. Above these levels the sunnier fields and fresher uplands lie wide and warm; and there the lord of the land should sit at peace among his good things. If a spirit by nature clear and high, a harmonious and a shining soul, does ever feel itself 'immured in the hot prison of the present,'[o] its fit work is not to hug but break its chain; and only by its own will or weakness can it remain ill at ease in a thick and difficult air. Of such poetry I would say what Joubert, as cited by Mr Arnold, says of all coarse and violent literature: it may be produced in any amount of supply to any excess of effect, but it is no proper matter of pure art, and 'the soul says all the while, You hurt me.'[o] Deep-reaching doubt and 'large discourse' are poetical; so is faith, so are sorrow and joy; but so are not the small troubles of spirits that nibble and quibble about beliefs living or dead; so are not those sickly moods which are warmed and weakened by feeding on the sullen drugs of dejection; and the savour of this disease and its medicines is enough to deaden the fresh air of poetry. Nothing which leaves us depressed is a true work of art. We must have light though it be lightning, and air though it be storm. [...]

# WILLIAM BLAKE.

A Critical Essay.

BY

ALGERNON CHARLES SWINBURNE.

*"Going to and fro in the Earth."*

WITH ILLUSTRATIONS FROM BLAKE'S DESIGNS IN FACSIMILE,

*COLOURED AND PLAIN.*

LONDON:
JOHN CAMDEN HOTTEN, PICCADILLY.
1868.



FIG. 5. Title page of *William Blake: A Critical Essay* (London: Hotten, 1868), a copy from the Brotherton Library, Special Collections, University of Leeds, reproduced with permission.

# FROM *WILLIAM BLAKE: A CRITICAL ESSAY* (1868)

## II.—Lyrical Poems

We must here be allowed space to interpolate a word of the briefest possible comment on the practical side of Blake's character. No man ever lived and laboured in hotter earnest; and the native energy in him had the property of making all his atmosphere of work intense and keen as fire—too sharp and rare in quality of heat to be a good working element for any more temperate intellect. Into every conceivable channel or byway of work he contrived to divert and infuse this overflowing fervour of mind; the least bit of engraving, the poorest scrap or scratch of drawing or writing traceable to his hands, has on it the mark of passionate labour and enjoyment; but of all this devotion of laborious life, the only upshot visible to most of us consists in a heap of tumbled and tangled relics, verse and prose mainly inexplicable, paintings and engravings mainly unacceptable if not unendurable. And if certain popular theories of the just aims of life, duties of an earnest-minded man, and meritorious nature of practical deeds and material services only, are absolutely correct—in that case the work of this man's life is certainly a sample of deplorable waste and failure. A religion which has for Walhalla some factory of the Titans, some prison fitted with moral cranks and divine treadmills of all the virtues, can have no place among its heroes for the most energetic of mere artists. To him, as to others of his kind, all faith, all virtue, all moral duty or religious necessity, was not so much abrogated or superseded as summed up, included and involved, by the one matter of art. To him, as to other such workmen, it seemed better to do this well and let all the rest drift than to do incomparably well in all other things and dispense with this one. For this was the thing he had to do; and this once well done, he had the assurance of a certain faith that other things could not be wrong with him. As long as two such parties exist among men who think and act, it must always be some pleasure to deal with a man of either party who has no faith or hope in compromise. These middle-men, with some admirable self-sufficient theory of reconciliation between two directly opposite aims and forces, are fit for no great work on either side. If it be in the interest of facts really desirable that 'the poor Fine Arts should take themselves away,'[o] let it be fairly avowed and preached in a distinct manner. That thesis, so delivered, is comprehensible, and deserves respect. One may add that if art can be destroyed it by all means ought to be. If for example the art of verse is not indispensable and indestructible, the sooner it is put out of the way the better. If anything can be done instead better worth doing than painting or poetry, let that preferable thing be done with all the might and haste that may be attainable. And if to live well be really better than to write or paint well, and a noble action more valuable than the greatest poem or most perfect picture, let us have done at once with the meaner things that stand in the way of the higher. For we cannot on any terms have everything; and assuredly no chief artist or poet has ever been fit to hold rank among the world's supreme benefactors in the way of doctrine, philanthropy, reform, guidance, or example: what is called the artistic faculty not being by any means the same thing as a general capacity for doing good work, diverted into this one strait or shallow in default of a better outlet. Even were this true for example of a man so imperfect as Burns, it would remain false of a man so perfect as Keats. The great men, on whichever side one finds them, are never found trying to take truce or patch up terms. Savonarola burnt Boccaccio;° Cromwell proscribed Shakespeare. The early Christians were not great at verse or sculpture. Men of immense capacity and energy who do seem to think or assert it possible to serve both masters—a Dante, a Shelley, a Hugo—poets whose work is mixed with and coloured by personal action or suffering for some cause moral or political—these even are no real exceptions. It is not as artists that they do or seem to do this. The work done may be, and in such high cases often must be, of supreme value to art; but not the moral implied. Strip the sentiments and re-clothe them in bad verse, what residue will be left of the slightest importance to art? Invert them, retaining the manner or form (supposing this feasible, which it might be), and art has lost nothing. Save the shape, and art will take care of the soul for you:[1] unless that is all right, she will refuse to run or start at all; but the shape or style of workmanship each artist is bound to look to, whether or no he may choose to trouble himself about the moral or other bearings of his work. This principle, which makes the manner of doing a thing the essence of the thing done, the purpose or result of it the accident, thus reversing the principle of moral or material duty, must inevitably expose art to the condemnation of the other party—the party of those who (as aforesaid) regard what certain of their leaders° call an earnest life or a great acted poem (that is, material virtue or the mere doing and saying of good or instructive deeds and words) as infinitely preferable to any possible feat of art. Opinion is free, and the choice always open; but if any man leaning on crutches of theory chooses to halt between the two camps, it shall be at his own peril—imminent peril of conviction as

[1] Of course, there can be no question here of bad art: which indeed is a non-entity or contradiction in terms, as to speak of good art is to run into tautology. It is assumed, to begin with, that the artist has something to say or do worth doing or saying in an artistic form.

one unfit for service on either side. For Puritanism is in this one thing absolutely right about art; they cannot live and work together, or the one under the other. All ages which were great enough to have space for both, to hold room for a fair fighting-field between them, have always accepted and acted upon this evident fact. Take the Renaissance age for one example; you must have Knox or Ronsard, Scotch or French; not both at once; there is no place under reformers for the singing of a 'Pléiade.'° Take the mediæval period in its broadest sense; not to speak of the notably heretical and immoral Albigeois with their exquisite school of heathenish verse, or of that other rebellious gathering under the great emperor Frederick II., a poet and pagan, when eastern arts and ideas began to look up westward at one man's bidding and open out Saracenic prospects in the very face and teeth of the Church—look at home into familiar things, and see by such poems as Chaucer's *Court of Love*, absolutely one in tone and handling as it is with the old Albigensian *Aucassin*° and all its paganism,[2] how the poets of the time, with their eager nascent worship of beautiful form and external nature, dealt with established opinion and the incarnate moralities of church or household. It is easy to see why the Church on its own principle found it (as in the Albigensian case) a matter of the gravest necessity to have such schools of art and thought cut down or burnt out. Priest and poet, all those times through, were proverbially on terms of reciprocal biting and striking. That magnificent invention of making 'Art the handmaid of Religion'° had not been stumbled upon in the darkness

[2] Observe especially in Chaucer's most beautiful of young poems that appalling passage,° where, turning the favourite edgetool of religious menace back with point inverted upon those who forged it, the poet represents men and women of religious habit or life as punished in the next world, beholding afar off with jealous regret the salvation and happiness of Venus and all her servants (converse of the Hörsel legend,° which shows the religious or anti-Satanic view of the matter; though there too there is some pity or sympathy implied for the pagan side of things, revealing in the tradition the presence and touch of some poet): expressly punished, these monks and nuns, for their continence and holiness of life, and compelled after death to an eternity of fruitless repentance for having wilfully missed of pleasure and made light of indulgence in this world; which is perfect Albigeois. Compare the famous speech° in *Aucassin et Nicolette*, where the typical hero weighs in a judicial manner the respective attractions of heaven and hell; deciding of course dead against the former on account of the deplorably bad company kept there; priests, hermits, saints, and such-like, in lieu of knights and ladies, painters and poets. One may remark also, the minute this pagan revival begins to get breathing-room, how there breaks at once into flower a most passionate and tender worship of nature, whether as shown in the bodily beauty of man and woman or in the outside loveliness of leaf and grass; both Chaucer and his anonymous southern colleague being throughout careful to decorate their work with the most delicate and splendid studies of colour and form. Either of the two choice morsels of doctrinal morality cited above would have exquisitely suited the palate of Blake. He in his time, one need not doubt, was considerably worried and gibbered at by 'monkeys in houses of brick,'° moral theorists, and 'pantopragmatic'° men of all sorts; what can we suppose he would have said or done in an epoch given over to preachers (lay, clerical, and mixed) who assert without fear or shame that you may demand, nay are bound to demand, of a picture or poem what message it has for you, what may be its moral utility or material worth? 'Poetry must conform itself to' &c.; 'art must have a mission and meaning appreciable by earnest men in an age of work,' and so forth. These be thy gods, O Philistia.

of those days. Neither minstrel nor monk would have caught up the idea with any rapture. As indeed they would have been unwise to do; for the thing is impossible. Art is not like fire or water, a good servant and bad master; rather the reverse. She will help in nothing, of her own knowledge or freewill: upon terms of service you will get worse than nothing out of her. Handmaid of religion, exponent of duty, servant of fact, pioneer of morality, she cannot in any way become; she would be none of these things though you were to bray her in a mortar. All the battering in the world will never hammer her into fitness for such an office as that. It is at her peril, if she tries to do good: one might say, borrowing terms from the other party, 'she shall not try that under penalty of death and damnation.' Her business is not to do good on other grounds, but to be good on her own: all is well with her while she sticks fast to that. To ask help or furtherance from her in any extraneous good work is exactly as rational as to expect lyrical beauty of form and flow in a logical treatise. The contingent result of having good art about you and living in a time of noble writing or painting may no doubt be this; that the spirit and mind of men then living will receive on some points a certain exaltation and insight caught from the influence of such forms and colours of verse or painting; will become for one thing incapable of tolerating bad work, and capable therefore of reasonably relishing the best; which of course implies and draws with it many other advantages of a sort you may call moral or spiritual. But if the artist does his work with an eye to such results or for the sake of bringing about such improvements, he will too probably fail even of them. Art for art's sake first of all, and afterwards we may suppose all the rest shall be added to her° (or if not she need hardly be overmuch concerned); but from the man who falls to artistic work with a moral purpose, shall be taken away even that which he has°—whatever of capacity for doing well in either way he may have at starting. A living critic[3] of incomparably delicate insight and subtly good sense, himself 'impeccable' as an artist, calls this 'the heresy of instruction'

[3] I will not resist the temptation to write a brief word of comment on this passage.° While my words of inadequate and now of joyless praise were in course of printing, I heard that a mortal illness had indeed stricken the illustrious poet, the faultless critic, the fearless artist; that no more of fervent yet of perfect verse, no more of subtle yet of sensitive comment, will be granted us at the hands of Charles Baudelaire: that now for ever we must fall back upon what is left us. It is precious enough. We may see again as various a power as was his, may feel again as fiery a sympathy, may hear again as strange a murmur of revelation, as sad a whisper of knowledge, as mysterious a music of emotion; we shall never find so keen, so delicate, so deep an unison of sense and spirit. What verse he could make, how he loved all fair and felt all strange things, with what infallible taste he knew at once the limit and the licence of his art, all may see at a glance. He could give beauty to the form, expression to the feeling, most horrible and most obscure to the senses or souls of lesser men. The chances of things parted us once and again; the admiration of some years, at last in part expressed, brought me near him by way of written or transmitted word; let it be an excuse for the insertion of this note, and for a desire, if so it must be, to repeat for once the immortal words which too often return upon our lips[:]

'Ergo in perpetuum, frater, ave atque vale!'°

(*l'hérésie de l'enseignement*):° one might call it, for the sake of a shorter and more summary name, the great moral heresy. Nothing can be imagined more futile; nothing so ruinous. Once let art humble herself, plead excuses, try at any compromise with the Puritan principle of doing good, and she is worse than dead. Once let her turn apologetic, and promise or imply that she really will now be 'loyal to fact' and useful to men in general (say, by furthering their moral work or improving their moral nature), she is no longer of any human use or value. The one fact for her which is worth taking account of is simply mere excellence of verse or colour, which involves all manner of truth and loyalty necessary to her well-being. That is the important thing; to have her work supremely well done, and to disregard all contingent consequences. You may extract out of Titian's work or Shakespeare's any moral or immoral inference you please; it is none of their business to see after that. Good painting or writing, on any terms, is a thing quite sufficiently in accordance with fact and reality for them. Supplant art by all means if you can; root it out and try to plant in its place something useful or at least safe, which at all events will not impede the noble moral labour and trammel the noble moral life of Puritanism. But in the name of sense and fact itself let us have done with all abject and ludicrous pretence of coupling the two in harness or grafting the one on the other's stock: let us hear no more of the moral mission of earnest art; let us no longer be pestered with the frantic and flatulent assumptions of quasi-secular clericalism willing to think the best of all sides, and ready even, with consecrating hand, to lend meritorious art and poetry a timely pat or shove. Philistia had far better (always providing it be possible) crush art at once, hang or burn it out of the way, than think of plucking out its eyes and setting it to grind moral corn in the Philistine mills;° which it is certain not to do at all well. Once and again the time has been that there was no art worth speaking of afloat anywhere in the world; but there never has been or can have been a time when art, or any kind of art worth having, took active service under Puritanism, or indulged for its part in the deleterious appetite of saving souls or helping humanity in general along the way of labour and progress.[4] Let no artist or poet listen to the bland bark of those porter dogs of the Puritan kingdom even when they fawn and flirt with tongue or tail. *Cave canem.*° That Cerberus of the portals of Philistia will swallow your honey-cake° to no purpose; if he does not turn and rend you, his slaver as he licks your hand will leave it impotent and palsied for all good work.

[4] There are exceptions, we are told from the first, to all rules; and the sole exception to this one is great enough to do all but establish a rival rule. But, as I have tried already to say, the work—all the work—of Victor Hugo is in its essence artistic, in its accident alone philanthropic or moral.° I call this the sole exception, not being aware that the written work of Dante or Shelley did ever tend to alter the material face of things; though they may have desired that it should, and though their unwritten work may have done so. Accidentally of course a poet's work may tend towards some moral or actual result; that is beside the question.

Thus much it seemed useful to premise, by way of exposition rather than excursion, so as once for all to indicate beyond chance of mistake the real point of view taken during life by Blake, and necessary to be taken by those who would appreciate his labours and purposes. Error on this point would be ruinous to any student. No one again need be misled by the artist's eager incursions into grounds of faith or principle; his design being merely to readjust all questions of such a kind by the light of art and law of imagination—to reduce all outlying provinces, and bring them under government of his own central empire—the 'fourfold spiritual city' of his vision.° Power of imaginative work and insight—'the Poetic Genius, as you now call it'—was in his mind, we shall soon have to see, 'the first principle' of all things moral or material, 'and all the others merely derivative;'° a hazardous theory in its results and corollaries, but one which Blake at all events was always ready to push to its utmost consequences and defend at its extreme outworks. Against all pretensions on the part of science or experimental reasoning to assume this post he was especially given to rebel and recalcitrate. Whether or no he were actually prepared to fight science in earnest on its own pitched field—to dispute seriously the conquest of facts achieved by it—may be questionable; I for one am inclined to disbelieve this, and to refer much of his verbal pugnacity on such matters to the strong irregular humour, rough and loose as that of children, and the half simple half scornful love of paradox, which were ingrained in the man. For argument and proof he had the contempt of a child or an evangelist. Not that he would have fallen back in preference upon the brute resource of thaumaturgy; the coarse and cheap machinery of material miracle was wholly insufficient and despicable to him. No wonder-monger of the low sort need here have hoped for a pupil, a colleague, or an authority. This the biographer has acutely noted, and taken well into account; as we must all do under pain of waste time and dangerous error. Let this too be taken note of; that to believe a thing is not necessarily to heed or respect it; to despise a thing is not the same as to disbelieve it. Those who argue against the reality of the meaner forms of 'spiritualism' in disembodied life, on the ground apparently that whatever is not of the patent tangible flesh must be of high imperishable importance, are merely acting on the old ascetic assumption that the body is of its nature base and the soul of its nature noble, and that between the two there is a great gulf fixed, neither to be bridged over nor filled up. Blake, as a mystic of the higher and subtler kind, would have denied this superior separate vitality of the spirit; but far from inferring thence that the soul must expire with the body, would have maintained that the essence of the body must survive with the essence of the soul: accepting thus (as we may have to observe he did), in its most absolute and profound sense, the doctrine of the Resurrection of the Flesh. As a temporary blind and bar to the soul while dwelling on earth, fit only (if so permitted) to impede the spiritual vision and hamper the spiritual feet, he did indeed appear to contemn the 'vegetable' and sensual nature of man; but on no ascetic grounds.

Admitting once for all that it was no fit or just judge of things spiritual, he claimed for the body on its own ground an equal honour and an equal freedom with the soul; denying the river's channel leave to be called the river—refusing to the senses the license claimed for them by materialism to decide by means of bodily insight or sensation questions removed from the sphere of sensual evidence—and reserving always the absolute assurance and certain faith that things do exist of which the flesh can take no account, but only the spirit—he would grant to the physical nature the full right to every form of physical indulgence: would allow the largest liberty to all powers and capacities of pleasure proper to the pure bodily life. In a word, translated into crude practical language, his creed was about this: as long as a man believes all things he may do any thing; scepticism (not sin) is alone damnable, being the one thing purely barren and negative; do what you will with your body, as long as you refuse it leave to disprove or deny the life eternally inherent in your soul. That we believe is what people call or have called by some such name as 'antinomian mysticism:'° do anything but doubt, and you shall not in the end be utterly lost. Clearly enough it was Blake's faith; and one assuredly grounded not on mere contempt of the body, but on an equal reverence for spirit and flesh as the two sides or halves of a completed creature: a faith which will allow to neither license to confute or control the other. The body shall not deny, and the spirit shall not restrain; the one shall not prescribe doubt through reasoning; the other shall not preach salvation through abstinence. A man holding such tenets sees no necessity to deny that the indulged soul may be in some men as ignoble as the indulged body in others may be noble; and that a spirit ignoble while embodied need not become noble or noticeable by the process of getting disembodied; in other words, that death or change need not be expected to equalize the unequal by raising or lowering spirits to one settled level. Much of the existing evidence as to baser spiritual matters, Blake, like other men of candid sense and insight, would we may suppose have accepted—and dropped with the due contempt into the mass of facts worth forgetting only, which the experience of every man must carry till his memory succeeds in letting go its hold of them. Nothing, he would doubtless have said, is worth disputing in disproof of, which if proved would not be worth giving thanks for. Let such things be or not be as the fates of small things please; but will any one prove or disprove for me the things I hold by warrant of imaginative knowledge? things impossible to discover, to analyze, to attest, to undervalue, to certify, or to doubt?

This old war—not (as some would foolishly have it defined) a war between facts and fancies, reason and romance, poetry and good sense, but simply between the imagination which apprehends the spirit of a thing and the understanding which dissects the body of a fact—this strife which can never be decided or ended—was for Blake the most important question possible. He for one, madman or no madman, had the sense to see that the one thing utterly futile to attempt was a reconciliation between two sides of life and thought which have no community of work or aim imaginable. This is no question of reconciling contraries.° Admit all the implied pretensions of art, they remain simply nothing to science; accept all the actual deductions of science, they simply signify nothing to art. The eternal 'Après?'° is answer enough for both in turn. 'True, then, if you will have it; but what have we to do with your good or bad poetries and paintings?' 'Undeniably; but what are we to gain by your deductions and discoveries, right or wrong?' The betrothal of art and science were a thing harder to bring about and more profitless to proclaim than 'the marriage of heaven and hell.' It were better not to fight, but to part in peace; but better certainly to fight than to temporize, where no reasonable truce can be patched up. Poetry or art based on loyalty to science is exactly as absurd (and no more) as science guided by art or poetry. Neither in effect can coalesce with the other and retain a right to exist. Neither can or (while in its sober senses) need wish to destroy the other; but they must go on their separate ways, and in this life their ways can by no possibility cross. Neither can or (unless in some fit of fugitive insanity) need wish to become valuable or respectable to the other: each must remain, on its own ground and to its own followers, a thing of value and deserving respect. To art, that is best which is most beautiful; to science, that is best which is most accurate; to morality, that is best which is most virtuous. Change or quibble upon the simple and generally accepted significance of these three words, 'beautiful,' 'accurate,' 'virtuous,' and you may easily (if you please, or think it worth while) demonstrate that the aim of all three is radically one and the same; but if any man be correct in thinking this exercise of the mind worth the expenditure of his time, that time must indeed be worth very little. You can say (but had perhaps better not say) that beauty is the truthfullest, accuracy the most poetic, and virtue the most beautiful of things; but a man of ordinary or decent insight will perceive that you have merely reduced an affair of things to an affair of words—shifted the body of one thing into the clothes of another—and proved actually nothing.

To attest by word or work the identity of things which never can become identical, was no part of Blake's object in life. What work it fell to his lot to do, that, having faith in the fates, he believed the best work possible, and performed to admiration. It is in consequence of this belief that, apart from all conjectural or problematic theory, the work he did is absolutely good. Intolerant he was by nature to a degree noticeable even among freethinkers and prophets; but the strange forms assumed by this intolerance are best explicable by the singular facts of his training—his perfect ignorance of well-known ordinary things and imperfect quaint knowledge of much that lay well out of the usual way. He retained always an excellent arrogance and a wholly laudable self-reliance; being incapable of weak-eyed doubts or any shuffling modesty. His great tenderness had a lining of contempt—his fiery self-assertion a kernel of loyalty. No one, it is evident, had ever a more intense and noble enjoyment of good or great works in other men—took sharper or deeper delight in the sense of a loyal admiration: being of his nature noble, fearless, and fond of all things good; a man made for believing. This royal temper of mind goes properly with a keen relish of what excellence or greatness a man may have in himself. Those must be readiest to feel and to express unalloyed and lofty pleasure in the great powers and deeds of a neighbour, who, while standing clear alike of reptile modesty and pretentious presumption, perceive and know in themselves such qualities as give them a right to admire and a right to applaud. If a man thinks meanly of himself, he can hardly in reason think much of his judgment; if he depreciates the value of his own work, he depreciates also the value of his praise. Those are loyallest who have most of a just self-esteem; and their applause is best worth having. It is scarcely conceivable that a man should take delight in the real greatness or merit of his own work for so pitiful and barren a reason as merely that it is his own; should be unable to pass with a fresh and equal enjoyment from the study and relish of his own capacities and achievements to the study and relish of another man's. A timid jealousy, easily startled into shrieks of hysterical malice and disloyal spite, is (wherever you may fall in with it) the property of base men and mean artists who, at sight of some person or thing greater than themselves, are struck sharply by unconscious self-contempt, and at once, whether they know it or not, lose heart or faith in their own applauded work. To recognize their equal, even their better when he does come, must be the greatest delight of great men. 'All the gods,' says a French essayist,° 'delight in worship: is one lesser for the other's godhead? Divine things give divine thanks for companionship; the stars sang not one at once, but all together.' Like all men great enough to enjoy greatness, Blake was born with the gift of admiration; and in his rapid and fervent nature it struck root and broke into flower at the least glimpse or chance of favourable weather. Therefore, if on no other ground, we may allow him his curious outbreaks of passionate dispraise and scorn against all such as seemed to stand in the way of his art. Again, as we have noted, he had a faith of his own, made out of art for art's sake, and worked by means of art; and whatever made against this faith was as hateful to him as any heresy to any pietist. In a rough and rapid way he chose to mass and sum up under some one or two types, comprehensible at first sight to few besides himself, the main elements of opposition which he conceived to exist. Thus for instance the names of Locke and Newton, of Bacon and Voltaire, recur with the most singular significance in his writings, as emblems or incarnate symbols of the principles opposite to his own: and when the clue is once laid hold of, and the ear once accustomed to the curious habit of direct mythical metaphor or figure peculiar to Blake—his custom of getting whole classes of men or opinions embodied, for purposes of swift irregular attack, in some one representative individual—much is at once clear and amenable to critical reason which seemed before mere tempestuous incoherence and clamour of bodiless rhetoric. There is also a certain half-serious perversity and wilful personal humour in the choice and use of these representative names, which must be taken into account by a startled reader unless he wishes to run off at a false tangent. After all, it is perhaps impossible for any one not specially qualified by nature for sympathy with such a man's kind of work, to escape going wrong in his estimate of Blake; to such excesses of paradox did the poet-painter push his favourite points, and in such singular attire did he bring forward his most serious opinions. But at least the principal and most evident chances of error may as well be indicated, by way of warning off the over-hasty critic from shoals on which otherwise he is all but certain to run.

It is a thing especially worth regretting that Balzac, in his Swedenborgian researches,° could not have fallen in with Blake's 'prophetic' works. Passed through the crucible of that supreme intellect—submitted to the test of that supple practical sense, that laborious apprehension, so delicate and so passionate at once, of all forms of thought or energy, which were the great latent gifts of the deepest and widest mind that ever worked within the limits of inventive prose—the strange floating forces of Blake's instinctive and imaginative work might have been explained and made applicable to direct ends in a way we cannot now hope for. The incomparable power of condensing apparent vapour into tangible and malleable form, of helping us to handle air and measure mist, which is so instantly perceptible whenever Balzac begins to open up any intricate point of physical or moral speculation, would here have been beyond price. He alone who could push analysis to the verge of creation, and with his marvellous clearness of eye and strength of hand turn discovery almost to invention; he who was not 'a prose Shakespeare'° merely, but rather perhaps a Shakespeare complete in all but the lyrical faculty; he alone could have brought a scale to weigh this water, a sieve to winnow this wind. That wonderful wisdom, never at fault on its own ground, which made him not simply the chief of dramatic story, but also the great master of morals,[5] would not

[5] The reader who cares to remember that everything here set down is of immediate importance and necessity for the understanding of the matter in hand (namely, the life of Blake, and the faith and works which made that life what it was) may as well take here a word of comment. It will soon be necessary for even the very hack-writers and ingenious people of ready pens and wits who now babble about Balzac in English and French as a splendid specimen of their craft, fertile but faulty, and so forth—to understand that they have nothing to do with Balzac; that he is not of their craft, nor of any but the common craft of all great men—the guild of godlike things and people; that a shelf holding 'all Balzac's novels—forty volumes long,' is not 'cabin-furniture' for any chance 'passenger' to select or reject.° Error and deficiency there may be in his work; but none such as they can be aware of. Of poetic form, for example, we know that he knew nothing; the error would be theirs who should think his kind of work the worse for that. Among men equally great, the distinctive supremacy of Balzac is this; that whereas the great men who are pure artists (Shakespeare for instance) work by implication only, and hardly care about descending to the level of a preacher's or interpreter's work, he is the only man not of their kind who is great enough to supply their place in his own way—to be their correlative in a different class

have failed of foothold or eyesight even in this cloudy and noisy borderland of vision and of faith. Even to him too, the supreme student and interpreter of things, our impulsive prophet with his plea of mere direct inspiration might have been of infinite help and use: to such an eye and brain as his, Blake might have made straight the ways which Swedenborg had left crooked,° set right the problems which mesmerism had set wrong. As however we cannot have this, we must do what share of interpreter's work falls to our lot as well as we can.

There are two points in the work of Blake which first claim notice and explanation; two points connected, but not inseparable; his mysticism and his mythology. This latter is in fact hardly more in its relation to the former, than the clothes to the body or the body to the soul. To make either comprehensible, it is requisite above all things to get sight of the man in whom they became incarnate and active as forces or as opinions. Now, to those who regard mysticism with distaste or contempt, as essentially in itself a vain or noxious thing—a sealed bag or bladder that can only be full either of wind or of poison—the man, being above all and beyond all a mystic in the most subtle yet most literal sense, must remain obscure and contemptible. Such readers—if indeed such men should choose or care to become readers at all—will be (for one thing) unable to understand that one may think it worth while to follow out and track to its root the peculiar faith or fancy of a mystic without being ready to accept his deductions and his assertions as absolute and durable facts. Servility of extended hand or passive brain is the last quality that a mystic of the nobler kind will demand or desire in his auditors. Councils and synods may put forth notes issued under their stamp, may exact of all recipients to play the part of clerks and indorse their paper with shut eyes: to the mystic such a way of doing spiritual business would seem the very frenzy of fatuity; whatever else may be profitable, that (he would say) is suicidal. And assuredly it is not to be expected that Blake's mystical creed, when once made legible and even partially coherent, should prove likely to win over proselytes. Nor can this be the wish or the object of a reasonable commentator, whose desire is merely to do art a good turn in some small way, by explaining the 'faith and

of workmen; being from his personal point of view simply impeccable and infallible. The pure artist never asserts;° he suggests, and therefore his meaning is totally lost upon moralists and sciolists—is indeed irreparably wasted upon the run of men who cannot work out suggestions. Balzac asserts; and Balzac cannot blunder or lie. So profound and extensive a capacity of moral apprehension no other prose writer, no man of mere analytic faculty, ever had or can have. This assuredly, when men become (as they will have to become) capable of looking beyond the mere clothes and skin of his work, will be always, as we said, his great especial praise; that he was, beyond any other man, the master of morals—the greatest direct expounder of actual moral fact. Once consent to forget or overlook the mere entourage and social habiliment of Balzac's intense and illimitable intellect, you cannot fail of seeing that he of all men was fittest to grapple with all strange things and words, and compel them by divine violence of spiritual rape to bring forth flowers and fruits good for food and available for use.

works' of a great artist. It is true that whatever a good poet or a good painter has thought worth representing by verse or design must probably be worth considering before one deliver judgment on it. But the office of an apostle of some new faith and the business of a commentator on some new evangel are two sufficiently diverse things. The present critic has not (happily) to preach the gospel as delivered by Blake; he has merely, if possible, to make the text of that gospel a little more readable. And this must be worth doing, if it be worth while to touch on Blake's work at all. What is true of all poets and artists worth judging is especially true of him; that critics who attempt to judge him piecemeal do not in effect judge him at all, but some one quite different from him, and some one (to any serious student) probably more inexplicable than the real man. For what are we to make of a man whose work deserves crowning one day and hooting the next? If the *Songs* be so good, are not those who praise them bound to examine and try what merit may be latent in the *Prophecies*?—bound at least to explain as best they may how the one comes to be worth so much and the other worth nothing? On this side alone the biography appears to us emphatically deficient; here only do we feel how much was lost, how much impaired by the untimely death of the writer.° Those who had to complete his work have done their part admirably well; but here they have not done enough. We are not bound to accept Blake's mysticism; we are bound to take some account of it. A disciple must take his master's word for proof of the thing preached. This it would be folly to expect of a biographer; even Boswell falls short of this, having courage on some points to branch off from the strait pathway of his teacher and strike into a small speculative track of his own. But a biographer must be capable of expounding the evangel (or, if such a word could be, 'dysangel') of his hero, however far he may be from thinking it worth acceptance. And this, one must admit, the writers on Blake have upon the whole failed of doing. Consequently their critical remarks on such specimens of Blake's more speculative and subtle work as did find favour in their sight have but a narrow range and a limited value. Some clue to the main character of the artist's habit of mind we may hope already to have put into the reader's hands—some frayed and ravelled 'end of the golden string,' which with due labour he may 'wind up into a ball.'° To pluck out the heart of Blake's mystery is a task which every man must be left to attempt for himself: for this prophet is certainly not 'easier to be played on than a pipe.'° Keeping fast in hand what clue we have, we may nevertheless succeed in making some further way among the clouds. One thing is too certain; if we insist on having hard ground under foot all the way we shall not get far. The land lying before us, bright with fiery blossom and fruit, musical with blowing branches and falling waters, is not to be seen or travelled in save by help of such light as lies upon dissolving dreams and dividing clouds. By moonrise, to the sound of wind at sunset, one may tread upon the limit of this land and gather as with muffled apprehension some soft remote sense of the singing of its birds and flowering of its fields.

This premised, we may start with a clear conscience. Of Blake's faith we have by this time endeavoured to give the reader some conception—if a faint one, yet at least not a false: of the form assumed by that faith (what we have called the mythology) we need not yet take cognizance. To follow out in full all his artistic and illustrative work, with a view to extract from each separate fruit of it some core of significance, would be an endless labour: and we are bound to consider what may be feasible rather than what, if it were feasible, might be worth doing. Therefore the purpose of this essay is in the main to deal with the artist's personal work in preference to what is merely illustrative and decorative. Designs, however admirable, made to order for the text of Blair, of Hayley, or of Young,° are in comparison with the designer's original and spontaneous work mere extraneous by-play. These also are if anything better known than Blake's other labours. Again, the mass of his surviving designs is so enormous and as yet (except for the inestimable Catalogue in Vol. 2 of the *Life*) so utterly chaotic and unarrangeable that in such an element one can but work as it were by fits and plunges. Of these designs there must always be many which not having seen we cannot judge; many too on which artists alone are finally competent to deliver sentence by authority. Moreover the supreme merits as well as the more noticeable qualities merely special and personal of Blake are best seen in his mixed work. Where both text and design are wholly his own, and the two forms or sides of his art so coalesce or overlap as to become inextricably interfused, we have the best chance of seeing and judging what the workman essentially was. In such an enterprise, we must be always duly grateful for any help or chance of help given us: and for one invaluable thing we have at starting to give due honour and thanks to the biographer. He has, one may rationally hope, finally beaten to powder the rickety and flaccid old theory of Blake's madness. Any one wishing to moot that question again will have to answer or otherwise get over the facts and inferences so excellently set out in Chap. xxxv:° to refute them we may fairly consider impossible. Here at least no funeral notice or obsequies will be bestowed on the unburied carcase of that forlorn fiction. Assuming as a reasonable ground for our present labour that Blake was superior to the run of men, we shall spend no minute of time in trying to prove that he was not inferior. Logic and sense alike warn us off such barren ground.

Of the editing of the present selections—a matter evidently of most delicate and infinite labour—we have here to say this only; that as far as one can see it could not have been done better: and indeed that it could only have been done so well by the rarest of happy chances. Even with the already published poems there was enough work to get through; for even these had suffered much from the curiously reckless and helpless neglect of form which was natural to Blake when his main work was done and his interest in the matter prematurely wound up. Those only who have dived after the original copies can fully appreciate or apprehend with what tenderness of justice and subtlety of sense these tumbled folds have been gathered up and these ragged edges smoothed off. As much power and labour has gone to the perfect adjustment of these relics of another man's work as a meaner man could have dreamed only of expending on his own. Nor can any one thoroughly enter into the value and excellence of the thing here achieved who has not in himself the impulsive instinct of form—the exquisite desire of just and perfect work. Alike to those who seem to be above it as to those who are evidently below, such work must remain always inappreciable and inexplicable. To the ingeniously chaotic intellect, with its admirable aptitude for all such feats of conjectural cleverness as are worked out merely by strain and spasm, it will seem an offensive waste of good work. But to all who relish work for work's sake and art for art's it will appear, as it is, simply invaluable—the one thing worth having yet not to be had at any price or by any means, except when it falls in your way by divine accident. True however as all this is of the earlier and easier part of the editor's task, it is incomparably more true of the arrangement and selection of poems fit for publishing out of the priceless but shapeless chaos of unmanageable MSS. The good work here done and good help here given it is not possible to over-estimate.° Every light slight touch of mere arrangement has the mark of a great art consummate in great things—the imprint of a sure and strong hand, in which the thing to be done lies safe and gathers faultless form. These great things too are so small in mere size and separate place that they can never get praised in due detail. They are great by dint of the achievement implied and the forbearance involved. Only a chief among lyric poets could so have praised the songs of Blake; only a leader among imaginative painters could so have judged his designs; only an artist himself supreme at once in lordship of colour and mastery of metre could so have spoken of Blake's gifts and feats in metre and colour. Reading these notes, one can rest with sufficient pleasure on the conviction that, wherever else there may be failure in attaining the right word of judgment or of praise, here certainly there is none. Here there is more than (what all critics may have) goodwill and desire to give just thanks; for here there is authority, and the right to seem right in delivering sentence.

But these notes, good as they are and altogether valuable, are the least part of the main work. To the beauty and nobility of style, the exquisite strength of sifted English, the keen vision and deep clearness of expression, which characterize as well these brief prefaces as the notes on *Job* and that critical summary in the final chapter of the *Life*, one need hardly desire men's attention; that splendid power of just language and gift of grace in detail stand out at once distinguishable from the surrounding work, praiseworthy as that also in the main is; neither from the matter nor the manner can any careful critic mistake the exact moment and spot where the editor of the poems has taken up any part of the business, laid any finger on the mechanism of the book. But this work, easier to praise, must have been also easier to perform than the more immediate editorial labours which were here found requisite. With care inappreciable and invaluable fidelity has the editing throughout been done. The selection must of necessity have been to a certain degree straitened and limited by many minor and temporary considerations; publishers, tasters, and such-like, must have fingered the work here and there, snuffing at this and nibbling at that as their manner is. For the work and workman have yet their way to make in the judicious reading world; and so long as they have, they are more or less in the lax limp clutch of that 'dieu ganache des bourgeois'° who sits nodding and ponderously dormant in the dust of publishing offices, ready at any jog of the elbow to snarl and start—a new Pan, feeding on the pastures of a fat and foggy land his Arcadian herds of review or magazine:

> ἔστι δὲ πικρός,
> καί οἱ ἀεὶ δριμεῖα χολὰ ποτὶ ῥινὶ κάθηται.°

Arcadian virtue and Bœotian brain, under the presidency of such a stertorous and splenetic goat-god, given to be sleepy in broadest noonday, are not the best crucibles for art to be tried in. Then, again, thought had to be taken for the poems themselves; not merely how to expose them in most acceptable form for public acceptance, but how at the same time to give them in the main all possible fullness of fair play. This too by dint of work and patience, still more by dint of pliable sense and taste, has been duly accomplished. Future editions may be, and in effect will have to be, altered and enlarged: it is as well for people to be aware that they have not yet a final edition of Blake; that will have to be some day completed on a due scale. But for the great mass of his lyrical verse all there was to do has been done here, and the ground-plan taken of a larger building to come. These preliminaries stated, we pass on to a rapid general review of those two great divisions which may be taken as resuming for us the ripe poetry of Blake's manhood. Two divisions, the one already published and partially known, the other now first brought into light and baptized with some legible name; the *Songs of Innocence and Experience*, and the *Ideas of Good and Evil.*° Under this latter head we will class for purposes of readier reference as well the smaller MS. volume of fairly transcribed verses as the great mass of more disorderly writing in verse and prose to which the name above given is attached in a dim broad scrawl of the pencil evidently meant to serve as general title, though set down only on the reverse page of the second MS. leaf. This latter and larger book, extending in date at least from 1789 to (August) 1811, but presumably beyond the later date, is the great source and treasure-house from which has been drawn out most of the fresh verse and all of the fresh prose here given us: and is of course among the most important relics left of Blake.

First then for the *Songs of Innocence and Experience*. These at a first naming recall only that incomparable charm of form in which they first came out clothed, and hence vex the souls of men with regretful comparison. For here by hard necessity we miss the lovely and luminous setting of designs, which makes the *Songs* precious and pleasurable to those who know or care for little else of the master's doing; the infinite delight of those drawings, sweeter to see than music to hear, where herb and stem break into grace of shape and blossom of form, and the branch-work is full of little flames and flowers, catching as it were from the verse enclosed the fragrant heat and delicate sound they seem to give back; where colour lapses into light and light assumes feature in colour. If elsewhere the artist's strange strength of thought and hand is more visible, nowhere is there such pure sweetness and singleness of design in his work. All the tremulous and tender splendour of spring is mixed into the written word and coloured draught; every page has the smell of April. Over all things given, the sleep of flocks and the growth of leaves, the laughter in dividing lips of flowers and the music at the moulded mouth of the flute-player, there is cast a pure fine veil of light, softer than sleep and keener than sunshine. The sweetness of sky and leaf, of grass and water—the bright light life of bird and child and beast—is so to speak kept fresh by some graver sense of faithful and mysterious love, explained and vivified by a conscience and purpose in the artist's hand and mind. Such a fiery outbreak of spring, such an insurrection of fierce floral life and radiant riot of childish power and pleasure, no poet or painter ever gave before: such lustre of green leaves and flushed limbs, kindled cloud and fervent fleece, was never wrought into speech or shape. Nevertheless this decorative work is after all the mere husk and shell of the *Songs*. These also, we may notice, have to some extent shared the comparative popularity of the designs which serve as framework to them. They have absolutely achieved the dignity of a reprint;° have had a chance before now of swimming for life; whereas most of Blake's offspring have been thrown into Lethe bound hand and foot, without hope of ever striking out in one fair effort. Perhaps on some accounts this preference has been not unreasonable. What was written for children can hardly offend men; and the obscurities and audacities of the prophet would here have been clearly out of place. It is indeed some relief to a neophyte serving in the outer courts of such an intricate and cloudy temple, to come upon this little side-chapel set about with the simplest wreaths and smelling of the fields rather than incense, where all the singing is done by clear children's voices to the briefest and least complex tunes. Not at first without a sense of release does the human mind get quit for a little of the clouds of Urizen, the fires of Orc, and all the Titanic apparatus of prophecy. And these poems are really unequalled in their kind. Such verse was never written for children since verse-writing began. Only in a few of those faultless fragments of childish rhyme which float without name or form upon the memories of men shall we find such a pure clear cadence of verse, such rapid ring and flow of lyric laughter, such sweet and direct choice of the just word and figure, such an impeccable simplicity; nowhere but here such a tender wisdom of holiness, such a light and perfume of innocence.

Nothing like this was ever written on that text of the lion and the lamb;° no such heaven of sinless animal life was ever conceived so intensely and sweetly.

> 'And there the lion's ruddy eyes
> Shall flow with tears of gold,
> And pitying the tender cries,
> And walking round the fold,
> Saying *Wrath by His meekness*
> *And by His health sickness*
> *Is driven away*
> *From our immortal day.*
> And now beside thee, bleating lamb,
> *I can lie down and sleep*,
> Or think on Him who bore thy name,
> *Graze after thee, and weep*.'°

The leap and fall of the verse is so perfect as to make it a fit garment and covering for the profound tenderness of faith and soft strength of innocent impulse embodied in it. But the whole of this hymn of *Night* is wholly beautiful; being perhaps one of the two poems of loftiest loveliness among all the *Songs of Innocence*. The other is that called *The Little Black Boy*; a poem especially exquisite for its noble forbearance from vulgar pathos and achievement of the highest and most poignant sweetness of speech and sense; in which the poet's mysticism is baptized with pure water and taught to speak as from faultless lips of children, to such effect as this.

> 'And we are put on earth a little space
> *That we may learn to bear the beams of love*;
> And these black bodies and this sunburnt face
> Are like a cloud and like a shady grove.'°

Other poems of a very perfect beauty are those of the Piper, the Lamb, the Chimney-sweeper, and the two-days-old baby; all, for the music in them, more like the notes of birds caught up and given back than the modulated measure of human verse. One cannot say, being so slight and seemingly wrong in metrical form, how they come to be so absolutely right; but right even in point of verses and words they assuredly are. Add fuller formal completion of rhyme and rhythm to that song of Infant Joy, and you have broken up the soft bird-like perfection of clear light sound which gives it beauty; the little bodily melody of soulless and painless laughter.

Against all articulate authority we do however class several of the *Songs of Experience* higher for the great qualities of verse than anything in the earlier division of these poems. If the *Songs of Innocence* have the shape and smell of leaves or buds, these have in them the light and sound of fire or the sea. Entering among them, a fresher savour and a larger breath strikes one upon the lips and forehead. In the first part we are shown who they are who have or who deserve the gift of spiritual sight: in the second, what things there are for them to see when that gift has been given. Innocence, the quality of beasts and children, has the keenest eyes; and such eyes alone can discern and interpret the actual mysteries of experience. It is natural that this second part, dealing as it does with such things as underlie the outer forms of the first part, should rise higher and dive deeper in point of mere words. These give the distilled perfume and extracted blood of the veins in the rose-leaf, the sharp, liquid, intense spirit crushed out of the broken kernel in the fruit. The last of the *Songs of Innocence*° is a prelude to these poems; in it the poet summons to judgment the young and single-spirited, that by right of the natural impulse of delight in them they may give sentence against the preachers of convention and assumption; and in the first poem of the second series° he, by the same 'voice of the bard,' calls upon earth herself, the mother of all these, to arise and become free: since upon her limbs also are bound the fetters, and upon her forehead also has fallen the shadow, of a jealous law: from which nevertheless, by faithful following of instinct and divine liberal impulse, earth and man shall obtain deliverance.

'Hear the voice of the bard!
Who present, past, and future sees:
Whose ears have heard
The ancient Word
That walked among the silent trees:
Calling the lapsèd soul
And weeping in the evening dew;
That might control
The starry pole
And fallen fallen light renew!'°

If they will hear the Word, earth and the dwellers upon earth shall be made again as little children;° shall regain the strong simplicity of eye and hand proper to the pure and single of heart; and for them inspiration shall do the work of innocence; let them but once abjure the doctrine by which comes sin and the law by which comes prohibition. Therefore must the appeal be made; that the blind may see and the deaf hear,° and the unity of body and spirit be made manifest in perfect freedom: and that to the innocent even the liberty of 'sin' may be conceded. For if the soul suffer by the body's doing, are not both degraded? and if the body be oppressed for the soul's sake, are not both the losers?

'O Earth, O Earth, return!
Arise from out the dewy grass!
Night is worn,
And the morn

Rises from the slumberous mass.
Turn away no more;
Why wilt thou turn away?
The starry shore,
The watery floor,
Are given thee till the break of day.'°

For so long, during the night of law and oppression of material form, the divine evidences hidden under sky and sea are left her; even 'till the break of day.' Will she not get quit of this spiritual bondage to the heavy body of things, to the encumbrance of deaf clay and blind vegetation, before the light comes that shall redeem and reveal? But the earth, being yet in subjection to the creator of men, the jealous God who divided nature against herself—father of woman and man, legislator of sex and race—makes blind and bitter answer as in sleep, 'her locks covered with grey despair.'

'Prisoned on this watery shore,
Starry Jealousy does keep my den;
Cold and hoar,
Weeping o'er,
I hear the father of the ancient men.'°

Thus, in the poet's mind, Nature and Religion are the two fetters of life, one on the right wrist, the other on the left; an obscure material force on this hand, and on that a mournful imperious law: the law of divine jealousy, the government of a God who weeps over his creature and subject with unprofitable tears, and rules by forbidding and dividing: the 'Urizen' of the prophetic books, clothed with the coldness and the grief of remote sky and jealous cloud. Here as always, the cry is as much for light as for license, the appeal not more against prohibition than against obscurity.

'Can the sower sow by night,
Or the ploughman in darkness plough?'°

In the *Songs of Innocence* there is no such glory of metre or sonorous beauty of lyrical work as here. No possible effect of verse can be finer in a great brief way than that given in the second and last stanzas of the first part of this poem. It recals within one's ear the long relapse of recoiling water and wash of the refluent wave;° in the third and fourth lines sinking suppressed as with equal pulses and soft sobbing noise of ebb, to climb again in the fifth line with a rapid clamour of ripples and strong ensuing strain of weightier sound, lifted with the lift of the running and ringing sea.

Here also is that most famous of Blake's lyrics, *The Tiger*; a poem beyond praise for its fervent beauty and vigour of music. It appears by the MS. that this was written with some pains;° the cancels and various readings bear marks of frequent rehandling. One of the latter is worth transcription for its own excellence and also in proof of the artist's real care for details, which his rapid instinctive way of work has induced some to disbelieve in.

'Burnt in distant deeps or skies
The cruel fire of thine eyes?
Could heart descend or wings aspire?[6]
What the hand dare seize the fire?'°

Nor has Blake left us anything of more profound and perfect value than *The Human Abstract*; a little mythical vision of the growth of error; through soft sophistries of pity and faith, subtle humility of abstinence and fear, under which the pure simple nature lies corrupted and strangled; through selfish loves which prepare a way for cruelty, and cruelty that works by spiritual abasement and awe.

'Soon spreads the dismal shade
Of Mystery over his head;
And the caterpillar and fly
Feed on the Mystery.

[6] Could God bring down his heart to the making of a thing so deadly and strong? or could any lesser dæmonic force of nature take to itself wings and fly high enough to assume power equal to such a creation? Could spiritual force so far descend or material force so far aspire? Or, when the very stars, and all the armed children of heaven, the 'helmed cherubim' that guide and the 'sworded seraphim' that guard their several planets, wept for pity and fear at sight of this new force of monstrous matter seen in the deepest night as a fire of menace to man—

'Did he smile his work to see?
Did he who made the lamb make thee?'°

We may add another cancelled reading to show how delicately the poem has been perfected; although by an oversight of the writer's most copies hitherto have retained some trace of the rough first draught, neglecting in one line a change necessary to save the sense as well as to complete the sentence.

'And when thy heart began to beat,
What dread hand and what dread feet

Could fetch it from the furnace deep
And in thy horrid ribs dare steep?
In what clay and in what mould
Were thine eyes of fury rolled?'

Having cancelled this stanza or sketched ghost of a stanza, Blake in his hurry of rejection did not at once remember to alter the last line of the preceding one; leaving thus a stone of some size and slipperiness for editorial feet to trip upon, until the recovery of that nobler reading—

'What dread hand *framed thy* dread feet?'

Nor was this little 'rock of offence'° cleared from the channel of the poem even by the editor of 1827, who was yet not afraid of laying hand upon the text. So grave a flaw in so short and so great a lyric was well worth the pains of removing and is yet worth the pains of accounting for; on which ground this note must be of value to all who take in verse with eye and ear instead of touching it merely with eyelash and finger-tip in the manner of sand-blind students.

And it bears the fruit of Deceit,
Ruddy and sweet to eat;
And the raven his nest has made
In the thickest shade.'°

Under the shadow of this tree of mystery,[7] rooted in artificial belief, all the meaner kind of devouring things take shelter and eat of the fruit of its branches; the sweet poison of false faith, painted on its outer husk with the likeness of all things noble and desirable; and in the deepest implication of barren branch and deadly leaf, the bird of death, with priests for worshippers ('the priests of the raven of dawn,'° loud of lip and hoarse of throat until the light of day have risen), finds house and resting-place. Only in the 'mis-creative brain'° of fallen men can such a thing strike its tortuous root and bring forth its fatal flower; nowhere else in all nature can the tyrants of divided matter and moral law, 'Gods of the earth and sea,'° find soil that will bear such fruit.

Nowhere has Blake set forth his spiritual creed more clearly and earnestly than in the last of the *Songs of Experience*. 'Tirzah,' in his mythology, represents the mere separate and human nature, mother of the perishing body and daughter of the 'religion' which occupies itself with laying down laws for the flesh; which, while pretending (and that in all good faith) to despise the body and bring it into subjection as with control of bit and bridle, does implicitly overrate its power upon the soul for evil or good, and thus falls foul of fact on all sides by assuming that spirit and flesh are twain, and that things pleasant and good for the one can properly be loathsome or poisonous to the other. This 'religion' or 'moral law,' the inexplicable prophet has chosen to baptize under the singular type of 'Rahab'—the 'harlot virgin-mother,' impure by dint of chastity and forbearance from such things as are pure to the pure of heart: for in this creed the one thing unclean is the belief in uncleanness, the one thing forbidden is to believe in the existence of forbidden things. Of this mystical mother and her daughter we shall have to take some further account when once fairly afloat on those windy waters of prophecy° through which all who would know Blake to any purpose must be content to steer with such pilotage as they can get. For the present it will be enough to note how eager and how direct is the appeal here made against any rule or reasoning based on reference to the mere sexual and external nature of man—the nature made for ephemeral life and speedy death, kept alive 'to work and weep' only through that mercy which 'changed death into sleep';° how intense the reliance on

[7] Compare the passage in *Ahania* where the growth of it is defined; rooted in the rock of separation, watered with the tears of a jealous God, shot up from sparks and fallen germs of material seed; being after all a growth of mere error, and vegetable (not spiritual) life; the topmost stem of it made into a cross whereon to nail the dead redeemer and friend of men.

redemption from such a law by the grace of imaginative insight and spiritual freedom, typified in 'the death of Jesus.'[8] Nor are any of these poems finer in structure or nobler in metrical form. [...]

[8] Compare again in the *Vision of the Last Judgment* (v.2, p.163), that definition of the 'Divine body of the Saviour, the true Vine of Eternity,' as 'the Human Imagination, who appeared to me as coming to judgment among his saints, and throwing off the Temporal that the Eternal might be established.' The whole of that subtle and eloquent rhapsody is about the best commentary attainable on Blake's mystical writings and designs. It is impossible to overstate the debt of gratitude due from all students of Blake to the transcriber and editor° of the *Vision*, whose indefatigable sense and patient taste have made it legible for all. To have extracted it piecemeal from the chaos of notes jotted down by Blake in the most inconceivable way, would have been a praiseworthy labour enough; but without addition or omission to have constructed these abortive fragments into a whole so available and so admirable, is a labour beyond praise.

# FROM 'NOTES ON DESIGNS OF THE OLD MASTERS AT FLORENCE' (1868)

In the spring of 1864 I had the chance of spending many days in the Uffizj° on the study of its several collections. Statues and pictures I found ranged and classed, as all the world knows they are, with full care and excellent sense; but one precious division of the treasury was then, and I believe is still, unregistered in catalogue or manual. The huge mass of original designs, in pencil or ink or chalk, swept together by Vasari and others, had then been but recently unearthed and partially assorted. Under former Tuscan governments this sacred deposit had lain unseen and unclassed in the lower chambers of the palace, heaped and huddled in portfolios by the loose stackful. A change of rule° had put the matter at length into the hands of official men gifted with something more of human reason and eyesight. Three rooms were filled with the select flower of the collection acquired and neglected by past Florentine governors. Each design is framed, glazed, labelled legibly outside with the designer's name: the arrangement is not too far from perfect for convenience of study. As there can be no collection of the kind more rich, more various, more singular in interest, I supplied for myself the want of a register by taking hasty memorial notes of all the important designs as they fell in my way. They are not ranged in any order of time, nor are all a painter's drawings kept together; some have samples scattered about various corners of different rooms, but all accessible and available. Space even there is bounded, and valued accordingly. In the under chambers there still remain piles of precious things but partially set in order. To these the public visitor has not access; but through the courtesy of their guardian I was offered admission and shown by him through the better part. There are many studies of the figure by Andrea del Sarto° which deserve and demand a public place; others also of interest which belong to the earlier Florentine school; many nameless but some recognisable by a student of that time of art. In such studies as these the collection is naturally richest; though, as will at once be seen, not poor in samples of Milanese or Venetian work. The fruitful vigour, the joyous and copious effusion of spirit and labour, which makes all early times of awakening art dear to all students and profitable to all, has left noble fragments and relics behind, the golden gleanings of a full harvest. In these desultory notes I desire only to guide the attention to what seems worthiest of notice, without more form of order than has been given by the framers and hangers; taking men and schools as they come to hand, giving precedence and prominence only to the more precious and significant. For guide I have but my own sense of interest and admiration; so that, while making the list of things remarkable as complete and careful as I can, I have aimed at nothing further than to cast into some legible form my impression of the designs registered in so rough and rapid a fashion; and shall begin my transcript with notices of such as first caught and longest fixed my attention.

Of Leonardo° the samples are choice and few; full of that indefinable grace and grave mystery which belong to his slightest and wildest work. Fair strange faces of women full of dim doubt and faint scorn; touched by the shadow of an obscure fate; eager and weary as it seems at once, pale and fervent with patience or passion; allure and perplex the eyes and thoughts of men. There is a study here of Youth and Age meeting; it may be, of a young man coming suddenly upon the ghostly figure of himself as he will one day be; the brilliant life in his face is struck into sudden pallor and silence, the clear eyes startled, the happy lips confused. A fair straight-featured face, with full curls fallen or blown against the eyelids; and confronting it, a keen, wan, mournful mask of flesh: the wise ironical face of one made subtle and feeble by great age. The vivid and various imagination of Leonardo never fell into a form more poetical than in this design. Grotesques of course are not wanting; and there is a noble sketch of a griffin and lion locked or dashed together in the hardest throes of a final fight, which is full of violent beauty; and again, a study of the painter's chosen type of woman: thin-lipped, with a forehead too high and weighty for perfection or sweetness of form; cheeks exquisitely carved, clear pure chin and neck, and grave eyes full of a cold charm; folded hands, and massive hair gathered into a net; shapely and splendid, as a study for Pallas or Artemis.

Here, as in his own palace° and wherever in Florence the shadow of his supreme presence has fallen and the mark of his divine hand been set, the work of Michel Angelo° for a time effaces all thought of other men or gods. Before the majesty of his imperious advent the lesser kings of time seem as it were men bidden to rise up from their thrones, to cover their faces and come down. Not gratitude, not delight, not sympathy, is the first sense excited in one suddenly confronted with his designs; fear rather, oppressive reverence, and well-nigh intolerable adoration. Their tragic beauty, their inexplicable strength and wealth of thought, their terrible and exquisite significance, all the powers they unveil and all the mysteries they reserve, all their suggestions and all their suppressions, are at first adorable merely. Delightful beyond words they become in time, as the subtler and weightier work of Æschylus or Shakespeare; but like these they first fill and exalt the mind with a strange and violent pleasure which is the highest mood of worship; reverence intensified to the last endurable degree. The mind, if then it enjoys at all or wonders at all, knows little of its own wonder or its own enjoyment; the air and light about it is too fine and pure to breathe or bear. The least thought of these men has in it something intricate and enormous, faultless as the formal work of their triumphant art must be. All mysteries of good and evil, all wonders of life and death, lie in their hands or at their feet. They have known the causes of things, and are not too happy. The fatal labour of the world, the clamour and hunger of the open-mouthed all-summoning grave, all fears and hopes of ephemeral men, are indeed made subject to them, and trodden by them underfoot; but the sorrow and strangeness of things are not lessened because to one or two their secret springs have been laid bare and the courses of their tides made known; refluent evil and good, alternate grief and joy, life inextricable from death, change inevitable and insuperable fate. Of the three, Michel Angelo is saddest; on his, the most various genius of the three, the weight of things lies heaviest. Glad or sad as the days of his actual life may have been, his work in the fulness of its might and beauty has most often a mournful meaning, some grave and subtle sorrow latent under all its life. Here in one design is the likeness of perishable pleasure; Vain Delight with all her children; one taller boy has drawn off a reverted and bearded mask, on which another lays hold with one hand, fingering it as with lust or curiosity; his other hand holds to the mother's knee; behind her a third child lurks and cowers; she with a hard broad smile of dull pleasure, feeds her eyes on the sight of her own face in a hand-mirror. Fear and levity, cruelty and mystery, make up their mirth; evil seems to impend over all these joyous heads, to hide behind all these laughing features: they are things too light for hell, too low for heaven; bubbles of the earth, brilliant and transient and poisonous, blown out of unclean foam by the breath of meaner spirits, to glitter and quiver for a little under the beams of a mortal sun. Cruel and curious and ignorant, all their faces are full of mean beauty and shallow delight. Hard by, a troop of Loves haul after them, with mocking mouths and straining arms, a live human mask, a hollow face shorn off from the head, old and grim and sad, worn through and through with pain and time, from the vexed forehead to the sharp chin which grates against the ground; the eyes and lips full of suffering, sardonic and helpless; the face of one knowing his own fate, who has resigned himself sadly and scornfully to the violence of base and light desires; the grave and great features all hardened into suffering and self-contempt.

But in one separate head there is more tragic attraction than in these: a woman's, three times studied, with divine and subtle care; sketched and resketched in youth and age, beautiful always beyond desire and cruel beyond words; fairer than heaven and more terrible than hell; pale with pride and weary with wrong-doing; a silent anger against God and man burns, white and repressed, through her clear features. In one drawing she wears a head-dress of eastern fashion rather than western, but in effect made out of the artist's mind only; plaited in the likeness of closely-welded scales as of a chrysalid serpent, raised and waved and rounded in the likeness of a sea-shell. In some inexplicable way all her ornaments seem to partake of her fatal nature, to bear upon them her brand of beauty fresh from hell; and this through no vulgar machinery of symbolism, no serpentine or otherwise bestial emblem: the bracelets and rings are innocent enough in shape and workmanship; but in touching her flesh they have become infected with deadly and malignant meaning. Broad bracelets divide the shapely splendour of her arms; over the nakedness of her firm and luminous breasts, just below the neck, there is passed a band as of metal. Her eyes are full of proud and passionless lust after gold and blood; her hair, close and curled, seems ready to shudder in sunder and divide into snakes. Her throat, full and fresh, round and hard to the eye as her bosom and arms, is erect and stately, the head set firm on it without any droop or lift of the chin; her mouth crueller than a tiger's, colder than a snake's, and beautiful beyond a woman's. She is the deadlier Venus incarnate;

πολλὴ μὲν ἐν Θεοῖσι κοὐκ ἀνώνυμος θεά·°

for upon earth also many names might be found for her: Lamia re-transformed, invested now with a fuller beauty, but divested of all feminine attributes not native to the snake—a Lamia loveless and unassailable by the sophist, readier to drain life out of her lover than to fade for his sake at his side; or the Persian Amestris,° watching the only breasts on earth more beautiful than her own cut off from her rival's living bosom; or Cleopatra,° not dying but turning serpent under the serpent's bite; or that queen of the extreme east who with her husband marked every day as it went by some device of a new and wonderful cruelty. In one design, where the cruel and timid face of a king rises behind her, this crowned and cowering head might stand for Ahab's, and hers for that of Jezebel.° Another study is in red chalk; in this the only ornaments are ear-rings. In a third, the serpentine hair is drawn up into a tuft at the crown with two ringlets hanging, heavy and deadly as small tired snakes. There is a drawing in the furthest room at the Buonarroti Palace which recalls and almost reproduces the design of these three. Here also the electric hair, which looks as though it would hiss and glitter with sparks if once touched, is wound up to a tuft with serpentine plaits and involutions; all that remains of it unbound falls in one curl, shaping itself into a snake's likeness as it unwinds, right against a living snake held to the breast and throat. This is rightly registered as a study for Cleopatra; but notice has not yet been accorded to the subtle and sublime idea which transforms her death by the aspic's bite into a meeting of serpents which recognise and embrace, an encounter between the woman and the worm of Nile,° almost as though this match for death were a monstrous love-match, or such a mystic marriage as that painted in the loveliest passage of *Salammbô*,° between the maiden body and the scaly coils of the serpent and the priestess alike made sacred to the moon; so closely do the snake and the queen of snakes caress and cling. Of this idea Shakespeare also had a vague and great glimpse when he made Antony 'murmur, *Where's my serpent of old Nile?*' mixing a foretaste of her death with the full sweet savour of her supple and amorous 'pride of life.' For what indeed is lovelier or more luxuriously loving than a strong and graceful snake of the nobler kind?

After this the merely terrible designs of Michel Angelo are shorn of half their horror; even the single face as of one suddenly caught and suddenly released from hell, with wild drapery blown behind it by a wind not of this world, strikes upon the sight and memory of a student less deeply and sharply. Certain of his slight and swift studies for damned souls and devils—designs probably for the final work in which he has embodied and made immortal the dream of a great and righteous judgment between soul and soul—resemble much at first sight, and more on longer inspection, the similar studies and designs of Blake. One devil indeed recalls at once the famous 'ghost of a flea,'° having much of the same dull and liquorish violence of expression. Other sketches in the small chamber of his palace bring also to mind his great English disciple: the angry angel poised as in fierce descent; the falling figure with drawn-up legs, splendidly and violently designed; the reverted head showing teeth and nostrils: the group of two old men in hell; one looks up howling, with level face; one looks down with lips drawn back. Nothing can surpass the fixed and savage agony of his face, immutable and imperishable. In this same room are other studies worth record: a Virgin and Child, unfinished, but of supreme strength and beauty; the child fully drawn, with small strong limbs outlined in faint red, rounded and magnificent; soft vigorous arms, and hands that press and cling. There is a design of a covered head, looking down; mournful, with nervous mouth, with clear and deep-set eyes; the nostril strong and curved. Another head, older, with thicker lips, is drawn by it in the same attitude.

Beside the Jezebel or Amestris of the Uffizj there is a figure of Fortune, with a face of cold exaltation and high clear beauty; strong wings expand behind her, or shadows rather of vast and veiled plumes; below her the wheel seems to pause, as in a lull of the perpetual race. This design was evidently the sketch out of which the picture of Fortune in the Corsini Palace was elaborated by some pupil of the master's. In that picture, as in the Venus and Cupid with mystic furniture of melancholy masks and emblems in the background, lodged now in the last Tuscan chamber but one of the Uffizj, the meaner hand of the executive workman has failed to erase or overlay the great and fruitful thought of that divine mind in which their first conceptions lay and gathered form. The strong and laughing God treading with a vigorous wantonness the fair flesh of his mother; the goddess languid and effused like a broad-blown flower, her soft bright side pressed hard under his foot and nestling heel, her large arm lifted to wrest the arrow from his hand, with a lazy and angry mirth; and at her feet the shelves full of masks, sad inverted faces, heads of men overset, blind strings of broken puppets forgotten where they fell; all these are as clearly the device of Michel Angelo's great sad mind as the handiwork is clearly none of his. Near the sketch of Fortune is a strange figure, probably worked up into some later design. A youth with reverted head, wearing furry drapery with plumy fringes, has one leg drawn up and resting on a step; the face, as it looks back, is laughing with fear; the hysterical horror of some unseen thing is branded into the very life of its fair features. This violent laugh as of a child scared into madness subjects the whole figure, brilliant and supple in youth as it seems, to the transformation of terror. Upon this design also much tragic conjecture of allegory or story might be spent, and wasted.

There are here no other sketches so terrible, except one of hell by Luca Signorelli,° rough and slight in comparison: a fierce chaos of figures fighting, falling, crushing and crushed together, their faces hissed at and their limbs locked round by lithe snakes, their eyes blasted and lidless from the hot wind and heaving flame; one lost face of a woman looks out between two curving bat's wings, deadlier than the devils about her who plunge and struggle and sink.

The sketches of Filippo Lippi° are exquisite and few. One above all, of Lucrezia Buti in her girlhood as the painter found her at Prato in the convent, is of a beauty so intolerable that the eyes can neither endure nor abstain from it without a pleasure acute even to pain which compels them to cease looking, or a desire which, as it compels them to return, relapses into delight. Her face is very young, more faultless and fresher than the first forms and colours of morning; her pure mouth small and curved, cold and tender; her eyes, set with an exquisite mastery of drawing in the clear and gracious face, seem to show actual colour of brilliant brown in their shapely and lucid pupils, under their chaste and perfect eyelids; her hair is deeply drawn backwards from the sweet low brows and small rounded cheeks, heaped and hidden away under a knotted veil whose flaps fall on either side of her bright round throat. The world has changed for painters and their Virgins since the lean school of Angelico° had its day and its way in art; this study assuredly was not made by a kneeling painter in the intervals of prayer. More vivid, more fertile, and more dramatic than Lippo, the great invention and various power of Benozzo° never produced a face like this. For pure and simple beauty it is absolutely unsurpassable: innocent enough also for a Madonna, but pure by nature, not chaste through religion. No creeds have helped to compose the holiness of her beauty. The meagre and arid sanctities of women ascetic by accident or abstemious by force have nothing in common with her chastity. She might be as well a virgin chosen of Artemis as consecrated to Christ. Mystic passions and fleshless visions have never taken hold upon her sense or faith. No flower and no animal is more innocent; none more capable of giving and of yielding to the pleasure that they give. Before the date of her immortal lover there was probably no artist capable of painting such a thing at all: and in none of his many paintings does the stolen nun look and smile with a more triumphant and serene supremacy of beauty. [...]

# FROM *NOTES ON THE ROYAL ACADEMY EXHIBITION, 1868* (1868)

[...] It is well known that the painter of whom I now propose to speak has never suffered exclusion or acceptance at the hand of any academy. To such acceptance or such rejection all other men of any note have been and maybe liable. It is not less well known that his work must always hold its place as second in significance and value to no work done by any painter of his time.° Among the many great works of Mr D. G. Rossetti, I know of none greater than his two latest. These are types of sensual beauty and spiritual, the siren and the sibyl. The one is a woman of the type of Adam's first wife; she is a living Lilith, with ample splendour of redundant hair;

> 'She excels
> All women in the magic of her locks;
> And when she winds them round a young man's neck
> She will not ever set him free again.'°

Clothed in soft white garments, she draws out through a comb the heavy mass of hair like thick spun gold to fullest length; her head leans back half sleepily, superb and satiate with its own beauty; the eyes are languid, without love in them or hate; the sweet luxurious mouth has the patience of pleasure fulfilled and complete, the warm repose of passion sure of its delight. Outside, as seen in the glimmering mirror, there is full summer; the deep and glowing leaves have drunk in the whole strength of the sun. The sleepy splendour of the picture is a fit raiment for the idea incarnate of faultless fleshly beauty and peril of pleasure unavoidable. For this serene and sublime sorceress there is no life but of the body; with spirit (if spirit there be) she can dispense. Were it worth her while for any word to divide those terrible tender lips, she too might say with the hero of the most perfect and exquisite book of modern times—*Mademoiselle de Maupin*—'Je trouve la terre aussi belle que le ciel, et je pense que la correction de la forme est la vertu.'° Of evil desire or evil impulse she has nothing; and nothing of good. She is indifferent, equable, magnetic; she charms and draws down the souls of men by pure force of absorption, in no wise wilful or malignant; outside herself she cannot live, she cannot even see: and because of this she attracts and subdues all men at once in body and in spirit. Beyond the mirror she cares not to look, and could not.

> 'Ma mia suora Rachel mai non si smaga
> Dal suo miraglio, e siede tutto 'l giorno.'°

So, rapt in no spiritual contemplation, she will sit to all time, passive and perfect: the outer light of a sweet spring day flooding and filling the massive gold of her hair. By the reflection in a deep mirror of fervent foliage from without, the chief chord of stronger colour is touched in this picture; next in brilliance and force of relief is the heap of curling and tumbling hair on which the sunshine strikes; the face and head of the siren are withdrawn from the full stroke of the light.°

After this faint essay at an exposition, the weighty and melodious words in which the painter has recast his thought (words inscribed on the frame of the picture) will be taken as full atonement for my shortcomings; I fear only that the presumption and insufficience of the commentator will now be but the more visible.

Lady Lilith

Of Adam's first wife, Lilith, it is told
  (The witch he loved before the gift of Eve)
  That, ere the snake's, her sweet tongue could deceive,
And her enchanted hair was the first gold.
And still she sits, young while the earth is old,
  And, subtly of herself contemplative,
  Draws men to watch the bright net she can weave,
Till heart and body and life are in its hold.

Rose, foxglove, poppy are her flowers: for where
  Is he not found, O Lilith, whom shed scent
And soft-shed fingers and soft sleep shall snare?
  Lo! as that youth's eyes burned at thine, so went
  Thy spell through him, and left his straight neck bent,
And round his heart one strangling golden hair.

The other picture gives the type opposite to this; a head of serene and spiritual beauty, severe and tender, with full and heavy hair falling straight in grave sweet lines, not, like Lilith's, exuberant of curl and coil; with carven column of throat, solid and round and flawless as living ivory; with still and sacred eyes and pure calm lips; an imperial votaress truly, in maiden meditation:° yet as true and tangible a woman of mortal mould, as ripe and firm of flesh as her softer and splendid sister. The mystic emblems in the background show her power upon love and death to make them loyal servants to the law of her lofty and solemn spirit. Here also the artist alone should first be heard; and I, having leave to act as his outrider, give him the due precedence.

Sibylla Palmifera

Under the arch of life, where love and death,
  Terror and mystery, guard her shrine, I saw

Beauty enthroned; and though her gaze struck awe,
I drew it in as simply as my breath.
Hers are the eyes which, over and beneath,
The sky and sea bend on thee,—which can draw,
By sea or sky or woman, to one law,
The allotted bondman of her palm and wreath.

This is that Lady Beauty, in whose praise
Thy voice and hand shake still,—long known to thee
By flying hair and fluttering hem,—the beat
Following her daily of thy heart and feet,
How passionately and irretrievably,
In what fond flight, how many ways and days!

After these all weaker words must fall flat enough; but something of further description may yet be allowed. Behind this figure of the ideal and inaccessible beauty, an inlaid wall of alternate alabaster and black marble bears inwrought on its upper part the rival twin emblems of love and death; over the bare carven skull poppies impend, and roses over the sweet head with bound blind eyes: in her hand is the palm-branch, a sceptre of peace and of power. The cadence of colour is splendid and simple, a double trinity of green and red, the dim red robe, the deep red poppies, the soft red roses; and again the green veil wound about with wild flowers, the green down of poppy-leaves, the sharper green of rose-leaves.

An unfinished picture of Beatrice (the Beata Beatrix of the Vita Nuova°), a little before death, is perhaps the noblest of Mr Rossetti's many studies after Dante. This work is wholly symbolic and ideal; a strange bird flown earthward from heaven brings her in its beak a full-blown poppy, the funereal flower of sleep. Her beautiful head lies back, sad and sweet, with fast-shut eyes in a death-like trance that is not death; over it the shadow of death seems to impend, making sombre the splendour of her ample hair and tender faultless features. Beyond her the city and the bridged river are seen as from far, dim and veiled with misty lights as though already 'sitting alone, made as a widow.'° Love, on one side, comes bearing in his hand a heart in flames, having his eyes bent upon Dante's; on the other side is Dante, looking sadly across the way towards Love. In this picture the light is subdued and soft, touching tenderly from behind the edges of Beatrice's hair and raiment; in the others there is a full fervour of daylight. The great picture of Venus Verticordia has now been in great measure recast; the head is of a diviner type of beauty; golden butterflies hover about the halo of her hair, alight upon the sweet supremacy of a beauty imperial and immortal; her glorious bosom seems to exult and expand as the roses on each side of it. The painting of leaf and fruit and flower in this picture is beyond my praise or any man's; but of one thing I will here take note; the flash of green brilliance from the upper leaves of the

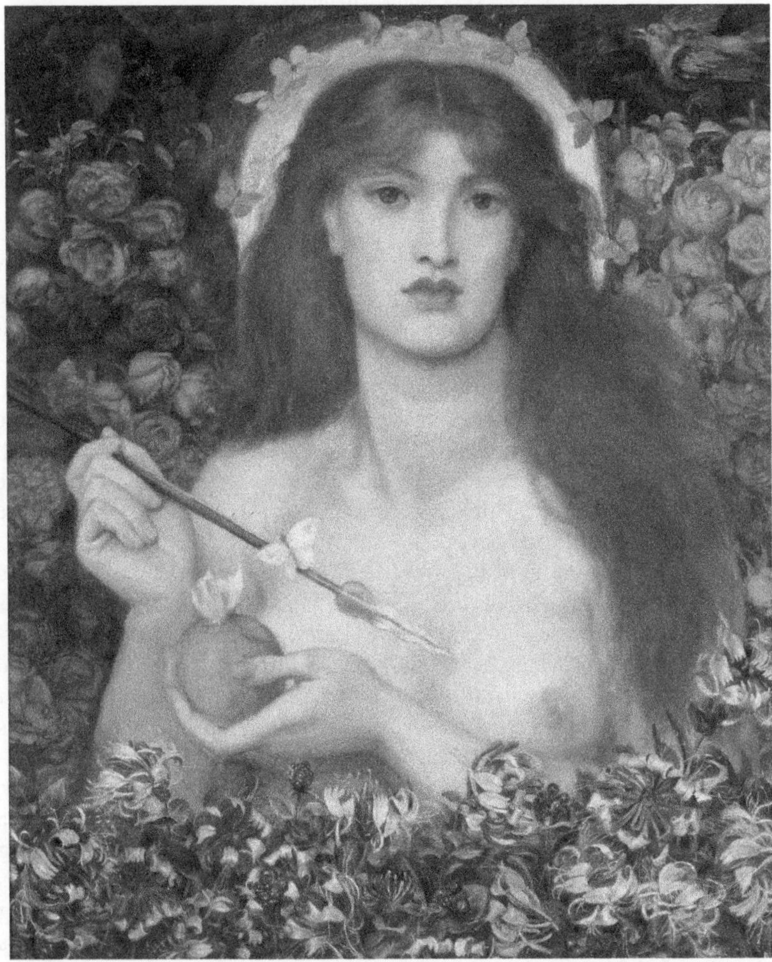

FIG. 6. Dante Gabriel Rossetti, *Venus Verticordia*. Photograph reproduced with the kind permission of the Russell-Cotes Art Gallery & Museum, Bournemouth.

trellis against the sombre green of the trees behind. Once more it must appear that the painter alone can translate into words as perfect in music and colour the sense and spirit of his work.

Venus Verticordia

She hath it in her hand to give it thee,
   Yet almost in her heart would hold it back;
   She muses, with her eyes upon the track
Of that which in thy spirit they can see.
Haply, 'Behold, he is at peace,' saith she:
'Alas! the apple for his lips—the dart
   That follows its brief sweetness to his heart—
The wandering of his feet perpetually!'

A little space her glance is still and coy;
   But if she give the fruit that works her spell,
Those eyes shall flame as for her Phrygian boy;
   Then shall her bird's strained throat the woe foretell,
   And her far seas moan as a single shell,
And through her dark grove strike the light of Troy.

Another work, as yet incomplete, is a study of La Pia; she is seen looking forth from the ramparts of her lord's castle, over the fatal lands without; her pallid splendid face hangs a little forward, wan and white against the mass of dark deep hair; under her hands is a work of embroidery, hanging still on the frame unfinished; just touched by the weak weary hands, it trails forward across the lap of her pale green raiment, into the foreground of the picture. In her eyes is a strange look of wonder and sorrow and fatigue, without fear and without pain, as though she were even now looking beyond earth into the soft and sad air of purgatory: she presses the deadly marriage-ring° into the flesh of her finger, so deep that the soft skin is bloodless and blanched from the intense imprint of it. Two other studies, as yet only sketched, give promise of no less beauty; the subject of one was long since handled by the artist in a slighter manner. It also is taken from the Vita Nuova; Dante in a dream beholding Beatrice dead, tended by handmaidens, and Love, with bow and dart in hand, in act to kiss her beautiful dead mouth. The other is a design of Perseus showing to Andromeda the severed head of Medusa, reflected in water; an old and well-worn subject, but renewed and reinformed with life by the vital genius of the artist. In the Pompeian picture we see the lovers at halt beside a stream, on their homeward way; here we see them in their house, bending over the central cistern or impluvium of the main court. The design is wonderful for grace and force; the picture will assuredly be one of the painter's greatest.

Wide and far apart as lie their provinces of work, their tones of thought and emotion, the two illustrious artists° of whom I have just said a short and inadequate word have in common one supreme quality of spirit and of work, coloured and moulded in each by his individual and inborn force of nature; the love of beauty for the very beauty's sake, the faith and trust in it as in a god indeed. This gift of love and faith, now rare enough, has been and should be ever the common apanage of artists. *Rien n'est vrai que le beau*;° this should be the beginning and the ending of their belief, held in no small or narrow sense, but in the largest and most liberal scope of meaning. Beauty may be strange, quaint, terrible, may play with pain as with pleasure, handle a horror till she leave it a delight; she forsakes not such among her servants as Webster or as Goya. No good art is unbeautiful; but much able and effective work may be, and is. Mere skill, mere thought and trouble, mere feeling or mere dexterity, will never on earth make a man painter or poet or artist in any kind. Hundreds of English pictures just now have but these to boast of; and with these even studious and able men are often now content; forgetful that art is no more a matter of mere brain-work than of mere handicraft. The worship of beauty, though beauty be itself transformed and incarnate in shapes diverse without end, must be simple and absolute; hence only must the believer expect profit or reward. Over every building made sacred to art of any sort, upon the hearts of all who strive after it to serve it, there should be written these words of the greatest master now living among us:—

La beauté est parfaite,
La beauté peut toute chose,
La beauté est la seule chose au monde qui n'existe pas à demi.°

# FROM 'THE POEMS OF DANTE GABRIEL ROSSETTI' (1870)

[...] In every age there is some question raised as to its wants and powers, its strength and weakness, its great or small worth and work; and in every age that question is waste of time and speech—of thought usually there is no waste, for the questioners have none to expend. There has never been an age that was not degenerate in the eyes of its own fools; the yelp of curtailed foxes in every generation is the same. To a small soul the age which has borne it can appear only as an age of small souls; the pigmy brain and emasculate spirit can perceive in its own time nothing but dwarfishness and emasculation. That the world has ever seen spirits of another sort, the poor heart of such creatures would fain deny and dares not; but to allow that the world does now is insufferable; at least they can 'swagger themselves out of their own eyes'° into the fond belief that they are but samples of their puny time, overtopped in spiritual stature by the spirits of times past alone. But not by blustering denial or blustering assertion of an age's greatness will the question be decided whether the age be great or not. Each century has seemed to some of its children an epoch of decadence and decline in national life and spiritual, in moral or material glory; each alike has heard the cry of degeneracy raised against it, the wail of emulous impotence set up against the weakness of the age; Dante's generation and Shakespeare's, Milton's and Shelley's, have all been ages of poetic decay in their turn, as the age of Hugo is now; there as here no great man was to be seen, no great work was to be done, no great cry was to be heard, no great impulse was to be felt, by those who could feel nothing, hear nothing, do nothing, and see nothing. To them the poor present has always been pitiable or damnable, the past which bore it divine. And other men than these have swelled the common cry of curs: Byron, himself in his better moments a witness against his own words, helped the fools of his hour to decry their betters and his own, by a pretence of wailing over the Augustan age of Anne, when 'it was all Horace with us; it is all Claudian now.'° His *now* has become our *then*, and the same whine is raised in its honour; for the cant of irritation and insincerity, hungry vanity and starving spite, can always be caught up and inherited by those who can inherit nothing of a strong man's but his weakness, of a wise man's but his folly; who can gather at a great man's board no sustenance from the meats and wines, but are proud to pilfer the soiled napkins and cracked platters from under his side-table. Whether there be any great work doing in our time, or any great man living, it is not worth while to debate; but if there be not, it is certain that no man living can know it; for to pass judgment worth heeding on any age and give sentence that shall last on any generation, a man must himself be great; and if no man on earth be great in our day, who on earth can be great enough to know and let us know it on better authority than a pigmy's? Such champions as please may fight out on either side their battle of the sandbags and windbags between this hour and the next; I am content to assume, and am not careful to dispute in defence of the assumption, that the qualities which make men great and the work of men famous are now what they were, and will be what they are: that there is no progress and no degeneracy traceable from Æschylus to Shakespeare, from Athenian sculptors to Venetian painters; that the gifts of genius are diverse, but the quality is one; and—though this be a paradox—that this quality does not wait till a man be dead to descend on him and belong to him; that his special working power does not of necessity begin with the cessation of it, and that the dawn of his faculty cannot reasonably be dated from the hour of its extinction. If this paradox be not utterly untenable, it follows that dead men of genius had genius even when yet alive, and did not begin to be great men by ceasing to be men at all; and that so far we have no cause to distrust the evidence of reason which proves us the greatness of men past when it proves to us by the same process of testimony the greatness of men present.

Here, for example, in the work of Mr Rossetti, besides that particular colour and flavour which distinguishes each master's work from that of all other masters, and by want of which you may tell merely good work from wholly great work, the general qualities of all great poetry are separately visible and divisible—strength, sweetness, affluence, simplicity, depth, light, harmony, variety, bodily grace and range of mind and force of soul and ease of flight, the scope and sweep of wing to impel the might and weight of thought through the air and light of speech with a motion as of mere musical impulse; and not less the live bloom of perfect words, warm as breath and fine as flower-dust, which lies light as air upon the parting of lyric leaves that open into song; the rare and ineffable mark of a supreme singing power, an element too subtle for solution in any crucible of analysis, though its presence or absence be patent at a first trial to all who have a sense of taste. All these this poet has, and the mastery over all these which melts and fuses all into form and use; the cunning to turn his own gifts to service which is the last great apanage of great workmen. Colour and sound are servants of his thought, and his thought is servant of his will; in him the will and the instinct are not two forces, but one strength; are not two leaders, but one guide; there is no shortcoming, no pain or compulsion in the homage of hand to soul. The subject-matter of his work is always great and fit; nothing trivial, nothing illicit, nothing unworthy the workmanship of a master-hand, is to be swept up from any comer of the floor; there is no misuse or waste of good work on stuff too light or hard to take the impression of his noble style. He builds up no statues of snow at the bidding of any fool, with the hand that can carve itself a godlike model in ivory or gold; not though all the fools of the place and hour should recommend snow as the best material, for its softness and purity. Time and work and art are too precious to him and too serious to be spent on anything less than the best. An artist worthy of the highest work will make his least work worthy of himself. In each line of labour which his spirit may strike into he will make his mark, and set his stamp on any metal he may take in hand to forge; for he can strike into no wrong line, and take in hand no base metal. So equal a balance of two great gifts, as we find in the genius of this artist is perhaps the greatest gift of all, as it is certainly the most singular. We cannot tell what jewels were lost to the treasure-house of time in that century of sonnets which held 'the bosom-beats of Raffael;'° we can but guess that they had somewhat, and doubt how nearly they had all, of his perfect grace and godhead of heavenly humanity. Even of the giant-god his rival° we cannot be sure that his divine faculties never clashed or crossed each other to their mutual hindrance.

But here, where both the sister powers serve in the temple of one mind and impel the work of one hand, their manner of service is smooth, harmonious, perfect; the splendid quality of painting and the subtle faculty of verse gain glory from each other without taking, reign side by side with no division of empire, yet with no confusion of claims, with no invasion of rights. No tongueless painter or handless poet could be safer from the perils of mixed art; his poems are not over pictorial or his pictures over poetical; his poetry has not the less depth and reach and force and height of spirit proper to poetry, his painting has not the less might and skill, the less excellence of form and colour or masterdom of design and handiwork proper to painting, for the double glory of his genius. Which of the two great men in him, the painter or the poet, be the greater, only another artist equal to him on either hand and taintless of jealousy or misconceit could say with authority worth a hearing; and such a judge he is not likely to find. But what is his relative rank among other men it needs no such rare union of faculties to perceive. His place among the painters of his century may be elsewhere debated and determined; but here and now the materials lie before us for decision as to his place among its poets. Of these there is but one alive whose name is already unamenable to any judgment of the hour's; whose supremacy, whether it be or be not a matter of question between insular and provincial circles of parasites or sectarians, is no more debatable before any graver tribunal than the motion of the earth round the sun. Upon him, as upon two or three other of the leaders of men in time past, the verdict of time has been given before his death. In our comparison of men with men for worse or better we do not now take into reckoning the name of Victor Hugo. The small gatherings or swollen assemblies of important ephemerals who met to dispute the respective claims and merits of Shakespeare and Jonson, Milton and Waller, Shelley and Byron, have on the whole fallen duly dumb: the one supreme figure of each time is as generally and openly acknowledged by all capable articulate creatures as need be desired. To sit in the seat of such disputants can be no present man's ambition. It ought to be, if it be not, superfluous to set down in words the assurance that we claim for no living poet a place beside the Master; that we know there is no lyrist alive but one who could have sung for us the cradle-song of death, the love-song madness, the sea-song of exile, the hunting-song of revolution;° that since the songs of Gretchen in 'Faust' and Beatrice in the 'Cenci,'° there have been no such songs heard among men as the least of these first four among all his lyrics that rise to recollection at the moment. Fantine's song or Gastibelza's, the 'Adieu, patrie!' or the 'Chasseur Noir,'° any one of these by itself would suffice to establish, beyond debate and beyond acclamation, the absolute sovereignty of the great poet whose glory could dispense even with any of these.

The claims to precedence of other men who stand in the vanguard of their time are open matters for the discussion of judgments to adjust or readjust. Among English-speaking poets of his age I know of none who can reasonably be said to have given higher proof of the highest qualities than Mr Rossetti—if the qualities we rate highest in poetry be imagination, passion, thought, harmony and variety of singing power. Each man who has anything has his own circle of work and realm of rule, his own field to till and to reign in; no rival can overmatch for firm completion of lyric line, for pathos made perfect and careful melody of high or of intimate emotion, 'New-Year's Eve' or 'The Grandmother,' 'Œnone' or 'Boadicea,' the majestic hymn or the rich lament for love won and lost in 'Maud;' none can emulate the fiery subtlety and sinuous ardour of spirit which penetrates and lights up all secret gulfs and glimmering heights of human evil and good in 'The Ring and the Book,'° making the work done live because 'the soul of man is precious to man:'° none can 'blow in power' again through the notched reed of Pan by the river,° to detain the sun on the hills with music; none can outrun that smooth speed of gracious strength which touched its Grecian goal in 'Thyrsis' and the 'Harp-player;'° none can light as with fires or lull as with flutes of magic the reaches of so full a stream of story as flows round the 'Earthly Paradise'° with ships of heroes afloat on it. But for height and range and depth, for diversity and perfection of powers, Mr Rossetti is abreast of elder poets not less surely than of younger. Again I take to witness, four singled poems; 'The Burden of Nineveh,' 'Sister Helen,' 'Jenny,' and 'Eden Bower.' Though there were not others as great as these to cite at need, we might be content to pass judgment on the strength of these only; but others as great there are. If he have not the full effluence of romance or the keen passion of human science that give power on this hand to Morris and on that to Browning, his work has form and voice, shapeliness and sweetness, unknown to the great analyst; it has weight and heat, gravity and intensity, wanting to the less serious and ardent work of the latest master of romance. Neither by any defect of form nor by any default of force does he ever fall short of either mark or fight with either hand 'as one that beateth the air.'° In sureness of choice and scope of interest, in solidity of subject and sublimity of object, the general worth of his work excels the rate of other men's; he wastes no breath and mistakes no distance, sets his genius to no tasks unfit for it, and spends his strength in the culture of no fruitless fields. What he would do is always what a poet should, and what he would do is always done. Born a light-bearer and leader of men,° he has always fulfilled his office with readiness and done his work with might. Help and strength and delight and fresh life have long been gifts of his giving, and freely given as only great gifts can be. And now that at length we receive from hands yet young and strong this treasure of many years, the gathered flower of youth and ripe firstlings of manhood, a fruit of the topmost branch 'more golden than gold,' all men may witness and assure themselves what manner of harvest the life of this man was to bear; all may see that although, in the perfect phrase of his own sonnet, the last birth of life be death,° as her three firstborn were love and art and song, yet two of these which she has borne to him, art namely and song, cannot now be made subject to that last; that life and love with it may pass away, but very surely no death that ever may be born shall have power upon these for ever.

# FROM *SONGS BEFORE SUNRISE*
# (1871)

# Super Flumina Babylonis

By the waters of Babylon we sat down and wept,
Remembering thee,
That for ages of agony hast endured, and slept,
And wouldst not see.

By the waters of Babylon we stood up and sang,
Considering thee,
That a blast of deliverance in the darkness rang,
To set thee free.

And with trumpets and thunderings and with morning song
Came up the light;
And thy spirit uplifted thee to forget thy wrong
As day doth night.

And thy sons were dejected not any more, as then
When thou wast shamed;
When thy lovers went heavily without heart, as men
Whose life was maimed.

In the desolate distances, with a great desire,
For thy love's sake,
With our hearts going back to thee, they were filled with fire,
Were nigh to break.

It was said to us: 'Verily ye are great of heart,
But ye shall bend;
Ye are bondsmen and bondswomen, to be scourged and smart,
To toil and tend.'

And with harrows men harrowed us, and subdued with spears,
And crushed with shame;
And the summer and winter was, and the length of years,
And no change came.

By the rivers of Italy, by the sacred streams,
By town, by tower,
There was feasting with revelling, there was sleep with dreams,
Until thine hour.

And they slept and they rioted on their rose-hung beds,
With mouths on flame,
And with love-locks vine-chapleted, and with rose-crowned heads
And robes of shame.

And they knew not their forefathers,° nor the hills and streams
And words of power,
Nor the gods that were good to them, but with songs and dreams
Filled up their hour.

By the rivers of Italy, by the dry streams' beds,
When thy time came,
There was casting of crowns from them, from their young men's heads,
The crowns of shame.

By the horn of Eridanus,° by the Tiber mouth,
As thy day rose,
They arose up and girded them to the north and south,
By seas, by snows.

As a water in January the frost confines,
Thy kings bound thee;
As a water in April is, in the new-blown vines,
Thy sons made free.

And thy lovers that looked for thee, and that mourned from far,
For thy sake dead,
We rejoiced in the light of thee, in the signal star
Above thine head.

In thy grief had we followed thee, in thy passion loved,
Loved in thy loss;
In thy shame we stood fast to thee, with thy pangs were moved,
Clung to thy cross.

By the hillside of Calvary we beheld thy blood,
Thy bloodred tears,
As a mother's in bitterness, an unebbing flood,
Years upon years.

And the north was Gethsemane, without leaf or bloom,
A garden sealed;
And the south was Aceldama,° for a sanguine fume
Hid all the field.

By the stone of the sepulchre we returned to weep,
From far, from prison;
And the guards by it keeping it we beheld asleep,
But thou wast risen.

And an angel's similitude by the unsealed grave,
And by the stone:°

And the voice was angelical, to whose words God gave
Strength like his own.

'Lo, the graveclothes of Italy that are folded up
In the grave's gloom!°
And the guards as men wrought upon with a charmed cup,
By the open tomb.

'And her body most beautiful, and her shining head,
These are not here;
For your mother, for Italy, is not surely dead:
Have ye no fear.

'As of old time she spake to you, and you hardly heard,
Hardly took heed,
So now also she saith to you, yet another word,
Who is risen indeed.°

'By my saying she saith to you, in your ears she saith,
Who hear these things,
Put no trust in men's royalties, nor in great men's breath,
Nor words of kings.°

'For the life of them vanishes and is no more seen,
Nor no more known;°
Nor shall any remember him if a crown hath been,
Or where a throne.

'Unto each man his handiwork, unto each his crown,
The just Fate gives;
Whoso takes the world's life on him and his own lays down,
He, dying so, lives.

'Whoso bears the whole heaviness of the wronged world's weight
And puts it by,
It is well with him suffering, though he face man's fate;
How should he die?

'Seeing death has no part in him any more, no power
Upon his head;
He has bought his eternity with a little hour,
And is not dead.

'For an hour, if ye look for him, he is no more found,
For one hour's space;
Then ye lift up your eyes to him and behold him crowned,
A deathless face.

'On the mountains of memory, by the world's wellsprings,
        In all men's eyes,
Where the light of the life of him is on all past things,
        Death only dies.

'Not the light that was quenched for us, nor the deeds that were,
        Nor the ancient days,
Nor the sorrows not sorrowful, nor the face most fair
        Of perfect praise.'

So the angel of Italy's resurrection said,
        So yet he saith;
So the son of her suffering, that from breasts nigh dead
        Drew life, not death.

That the pavement of Golgotha should be white as snow,[°]
        Not red, but white;
That the waters of Babylon should no longer flow,
        And men see light.

# Mentana: First Anniversary

At the time when the stars are grey,
  And the gold of the molten moon
Fades, and the twilight is thinned,
And the sun leaps up, and the wind,
A light rose, not of the day,
  A stronger light than of noon.

As the light of a face much loved
  Was the face of the light that clomb;
As a mother's whitened with woes
Her adorable head that arose;
As the sound of a god that is moved,
  Her voice went forth upon Rome.

At her lips it fluttered and failed
  Twice, and sobbed into song,
And sank as a flame sinks under;
Then spake, and the speech was thunder,
And the cheek as he heard it paled
  Of the wrongdoer grown grey with the wrong.

'Is it time, is it time appointed,
  Angel of time, is it near?
For the spent night aches into day
When the kings shall slay not or pray,
And the high-priest,° accursed and anointed,
  Sickens to deathward with fear.

'For the bones of my slain are stirred,
  And the seed of my earth in her womb
Moves as the heart of a bud
Beating with odorous blood
To the tune of the loud first bird
  Burns and yearns into bloom.

'I lay my hand on her bosom,
  My hand on the heart of my earth,
And I feel as with shiver and sob
The triumphant heart in her throb,
The dead petals dilate into blossom,
  The divine blood beat into birth.

'O my earth, are the springs in thee dry?
  O sweet, is thy body a tomb?
Nay, springs out of springs derive,
And summers from summers alive,
And the living from them that die;
  No tomb is here, but a womb.

'O manifold womb and divine,
  Give me fruit of my children, give!
I have given thee my dew for thy root,
Give thou me for my mouth of thy fruit;
Thine are the dead that are mine,
  And mine are thy sons that live.

'O goodly children, O strong
  Italian spirits, that wear
My glories as garments about you,
Could time or the world misdoubt you,
Behold, in disproof of the wrong,
  The field of the grave-pits there.

'And ye that fell upon sleep,
  We have you too with us yet.
Fairer than life or than youth
Is this, to die for the truth:
No death can sink you so deep
  As their graves whom their brethren forget.

'Were not your pains as my pains?
  As my name are your names not divine?
Was not the light in your eyes
Mine, the light of my skies,
And the sweet shed blood of your veins,
  O my beautiful martyrs, mine?

'Of mine earth were your dear limbs made,
  Of mine air was your sweet life's breath;
At the breasts of my love ye were fed,
O my children, my chosen, my dead,
At my breasts where again ye are laid,
  At the old mother's bosom, in death.

'But ye that live, O their brothers,
  Be ye to me as they were;
Give me, my children that live,

What these dead grudged not to give,
Who alive were sons of your mother's,
Whose lips drew breath of your air.

'Till darkness by dawn be cloven,
Let youth's self mourn and abstain;
And love's self find not an hour,
And spring's self wear not a flower,
And Lycoris,° with hair unenwoven,
Hail back to the banquet in vain.

'So sooner and surer the glory
That is not with us shall be,
And stronger the hands that smite
The heads of the sons of night,
And the sound throughout earth of our story
Give all men heart to be free.'

# The Litany of Nations

μᾶ Γᾶ, μᾶ Γᾶ, βοὰν
φοβερὸν ἀπότρεπε.°
Æsch. *Supp.* 890.

CHORUS If with voice of words or prayers thy sons may reach thee,
We thy latter sons, the men thine after-birth,
We the children of thy grey-grown age, O Earth,
O our mother everlasting, we beseech thee,
By the sealed and secret ages of thy life;
By the darkness wherein grew thy sacred forces;
By the songs of stars thy sisters in their courses;
By thine own song hoarse and hollow and shrill with strife;
By thy voice distuned and marred of modulation;
By the discord of thy measure's march with theirs;
By the beauties of thy bosom, and the cares;
By thy glory of growth, and splendour of thy station;
By the shame of men thy children, and the pride;
By the pale-cheeked hope that sleeps and weeps and passes,
As the grey dew from the morning mountain-grasses;
By the white-lipped sightless memories that abide;
By the silence and the sound of many sorrows;
By the joys that leapt up living and fell dead;
By the veil that hides thy hands and breasts and head,
Wrought of divers-coloured days° and nights and morrows;
Isis,° thou that knowest of God what worlds are worth,
Thou the ghost of God, the mother uncreated,
Soul for whom the floating forceless ages waited
As our forceless fancies wait on thee, O Earth;
Thou the body and soul, the father-God and mother,
If at all it move thee, knowing of all things done
Here where evil things and good things are not one,
But their faces are as fire against each other;
By thy morning and thine evening, night and day;
By the first white light that stirs and strives and hovers
As a bird above the brood her bosom covers,
By the sweet last star that takes the westward way;
By the night whose feet are shod with snow or thunder,
Fledged with plumes of storm, or soundless as the dew;
By the vesture bound of many-folded blue
Round her breathless breasts, and all the woven wonder;

By the golden-growing eastern stream of sea;
By the sounds of sunrise moving in the mountains;
By the forces of the floods and unsealed fountains;
Thou that badest man be born, bid man be free.

GREECE I am she that made thee lovely with my beauty
From north to south:
Mine, the fairest lips, took first the fire of duty
From thine own mouth.
Mine, the fairest eyes, sought first thy laws and knew them
Truths undefiled;
Mine, the fairest hands, took freedom first into them,
A weanling child.
By my light, now he lies sleeping, seen above him
Where none sees other;
By my dead that loved and living men that love him;
(*Cho.*) Hear us, O mother.

ITALY I am she that was the light of thee enkindled
When Greece grew dim;
She whose life grew up with man's free life, and dwindled
With wane of him.
She that once by sword and once by word imperial
Struck bright thy gloom;
And a third time, casting off these years funereal,
Shall burst thy tomb.
By that bond 'twixt thee and me whereat affrighted
Thy tyrants fear us;
By that hope and this remembrance reunited;
(*Cho.*) O mother, hear us.

SPAIN I am she that set my seal upon the nameless
West worlds of seas;
And my sons as brides took unto them the tameless
Hesperides.
Till my sins and sons through sinless lands dispersèd,
With red flame shod,
Made accurst the name of man, and thrice accursed
The name of God.
Lest for those past fires the fires of my repentance
Hell's fume yet smother,
Now my blood would buy remission of my sentence;
(*Cho.*) Hear us, O mother.

FRANCE I am she that was thy sign and standard-bearer,
Thy voice and cry;
She that washed thee with her blood and left thee fairer,
The same was I.
Were not these the hands that raised thee fallen and fed thee,
These hands defiled?
Was not I thy tongue that spake, thine eye that led thee,
Not I thy child?
By the darkness on our dreams, and the dead errors
Of dead times near us;°
By the hopes that hang around thee, and the terrors;
(*Cho.*) O mother, hear us.

RUSSIA I am she whose hands are strong and her eyes blinded
And lips athirst
Till upon the night of nations many-minded
One bright day burst:
Till the myriad stars be molten into one light,
And that light thine;
Till the soul of man be parcel of the sunlight,
And thine of mine.
By the snows that blanch not him nor cleanse from slaughter
Who slays his brother;
By the stains and by the chains on me thy daughter;
(*Cho.*) Hear us, O mother.

SWITZERLAND I am she that shews on mighty limbs and maiden
Nor chain nor stain;
For what blood can touch these hands with gold unladen,
These feet what chain?
By the surf of spears one shieldless bosom breasted
And was my shield,
Till the plume-plucked Austrian vulture-heads twin-crested
Twice drenched the field;
By the snows and souls untrampled and untroubled
That shine to cheer us,
Light of those to these responsive and redoubled;
(*Cho.*) O mother, hear us.

GERMANY I am she beside whose forest-hidden fountains
Slept freedom armed,
By the magic born to music in my mountains
Heart-chained and charmed.
By those days the very dream whereof delivers

My soul from wrong;
By the sounds that make of all my ringing rivers
None knows what song;
By the many tribes and names of my division
One from another;
By the single eye of sun-compelling vision;
(*Cho.*) Hear us, O mother.

ENGLAND I am she that was and was not of thy chosen,
Free, and not free;
She that fed thy springs, till now her springs are frozen;
Yet I am she.
By the sea that clothed and sun that saw me splendid
And fame that crowned,
By the song-fires and the sword-fires mixed and blended
That robed me round;
By the star that Milton's soul for Shelley's lighted,
Whose rays insphere us;
By the beacon-bright Republic far-off sighted;
(*Cho.*) O mother, hear us.

CHORUS Turn away from us the cross-blown blasts of error,
That drown each other;
Turn away the fearful cry, the loud-tongued terror,
O Earth, O mother.
Turn away their eyes who track, their hearts who follow,
The pathless past;
Shew the soul of man, as summer shews the swallow,
The way at last.
By the sloth of men that all too long endure men
On man to tread;
By the cry of men, the bitter cry of poor men
That faint for bread;
By the blood-sweat of the people in the garden
Inwalled of kings;
By his passion interceding for their pardon
Who do these things;
By the sightless souls and fleshless limbs that labour
For not their fruit;
By the foodless mouth with foodless heart for neighbour,
That, mad, is mute;
By the child that famine eats as worms the blossom
—Ah God, the child!

By the milkless lips that strain the bloodless bosom
        Till woe runs wild;
By the pastures that give grass to feed the lamb in,
        Where men lack meat;
By the cities clad with gold and shame and famine;
        By field and street;
By the people, by the poor man, by the master
        That men call slave;
By the cross-winds of defeat and of disaster,
        By wreck, by wave;
By the helm that keeps us still to sunwards driving,
        Still eastward bound,
Till, as night-watch ends, day burn on eyes reviving,
        And land be found:
We thy children, that arraign not nor impeach thee
        Though no star steer us,
By the waves that wash the morning we beseech thee,
        O mother, hear us.

## Hertha

I am that which began;
Out of me the years roll;
Out of me God and man;
I am equal and whole;
God changes, and man, and the form of them bodily; I am the soul.

Before ever land was,
Before ever the sea,
Or soft hair of the grass,
Or fair limbs of the tree,
Or the flesh-coloured fruit of my branches, I was, and thy soul
was in me.

First life on my sources
First drifted and swam;
Out of me are the forces
That save it or damn;
Out of me man and woman, and wild-beast and bird; before
God was, I am.°

Beside or above me
Nought is there to go;
Love or unlove me,
Unknow me or know,
I am that which unloves me and loves; I am stricken, and
I am the blow.

I the mark that is missed
And the arrows that miss,
I the mouth that is kissed
And the breath in the kiss,
The search, and the sought, and the seeker, the soul and
the body that is.°

I am that thing which blesses
My spirit elate;
That which caresses
With hands uncreate
My limbs unbegotten that measure the length of the
measure of fate.

But what thing dost thou now,
Looking Godward, to cry

'I am I, thou art thou,
I am low, thou art high'?
I am thou, whom thou seekest to find him; find thou but thyself,
thou art I.

I the grain and the furrow,
The plough-cloven clod
And the ploughshare drawn thorough,
The germ and the sod,
The deed and the doer, the seed and the sower, the dust
which is God.

Hast thou known how I fashioned thee,°
Child, underground?
Fire that impassioned thee,
Iron that bound,
Dim changes of water, what thing of all these hast thou
known of or found?

Canst thou say in thine heart
Thou hast seen with thine eyes
With what cunning of art
Thou wast wrought in what wise,
By what force of what stuff thou wast shapen, and shown on
my breast to the skies?

Who hath given, who hath sold it thee,
Knowledge of me?
Hath the wilderness told it thee?
Hast thou learnt of the sea?
Hast thou communed in spirit with night? have the winds
taken counsel with thee?

Have I set such a star
To show light on thy brow
That thou sawest from afar
What I show to thee now?
Have ye spoken as brethren together, the sun and the
mountains and thou?

What is here, dost thou know it?
What was, hast thou known?
Prophet nor poet
Nor tripod° nor throne
Nor spirit nor flesh can make answer, but only thy
mother alone.

Mother, not maker,
Born, and not made;°
Though her children forsake her,
Allured or afraid,
Praying prayers to the God of their fashion, she stirs not for all that have prayed.

A creed is a rod,
And a crown is of night;
But this thing is God,
To be man with thy might,
To grow straight in the strength of thy spirit, and live out thy life as the light.

I am in thee to save thee,
As my soul in thee saith;
Give thou as I gave thee,
Thy life-blood and breath,
Green leaves of thy labour, white flowers of thy thought, and red fruit of thy death.°

Be the ways of thy giving
As mine were to thee;
The free life of thy living,
Be the gift of it free;
Not as servant to lord, nor as master to slave, shalt thou give thee to me.

O children of banishment,
Souls overcast,
Were the lights ye see vanish meant
Alway to last,
Ye would know not the sun overshining the shadows and stars overpast.

I that saw where ye trod
The dim paths of the night
Set the shadow called God
In your skies to give light;
But the morning of manhood is risen, and the shadowless soul is in sight.

The tree many-rooted°
That swells to the sky
With frondage red-fruited,
The life-tree am I;
In the buds of your lives is the sap of my leaves: ye shall live and not die.°

But the Gods of your fashion
  That take and that give,
In their pity and passion
  That scourge and forgive,
They are worms that are bred in the bark that falls off; they shall die and not live.

My own blood is what stanches
  The wounds in my bark;
Stars caught in my branches
  Make day of the dark,
And are worshipped as suns till the sunrise shall tread out their fires as a spark.

Where dead ages hide under
  The live roots of the tree,
In my darkness the thunder
  Makes utterance of me;
In the clash of my boughs with each other ye hear the waves sound of the sea.

That noise is of Time,
  As his feathers are spread
And his feet set to climb
  Through the boughs overhead,
And my foliage rings round him and rustles, and branches are bent with his tread.

The storm-winds of ages
  Blow through me and cease,
The war-wind that rages,
  The spring-wind of peace,
Ere the breath of them roughen my tresses, ere one of my blossoms increase.

All sounds of all changes,
  All shadows and lights
On the world's mountain-ranges
  And stream-riven heights,
Whose tongue is the wind's tongue and language of storm-clouds on earth-shaking nights;

All forms of all faces,
  All works of all hands
In unsearchable places
  Of time-stricken lands,

All death and all life, and all reigns and all ruins, drop through
me as sands.

Though sore be my burden
And more than ye know,
And my growth have no guerdon
But only to grow,
Yet I fail not of growing for lightnings above me or
deathworms below.

These too have their part in me,
As I too in these;
Such fire is at heart in me,
Such sap is this tree's,
Which hath in it all sounds and all secrets of infinite lands
and of seas.

In the spring-coloured hours
When my mind was as May's,
There brake forth of me flowers
By centuries of days,
Strong blossoms with perfume of manhood, shot out from
my spirit as rays.

And the sound of them springing
And smell of their shoots
Were as warmth and sweet singing
And strength to my roots;
And the lives of my children made perfect with freedom of
soul were my fruits.

I bid you but be;
I have need not of prayer;
I have need of you free
As your mouths of mine air;
That my heart may be greater within me, beholding the
fruits of me fair.

More fair than strange fruit is
Of faiths ye espouse;
In me only the root is
That blooms in your boughs;
Behold now your God that ye made you, to feed him with
faith of your vows.

In the darkening and whitening
Abysses adored,

With dayspring and lightning
For lamp and for sword,
God thunders in heaven, and his angels are red with the wrath of the Lord.

O my sons, O too dutiful
Toward Gods not of me,
Was not I enough beautiful?
Was it hard to be free?
For behold, I am with you, am in you and of you; look forth now and see.

Lo, winged with world's wonders,
With miracles shod,
With the fires of his thunders
For raiment and rod,
God trembles in heaven, and his angels are white with the terror of God.

For his twilight is come on him,
His anguish is here;
And his spirits gaze dumb on him,
Grown grey from his fear;
And his hour taketh hold on him stricken, the last of his infinite year.

Thought made him and breaks him,
Truth slays and forgives;
But to you, as time takes him,
This new thing it gives,
Even love, the beloved Republic, that feeds upon freedom and lives.

For truth only is living,
Truth only is whole,
And the love of his giving
Man's polestar and pole;
Man, pulse of my centre, and fruit of my body, and seed of my soul.

One birth of my bosom;
One beam of mine eye;
One topmost blossom
That scales the sky;
Man, equal and one with me, man that is made of me, man that is I.

## Before a Crucifix

Here, down between the dusty trees,
   At this lank edge of haggard wood,
Women with labour-loosened knees,
   With gaunt backs bowed by servitude,
Stop, shift their loads, and pray, and fare
Forth with souls easier for the prayer.

The suns have branded black, the rains
   Striped grey this piteous God of theirs;
The face is full of prayers and pains,
   To which they bring their pains and prayers;
Lean limbs that shew the labouring bones,
And ghastly mouth that gapes and groans.

God of this grievous people, wrought
   After the likeness of their race,[o]
By faces like thine own besought,
   Thine own blind helpless eyeless face,
I too, that have nor tongue nor knee
For prayer, I have a word to thee.

It was for this then, that thy speech
   Was blown about the world in flame,
And men's souls shot up out of reach
   Of fear or lust or thwarting shame—
That thy faith over souls should pass
As sea-winds burning the grey grass?

It was for this, that prayers like these
   Should spend themselves about thy feet,
And with hard overlaboured knees
   Kneeling, these slaves of men should beat
Bosoms too lean to suckle sons
And fruitless as their orisons?

It was for this, that men should make
   Thy name a fetter on men's necks,
Poor men's made poorer for thy sake,
   And women's withered out of sex?
It was for this, that slaves should be,
Thy word was passed to set men free?

The nineteenth wave of the ages rolls
   Now deathward since thy death and birth.
Hast thou fed full men's starved-out souls?
   Hast thou brought freedom upon earth?[o]
Or are there less oppressions done
In this wild world under the sun?

Nay, if indeed thou be not dead,
   Before thy terrene shrine be shaken,
Look down, turn usward, bow thine head;
   O thou that wast of God forsaken,
Look on thine household here, and see
These that have not forsaken thee.[o]

Thy faith is fire upon their lips,
   Thy kingdom golden in their hands;
They scourge us with thy words for whips,
   They brand us with thy words for brands;
The thirst that made thy dry throat shrink
To their moist mouths commends the drink.

The toothèd thorns that bit thy brows
   Lighten the weight of gold on theirs;
Thy nakedness enrobes thy spouse
   With the soft sanguine stuff she wears
Whose old limbs use for ointment yet
Thine agony and bloody sweat.

The blinding buffets on thine head
   On their crowned heads confirm the crown;[o]
Thy scourging dyes their raiment red,
   And with thy bands they fasten down
For burial in the blood-bought field[o]
The nations by thy stripes unhealed.[o]

With iron for thy linen bands
   And unclean cloths for winding-sheet
They bind the people's nail-pierced hands,
   They hide the people's nail-pierced feet;
And what man or what angel known
Shall roll back the sepulchral stone?[o]

But these have not the rich man's grave[o]
   To sleep in when their pain is done.
These were not fit for God to save.

As naked hell-fire is the sun
In their eyes living, and when dead
These have not where to lay their head.°

They have no tomb to dig, and hide;
Earth is not theirs, that they should sleep.
On all these tombless crucified
No lovers' eyes have time to weep.
So still, for all man's tears and creeds,
The sacred body hangs and bleeds.

Through the left hand a nail is driven,
Faith, and another through the right,
Forged in the fires of hell and heaven,
Fear that puts out the eye of light:
And the feet soiled and scarred and pale
Are pierced with falsehood for a nail.

And priests against the mouth divine
Push their sponge full of poison° yet
And bitter blood for myrrh and wine,
And on the same reed is it set
Wherewith before they buffeted
The people's disanointed head.

O sacred head, O desecrate,
O labour-wounded feet and hands,
O blood poured forth in pledge to fate
Of nameless lives in divers lands,
O slain and spent and sacrificed
People, the grey-grown speechless Christ!

Is there a gospel in the red
Old witness of thy wide-mouthed wounds?
From thy blind stricken tongueless head
What desolate evangel sounds
A hopeless note of hope deferred?
What word, if there be any word?

O son of man, beneath man's feet
Cast down, O common face of man
Whereon all blows and buffets meet,
O royal, O republican
Face of the people bruised and dumb
And longing till thy kingdom come!°

The soldiers and the high priests part
  Thy vesture: all thy days are priced,
And all the nights that eat thine heart.
  And that one seamless coat of Christ,
The freedom of the natural soul,
They cast their lots for to keep whole.°

No fragment of it save the name
  They leave thee for a crown of scorns
Wherewith to mock thy naked shame
  And forehead bitten through with thorns
And, marked with sanguine sweat and tears,
The stripes of eighteen hundred years.

And we seek yet if God or man
  Can loosen thee as Lazarus,
Bid thee rise up republican°
  And save thyself and all of us;°
But no disciple's tongue can say
When thou shalt take our sins away.°

And mouldering now and hoar with moss
  Between us and the sunlight swings
The phantom of a Christless cross
  Shadowing the sheltered heads of kings
And making with its moving shade
The souls of harmless men afraid.

It creaks and rocks to left and right,
  Consumed of rottenness and rust,
Worm-eaten of the worms of night,
  Dead as their spirits who put trust,
Round its base muttering as they sit,
In the time-cankered name of it.

Thou, in the day that breaks thy prison,
  People, though these men take thy name,
And hail and hymn thee rearisen,
  Who made songs erewhile of thy shame,
Give thou not ear; for these are they
Whose good day was thine evil day.

Set not thine hand unto their cross.
  Give not thy soul up sacrificed.
Change not the gold of faith for dross

  Of Christian creeds that spit on Christ.
Let not thy tree of freedom be
Regrafted from that rotting tree.

This dead God here against my face
  Hath help for no man; who hath seen
The good works of it, or such grace
  As thy grace in it, Nazarene,
As that from thy live lips which ran
For man's sake, O thou son of man?

The tree of faith ingraffed° by priests
  Puts its foul foliage out above thee,
And round it feed man-eating beasts
  Because of whom we dare not love thee;
Though hearts reach back and memories ache,
We cannot praise thee for their sake.

O hidden face of man, whereover
  The years have woven a viewless veil,
If thou wast verily man's lover,
  What did thy love or blood avail?
Thy blood the priests make poison of,
And in gold shekels coin thy love.

So when our souls look back to thee
  They sicken, seeing against thy side,
Too foul to speak of or to see,
  The leprous likeness of a bride,°
Whose kissing lips through his lips grown
Leave their God rotten to the bone.

When we would see thee man, and know
  What heart thou hadst toward men indeed,
Lo, thy blood-blackened altars; lo,
  The lips of priests that pray and feed
While their own hell's worm curls and licks
The poison of the crucifix.

Thou bad'st let children come to thee;°
  What children now but curses come?
What manhood in that God can be
  Who sees their worship, and is dumb?
No soul that lived, loved, wrought, and died,
Is this their carrion crucified.

Nay, if their God and thou be one,
  If thou and this thing be the same,
Thou shouldst not look upon the sun;
  The sun grows haggard at thy name.
Come down, be done with, cease, give o'er;
Hide thyself, strive not, be no more.

# Tenebræ

At the chill high tide of the night,
   At the turn of the fluctuant hours,
When the waters of time are at height,
In a vision arose on my sight
   The kingdoms of earth and the powers.

In a dream without lightening of eyes
   I saw them, children of earth,
Nations and races arise,
Each one after his wise,
   Signed with the sign of his birth.

Sound was none of their feet,
   Light was none of their faces;
In their lips breath was not, or heat,
But a subtle murmur and sweet
   As of water in wan waste places.

Pale as from passionate years,
   Years unassuaged of desire,
Sang they soft in mine ears,
Crowned with jewels of tears,
   Girt with girdles of fire.

A slow song beaten and broken,
   As it were from the dust and the dead,
As of spirits athirst unsloken,[o]
As of things unspeakable spoken,
   As of tears unendurable shed.

In the manifold sound remote,
   In the molten murmur of song,
There was but a sharp sole note
Alive on the night and afloat,
   The cry of the world's heart's wrong.

As the sea in the strait sea-caves,
   The sound came straitened and strange;
A noise of the rending of graves,
A tidal thunder of waves,
   The music of death and of change.

'We have waited so long,' they say,
'For a sound of the God, for a breath,
For a ripple of the refluence of day,
For the fresh bright wind of the fray,
For the light of the sunrise of death.

'We have prayed not, we, to be strong,
To fulfil the desire of our eyes;°
—Howbeit they have watched for it long,
Watched, and the night did them wrong,
Yet they say not of day, shall it rise?

'They are fearful and feeble with years,
Yet they doubt not of day if it be;
Yea, blinded and beaten with tears,
Yea, sick with foresight of fears,
Yet a little, and hardly, they see.

'We pray not, we, for the palm,
For the fruit ingraffed of the fight,
For the blossom of peace and the balm,
And the tender triumph and calm
Of crownless and weaponless right.

'We pray not, we, to behold
The latter august new birth,
The young day's purple and gold,
And divine, and rerisen as of old,
The sun-god of Freedom on earth.

'Peace, and world's honour, and fame,
We have sought after none of these things;
The light of a life like flame
Passing, the storm of a name
Shaking the strongholds of kings:

'Nor, fashioned of fire and of air,
The splendour that burns on his head
Who was chiefest in ages that were,
Whose breath blew palaces bare,
Whose eye shone tyrannies dead:

'All these things in your day
Ye shall see, O our sons, and shall hold
Surely; but we, in the grey
Twilight, for one thing we pray,
In that day though our memories be cold:

'To feel on our brows as we wait
An air of the morning, a breath
From the springs of the east, from the gate
Whence freedom issues, and fate,
Sorrow, and triumph, and death:

'From a land whereon time hath not trod,
Where the spirit is bondless and bare,
And the world's rein breaks, and the rod,
And the soul of a man, which is God,
He adores without altar or prayer:

'For alone of herself and her right
She takes, and alone gives grace:
And the colours of things lose light,
And the forms, in the limitless white
Splendour of space without space:

'And the blossom of man from his tomb
Yearns open, the flower that survives;
And the shadows of changes consume
In the colourless passionate bloom
Of the live light made of our lives:

'Seeing each life given is a leaf
Of the manifold multiform flower,
And the least among these, and the chief,
As an ear in the red-ripe sheaf
Stored for the harvesting hour.

'O spirit of man, most holy,
The measure of things and the root,
In our summers and winters a lowly
Seed, putting forth of them slowly
Thy supreme blossom and fruit;

'In thy sacred and perfect year,
The souls that were parcel of thee
In the labour and life of us here
Shall be rays of thy sovereign sphere,
Springs of thy motion shall be.

'There is the fire that was man,
The light that was love, and the breath
That was hope ere deliverance began,
And the wind that was life for a span,
And the birth of new things, which is death.

'There, whosoever had light,
And, having, for men's sake gave;
All that warred against night;
All that were found in the fight
Swift to be slain and to save;

'Undisbranched of the storms that disroot us,
Of the lures that enthrall unenticed;
The names that exalt and transmute us;
The blood-bright splendour of Brutus,°
The snow-bright splendour of Christ.

'There all chains are undone;
Day there seems but as night;
Spirit and sense are as one
In the light not of star nor of sun;
Liberty there is the light.

'She, sole mother and maker,
Stronger than sorrow, than strife;
Deathless, though death overtake her;
Faithful, though faith should forsake her;
Spirit, and saviour, and life.'

# Cor Cordium

O heart of hearts, the chalice of love's fire,
  Hid round with flowers and all the bounty of bloom;
  O wonderful and perfect heart, for whom
The lyrist liberty made life a lyre;
O heavenly heart, at whose most dear desire
  Dead love, living and singing, cleft his tomb,
  And with him risen and regent in death's room
All day thy choral pulses rang full choir;
O heart whose beating blood was running song,
  O sole thing sweeter than thine own songs were,
    Help us for thy free love's sake to be free,
True for thy truth's sake, for thy strength's sake strong,
  Till very liberty make clean and fair
    The nursing earth as the sepulchral sea.°

## In San Lorenzo

Is thine hour come to wake, O slumbering Night?
  Hath not the Dawn a message in thine ear?
  Though thou be stone and sleep, yet shalt thou hear
When the word falls from heaven—Let there be light.°
Thou knowest we would not do thee the despite
  To wake thee while the old sorrow and shame were near;
  We spake not loud for thy sake, and for fear
Lest thou shouldst lose the rest that was thy right,
The blessing given thee that was thine alone,
The happiness to sleep and to be stone:
  Nay, we kept silence of thee for thy sake
Albeit we knew thee alive, and left with thee
The great good gift to feel not nor to see;
  But will not yet thine Angel bid thee wake?

## On the Downs

A faint sea without wind or sun;
A sky like flameless vapour dun;
  A valley like an unsealed grave
That no man cares to weep upon,
  Bare, without boon to crave,
    Or flower to save.

And on the lip's edge of the down,
Here where the bent-grass burns to brown
  In the dry sea-wind, and the heath
Crawls to the cliff-side and looks down,
  I watch, and hear beneath
    The low tide breathe.

Along the long lines of the cliff,
Down the flat sea-line without skiff
  Or sail or back-blown fume for mark,
Through wind-worn heads of heath and stiff
  Stems blossomless and stark
    With dry sprays dark,

I send mine eyes out as for news
Of comfort that all these refuse,
  Tidings of light or living air
From windward where the low clouds muse
  And the sea blind and bare
    Seems full of care.

So is it now as it was then,
And as men have been such are men.
  There as I stood I seem to stand,
Here sitting chambered, and again
  Feel spread on either hand
    Sky, sea, and land.

As a queen taken and stripped and bound
Sat earth, discoloured and discrowned;
  As a king's palace empty and dead
The sky was, without light or sound;
  And on the summer's head
    Were ashes shed.

Scarce wind enough was on the sea,
Scarce hope enough there moved in me,
  To sow with live blown flowers of white
The green plain's sad serenity,
  Or with stray thoughts of light
    Touch my soul's sight.

By footless ways and sterile went
My thought unsatisfied, and bent
  With blank unspeculative eyes
On the untracked sands of discontent
  Where, watched of helpless skies,
    Life hopeless lies.

East and west went my soul to find
Light, and the world was bare and blind
  And the soil herbless where she trod
And saw men laughing scourge mankind,
  Unsmitten by the rod
    Of any God.

Out of time's blind old eyes were shed
Tears that were mortal, and left dead
  The heart and spirit of the years,
And on man's fallen and helmless head
  Time's disanointing tears
    Fell cold as fears.

Hope flowering had but strength to bear
The fruitless fruitage of despair;
  Grief trod the grapes of joy for wine,
Whereof love drinking unaware
  Died as one undivine
    And made no sign.

And soul and body dwelt apart;
And weary wisdom without heart
  Stared on the dead round heaven and sighed,
'Is death too hollow as thou art
  Or as man's living pride?'
    And saying so died.

And my soul heard the songs and groans
That are about and under thrones,

And felt through all time's murmur thrill
Fate's old imperious semitones
That made of good and ill
One same tune still.

Then 'Where is God? and where is aid?
Or what good end of these?' she said;
'Is there no God or end at all,
Nor reason with unreason weighed,
Nor force to disenthral
Weak feet that fall?

'No light to lighten and no rod
To chasten men? Is there no God?'
So girt with anguish, iron-zoned,°
Went my soul weeping as she trod
Between the men enthroned
And men that groaned.

O fool, that for brute cries of wrong
Heard not the grey glad mother's song
Ring response from the hills and waves,
But heard harsh noises all day long
Of spirits that were slaves
And dwelt in graves.

The wise word of the secret earth
Who knows what life and death are worth,
And how no help and no control
Can speed or stay things come to birth,
Nor all worlds' wheels that roll
Crush one born soul.

With all her tongues of life and death,
With all her bloom and blood and breath,
From all years dead and all things done,
In the ear of man the mother saith,
'There is no God, O son,
If thou be none.'

So my soul sick with watching heard
That day the wonder of that word,
And as one springs out of a dream
Sprang, and the stagnant wells were stirred

Whence flows through gloom and gleam
Thought's soundless stream.

Out of pale cliff and sunburnt heath,
Out of the low sea curled beneath
In the land's bending arm embayed,
Out of all lives that thought hears breathe
Life within life inlaid,
Was answer made.

A multitudinous monotone
Of dust and flower and seed and stone,
In the deep sea-rock's mid-sea sloth,
In the live water's trembling zone,
In all men love and loathe,
One God at growth.

One forceful nature uncreate
That feeds itself with death and fate,
Evil and good, and change and time,
That within all men lies at wait
Till the hour shall bid them climb
And live sublime.

For all things come by fate to flower
At their unconquerable hour,
And time brings truth, and truth makes free,°
And freedom fills time's veins with power,
As, brooding on that sea,
My thought filled me.

And the sun smote the clouds and slew,
And from the sun the sea's breath blew,
And white waves laughed and turned and fled
The long green heaving sea-field through,
And on them overhead
The sky burnt red.

Like a furled flag that wind sets free,
On the swift summer-coloured sea
Shook out the red lines of the light,
The live sun's standard, blown to lee
Across the live sea's white
And green delight.°

And with divine triumphant awe
My spirit moved within me saw,
  With burning passion of stretched eyes,
Clear as the light's own firstborn law,
  In windless wastes of skies
    Time's deep dawn rise.

## An Appeal

Art thou indeed among these,
Thou of the tyrannous crew,
The kingdoms fed upon blood,
O queen from of old of the seas,
England, art thou of them too
That drink of the poisonous flood,
That hide under poisonous trees?

Nay, thy name from of old,
Mother, was pure, or we dreamed;
Purer we held thee than this,
Purer fain would we hold;
So goodly a glory it seemed,
A fame so bounteous of bliss,
So more precious than gold.

A praise so sweet in our ears,
That thou in the tempest of things
As a rock for a refuge shouldst stand,
In the bloodred river of tears
Poured forth for the triumph of kings;
A safeguard, a sheltering land,
In the thunder and torrent of years.

Strangers came gladly to thee,
Exiles,° chosen of men,
Safe for thy sake in thy shade,
Sat down at thy feet and were free.
So men spake of thee then;
Now shall their speaking be stayed?
Ah, so let it not be!

Not for revenge or affright,
Pride, or a tyrannous lust,
Cast from thee the crown of thy praise.
Mercy was thine in thy might;
Strong when thou wert, thou wert just;
Now, in the wrong-doing days,
Cleave thou, thou at least, to the right.

How should one charge thee, how sway,
Save by the memories that were?

Not thy gold nor the strength of thy ships,
Nor the might of thine armies at bay,
Made thee, mother, most fair;
But a word from republican lips
Said in thy name in thy day.

Hast thou said it, and hast thou forgot?
Is thy praise in thine ears as a scoff?
Blood of men guiltless was shed,
Children, and souls without spot,
Shed, but in places far off;
*Let slaughter no more be*, said
Milton; and slaughter was not.°

Was it not said of thee too,
Now, but now, by thy foes,
By the slaves that had slain their France,°
And thee would slay as they slew—
'Down with her walls that enclose
Freemen that eye us askance,
Fugitives, men that are true!'

This was thy praise or thy blame
From bondsman or freeman—to be
Pure from pollution of slaves,
Clean of their sins, and thy name
Bloodless, innocent, free;
Now if thou be not, thy waves
Wash not from off thee thy shame.

Freeman he is not, but slave,
Whoso in fear for the State
Cries for surety of blood,
Help of gibbet and grave;
Neither is any land great
Whom, in her fear-stricken mood,
These things only can save.

Lo, how fair from afar,
Taintless of tyranny, stands
Thy mighty daughter, for years
Who trod the winepress of war;°
Shines with immaculate hands;
Slays not a foe, neither fears;
Stains not peace with a scar.

Be not as tyrant or slave,
England; be not as these,
Thou that wert other than they.
Stretch out thine hand, but to save;°
Put forth thy strength, and release;
Lest there arise, if thou slay,
Thy shame as a ghost from the grave.°

*November 20, 1867.*

# FROM 'SIMEON SOLOMON: NOTES ON HIS "VISION OF LOVE AND OTHER STUDIES"' (1871)

If it may be said with perfect accuracy that in all plastic art, whether the language chosen be of words or forms, of sounds or colours, beauty is the only truth, and nothing not beautiful is true; yet this axiom of a great living artist and critic° must not be so construed as to imply forgetfulness of the manifold and multiform nature of beauty. To one interpreter the terror or the pity° of it, the shadow or the splendour, will appear as its main aspect, as that which gives him his fittest material for work or speech, the substance most pliable to his spirit, the form most suggestive to his hand; to another its simplicity or its mystery, its community or its specialty of gifts. Each servant serves under the compulsion of his own charm; each spirit has its own chain. Upon men in whom there is, so to speak, a compound genius, an intermixture of spiritual forces, a confluence of separate yet conspiring influences, diverse in source yet congruous in result upon men in whose eyes the boundary lines of the several conterminous arts appear less as lines of mere distinction than as lines of mutual alliance the impression of the mystery in all beauty, and in all defects that fall short of it, and in all excesses that overbear it, is likely to have a special hold. The subtle interfusion of art with art, of sound with form, of vocal words with silent colours, is as perceptible to the sense and as inexplicable to the understanding of such men as the interfusion of spirit with flesh is to all men in common; and in fact when perceived of no less significance than this, but rather a part and complement of the same truth. One of such artists, and at once recognisable as such, is Mr Simeon Solomon. There is not, for instance, more of the painter's art in the verse of Keats than of the musician's in Solomon's designs. As surely as the mystery of beauty a mystery 'most glad and sad' as Chaucer says of a woman's mouth° was done into colour of verse for ever unsurpassable in the odes 'To a Nightingale' and on 'Melancholy,' so is the same secret wrought into perfect music of outline by the painter. The 'unheard melodies,' which Keats, with a sense beyond the senses, perceived and enjoyed in the forms of his Grecian urn, vibrate in the forms of this artist's handiwork; and all their lines and colours,

> Not to the sensual ear, but more endeared,
> Pipe to the spirit ditties of no tone.°

Since the first years of his very early and brilliant celebrity° as a young artist of high imaginative power and promise, Mr Solomon has been at work long enough to enable us to define at least certain salient and dominant points of his genius. It holds at once of east and west, of Greek and Hebrew. So much indeed does this fresh interfusion of influences give tone and shape to his imagination that I have heard him likened on this ground to Heine,° as a kindred Hellenist of the Hebrews. Grecian form and beauty divide the allegiance of his spirit with Hebraic shadow and majesty: depths of cloud unsearchable and summits unsurmountable of fire darken and lighten before the vision of a soul enamoured of soft light and clear water, of leaves and flowers and limbs more lovely than these. For no painter has more love of loveliness; but the fair forms of godhead and manhood which in ancient art are purely and merely beautiful rise again under his hand with the likeness on them of a new thing, the shadow of a new sense, the hint of a new meaning; their eyes have seen in sleep or waking, in substance or reflection, some change now past or passing or to come; their lips have tasted a new savour in the wine of life, one strange and alien to the vintage of old; they know of something beyond form and outside of speech. There is a questioning wonder in their faces, a fine joy and a faint sorrow, a trouble as of water stirred, a delight as of thirst appeased. Always, at feast or sacrifice, in chamber or in field, the air and carriage of their beauty has something in it of strange: hardly a figure but has some touch, though never so delicately slight, either of eagerness or of weariness, some note of expectancy or of satiety, some semblance of outlook or inlook: but prospective or introspective, an expression is there which is not pure Greek, a shade or tone of thought or feeling beyond Hellenic contemplation; whether it be oriental or modern in its origin, and derived from national or personal sources. This passionate sentiment of mystery seems at times to 'o'er inform its tenement'° of line and colour, and impress itself even to perplexity upon the sense of the spectator. The various studies, all full of subtleties and beauties definable and not definable, to which the artist has given for commentary the graceful mysticism of a symbolic rhapsody in prose, are also full to overflowing of such sentiment. Read by itself as a fragment of spiritual allegory, this written 'Vision of Love revealed in Sleep' seems to want even that much coherence which is requisite to keep symbolic or allegoric art from absolute dissolution and collapse; that unity of outline and connection of purpose, that gradation of correlative parts and significance of corresponsive details, without which the whole aerial and tremulous fabric of symbolism must decompose into mere confusion of formless and fruitless chaos. Even allegory or prophecy must live and work by rule as well as by rapture; transparent it need not be, but it must be translucent. And translucent the fluctuating twilight of this rhapsody does become in time, with the light behind it of the designs; though at first it seems as hard to distinguish one incarnation of love or sleep or charity from the next following as to disentangle the wings and wheels of

Ezekiel's cherubim,[o] or to discover and determine the respective properties and qualities of Blake's 'emanations' and 'spectres.' The style is soft, fluent, genuinely melodious; it has nothing of inflation or constraint. There is almost a superflux of images full of tender colour and subtle grace, which is sure to lead the writer into some danger of confusion and repetition; and in such vague and uncertain ground any such stumbling-blocks are likely to be especial rocks of offence[o] to the feet of the traveller. Throughout the whole there is as it were a suffusion of music, a transpiration of light and sound, very delicately and surely sustained. There are thoughts and fragments of thoughts, fancies and fantastic symbols, sometimes of rare beauty and singular force; in this for instance, of Night as a mother watching Sleep her child, there is a greater height and sweetness of imagination than in any but the sweetest and highest poetic allegories. 'And she, to whom all was as an open scroll, wept when she looked upon him whose heart was as the heart of a little child.'[o]

The depth[o] and tenderness of this conception of Night, omniscient with the conscience of all things wrought under her shadow, world-wide of sight and sway, and wise with all the world's wisdom, weeping for love over the innocence of her first-born, is great and perfect enough for the noblest verse of a poet. The same affluence and delicacy of emblems interwoven with every part of the allegory is kept up from the first dawn of memory to the last transfiguration of love. There is an exquisite touch in the first vision of Memory standing by the sea-side with the shell held to her ear whose voice 'unburied the dead cycles of the soul,' with autumn leaves showered on head and breast, 'and upon her raiment small flecks of foam had already dried;'[o] this last emblem of the salt small foam-flecks, sharp and arid waifs of the unquiet sea of life, light and bitter strays of barren thought and remembrance with the freshness dried out of them, is beautiful and new. Dim and vague as the atmosphere of such work should be, this vision would be more significant, and not less suggestive of things hidden in secret places of spiritual reserve, if it had more body of drawing, more shapeliness of thought and fixity of outline. Not that we would seek for solidity in shadow, or blame the beauty of luminous clouds for confusion of molten outlines; but even in cloud there is some law of form, some continuous harmony of line and mass, that only dissolves and changes 'as a tune into a tune.'[o] To invigorate and support this fair frame of allegory there should be some clearer infusion of a purpose; there should be some thread of clearer connection, some filament, though never so slender, to link vision again to vision, some clue, 'as subtle as Arachne's broken woof,'[o] to lead the reader's perception through the labyrinth of sounds and shapes. Each new revelation and change of aspect has beauty and meaning of its own; but even in a dream the steps of progress seem clearer than here, and the process from stage to stage of action or passion is ruled after some lawless law and irrational reason of its own. Such process as this at least we might hope to find even in the records of allegoric vision; in this mystery or tragedy of the passion of a divine sufferer 'wounded in the house of his friends'° and bleeding from the hands of men, those who follow the track of his pilgrimage might desire at least to be shown the stations of his cross.° We miss the thread of union between the varying visions of love forsaken and shamed, wounded and forgotten; of guileless and soulless pleasure in its naked and melodious maidenhood, and passion that makes havoc of love, and after that even of itself also; of death and silence, and of sleep and time. Many of these have in them the sweetness and depth of good dreams, and much subtle and various beauty; and had we but some clue to the gradations of its course, we might thread our way through the Daedalian maze° with a free sense of gratitude to the artificer whose cunning reared it to hide no monstrous thing, but one of divine likeness. It might have been well to issue with the text some further reproductions of the designs: those especially of the wounded Love from whose heart's blood the roses break into blossom, of Desire with body and raiment dishevelled and deformed from self-inflicted strokes, of Divine Charity bearing Sleep down to the dark earth among men that suffer, of Love upborne by the strong arms and wings of Time, of the spirit that watches in the depth of its crystal sphere the mutable reflections of the world and the revolutions of its hidden things; all designs full of mystical attraction and passion, of bitter sweetness and burning beauty.

Outside the immediate cycle of this legend of love divine and human, the artist has done much other work of a cognate kind; his sketches and studies in this line have always the charm of a visible enjoyment in the vigorous indulgence of a natural taste and power. One of these, a noble study of 'Sleepers and One that Watches,' has been translated into verse of kindred strength and delicacy, in three fine sonnets of high rank among the clear-cut and exquisite 'Intaglios' of Mr John Payne.° But the artist is not a mere cloud-compeller,° a dreamer on the wing who cannot use his feet for good travelling purpose on hard ground; witness the admirable picture of Roman ladies at a show of gladiators, exhibited in 1865, which remains still his masterpiece of large dramatic realism and live imagination.° All the heads are full of personal force and character, especially the woman's with heavy brilliant hair and glittering white skin, like hard smooth snow against the sunlight, the delicious thirst and subtle raving of sensual hunger for blood visibly enkindled in every line of the sweet fierce features. Mr Solomon apparently has sufficient sense of physiology to share the theory which M. Alphonse Karr° long since proposed to develope at length in a systematic treatise 'sur la férocité des blondes.' The whole spirit of this noble picture is imbued with the proper tragic beauty and truth and terror. [...]

# 'TRISTRAM AND ISEULT: PRELUDE OF AN UNFINISHED POEM' (1871)

Love, that is first and last of all things made,
The light that moving has man's life for shade,
The spirit that for temporal veil has on
The souls of all men woven in unison,
One fiery raiment with all lives inwrought
And lights of sunny and starry deed and thought,
And alway through new act and passion new
Shines the divine same body and beauty through,
The body spiritual of fire and light
That is to worldly noon as noon to night;
Love, that is flesh upon the spirit of man
And spirit within the flesh whence breath began;
Love, that keeps all the choir of lives in chime;
Love, that is blood within the veins of time;
That wrought the whole world without stroke of hand,
Shaping the breadth of sea, the length of land,
And with the pulse and motion of his breath
Through the great heart of the earth strikes life and death,
The sweet twain chords that make the sweet time live
Through day and night of things alternative,
Through silence and through sound of stress and strife,
And ebb and flow of dying death and life;
Love, that sounds loud or light in all men's ears,
Whence all men's eyes take fire from sparks of tears;
That binds on all men's feet or chains or wings,
Love that is root and fruit of terrene things;
Love, that the whole world's waters shall not drown,
The whole world's fiery forces not burn down;
Love, that what time his own hands guard his head
The whole world's wrath and strength shall not strike dead;
Love, that if once his own hands make his grave
The whole world's pity and sorrow shall not save;
Love, that for every life shall not be sold,
Nor bought nor bound with iron nor with gold;
So strong that heaven, could love bid heaven farewell,
Would turn to fruitless and unflowering hell;
So sweet that hell, to hell could love be given,
Would turn to splendid and sonorous heaven.
Love that is fire within thee and light above,
And lives by grace of nothing but of love;
Through many and lovely thoughts and much desire
Led these twain to the life of tears and fire;
Through many and lovely days and much delight

Led these twain to the lifeless life of night.
   Yea, but what then? albeit all this were thus,
And soul smote soul and left it ruinous,
And love led love as eyeless men lead men,
Through chance by chance to deathward,—Ah, what then?
Hath love not likewise led them further yet,
Out through the years where memories rise and set,
Some large as suns, some moon-like warm and pale,
Some starry-sighted, some through, clouds that sail
Seen as red flame through spectral float of fume,
Each with the blush of its own special bloom
On the fair face of its own coloured light,
Distinguishable in all the host of night,
Divisible from all the radiant rest
And separable in splendour? Hath the best
Light of love's all, of all that burn and move,
A better heaven than heaven is? Hath not love
Made for all these their sweet particular air
To shine in, their own beams and names to bear,
Their ways to wander and their wards to keep,
Till story and song and glory and all things sleep?
Hath he not plucked from death of lovers dead
Their musical sweet memories, and kept red
The rose of their remembrance in men's eyes,
The sunsets of their stories in his skies,
The blush of their dead blood in lips that speak
Of their dead lives, and in the listener's cheek
That trembles with the kindling pity lit
In gracious hearts for a sweet fever-fit,
A fiery pity enkindled of pure thought
By tales that make their honey out of nought,
The faithless faith that lives without belief
Its light life through, the griefless ghost of grief?
Yea, as warm night refashions the sere blood
In storm-struck petal or in sun-struck bud,
With tender hours and tempering dew to cure
The hunger and thirst of day's distemperature
And ravin of the dry discolouring hours,
Hath he not bid relume° their flameless flowers
With summer fire and heat of lamping song,
And bid the short-lived things, long dead, live long,
And thought remake their wan funereal fames,
And the sweet shining signs of women's names

That mark the months out and the weeks anew
He moves in changeless change of seasons through
To make the days up of his dateless year,
Flame from Queen Helen to Queen Guenevere?
For first of all the spherèd signs whereby
Love severs light from darkness, and most high
In the white front of January there glows
The rose-red sign of Helen° like a rose:
And gold-eyed as the shore-flower shelterless
Whereon the sharp-breathed sea blows bitterness,
A storm-star that the seafarers of love
Strain their wind-wearied eyes for glimpses of,
Shoots keen through February's grey frost and damp
The lamp-like star of Hero for a lamp;
The star that Marlowe° sang into our skies
With mouth of gold, and morning in his eyes;
And in clear March across the rough blue sea
The spherèd sapphire of Alcyone°
Makes bright the blown brows of the wind-foot year;
And shining like a sunbeam-smitten tear
Full ere it fall, the fair next sign in sight
Burns opal-wise with April-coloured light
When air is quick with song and rain and flame,
My birth-month° star that in love's heaven hath name
Iseult, a light of blossom and beam and shower,
My Singing sign that makes the song-tree flower;
Next like a pale and burning pearl beyond
The rose-white sphere of flower-named Rosamond°
Signs the sweet head of Maytime; and for June
Flares like an angered and storm-reddening moon
Her signal sphere, whose Carthaginian pyre
Shadowed her traitor's flying sail with fire;°
Next, glittering as the wine-bright jacinth-stone,
A star south-risen that first to music shone,
The keen girl-star of golden Juliet bears
Light northward to the month whose forehead wears
Her name for flower upon it, and his trees
Mix their deep English song with Veronese;°
And like an awful sovereign chrysolite
Burning, the supreme fire that blinds the night
The hot gold head of Venus kissed by Mars,
A sun-flower among small sphered flowers of stars,
The light of Cleopatra° fills and burns

The hollow of heaven whence ardent August yearns;
And fixed and shining as the sister-shed
Sweet tears for Phaethon° disorbed and dead,
The pale bright autumn's amber-coloured sphere,
That through September sees the saddening year
As love sees change through sorrow, hath to name
Francesca's;° and the star that watches flame
The embers of the harvest overgone
Is Thisbe's,° slain of love in Babylon,
Set in the golden girdle of sweet signs
A blood-bright ruby; last save one light shines
An eastern wonder of sphery chrysopras,
The star that made men mad, Angelica's;
And latest named and lordliest, with a sound
Of swords and harps in heaven that ring it round,
Last love-light and last love-song of the year's,
Gleams like a glorious emerald Guenevere's.
These are the signs wherethrough the year sees move,
Full of the sun, the sun-god which is love,
A fiery body blood-red from the heart
Outward, with fire-white wings made wide apart,
That close not and unclose not, but upright
Steered without wind by their own light and might,
Sweep through the flameless fire of air that rings
From heaven to heaven with thunder of wheels and wings
And antiphones of motion-moulded rhyme
Through spaces out of space and timeless time.
 So shine above dead chance and conquered change
The spherèd signs, and leave without their range
Doubt and desire, and hope with fear for wife,
Pale pains, and pleasures long worn out of life.
Yea, even the shadows of them spiritless,
Through the dim door of sleep that seem to press,
Forms without form, a piteous people and blind,
Men and no men, whose lamentable kind
The shadow of death and shadow of life compel
Through semblances of heaven and false-faced hell,
Through dreams of light and dreams of darkness tost
On waves unnavigable, are these so lost?
Shapes that wax pale and shift in swift strange wise,
Void faces with unspeculative eyes,
Dim things that gaze and glare, dead mouths that move,
Featureless heads discrowned of hate and love,

Mockeries and masks of motion and mute breath,
Leavings of life, the superflux of death—
If these things and no more than these things be
Left when man ends or changes, who can see?
Or who can say with what more subtle sense
Their subtler natures taste in air less dense
A life less thick and palpable than ours,
Warmed with faint fires and sweetened with dead flowers
And measured by low music? how time fares
In that wan time-forgotten world of theirs,
Their pale poor world too deep for sun or star
To live in, where the eyes of Helen are,
And hers° who made as God's own eyes to shine
The eyes that met them of the Florentine,
Eyes heavenly ere they knew her, but when they knew
Heavenly past name of heaven their godhead grew,
Grew great and waxed and wonderfully lit°
All time for all men with the shadow of it;
Ah, and those too felt on them as God's grace
The pity and glory of this man's breathing face—
For these too, these my lovers, these my twain,
Saw Dante,° saw God visible by pain,
With lips that thundered and with feet that trod
Before men's eyes incognisable God—
Saw love and wrath and light and night and fire
Live with one life and at one mouth respire,
And in one golden sound their whole soul heard
Sounding, one sweet immitigable word.
  They have the night, who had like us the day;
We, whom day binds, shall have the night as they.
We, from the fetters of the light unbound,
Healed of our wound of living, shall sleep sound.
All gifts but one the jealous God may keep
From our soul's longing, one he cannot—sleep.
This, though he grudge all other grace to prayer,
This grace his closed hand cannot choose but spare.
This, though his ear be sealed to all that live,
Be it lightly given or lothly, God must give.
We, as the men our memory sleeps upon,
We too shall surely pass out of the sun;
Out of the sound and eyeless light of things,
Wide as the stretch of life's time-wandering wings,
Wide as the naked world and shadowless,

And long-lived as the world's own weariness.
Us too, when all the fires of time are cold,
The heights shall hide us and the depths shall hold.
Us too, when all the tears of time are dry,
The night shall lighten from her tearless eye.
Blind is the day and eyeless all its light,
But the large unbewildered eye of night
Hath sense and speculation; and the sheer
Limitless length of lifeless life and clear,
The timeless space wherein the brief worlds move
Clothed with light life and fruitful with light love,
With hopes that threaten, and with fears that cease,
Past fear and hope, hath in it only peace.
  Yet of these lives inlaid with hopes and fears,
Spun fine as fire and jewelled thick with tears,
These lives made out of loves that long since were,
Lives made as ours of earth and burning air,
Fugitive flame, and water of secret springs,
And clothed with joys and sorrows as with wings,
Some yet are good, if aught be good, to save
Some while from washing wreck and wrecking wave.
Was such not theirs, the twain I take, and give
Out of my life to make their dead life live
Some days of mine, and blow my living breath
Between the lips for their sake of their death?°
So many and many ere me have given my twain
Love and live song and honey-hearted pain,
Whose root is sweetness and whose fruit is sweet,
So many and with such joy have tracked their feet,
What should I do to follow? yet I too,
I have the heart to follow, many or few
Be the feet gone before me; for the way,
Rose-red with remnant roses of the day
Westward, and eastward white with stars that break,
Between the green and foam is fair to take
For any sail the sea-wind steers for me
From morning into morning, sea to sea.

# FROM 'VICTOR HUGO'S *L'ANNÉE TERRIBLE*' (1872)

[...] A poem having in it any element of greatness is likely to arouse many questions with regard to the poetic art in general, and certain in that case to illustrate them with fresh lights of its own. This of Victor Hugo's at once suggests two points of frequent and fruitless debate between critics of the higher kind. The first, whether poetry and politics are irreconcilable or not; the second, whether art should prefer to deal with things immediate or with things remote. Upon both sides of either question it seems to me that even wise men have ere now been led from errors of theory to errors of decision. The well-known formula of art for art's sake, opposed as it has ever been to the practice of the poet who was so long credited with its authorship,° has like other doctrines a true side to it and an untrue. Taken as an affirmative, it is a precious and everlasting truth. No work of art has any worth or life in it that is not done on the absolute terms of art; that is not before all things and above all things a work of positive excellence as judged by the laws of the special art to whose laws it is amenable. If the rules and conditions of that art be not observed, or if the work done be not great and perfect enough to rank among its triumphs, the poem, picture, statue, is a failure irredeemable and inexcusable by any show or any proof of high purpose and noble meaning. The rule of art is not the rule of morals; in morals the action is judged by the intention, the doer is applauded, excused, or condemned, according to the motive which induced his deed; in art, the one question is not what you mean but what you do. Therefore, as I have said elsewhere, the one primary requisite of art is artistic worth; 'art for art's sake first, and then all things shall be added to her°—or if not, it is a matter of quite secondary importance; but from him that has not this one indispensable quality of the artist, shall be taken away even that which he has; whatever merit of aspiration, sentiment, sincerity, he may naturally possess, admirable and serviceable as in other lines of work it might have been and yet may be, is here unprofitable and unpraiseworthy.' Thus far we are at one with the preachers of 'art for art;' we prefer for example Goethe to Körner and Sappho to Tyrtæus;° we would give many patriots for one artist, considering that civic virtue is more easily to be had than lyric genius, and that the hoarse monotony of verse lowered to the level of a Spartan understanding, however commendable such verse may be for the doctrine delivered and the duty inculcated upon all good citizens, is of less than no value to art, while there is a value beyond price and beyond thought in the

Lesbian music° which spends itself upon the record of fleshly fever and amorous malady. We admit then that the worth of a poem has properly nothing to do with its moral meaning or design; that the praise of a Caesar as sung by Virgil, of a Stuart as sung by Dryden, is preferable to the most magnanimous invective against tyranny which love of country and of liberty could wring from a Bavius or a Shadwell;° but on the other hand we refuse to admit that art of the highest kind may not ally itself with moral or religious passion, with the ethics or the politics of a nation or an age. It does not detract from the poetic supremacy of Æschylus and of Dante, of Milton and of Shelley, that they should have been pleased to put their art to such use; nor does it detract from the sovereign greatness of other poets that they should have had no note of song for any such theme. In a word, the doctrine of art for art is true in the positive sense, false in the negative; sound as an affirmation, unsound as a prohibition. If it be not true that the only absolute duty of art is the duty she owes to herself, then must art be dependent on the alien conditions of subject and of aim; whereas she is dependent on herself alone, and on nothing above her or beneath; by her own law she must stand or fall, and to that alone she is responsible; by no other law can any work of art be condemned, by no other plea can it be saved. But while we refuse to any artist on any plea the license to infringe in the least article the letter of this law, to overlook or overpass it in the pursuit of any foreign purpose, we do not refuse to him the liberty of bringing within the range of it any subject that under these conditions may be so brought and included within his proper scope of work. This liberty the men who take 'art for art' as their motto, using the words in an exclusive sense, would refuse to concede. They see with perfect clearness and accuracy that art can never be a 'handmaid'° of any 'lord,' as the moralist, pietist, or politician would fain have her be, and therefore they will not allow that she can properly be even so much as an ally of anything else. So on the one side we have the judges who judge of art by her capacity to serve some other good end than the production of good work; these would leave us for instance *King John*, but would assuredly deprive us of *As You Like It*; the national devotion and patriotic fire of *King Henry V* would suffice in their estimation to set it far above the sceptic and inconclusive meditations of *Hamlet*, the pointless and aimless beauty of *A Midsummer Night's Dream*. On the other side we have the judges who would ostracise every artist found guilty of a moral sense, of the political faith or the religious emotion of patriots and heroes; whose theory would raze the Persæ from the scroll of Æschylus, and leave us nothing of Dante but the Vita Nuova,° of Milton but the Allegro and Penseroso, of Shelley but the Skylark and the Cloud. In consistency the one order of fanatics would expel from the poetic commonwealth such citizens as Coleridge and Keats, the other would disfranchise such as Burns and Byron. The simple truth is that the question at issue between them is that illustrated by the old child's parable of the gold and silver shield. Art is one, but the service of art is diverse. It is equally foolish to demand of a Goethe, a Keats, or a Coleridge, the proper and natural work of a Dante, a Milton, or a Shelley, as to invert the demand; to arraign the Divina Commedia in the name of Faust, the Sonnet on the Massacres in Piedmont in the name of the Ode on a Grecian Urn, or the Ode to Liberty in the name of Kubla Khan. I know nothing stranger in the history of criticism than the perversity even of eminent and exquisite critics in persistent condemnation of one great artist for his deficiency in the qualities of another. It is not that critics of the higher kind expect to gather grapes of thorns or figs of thistles; but they are too frequently surprised and indignant that they cannot find grapes on a fig-tree or figs on a vine. M. Auguste Vacquerie° has remarked before me on this unreasonable expectation and consequent irritation of the critical mind, with his usual bright and swift sense of the truth—a quality which we are sure to find when a good artist has occasion to speak of his own art and the theories current with respect to it. In this matter proscription and prescription are alike unavailing; it is equally futile to bid an artist forego the natural bent of his genius or to bid him assume the natural office of another. If the spirit or genius proper to himself move him for instance to write political poetry, he will write it; if it bid him abstain from any such theme and write only on personal or ideal subjects, then also he will obey; or if ever he attempt to force his genius into unnatural service, constrain it to some alien duty, the most praiseworthy purpose imaginable will not suffice to put life or worth into the work so done. Art knows nothing of choice between the two kinds or preference of the one to the other; she asks only that the artist shall 'follow his star' with the faith and the fervour of Dante, whether it lead him on a path like or unlike the way of Dante's work; the ministers of either tribe, the savours of either sacrifice, are equally excellent in her sight.

The question whether past or present afford the highest matter for high poetry and offer the noblest reward to the noble workman has been as loudly and as long debated, but is really less debateable on any rational ground than the question of the end and aim of art. It is but lost labour that the champions on one side summon us to renounce the present and all its works,° and return to bathe our spirits in the purer air and living springs of the past; it is but waste of breath for the champions of the other party to bid us break the yoke and cast off the bondage of that past, leave the dead to bury their dead,° and turn from the dust and rottenness of old-world themes, epic or romantic, classical or feudal, to face the age wherein we live and move and have our being,° to send forth our souls and songs in search of the wonderful and doubtful future. Art knows nothing of time; for her there is but one tense, and all ages in her sight are alike present; there is nothing old in her sight, and nothing new. It is true, as the one side urges, that she fears not to face the actual aspect of the hour, to handle if it please her the immediate matters of the day; it is true, as the other side insists, that she is free to go back when she will to the very beginnings of tradition and fetch her subject from the furthest of ancient days; she cannot be vulgarised by the touch of the present or deadened by the contact of the past. In vain, for instance, do the first poetess of England and the first poet of America° agree to urge upon their fellows or their followers the duty of confronting and expressing the spirit and the secret of their own time, its meaning and its need; such work is worthy of a poet, but no worthier than any other work that has in it the principle of life.° And a poem of the past, if otherwise as good, has in it as much of this principle as a poem of the present. If a poem cast in the mould of classic or feudal times, of Greek drama° or mediæval romance, be lifeless and worthless, it is not because the subject or the form was ancient, but because the poet was inadequate to his task, incompetent to do better than a flat and feeble imitation; had he been able to fill the old types of art with new blood and breath, the remoteness of subject and the antiquity of form would in no wise have impaired the worth and reality of his work; he would have brought close to us the far-off loveliness and renewed for us the ancient life of his models, not by mechanical and servile transcript as of a copying clerk, but by loving and reverent emulation as of an original fellow-craftsman. No form is obsolete, no subject out of date, if the right man be there to rehandle it. To the question 'Can these bones live?' there is but one answer. If the spirit and breath of art be breathed upon them indeed, and the voice prophesying upon them be indeed the voice of a prophet, then assuredly will the bones 'come together, bone to his bone;'° and the sinews and the flesh will come up upon them, and the skin cover them above, and the breath come into them, and they will live. For art is very life itself, and knows nothing of death; she is absolute truth, and takes no care of fact; she sees that Achilles and Ulysses are even now more actual by far than Wellington and Talleyrand;° not merely more noble and more interesting as types and figures, but more positive and real; and thus it is (as Victor Hugo has himself so finely instanced it) 'that Trimalchio is alive, while the late M. Romieu is dead.'° Vain as is the warning of certain critics to beware of the present and abstain from its immediate vulgarities and realities, not less vain, however nobly meant or nobly worded, is the counter admonition to 'mistrust the poet' who 'trundles back his soul' some centuries to sing of chiefs and ladies 'as dead as must be, for the greater part, the poems made on their heroic bones;'° for if he be a poet indeed, these will at once be reclothed with instant flesh and reinspired with immediate breath, as present and as true, as palpable and as precious, as anything most near and real; and if the heroic bones be still fleshless and the heroic poems lifeless, the fault is not in the bones but in the poems, not in the theme but in the singer. As vain it is, not indeed to invite the muse to new spheres and fresher fields whither also she will surely and gladly come, but to bid her 'migrate from Greece and Ionia, cross out those immensely overpaid accounts, that matter of Troy, and Achilles' wrath, and Æneas', Odysseus' wanderings;'° forsake her temples and castles of old for the new quarters which doubtless, also suit her well and make her welcome; for neither epic nor romance of chivalrous quest or classic war is obsolete yet, or ever can be; there is nothing in the past extinct; no scroll is 'closed for ever,'° no legend or vision of Hellenic or feudal faith 'dissolved utterly like an exhalation:'° all that ever had life in it has life in it for ever; those themes only are dead which never were other than dead. 'She has left them all, and is here;'° so the prophet of the new world vaunts himself in vain; she is there indeed, as he says, 'by thud of machinery and shrill steam-whistle undismayed—smiling and pleased, with palpable intent to stay;'° but she has not needed for that to leave her old abodes; she is not a dependent creature of time or place, 'servile to all the skiey influences;'° she need not climb mountains or cross seas to bestow on all nations at once the light of her countenance;° she is omnipresent and eternal, and forsakes neither Athens nor Jerusalem, Camelot nor Troy, Argonaut nor Crusader, to dwell as she does with equal good-will among modern appliances in London and New York. All times and all places are one to her; the stuff she deals with is eternal, and eternally the same; no time or theme is inapt for her, no past or present preferable.

We do not therefore rate this present book higher or lower because it deals with actual politics and matter of the immediate day. It is true that to all who put their faith and hope in the republican principle it must bring comfort and encouragement, a sense of strength and a specialty of pleasure, quite apart from the delight in its beauty and power; but it is not on this ground that we would base its claim to the reverent study and thankful admiration of men. The first and last thing to be noted in it is the fact of its artistic price and poetic greatness. Those who share the faith and the devotion of the writer have of course good reason to rejoice that the first poet of a great age, the foremost voice of a great nation, should speak for them in the ears of the world; that the highest poetry of their time should take up the cause they have at heart, and set their belief to music. To have with us Victor Hugo in the present as we have Milton and Shelley in the past is not a matter to be lightly prized. Whether or not we may be at one with the master-singer on all points is a matter of less weight; whether we have learnt to look to Rome or to Paris, regenerate and redeemed from imperial or sacerdotal damnation, for the future light and model of republican Europe,° we can receive with equal sympathy the heroic utterance of the greatest Frenchman's trust in the country and the city of the Revolution. Not now, after so many days of darkness, after so many stages of terror and pity, can any lover of France be inclined to cavil at the utmost expression of loyalty, the utmost passion of worship, which the first of her sons may offer in the time of her sore need. [...]

## FROM *BOTHWELL: A TRAGEDY*, Act 5, sc. 13

The Shore of Solway Firth. [16 May 1568]

*The* QUEEN, MARY BEATON, HERRIES, GEORGE DOUGLAS, *Page and Attendants.*

QUEEN

Is not the tide yet full?

HERRIES

Come half an hour,
And it will turn; but ere that ebb begin,
Let me once more desire your pardon, though
I plead against your pleasure. Here you stand
Not yet dethroned from royal hope, not yet
Discrowned of your great name, whose natural power
Faith here forgets not, nor man's loyal love
Leaves off to honour; but gone hence, your name
Is but a stranger's, subject to men's laws,
Alien and liable to control and chance
That are the lords of exile, and command
The days and nights of fugitives; your hope
Dies of strange breath or lives between strange lips,
And nor your will nor only God's beside
Is master of your peace of life, but theirs
Who being the lords of land that harbours you
Give your life leave to endure their empire: what
Can man do to you that a rebel may,
Which fear might deem as bad as banishment?
Not death, not bonds are bitterer than his day
On whom the sun looks forth of a strange sky,
Whose thirst drinks water from strange hands, whose lips
Eat stranger's bread for hunger; who lies down
In a strange dark and sleeps not, and the light
Makes his eyes weep for their own morning, seen
On hills that helped to make him man, and fields

Whose flowers grew round his heart's root; day like night
Denies him, and the stars and airs of heaven
Are as their eyes and tongues who know him not.
Go not to banishment; the world is great,
But each has but his own land in the world.
There is one bosom that gives each man milk,
One country like one mother: none sleeps well
Who lies between strange breasts; no lips drink life
That seek it from strange fosters. Go not hence;
You shall find no man's faith or love on earth
Like theirs that here cleave to you.

QUEEN

I have found
And think to find no hate of men on earth
Like theirs that here beats on me. Hath this earth
Which sent me forth a five-years' child,° and queen
Not even of mine own sorrows, to come back°
A widowed girl out of the fair warm sun
Into the grave's mouth of a dolorous land
And life like death's own shadow, that began
With three day's darkness—hath this earth of yours
That made mine enemies, at whose iron breast
They drank the milk of treason—this hard nurse,
Whose rocks and storms have reared no violent thing
So monstrous as men's angers, whose wild minds
Were fed from hers and fashioned—this that bears
None but such sons as being my friends are weak,
And strong, being most my foes—hath it such grace
As I should cling to, or such virtue found
In some part of its evil as my heart
Should fear, being free, to part from? Have I lived,
Since I came here in shadow and storm, three days
Out of the storm and shadow? Have I seen
Such rest, such hope, such respite from despair,
As thralls and prisoners in strong darkness may
Before the light look on them? Hath there come
One chance on me of comfort, one poor change,
One possible content that was not born
Of hope to break forth of these bonds, or made
Of trust in foreign fortune? Here, I knew,
Could never faith nor love nor comfort breed
While I sat fast in prison; ye, my friends,

The few men and the true men that were mine,
What were ye but what I was, and what help
Hath each love had of other, yours of mine,
Mine of your faith, but change of fight and flight,
Fear and vain hope and ruin? Let me go,
Who have been but grief and danger to my friends;
It may be I shall come with power again
To give back all their losses, and build up
What for my sake was broken.

HERRIES

Did I know it,
Yet were I loth to bid you part, and find
What there you go to seek; but knowing it not,
My heart sinks in me and my spirit is sick
To think how this fair foot once parted hence
May rest thus light on Scottish ground no more.

QUEEN

It shall tread heavier when it steps again
On earth which now rejects it; I shall live
To bruise their heads who wounded me at heel,°
When I shall set it on their necks. Come, friends,
I think the fisher's boat hath hoised up sail
That is to bear none but one friend and me:
Here must my true men and their queen take leave,
And each keep thought of other. My fair page,
Before the man's change darken on your chin
I may come back to ride with you at rein
To a more fortunate field: howe'er that be,
Ride you right on with better hap, and live
As true to one of merrier days than mine
As on that night to Mary once your queen.
Douglas, I have not won a word of you;
What would you do to have me tarry?

GEORGE DOUGLAS

Die.

QUEEN

I lack not love it seems then at my last
That word was bitter; yet I blame it not,
Who would not have sweet words upon my lips

Nor in mine ears at parting. I should go
And stand not here as on a stage to play
My last part out in Scotland; I have been
Too long a queen too little. By my life,
I know not what should hold me here or turn
My foot back from the boat-side, save the thought
How at Lochleven I last set foot aboard,
And with what hope, and to what end; and now
I pass not out of prison to my friends,
But out of all friends' help to banishment.
Farewell, Lord Herries.

HERRIES

God go with my queen,
And bring her back with better friends than I.

QUEEN

Methinks the sand yet cleaving to my foot
Should not with no more words be shaken off,
Nor this my country from my parting eyes
Pass unsaluted; for who knows what year
May see us greet hereafter? Yet take heed,
Ye that have ears, and hear me; and take note,
Ye that have eyes, and see with what last looks
Mine own take leave of Scotland; seven years since
Did I take leave of my fair land of France,
My joyous mother, mother of my joy,
Weeping; and now with many a woe between
And space of seven years' darkness, I depart
From this distempered and unnatural earth
That casts me out unmothered, and go forth
On this grey sterile bitter gleaming sea
With neither tears nor laughter, but a heart
That from the softest temper of its blood
Is turned to fire and iron. If I live,
If God pluck not all hope out of my hand,
If aught of all mine prosper, I that go
Shall come back to men's ruin, as a flame
The wind bears down, that grows against the wind,
And grasps it with great hands, and wins its way,
And wins its will, and triumphs; so shall I
Let loose the fire of all my heart to feed
On these that would have quenched it I will make

From sea to sea one furnace of the land
Whereon the wind of war shall beat its wings
Till they wax faint with hopeless hope of rest,
And with one rain of men's rebellious blood
Extinguish the red embers. I will leave
No living soul of their blaspheming faith
Who war with monarchs; God shall see me reign
As he shall reign beside me, and his foes
Lie at my foot with mine; kingdoms and kings
Shall from my heart take spirit, and at my soul
Their souls be kindled to devour for prey
The people that would make its prey of them
And leave God's altar stripped of sacrament
As all king's heads of sovereignty, and make
Bare as their thrones his temples; I will set
Those old things of his holiness on high
That are brought low, and break beneath my feet
These new things of men's fashion; I will sit
And see tears flow from eyes that saw me weep
And dust and ashes and the shadow of death
Cast from the block beneath the axe that falls
On heads that saw me humbled; I will do it,
Or bow mine own down to no royal end
And give my blood for theirs if God's will be,
But come back never as I now go forth
With but the hate of men to track my way
And not the face of any friend alive.

MARY BEATON

But I will never leave you till you die.

# FROM *SONGS OF TWO NATIONS* (1875)

# *From* Diræ

## VII. Celæno

The blind king hides his weeping eyeless head,
Sick with the helpless hate and shame and awe,
Till food have choked the glutted hell-bird's craw
And the foul cropful creature lie as dead
And soil itself with sleep and too much bread:
So the man's life serves under the beast's law,
And things whose spirit lives in mouth and maw
Share shrieking the soul's board and soil her bed,
Till man's blind spirit, their sick slave, resign
Its kingdom to the priests whose souls are swine,
And the scourged serf lie reddening from their rod,
Discrowned, disrobed, dismantled, with lost eyes
Seeking where lurks in what conjectural skies
That triple-headed hound of hell their God.°

## VIII. A Choice

Faith is the spirit that makes man's body and blood
Sacred, to crown when life and death have ceased
His heavenward head for high fame's holy feast;
But as one swordstroke swift as wizard's rod
Made Cæsar carrion and made Brutus God,
Faith false or true, born patriot or born priest,
Smites into semblance or of man or beast
The soul that feeds on clean or unclean food.
Lo here the faith that lives on its own light,
Visible music; and lo there, the foul
Shape without shape, the harpy throat and howl.
Sword of the spirit of man! arise and smite,
And sheer through throat and claw and maw and tongue
Kill the beast faith that lives on its own dung.

## IX. The Augurs

Lay the corpse out on the altar; bid the elect
Slaves clear the ways of service spiritual,
Sweep clean the stalled soul's serviceable stall,
Ere the chief priest's° dismantling hands detect

The ulcerous flesh of faith all scaled and specked
  Beneath the bandages that hid it all,
  And with sharp edgetools œcumenical
The leprous carcases of creeds dissect.
As on the night ere Brutus grew divine
The sick-souled augurs found their ox or swine
  Heartless;° so now too by their after art
In the same Rome, at an uncleaner shrine,
  Limb from rank limb, and putrid part from part,
  They carve the corpse a beast without a heart.

## X. A Counsel

O strong Republic of the nobler years
  Whose white feet shine beside time's fairer flood
  That shall flow on the clearer for our blood
Now shed, and the less brackish for our tears;
When time and truth have put out hopes and fears
  With certitude, and love has burst the bud,
  If these whose powers then down the wind shall scud
Still live to feel thee smite their eyes and ears,
When thy foot's tread hath crushed their crowns and creeds,
Care thou not then to crush the beast that bleeds,
  The snake whose belly cleaveth to the sod,
Nor set thine heel on men as on their deeds;°
  But let the worm Napoleon crawl untrod,
  Nor grant Mastai the gallows of his God.

1869.

# FROM 'REPORT OF THE FIRST ANNIVERSARY MEETING OF THE NEWEST SHAKESPEARE SOCIETY: 1 APRIL 1876' (1876/1880)

A paper was read by Mr A. on the disputed authorship of *A Midsummer Night's Dream*. He was decidedly of opinion that this play was to be ascribed to George Chapman. He based this opinion principally on the ground of style. From its similarity of subject he had at first been disposed to assign it to Cyril Tourneur, author of *The Revenger's Tragedy*;° and he had drawn up in support of this theory a series of parallel passages extracted from the speeches of Vindice in that drama and of Oberon in the present play. He pointed out however that the character of Puck could hardly have been the work of any English poet but the author of *Bussy d'Ambois*.° There was here likewise that gravity and condensation of thought conveyed through the medium of the 'full and heightened style' commended by Webster,° and that preponderance of philosophic or political discourse over poetic interest and dramatic action for which the author in question had been justly censured.

Some of the audience appearing slightly startled by this remark (indeed it afterwards appeared that the Chairman had been on the point of asking the learned member whether he was not thinking rather of *Love's Labour's Lost*?), Mr A. cited the well-known scene in which Oberon discourses with Puck on matters concerning Mary Stuart and Queen Elizabeth, instead of despatching him at once on his immediate errand. This was universally accepted as proof positive, and the reading concluded amid signs of unanimous assent, when[:]°

Mr B. had nothing to urge against the argument they had just heard, but he must remind them that there was a more weighty kind of evidence than that adduced by Mr A.; and to this he doubted not they would all defer. He could prove by a tabulated statement that the words 'to' and 'from' occurred on an average from seven to nine times in every play of Chapman; whereas in the play under consideration the word 'to' occurred exactly twelve times and the word 'from' precisely ten. He was therefore of opinion that the authorship should in all probability be assigned to Anthony Munday.°

As nobody present could dispute this conclusion, Mr C. proceeded to read the argument by which he proposed to establish the fact, hitherto unaccountably overlooked by all preceding commentators, that the character of Romeo was obviously designed as a satire on Lord Burghley.° The first and perhaps the strongest evidence in favour of this proposition was the extreme difficulty, he might almost say the utter impossibility, of discovering a single point of likeness between the two characters. This would naturally be the first precaution taken by a poor player who designed to attack an all-powerful Minister. But more direct light was thrown upon the subject by a passage in which 'that kind of fruit that maids call medlars when they laugh alone'° is mentioned in connection with a wish of Romeo's regarding his mistress. This must evidently be taken to refer to some recent occasion on which the policy of Lord Burghley (possibly in the matter of the Anjou marriage°) had been rebuked in private by the Maiden Queen, 'his mistress,' as meddling, laughable, and fruitless.

This discovery seemed to produce a great impression till the Chairman reminded the Society that the play in question was now generally ascribed to George Peele, who was notoriously the solicitor of Lord Burghley's patronage and the recipient of his bounty.° That this poet was the author of *Romeo and Juliet* could no longer be a matter of doubt, as he was confident they would all agree with him on hearing that a living poet of note had positively assured him of the fact; adding that he had always thought so when at school. The plaudits excited by this announcement had scarcely subsided, when the Chairman clenched the matter by observing that he rather thought the same opinion had ultimately been entertained by his own grandmother.

Mr D. then read a paper on the authorship and the hidden meaning of two contemporary plays which, he must regretfully remark, were too obviously calculated to cast a most unfavourable and even sinister light on the moral character of the new Shakespeare; whose possibly suspicious readiness to attack the vices of others with a view to diverting attention from his own was signally exemplified in the well-known fact that, even while putting on a feint of respect and tenderness for his memory, he had exposed the profligate haunts and habits of Christopher Marlowe under the transparent pseudonym of Christopher Sly.° To the first of these plays attention had long since been drawn by a person of whom it was only necessary to say that he had devoted a long life to the study and illustration of Shakespeare and his age, and had actually presumed to publish a well-known edition of the poet at a date previous to the establishment of the present Society. He (Mr D.) was confident that not another syllable could be necessary to expose that person to the contempt of all present. He proceeded, however, with the kind encouragement of the Chairman, to indulge at that editor's expense in sundry personalities both 'loose and humorous,"° which being totally unfit for publication here are reserved for a private issue of 'Loose and Humorous Papers' to be edited, with a running marginal commentary or illustrative and explanatory version of the utmost possible fullness,[1] by the Founder and another member of the

[1] This word was incomprehensibly misprinted in the first issue of the Society's Report, where it appeared as 'foulness.' To prevent misapprehension, the whole staff of printers was at once discharged.

Society. To these it might possibly be undesirable for them to attract the notice of the outside world. Reverting therefore to his first subject from various references to the presumed private character, habits, gait, appearance, and bearing of the gentleman in question, Mr D. observed that the ascription of a share in the *Taming of the Shrew* to William Haughton (hitherto supposed the author of a comedy called *Englishmen for my Money*)° implied a doubly discreditable blunder. The real fact, as he would immediately prove, was not that Haughton was joint author with Shakespeare of the *Taming of the Shrew*, but that Shakespeare was joint author with Haughton of *Englishmen for my Money*. He would not enlarge on the obvious fact that Shakespeare, so notorious a plunderer of others, had actually been reduced to steal from his own poor store an image transplanted from the last scene of the third act of *Romeo and Juliet* into the last scene of the third act of *Englishmen for my Money*; where the well-known and pitiful phrase—'Night's candles are burnt out'°—reappears in all its paltry vulgarity as follows;—'Night's candles burn obscure.'° Ample as was the proof here supplied, he would prefer to rely exclusively upon such further evidence as might be said to lie at once on the surface and in a nutshell.

The second title of this play, by which the first title was in a few years totally superseded, ran thus: *A Woman will have her Will*. Now even in an age of punning titles such as that of a well-known and delightful treatise by Sir John Harrington,° the peculiar fondness of Shakespeare for puns was notorious; but especially for puns on names, as in the proverbial case of Sir Thomas Lucy;° and above all for puns on his own Christian name, as in his 135th, 136th, and 143rd sonnets.° It must now be but too evident to the meanest intelligence—to the meanest intelligence, he repeated; for to such only did he or would he then and there or ever or anywhere address himself—(loud applause) that the graceless author, more utterly lost to all sense of shame than any Don Juan or other typical libertine of fiction, had come forward to placard by way of self-advertisement on his own stage, and before the very eyes of a Maiden Queen, the scandalous confidence in his own powers of fascination and seduction so cynically expressed in the too easily intelligible vaunt—A Woman will have her Will [Shakespeare].° In the penultimate line of the hundred and forty-third sonnet the very phrase might be said to occur:

So will I pray that thou mayst have thy Will.

Having thus established his case in the first instance to the satisfaction, as he trusted, not only of the present Society, but of any asylum for incurables in any part of the country, the learned member now passed on to the consideration of the allusions at once to Shakespeare and to a celebrated fellow-countryman, fellow-poet, and personal friend of his—Michael Drayton—contained in a play which had been doubtfully attributed to Shakespeare himself by such absurd idiots as looked rather to the poetical and dramatic quality of a poem or a play than to such tests as those to which alone any member ofthat Society would ever dream of appealing. What these were he need not specify; it was enough to say in recommendation of them that they had rather less to do with any question of dramatic or other poetry than with the differential calculus or the squaring of the circle. It followed that only the most perversely ignorant and æsthetically presumptuous of readers could imagine the possibility of Shakespeare's concern or partnership in a play which had no more Shakespearean quality about it than mere poetry, mere passion, mere pathos, mere beauty and vigour of thought and language, mere command of dramatic effect, mere depth and subtlety of power to read, interpret, and reproduce the secrets of the heart and spirit. Could any further evidence be required of the unfitness and unworthiness to hold or to utter any opinion on the matter in hand which had consistently been displayed by the poor creatures to whom he had just referred, it would be found, as he felt sure the Founder and all worthy members of their Society would be the first to admit, in the despicable diffidence, the pitiful modesty, the contemptible deficiency in common assurance, with which the suggestion of Shakespeare's partnership in this play had generally been put forward and backed up. The tragedy of *Arden of Feversham* was indeed connected with Shakespeare—and that, as he should proceed to show, only too intimately; but Shakespeare was not connected with it—that is, in the capacity of its author. In what capacity would be but too evident when he mentioned the names of the two leading ruffians concerned in the murder of the principal character—Black Will and Shakebag.° The single original of these two characters he need scarcely pause to point out. It would be observed that a double precaution had been taken against any charge of libel or personal attack which might be brought against the author and supported by the all-powerful court influence of Shakespeare's two principal patrons, the Earls of Essex and Southampton. Two figures were substituted for one, and the unmistakable name of Will Shakebag was cut in half and divided between them. Care had moreover been taken to disguise the person by altering the complexion of the individual aimed at. That the actual Shakespeare was a fair man they had the evidence of the coloured bust at Stratford.° Could any capable and fair-minded man—he would appeal to their justly honoured Founder—require further evidence as to the original of Black Will Shakebag? Another important character in the play was Black Will's accomplice and Arden's servant—Michael, after whom the play had also at one time been called *Murderous Michael*. The single fact that Shakespeare and Drayton were both of them Warwickshire men would suffice, he could not doubt, to carry conviction with it to the mind of every member present, with regard to the original of this personage. It now only remained for him to produce the name of the real author of this play. He would do so at once—Ben Jonson. About the time of its production Jonson was notoriously engaged in writing those additions to the *Spanish Tragedy*° of which a preposterous attempt had been made to deprive him on the paltry ground that the style (forsooth) of these additional scenes was very like the style of Shakespeare and utterly unlike the style of Jonson. To dispose for ever of this pitiful argument it would be sufficient to mention the names of its two first and principal supporters—Charles Lamb and Samuel Taylor Coleridge (hisses and laughter). Now, in these 'adycions to Jeronymo'° a painter was introduced complaining of the murder of his son. In the play before them a painter was introduced as an accomplice in the murder of Arden. It was unnecessary to dwell upon so trivial a point of difference as that between the stage employment or the moral character of the one artist and the other. In either case they were as closely as possible connected with a murder. There was a painter in the *Spanish Tragedy*, and there was also a painter in *Arden of Feversham*. He need not—he would not add another word in confirmation of the now established fact, that Ben Jonson had in this play held up to perpetual infamy—whether deserved or undeserved he would not pretend to say—the names of two poets who afterwards became his friends, but whom he had previously gibbeted or at least pilloried in public as Black Will Shakespeare and Murderous Michael Drayton.

Mr E. then brought forward a subject of singular interest and importance—'The lameness° of Shakespeare—was it moral or physical?' He would not insult their intelligence by dwelling on the absurd and exploded hypothesis that this expression was allegorical, but would at once assume that the infirmity in question was physical. Then arose the question—In which leg? He was prepared, on the evidence of an early play, to prove to demonstration that the injured and interesting limb was the left. 'This shoe is my father,' says Launce in the *Two Gentlemen of Verona*; 'no, this left shoe is my father; no, no, this left shoe is my mother; nay, that cannot be so neither; yes, it is so, it is so; *it hath the worser sole*.'° This passage was not necessary either to the progress of the play or to the development of the character; he believed he was justified in asserting that it was not borrowed from the original novel° on which the play was founded; the inference was obvious, that without some personal allusion it must have been as unintelligible to the audience as it had hitherto been to the commentators. His conjecture was confirmed, and the whole subject illustrated with a new light, by the well-known line in one of the Sonnets, in which the poet describes himself as 'made lame by Fortune's dearest spite':° a line of which the inner meaning and personal application had also by a remarkable chance been reserved for him (Mr E.) to discover. There could be no doubt that we had here a clue to the origin of the physical infirmity referred to; an accident which must have befallen Shakespeare in early life while acting at the Fortune theatre, and consequently before his connection with a rival company; a fact of grave importance till now unverified. The epithet 'dearest,' like so much else in the Sonnets, was evidently susceptible of a double interpretation. The first and most natural explanation of the term would at once suggest itself; the playhouse would of necessity be dearest to the actor dependent on it for subsistence, as the means of getting his bread; but he thought it not unreasonable to infer from this unmistakable allusion that the entrance fee charged at the Fortune may probably have been higher than the price of seats in any other house. Whether or not this fact, taken in conjunction with the accident already mentioned, should be assumed as the immediate cause of Shakespeare's subsequent change of service, he was not prepared to pronounce with such positive confidence as they might naturally expect from a member of the Society; but he would take upon himself to affirm that his main thesis was now and for ever established on the most irrefragable evidence, and that no assailant could by any possibility dislodge by so much as a hair's breadth the least fragment of a single brick in the impregnable structure of proof raised by the argument to which they had just listened.

This demonstration being thus satisfactorily concluded, Mr F. proceeded to read his paper on the date of *Othello*, and on the various parts of that play respectively assignable to Samuel Rowley, to George Wilkins, and to Robert Daborne. It was evident that the story of Othello and Desdemona was originally quite distinct from that part of the play in which Iago was a leading figure. This he was prepared to show at some length by means of the weak-ending test, the light-ending test, the double-ending test, the triple-ending test, the heavy-monosyllabic-eleventh-syllable-of-the-double-ending test, the run-on-line test, and the central-pause test. [...]

# FROM *NOTE OF AN ENGLISH REPUBLICAN ON THE MUSCOVITE CRUSADE* (1876)

Amid and above the many voices now jangling around what is called the Eastern Question, the sound of one voice like the blast of a trumpet has at length rung its message in all English ears after a sufficiently well-known fashion to a sufficiently unmistakable purport. A preacher who defends the gallows, an apostle who approves the lash, has lifted up his voice against oppression, and has cursed 'the unspeakable Turk' by all his gods: in the name of Francia° and in the name of Mouravieff° the champion of Eyre Pasha in Jamaica has uttered his sonorous note of protest against the misdeeds of Achmet Aga in Bulgaria. For all sincere and lifelong admirers of the greatest English writer° now living among us in an old age more peaceful though not more noble than was granted to the one Englishman° we can remember yet greater in genius and in heart than he, it must be no small satisfaction, though it cannot but be no small surprise, to discover that there is actually some limit, however indefinable, to Mr Carlyle's admiration of the strongest hand. But why the single exception which is to prove the else universal rule should be that particular instance which apparently it is, we may surely be permitted in all loyalty and humility to inquire. What is the peculiar sanctifying quality in the Bulgarian which is to exempt him at need from the good offices of 'beneficent whip' and 'portable gallows,' as from things insupportable and maleficent to him alone of human kind? What tie can it be which binds together such allies as Mr Gladstone and Mr Carlyle on a question of political philanthropy?° Misery, we all know, makes strange bedfellows; but there would seem to be sympathies, religious or political, which bring stranger matches about than ever were made by misery. Is it a common love of liberty which links the veteran of letters to the veteran of politics? In this very epistle published by the *Times* of November 28 we see that the new champion of oppressed Christendom cannot resist the overwhelming temptation to turn aside and spit on the very name of liberty—'divine freedom, &c.'° His innate loathing of the mere word is too rabid and ungovernable an appetite to be suppressed or disguised for an instant. And yet it is not of conceding to their subjects too much of that mortal poison, of that damnable dissolvent, that the Turks now stand accused. Their Bashi-Bazouks are shamefully and incredibly maligned if they have earned no right to claim fellowship with the torturers, the hangmen, and the women-whippers of Hungary, of Poland,° and of Jamaica. What then can Mr Carlyle see in them deserving thus far of his reprobation, or undeserving thus far of his applause? For we all remember what largesse of full-mouthed obloquy, what wealth of free-handed disdain, was lavished from a quarter so fruitful of perennial insult on the 'small loud group or knot of rabid Nigger-Philanthropists, barking furiously in the gutter,'° and headed by John Stuart Mill, who ventured to question the excellence of such now discredited methods of government as were applied not long since to his victims by a satrap° of English birth. It cannot be tyranny, it cannot be torture, it cannot be massacre to which Mr Carlyle now objects. His daring has always approved itself as great as even his genius, as unquestionable as even his honesty; but there is a point at which daring, like all other human qualities, loses its virtue and changes its likeness and [forgoes]° its name. And the repudiation in any one case of a principle avowed as righteous and cherished as sacred in every case but one is usually and naturally considered as evidence of a quality which cannot accurately be defined as mere daring. We cannot therefore insult the great age and the great character of Mr Carlyle by the supposition that he could now desire to come forward at the long last as a preacher of philanthropy or mercy, as a pleader for the laws of equity or the rights of man, as a champion of all things or of any one thing which it has been a main object of his lifelong energy to denounce alike in the rare moments of its triumph and through the prolonged years of its defeat. For so much at least the sternest republican must concede to this illustrious enemy of all freedom; that he has not hated it only when unsuccessful, nor reviled it only when out of fashion. Liberty and justice, equality and equity, fraternity and mercy, have had but few enemies in our day for whom as much can honestly be said. This credit is Mr Carlyle's; *hoc habeat secum, servetque sepulchro*.° It is not only on truth in the hour of its overthrow that he has ever sought to set his heel. No man has a right to suspect him of even a partial or a passing apostasy from the great consistent principle of his prophecies and his gospel. He has always hated the very thought of liberty, abhorred the very notion of equality, abjured the very idea of fraternity, as he hates, abhors, and abjures them now. No man can doubt on which side or to what effect his potent voice would have been lifted at its utmost pitch before the throne of Herod or the judgment-seat of Pilate. No tetrarch or pro-consul, no Mouravieff or Eyre of them all, would have been swifter to inflict or louder to invoke the sentence of beneficent whip, the doom of beneficent gallows, on the communist and stump-orator of Nazareth. Had there but lived and written under the shadow of the not as yet divine emperor Tiberius,° doubtless as 'strictly honest and just a man' as any 'present Czar' or emperor of his kind, a pamphleteer as eloquent and as ardent an imperialist as these pitiful times of 'ballot-box, divine freedom, &c.' have brought forth even 'in this distracted country,' what a Latter-day Pamphlet on the Crucifixion, what an Occasional Discourse on the Nazarene Question,° might we not now possess, whereby to lighten the darkness of history and adjust the balance of judgment! To the regretful disciple of Mr Carlyle, considering duly of this matter, it must seem wellnigh as though nature were sparing of her greatest men at the right time, and again were lavish at the wrong. Happily, however, it can be no hard task, for any disciple that way given, to reconstruct in fancy from the many models before him the perfect scheme and argument of such possible pamphlet or discourse. For if ever a life was lived on earth, if ever a word was preached, if ever a death was died, most utterly in all points deserving of abhorrence from all who abhor the thought of freedom, of contempt from all who contemn the notion of equality, of hatred from all who hate the name of brotherhood, that life was assuredly the life, that word was the Gospel, that death was the death of Jesus. It cannot be therefore in his most undeserving name that we hear this protest on behalf of suffering Christians put forth by the worshipper of every gallows on earth but one—and that one the cross of Christ.

We may then presumably be permitted to dismiss without further discussion any possible theory of Christian sympathy with Christians on the part of a preacher to whom the spirit of every saying yet fathered on the Founder of Christianity should seem incomparably more hateful and contemptible than ever did the letter of any to Diderot or Voltaire. And with it we may joyfully discard any possible apprehension of seeing a catechumen of his years and antecedents received at the eleventh hour into the fold or vineyard of the Eastern Church; a sight which could be profitable for edification to no mortal. Is it then in the mere secular name of mercy or of chivalry, of decency or of manhood, that 'the unspeakable Turk should be immediately struck out of the question'° to make room for the unspeakable Muscovite? Nay, for very shame,°—in Shakespeare's phrase, if aught so despicable as the phrase of a mere poet and player may here be cited without offence, 'for godly shame'—it cannot be on any such plea as this that the sympathy or the indignation of any creature is now invoked by the patron of Eyre Pasha, the champion of Mouravieff Bey. Not all Englishmen have yet forgotten the horror of shame, the sickness of disgust, with which they learnt how the accomplices and the satellites of the former had devised and carried out such ultra-Bulgarian atrocities as the stripping and whipping of women by men in public with scourges of 'pianoforte wire.' It was the infliction of such tortures and such outrages as these by English Bashi-Bazouks, that set those to whom the honour of humanity and of England was more than a mockery and a byword 'barking furiously in the gutter' under the guidance of the best and wisest among English philosophers° and statesmen; and this also it was which evoked the vociferous acclamations and inflamed the tempestuous applause of Mr Carlyle and his tail. We must not therefore now insult him by the imputation of a tardy apostasy from the persistent principles of his life. We must not assume that some afterthought has brought over from the natural side of his sympathy and his service a pervert so illustrious as the prophet who long since denounced 'the soft quality of mercy' as 'thrice accursed'° in all cases where it was not 'permissible,' and who in the same breath referred the question of when and where, if ever, it might be, to the ultimate and indisputable decision of a drunken murderer and of a whipper of women. Nor, again, unless the meaning of words can be juggled into its exact reverse by the most able and audacious of special pleaders, can it be out of respect for 'the hard quality of justice' that the adoring biographer of Frederic William° would imprecate our execration on the Turk. For in this very instance of judicial murder he admits, with quaint and admirable candour, that the royal hangman was indeed a mere assassin of the innocent, his 'poor old'° victim being afterwards proved to have been wholly and demonstrably, morally and legally, guiltless of the charge on which he was murdered. Really it grows more and more difficult for the sharpest eye of the most devout disciple to detect whereabouts in the prophetic mind of the North British evangelist he may discern the exact point at which tyranny or cruelty, torture or murder, violence or injustice, ceases to be something admirable and is transmuted as by witchcraft into something unspeakable. Cruelty in Ireland, cruelty in Jamaica, cruelty in the plantation, cruelty in the jail, each of these in turn has naturally provoked the stigmatic brand of his approbation, each in turn has deservedly incurred the indelible condemnation of his praise.

Is it then to the anarchy, the lack of 'rhythmic drill,'° the prevalence of democratic principles and the insurrection of republican ideas, that he objects as to a dominant and perceptible element of evil and of danger among the soldiers of the unspeakable Turk? But never, if we may take the word of all who have fought beside and all who have fought against them, were there better soldiers upon earth; never men more loyal to their flag, more patient and faithful and laborious, more impermeable in wartime to any breath of insubordination, more impenetrable on campaign by any suggestion of revolt; no, not among the Bashi-Bazouks let loose by a strictly honest Czar on Khiva or Poland or Circassia. That unlucky word 'honest,' I may remark by the way, has always, when applied to emperors or kings, a perilous tendency to remind his idle admirers with which in particular among all the fantastic creatures of his unprofitable brain this especial epithet was associated by the author of *Othello*.°

It could not be therefore because the Turk is cruel, though he were seventy times seven times° as cruel as he is—it cannot be because he is insubordinate in wartime, for insubordinate in war time he is not—that we are invited on such authority as this to gather grapes of Russian thorns or figs of Pan-slavistic thistles. It is simply, to all appearance, because the Russians 'in our own time have done signal service to God and man in drilling into order and peace anarchic populations all over their side of the world.'° To what manner of God and what type of man, if there be any reader that remembers not, yet Hungary remembers and Poland knows; to the God of the worshippers of Moloch,°

and to men of the kindred of his priests. But in this case, when 'the Czar, whose serious task it is to protect the Christian subjects in Turkey proper,' shall practically have established his most righteous 'claim to territorial footing in the recovered country,' then 'the peaceful Mongol inhabitants' will 'of course be left in peace, and treated with perfect equity, and even friendly consideration.' Of course they will: about this at least there can be no debate possible among honest men—men as strictly 'honest and just, who have such noble sense of their friends' wrongs,'° as even Czar Alexander and Ancient Iago themselves. The man who could doubt this might be capable of doubting the sacred word of an emperor or the plighted honour of a king. Seriously let me ask, for what imaginable or imaginary class of readers can such a sentence as this be written? Mr Carlyle has shewn himself always the greatest and sometimes the uncleanliest of all great English humourists since Swift; but the gravely indecent irony of this hideous jest might have disconcerted Aristophanes and made Rabelais think twice. [...]

# 'THE SAILING OF THE SWALLOW' (1877)

About the middle music of the spring
Came from the green shore of the Irish king
A fair ship stoutly sailing, eastward bound
And south by Wales and its grey land-line round
To the loud rocks and ringing reaches home
That take the wild wrath of the Cornish foam,
Past Lyonesse unswallowed of the tides
And high Carlion that now the steep sea hides
To the wind-hollowed heights and gusty bays
Of sheer Tintagel, fair with famous days.
Above the stem a gilded swallow shone,
Wrought with straight wings and eyes of glittering stone
As flying sunward oversea, to bear
Green summer with it through the singing air.
And on the deck between the rowers at dawn,
As the bright sail with brightening wind was drawn,
Sat with full face against the strengthening light
Iseult, more fair than foam or dawn was white.
Her gaze was glad past love's own singing of,
And her face lovely past desire of love.
Past thought and speech her maiden motions were,
And a more golden sunrise was her hair.
The very veil of her bright flesh was made
As of light woven and moonbeam-coloured shade
More fine than moonbeams; her warm eyelids shone
As snow sun-stricken that endures the sun,
And through their curled and coloured clouds of deep
Luminous lashes thick as dreams in sleep
Shone as the sea's depth swallowing up the sky's
The springs of unimaginable eyes.
As the wave's subtler emerald is pierced through
With the utmost heaven's inextricable blue,
And both are woven and molten in one sleight
Of amorous colour and implicated light
Under the golden guard and gaze of noon,

So glowed their awless amorous plenilune,
Azure and gold and ardent grey, made strange
With fiery difference and deep interchange
Inexplicable of glories multiform;
Now as the sullen sapphire swells toward storm
Foamless, their bitter beauty grew acold,
And now afire with ardour of fine gold.
Her flower-soft lips were meek and passionate,
For love upon them like a shadow sate
Patient, a foreseen vision of sweet things,
A dream with eyes fast shut and plumeless wings
That knew not what man's love or life should be,
Nor had it sight nor heart to hope or see
What thing should come, but childlike satisfied
Watched out its virgin vigil in soft pride
And unkissed expectation; and the glad
Clear cheeks and throat and tender temples had
Such maiden heat as if a rose's blood
Beat in the live heart of a lily-bud.
Between the small round breasts a white way led
Heavenward, and from slight foot to slender head
The whole fair body flower-like swayed and shone
Moving, and what her light hand leant upon
Grew blossom-scented: her warm arms began
To round and ripen for delight of man
That they should clasp and circle: her fresh hands,
Like regent lilies of reflowering lands
Whose vassal firstlings, crown and star and plume,
Bow down to the empire of that sovereign bloom,
Shone sceptreless, and from her face there went
A silent light as of a God content;
Save when, more swift and keen than love or shame,
Some flash of blood, light as the laugh of flame,
Broke it with sudden beam and shining speech,
As dream by dream shot through her eyes, and each
Outshone the last that lightened, and not one
Shewed her such things as should be borne and done.
Though hard against her shone the sunlike face
That in all change and wreck of time and place
Should be the star of her sweet living soul.
Nor had love made it as his written scroll
For evil will and good to read in yet;
But smooth and mighty, without scar or fret,

Fresh and high-lifted was the helmless brow
As the oak-tree flower that tops the topmost bough,
Ere it drop off before the perfect leaf;
And nothing save his name he had of grief,
The name his mother,° dying as he was born,
Made out of sorrow in very sorrow's scorn,
And set it on him smiling in her sight,
Tristram; who now, clothed with sweet youth and might,
As a glad witness wore that bitter name,°
The second symbol of the world for fame.°
Famous and full of fortune was his youth
Ere the beard's bloom had left his check unsmooth,
And in his face a lordship of strong joy
And height of heart no chance could curb or cloy
Lightened, and all that warmed them at his eyes
Loved them as young larks love the blue strong skies.
So like the morning through the morning moved
Tristram, a light to look on and be loved.
Song sprang between his lips and hands, and shone
Singing, and strengthened and sank down thereon
As a bird settles to the second flight,
Then from beneath his harping hands with might
Leapt, and made way and had its fill and died,
And all whose hearts were fed upon it sighed
Silent, and in their hearts the fire of tears
Burned as wine drunken not with lips but ears.
And gazing on his fervent hands that made
The might of music all their souls obeyed
With trembling strong subservience of delight,
Full many a queen that had him once in sight
Thought in the secret place of her hot heart
In what strong battle had these hands borne part
How oft, and were so young and sweet of skill;
And those red lips whereon the song burned still,
What words and cries of battle had they flung
Athwart the swing and shriek of swords, so young;
And eyes as glad as summer, what strange youth
Fed them so full of happy heart and truth,
That had seen sway from side to sundering side
The steel flow of that terrible springtide
That the moon rules not, but the fire and light
Of men's hearts mixed in the mid mirth of fight.
Therefore the joy and love of him they had

Made thought more amorous in them and more glad
For his fame's sake remembered, and his youth
Gave his fame flowerlike fragrance and soft growth
As of a rose requickening, when he stood
Fair in their eye, a flower of faultless blood.
And that sad queen° to whom his life was death,
A rose plucked forth of summer in mid breath,
A star fall'n out of season in mid throe
Of that life's joy that makes the star's life glow,
Made their love sadder toward him and more strong.
And in mid change of time and fight and song
Chance cast him westward on the low sweet strand
Where songs are sung of the green Irish land,
And the sky loves it, and the sea loves best,
And as a bird is taken to man's breast
The sweet-souled land where sorrow sweetest sings
Is wrapt round with them as with hands and wings
And taken to the sea's heart as a flower.
There in the luck and light of his good hour
Came to the king's court like a noteless man
Tristram, and while some half a season ran
Abode before him harping in his hall,
And taught sweet craft of new things musical
To the dear maiden mouth and innocent hands
That for his sake are famous in all lands.
Yet was not love between them, for their fate
Lay wrapt in its appointed hour at wait,
And had no flower to show yet, and no sting.
But once being vexed with some past wound the king
Bade give him comfort of sweet baths, and then
Should Iseult watch him as his handmaiden,
For his more honour in men's sight, and ease
The hurts he had with holy remedies
Made by her mother's magic° in strange hours
Out of live roots and life-compelling flowers.
And finding by the wound's shape in his side
This was the knight by whom their strength had died
And all their might in one man overthrown
Had left their shame in sight of all men shown,
She would have slain him swordless with his sword;
Yet seemed he to her so great and fair a lord
She heaved up hand and smote not; and he said,
Laughing—'What comfort shall this man be dead,

Damsel? what hurt is for my blood to heal?
But set your hand not near the toothèd steel
Lest the fang strike it.'—'Yea, the fang,' she said,
'Should it not sting the very serpent dead
That stung mine uncle? for his slayer art thou,
And half my mother's heart is bloodless now
Through thee, that mad'st the veins of all her kin
Bleed in his wounds whose veins through thee ran thin.'
Yet thought she how their hot chief's violent heart
Had flung the fierce word forth upon their part
That bade to battle the best knight that stood
On Arthur's, and so dying of his wild mood
Had set upon his conqueror's flesh the seal
Of his mishallowed and anointed steel,
Whereof the venom and enchanted might
Made the sign burn here branded in her sight.
These things she stood recasting, and her soul
Subsiding in her, thought like thin flame stole
Through all its maiden courses, and filled up
Its hidden ways as wine fulfils a cup.
So past she from him humbly, and he went
Home with hands reconciled and heart content,
To bring fair peace between the Cornish strand
And the long wrangling wars of that loud land.
And when the peace was struck between them twain
Forth must he fare by those green straits again,
And bring back Iseult for a plighted bride
And set to reign at Mark his uncle's side.
So now with feast made and all triumphs done
They sailed between the moonfall and the sun
Under the spent stars eastward; but the queen
Out of wise heart and subtle love had seen
Such things as might be, dark as in a glass,
And lest some doom of these should come to pass
Bethought her with her secret soul alone
To work some charm for marriage unison
And strike the heart of Iseult to her lord
With a spell stronger than the stroke of sword.
Therefore with marvellous herbs and spells she wrought
To win the very wonder of her thought,
And brewed it with her secret hands and blest
And drew and gave out of her secret breast
To one her chosen and Iseult's handmaiden,

Brangwain, and bade her hide from sight of men
This marvel covered in a golden cup,
So covering in her heart the counsel up
As in the gold the wondrous wine lay close;
And when the last shout with the last cup rose
About the bride and bridegroom bound to bed,
Then should this one word of her will be said
To her new-married maiden child, that she
Should drink with Mark this draught in unity,
And no lip touch it for her sake but theirs:
For with long love and consecrating prayers
The wine was hallowed for their mouths to pledge,
And if a drop fell from the beaker's edge
That drop should Iseult hold as dear as blood
Shed from her mother's heart to do her good.
And having drunk they twain should be one heart
Who were one flesh till fleshly death should part—
Death, who parts all. So Brangwain swore, and kept
The hid thing by her while she waked or slept.
And now they sat to see the sun again
Whose light of eye had looked on no such twain
Since Galahault° in the rose-time of the year
Brought Launcelot first to sight of Guenevere.
    And Tristram caught her changing eyes and said:
'As this day raises daylight from the dead
Might not this face the life of a dead man?'
    And Iseult, gazing where the sea was wan
Out of the sun's way, said; 'I pray you not
Praise me, but tell me there in Camelot,
Saving the queen, who hath most name of fair?
I would I were a man and dwelling there,
That I might win me better praise than yours,
Even such as you have; for your praise endures,
That with great deeds ye wring from mouths of men,
But ours—for shame, where is it? Tell me then,
Since woman may not wear a better here,
Who of this praise hath most save Guenevere?'
    And Tristram, lightening with a laugh held in—
'Surely a little praise is this to win,
A poor praise and a little! but of these
Hapless, whom love serves only with bowed knees,
Of such poor women fairer face hath none
That lifts her eyes against the eye o' the sun

Than Arthur's sister,° whom the north seas call
Mistress of isles; so yet majestical
Above the crowns on younger heads she moves,
Outlightening with her eyes our late-born loves.'
'Ah,' said Iseult, 'is she more tall than I?
Look, I am tall;' and touched the mast hard by,
Reaching far up the flower that was her hand;
'And look, fair lord, now, when I rise and stand,
How high with feet unlifted I can touch
Standing straight up; could this queen do thus much?
Nay, over tall she must be then, like me:
I should love lesser women. May this be,
That she is still the second stateliest there,
So more than many so much younger fair,
She, born before the king too, was she not?
And has the third knight after Launcelot°
And after you to serve her? nay, sir, then
God made her for a love-sign among men.'
'Ay,' Tristram answered, 'for a sign, a sign—
Would God it were not! for no planets shine
With half such fearful forecast of men's fate
As a fair face so more unfortunate.'
Then with a smile that lit not on her brows
But moved upon her red mouth tremulous
Light as a sea-bird's motion oversea,
'Yea,' quoth Iseult, 'the happier hap for me,
With no such face to bring men no such fate.
Yet her might all we women born too late
Praise for good hap, who so enskied above
Not more in age excels us than man's love.'
There came a glooming light on Tristram's face
Answering: 'God keep you better in His grace
Than to sit down beside her in men's sight.
For if men be not blind whom God gives light
And lie not in whose lips he bids truth live,
Great grief shall she be given, and greater give.
For Merlin witnessed of her years ago
That she should work woe and should suffer woe
Beyond the race of women: and in truth
Her face, too bright and dark for age or youth,
Hath on it such a light of cloud and fire,
With charm and change of keen or dim desire,
And over all a fearless look of fear

Hung like a veil across its changing cheer,
Made up of fierce foreknowledge and sharp scorn,
That it were better she had not been born.
For not love's self can help a face which hath
Such insubmissive anguish of wan wrath,
Blind prescience and self-contemptuous hate
Of her own soul and heavy-footed fate,
Writ broad upon its beauty: none the less
Its fire of bright and burning bitterness
Takes with as quick a flame the sense of men
As any sunbeam, nor is quenched again
With any drop of dewfall; yea, I think
No herb of force or blood-compelling drink°
Would heal a heart that ever it made hot.
Ay, and men too that greatly love her not,
Seeing the great love of her and Lamoracke,
Make no great marvel, nor look strangely back
When with his gaze about her she goes by
Pale as a breathless and star-quickening sky
Between moonrise and sunset, and moves out
Clothed with the passion of his eyes about
As night with all her stars, yet night is black;
And she, clothed warm with love of Lamoracke,
Girt with his worship as with girdling gold,
Seems all at heart anhungered and acold,
Seems sad at heart and loveless of the light,
As night, star-clothed or naked, is but night.'
  And with her sweet eyes sunken, and the mirth
Dead in their look as earth lies dead in earth
That reigned on earth and triumphed, Iseult said;
'Is it her shame of something done and dead
Or fear of something to be born and done
That so in her soul's eye puts out the sun?'
  And Tristram answered: 'Surely, as I think,
This gives her soul such bitterness to drink,
The sin born blind, the sightless sin unknown,
Wrought when the summer in her blood was blown,
But scarce aflower, and spring first flushed her will
With bloom of dreams no fruitage should fulfil,
When out of vision and desire was wrought
The sudden sin that from the living thought
Leaps a live deed and dies not: then there came
On that blind sin swift eyesight like a flame

Touching the dark to death, and made her mad
With helpless knowledge that too late forbade
What was before the bidding; and she knew
How sharp a life dead love should lead her through
To what sure end how fearful; and though yet
Nor with her blood nor tears her way be wet
And she look bravely with set face on fate,
Yet she knows well the serpent hour at wait
Somewhere to sting and spare not; ay, and he,
Arthur'——
'The king,' quoth Iseult suddenly,
'Doth the king too live so in sight of fear?
They say sin touches not a man so near
As shame a woman; yet he too should be
Part of the penance, being more deep than she
Set in the sin.'
'Nay,' Tristram said, 'for thus
It fell by wicked hap and hazardous,
That wittingly he sinned[o] no more than youth
May sin and be assoiled of God and truth,
Repenting; for in his first year of reign
As he stood splendid with his foemen slain
And light of new-blown battles, flushed and hot
With hope and life, came greeting from King Lot
Out of his wind-worn islands oversea,
And homage to my king and fealty
Of those north seas wherein the strange shapes swim,
As from his man; and Arthur greeted him
As his good lord and courteously, and bade
To his high feast; who coming with him had
This Queen Morgause of Orkney,[o] his fair wife,
In the green middle Maytime of her life,
And in scarce April was our king's as then
And goodliest was he of all flowering men,
And of what graft as yet himself knew not;
But cold as rains in autumn was King Lot
And grey-grown out of season: so there sprang
Swift love between them, and all spring through sang
Light in their joyous hearing; for none knew
The bitter bond of blood between them two,
Twain fathers but one mother,[o] till too late
The sacred mouth of Merlin set forth fate
And brake the secret seal on Arthur's birth,

And shewed his ruin and his rule on earth
Inextricable, and light on lives to be.
For surely, though time slay us, yet shall we
Have such high name and lordship of good days
As shall sustain us living, and men's praise
Shall burn a beacon lit above us dead.
And of the king how shall not this be said
When any of us from any mouth has praise,
That such were men in only this king's days,
In Arthur's? yea, come shine or shade, no less
His name shall be one name with knightliness,
His fame one light with sunlight. Yet in sooth
His age shall bear the burdens of his youth
And bleed from his own bloodshed; for indeed
Blind to him blind his sister brought forth seed,
And of the child between them shall be born
Destruction: so shall God not suffer scorn,
Nor in men's souls and lives his law lie dead.'
  And as one moved and marvelling Iseult said:
'Great pity it is and strange it seems to me
God could not do them so much right as we,
Who slay not men for witless evil done;
And these the noblest under the great sun
For sin they knew not he that knew shall slay,
And smite blind men for stumbling in fair day.
What good is it to God that such should die?
Shall the sun's light grow sunnier in the sky
Because their light of spirit is put out?'
  And sighing, she looked from wave to cloud about,
And even with that the full-grown feet of day
Sprang upright on the quivering water-way,
And his face burned against her meeting face
Most like a lover's lightening from his place
Who gazes to his bride-ward; the sea shone
And shivered like spread wings of angels blown
By the sun's breath before him; and a low
Sweet gale shook all the foam-flowers of thin snow
As into rainfall of sea-roses shed
Leaf by wild leaf on the green garden-bed
That tempests till and sea-winds turn and plough:
For rosy and fiery round the running prow
Fluttered the flakes and feathers of the spray,
And bloomed like blossoms cast by God away

To waste on the ardent water; the wan moon
Withered to westward as a face in swoon
Death-stricken by glad tidings: and the height
Throbbed and the centre quivered with delight
And the depth quailed with passion as of love,
Till like the heart of a new-mated dove
Air, light, and wave seemed full of burning rest,
With motion as of one God's beating breast.
   And her heart sprang in Iseult, and she drew
With all her spirit and life the sunrise through,
And through her lips the keen triumphant air
Sea-scented, sweeter than land-roses were,
And through her eyes the whole rejoicing east
Sun-satisfied, and all the heaven at feast
Spread for the morning; and the imperious mirth
Of wind and light that moved upon the earth,
Making the spring, and all the fruitful might
And strong regeneration of delight
That swells the seedling leaf and sapling man,
Since the first life in the first world began
To burn and burgeon through void limbs and veins,
And the first love with sharp sweet procreant pains
To pierce and bring forth roses: nay, she felt
Through her own soul the sovereign morning melt,
And all the sacred passion of the sun;
And as the young clouds flamed and were undone
About him coming, touched and burnt away
In rosy ruin and yellow spoil of day,
The sweet veil of her body and corporal sense
Felt the dawn also cleave it, and incense
With light from inward and with effluent heat
The kindling soul through fleshly hands and feet.
And as the august great blossom of the dawn
Burst, and the full sun scarce from sea withdrawn
Seemed on the fiery water a flower afloat,
So as a fire the mighty morning smote
Throughout her, and incensed with the influent hour
Her whole soul's one great mystical red flower
Burst, and the bud of her sweet spirit broke
Rose-fashion, and the strong spring at a stroke
Thrilled, and was cloven, and from the full sheath came
The whole rose of the woman red as flame:
And all her Mayday blood as from a swoon

Flushed, and May rose up in her and was June.
So for a space the morning in her burned:
Then with half summer in her eyes she turned,
And on her lips was April yet,° and smiled,
In the eyes all woman, in the lips half child.
  And the soft speech between them grew again
With questionings and records of what men
Were mightiest, and what names for love or fight
Shone starriest overhead of queen or knight.
There Tristram spake of many a noble thing,
High feast and storm of tournay round the king,
Strange quest by perilous lands of marsh and brake
And circling woods branch-knotted like a snake
And places pale with sins that they had seen
Where was no life of red fruit or of green
But all was as a dead face wan and dun;
And bowers of evil builders whence the sun
Turns silent, and the moon moves without light
Above them through the sick and star-crossed night;
And of their hands through whom such holds lay waste,
And all their strengths dishevelled and defaced
Fell ruinous, and were not from north to south:
And of the might of Merlin's ancient mouth,
The son of no man's loins,° begot by doom
In speechless sleep out of a spotless womb;
For sleeping among graves where none had rest
And ominous houses of dead bones unblest
Among the grey grass rough as old rent hair
And wicked herbage whitening like despair
And blown upon with blasts of dolorous breath
From the gaunt openings and rare doors of death,
A maid unspotted, senseless of the spell,
Felt not about her breathe some thing of hell
Whose child and hers was Merlin; and to him
Great light from God gave sight of all things dim
And wisdom of all wondrous things, to say
What root should bear what fruit of night or day,
And sovereign speech and counsel above man;
Wherefore his youth like age was wise and wan,
And his age sorrowful and fain to sleep;
Yet should sleep never, neither laugh nor weep,
Till in some deep place of some land or sea
The heavenly hands of holier Nimue°

That was the nurse of Launcelot, and most sweet
Of all that move with magical soft feet
Among us, being of lovelier blood and breath,
Should shut him in with sleep as kind as death,
For she could pass between the quick and dead;
And of her love toward Pelleas, for whose head
Love-wounded and world-wearied she had won
A place beyond all pain in Avalon;
And of the fire that wasted afterward
The loveless eyes and bosom of Ettarde,°
In whose false love his faultless heart had burned;
And now being rapt from her, her lost heart yearned
To seek him, and passed hungering out of life:
And after all the thunder-hours of strife
That roared between King Claudas and King Ban,°
How Nimue's mighty nursling waxed to man,
And how from his first field such grace he got
That all men's hearts bowed down to Launcelot,
And how the high prince Galahault held him dear
And led him even to love of Guenevere
And to that kiss which made break forth as fire
The laugh that was the flower of his desire,
The laugh that lightened at her lips for bliss
To win from Love so great a lover's kiss:
And of the toil of Balen° all his days
To reap but thorns for fruit and tears for praise,
Whose hap was evil as his heart was good,
And all his works and ways by wold and wood
Led through much pain to one last labouring day
When the blood washed the tears out from his way:
And of the kin of Arthur, and their might;
The misborn head of Mordred,° sad as night,
With cold waste cheeks and eyes as keen as pain,
And the close angry lips of Agravaine;
And gracious Gawain,° scattering words as flowers,
The kindliest head of worldly paramours;
And the fair hand of Gareth,° found in fight
Strong as a sea-beast's tushes and as white:
And of the king's self, glorious yet and glad
For all the toil and doubt of doom he had,
Clothed with men's loves and full of kingly days.
  Then Iseult said: 'Let each knight have his praise
And each good man good witness of his worth;

But when men laud the second name on earth,
Whom would they praise to have no worldly peer
Save him whose love makes glorious Guenevere?'
'Nay,' Tristram said, 'such man as he is none.'
'What,' said she, 'there is none such under sun
Of all the large earth's living? yet I deemed
Men spake of one—but maybe men that dreamed,
Fools and tongue-stricken, witless, babbler's breed—
That for all high things was his peer indeed
Save this one highest, to be so loved and love.'
And Tristram: 'Little wit had these thereof;
For there is none such in the world as this.'
'Ay, upon land,' quoth Iseult, 'none such is,
I doubt not, nor where fighting folk may be;
But were there none such between sky and sea,
The world's whole worth were poorer than I wist.'
And Tristram took her flower-white hand and kissed,
Laughing; and through his fair face as in shame
The light blood lightened. 'Hear ye no such name?'
She said; and he, 'If there be such a word,
I wot the queen's poor harper hath not heard.'
Then, as the fuller-feathered hours grew long,
Began to speed their warm slow feet with song.

'Love, is it morning risen or night deceased
That makes the mirth of the triumphant east?
Is it joy given or bitterness put by
That makes the sweetest drinking at love's feast?
O love, love, love, that day should live and die!
'Is it with soul's thirst or with body's drouth
That summer yearns out sunward to the south,
With all the flowers that when thy birth drew nigh
Were molten in one rose to make thy mouth?
O love, what care though day should live and die?
'Is the sun glad of all the love on earth,
The spirit and sense and work of things and worth?
Is the moon sad because the month must fly
And bring her death that can but bring back birth?
For all these things as day must live and die.
'Love, is it day that makes thee thy delight
Or thou that seest day made out of thy light?
Love, as the sun and sea are thou and I,
Sea without sun dark, sun without sea bright;

The sun is one though day should live and die.
'O which is elder, night or light, who knows?
And life and love, which first of these twain grows?
For life is born of love to wail and cry,
And love is born of life to heal his woes,
And light of night, that day should live and die.
'O sun of heaven above the worldly sea,
O very love, what light is this of thee!
My sea of soul is deep as thou art high,
But all thy light is shed through all of me,
As love through love, while day shall live and die.'

'Nay,' said Iseult, 'your song is hard to read.'
'Ay?' said he: 'or too light a song to heed,
Too slight to follow, it may be? Who shall sing
Of love but as a churl before a king
If by love's worth men rate his worthiness?
Yet as the poor churl's worth to sing is less,
Surely the more shall be the great king's grace
To shew for churlish love a kindlier face.'
'No churl,' she said, 'but one in soothsayer's wise
Who says true things that help no more than lies.
I have heard men sing of love a simpler way
Than these wrought riddles made of night and day,
Like jewelled reins whereon the rhyme-bells hang.'
And Tristram smiled and changed his song and sang.

'The breath between my lips of lips not mine,
Like spirit in sense that makes pure sense divine,
Is as life in them from the living sky
That entering fills my heart with blood of thine
And thee with me, while day shall live and die.°
'Thy soul is shed into me with thy breath,
And in my heart each heartbeat of thee saith
How in thy life the life-springs of me lie,
Even one life to be gathered of one death
In me and thee, though day may live and die.
'Ah, who knows now if in my veins it be
My blood that feels life sweet, or blood of thee,
And this thine eyesight kindled in mine eye
That shews me in thy flesh the soul of me,
For thine made mine, while day may live and die?
'Ah, who knows yet if one be twain or one,
And sunlight separable again from sun,

And I from thee with all my lifesprings dry,
And thou from me with all thine heartbeats done,
Dead separate souls while day shall live and die?
'I see my soul within thine eyes, and hear
My spirit in all thy pulses thrill with fear,
And in my lips the passion of thee sigh,
And music of me made in mine own ear;
Am I not thou while day shall live and die?
'Art thou not I as I thy love am thou?
So let all things pass from us; we are now,
For all that was and will be, who knows why?
And all that is and is not, who knows how?
Who knows? God knows why day should live and die.'

And Iseult mused and spake no word, but sought
Through all the hushed ways of her tongueless thought
What face or covered likeness of a face
In what veiled hour or dream-determined place
She seeing might take for love's face, and believe
This was the spirit to whom all spirits cleave.
For that sweet wonder of the twain made one
And each one twain, incorporate sun with sun,
Star with star molten, soul with soul imbued,
And all the soul's works, all their multitude,
Made one thought and one vision and one song,
Love—this thing, this, laid hand on her so strong
She could not choose but yearn till she should see.
So went she musing down her thoughts; but he,
Sweet-hearted as a bird that takes the sun
With his clear eyes, and feels the glad god run
Through his bright blood and his rejoicing wings,
And opens all himself to heaven and sings,
Made her mind light and full of noble mirth
With words and songs the gladdest grown on earth,
Till she was blithe and high of heart as he.
So swam the Swallow through the springing sea.

And while they sat at speech as at a feast,
There came a light wind hardening from the east
And blackening, and made comfortless the skies;
And the sea thrilled as with heart-sundering sighs
One after one drawn, with each breath it drew,
And the green hardened into iron blue,
And the soft light went out of all its face.

Then Tristram girt him for an oarsman's place
And took his oar and smote, and toiled with might
In the east wind's full face and the strong sea's spite
Labouring; and all the rowers rowed hard, but he
More mightily than any wearier three.
And Iseult watched him rowing with sinless eyes
That loved him but in holy girlish wise
For noble joy in his fair manliness
And trust and tender wonder; none the less
She thought if God had given her grace to be
Man, and make war on danger of earth and sea,
Even such a man she would be; for his stroke
Was mightiest as the mightier water broke,
And in sheer measure like strong music drave
Clean through the wet weight of the wallowing wave,
And as a tune before a great king played
For triumph was the tune their strong strokes made,
And sped the ship through with smooth strife of oars
Over the mid sea's grey foam-paven floors,
For all the loud breach of the waves at will.
So for an hour they fought the storm out still,
And the shorn foam spun from the blades, and high
The keel sprang from the wave-ridge, and the sky
Glared at them for a breath's space through the rain;
Then the bows with a sharp shock plunged again
Down, and the sea clashed on them, and so rose
The bright stem like one panting from swift blows,
And as a swimmer's joyous beaten head
Rears itself laughing, so in that sharp stead
The light ship lifted her long quivering bows
As might the man his buffeted strong brows
Out of the wave-breach; for with one stroke yet
Went all men's oars together, strongly set
As to loud music, and with hearts uplift
They smote their strong way through the drench and drift.
Till the keen hour had chafed itself to death
And the east wind fell fitfully, breath by breath,
Tired; and across the thin and slackening rain
Sprang the face southward of the sun again.
Then all they rested and were eased at heart,
And Iseult rose up where she sat apart,
And with her sweet soul deepening her deep eyes
Cast the furs from her and subtle embroideries

That wrapped her from the storming rain and spray,
And shining like all April in one day,
Hair, face, and throat dashed with the straying showers,
She turned, a sunbeam-coloured flower of flowers,
And laughed on Tristram with her eyes, and said
'I too have heart then, I was not afraid.'
And answering some light courteous word of grace
He saw her clear face lighten on his face
Unwittingly, with unenamoured eyes,
For the last time. A live man in such wise
Looks in the deadly face of his fixed hour
And laughs with lips wherein he hath no power
To keep the life yet some five minutes' space.
So Tristram looked on Iseult face to face
And knew not, and she knew not. The last time—
The last that should be told in any rhyme
Heard anywhere on mouths of singing men
That ever should sing praise of them again;
The last hour of their hurtless hearts at rest,
The last that peace should touch them breast to breast,
The last that sorrow far from them should sit.
This last was with them, and they knew not it.
    For Tristram being athirst with strong toil spake,
Saying:— 'Iseult, for all dear love's labour's sake
Give me to drink, and give me for a pledge
The touch of four lips on the beaker's edge.'
And Iseult sought and would not wake Brangwain
Who slept as one half dead with fear and pain,
Being tender-natured; so with hushed light feet
Went Iseult round her, with soft looks and sweet
Pitying her pain; so sweet a spirited thing
She was, and daughter of a kindly king.
And spying what strange bright secret charge was kept
Fast in that maid's white bosom while she slept,
She sought and drew the gold cup forth and smiled
Marvelling, with such light wonder as a child
That hears of glad sad life in magic lands;
And bare it back to Tristram with pure hands
Holding the love-draught that should be for flame
To burn out of them fear and faith and shame,
And lighten all their life up in men's sight,
And make them sad for ever. Then the knight
Bowed toward her and craved whence had she this strange thing

That might be spoil of some dim Asian king,
By starlight stolen from some waste place of sands,
And a maid bore it here in harmless hands.
And Iseult, laughing—'Other lords that be
Feast, and their men feast after them; but we,
Our men must keep the best wine back to feast
Till they be full and we of all men least
Feed after them and fain to fare so well:°
So with mine handmaid and your squire it fell
That hid this bright thing from us in a wile:'
And with light lips yet full of their swift smile
And hands that wist not though they dug a grave,
Undid the hasps of gold, and drank, and gave,
And he drank after, a deep glad kingly draught:
And all their life changed in them, for they quaffed
Death; if it be death so to drink, and fare
As men who change and are what these twain were.
And shuddering with eyes full of fear and fire
And heart-stung with a serpentine desire
He turned and saw the terror in her eyes
That yearned upon him shining in such wise
As a star midway in the midnight fixed.
  Their Galahault was the cup,° and she that mixed;
Nor other hand there needed, nor sweet speech
To lure their lips together; each on each
Hung with strange eyes and hovered as a bird
Wounded, and each mouth trembled for a word;
Their heads neared, and their hands were drawn in one,
And they saw dark, though still the unsunken sun
Far through fine rain shot fire into the south,
And their four lips became one burning mouth.

# POEMS AND BALLADS

*SECOND SERIES*

BY

ALGERNON CHARLES SWINBURNE

London

CHATTO AND WINDUS, PICCADILLY

1878

[*The right of translation is reserved*]

FIG. 7. Title page of *Poems and Ballads, Second Series* (London: Chatto & Windus, 1878), a copy from the Brotherton Library, Special Collections, University of Leeds, reproduced with permission.

# FROM *POEMS AND BALLADS, SECOND SERIES* (1878)

# The Last Oracle (A.D. 361)

*εἴπατε τῷ βασιλῆϊ, χαμαὶ πέσε δαίδαλος αὐλά·*
*οὐκέτι Φοῖβος ἔχει καλύβαν, οὐ μάντιδα δάφνην,*
*οὐ παγὰν λαλέουσαν· ἀπέσβετο καὶ λάλον ὕδωρ.*°

Years have risen and fallen in darkness or in twilight,
  Ages waxed and waned that knew not thee nor thine,
While the world sought light by night and sought not thy light,
  Since the sad last pilgrim left thy dark mid shrine.°
Dark the shrine and dumb the fount of song thence welling,
  Save for words more sad than tears of blood, that said:
*Tell the king, on earth has fallen the glorious dwelling,*
  *And the watersprings that spake are quenched and dead*
*Not a cell is left the God, no roof, no cover;*
  *In his hand the prophet laurel flowers no more.*
And the great king's high sad heart, thy true last lover,
  Felt thine answer pierce and cleave it to the core.
    And he bowed down his hopeless head°
      In the drift of the wild world's tide,
    And dying, *Thou hast conquered*, he said,
      *Galilean*;° he said it, and died.
    And the world that was thine and was ours
    When the Graces took hands with the Hours
    Grew cold as a winter wave
    In the wind from a wide-mouthed grave,
    As a gulf wide open to swallow
      The light that the world held dear.
  O father of all of us, Paian,° Apollo,
      Destroyer and healer, hear!

Age on age thy mouth was mute, thy face was hidden,
  And the lips and eyes that loved thee blind and dumb;
Song forsook their tongues that held thy name forbidden,
  Light their eyes that saw the strange God's kingdom come.
Fire for light and hell for heaven and psalms for paeans°
  Filled the clearest eyes and lips most sweet of song,
When for chant of Greeks the wail of Galileans
  Made the whole world moan with hymns of wrath and wrong.
Yea, not yet we see thee, father, as they saw thee,
  They that worshipped when the world was theirs and thine,
They whose words had power by thine own power to draw thee
  Down from heaven till earth seemed more than heaven divine.

For the shades are about us that hover
When darkness is half withdrawn
And the skirts of the dead night cover
The face of the live new dawn.
For the past is not utterly past
Though the word on its lips be the last,
And the time be gone by with its creed
When men were as beasts that bleed,
As sheep or as swine that wallow,
In the shambles of faith and of fear.
O father of all of us, Paian, Apollo,
Destroyer and healer, hear!

Yet it may be, lord and father, could we know it,
We that love thee for our darkness shall have light
More than ever prophet hailed of old or poet
Standing crowned and robed and sovereign in thy sight.
To the likeness of one God their dreams enthralled thee,
Who wast greater than all Gods that waned and grew;
Son of God° the shining son of Time they called thee,
Who wast older, O our father, than they knew.
For no thought of man made Gods to love or honour
Ere the song within the silent soul began,
Nor might earth in dream or deed take heaven upon her
Till the word was clothed with speech by lips of man.
And the word and the life wast thou,
The spirit of man and the breath;
And before thee the Gods that bow
Take life at thine hands and death.
For these are as ghosts that wane,
That are gone in an age or twain;
Harsh, merciful, passionate, pure,
They perish, but thou shalt endure;
Be their flight with the swan or the swallow,
They pass as the flight of a year.
O father of all of us, Paian, Apollo,
Destroyer and healer, hear!

Thou the word, the light, the life,° the breath, the glory,
Strong to help and heal, to lighten and to slay,
Thine is all the song of man, the world's whole story;
Not of morning and of evening is thy day.
Old and younger Gods are buried or begotten
From uprising to downsetting of thy sun,

Risen from eastward, fallen to westward and forgotten,
  And their springs are many, but their end is one.
Divers births of godheads find one death appointed,
  As the soul whence each was born makes room for each;
God by God goes out, discrowned and disanointed,
  But the soul stands fast that gave them shape and speech.
    Is the sun yet cast out of heaven?
      Is the song yet cast out of man?
    Life that had song for its leaven
      To quicken the blood that ran
    Through the veins of the songless years
    More bitter and cold than tears,
    Heaven that had thee for its one
    Light, life, word, witness, O sun,
    Are they soundless and sightless and hollow,
      Without eye, without speech, without ear?
  O father of all of us, Paian, Apollo,
      Destroyer and healer, hear!

Time arose and smote thee silent at his warning,
  Change and darkness fell on men that fell from thee;
Dark thou satest, veiled with light, behind the morning,
  Till the soul of man should lift up eyes and see.
Till the blind mute soul get speech again and eyesight,
  Man may worship not the light of life within;
In his sight the stars whose fires grow dark in thy sight
  Shine as sunbeams on the night of death and sin.
Time again is risen with mightier word of warning,
  Change hath blown again a blast of louder breath;
Clothed with clouds and stars and dreams that melt in morning,
  Lo, the Gods that ruled by grace of sin and death!
    They are conquered, they break, they are stricken,
      Whose might made the whole world pale;
    They are dust that shall rise not or quicken
      Though the world for their death's sake wail.
    As a hound on a wild beast's trace,
    So time has their godhead in chase;
    As wolves when the hunt makes head,
    They are scattered, they fly, they are fled;
    They are fled beyond hail, beyond hollo,
      And the cry of the chase, and the cheer.
  O father of all of us, Paian, Apollo,
      Destroyer and healer, hear!

Day by day° thy shadow shines in heaven beholden,
Even the sun, the shining shadow of thy face:
King, the ways of heaven before thy feet grow golden;
God, the soul of earth is kindled with thy grace.
In thy lips the speech of man whence Gods were fashioned,
In thy soul the thought that makes them and unmakes;
By thy light and heat incarnate and impassioned,
Soul to soul of man gives light for light and takes.
As they knew thy name of old time could we know it,
Healer called of sickness, slayer invoked of wrong,
Light of eyes that saw thy light, God, king, priest, poet,
Song should bring thee back to heal us with thy song.
For thy kingdom is past not away,
Nor thy power from the place thereof hurled;
Out of heaven they shall cast not the day,
They shall cast not out song from the world.
By the song and the light they give
We know thy works that they live;
With the gift thou hast given us of speech
We praise, we adore, we beseech,
We arise at thy bidding and follow,
We cry to thee, answer, appear,
O father of all of us, Paian, Apollo,
Destroyer and healer, hear!

## A Forsaken Garden

In a coign of the cliff between lowland and highland,
  At the sea-down's edge between windward and lee,
Walled round with rocks as an inland island,
  The ghost of a garden fronts the sea.
A girdle of brushwood and thorn encloses
  The steep square slope of the blossomless bed
Where the weeds that grew green from the graves of its roses
    Now lie dead.

The fields fall southward, abrupt and broken,
  To the low last edge of the long lone land.
If a step should sound or a word be spoken,
  Would a ghost not rise at the strange guest's hand?
So long have the grey bare walks lain guestless,
  Through branches and briars if a man make way,
He shall find no life but the sea-wind's, restless
    Night and day.

The dense hard passage is blind and stifled
  That crawls by a track none turn to climb
To the strait waste place that the years have rifled
  Of all but the thorns that are touched not of time.
The thorns he spares when the rose is taken;
  The rocks are left when he wastes the plain.
The wind that wanders, the weeds wind-shaken,
    These remain.

Not a flower to be pressed of the foot that falls not;
  As the heart of a dead man the seed-plots are dry;
From the thicket of thorns whence the nightingale calls not,
  Could she call, there were never a rose to reply.
Over the meadows that blossom and wither
  Rings but the note of a sea-bird's song;
Only the sun and the rain come hither
    All year long.

The sun burns sere and the rain dishevels
  One gaunt bleak blossom of scentless breath.
Only the wind here hovers and revels
  In a round where life seems barren as death.
Here there was laughing of old, there was weeping
  Haply, of lovers none ever will know,

Whose eyes went seaward a hundred sleeping
Years ago.

Heart handfast in heart as they stood, 'Look thither,'
Did he whisper? 'Look forth from the flowers to the sea;
For the foam-flowers endure when the rose-blossoms wither,
And men that love lightly may die—but we?'
And the same wind sang and the same waves whitened,
And or ever the garden's last petals were shed,
In the lips that had whispered, the eyes that had lightened,
Love was dead.

Or they loved their life through, and then went whither?
And were one to the end—but what end who knows?
Love deep as the sea as a rose must wither,
As the rose-red seaweed that mocks the rose.
Shall the dead take thought for the dead to love them?
What love was ever as deep as a grave?
They are loveless now as the grass above them
Or the wave.

All are at one now, roses and lovers,
Not known of the cliffs and the fields and the sea.
Not a breath of the time that has been hovers
In the air now soft with a summer to be.
Not a breath shall there sweeten the seasons hereafter
Of the flowers or the lovers that laugh now or weep,
When as they that are free now of weeping and laughter
We shall sleep.°

Here death may deal not again for ever;
Here change may come not till all change end.
From the graves they have made they shall rise up never,
Who have left nought living to ravage and rend.
Earth, stones, and thorns of the wild ground growing,
While the sun and the rain live, these shall be;
Till a last wind's breath upon all these blowing
Roll the sea.

Till the slow sea rise and the sheer cliff crumble,
Till terrace and meadow the deep gulfs drink,
Till the strength of the waves of the high tides humble
The fields that lessen, the rocks that shrink,
Here now in his triumph where all things falter,
Stretched out on the spoils that his own hand spread,
As a god self-slain on his own strange altar,
Death lies dead.

## Relics

This flower that smells of honey and the sea,
White laurustine, seems in my hand to be
  A white star made of memory long ago
Lit in the heaven of dear times dead to me.

A star out of the skies love used to know
Here held in hand, a stray left yet to show
  What flowers my heart was full of in the days
That are long since gone down dead memory's flow.

Dead memory that revives on doubtful ways,
Half hearkening what the buried season says
  Out of the world of the unapparent dead
Where the lost Aprils are, and the lost Mays.

Flower, once I knew thy star-white brethren bred
Nigh where the last of all the land made head
  Against the sea, a keen-faced promontory,
Flowers on salt wind and sprinkled sea-dews fed.

Their hearts were glad of the free place's glory;
The wind that sang them all his stormy story
  Had talked all winter to the sleepless spray,
And as the sea's their hues were hard and hoary.

Like things born of the sea and the bright day,
They laughed out at the years that could not slay,
  Live sons and joyous of unquiet hours,
And stronger than all storms that range for prey.

And in the close indomitable flowers
A keen-edged odour of the sun and showers
  Was as the smell of the fresh honeycomb
Made sweet for mouths of none but paramours.

Out of the hard green wall of leaves that clomb
They showed like windfalls of the snow-soft foam,
  Or feathers from the weary south-wind's wing,
Fair as the spray that it came shoreward from.

And thou, as white, what word hast thou to bring?
If my heart hearken, whereof wilt thou sing?
  For some sign surely thou too hast to bear,
Some word far south was taught thee of the spring.

White like a white rose, not like these that were
Taught of the wind's mouth and the winter air,
  Poor tender thing of soft Italian bloom,
Where once thou grewest, what else for me grew there?

Born in what spring and on what city's tomb,
By whose hand wast thou reached, and plucked for whom?
  There hangs about thee, could the soul's sense tell,
An odour as of love and of love's doom.

Of days more sweet than thou wast sweet to smell,
Of flower-soft thoughts that came to flower and fell,
  Of loves that lived a lily's life and died,
Of dreams now dwelling where dead roses dwell.

O white birth of the golden mountain-side
That for the sun's love makes its bosom wide
  At sunrise, and with all its woods and flowers
Takes in the morning to its heart of pride!

Thou hast a word of that one land of ours,
And of the fair town called of the fair towers,
  A word for me of my San Gimignan,
A word of April's greenest-girdled hours.

Of the old breached walls whereon the wallflowers ran
Called of Saint Fina, breachless now of man,
  Though time with soft feet break them stone by stone,
Who breaks down hour by hour his own reign's span.

Of the old cliff overcome and overgrown
That all that flowerage clothed as flesh clothes bone,
  That garment of acacias made for May,
Whereof here lies one witness overblown.

The fair brave trees with all their flowers at play,
How king-like they stood up into the day!
  How sweet the day was with them, and the night!
Such words of message have dead flowers to say.

This that the winter and the wind made bright,
And this that lived upon Italian light,
  Before I throw them and these words away,
Who knows but I what memories too take flight?

## *Ave Atque Vale*: In Memory of Charles Baudelaire

Nous devrions pourtant lui porter quelques fleurs;
Les morts, les pauvres morts, ont de grandes douleurs,
Et quand Octobre souffle, émondeur des vieux arbres,
Son vent mélancolique à l'entour de leurs marbres,
[Certes],° ils doivent trouver les vivants bien ingrats.°

*Les Fleurs du mal.*

Shall I strew on thee rose or rue or laurel,
Brother, on this that was the veil of thee?
Or quiet sea-flower moulded by the sea,
Or simplest growth of meadow-sweet or sorrel,
Such as the summer-sleepy Dryads weave,
Waked up by snow-soft sudden rains at eve?
Or wilt thou rather, as on earth before,
Half-faded fiery blossoms, pale with heat
And full of bitter summer, but more sweet
To thee than gleanings of a northern shore
Trod by no tropic feet?

For always thee the fervid languid glories
Allured of heavier suns in mightier skies;
Thine ears knew all the wandering watery sighs
Where the sea sobs round Lesbian promontories,
The barren kiss of piteous wave to wave
That knows not where is that Leucadian grave°
Which hides too deep the supreme head of song.
Ah, salt and sterile as her kisses were,
The wild sea winds her and the green gulfs bear
Hither and thither, and vex and work her wrong,
Blind gods that cannot spare.

Thou sawest, in thine old singing season, brother,
Secrets and sorrows unbeheld of us:
Fierce loves, and lovely leaf-buds poisonous,
Bare to thy subtler eye, but for none other
Blowing by night in some unbreathed-in clime;
The hidden harvest of luxurious time,
Sin without shape, and pleasure without speech;
And where strange dreams in a tumultuous sleep
Make the shut eyes of stricken spirits weep;

And with each face thou sawest the shadow on each,
  Seeing as men sow men reap.°

O sleepless heart and sombre soul unsleeping,
  That were athirst for sleep and no more life
  And no more love, for peace and no more strife!
Now the dim gods of death have in their keeping
  Spirit and body and all the springs of song,
  Is it well now where love can do no wrong,
Where stingless pleasure has no foam or fang
  Behind the unopening closure of her lips?
  Is it not well where soul from body slips
And flesh from bone divides without a pang
  As dew from flower-bell drips?

It is enough;° the end and the beginning
  Are one thing to thee, who art past the end.
  O hand unclasped of unbeholden friend,
For thee no fruits to pluck, no palms for winning,
  No triumph and no labour and no lust,
  Only dead yew-leaves and a little dust.
O quiet eyes wherein the light saith nought,
  Whereto the day is dumb, nor any night
  With obscure finger silences your sight,
Nor in your speech the sudden soul speaks thought,
  Sleep, and have sleep for light.

Now all strange hours and all strange loves are over,
  Dreams and desires and sombre songs and sweet,
  Hast thou found place at the great knees and feet
Of some pale Titan-woman like a lover,
  Such as thy vision here solicited,
  Under the shadow of her fair vast head,
The deep division of prodigious breasts,
  The solemn slope of mighty limbs asleep,
  The weight of awful tresses that still keep
The savour and shade of old-world pine-forests
  Where the wet hill-winds weep?

Hast thou found any likeness for thy vision?
  O gardener of strange flowers, what bud, what bloom,
  Hast thou found sown, what gathered in the gloom?
What of despair, of rapture, of derision,
  What of life is there, what of ill or good?
  Are the fruits grey like dust or bright like blood?

Does the dim ground grow any seed of ours,
  The faint fields quicken any terrene root,
  In low lands where the sun and moon are mute
And all the stars keep silence? Are there flowers
  At all, or any fruit?

Alas, but though my flying song flies after,
  O sweet strange elder singer, thy more fleet
  Singing, and footprints of thy fleeter feet,
Some dim derision of mysterious laughter
  From the blind tongueless warders of the dead,
  Some gainless glimpse of Proserpine's veiled head,
Some little sound of unregarded tears
  Wept by effaced unprofitable eyes,
  And from pale mouths some cadence of dead sighs—
These only, these the hearkening spirit hears,
  Sees only such things rise.

Thou art far too far for wings of words to follow,
  Far too far off for thought or any prayer.
  What ails us with thee, who art wind and air?
What ails us gazing where all seen is hollow?
  Yet with some fancy, yet with some desire,
  Dreams pursue death as winds a flying fire,
Our dreams pursue our dead and do not find.
  Still, and more swift than they, the thin flame flies,
  The low light fails us in elusive skies,
Still the foiled earnest ear is deaf, and blind
  Are still the eluded eyes.

Not thee, O never thee, in all time's changes,
  Not thee, but this the sound of thy sad soul,
  The shadow of thy swift spirit, this shut scroll
I lay my hand on, and not death estranges
  My spirit from communion of thy song—
  These memories and these melodies that throng
Veiled porches of a Muse funereal—
  These I salute, these touch, these clasp and fold
  As though a hand were in my hand to hold,
Or through mine ears a mourning musical
  Of many mourners rolled.

I among these, I also, in such station
  As when the pyre was charred, and piled the sods,
  And offering to the dead made, and their gods,
The old mourners had, standing to make libation,

I stand, and to the gods and to the dead
Do reverence without prayer or praise, and shed
Offering to these unknown, the gods of gloom,
And what of honey and spice my seedlands bear,
And what I may of fruits in this chilled air,
And lay, Orestes-like, across the tomb
A curl of severed hair.°

But by no hand nor any treason stricken,°
Not like the low-lying head of Him, the King,
The flame that made of Troy a ruinous thing,
Thou liest and on this dust no tears could quicken
There fall no tears like theirs that all men hear
Fall tear by sweet imperishable tear
Down the opening leaves of holy poets' pages.
Thee not Orestes, not Electra mourns;
But bending us-ward with memorial urns
The most high Muses that fulfil all ages
Weep, and our God's heart yearns.

For, sparing of his sacred strength, not often
Among us darkling here the lord of light°
Makes manifest his music and his might
In hearts that open and in lips that soften
With the soft flame and heat of songs that shine
Thy lips indeed he touched with bitter wine,
And nourished them indeed with bitter bread;
Yet surely from his hand thy soul's food came,
The fire that scarred thy spirit at his flame
Was lighted, and thine hungering heart he fed
Who feeds our hearts with fame.

Therefore he too now at thy soul's sunsetting,
God of all suns and songs, he too bends down
To mix his laurel with thy cypress crown.°
And save thy dust from blame and from forgetting.
Therefore he too, seeing all thou wert and art,
Compassionate, with sad and sacred heart,
Mourns thee of many his children the last dead,
And hallows with strange tears and alien sighs
Thine unmelodious mouth and sunless eyes,
And over thine irrevocable head
Sheds light from the under skies.

And one weeps with him in the ways Lethean,
And stains with tears her changing bosom chill:

That obscure Venus of the hollow hill,°
That thing transformed which was the Cytherean,
With lips that lost their Grecian laugh divine
Long since, and face no more called Erycine;°
A ghost, a bitter and luxurious god.
Thee also with fair flesh and singing spell
Did she, a sad and second prey, compel
Into the footless places once more trod,
And shadows hot from hell.

And now no sacred staff shall break in blossom,°
No choral salutation lure to light
A spirit sick with perfume and sweet night
And love's tired eyes and hands and barren bosom.
There is no help for these things; none to mend,
And none to mar; not all our songs, O friend,
Will make death clear or make life durable.
Howbeit with rose and ivy and wild vine
And with wild notes about this dust of thine
At least I fill the place where white dreams dwell
And wreathe an unseen shrine.

Sleep; and if life was bitter to thee, pardon,
If sweet, give thanks; thou hast no more to live;
And to give thanks is good, and to forgive.
Out of the mystic and the mournful garden
Where all day through thine hands in barren braid
Wove the sick flowers of secrecy and shade,
Green buds of sorrow and sin, and remnants grey,
Sweet-smelling, pale with poison, sanguine-hearted,
Passions that sprang from sleep and thoughts that started,
Shall death not bring us all as thee one day
Among the days departed?

For thee, O now a silent soul, my brother,
Take at my hands this garland, and farewell.
Thin is the leaf, and chill the wintry smell,
And chill the solemn earth, a fatal mother,
With sadder than the Niobean womb,°
And in the hollow of her breasts a tomb.
Content thee, howsoe'er, whose days are done;
There lies not any troublous thing before,
Nor sight nor sound to war against thee more,
For whom all winds are quiet as the sun,
All waters as the shore.

# Memorial Verses

## On the Death of Théophile Gautier

Death, what hast thou to do with me? So saith
Love, with eyes set against the face of Death;
 What have I done, O thou strong Death, to thee,
That mine own lips should wither from thy breath?

Though thou be blind as fire or as the sea,
Why should thy waves and storms make war on me?
 Is it for hate thou hast to find me fair,
Or for desire to kiss, if it might be,

My very mouth of song, and kill me there?
So with keen rains vexing his crownless hair,
 With bright feet bruised from no delightful way,
Through darkness and the disenchanted air,

Lost Love went weeping half a winter's day.
And the armèd wind that smote him seemed to say,
 How shall the dew live when the dawn is fled,
Or wherefore should the Mayflower outlast May?

Then Death took Love by the right hand and said,
Smiling: Come now and look upon thy dead.
 But Love cast down the glories of his eyes,
And bowed down like a flower his flowerless head.

And Death spake, saying: What ails thee in such wise,
Being god, to shut thy sight up from the skies?
 If thou canst see not, hast thou ears to hear?
Or is thy soul too as a leaf that dies?

Even as he spake with fleshless lips of fear,
But soft as sleep sings in a tired man's ear,
 Behold, the winter was not, and its might
Fell, and fruits broke forth of the barren year.

And upon earth was largess of great light,
And moving music winged for worldwide flight,
 And shapes and sounds of gods beheld and heard,
And day's foot set upon the neck of night.

And with such song the hollow ways were stirred
As of a god's heart hidden in a bird,

Or as the whole soul of the sun in spring
Should find full utterance in one flower-soft word,

And all the season should break forth and sing
From one flower's lips, in one rose triumphing;
Such breath and light of song as of a flame
Made ears and spirits of them that heard it ring.

And Love beholding knew not for the same
The shape that led him, nor in face nor name,
For he was bright and great of thews and fair,
And in Love's eyes he was not Death, but Fame.

Not that grey ghost whose life is empty and bare
And his limbs moulded out of mortal air,
A cloud of change that shifts into a shower
And dies and leaves no light for time to wear:

But a god clothed with his own joy and power,
A god re-risen out of his mortal hour
Immortal, king and lord of time and space,
With eyes that look on them as from a tower.

And where he stood the pale sepulchral place
Bloomed, as new life might in a bloodless face,
And where men sorrowing came to seek a tomb
With funeral flowers and tears for grief and grace,

They saw with light as of a world in bloom
The portal of the House of Fame° illume
The ways of life wherein we toiling tread,
And watched the darkness as a brand consume.°

And through the gates where rule the deathless dead
The sound of a new singer's soul was shed
That sang among his kinsfolk, and a beam
Shot from the star on a new ruler's head.

A new star lighting the Lethean stream,
A new song mixed into the song supreme
Made of all souls of singers and their might,
That makes of life and time and death a dream.

Thy star, thy song, O soul that in our sight
Wast as a sun that made for man's delight
Flowers and all fruits in season, being so near
The sun-god's face, our god that gives us light.

To him of all gods that we love or fear
Thou among all men by thy name wast dear,
  Dear to the god that gives us spirit of song
To bind and burn all hearts of men that hear.

The god that makes men's words too sweet and strong
For life or time or death to do them wrong,
  Who sealed with his thy spirit for a sign
And filled it with his breath thy whole life long.

Who made thy moist lips fiery with new wine
Pressed from the grapes of song the sovereign vine,
  And with all love of all things loveliest
Gave thy soul power to make them more divine.

That thou might'st breathe upon the breathless rest
Of marble, till the brows and lips and breast
  Felt fall from off them as a cancelled curse
That speechless sleep wherewith they lived opprest.

Who gave thee strength and heat of spirit to pierce
All clouds of form and colour that disperse,
  And leave the spirit of beauty to remould
In types of clean chryselephantine° verse.

Who gave thee words more golden than fine gold
To carve in shapes more glorious than of old,
  And build thy songs up in the sight of time
As statues set in godhead manifold:

In sight and scorn of temporal change and clime
That meet the sun re-risen with refluent rhyme
—As god to god might answer face to face—
From lips whereon the morning strikes sublime.

Dear to the god, our god who gave thee place
Among the chosen of days, the royal race,
  The lords of light, whose eyes of old and ears
Saw even on earth and heard him for a space.

There are the souls of those once mortal years
That wrought with fire of joy and light of tears
  In words divine as deeds that grew thereof
Such music as he swoons with love who hears.

There are the lives that lighten from above
Our under lives, the spheral souls that move

Through the ancient heaven of song-illumined air
Whence we that hear them singing die with love.

There all the crowned Hellenic heads, and there
The old gods who made men godlike as they were,
The lyric lips wherefrom all songs take fire,
Live eyes, and light of Apollonian hair.

There, round the sovereign passion of that lyre
Which the stars hear and tremble with desire,
The ninefold light Pierian° is made one
That here we see divided, and aspire,

Seeing, after this or that crown to be won;
But where they hear the singing of the sun,
All form, all sound, all colour, and all thought
Are as one body and soul in unison.

There the song sung shines as a picture wrought,
The painted mouths sing that on earth say nought,
The carven limbs have sense of blood and growth
And large-eyed life that seeks nor lacks not aught.

There all the music of thy living mouth
Lives, and all loves wrought of thine hand in youth
And bound about the breasts and brows with gold
And coloured pale or dusk from north or south.

Fair living things made to thy will of old,
Born of thy lips, no births of mortal mould,
That in the world of song about thee wait
Where thought and truth are one and manifold.

Within the graven lintels of the gate
That here divides our vision and our fate,
The dreams we walk in and the truths of sleep,
All sense and spirit have life inseparate.

There what one thinks, is his to grasp and keep;
There are no dreams, but very joys to reap,
No foiled desires that die before delight,
No fears to see across our joys and weep.

There hast thou all thy will of thought and sight,
All hope for harvest, and all heaven for flight;
The sunrise of whose golden-mouthed glad head
To paler songless ghosts was heat and light.

Here where the sunset of our year is red
Men think of thee as of the summer dead,
  Gone forth before the snows, before thy day,
With unshod feet, with brows unchapleted.

Couldst thou not wait till age had wound, they say,
Round those wreathed brows his soft white blossoms?° Nay,
  Why shouldst thou vex thy soul with this harsh air,
Thy bright-winged soul, once free to take its way?

Nor for men's reverence hadst thou need to wear
The holy flower of grey time-hallowed hair;
  Nor were it fit that aught of thee grew old,
Fair lover all thy days of all things fair.

And hear we not thy words of molten gold
Singing? or is their light and heat acold
  Whereat men warmed their spirits? Nay, for all
These yet are with us, ours to hear and hold.

The lovely laughter, the clear tears, the call
Of love to love on ways where shadows fall,
  Through doors of dim division and disguise,
And music made of doubts unmusical;

The love that caught strange light from death's own eyes,[1]
And filled death's lips with fiery words and sighs,
  And half asleep let feed from veins of his
Her close red warm snake's mouth, Egyptian-wise:

And that great night of love more strange than this,[2]
When she that made the whole world's bale and bliss
  Made king of all the world's desire a slave,
And killed him in mid kingdom with a kiss;

Veiled loves that shifted shapes and shafts, and gave,[3]
Laughing, strange gifts to hands that durst not crave,
  Flowers double-blossomed, fruits of scent and hue
Sweet as the bride-bed, stranger than the grave;

All joys and wonders of old lives and new
That ever in love's shine or shadow grew,
  And all the grief whereof he dreams and grieves,
And all sweet roots fed on his light and dew;

[1] *La Morte Amoureuse.* [2] *Une Nuit de Cléopâtre.*
[3] *Mademoiselle de Maupin.*°

All these through thee our spirit of sense perceives,
As threads in the unseen woof thy music weaves,
  Birds caught and snared that fill our ears with thee,
Bay-blossoms in thy wreath of brow-bound leaves.

Mixed with the masque of death's old comedy
Though thou too pass, have here our flowers, that we
  For all the flowers thou gav'st upon thee shed,
And pass not crownless to Persephone.

Blue lotus-blooms and white and rosy-red
We wind with poppies for thy silent head,
  And on this margin of the sundering sea
Leave thy sweet light to rise upon the dead.

## Sonnet

### (with a copy of *Mademoiselle de Maupin*)

This is the golden book of spirit and sense,
The holy writ of beauty; he that wrought
Made it with dreams and faultless words and thought
That seeks and finds and loses in the dense
Dim air of life that beauty's excellence
Wherewith love makes one hour of life distraught
And all hours after follow and find not aught.
Here is that height of all love's eminence
Where man may breathe but for a breathing-space
And feel his soul burn as an altar-fire
To the unknown God of unachieved desire,
And from the middle mystery of the place
Watch lights that break, hear sounds as of a quire,
But see not twice unveiled the veiled God's face.

## In Memory of Barry Cornwall

### (October 4, 1874)

In the garden of death, where the singers whose names are deathless
   One with another make music unheard of men,
Where the dead sweet roses fade not of lips long breathless,
   And the fair eyes shine that shall weep not or change again,
Who comes now crowned with the blossom of snow-white years?
What music is this that the world of the dead men hears?

Beloved of men, whose words on our lips were honey,
   Whose name in our ears and our fathers' ears was sweet,
Like summer gone forth of the land his songs made sunny,
   To the beautiful veiled bright world where the glad ghosts meet,
Child, father, bridegroom and bride, and anguish and rest,
No soul shall pass of a singer than this more blest.

Blest for the years' sweet sake that were filled and brightened,
   As a forest with birds, with the fruit and the flower of his song;
For the souls' sake blest that heard, and their cares were lightened,
   For the hearts' sake blest that have fostered his name so long;
By the living and dead lips blest that have loved his name,
And clothed with their praise and crowned with their love for fame.

Ah, fair and fragrant his fame as flowers that close not,
   That shrink not by day for heat or for cold by night,
As a thought in the heart shall increase when the heart's self knows not,
   Shall endure in our ears as a sound, in our eyes as a light;
Shall wax with the years that wane and the seasons' chime,
As a white rose thornless that grows in the garden of time.

The same year calls, and one goes hence with another,°
   And men sit sad that were glad for their sweet songs' sake;
The same year beckons, and elder with younger brother
   Takes mutely the cup from his hand that we all shall take.[1]
They pass ere the leaves be past or the snows be come;
And the birds are loud, but the lips that outsang them dumb.

Time takes them home that we loved, fair names and famous,
   To the soft long sleep, to the broad sweet bosom of death;
But the flower of their souls he shall take not away to shame us,
   Nor the lips lack song for ever that now lack breath.
For with us shall the music and perfume that die not dwell,
Though the dead to our dead bid welcome, and we farewell.

[1] Sydney Dobell died August 22, 1874.

# Inferiae

Spring, and the light and sound of things on earth
Requickening, all within our green sea's girth;
A tune of passage or a time of birth
   Fourscore years since as this year, first and last.

The sun is all about the world we see,
The breath and strength of very spring; and we
Live, love, and feed on our own hearts; but he
   Whose heart fed mine has passed into the past.

Past, all things born with sense and blood and breath;
The flesh hears nought that now the spirit saith.
If death be like as birth and birth as death,
   The first was fair more fair should be the last.

Fourscore years since, and come but one month more
The count were perfect of his mortal score
Whose sail went seaward yesterday from shore
   To cross the last of many an unsailed sea.

Light, love and labour up to life's last height,
These three were stars unsetting in his sight;
Even as the sun is life and heat and light
   And sets not nor is dark when dark are we.

The life, the spirit, and the work were one
That here ah, who shall say, that here are done?
Not I, that know not; father, not thy son,
   For all the darkness of the night and sea.

*March 5, 1877.*

# Cyril Tourneur

A sea that heaves with horror of the night,
  As maddened by the moon that hangs aghast
  With strain and torment of the ravening blast,
Haggard as hell, a bleak blind bloody light;
No shore but one red reef of rock in sight,
  Whereon the waifs of many a wreck were cast
  And shattered in the fierce nights overpast
Wherein more souls toward hell than heaven took flight;
And 'twixt the shark-toothed rocks and swallowing shoals
A cry as out of hell from all these souls
  Sent through the sheer gorge of the slaughtering sea,
Whose thousand throats, full-fed with life by death,
Fill the black air with foam and furious breath;
  And over all these one star—Chastity.°

# A Ballad of François Villon

## Prince of All Ballad-Makers

Bird of the bitter bright grey golden morn
   Scarce risen upon the dusk of dolorous years,
First of us all and sweetest singer born
   Whose far shrill note the world of new men hears
   Cleave the cold shuddering shade as twilight clears;
When song new-born put off the old world's attire
And felt its tune on her changed lips expire,
   Writ foremost on the roll of them that came
Fresh girt for service of the latter lyre,
   Villon, our sad bad glad mad brother's name!

Alas the joy, the sorrow, and the scorn,
   That clothed thy life with hopes and sins and fears,
And gave thee stones for bread and tares for corn
   And plume-plucked gaol-birds for thy starveling peers
   Till death clipt close their flight with shameful shears;
Till shifts came short and loves were hard to hire,
When lilt of song nor twitch of twangling wire
   Could buy thee bread or kisses; when light fame
Spurned like a ball and haled through brake and briar,
   Villon, our sad bad glad mad brother's name!

Poor splendid wings so frayed and soiled and torn!
   Poor kind wild eyes so dashed with light quick tears!
Poor perfect voice, most blithe when most forlorn,
   That rings athwart the sea whence no man steers
   Like joy-bells crossed with death-bells in our ears!
What far delight has cooled the fierce desire
That like some ravenous bird was strong to tire
   On that frail flesh and soul consumed with flame,
But left more sweet than roses to respire,
   Villon, our sad bad glad mad brother's name?

*Envoi.*

Prince of sweet songs made out of tears and fire,
A harlot was thy nurse, a God thy sire;
   Shame soiled thy song, and song assoiled thy shame.
But from thy feet now death has washed the mire,
   Love reads out first at head of all our quire,
Villon, our sad bad glad mad brother's name.

# A Vision of Spring in Winter

O tender time that love thinks long to see,
  Sweet foot of spring that with her footfall sows
  Late snowlike flowery leavings of the snows,
Be not too long irresolute to be;
O mother-month, where have they hidden thee?
  Out of the pale time of the flowerless rose
I reach my heart out toward the springtime lands,
  I stretch my spirit forth to the fair hours,
    The purplest of the prime;
I lean my soul down over them, with hands
  Made wide to take the ghostly growths of flowers;
    I send my love back to the lovely time.

Where has the greenwood° hid thy gracious head?
  Veiled with what visions while the grey world grieves,
  Or muffled with what shadows of green leaves,
What warm intangible green shadows spread
To sweeten the sweet twilight for thy bed?
  What sleep enchants thee? what delight deceives?
Where the deep dreamlike dew before the dawn
  Feels not the fingers of the sunlight yet
    Its silver web unweave,
Thy footless ghost on some unfooted lawn
  Whose air the unrisen sunbeams fear to fret
    Lives a ghost's life of daylong dawn and eve.

Sunrise it sees not, neither set of star,
  Large nightfall, nor imperial plenilune,
  Nor strong sweet shape of the full-breasted noon;
But where the silver-sandalled shadows are,
Too soft for arrows of the sun to mar,
  Moves with the mild gait of an ungrown moon:
Hard overhead the half-lit crescent swims,
  The tender-coloured night draws hardly breath,
    The light is listening;
They watch the dawn of slender-shapen limbs,
  Virginal, born again of doubtful death,
    Chill foster-father of the weanling spring.°

As sweet desire of day before the day,
  As dreams of love before the true love born,

  From the outer edge of winter overworn
The ghost arisen of May before the May
Takes through dim air her unawakened way,
  The gracious ghost of morning risen ere morn.
With little unblown breasts and child-eyed looks
  Following, the very maid, the girl-child spring,
    Lifts windward her bright brows,
Dips her light feet in warm and moving brooks,
  And kindles with her own mouth's colouring
    The fearful firstlings of the plumeless boughs.

I seek thee sleeping, and awhile I see,
  Fair face that art not, how thy maiden breath
  Shall put at last the deadly days to death
And fill the fields and fire the woods with thee
And seaward hollows where my feet would be
  When heaven shall hear the word that April saith
To change the cold heart of the weary time,
  To stir and soften all the time to tears,
    Tears joyfuller than mirth;
As even to May's clear height the young days climb
  With feet not swifter than those fair first years
    Whose flowers revive not with thy flowers on earth.

I would not bid thee, though I might, give back
  One good thing youth has given and borne away;
  I crave not any comfort of the day
That is not, nor on time's retrodden track
Would turn to meet the white-robed hours or black
  That long since left me on their mortal way;
Nor light nor love that has been, nor the breath
  That comes with morning from the sun to be
    And sets light hope on fire;
No fruit, no flower thought once too fair for death,
  No flower nor hour once fallen from life's green tree,
    No leaf once plucked or once fulfilled desire.

The morning song beneath the stars that fled
  With twilight through the moonless mountain air,
  While youth with burning lips and wreathless hair
Sang toward the sun that was to crown his head,
Rising; the hopes that triumphed and fell dead,
  The sweet swift eyes and songs of hours that were;
These may'st thou not give back for ever; these,

As at the sea's heart all her wrecks lie waste,
Lie deeper than the sea;
But flowers thou may'st, and winds, and hours of ease,
And all its April to the world thou may'st
Give back, and half my April back to me.

# The Epitaph in Form of a Ballad Which Villon made for Himself and his Comrades, Expecting to be Hanged along with them

Men, brother men, that after us yet live,
Let not your hearts too hard against us be;
For if some pity of us poor men ye give,
The sooner God shall take of you pity.
Here are we five or six strung up, you see,
And here the flesh that all too well we fed
Bit by bit eaten and rotten, rent and shred,
And we the bones grow dust and ash withal;
Let no man laugh at us discomforted,
But pray to God that he forgive us all.

If we call on you, brothers, to forgive,
Ye should not hold our prayer in scorn, though we
Were slain by law; ye know that all alive
Have not wit alway to walk righteously;
Make therefore intercession heartily
With him that of a virgin's womb was bred,
That his grace be not as a dry well-head
For us, nor let hell's thunder on us fall;
We are dead, let no man harry or vex us dead,
But pray to God that he forgive us all.

The rain has washed and laundered us all five,
And the sun dried and blackened; yea, perdie,
Ravens and pies with beaks that rend and rive
Have dug our eyes out, and plucked off for fee
Our beards and eyebrows; never are we free,
Not once, to rest; but here and there still sped,
Drive at its wild will by the wind's change led,
More pecked of birds than fruits on garden-wall;
Men, for God's love, let no gibe here be said,
But pray to God that he forgive us all.

Prince Jesus, that of all art lord and head,
Keep us, that hell be not our bitter bed;
We have nought to do in such a master's hall.
Be not ye therefore of our fellowhead,
But pray to God that he forgive us all.

# FROM *A STUDY OF SHAKESPEARE* (1880)

[...] The entrance to the third period of Shakespeare is like the entrance to that lost and lesser Paradise of old,

> With dreadful faces thronged, and fiery arms.°

Lear, Othello, Macbeth, Coriolanus, Antony, Timon, these are names indeed of something more than tragic purport. Only in the sunnier distance beyond, where the sunset of Shakespeare's imagination seems to melt or flow back into the sunrise, do we discern Prospero beside Miranda, Florizel by Perdita, Palamon with Arcite, the same knightly and kindly Duke Theseus as of old; and above them all, and all others of his divine and human children, the crowning and final and ineffable figure of Imogen.

Of all Shakespeare's plays, *King Lear* is unquestionably that in which he has come nearest to the height and to the likeness of the one tragic poet on any side greater than himself whom the world in all its ages has ever seen born of time. It is by far the most Æschylean of his works;° the most elemental and primæval, the most oceanic and Titanic in conception. He deals here with no subtleties as in *Hamlet*, with no conventions as in *Othello*: there is no question of 'a divided duty' or a problem half insoluble, a matter of country and connection, of family or of race; we look upward and downward, and in vain, into the deepest things of nature, into the highest things of providence; to the roots of life, and to the stars; from the roots that no God waters to the stars which give no man light; over a world full of death and life without resting-place or guidance.

But in one main point it differs radically from the work and the spirit of Æschylus. Its fatalism is of a darker and harder nature. To Prometheus the fetters of the lord and enemy of mankind were bitter; upon Orestes° the hand of heaven was laid too heavily to bear; yet in the not utterly infinite or everlasting distance we see beyond them the promise of the morning on which mystery and justice shall be made one; when righteousness and omnipotence at last shall kiss each other. But on the horizon of Shakespeare's tragic fatalism we see no such twilight of atonement, such pledge of reconciliation as this. Requital, redemption, amends, equity, explanation, pity and mercy, are words without a meaning here.

> As flies to wanton boys are we to the gods;
> They kill us for their sport.°

Here is no need of the Eumenides,° children of Night everlasting; for here is very Night herself.

The words just cited are not casual or episodical; they strike the keynote of the whole poem, lay the keystone of the whole arch of thought. There is no contest of conflicting forces, no judgment so much as by casting of lots: far less is there any light of heavenly harmony or of heavenly wisdom, of Apollo or Athene from above. We have heard much and often from theologians of the light of revelation: and some such thing indeed we find in Æschylus: but the darkness of revelation is here.

For in this the most terrible work of human genius it is with the very springs and sources of nature that her student has set himself to deal. The veil of the temple of our humanity is rent in twain.° Nature herself, we might say, is revealed—and revealed as unnatural. In face of such a world as this a man might be forgiven who should pray that chaos might come again.° Nowhere else in Shakespeare's work or in the universe of jarring lives are the lines of character and event so broadly drawn or so sharply cut. Only the supreme self-command of this one poet could so mould and handle such types as to restrain and prevent their passing from the abnormal into the monstrous: yet even as much as this, at least in all cases but one, it surely has accomplished. In Regan alone would it be, I think, impossible to find a touch or trace of anything less vile than it was devilish. Even Goneril has her one splendid hour, her fire-flaught° of hellish glory; when she treads under foot the half-hearted goodness, the wordy and windy though sincere abhorrence, which is all that the mild and impotent revolt of Albany can bring to bear against her imperious and dauntless devilhood; when she flaunts before the eyes of her 'milk-livered' and 'moral fool' the coming banners of France about the 'plumed helm' of his slayer.°

On the other side, Kent is the exception which answers to Regan on this. Cordelia, the brotherless Antigone of our stage, has one passing touch of intolerance for what her sister was afterwards to brand as indiscretion and dotage in their father, which redeems her from the charge of perfection. Like Imogen, she is not too inhumanly divine for the sense of divine irritation. Godlike though they be, their very godhead is human and feminine; and only therefore credible, and only therefore adorable. Cloten and Regan, Goneril and Iachimo, have power to stir and embitter the sweetness of their blood. But for the contrast and even the contact of antagonists as abominable as these, the gold of their spirit would be too refined, the lily of their holiness too radiant, the violet of their virtue too sweet. As it is, Shakespeare has gone down perforce among the blackest and the basest things of nature to find anything so equally exceptional in evil as properly to counterbalance and make bearable the excellence and extremity of their goodness. No otherwise could either angel have escaped the blame implied in the very attribute and epithet of blameless. But where the possible depth of human hell is so foul and unfathomable as it appears in the spirits which serve as foils to these, we may endure that in them the inner height of heaven should be no less immaculate and immeasurable.

It should be a truism wellnigh as musty as Hamlet's half cited proverb,° to enlarge upon the evidence given in *King Lear* of a sympathy with the mass of social misery more wide and deep and direct and bitter and tender than Shakespeare has shown elsewhere. But as even to this day and even in respectable quarters the murmur is not quite duly extinct which would charge on Shakespeare a certain share of divine indifference to suffering, of godlike satisfaction and a less than compassionate content, it is not yet perhaps utterly superfluous to insist on the utter fallacy and falsity of their creed who whether in praise or in blame would rank him to his credit or discredit among such poets as on this side at least may be classed rather with Goethe than with Shelley and with Gautier than with Hugo. A poet of revolution he is not, as none of his country in that generation could have been: but as surely as the author of *Julius Cæsar* has approved himself in the best and highest sense of the word at least potentially a republican, so surely has the author of *King Lear* avowed himself in the only good and rational sense of the words a spiritual if not a political democrat and socialist.

It is only, I think, in this most tragic of tragedies that the sovereign lord and incarnate god of pity and terror can be said to have struck with all his strength a chord of which the resonance could excite such angry agony and heartbreak of wrath as that of the brother kings when they smote their staffs against the ground in fierce imperious anguish of agonised and rebellious compassion, at the oracular cry of Calchas for the innocent blood of Iphigenia.° The doom even of Desdemona seems as much less morally intolerable as it is more logically inevitable than the doom of Cordelia. But doubtless the fatalism of *Othello* is as much darker and harder than that of any third among the plays of Shakespeare, as it is less dark and hard than the fatalism of *King Lear*. For upon the head of the very noblest man whom even omnipotence or Shakespeare could ever call to life he has laid a burden in one sense yet heavier than the burden of Lear, insomuch as the sufferer can with somewhat less confidence of universal appeal proclaim himself a man more sinned against than sinning.°

And yet, if ever man after Lear might lift up his voice in that protest, it would assuredly be none other than Othello. He is in all the prosperous days of his labour and his triumph so utterly and wholly nobler than the self-centred and wayward king, that the capture of his soul and body in the unimaginable snare of Iago seems a yet blinder and more unrighteous blow

> Struck by the envious wrath of man or God°

than ever fell on the old white head of that child-changed father. But at least he is destroyed by the stroke of a mightier hand than theirs who struck down

Lear. As surely as Othello is the noblest man of man's making, Iago is the most perfect evildoer, the most potent demi-devil. It is of course the merest commonplace to say as much, and would be no less a waste of speech to add the half comfortable reflection that it is in any case no shame to fall by such a hand. But this subtlest and strangest work of Shakespeare's admits and requires some closer than common scrutiny. Coleridge has admirably described the first great soliloquy which opens to us the pit of hell within as 'the motive-hunting of a motiveless malignity.'° But subtle and profound and just as is this definitive appreciation, there is more in the matter yet than even this. It is not only that Iago, so to speak, half tries to make himself half believe that Othello has wronged him, and that the thought of it gnaws him inly like a poisonous mineral: though this also be true, it is not half the truth—nor half that half again. Malignant as he is, the very subtlest and strongest component of his complex nature is not even malignity. It is the instinct of what Mr Carlyle would call an inarticulate poet.° In his immortal study on the affair of the diamond necklace, the most profound and potent humourist of his country in his century has unwittingly touched on the mainspring of Iago's character—'the very pulse of the machine.'° He describes his Circe de la Mothe-Valois° as a practical dramatic poet or playwright at least in lieu of play-writer: while indicating how and wherefore, with all her constructive skill and rhythmic art in action, such genius as hers so differs from the genius of Shakespeare that she undeniably could not have written a *Hamlet*.° Neither could Iago have written an *Othello*. (From this theorem, by the way, a reasoner or a casuist benighted enough to prefer articulate poets to inarticulate, Shakespeare to Cromwell, a fair Vittoria Colonna to a 'foul Circe-Megæra,' and even such a strategist as Homer to such a strategist as Frederic-William,° would not illogically draw such conclusions or infer such corollaries as might result in opinions hardly consonant with the Teutonic-Titanic evangel of the preacher who supplied him with his thesis.) 'But what he can do, that he will': and if it be better to make a tragedy than to write one, to act a poem than to sing it, we must allow to Iago a station in the hierarchy of poets very far in advance of his creator's. None of the great inarticulate may more justly claim place and precedence. With all his poetic gift, he has no poetic weakness. Almost any creator but his would have given him some grain of spite or some spark of lust after Desdemona. To Shakespeare's Iago she is no more than is a rhyme to another and articulate poet. His stanza must at any rate and at all costs be polished:° to borrow the metaphor used by Mr Carlyle in apologetic illustration of a royal hero's peculiar system of levying recruits for his colossal brigade. He has within him a sense or conscience of power incomparable: and this power shall not be left, in Hamlet's phrase, 'to fust in him unused.'° A genuine and thorough capacity for human lust or hate would diminish and degrade the supremacy of his evil. He is almost as far above or beyond vice as he is beneath or beyond virtue. And this it is that makes him impregnable and invulnerable. When once he has said it, we know as well as he that thenceforth he never will speak word. We could smile almost as we can see him to have smiled at Gratiano's most ignorant and empty threat, being well assured that torments will in no wise ope his lips:[o] that as surely and as truthfully as ever did the tortured philosopher before him, he might have told his tormentors that they did but bruise the coating, batter the crust, or break the shell of Iago. Could we imagine a far other lost spirit than Farinata degli Uberti's[o] endowed with Farinata's might of will, and transferred from the sepulchres of fire to the dykes of Malebolge,[o] we might conceive something of Iago's attitude in hell—of his unalterable and indomitable posture for all eternity. As though it were possible and necessary that in some one point the extremities of all conceivable good and of all imaginable evil should meet and mix together in a new 'marriage of heaven and hell,'[o] the action in passion of the most devilish among all the human damned could hardly be other than that of the most godlike among all divine saviours—the figure of Iago than a reflection by hell-fire of the figure of Prometheus.

Between Iago and Othello the position of Desdemona is precisely that defined with such quaint sublimity of fancy in the old English byword—'between the devil and the deep sea.' Deep and pure and strong and adorable always and terrible and pitiless on occasion as the sea is the great soul of the glorious hero to whom she has given herself; and what likeness of man's enemy from Satan down to Mephistopheles could be matched for danger and for dread against the good bluff soldierly trustworthy figure of honest Iago? The rough license of his tongue at once takes warrant from his good soldiership and again gives warrant for his honesty: so that in a double sense it does him yeoman's service, and that twice told. It is pitifully ludicrous to see him staged to the show like a member—and a very inefficient member—of the secret police. But it would seem impossible for actors to understand that he is not a would-be detective, an aspirant for the honours of a Vidocq, a candidate for the laurels of a Vautrin:[o] that he is no less than Lepidus,[o] or than Antony's horse, 'a tried and valiant soldier.'[o] It is perhaps natural that the two deepest and subtlest of all Shakespeare's intellectual studies in good and evil should be the two most painfully misused and misunderstood alike by his commentators and his fellows of the stage: it is certainly undeniable that no third figure of his creation has ever been on both sides as persistently misconceived and misrepresented with such desperate pertinacity as Hamlet and Iago.

And it is only when Iago is justly appreciated that we can justly appreciate either Othello or Desdemona. This again should surely be no more than the truism that it sounds; but practically it would seem to be no less than an adventurous and audacious paradox. Remove or deform or diminish or modify the dominant features of the destroyer, and we have but the eternal and vulgar figures of jealousy and innocence, newly vamped and veneered and padded and patched up for the stalest purposes of puppetry. As it is, when Coleridge asks 'which do we pity the most'° at the fall of the curtain, we can surely answer, Othello. Noble as are the 'most blessed conditions'° of 'the gentle Desdemona,'° he is yet the nobler of the two; and has suffered more in one single pang than she could suffer in life or in death. [...]

# FROM *SONGS OF THE SPRINGTIDES* (1880)

## Thalassius

Upon the flowery forefront of the year,
One wandering by the grey-green April sea
Found on a reach of shingle and shallower sand
Inlaid with starrier glimmering jewellery
Left for the sun's love and the light wind's cheer
Along the foam-flowered strand
Breeze-brightened, something nearer sea than land
Though the last shoreward blossom-fringe was near,
A babe asleep with flower-soft face that gleamed
To sun and seaward as it laughed and dreamed,
Too sure of either love for either's fear,
Albeit so birdlike slight and light, it seemed
Nor man nor mortal child of man, but fair
As even its twin-born tenderer spray-flowers were,
That the wind scatters like an Oread's hair.

For when July strewed fire on earth and sea
The last time ere that year,
Out of the flame of morn Cymothoe°
Beheld one brighter than the sunbright sphere
Move toward her from its fieriest heart, whence trod
The live sun's very God,
Across the foam-bright water-ways that are
As heavenlier heavens with star for answering star,
And on her eyes and hair and maiden mouth
Felt a kiss falling fierier than the South,
And heard above afar
A noise of songs and wind-enamoured wings
And lutes and lyres of milder and mightier strings,
And round the resonant radiance of his car
Where depth is one with height,
Light heard as music, music seen as light
And with that second moondawn of the spring's
That fosters the first rose,

A sun-child whiter than the sunlit snows
Was born out of the world of sunless things
That round the round earth flows and ebbs and flows.

But he that found the sea-flower by the sea
And took to foster like a graft of earth
Was born of man's most highest and heavenliest birth,
Free-born as winds and stars and waves are free;
A warrior grey with glories more than years,
Though more of years than change the quick to dead
Had rained their light and darkness on his head;
A singer that in time's and memory's ears
Should leave such words to sing as all his peers
Might praise with hallowing heat of rapturous tears
Till all the days of human flight were fled.
And at his knees his fosterling was fed
Not with man's wine and bread
Nor mortal mother-milk of hopes and fears,
But food of deep memorial days long sped;
For bread with wisdom and with song for wine
Clear as the full calm's emerald hyaline.°
And from his grave glad lips the boy would gather
Fine honey of song-notes goldener than gold,
More sweet than bees make of the breathing heather,
That he, as glad and bold,
Might drink as they, and keep his spirit from cold.
And the boy loved his laurel-laden hair
As his own father's risen on the eastern air,
And that less white brow-binding bayleaf bloom
More than all flowers his father's eyes relume;
And those high songs he heard,
More than all notes of any landward bird,
More than all sounds less free
Than the wind's quiring to the choral sea.

High things the high song taught him; how the breath
Too frail for life may be more strong than death;
And this poor flash of sense in life, that gleams
As a ghost's glory in dreams,
More stabile than the world's own heart's root seems,
By that strong faith of lordliest love which gives
To death's own sightless-seeming eyes a light
Clearer, to death's bare bones a verier might,
Than shines or strikes from any man that lives.

How he that loves life overmuch shall die
The dog's death, utterly:
And he that much less loves it than he hates
All wrongdoing that is done
Anywhere always underneath the sun
Shall live a mightier life than time's or fate's.
One fairer thing he shewed him, and in might
More strong than day and night
Whose strengths build up time's towering period:
Yea, one thing stronger and more high than God,
Which if man had not, then should God not be:
And that was Liberty.
And gladly should man die to gain, he said,
Freedom; and gladlier, having lost, lie dead.
For man's earth was not, nor the sweet sea-waves
His, nor his own land, nor its very graves,
Except they bred not, bore not, hid not slaves:
But all of all that is,
Were one man free in body and soul, were his.

And the song softened, even as heaven by night
Softens, from sunnier down to starrier light,
And with its moonbright breath
Blessed life for death's sake, and for life's sake death.
Till as the moon's own beam and breath confuse
In one clear hueless haze of glimmering hues
The sea's line and the land's line and the sky's,
And light for love of darkness almost dies,
As darkness only lives for light's dear love,
Whose hands the web of night is woven of,
So in that heaven of wondrous words were life
And death brought out of strife;
Yea, by that strong spell of serene increase
Brought out of strife to peace.

And the song lightened, as the wind at morn
Flashes, and even with lightning of the wind
Night's thick-spun web is thinned
And all its weft unwoven and overworn
Shrinks, as might love from scorn.
And as when wind and light on water and land
Leap as twin gods from heavenward hand in hand,
And with the sound and splendour of their leap
Strike darkness dead, and daunt the spirit of sleep,

And burn it up with fire;
So with the light that lightened from the lyre
Was all the bright heat in the child's heart stirred
And blown with blasts of music into flame
Till even his sense became
Fire, as the sense that fires the singing bird
Whose song calls night by name.
And in the soul within the sense began
The manlike passion of a godlike man,
And in the sense within the soul again
Thoughts that make men of gods and gods of men.

For love the high song taught him: love that turns
God's heart toward man as man's to Godward; love
That life and death and life are fashioned of,
From the first breath that burns
Half kindled on the flowerlike yeanling's lip,
So light and faint that life seems like to slip,
To that yet weaklier drawn
When sunset dies of night's devouring dawn;
But the man dying not wholly as all men dies
If aught be left of his in live men's eyes
Out of the dawnless dark of death to rise;
If aught of deed or word
Be seen for all time or of all time heard.
Love, that though body and soul were overthrown
Should live for love's sake of itself alone,
Though spirit and flesh were one thing doomed and dead,
Not wholly annihilated.
Seeing even the hoariest ash-flake that the pyre
Drops, and forgets the thing was once afire
And gave its heart to feed the pile's full flame
Till its own heart its own heat overcame,
Outlives its own life, though by scarce a span,
As such men dying outlive themselves in man,
Outlive themselves for ever; if the heat
Outburn the heart that kindled it, the sweet
Outlast the flower whose soul it was, and flit
Forth of the body of it
Into some new shape of a strange perfume
More potent than its light live spirit of bloom,
How shall not something of that soul relive,
That only soul that had such gifts to give

As lighten something even of all men's doom
Even from the labouring womb
Even to the seal set on the unopening tomb?
And these the loving light of song and love
Shall wrap and lap round and impend above,
Imperishable; and all springs born illume
Their sleep with brighter thoughts than wake the dove
To music, when the hillside winds resume
The marriage-song of heather-flower and broom
And all the joy thereof.

And hate the song too taught him: hate of all
That brings or holds in thrall
Of spirit or flesh, free-born ere God began,
The holy body and sacred soul of man.
And wheresoever a curse was or a chain,
A throne for torment or a crown for bane
Rose, moulded out of poor men's molten pain,
There, said he, should man's heaviest hate be set
Inexorably, to faint not or forget
Till the last warmth bled forth of the last vein
In flesh that none should call a king's again,
Seeing wolves and dogs and birds that plague-strike air
Leave the last bone of all the carrion bare.

And hope the high song taught him: hope whose eyes
Can sound the seas unsoundable, the skies
Inaccessible of eyesight; that can see
What earth beholds not, hear what wind and sea
Hear not, and speak what all these crying in one
Can speak not to the sun.
For in her sovereign eyelight all things are
Clear as the closest seen and kindlier star
That marries morn and even and winter and spring
With one love's golden ring.
For she can see the days of man, the birth
Of good and death of evil things on earth
Inevitable and infinite, and sure
As present pain is, or herself is pure.
Yea, she can hear and see, beyond all things
That lighten from before Time's thunderous wings
Through the awful circle of wheel-winged periods,
The tempest of the twilight of all Gods:

And higher than all the circling course they ran
The sundawn of the spirit that was man.

And fear the song too taught him; fear to be
Worthless the dear love of the wind and sea
That bred him fearless, like a sea-mew reared
In rocks of man's foot feared,
Where nought of wingless life may sing or shine.
Fear to wax worthless of that heaven he had
When all the life in all his limbs was glad
And all the drops in all his veins were wine
And all the pulses music; when his heart,
Singing, bade heaven and wind and sea bear part
In one live song's reiterance, and they bore:
Fear to go crownless of the flower he wore
When the winds loved him and the waters knew,
The blithest life that clove their blithe life through
With living limbs exultant, or held strife
More amorous than all dalliance aye anew
With the bright breath and strength of their large life,
With all strong wrath of all sheer winds that blew,
All glories of all storms of the air that fell
Prone, ineluctable,°
With roar from heaven of revel, and with hue
As of a heaven turned hell.
For when the red blast of their breath had made
All heaven aflush with light more dire than shade,
He felt it in his blood and eyes and hair
Burn as if all the fires of the earth and air
Had laid strong hold upon his flesh, and stung
The soul behind it as with serpent's tongue,
Forked like the loveliest lightnings: nor could bear
But hardly, half distraught with strong delight,
The joy that like a garment wrapped him round
And lapped him over and under
With raiment of great light
And rapture of great sound
At every loud leap earthward of the thunder
From heaven's most furthest bound:
So seemed all heaven in hearing and in sight,
Alive and mad with glory and angry joy,
That something of its marvellous mirth and might

Moved even to madness, fledged as even for flight,
The blood and spirit of one but mortal boy.

So, clothed with love and fear that love makes great,
And armed with hope and hate,
He set first foot upon the spring-flowered ways
That all feet pass and praise.
And one dim dawn between the winter and spring,
In the sharp harsh wind harrying heaven and earth
To put back April that had borne his birth
From sunward on her sunniest shower-struck wing,
With tears and laughter for the dew-dropt thing,
Slight as indeed a dew-drop, by the sea
One met him lovelier than all men may be,
God-featured, with god's eyes; and in their might
Somewhat that drew men's own to mar their sight,
Even of all eyes drawn toward him: and his mouth
Was as the very rose of all men's youth,
One rose of all the rose-beds in the world:
But round his brows the curls were snakes that curled,
And like his tongue a serpent's; and his voice
Speaks death, and bids rejoice.
Yet then he spake no word, seeming as dumb,
A dumb thing mild and hurtless; nor at first
From his bowed eyes seemed any light to come,
Nor his meek lips for blood or tears to thirst:
But as one blind and mute in mild sweet wise
Pleading for pity of piteous lips and eyes,
He strayed with faint bare lily-lovely feet
Helpless, and flowerlike sweet:
Nor might man see, not having word hereof,
That this of all gods was the great god Love.

And seeing him lovely and like a little child
That wellnigh wept for wonder that it smiled
And was so feeble and fearful, with soft speech
The youth bespake him softly; but there fell
From the sweet lips no sweet word audible
That ear or thought might reach:
No sound to make the dim cold silence glad,
No breath to thaw the hard harsh air with heat;
Only the saddest smile of all things sweet,
Only the sweetest smile of all things sad.

And so they went together one green way
Till April dying made free the world for May;
And on his guide suddenly Love's face turned,
And in his blind eyes burned
Hard light and heat of laughter; and like flame
That opens in a mountain's ravening mouth
To blear and sear the sunlight from the south,
His mute mouth opened, and his first word came:
'Knowest thou me now by name?'
And all his stature waxed immeasurable,
As of one shadowing heaven and lightening hell;
And statelier stood he than a tower that stands
And darkens with its darkness far-off sands
Whereon the sky leans red;
And with a voice that stilled the winds he said:
'I am he that was thy lord before thy birth,
I am he that is thy lord till thou turn earth:
I make the night more dark, and all the morrow
Dark as the night whose darkness was my breath:
O fool, my name is sorrow;
Thou fool, my name is death.'

And he that heard spake not, and looked right on
Again, and Love was gone.

Through many a night toward many a wearier day
His spirit bore his body down its way.
Through many a day toward many a wearier night
His soul sustained his sorrows in her sight.
And earth was bitter, and heaven, and even the sea
Sorrowful even as he.
And the wind helped not, and the sun was dumb;
And with too long strong stress of grief to be
His heart grew sere and numb.

And one bright eve ere summer in autumn sank
At stardawn standing on a grey sea-bank
He felt the wind fitfully shift and heave
As toward a stormier eve;
And all the wan wide sea shuddered; and earth
Shook underfoot as toward some timeless birth,
Intolerable and inevitable; and all
Heaven, darkling, trembled like a stricken thrall.

And far out of the quivering east, and far
From past the moonrise and its guiding star,
Began a noise of tempest and a light
That was not of the lightning; and a sound
Rang with it round and round
That was not of the thunder; and a flight
As of blown clouds by night,
That was not of them; and with songs and cries
That sang and shrieked their soul out at the skies
A shapeless earthly storm of shapes began
From all ways round to move in on the man,
Clamorous against him silent; and their feet
Were as the wind's are fleet,
And their shrill songs were as wild birds' are sweet.

And as when all the world of earth was wronged
And all the host of all men driven afoam
By the red hand of Rome,
Round some fierce amphitheatre overthronged
With fair clear faces full of bloodier lust
Than swells and stings the tiger when his mood
Is fieriest after blood
And drunk with trampling of the murderous must
That soaks and stains the tortuous close-coiled wood
Made monstrous with its myriad-mustering brood,
Face by fair face panted and gleamed and pressed,
And breast by passionate breast
Heaved hot with ravenous rapture, as they quaffed
The red ripe full fume of the deep live draught,
The sharp quick reek of keen fresh bloodshed, blown
Through the dense deep drift up to the emperor's throne
From the under steaming sands
With clamour of all-applausive throats and hands,
Mingling in mirthful time
With shrill blithe mockeries of the lithe-limbed mime:
So from somewhence far forth of the unbeholden,
Dreadfully driven from over and after and under,
Fierce, blown through fifes of brazen blast and golden,
With sound of chiming waves that drown the thunder
Or thunder that strikes dumb the sea's own chimes,
Began the bellowing of the bull-voiced mimes,
Terrible; firs bowed down as briars or palms
Even at the breathless blast as of a breeze

Fulfilled with clamour and clangour and storms of psalms;
Red hands rent up the roots of old-world trees,
Thick flames of torches tossed as tumbling seas
Made mad the moonless and infuriate air
That, ravening, revelled in the riotous hair
And raiment of the furred Bassarides.°

So came all those in on him; and his heart,
As out of sleep suddenly struck astart,
Danced, and his flesh took fire of theirs, and grief
Was as a last year's leaf
Blown dead far down the wind's way; and he set
His pale mouth to the brightest mouth it met
That laughed for love against his lips, and bade
Follow; and in following all his blood grew glad
And as again a sea-bird's; for the wind
Took him to bathe him deep round breast and brow
Not as it takes a dead leaf drained and thinned,
But as the brightest bay-flower blown on bough,
Set springing toward it singing: and they rode
By many a vine-leafed, many a rose-hung road,
Exalt with exultation; many a night
Set all its stars upon them as for spies
On many a moon-bewildering mountain-height
Where he rode only by the fierier light
Of his dread lady's hot sweet hungering eyes.
For the moon wandered witless of her way,
Spell-stricken by strong magic in such wise
As wizards use to set the stars astray.
And in his ears the music that makes mad
Beat always; and what way the music bade,
That alway rode he; nor was any sleep
His, nor from height nor deep.
But heaven was as red iron, slumberless,
And had no heart to bless;
And earth lay sere and darkling as distraught,
And help in her was nought.

Then many a midnight, many a morn and even,
His mother, passing forth of her fair heaven,
With goodlier gifts than all save gods can give
From earth or from the heaven where sea-things live,
With shine of sea-flowers through the bay-leaf braid
Woven for a crown her foam-white hands had made

To crown him with land's laurel and sea-dew,
Sought the sea-bird that was her boy: but he
Sat panther-throned beside Erigone,°
Riding the red ways of the revel through
Midmost of pale-mouthed passion's crownless crew.
Till on some winter's dawn of some dim year
He let the vine-bit on the panther's lip
Slide, and the green rein slip,
And set his eyes to seaward, nor gave ear
If sound from landward hailed him, dire or dear;
And passing forth of all those fair fierce ranks
Back to the grey sea-banks,
Against a sea-rock lying, aslant the steep,
Fell after many sleepless dreams on sleep.

And in his sleep the dun green light was shed
Heavily round his head
That through the veil of sea falls fathom-deep,
Blurred like a lamp's that when the night drops dead
Dies; and his eyes gat grace of sleep to see
The deep divine dark dayshine of the sea,
Dense water-walls and clear dusk water-ways,
Broad-based, or branching as a sea-flower sprays
That side or this dividing; and anew
The glory of all her glories that he knew.
And in sharp rapture of recovering tears
He woke on fire with yearnings of old years,
Pure as one purged of pain that passion bore,
Ill child of bitter mother; for his own
Looked laughing toward him from her midsea throne,
Up toward him there ashore.

Thence in his heart the great same joy began,
Of child that made him man:
And turned again from all hearts else on quest,
He communed with his own heart, and had rest.
And like sea-winds upon loud waters ran
His days and dreams together, till the joy
Burned in him of the boy.
Till the earth's great comfort and the sweet sea's breath
Breathed and blew life in where was heartless death,
Death spirit-stricken of soul-sick days, where strife
Of thought and flesh made mock of death and life.
And grace returned upon him of his birth

Where heaven was mixed with heavenlike sea and earth;
And song shot forth strong wings that took the sun
From inward, fledged with might of sorrow and mirth
And father's fire made mortal in his son.
Nor was not spirit of strength in blast and breeze
To exalt again the sun's child and the sea's;
For as wild mares in Thessaly° grow great
With child of ravishing winds, that violate
Their leaping length of limb with manes like fire
And eyes outburning heaven's
With fires more violent than the lightning levin's°
And breath drained out and desperate of desire,
Even so the spirit in him, when winds grew strong,
Grew great with child of song.
Nor less than when his veins first leapt for joy
To draw delight in such as burns a boy,
Now too the soul of all his senses felt
The passionate pride of deep sea-pulses dealt
Through nerve and jubilant vein
As from the love and largess of old time,
And with his heart again
The tidal throb of all the tides keep rhyme
And charm him from his own soul's separate sense
With infinite and invasive influence
That made strength sweet in him and sweetness strong,
Being now no more a singer, but a song.

Till one clear day when brighter sea-wind blew
And louder sea-shine lightened, for the waves
Were full of godhead and the light that saves,
His father's, and their spirit had pierced him through,
He felt strange breath and light all round him shed
That bowed him down with rapture; and he knew
His father's hand, hallowing his humbled head,
And the old great voice of the old good time, that said:

'Child of my sunlight and the sea, from birth
A fosterling and fugitive on earth;
Sleepless of soul as wind or wave or fire,
A manchild with an ungrown God's desire;
Because thou hast loved nought mortal more than me,
Thy father, and thy mother-hearted sea;
Because thou hast set thine heart to sing, and sold
Life and life's love for song, God's living gold;

Because thou hast given thy flower and fire of youth
To feed men's hearts with visions, truer than truth;
Because thou hast kept in those world-wandering eyes
The light that makes me music of the skies;
Because thou hast heard with world-unwearied ears
The music that puts light into the spheres;
Have therefore in thine heart and in thy mouth
The sound of song that mingles north and south,
The song of all the winds that sing of me,
And in thy soul the sense of all the sea.'

# On the Cliffs

ἱμερόφωνος ἀήδων.°
Sappho

Between the moondawn and the sundown here
The twilight hangs half starless; half the sea
Still quivers as for love or pain or fear
Or pleasure mightier than these all may be
A man's live heart might beat
Wherein a God's with mortal blood should meet
And fill its pulse too full to bear the strain
With fear or love or pleasure's twin-born, pain.
Fiercely the gaunt woods to the grim soil cling
That bears for all fair fruits
Wan wild sparse flowers of windy and wintry spring
Between the tortive° serpent-shapen roots
Wherethrough their dim growth hardly strikes and shoots
And shews one gracious thing
Hardly, to speak for summer one sweet word
Of summer's self scarce heard.
But higher the steep green sterile fields, thick-set
With flowerless hawthorn even to the upward verge
Whence the woods gathering watch new cliffs emerge
Higher than their highest of crowns that sea-winds fret,
Hold fast, for all that night or wind can say,
Some pale pure colour yet,
Too dim for green and luminous for grey.
Between the climbing inland cliffs above
And these beneath that breast and break the bay,
A barren peace too soft for hate or love
Broods on an hour too dim for night or day.

O wind, O wingless wind that walk'st the sea,
Weak wind, wing-broken, wearier wind than we,
Who are yet not spirit-broken, maimed like thee
Who wail not in our inward night as thou
In the outer darkness now,
What word has the old sea given thee for mine ear
From thy faint lips to hear?
For some word would she send me, knowing not how.

Nay, what far other word
Than ever of her was spoken, or of me

Or all my winged white kinsfolk of the sea
Between fresh wave and wave was ever heard,
Cleaves the clear dark enwinding tree with tree
Too close for stars to separate and to see
Enmeshed in multitudinous unity?
What voice of what strong God hath stormed and stirred
The fortressed rock of silence, rent apart
Even to the core Night's all-maternal heart?
What voice of God grown heavenlier in a bird,
Made keener of edge to smite
Than lightning,—yea, thou knowest, O mother Night,
Keen as that cry from thy strange children[o] sent
Wherewith the Athenian judgment-shrine was rent,
For wrath that all their wrath was vainly spent,
Their wrath for wrong made right
By justice in her own divine despite
That bade pass forth unblamed
The sinless matricide and unashamed?
Yea, what new cry is this, what note more bright
Than their song's wing of words was dark of flight,
What word is this thou hast heard,
Thine and not thine or theirs, O Night, what word
More keen than lightning and more sweet than light?
As all men's hearts grew godlike in one bird
And all those hearts cried on thee, crying with might,
Hear us, O mother Night![o]

Dumb is the mouth of darkness as of death:
Light, sound and life are one
In the eyes and lips of dawn that draw the sun
To hear what first child's word with glimmering breath
Their weak wan weanling child the twilight saith;
But night makes answer none.

God, if thou be God,—bird, if bird thou be,—
Do thou then answer me.
For but one word, what wind soever blow,
Is blown up usward ever from the sea.
In fruitless years of youth dead long ago
And deep beneath their own dead leaves and snow
Buried, I heard with bitter heart and sere
The same sea's word unchangeable, nor knew
But that mine own life-days were changeless too
And sharp and salt with unshed tear on tear

And cold and fierce and barren; and my soul,
Sickening, swam weakly with bated breath
In a deep sea like death,
And felt the wind buffet her face with brine
Hard, and harsh thought on thought in long bleak roll
Blown by keen gusts of memory sad as thine
Heap the weight up of pain, and break, and leave
Strength scarce enough to grieve
In the sick heavy spirit, unmanned with strife
Of waves that beat at the tired lips of life.

Nay, sad may be man's memory, sad may be
The dream he weaves him as for shadow of thee,
But scarce one breathing-space, one heartbeat long,
Wilt thou take shadow of sadness on thy song.
Not thou, being more than man or man's desire,
Being bird and God in one,
With throat of gold and spirit of the sun;
The sun whom all our souls and songs call sire,
Whose godhead gave thee, chosen of all our quire,
Thee only of all that serve, of all that sing
Before our sire and king,
Borne up some space on time's world-wandering wing,
This gift, this doom, to bear till time's wing tire—
Life everlasting of eternal fire.

Thee only of all; yet can no memory say
How many a night and day
My heart has been as thy heart, and my life
As thy life is, a sleepless hidden thing,
Full of the thirst and hunger of winter and spring,
That seeks its food not in such love or strife
As fill men's hearts with passionate hours and rest.
From no loved lips and on no loving breast
Have I sought ever for such gifts as bring
Comfort, to stay the secret soul with sleep.
The joys, the loves, the labours, whence men reap
Rathe fruit of hopes and fears,
I have made not mine; the best of all my days
Have been as those fair fruitless summer strays,
Those water-waifs that but the sea-wind steers,
Flakes of glad foam or flowers on footless ways
That take the wind in season and the sun,
And when the wind wills is their season done.

For all my days as all thy days from birth
My heart as thy heart was in me as thee,
Fire; and not all the fountains of the sea
Have waves enough to quench it, nor on earth
Is fuel enough to feed,
While day sows night and night sows day for seed.

We were not marked for sorrow, thou nor I,
For joy nor sorrow, sister, were we made,
To take delight and grief to live and die,
Assuaged by pleasures or by pains affrayed
That melt men's hearts and alter; we retain
A memory mastering pleasure and all pain,
A spirit within the sense of ear and eye,
A soul behind the soul, that seeks and sings
And makes our life move only with its wings
And feed but from its lips, that in return
Feed of our hearts wherein the old fires that burn
Have strength not to consume
Nor glory enough to exalt us past our doom.

*Ah, ah, the doom*[o] (thou knowest whence rang that wail)
*Of the shrill nightingale!*
(From whose wild lips, thou knowest, that wail was thrown)
*For round about her have the great gods cast*
*A wing-borne body, and clothed her close and fast*
*With a sweet life that hath no part in moan.*
*But me, for me* (how hadst thou heart to hear?)
*Remains a sundering with the two-edged spear.*

*Ah, for her doom!* so cried in presage then
The bodeful bondslave[o] of the king of men,
And might not win her will.
Too close the entangling dragnet[o] woven of crime,
The snare of ill new-born of elder ill,
The curse of new time for an elder time,
Had caught, and held her yet,
Enmeshed intolerably in the intolerant net,
Who thought with craft to mock the God most high,
And win by wiles his crown of prophecy
From the Sun's hand sublime,
As God were man, to spare or to forget.

But thou,[o]—the gods have given thee and forgiven thee
More than our master gave

That strange-eyed spirit-wounded strange-tongued slave°
There questing houndlike° where the roofs red-wet
Reeked as a wet red grave.
Life everlasting has their strange grace given thee,
Even hers° whom thou wast wont to sing and serve
With eyes, but not with song, too swift to swerve;
Yet might not even thine eyes estranged estrange her,
Who seeing thee too, but inly, burn and bleed
Like that pale princess-priest of Priam's seed,°
For stranger service gave thee guerdon stranger;
If this indeed be guerdon, this indeed
Her mercy, this thy meed—
That thou, being more than all we born, being higher
Than all heads crowned of him° that only gives
The light whereby man lives,
The bay that bids man moved of God's desire
Lay hand on lute or lyre,
Set lip to trumpet or deflowered green reed—
If this were given thee for a grace indeed,
That thou, being first of all these, thou alone
Shouldst have the grace to die not, but to live
And lose nor change one pulse of song, one tone
Of all that were thy lady's and thine own,
Thy lady's whom thou criedst on to forgive,
Thou, priest and sacrifice on the altar-stone
Where none may worship not of all that live,
Love's priestess, errant on dark ways diverse;
If this were grace indeed for Love to give,
If this indeed were blessing and no curse.

Love's priestess, mad with pain and joy of song,
Song's priestess, mad with joy and pain of love,
Name above all names° that are lights above,
We have loved, praised, pitied, crowned and done thee wrong,
O thou past praise and pity; thou the sole
Utterly deathless, perfect only and whole
Immortal, body and soul.
For over all whom time hath overpast
The shadow of sleep inexorable is cast,
The implacable sweet shadow of perfect sleep
That gives not back what life gives death to keep;
Yea, all that lived and loved and sang and sinned

Are all borne down death's cold sweet soundless wind
That blows all night and knows not whom its breath,
Darkling, may touch to death:
But one that wind hath touched and changed not,—one
Whose body and soul are parcel of the sun;
One that earth's fire could burn not, nor the sea
Quench; nor might human doom take hold on thee;
All praise, all pity, all dreams have done thee wrong,
All love, with eyes love-blinded from above;
Song's priestess, mad with joy and pain of love,
Love's priestess, mad with pain and joy of song.

Hast thou none other answer then for me
Than the air may have of thee,
Or the earth's warm woodlands girdling with green girth
Thy secret sleepless burning life on earth,
Or even the sea that once, being woman crowned
And girt with fire and glory of anguish round,
Thou wert so fain to seek to, fain to crave
If she would hear thee and save
And give thee comfort of thy great green grave?
Because I have known thee always who thou art,
Thou knowest, have known thee to thy heart's own heart,
Nor ever have given light ear to storied song
That did thy sweet name sweet unwitting wrong,
Nor ever have called thee nor would call for shame,
Thou knowest, but inly by thine only name,
Sappho—because I have known thee and loved, hast thou
None other answer now?
As brother and sister were we, child and bird,
Since thy first Lesbian word
Flamed on me,° and I knew not whence I knew
This was the song that struck my whole soul through,
Pierced my keen spirit of sense with edge more keen,
Even when I knew not, even ere sooth was seen,—
When thou wast but the tawny sweet winged thing
Whose cry was but of spring.

And yet even so thine ear should hear me—yea,
Hear me this nightfall by this northland bay,
Even for their sake whose loud good word I had,
Singing of thee in the all-beloved clime
Once, where the windy wine of spring makes mad
Our sisters of Majano,° who kept time

Clear to my choral rhyme.
Yet was the song acclaimed of these aloud
Whose praise had made mute humbleness misproud,
The song with answering song applauded thus,
But of that Daulian dream of Itylus.°
So but for love's love haply was it—nay,
How else?—that even their song took my song's part,
For love of love and sweetness of sweet heart,
Or god-given glorious madness of mid May
And heat of heart and hunger and thirst to sing,
Full of the new wine of the wind of spring.

Or if this were not, and it be not sin
To hold myself in spirit of thy sweet kin,
In heart and spirit of song;
If this my great love do thy grace no wrong,
Thy grace that gave me grace to dwell therein;
If thy gods thus be my gods, and their will
Made my song part of thy song—even such part
As man's hath of God's heart—
And my life like as thy life to fulfil;
What have our gods then given us? Ah, to thee,
Sister, much more, much happier than to me,
Much happier things they have given, and more of grace
Than falls to man's light race;
For lighter are we, all our love and pain
Lighter than thine, who knowest of time or place
Thus much, that place nor time
Can heal or hurt or lull or change again
The singing soul that makes his soul sublime
Who hears the far fall of its fire-fledged rhyme
Fill darkness as with bright and burning rain
Till all the live gloom inly glows, and light
Seems with the sound to cleave the core of night.

The singing soul that moves thee, and that moved
When thou wast woman, and their songs divine
Who mixed for Grecian mouths heaven's lyric wine
Fell dumb, fell down reproved
Before one sovereign Lesbian song of thine.
That soul, though love and life had fain held fast,
Wind-winged with fiery music, rose and past
Through the indrawn hollow of earth and heaven and hell,
As through some strait sea-shell

The wide sea's immemorial song,—the sea
That sings and breathes in strange men's ears of thee
How in her barren bride-bed, void and vast,
Even thy soul sang itself to sleep at last.

To sleep? Ah, then, what song is this, that here
Makes all the night one ear,
One ear fulfilled and mad with music, one
Heart kindling as the heart of heaven, to hear
A song more fiery than the awakening sun
Sings, when his song sets fire
To the air and clouds that build the dead night's pyre?
*O thou of divers-coloured mind, O thou*
*Deathless, God's daughter subtle-souled*°—lo, now,
Now too the song above all songs, in flight
Higher than the day-star's height,
And sweet as sound the moving wings of night!
*Thou of the divers-coloured seat*—behold,
Her very song of old!—
*O deathless, O God's daughter subtle-souled!*
That same cry through this boskage° overhead
Rings round reiterated,
Palpitates as the last palpitated,
The last that panted through her lips and died
Not down this grey north sea's half sapped cliff-side
That crumbles toward the coastline, year by year
More near the sands and near;
The last loud lyric fiery cry she cried,
Heard once on heights Leucadian,°—heard not here.

Not here; for this that fires our northland night,
This is the song that made
Love fearful, even the heart of love afraid,
With the great anguish of its great delight.
No swan-song, no far-fluttering half-drawn breath,
No word that love of love's sweet nature saith,
No dirge that lulls the narrowing lids of death,
No healing hymn of peace-prevented strife,—
This is her song of life.

*I loved thee*,°—hark, one tenderer note than all—
*Atthis, of old time, once*—one low long fall,
Sighing—one long low lovely loveless call,
Dying—one pause in song so flamelike fast—

*Atthis, long since in old time overpast*—
One soft first pause and last.
One,—then the old rage of rapture's fieriest rain
Storms all the music-maddened night again.

*Child of God,*° *close craftswoman, I beseech thee,*
*Bid not ache nor agony break nor master,*
*Lady, my spirit*—
O thou her mistress, might her cry not reach thee?
Our Lady of all men's loves, could Love go past her,
Pass, and not hear it?

She hears not as she heard not; hears not me,
O treble-natured mystery,—how should she
Hear, or give ear?—who heard and heard not thee;
Heard, and went past, and heard not; but all time
Hears all that all the ravin of his years
Hath cast not wholly out of all men's ears
And dulled to death with deep dense funeral chime
Of their reiterate rhyme.
And now of all songs uttering all her praise,
All hers who had thy praise and did thee wrong,
Abides one song yet of her lyric days,
Thine only, this thy song.

O soul triune, woman and god and bird,
Man, man at least has heard.
All ages call thee conqueror, and thy cry
The mightiest as the least beneath the sky
Whose heart was ever set to song, or stirred
With wind of mounting music blown more high
Than wildest wing may fly,
Hath heard or hears,—even Æschylus as I.
But when thy name was woman, and thy word
Human,—then haply, surely then meseems
This thy bird's note was heard on earth of none,
Of none save only in dreams.
In all the world then surely was but one
Song; as in heaven at highest one sceptred sun
Regent, on earth here surely without fail
One only, one imperious nightingale.
Dumb was the field, the woodland mute, the lawn
Silent; the hill was tongueless as the vale
Even when the last fair waif of cloud that felt

Its heart beneath the colouring moonrays melt,
At high midnoon of midnight half withdrawn,
Bared all the sudden deep divine moondawn.
Then, unsaluted by her twin-born tune,
That latter timeless morning of the moon
Rose past its hour of moonrise; clouds gave way
To the old reconquering ray,
But no song answering made it more than day;
No cry of song by night
Shot fire into the cloud-constraining light.
One only, one Æolian° island heard
Thrill, but through no bird's throat,
In one strange manlike maiden's godlike note,
The song of all these as a single bird.
Till the sea's portal was as funeral gate
For that sole singer in all time's ageless date
Singled and signed for so triumphal fate,
All nightingales but one in all the world
All her sweet life were silent; only then,
When her life's wing of womanhood was furled,
Their cry, this cry of thine was heard again,
As of me now, of any born of men.

Through sleepless clear spring nights filled full of thee,
Rekindled here, thy ruling song has thrilled
The deep dark air and subtle tender sea
And breathless hearts with one bright sound fulfilled.
Or at midnoon to me
Swimming, and birds about my happier head
Skimming, one smooth soft way by water and air,
To these my bright born brethren and to me
Hath not the clear wind borne or seemed to bear
A song wherein all earth and heaven and sea
Were molten in one music made of thee
To enforce us, O our sister of the shore,
Look once in heart back landward and adore?
For songless were we sea-mews, yet had we
More joy than all things joyful of thee—more,
Haply, than all things happiest; nay, save thee,
In thy strong rapture of imperious joy
Too high for heart of sea-borne bird or boy,
What living things were happiest if not we?

But knowing not love nor change nor wrath nor wrong,
No more we knew of song.

Song, and the secrets of it, and their might,
What blessings curse it and what curses bless,
I know them since my spirit had first in sight,
Clear as thy song's words or the live sun's light,
The small dark body's Lesbian loveliness
That held the fire eternal; eye and ear
Were as a god's to see, a god's to hear,
Through all his hours of daily and nightly chime,
The sundering of the two-edged spear of time:
The spear that pierces even the sevenfold shields°
Of mightiest Memory, mother of all songs made,
And wastes all songs as roseleaves kissed and frayed
As here the harvest of the foam-flowered fields;
But thine the spear may waste not that he wields
Since first the God whose soul is man's live breath,
The sun whose face hath our sun's face for shade,
Put all the light of life and love and death
Too strong for life, but not for love too strong,
Where pain makes peace with pleasure in thy song,
And in thine heart, where love and song make strife,
Fire everlasting of eternal life.

# FROM *SPECIMENS OF MODERN POETS: THE HEPTALOGIA OR THE SEVEN AGAINST SENSE: A CAP WITH SEVEN BELLS* (1880)

# The Higher Pantheism in a Nutshell

One, who is not, we see: but one, whom we see not, is:
Surely this is not that: but that is assuredly this.

What, and wherefore, and whence? for under is over and under:
If thunder could be without lightning, lightning could be without
thunder.

Doubt is faith in the main: but faith, on the whole, is doubt:
We cannot believe by proof: but could we believe without?

Why, and whither, and how? for barley and rye are not clover:
Neither are straight lines curves: yet over is under and over.

Two and two may be four: but four and four are not eight:
Fate and God may be twain: but God is the same thing as fate.

Ask a man what he thinks, and get from a man what he feels:
God, once caught in the fact, shows you a fair pair of heels.

Body and spirit are twins: God only knows which is which:
The soul squats down in the flesh, like a tinker drunk in a ditch.°

One and two are not one: but one and nothing is two:
Truth can hardly be false, if falsehood cannot be true.

Once the mastodon was: pterodactyls were common as cocks:
Then the mammoth was God: now is He a prize ox.

Parallels all things are: yet many of these are askew:
You are certainly I: but certainly I am not you.

Springs the rock from the plain, shoots the stream from the rock:
Cocks exist for the hen: but hens exist for the cock.

God, whom we see not, is: and God, who is not, we see:
Fiddle, we know, is diddle: and diddle, we take it, is dee.

## Nephelidia

From the depth of the dreamy decline of the dawn through
a notable nimbus of nebulous noonshine,
Pallid and pink as the palm of the flag-flower that flickers with
fear of the flies as they float,
Are they looks of our lovers that lustrously lean from a marvel
of mystic miraculous moonshine,
These that we feel in the blood of our blushes that thicken
and threaten with throbs through the throat?
Thicken and thrill as a theatre thronged at appeal of an actor's
appalled agitation,
Fainter with fear of the fires of the future than pale with the
promise of pride in the past;
Flushed with the famishing fullness of fever that reddens with
radiance of rathe recreation,
Gaunt as the ghastliest of glimpses that gleam through the gloom
of the gloaming when ghosts go aghast?
Nay, for the nick of the tick of the time is a tremulous touch on
the temples of terror,
Strained as the sinews yet strenuous with strife of the dead
who is dumb as the dust-heaps of death:
Surely no soul is it, sweet as the spasm of erotic emotional
exquisite error,
Bathed in the balms of beatified bliss, beatific itself by
beatitude's breath.
Surely no spirit or sense of a soul that was soft to the spirit and
soul of our senses
Sweetens the stress of suspiring suspicion that sobs in the
semblance and sound of a sigh;
Only this oracle opens Olympian, in mystical moods and
triangular tenses—
'Life is the lust of a lamp for the light that is dark till the
dawn of the day when we die.'
Mild is the mirk and monotonous music of memory,
melodiously mute as it may be,
While the hope in the heart of a hero is bruised by the
breach of men's rapiers, resigned to the rod;
Made meek as a mother whose bosom-beats bound with
the bliss-bringing bulk of a balm-breathing baby,
As they grope through the grave-yard of creeds, under
skies growing green at a groan for the grimness of God.°

# Poeta Loquitur (c.1880?)

If a person conceives an opinion
  That my verses are stuff that will wash,
Or my Muse has one plume on her pinion,
  That person's opinion is bosh.
My philosophy, politics, free-thought!
  Are worth not three skips of a flea,
And the emptiest of thoughts that can be thought
  Are mine on the sea.

In a maze of monotonous murmur
  Where reason roves ruined by rhyme,
In a voice neither graver nor firmer
  Than the bells on a fool's cap chime,
A party pretentiously pensive,
  With a Muse that deserves to be skinned,
Makes language and metre offensive
  With rhymes on the wind.

A perennial procession of phrases
  Pranked primly, though pruriently prime,
Precipitates preachings on praises
  In a ruffianly riot of rhyme
Through the pressure of print on my pages:
  But reckless the reader must be
Who imagines no one of the sages
  That steer through Time's sea.

Mad mixtures of Frenchified offal
  With insults to Christendom's creed,
Blind blasphemy, schoolboylike scoff, all
  These blazon me blockhead indeed.
I conceive myself obviously some one
  Whose audience will never be thinned,
But the pupil must needs be a rum one
  Whose teacher is wind.

In my poems, with ravishing rapture
  Storm strikes me and strokes me and stings:
But I'm scarcely the bird you might capture
  Out of doors in the thick of such things.
I prefer to be well out of harm's way
  When tempest makes tremble the tree,

And the wind with armipotent arm-sway
Makes soap of the sea.

Hanging hard on the rent rags of others,
Who before me did better, I try
To believe them my sisters and brothers,
Though I know what a low lot am I.
The mere sight of a church sets me yelping
Like a boy that at football is shinned!
But the cause must indeed be past helping
Whose gospel is wind!

All the pale past's red record of history
Is dusty with damnable deeds;
But the future's mild motherly mystery
Peers pure of all crowns and all creeds.
Truth dawns on time's resonant ruin,
Frank, fulminant, fragrant, and free
And apparently this is the doing
Of wind on the sea.

Fame flutters in front of pretension
Whose flagstaff is flagrantly fine
And it cannot be needful to mention
That such beyond question is mine.
Some singers indulging in curses,
Though sinful, have splendidly sinned:
But my would-be maleficent verses
Are nothing but wind.

# FROM *STUDIES IN SONG* (1880)

# After Nine Years:

## To Joseph Mazzini

*Primâ dicte mihi, summâ dicende Camenâ.*°

The shadows fallen of years are nine
Since heaven grew seven times more divine
With thy soul entering, and the dearth
Of souls on earth
Grew sevenfold sadder, wanting One
Whose light of life, quenched here and done,
Burns there eternal as the sun.

Beyond all word, beyond all deed,
Beyond all thought beloved, what need
Has death or love that speech should be,
Hast thou of me?
I had no word, no prayer, no cry,
To praise or hail or mourn thee by,
As when thou too wast man as I.

Nay, never, nor as any born
Save one whose name priests turn to scorn,
Who haply, though we know not now,
Was man as thou,
A wanderer branded with men's blame,
Loved past man's utterance: yea, the same,
Perchance, and as his name thy name.

Thou wast as very Christ—not he
Degraded into Deity,
And priest-polluted by such prayer
As poisons air,
Tongue-worship of the tongue that slays,
False faith and parricidal praise:
But the man crowned with suffering days.

God only, being of all mankind
Most manlike, of most equal mind
And heart most perfect, more than can
Be heart of man
Once in ten ages, born to be
As haply Christ was, and as we
Knew surely, seeing, and worshipped thee.

To know thee—this at least was ours,
God, clothed upon with human hours,
O face beloved, spirit adored,
Saviour and lord!
That wast not only for thine own
Redeemer—not of these alone
But all to whom thy word was known.

Ten years have wrought their will with me
Since last my words took wing for thee
Who then wast even as now above
Me, and my love.
As then thou knewest not scorn, so now
With that beloved benignant brow
Take these of him whose light wast thou.

# Evening on the Broads

Over two shadowless waters, adrift as a pinnace in peril,
  Hangs as in heavy suspense, charged with irresolute light,
Softly the soul of the sunset upholden awhile on the sterile
  Waves and wastes of the land, half repossessed by the night.
Inland glimmer the shallows asleep and afar in the breathless
  Twilight: yonder the depths darken afar and asleep.
Slowly the semblance of death out of heaven descends on the deathless
  Waters: hardly the light lives on the face of the deep—
Hardly, but here for awhile. All over the grey soft shallow
  Hover the colours and clouds of the twilight, void of a star.
As a bird unfledged is the broad-winged night, whose winglets are callow
  Yet, but soon with their plumes will she cover her brood from afar,
Cover the brood of her worlds that cumber the skies with their blossom
  Thick as the darkness of leaf-shadowed spring is encumbered with flowers.
World upon world is enwound in the bountiful girth of her bosom,
  Warm and lustrous with life lovely to look on as ours.
Still is the sunset adrift as a spirit in doubt that dissembles
  Still with itself, being sick of division and dimmed by dismay—
Nay, not so; but with love and delight beyond passion it trembles,
  Fearful and fain of the night, lovely with love of the day:
Fain and fearful of rest that is like unto death, and begotten
  Out of the womb of the tomb, born of the seed of the grave:
Lovely with shadows of loves that are only not wholly forgotten,
  Only not wholly suppressed by the dark as a wreck by the wave.
Still there linger the loves of the morning and noon, in a vision
  Blindly beheld, but in vain: ghosts that are tired, and would rest.
But the glories beloved of the night rise all too dense for division,
  Deep in the depth of her breast sheltered as doves in a nest.
Fainter the beams of the loves of the daylight season enkindled
  Wane, and the memories of hours that were fair with the love of them fade:
Loftier, aloft of the lights of the sunset stricken and dwindled,
  Gather the signs of the love at the heart of the night new-made.
New-made night, new-born of the sunset, immeasurable, endless,
  Opens the secret of love hid from of old in her heart,

In the deep sweet heart full-charged with faultless love of the
friendless
  Spirits of men that are eased when the wheels of the sun depart.
Still is the sunset afloat as a ship on the waters upholden
  Full-sailed, wide-winged, poised softly for ever asway—
Nay, not so, but at least for a little, awhile at the golden
  Limit of arching air fain for an hour to delay.
Here on the bar of the sand-bank, steep yet aslope to the gleaming
  Waste of the water without, waste of the water within,
Lights overhead and lights underneath seem doubtfully dreaming
  Whether the day be done, whether the night may begin.
Far and afar and farther again they falter and hover,
  Warm on the water and deep in the sky and pale on the cloud:
Colder again and slowly remoter, afraid to recover
  Breath, yet fain to revive, as it seems, from the skirt of the shroud.
Faintly the heartbeats shorten and pause of the light in the westward
  Heaven, as eastward quicken the paces of star upon star
Hurried and eager of life as a child that strains to the breast-ward
  Eagerly, yearning forth of the deeps where the ways of them are,
Glad of the glory of the gift of their life and the wealth of its wonder,
  Fain of the night and the sea and the sweet wan face of the earth.
Over them air grows deeper, intense with delight in them: under
  Things are thrilled in their sleep as with sense of a sure
new birth.
But here by the sand-bank watching, with eyes on the sea-line,
stranger
  Grows to me also the weight of the sea-ridge gazed on of me,
Heavily heaped up, changefully changeless, void though of danger
  Void not of menace, but full of the might of the dense dull sea.
Like as the wave is before me, behind is the bank deep-drifted;
  Yellow and thick as the bank is behind me in front is the wave.
As the wall of a prison imprisoning the mere is the girth of it lifted:
  But the rampire° of water in front is erect as the wall of a grave.
And the crests of it crumble and topple and change, but the
wall is not broken:
  Standing still dry-shod, I see it as higher than my head,
Moving inland alway again, reared up as in token
  Still of impending wrath still in the foam of it shed.
And even in the pauses between them, dividing the rollers in sunder,
  High overhead seems ever the sea-line fixed as a mark,
And the shore where I stand as a valley beholden of hills
whence thunder
  Cloud and torrent and storm, darkening the depths of the dark.
Up to the sea, not upon it or over it, upward from under

Seems he to gaze, whose eyes yearn after it here from the shore:
A wall of turbid water, aslope to the wide sky's wonder
Of colour and cloud, it climbs, or spreads as a slanted floor.
And the large lights change on the face of the mere like things that were living,
Winged and wonderful, beams like as birds are that pass and are free:
But the light is dense as darkness, a gift withheld in the giving,
That lies as dead on the fierce dull face of the landward sea.
Stained and stifled and soiled, made earthier than earth is and duller,
Grimly she puts back light as rejected, a thing put away:
No transparent rapture, a molten music of colour;
No translucent love taken and given of the day.
Fettered and marred and begrimed is the light's live self on her falling,
As the light of a man's life lighted the fume of a dungeon mars:
Only she knows of the wind, when her wrath gives ear to him calling;
The delight of the light she knows not, nor answers the sun or the stars.
Love she hath none to return for the luminous love of their giving:
None to reflect from the bitter and shallow response of her heart
Yearly she feeds on her dead, yet herself seems dead and not living,
Or confused as a soul heavy-laden with trouble that will not depart.
In the sound of her speech to the darkness the moan of her evil remorse is,
Haply, for strong ships gnawed by the dog-toothed sea-bank's fang
And trampled to death by the rage of the feet of her foam-lipped horses
Whose manes are yellow as plague, and as ensigns of pestilence hang,
That wave in the foul faint air of the breath of a death-stricken city;
So menacing heaves she the manes of her rollers knotted with sand,
Discoloured, opaque, suspended in sign as of strength without pity,
That shake with flameless thunder the low long length of the strand.
Here, far off in the farther extreme of the shore as it lengthens
Northward, lonely for miles, ere ever a village begin,
On the lapsing land that recedes as the growth of the strong sea strengthens
Shoreward, thrusting further and further its outworks in,
Here in Shakespeare's vision, a flower of her kin forsaken,
Lay in her golden raiment alone on the wild wave's edge,
Surely by no shore else, but here on the bank storm-shaken,
Perdita, bright as a dew-drop engilt of the sun on the sedge.
Here on a shore unbeheld of his eyes in a dream he beheld her
Outcast, fair as a fairy, the child of a far-off king:
And over the babe-flower gently the head of a pastoral elder

Bowed, compassionate, hoar as the hawthorn-blossom in spring,
And kind as harvest in autumn: a shelter of shade on the lonely
Shelterless unknown shore scourged of implacable waves:
Here, where the wind walks royal, alone in his kingdom, and only
Sounds to the sedges a wail as of triumph that conquers and craves.
All these waters and wastes are his empire of old, and awaken
From barren and stagnant slumber at only the sound of his breath:
Yet the hunger is eased not that aches in his heart, nor the goal overtaken
That his wide wings yearn for and labour as hearts that yearn after death.
All the solitude sighs and expects with a blind expectation
Somewhat unknown of its own sad heart, grown heart-sick of strife:
Till sometime its wild heart maddens, and moans, and the vast ululation
Takes wing with the clouds on the waters, and wails to be quit of its life.
For the spirit and soul of the waste is the wind, and his wings with their waving.
Darken and lighten the darkness and light of it thickened or thinned;
But the heart that impels them is even as a conqueror's insatiably craving
That victory can fill not, as power cannot satiate the want of the wind.
All these moorlands and marshes are full of his might, and oppose not
Aught of defence nor of barrier, of forest or precipice piled:
But the will of the wind works ever as his that desires what he knows not,
And the wail of his want unfulfilled is as one making moan for her child.
And the cry of his triumph is even as the crying of hunger that maddens
The heart of a strong man aching in vain as the wind's heart aches
And the sadness itself of the land for its infinite solitude saddens
More for the sound than the silence athirst for the sound that slakes.
And the sunset at last and the twilight are dead: and the darkness is breathless
With fear of the wind's breath rising that seems and seems not to sleep:
But a sense of the sound of it alway, a spirit unsleeping and deathless,
Ghost or God, evermore moves on the face of the deep.°

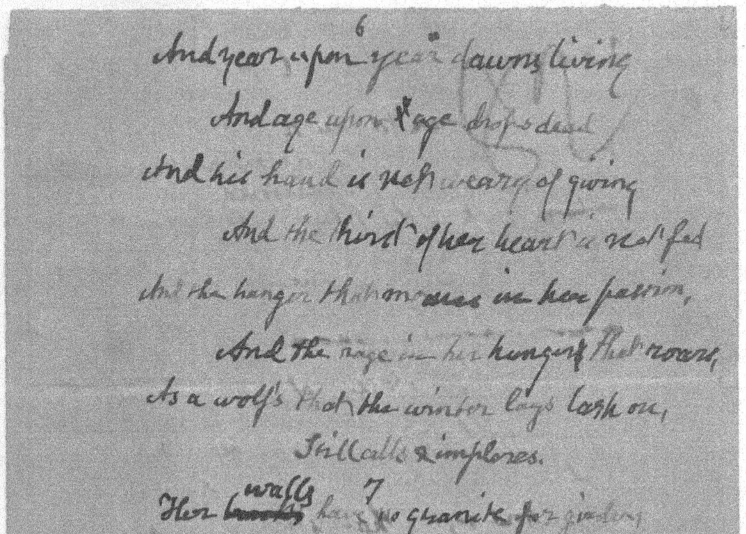

6

And year upon year dawns living,
And age upon age drops dead:
And his hand is not weary of giving,
And the thirst of her heart is not fed:
And the hunger that moans in her passion,
And the rage in her hunger that roars,
As a wolf's that the winter lays lash on,
Still calls & implores.

7

Her walls have no granite for girder,
No fortalice fronting her stands:
But reefs the bloodguiltiest of murder
Are less than the banks of her sands:
These number their slain by the thousand;
For the ship hath no surety to be,
When the bank is abreast of her bows &
Aflush with the sea.

8

No surety to stand, & no shelter
To dawn out of darkness but one,

FIG. 8. Stanza 6 of the MS of 'By the North Sea', reproduced by kind permission of the Master and Fellows of Balliol College Oxford.

# By the North Sea

To Walter Theodore Watts

'We are what suns and winds and waters make us.'°

—Landor.

*Sea, wind, and sun, with light and sound and breath*
*The spirit of man fulfilling—these create*
*That joy wherewith man's life grown passionate*
*Gains heart to hear and sense to read and faith*
*To know the secret word our Mother saith*
*In silence, and to see, though doubt wax great,*
*Death as the shadow cast by life on fate,*
*Passing, whose shade we call the shadow of death.*

*Brother, to whom our Mother as to me*
*Is dearer than all dreams of days undone,*
*This song I give you of the sovereign three*
*That are as life and sleep and death are, one:*
*A song the sea-wind gave me from the sea,*
*Where nought of man's endures before the sun.*

## I

A land that is lonelier than ruin;
A sea that is stranger than death:
Far fields that a rose never blew in,
Wan waste where the winds lack breath;
Waste endless and boundless and flowerless
But of marsh-blossoms fruitless as free:
Where earth lies exhausted, as powerless
To strive with the sea.

Far flickers the flight of the swallows,
Far flutters the weft of the grass
Spun dense over desolate hollows
More pale than the clouds as they pass:
Thick woven as the weft of a witch is
Round the heart of a thrall that hath sinned,
Whose youth and the wrecks of its riches
Are waifs on the wind.

The pastures are herdless and sheepless,
No pasture or shelter for herds:
The wind is relentless and sleepless.
And restless and songless the birds;
Their cries from afar fall breathless,
Their wings are as lightnings that flee;
For the land has two lords that are deathless:
Death's self, and the sea.

These twain, as a king with his fellow,
Hold converse of desolate speech:
And her waters are haggard and yellow
And crass with the scurf of the beach:
And his garments are grey as the hoary
Wan sky where the day lies dim;
And his power is to her, and his glory,
As hers unto him.

In the pride of his power she rejoices,
In her glory he glows and is glad:
In her darkness the sound of his voice is,
With his breath she dilates and is mad:
'If thou slay me, O death, and outlive me,
Yet thy love hath fulfilled me of thee.'
'Shall I give thee not back if thou give me,
O sister, O sea?'

And year upon year dawns living,
And age upon age drops dead:
And his hand is not weary of giving,
And the thirst of her heart is not fed:
And the hunger that moans in her passion,
And the rage in her hunger that roars,
As a wolf's that the winter lays lash on,
Still calls and implores.

Her walls have no granite for girder,
No fortalice fronting her stands:
But reefs the blood guiltiest of murder
Are less than the banks of her sands:
These number their slain by the thousand;
For the ship hath no surety to be,
When the bank is abreast of her bows and
Aflush with the sea.

No surety to stand, and no shelter
  To dawn out of darkness but one,
Out of waters that hurtle and welter
  No succour to dawn with the sun
But a rest from the wind as it passes,
  Where, hardly redeemed from the waves,
Lie thick as the blades of the grasses
    The dead in their graves.

A multitude noteless of numbers,
  As wild weeds cast on an heap:
And sounder than sleep are their slumbers,
  And softer than song is their sleep;
And sweeter than all things and stranger
  The sense, if perchance it may be,
That the wind is divested of danger
    And scatheless the sea.

That the roar of the banks they breasted
  Is hurtless as bellowing of herds,
And the strength of his wings that invested
  The wind, as the strength of a bird's;
As the sea-mew's might or the swallow's
  That cry to him back if he cries,
As over the graves and their hollows
    Days darken and rise.

As the souls of the dead men disburdened
  And clean of the sins that they sinned,
With a lovelier than man's life guerdoned
  And delight as a wave's in the wind,
And delight as the wind's in the billow,
  Birds pass, and deride with their glee
The flesh that has dust for its pillow
    As wrecks have the sea.

When the ways of the sun wax dimmer,
  Wings flash through the dusk like beams;
As the clouds in the lit sky glimmer,
  The bird in the graveyard gleams;
As the cloud at its wing's edge whitens
  When the clarions of sunrise are heard,
The graves that the bird's note brightens
    Grow bright for the bird.

As the waves of the numberless waters
  That the wind cannot number who guides
Are the sons of the shore and the daughters
  Here lulled by the chime of the tides:
And here in the press of them standing
  We know not if these or if we
Live truliest, or anchored to landing
    Or drifted to sea.

In the valley he named of decision
  No denser were multitudes met
When the soul of the seer in her vision
  Saw nations for doom of them set;°
Saw darkness in dawn, and the splendour
  Of judgment, the sword and the rod;
But the doom here of death is more tender
    And gentler the god.°

And gentler the wind from the dreary
  Sea-banks by the waves overlapped,
Being weary, speaks peace to the weary
  From slopes that the tide-stream hath sapped;
And sweeter than all that we call so
  The seal of their slumber shall be
Till the graves that embosom them also
  Be sapped of the sea.

II

For the heart of the waters is cruel,
  And the kisses are dire of their lips,
And their waves are as fire is to fuel
  To the strength of the sea-faring ships,
Though the sea's eye gleam as a jewel
  To the sun's eye back as he dips.

Though the sun's eye flash to the sea's
  Live light of delight and of laughter,
And her lips breathe back to the breeze
  The kiss that the wind's lips waft her
From the sun that subsides, and sees
  No gleam of the storm's dawn after.

And the wastes of the wild sea-marches
  Where the borderers are matched in their might—

Bleak fens that the sun's weight parches,
Dense waves that reject his light—
Change under the change-coloured arches
Of changeless morning and night.

The waves are as ranks enrolled
Too close for the storm to sever:
The fens lie naked and cold,
But their heart fails utterly never:
The lists are set from of old,
And the warfare endureth for ever.

III

Miles, and miles, and miles of desolation!
Leagues on leagues on leagues without a change!
Sign or token of some eldest nation
Here would make the strange land not so strange.
Time-forgotten, yea since time's creation,
Seem these borders where the sea-birds range.

Slowly, gladly, full of peace and wonder
Grows his heart who journeys here alone.
Earth and all its thoughts of earth sink under
Deep as deep in water sinks a stone.
Hardly knows it if the rollers thunder,
Hardly whence the lonely wind is blown.

Tall the plumage of the rush-flower tosses,
Sharp and soft in many a curve and line
Gleam and glow the sea-coloured marsh-mosses,
Salt and splendid from the circling brine.
Streak on streak of glimmering seashine crosses
All the land sea-saturate as with wine.

Far, and far between, in divers orders,
Clear grey steeples cleave the low grey sky;
Fast and firm as time-unshaken warders,
Hearts made sure by faith, by hope made high.
These alone in all the wild sea-borders
Fear no blast of days and nights that die.

All the land is like as one man's face is,
Pale and troubled still with change of cares.
Doubt and death pervade her clouded spaces:

Strength and length of life and peace are theirs;
Theirs alone amid these weary places,
Seeing not how the wild world frets and fares.

Firm and fast where all is cloud that changes
Cloud-clogged sunlight, cloud by sunlight thinned,
Stern and sweet, above the sand-hill ranges
Watch the towers and tombs of men that sinned
Once, now calm as earth whose only change is
Wind, and light, and wind, and cloud, and wind.

Out and in and out the sharp straits wander,
In and out and in the wild way strives,
Starred and paved and lined with flowers that squander
Gold as golden as the gold of hives,
Salt and moist and multiform: but yonder,
See, what sign of life or death survives?

Seen then only when the songs of olden
Harps were young whose echoes yet endure,
Hymned of Homer when his years were golden,
Known of only when the world was pure,
Here is Hades, manifest, beholden,
Surely, surely here, if aught be sure!

Where the border-line was crossed, that, sundering
Death from life, keeps weariness from rest,
None can tell, who fares here forward wondering;
None may doubt but here might end his quest.
Here life's lightning joys and woes once thundering
Sea-like round him cease like storm suppressed.

Here the wise wave-wandering steadfast-hearted
Guest of many a lord of many a land
Saw the shape or shade of years departed,
Saw the semblance risen and hard at hand,
Saw the mother long from love's reach parted,
Anticleia,° like a statue stand.

Statue? nay, nor tissued image woven
Fair on hangings in his father's hall;
Nay, too fast her faith of heart was proven,
Far too firm her loveliest love of all;
Love wherethrough the loving heart was cloven,
Love that hears not when the loud Fates call.

Love that lives and stands up re-created
  Then when life has ebbed and anguish fled;
Love more strong than death° or all things fated,
  Child's and mother's, lit by love and led;
Love that found what life so long awaited
  Here, when life came down among the dead.

Here, where never came alive another,
  Came her son across the sundering tide
Crossed before by many a warrior brother
  Once that warred on Ilion at his side;
Here spread forth vain hands° to clasp the mother
  Dead, that sorrowing for his love's sake died.

Parted, though by narrowest of divisions,
  Clasp he might not, only might implore,°
Sundered yet by bitterest of derisions,
  Son, and mother from the son she bore—
Here? But all dispeopled here of visions
  Lies, forlorn of shadows even, the shore.

All too sweet such men's Hellenic speech is,
  All too fain they lived of light to see,
Once to see the darkness of these beaches,
  Once to sing this Hades found of me
Ghostless, all its gulfs and creeks and reaches,
  Sky, and shore, and cloud, and waste, and sea.

IV

But aloft and afront of me faring
  Far forward as folk in a dream
That strive, between doubting and daring
  Right on till the goal for them gleam,
Full forth till their goal on them lighten,
  The harbour where fain they would be,
What headlands there darken and brighten?
  What change in the sea?

What houses and woodlands that nestle
  Safe inland to lee of the hill
As it slopes from the headlands that wrestle
  And succumb to the strong sea's will?
Truce is not, nor respite, nor pity,
  For the battle is waged not of hands

Where over the grave of a city
  The ghost of it stands.

Where the wings of the sea-wind slacken,
  Green lawns to the landward thrive,
Fields brighten and pine-woods blacken,
  And the heat in their heart is alive;
They blossom and warble and murmur,
  For the sense of their spirit is free:
But harder to shoreward and firmer
  The grasp of the sea.

Like ashes the low cliffs crumble,
  The banks drop down into dust,
The heights of the hills are made humble,
  As a reed's is the strength of their trust:
As a city's that armies environ,
  The strength of their stay is of sand:
But the grasp of the sea is as iron,
  Laid hard on the land.

A land that is thirstier than ruin;
  A sea that is hungrier than death;
Heaped hills that a tree never grew in;
  Wide sands where the wave draws breath;
All solace is here for the spirit
  That ever for ever may be
For the soul of thy son to inherit,
  My mother, my sea.

O delight of the headlands and beaches!
  O desire of the wind on the wold,
More glad than a man's when it reaches
  That end which it sought from of old
And the palm of possession is dreary
  To the sense that in search of it sinned;
But nor satisfied ever nor weary
  Is ever the wind.

The delight that he takes but in living
  Is more than of all things that live:
For the world that has all things for giving
  Has nothing so goodly to give:
But more than delight his desire is,
  For the goal where his pinions would be

Is immortal as air or as fire is,
  Immense as the sea.

Though hence come the moan that he borrows
  From darkness and depth of the night,
Though hence be the spring of his sorrows,
  Hence too is the joy of his might;
The delight that his doom is for ever
  To seek and desire and rejoice,
And the sense that eternity never
  Shall silence his voice.

That satiety never may stifle
  Nor weariness ever estrange
Nor time be so strong as to rifle
  Nor change be so great as to change
His gift that renews in the giving,
  The joy that exalts him to be
Alone of all elements living
  The lord of the sea.

What is fire, that its flame should consume her?
  More fierce than all fires are her waves:
What is earth, that its gulfs should entomb her?
  More deep are her own than their graves.
Life shrinks from his pinions that cover
  The darkness by thunders bedinned:
But she knows him, her lord and her lover,
  The godhead of wind.

For a season his wings are about her,
  His breath on her lips for a space;
Such rapture he wins not without her
  In the width of his worldwide race.
Though the forests bow down, and the mountains
  Wax dark, and the tribes of them flee,
His delight is more deep in the fountains
  And springs of the sea.

There are those too of mortals that love him,
  There are souls that desire and require,
Be the glories of midnight above him
  Or beneath him the daysprings of fire:
And their hearts are as harps that approve him
  And praise him as chords of a lyre

That were fain with their music to move him
 To meet their desire.

To descend through the darkness to grace them,
 Till darkness were lovelier than light:
To encompass and grasp and embrace them,
 Till their weakness were one with his might:
With the strength of his wings to caress them,
 With the blast of his breath to set free;
With the mouths of his thunders to bless them
 For sons of the sea.

For these have the toil and the guerdon
 That the wind has eternally: these
Have part in the boon and the burden
 Of the sleepless unsatisfied breeze,
That finds not, but seeking rejoices
 That possession can work him no wrong:
And the voice at the heart of their voice is
 The sense of his song.

For the wind's is their doom and their blessing;
 To desire, and have always above
A possession beyond their possessing,
 A love beyond reach of their love.
Green earth has her sons and her daughters,
 And these have their guerdons; but we
Are the wind's and the sun's and the water's,
 Elect of the sea.

## V

For the sea too seeks and rejoices,
 Gains and loses and gains,
And the joy of her heart's own choice is
 As ours, and as ours are her pains:
As the thoughts of our hearts are her voices,
 And as hers is the pulse of our veins.

Her fields that know not of dearth
 Nor lie for their fruit's sake fallow
Laugh large in the depth of their mirth
 But inshore here in the shallow,
Embroiled with encumbrance of earth,
 Their skirts are turbid and yellow.

The grime of her greed is upon her,
  The sign of her deed is her soil;
As the earth's is her own dishonour,
  And corruption the crown of her toil:
She hath spoiled and devoured, and her honour
  Is this, to be shamed by her spoil.

But afar where pollution is none,
  Nor ensign of strife nor endeavour,
Where her heart and the sun's are one,
  And the soil of her sin comes never,
She is pure as the wind and the sun,
  And her sweetness endureth for ever.

## VI

Death, and change, and darkness everlasting,
  Deaf, that hears not what the daystar saith,
Blind, past all remembrance and forecasting,
  Dead, past memory that it once drew breath;
These, above the washing tides and wasting,
  Reign, and rule this land of utter death.

Change of change, darkness of darkness, hidden,
  Very death of very death, begun
When none knows,—the knowledge is forbidden—
  Self-begotten, self-proceeding, one,
Born, not made°—abhorred, unchained, unchidden,
  Night stands here defiant of the sun.

Change of change, and death of death begotten,
  Darkness born of darkness, one and three,
Ghostly godhead of a world forgotten,
  Crowned with heaven, enthroned on land and sea,
Here, where earth with dead men's bones is rotten,
  God of Time, thy likeness worships thee.

Lo, thy likeness of thy desolation,
  Shape and figure of thy might, O Lord,
Formless form, incarnate miscreation,
  Served of all things living and abhorred;
Earth herself is here thine incarnation,
  Time, of all things born on earth adored.

All that worship thee are fearful of thee;
  No man may not worship thee for fear:

Prayers nor curses prove not nor disprove thee,
  Move nor change thee with our change of cheer:
All at last, though all abhorred thee, love thee,
  God, the sceptre of whose throne is here.

Here thy throne and sceptre of thy station,
  Here the palace paven for thy feet;
Here thy sign from nation unto nation
  Passed as watchword for thy guards to greet,
Guards that go before thine exaltation,
  Ages, clothed with bitter years and sweet.

Here, where sharp the sea-bird shrills his ditty,
  Flickering flame-wise through the clear live calm,
Rose triumphal, crowning all a city,
  Roofs exalted once with prayer and psalm,
Built of holy hands for holy pity,
  Frank and fruitful as a sheltering palm.

Church and hospice wrought in faultless fashion,
  Hall and chancel bounteous and sublime,
Wide and sweet and glorious as compassion,
  Filled and thrilled with force of choral chime,
Filled with spirit of prayer and thrilled with passion
  Hailed a God more merciful than Time.

Ah, less mighty, less than Time prevailing,
  Shrunk, expelled, made nothing at his nod,
Less than clouds across the sea-line sailing,
  Lies he, stricken by his master's rod.
'Where is man?' the cloister murmurs wailing;
  Back the mute shrine thunders—'Where is God?'

Here is all the end of all his glory—
  Dust, and grass, and barren silent stones.
Dead, like him, one hollow tower and hoary
  Naked in the sea-wind stands and moans,
Filled and thrilled with its perpetual story:
  Here, where earth is dense with dead men's bones.

Low and loud and long, a voice for ever,
  Sounds the wind's clear story like a song.
Tomb from tomb the waves devouring sever,
  Dust from dust as years relapse along;
Graves where men made sure to rest, and never
  Lie dismantled by the seasons' wrong.

Now displaced, devoured and desecrated,
  Now by Time's hands darkly disinterred,
These poor dead that sleeping here awaited
  Long the archangel's re-creating word,
Closed about with roofs and walls high-gated
  Till the blast of judgment should be heard,

Naked, shamed, cast out of consecration,
  Corpse and coffin, yea the very graves,
Scoffed at, scattered, shaken from their station,
  Spurned and scourged of wind and sea like slaves,
Desolate beyond man's desolation,
  Shrink and sink into the waste of waves.

Tombs, with bare white piteous bones protruded,
  Shroudless, down the loose collapsing banks,
Crumble, from their constant place detruded,
  That the sea devours and gives not thanks.
Graves where hope and prayer and sorrow brooded
  Gape and slide and perish, ranks on ranks.

Rows on rows and line by line they crumble,
  They that thought for all time through to be.
Scarce a stone whereon a child might stumble
  Breaks the grim field paced alone of me.
Earth, and man, and all their gods wax humble
  Here, where Time brings pasture to the sea.

VII

But afar on the headland exalted,
  But beyond in the curl of the bay,
From the depth of his dome deep-vaulted
  Our father is lord of the day.
Our father and lord that we follow,
  For deathless and ageless is he;
And his robe is the whole sky's hollow,
    His sandal the sea.

Where the horn of the headland is sharper,
  And her green floor glitters with fire,
The sea has the sun for a harper,
  The sun has the sea for a lyre.
The waves are a pavement of amber,
  By the feet of the sea-winds trod

To receive in a god's presence-chamber
 Our father, the God.

Time, haggard and changeful and hoary,
 Is master and God of the land:
But the air is fulfilled of the glory
 That is shed from our lord's right hand.
O father of all of us ever,
 All glory be only to thee
From heaven, that is void of thee never,
 And earth, and the sea.

O Sun, whereof all is beholden,
 Behold now the shadow of this death,
This place of the sepulchres, olden
 And emptied and vain as a breath.
The bloom of the bountiful heather
 Laughs broadly beyond in thy light
As dawn, with her glories to gather,
 At darkness and night.

Though the Gods of the night lie rotten
 And their honour be taken away
And the noise of their names forgotten,
 Thou, Lord, art God of the day.
Thou art father and saviour and spirit,
 O Sun, of the soul that is free
And hath grace of thy grace to inherit
 Thine earth and thy sea.

The hills and the sands and the beaches,
 The waters adrift and afar,
The banks and the creeks and the reaches.
 How glad of thee all these are!
The flowers, overflowing, overcrowded,
 Are drunk with the mad wind's mirth:
The delight of thy coming unclouded
 Makes music of earth.

I, last least voice of her voices,
 Give thanks that were mute in me long
To the soul in my soul that rejoices
 For the song that is over my song.
Time gives what he gains for the giving
 Or takes for his tribute of me;
My dreams to the wind everliving,
 My song to the sea.

# 'EMILY BRONTË' (1883)

To the England of our own time, it has often enough been remarked, the novel is what the drama was to the England of Shakespeare's. The same general interest produces the same incessant demand for the same inexhaustible supply of imaginative produce, in a shape more suited to the genius of a later day and the conditions of a changed society. Assuming this simple explanation to be sufficient for the obvious fact that in the modern world of English letters the novel is everywhere and the drama is nowhere, we may remark one radical point of difference between the taste of play-goers in the age of Shakespeare and the taste of novel-readers in our own. Tragedy was then at least as popular as either romantic or realistic comedy; whereas nothing would seem to be more unpopular with the run of modern readers than the threatening shadow of tragedy projected across the whole length of a story, inevitable and unmistakable from the lurid harshness of its dawn to the fiery softness of its sunset. The objection to a novel in which the tragic element has an air of incongruity and caprice—in which a tragic surprise is, as it were, sprung upon the reader, with a jarring shock such as might be given by the actual news of some unforeseen and grievous accident—this objection seems to me thoroughly reasonable, grounded on a true critical sense of fitness and unfitness; but the distaste for high and pure tragedy, where the close is in perfect and simple harmony with the opening, seems not less thoroughly pitiable and irrational.

A later work of indisputable power, in which the freshness of humour is as real and vital as the fervour of passion, was at once on its appearance compared with Emily Brontë's now famous story. And certainly not without good cause; for in point of local colour *Mehalah*° is, as far as I know, the one other book which can bear and may challenge the comparison. Its pages, for one thing, reflect the sterile glitter and desolate fascination of the salt marshes, their minute splendours and barren beauties and multitudinous monotony of measureless expanse, with the same instinctive and unlaborious accuracy which brings all the moorland before us in a breath when we open any chapter of *Wuthering Heights*. But the accumulated horrors of the close, however possible in fact, are wanting in the one quality which justifies and ennobles all admissible horror in fiction: they hardly seem inevitable; they lack the impression of logical and moral certitude. All the realism in the world will not suffice to convey this impression: and a work of art which wants it wants the one final and irreplaceable requisite of inner harmony. Now in *Wuthering Heights* this one thing needful is as perfectly and triumphantly attained as in *King Lear* or *The Duchess of Malfy*, in *The Bride of Lammermoor* or *Notre-Dame de Paris*.

From the first we breathe the fresh dark air of tragic passion and presage; and to the last the changing wind and flying sunlight are in keeping with the stormy promise of the dawn. There is no monotony, there is no repetition, but there is no discord. This is the first and last necessity, the foundation of all labour and the crown of all success, for a poem worthy of the name; and this it is that distinguishes the hand of Emily from the hand of Charlotte Brontë. All the works of the elder sister are rich in poetic spirit, poetic feeling, and poetic detail; but the younger sister's work is essentially and definitely a poem in the fullest and most positive sense of the term. It was therefore all the more proper that the honour of raising a biographical and critical monument to the author of *Wuthering Heights* should have been reserved for a poetess of the next generation to her own. And those who had already in their mind's eye the clearest and most definite conception of Emily Brontë will be the readiest to acknowledge their obligation and express their gratitude to Miss Robinson for the additional light which she has been enabled to throw upon a great and singular character. It is true that when all has been said the main features of that character stand out before us unchanged. The sweet and noble genius of Mrs Gaskell did not enable her to see far into so strange and sublime a problem;° but, after all, the main difference between the biographer of Emily and the biographer of Charlotte is that Miss Robinson has been interested and attracted where Mrs Gaskell was scared and perplexed. On one point, however, the new light afforded us is of the very utmost value and interest. We all knew how great was Emily Brontë's tenderness for the lower animals; we find, with surprise as well as admiration, that the range of this charity was so vast as to include even her own miserable brother. Of that lamentable and contemptible caitiff—contemptible not so much for his commonplace debauchery as for his abject selfishness, his lying pretention, and his nerveless cowardice—there is far too much in this memoir: it is inconceivable how any one can have put into a lady's hand such a letter as one which defaces two pages of the volume, and it may be permissible to regret that a lady should have made it public;° but this error is almost atoned for by the revelation that of all the three sisters in that silent home 'it was the silent Emily who had ever a cheering word for Branwell; it was Emily who still remembered that he was her brother, without that remembrance freezing her heart to numbness.'° That she saved his life from fire, and hid from their father the knowledge of her heroism, no one who knows anything of Emily Brontë will learn with any mixture of surprise in his sense of admiration; but it gives a new tone and colour to our sympathetic and reverent regard for her noble memory when we find in the depth of that self-reliant and stoic nature a fountain so inexhaustible of such Christlike longsuffering and compassion.

I cannot however but think that Miss Robinson makes a little too much of the influence exercised on Emily Brontë's work by the bitter, narrow, and ignoble misery of the life which she had watched burn down into such pitiful ruin that its memory is hardly redeemed by the last strange and inconsistent flash of expiring manhood which forbids us to regard with unmixed contempt the sufferer who had resolution enough to die standing° if he had lived prostrate, and so make at the very last a manful end of an abject history. The impression of this miserable experience is visible only in Anne Brontë's second work, *The Tenant of Wildfell Hall*; which deserves perhaps a little more notice and recognition than it has ever received. It is ludicrously weak, palpably unreal, and apparently imitative, whenever it reminds the reader that it was written by a sister of Charlotte and Emily Brontë; but as a study of utterly flaccid and invertebrate immorality it bears signs of more faithful transcription from life than anything in *Jane Eyre* or *Wuthering Heights*. On the other hand, the intelligent reader of *Wuthering Heights* cannot fail to recognize that what he is reading is a tragedy simply because it is the work of a writer whose genius is essentially tragic. Those who believe that Heathcliff was called into existence by the accident that his creator had witnessed the agonies of a violent weakling in love and in disgrace might believe that Shakespeare wrote *King Lear* because he had witnessed the bad effects of parental indulgence, and that Æschylus wrote the *Eumenides* because he had witnessed the uncomfortable results of matricide. The book is what it is because the author was what she was; this is the main and central fact to be remembered. Circumstances have modified the details; they have not implanted the conception. If there were any need for explanation there would be no room for apology. As it is, the few faults of design or execution leap to sight at a first glance, and vanish in the final effect and unimpaired impression of the whole; while those who object to the violent illegalities of conduct with regard to real or personal property on which the progress of the story does undeniably depend—'a senseless piece of glaring folly,' it was once called by some critic learned in the law°—might as well complain, in Carlylesque phrase, that the manners are quite other than Belgravian.

It is a fine and accurate instinct that has inevitably led Miss Robinson to cite in chosen illustration of the book's quality at its highest those two incomparable pictures of dreamland and delirium° which no poet that ever lived has ever surpassed for passionate and lifelike beauty of imaginative truth. But it is even somewhat less than exact to say that the latter scene 'is given with a masterly pathos that Webster need not have made more strong, nor Fletcher more lovely and appealing.'° Fletcher could not have made it as lovely and appealing as it is; he would have made it exquisitely pretty and effectively theatrical; but the depths the force, the sincerity, recalling here so vividly the 'several forms of distraction' through which Webster's Cornelia° passes after the murder of her son by his brother, excel everything else of the kind in imaginative art; not excepting, if truth may be spoken on such a subject, the madness of Ophelia or even of Madge Wildfire.° It is hardly ever safe to say dogmatically what can or cannot be done by the rarest and highest genius; yet it must surely be borne in upon us all that these two crowning passages could never have been written by any one to whom the motherhood of earth was less than the brotherhood of man—to whom the anguish, the intolerable and mortal yearning, of insatiate and insuppressible homesickness, was less than the bitterest of all other sufferings endurable or conceivable in youth. But in Emily Brontë this passion was twin-born with the passion for truth and rectitude. The stale and futile epithet of Titaness has in this instance a deeper meaning than appears; her goddess mother was in both senses the same who gave birth to the divine martyr of Æschylean legend:° Earth under one aspect and one name, but under the other Righteousness. And therefore was the first and last word uttered out of the depth of her nature a cry for that one thing needful without which all virtue is as worthless as all pleasure is vile, all hope as shameful as all faith is abject—a cry for liberty.

And therefore too, perhaps we may say, it is that any seeming confusion or incoherence in her work is merely external and accidental, not inward and spiritual. Belief in the personal or positive immortality of the individual and indivisible spirit was not apparently, in her case, swallowed up or nullified or made nebulous by any doctrine or dream of simple reabsorption into some indefinite infinity of eternal life. So at least it seems to me that her last ardent confession of dauntless and triumphant faith should properly be read,° however capable certain phrases in it may seem of the vaguer and more impersonal interpretation. For surely no scornfuller or stronger comment on the 'unutterable' vanity of creeds° could pass more naturally into a chant expressive of more profound and potent faith; a song of spiritual trust more grave and deep and passionate in the solemn ardour of its appeal than the Hymn to God of Cleanthes.° Her infrangible self-reliance and lonely sublimity of spirit she had in common with him and his fellows of the Porch;° it was much more than 'some shy ostrich prompting'° which bade her assign to an old Stoic the most personal and characteristic utterance in all her previous poems; but the double current of imaginative passion and practical compassion which made her a tragic poet and proved her a perfect woman gives as it were a living warmth and sweetness to her memory, such as might well have seemed incompatible with that sterner and colder veneration so long reserved for her spiritual kinsmen of the past. As a woman we never knew her so well as now that we have to welcome this worthy record of her life, with deeper thanks and warmer congratulations to the writer than can often be due even to the best of biographers and critics. As an author she has not perhaps even yet received her full due or taken her final place. Again and again has the same obvious objection been taken to that awkwardness of construction or presentation which no reader of *Wuthering Heights* can undertake to deny. But, to judge by the vigour with which this objection is urged, it might be supposed that the rules of narrative observed by all great novelists were of an almost legal or logical strictness and exactitude with regard to probability of detail. Now most assuredly the indirect method of relation through which the story of Heathcliff is conveyed, however unlikely or clumsy it may seem from the realistic point of view, does not make this narrative more liable to the charge of actual impossibility than others of the kind. Defoe still remains the one writer of narrative in the first person who has always kept the stringent law of possibilities before the eye of his invention. Even the admirable ingenuity and the singular painstaking which distinguish the method of Mr Wilkie Collins° can only give external and transient plausibility to the record of long conversations overheard or shared in by the narrator only a few hours before the supposed date of the report drawn up from memory. The very greatest masters in their kind, Walter Scott and Charles Dickens, are of all narrators the most superbly regardless of this objection. From *Rob Roy* and *Redgauntlet*, from *David Copperfield* and *Bleak House*, we might select at almost any stage of the autobiographic record some instance of detail in which the violation of plausibility, probability, or even possibility, is at least as daring and as glaring as any to be found in the narrative of Nelly Dean. Even when that narrative is removed, so to speak, yet one degree further back—even when we are supposed to be reading a minute detail of incident and dialogue transcribed by the hand of the lay figure Mr Lockwood from Nelly Dean's report of the account conveyed to her years ago by Heathcliff's fugitive wife or gadding servant, each invested for the nonce with the peculiar force and distinctive style of the author—even then we are not asked to put such an overwhelming strain on our faculty of imaginative belief as is exacted by the great writer who invites us to accept the report drawn up by Mr Pendennis of everything that takes place—down even to the minutest points of dialogue, accent, and gesture—in the household of the Newcomes or the Firmins° during the absence no less than in the presence of their friend the reporter. Yet all this we gladly and gratefully admit, without demur or cavil, to be thoroughly authentic and credible, because the whole matter of the report, however we get at it, is found when we do get at it to be vivid and lifelike as an actual experience of living fact. Here, if ever anywhere, the attainment of the end justifies the employment of the means. If we are to enjoy imaginative work at all, we must 'assume the virtue'° of imagination, even if we have it not; we must, as children say, 'pretend' or make believe a little as a very condition of the game.

A graver and perhaps a somewhat more plausible charge is brought against the author of *Wuthering Heights* by those who find here and there in her book the savage note or the sickly symptom of a morbid ferocity. Twice or thrice especially the details of deliberate or passionate brutality in Heathcliff's treatment of his victims make the reader feel for a moment as though he were reading a police report or even a novel by some French 'naturalist'° of the latest and brutallest order. But the pervading atmosphere of the book is so high and healthy that the effect even of those 'vivid and fearful scenes'° which impaired the rest for Charlotte Brontë is almost at once neutralized—we may hardly say softened, but sweetened, dispersed, and transfigured—by the general impression of noble purity and passionate straightforwardness, which removes it at once and for ever from any such ugly possibility of association or comparison. The whole work is not more incomparable in the effect of its atmosphere or landscape than in the peculiar note of its wild and bitter pathos; but most of all is it unique in the special and distinctive character of its passion. The love which devours life itself, which devastates the present and desolates the future with unquenchable and raging fire, has nothing less pure in it than flame or sunlight. And this passionate and ardent chastity is utterly and unmistakably spontaneous and unconscious. Not till the story is ended, not till the effect of it has been thoroughly absorbed and digested, does the reader even perceive the simple and natural absence of any grosser element, any hint or suggestion of a baser alloy in the ingredients of its human emotion than in the splendour of lightning or the roll of a gathered wave. Then, as on issuing sometimes from the tumult of charging waters, he finds with something of wonder how absolutely pure and sweet was the element of living storm with which his own nature has been for awhile made one; not a grain in it of soiling sand, not a waif of clogging weed. As was the author's life, so is her book in all things: troubled and taintless, with little of rest in it, and nothing of reproach. It may be true that not many will ever take it to their hearts; it is certain that those who do like it will like nothing very much better in the whole world of poetry or prose.

# FROM *A CENTURY OF ROUNDELS* (1883)

# In Harbour°

## I

Goodnight and goodbye to the life whose signs denote us
As mourners clothed with regret for the life gone by;
To the waters of gloom whence winds of the dayspring float us
    Goodnight and goodbye.

A time is for mourning, a season for grief to sigh;
But were we not fools and blind, by day to devote us
As thralls to the darkness, unseen of the sundawn's eye?

We have drunken of Lethe at length, we have eaten of lotus;
What hurts it us here that sorrows are born and die?
We have said to the dream that caressed and the dread
        that smote us
    Goodnight and goodbye.

## II

Outside of the port ye are moored in, lying
Close from the wind and at ease from the tide,
What sounds come swelling, what notes fall dying
    Outside?

They will not cease, they will not abide:
Voices of presage in darkness crying
Pass and return and relapse aside.

Ye see not, but hear ye not wild wings flying
To the future that wakes from the past that died?
Is grief still sleeping, is joy not sighing
    Outside?

## Plus Ultra°

Far beyond the sunrise and the sunset rises
Heaven, with worlds on worlds that lighten and respond:
Thought can see not thence the goal of hope's surmises
    Far beyond.

Night and day have made an everlasting bond
Each with each to hide in yet more deep disguises
Truth, till souls of men that thirst for truth despond.

All that man in pride of spirit slights or prizes,
All the dreams that make him fearful, fain, or fond,
Fade at forethought's touch of life's unknown surprises
    Far beyond.

## The Death of Richard Wagner°

I

Mourning on earth, as when dark hours descend,
Wide-winged with plagues, from heaven; when hope and mirth
Wane, and no lips rebuke or reprehend
    Mourning on earth.

The soul wherein her songs of death and birth,
Darkness and light, were wont to sound and blend,
Now silent, leaves the whole world less in worth.

Winds that make moan and triumph, skies that bend,
Thunders, and sound of tides in gulf and firth,
Spake through his spirit of speech, whose death should send
    Mourning on earth.

II

The world's great heart, whence all things strange and rare
Take form and sound, that each inseparate part
May bear its burden in all tuned thoughts that share
    The world's great heart—

The fountain forces, whence like steeds that start
Leap forth the powers of earth and fire and air,
Seas that revolve and rivers that depart—

Spake, and were turned to song: yea, all they were,
With all their works, found in his mastering art
Speech as of powers whose uttered word laid bare
    The world's great heart.

III

From the depths of the sea, from the wellsprings of earth,
from the wastes of the midmost night,
From the fountains of darkness and tempest and thunder,
from heights where the soul would be,
The spell of the mage of music evoked their sense, as an
        unknown light
    From the depths of the sea.

As a vision of heaven from the hollows of ocean, that none
but a god might see,
Rose out of the silence of things unknown of a presence,
a form, a might,
And we heard as a prophet that hears God's message against
him, and may not flee.

Eye might not endure it, but ear and heart with a rapture of
dark delight,
With a terror and wonder whose core was joy, and a passion
of thought set free,
Felt inly the rising of doom divine as a sundawn risen to sight
From the depths of the sea.

# Plus Intra°

Soul within sense, immeasurable, obscure,
Insepulchred and deathless, through the dense
Deep elements may scarce be felt as pure
    Soul within sense.

From depth and height by measurers left immense,
Through sound and shape and colour, comes the unsure
Vague utterance, fitful with supreme suspense.

All that may pass, and all that must endure,
Song speaks not, painting shews not: more intense
And keen than these, art wakes with music's lure
    Soul within sense.

## The Roundel

A roundel is wrought as a ring or a starbright sphere,
With craft of delight and with cunning of sound unsought,
That the heart of the hearer may smile if to pleasure his ear
A roundel is wrought.

Its jewel of music is carven of all or of aught—
Love, laughter, or mourning—remembrance of rapture or fear—
That fancy may fashion to hang in the ear of thought.

As a bird's quick song runs round, and the hearts in us hear
Pause answer to pause, and again the same strain caught,
So moves the device whence, round as a pearl or tear,
A roundel is wrought.

## Wasted Love

What shall be done for sorrow
  With love whose race is run?
Where help is none to borrow,
  What shall be done?

In vain his hands have spun
  The web, or drawn the furrow:
No rest their toil hath won.

His task is all gone thorough,
  And fruit thereof is none:
And who dare say to-morrow
  What shall be done?

## Before Sunset

Love's twilight wanes in heaven above,
  On earth ere twilight reigns:
Ere fear may feel the chill thereof,
  Love's twilight wanes.

Ere yet the insatiate heart complains
  'Too much, and scarce enough,'
The lip so late athirst refrains.

Soft on the neck of either dove
  Love's hands let slip the reins:
And while we look for light of love
  Love's twilight wanes.

## A Flower-piece by Fantin°

Heart's ease or pansy, pleasure or thought,
Which would the picture us of these?
Surely the heart that conceived it sought
        Heart's ease.

Surely by glad and divine degrees
The heart impelling the hand that wrought
Wrought comfort here for a soul's disease.

Deep flowers, with lustre and darkness fraught,
From glass that gleams as the chill still seas
Lean and lend for a heart distraught
        Heart's ease.

## To Catullus°

My brother, my Valerius, dearest head
Of all whose crowning bay-leaves crown their mother
Rome, in the notes first heard of thine I read
        My brother.

No dust that death or time can strew may smother
Love and the sense of kinship inly bred
From loves and hates at one with one another.

To thee was Cæsar's self nor dear nor dread,°
Song and the sea were sweeter each than other:
How should I living fear to call thee dead
        My brother?

## 'Insularum Ocelle'°

Sark, fairer than aught in the world that the lit skies cover,
Laughs inly behind her cliffs, and the seafarers mark
As a shrine where the sunlight serves, though the blown
        clouds hover,
    Sark.

We mourn, for love of a song that outsang the lark,
That nought so lovely beholden of Sirmio's lover
Made glad in Propontis the flight of his Pontic bark.°

Here earth lies lordly, triumphal as heaven is above her,
And splendid and strange as the sea that upbears as an ark,
As a sign for the rapture of storm-spent eyes to discover,
    Sark.

# FROM *A MIDSUMMER HOLIDAY AND OTHER POEMS* (1884)

## IX. On the Verge

Here begins the sea that ends not till the world's end. Where we stand,
Could we know the next high sea-mark set beyond these waves that gleam,
We should know what never man hath known, nor eye of man hath scanned.
Nought beyond these coiling clouds that melt like fume of shrines that steam
Breaks or stays the strength of waters till they pass our bounds of dream.
Where the waste Land's End leans westward, all the seas it watches roll
Find their border fixed beyond them, and a worldwide shore's control:
These whereby we stand no shore beyond us limits; these are free.
Gazing hence, we see the water that grows iron round the Pole,
From the shore that hath no shore beyond it set in all the sea.

Sail on sail along the sea-line fades and flashes; here on land
Flash and fade the wheeling wings on wings of mews that plunge and scream.
Hour on hour along the line of life and time's evasive strand
Shines and darkens, wanes and waxes, slays and dies: and scarce they seem
More than motes that thronged and trembled in the brief noon's breath and beam.
Some with crying and wailing, some with notes like sound of bells that toll,
Some with sighing and laughing, some with words that blessed and made us whole,
Passed, and left us, and we know not what they were, nor what were we.
Would we know, being mortal? Never breath of answering whisper stole
From the shore that hath no shore beyond it set in all the sea.

Shadows, would we question darkness? Ere our eyes and brows be fanned
Round with airs of twilight, washed with dews from sleep's eternal stream,

Would we know sleep's guarded secret? Ere the fire consume
 the brand,°
Would it know if yet its ashes may requicken? yet we deem
Surely man may know, or ever night unyoke her starry team,
What the dawn shall be, or if the dawn shall be not: yea, the scroll
Would we read of sleep's dark scripture, pledge of peace or
 doom of dole.
Ah, but here man's heart leaps, yearning toward the gloom
 with venturous glee,
Though his pilot eye behold nor bay nor harbour, rock nor shoal,
From the shore that hath no shore beyond it set in all the sea.

Friend, who knows if death indeed have life or life have death
 for goal?
Day nor night can tell us, nor may seas declare nor skies unroll
What has been from everlasting, or if aught shall alway be.
Silence answering only strikes response reverberate on the soul
From the shore that hath no shore beyond it set in all the sea.

# Lines on the Monument of Giuseppe Mazzini

Italia, mother of the souls of men,
  Mother divine,
Of all that served thee best with sword or pen,
  All sons of thine,

Thou knowest that here the likeness of the best
  Before thee stands;
The head most high, the heart found faithfullest,
  The purest hands.

Above the fume and foam of time that flits,
  The soul, we know,
Now sits on high where Alighieri sits
  With Angelo.°

Not his own heavenly tongue hath heavenly speech
  Enough to say
What this man was, whose praise no thought may reach,
  No words can weigh.

Since man's first mother brought to mortal birth
  Her first-born son,°
Such grace befell not ever man on earth
  As crowns this one.

Of God nor man was ever this thing said,
  That he could give
Life back to her who gave him, whence his dead
  Mother might live.

But this man found his mother dead and slain,
  With fast sealed eyes,
And bade the dead rise up and live again,°
  And she did rise.

And all the world was bright with her through him;
  But dark with strife,
Like heaven's own sun that storming clouds bedim,
  Was all his life.

Life and the clouds are vanished: hate and fear
  Have had their span

Of time to hurt, and are not: he is here,
The sunlike man.

City superb° that hadst Columbus first
For sovereign son,
Be prouder that thy breast hath later nurst
This mightier one.

Glory be his for ever, while his land
Lives and is free,
As with controlling breath and sovereign hand
He bade her be.

Earth shows to heaven the names by thousands told
That crown her fame,
But highest of all that heaven and earth behold
Mazzini's name.

## Les Casquets

From the depths of the waters that lighten and darken
With change everlasting of life and of death,
Where hardly by noon if the lulled ear hearken
It hears the sea's as a tired child's breath,
Where hardly by night if an eye dare scan it
The storm lets shipwreck be seen or heard,
As the reefs to the waves and the foam to the granite
Respond one merciless word,

Sheer seen and far, in the sea's live heaven,
A seamew's flight from the wild sweet land,
White-plumed with foam if the wind wake, seven
Black helms as of warriors that stir not stand.
From the depths that abide and the waves that environ
Seven rocks rear heads that the midnight masks;
And the strokes of the swords of the storm are as iron
On the steel of the wave-worn casques.

Be night's dark word as the word of a wizard,
Be the word of dawn as a god's glad word,
Like heads of the spirits of darkness visored
That see not for ever, nor ever have heard,
These basnets,° plumed as for fight or plumeless,
Crowned of the storm and by storm discrowned,
Keep ward of the lists where the dead lie tombless
And the tale of them is not found.

Nor eye may number nor hand may reckon°
The tithes that are taken of life by the dark,
Or the ways of the path, if doom's hand beckon,
For the soul to fare as a helmless bark—
Fare forth on a way that no sign showeth,
Nor aught of its goal or of aught between;
A path for her flight which no fowl knoweth,
Which the vulture's eye hath not seen.

Here still, though the wave and the wind seem lovers
Lulled half asleep by their own soft words,
A dream as of death in the sun's light hovers,
And a sign in the motions and cries of the birds.
Dark auguries and keen from the sweet sea-swallows
Strike noon with a sense as of midnight's breath,

And the wing that flees and the wing that follows
Are as types of the wings of death.

For here, when the night roars round, and under
The white sea lightens and leaps like fire,
Acclaimed of storm and applauded in thunder,
Sits death on the throne of his crowned desire.
Yea, hardly the hand of the god might fashion
A seat more strong for his strength to take,
For the might of his heart and the pride of his passion
To rejoice in the wars they make.

When the heart in him brightens with blitheness of battle
And the depth of its thirst is fulfilled with strife,
And his ear with the ravage of bolts that rattle,
And the soul of death with the pride of life,
Till the darkness is loud with his dark thanksgiving
And wind and cloud are as chords of his hymn,
There is nought save death in the deep night living
And the whole night worships him.

Heaven's height bows down to him, signed with his token,
And the sea's depth, moved as a heart that yearns,
Heaves up to him, strong as a heart half broken,
A heart that breaks in a prayer that burns.
Of cloud is the shrine of his worship moulded,
But the altar therein is of sea-shaped stone,
Whereon, with the strength of his wide wings folded,
Sits death in the dark, alone.

He hears the word of his servant spoken,
The word that the wind his servant saith;
Storm writes on the front of the night his token,
That the skies may seem to bow down to death.
But the clouds that stoop and the storms that minister
Serve but as thralls that fulfil their tasks;
And his seal is not set save here on the sinister
Crests reared of the crownless casques.

Nor flame nor plume of the storm that crowned them
Gilds or quickens their stark black strength.
Life lightens and murmurs and laughs right round them,
At peace with the noon's whole breadth and length,
At one with the heart of the soft-souled heaven,
At one with the life of the kind wild land:

But its touch may unbrace not the strengths of the seven
    Casques hewn of the storm-wind's hand.

No touch may loosen the black braced helmlets
  For the wild elves' heads of the wild waves wrought.
As flowers on the sea are her small green realmlets,
  Like heavens made out of a child's heart's thought;
But these as thorns of her desolate places,
  Strong fangs that fasten and hold lives fast:
And the vizors are framed as for formless faces
    That a dark dream sees go past[.]°

Of fear and of fate are the frontlets fashioned,
  And the heads behind them are dire and dumb.
When the heart of the darkness is scarce impassioned,
  Thrilled scarce with sense of the wrath to come,
They bear the sign from of old engraven,
  Though peace be round them and strife seem far,
That here is none but the night-wind's haven,
    With death for the harbour bar.

Of the iron of doom are the casquets carven,
  That never the rivets thereof should burst.
When the heart of the darkness is hunger-starven,
  And the throats of the gulfs are agape for thirst,
And stars are as flowers that the wind bids wither,
  And dawn is as hope struck dead by fear,
The rage of the ravenous night sets hither,
    And the crown of her work is here.

All shores about and afar lie lonely,
  But lonelier are these than the heart of grief,
These loose-linked rivets of rock, whence only
  Strange life scarce gleams from the sheer main reef,
With a blind wan face in the wild wan morning,
  With a live lit flame on its brows by night,
That the lost may lose not its word's mute warning
    And the blind by its grace have sight.

Here, walled in with the wide waste water,
  Grew the grace of a girl's lone life,°
The sea's and the sea-wind's foster-daughter,
  And peace was hers in the main mid strife.
For her were the rocks clothed round with thunder,
  And the crests of them carved by the storm-smith's craft

For her was the mid storm rent in sunder
As with passion that wailed and laughed.

For her the sunrise kindled and scattered
The red rose-leaflets of countless cloud:
For her the blasts of the springtide shattered
The strengths reluctant of waves back-bowed.
For her would winds in the mid sky levy
Bright wars that hardly the night bade cease:
At noon, when sleep on the sea lies heavy,
For her would the sun make peace.

Peace rose crowned with the dawn on golden
Lit leagues of triumph that flamed and smiled:
Peace lay lulled in the moon-beholden
Warm darkness making the world's heart mild.
For all the wide waves' troubles and treasons,
One word only her soul's ear heard
Speak from stormless and storm-rent seasons,
And nought save peace was the word.

All her life waxed large with the light of it,
All her heart fed full on the sound:
Spirit and sense were exalted in sight of it,
Compassed and girdled and clothed with it round.
Sense was none but a strong still rapture,
Spirit was none but a joy sublime,
Of strength to curb and of craft to capture
The craft and the strength of Time.

Time lay bound as in painless prison
There, closed in with a strait small space.
Never thereon as a strange light risen
Change had unveiled for her grief's far face.
Three white walls flung out from the basement
Girt the width of the world whereon
Gazing at night from her flame-lit casement
She saw where the dark sea shone.

Hardly the breadth of a few brief paces,
Hardly the length of a strong man's stride,
The small court flower-lit with children's faces
Scarce held scope for a bird to hide.
Yet here was a man's brood reared and hidden
Between the rocks and the towers and the foam,

Where peril and pity and peace were bidden
As guests to the same sure home.

Here would pity keep watch for peril,
And surety comfort his heart with peace.
No flower save one, where the reefs lie sterile,
Gave of the seed of its heart's increase.
Pity and surety and peace most lowly
Were the root and the stem and the bloom of the flower:
And the light and the breath of the buds kept holy
That maid's else blossomless bower.

With never a leaf but the seaweed's tangle,
Never a bird's but the seamew's note,
It heard all round it the strong storms wrangle,
Watched far past it the waste wrecks float.
But her soul was stilled by the sky's endurance,
And her heart made glad with the sea's content;
And her faith waxed more in the sun's assurance
For the winds that came and went.

Sweetness was brought for her forth of the bitter
Sea's strength, and light of the deep sea's dark,
From where green lawns on Alderney glitter
To the bastioned crags of the steeps of Sark.
These she knew from afar beholden,
And marvelled haply what life would be
On moors that sunset and dawn leave golden,
In dells that smile on the sea.

And forth she fared as a stout-souled rover,
For a brief blithe raid on the bounding brine:
And light winds ferried her light bark over
To the lone soft island of fair-limbed kine.
But the league-long length of its wild green border,
And the small bright streets of serene St Anne,
Perplexed her sense with a strange disorder
At sight of the works of man.

The world was here, and the world's confusion,
And the dust of the wheels of revolving life,
Pain, labour, change, and the fierce illusion
Of strife more vain than the sea's old strife.
And her heart within her was vexed, and dizzy
The sense of her soul as a wheel that whirled:

She might not endure for a space that busy
Loud coil of the troublous world.

Too full, she said, was the world of trouble,
Too dense with noise of contentious things,
And shews less bright than the blithe foam's bubble
As home she fared on the smooth wind's wings.
For joy grows loftier in air more lonely,
Where only the sea's brood fain would be;
Where only the heart may receive in it only
The love of the heart of the sea.

# In Sepulcretis

'Vidistis ipso rapere de rogo cœnam.'[o]
—Catullus, LIX. 3.

'To publish even one line of an author which he himself has not intended for the public at large—especially letters which are addressed to private persons—is to commit a despicable act of felony.'[o]
—Heine.

## I

It is not then enough that men who give
  The best gifts given of man to man should feel,
  Alive, a snake's head ever at their heel:
Small hurt the worms may do them while they live—
Such hurt as scorn for scorn's sake may forgive.
  But now, when death and fame have set one seal
  On tombs whereat Love, Grief, and Glory kneel,
Men sift all secrets, in their critic sieve,
Of graves wherein the dust of death might shrink
  To know what tongues defile the dead man's name
  With loathsome love, and praise that stings like shame.
Rest once was theirs, who had crossed the mortal brink:
  No rest, no reverence now: dull fools undress
  Death's holiest shrine, life's veriest nakedness.

## II

A man was born, sang, suffered, loved, and died.
  Men scorned him living: let us praise him dead.
  His life was brief and bitter, gently led
And proudly, but with pure and blameless pride.
He wrought no wrong toward any; satisfied
  With love and labour, whence our souls are fed
  With largesse yet of living wine and bread.
Come, let us praise him: here is nought to hide.
Make bare the poor dead secrets of his heart,
  Strip the stark-naked soul, that all may peer,
  Spy, smirk, sniff, snap, snort, snivel, snarl, and sneer:
Let none so sad, let none so sacred part
  Lie still for pity, rest unstirred for shame,
  But all be scanned of all men. This is fame.

### III

'Now, what a thing it is to be an ass!'[1]
  If one, that strutted up the brawling streets
  As foreman of the flock° whose concourse greets
Men's ears with bray more dissonant than brass,
Would change from blame to praise as coarse and crass
  His natural note, and learn the fawning feats
  Of lapdogs, who but knows what luck he meets?
But all in vain old fable holds her glass.

Mocked and reviled by men of poisonous breath,
  A great man dies: but one thing worst was spared;
  Not all his heart by their base hands lay bared.
One comes to crown with praise the dust of death;
  And lo, through him this worst is brought to pass.
  Now, what a thing it is to be an ass!

### IV

Shame, such as never yet dealt heavier stroke
  On heads more shameful, fall on theirs through whom
  Dead men may keep inviolate not their tomb,
But all its depths these ravenous grave-worms choke.
And yet what waste of wrath were this, to invoke
  Shame on the shameless? Even their twin-born doom,
  Their native air of life, a carrion fume,
Their natural breath of love, a noisome smoke,
The bread they break, the cup whereof they drink,
  The record whose remembrance damns their name,
  Smells, tastes, and sounds of nothing but of shame.
If thankfulness nor pity bids them think
  What work is this of theirs, and pause betimes,
  Not Shakespeare's grave would scare them off with rhymes.°

[1] *Titus Andronicus*, Act iv, Scene 2 [l.25].

# On the Death of Richard Doyle

A light of blameless laughter, fancy-bred,
  Soft-souled and glad and kind as love or sleep,
  Fades, and sweet mirth's own eyes are fain to weep
Because her blithe and gentlest bird is dead.
Weep, elves and fairies all, that never shed
  Tear yet for mortal mourning: you that keep
  The doors of dreams whence nought of ill may creep,
Mourn once for one whose lips your honey fed.
Let waters of the Golden River steep
  The rose-roots whence his grave blooms rosy-red
And murmuring of Hyblæan° hives be deep
  About the summer silence of its bed,
And nought less gracious than a violet peep
  Between the grass grown greener round his head.

# A Solitude

Sea beyond sea, sand after sweep of sand,
  Here ivory smooth, here cloven and ridged with flow
  Of channelled waters soft as rain or snow,
Stretch their lone length at ease beneath the bland
Grey gleam of skies whose smile on wave and strand
  Shines weary like a man's who smiles to know
  That now no dream can mock his faith with show,
Nor cloud for him seem living sea or land.

Is there an end at all of all this waste,
These crumbling cliffs defeatured and defaced,
These ruinous heights of sea-sapped walls that slide
  Seaward with all their banks of bleak blown flowers
Glad yet of life, ere yet their hope subside
  Beneath the coil of dull dense waves and hours?

# Clear the Way!

Clear the way, my lords and lackeys! you have had your day.
Here you have your answer—England's yea against your nay:
Long enough your house° has held you; up, and clear the way!

Lust and falsehood, craft and traffic, precedent and gold,
Tongue of courtier, kiss of harlot, promise bought and sold,
Gave you heritage of empire over thralls of old.

Now that all these things are rotten, all their gold is rust,
Quenched the pride they lived by, dead the faith and cold the lust,
Shall their heritage not also turn again to dust?

By the grace of these they reigned, who left their sons their sway:
By the grace of these, what England says her lords unsay:
Till at last her cry go forth against them—Clear the way!

By the grace of trust in treason knaves have lived and lied:
By the force of fear and folly fools have fed their pride:
By the strength of sloth and custom reason stands defied.

Lest perchance your reckoning on some latter day be worse,
Halt and hearken, lords of land and princes of the purse,
Ere the tide be full that comes with blessing and with curse.

Where we stand, as where you sit, scarce falls a sprinkling spray;
But the wind that swells, the wave that follows, none shall stay:
Spread no more of sail for shipwreck: out, and clear the way!

# FROM *POEMS AND BALLADS, THIRD SERIES* (1889)

# March: An Ode

1887

Ere frost-flower and snow-blossom faded and fell, and the
 splendour of winter had passed out of sight,
The ways of the woodlands were fairer and stranger than
 dreams that fulfil us in sleep with delight;
The breath of the mouths of the winds had hardened on
 tree-tops and branches that glittered and swayed
Such wonders and glories of blossomlike snow or of frost that
 outlightens all flowers till it fade
That the sea was not lovelier than here was the land, nor the
 night than the day, nor the day than the night,
Nor the winter sublimer with storm than the spring: such
 mirth had the madness and might in thee made,
March, master of winds, bright minstrel and marshal of
 storms that enkindle the season they smite.

And now that the rage of thy rapture is satiate with revel and
 ravin and spoil of the snow,
And the branches it brightened are broken, and shattered the
 tree-tops that only thy wrath could lay low,
How should not thy lovers rejoice in thee, leader and lord of
 the year that exults to be born
So strong in thy strength and so glad of thy gladness whose
 laughter puts winter and sorrow to scorn?
Thou hast shaken the snows from thy wings, and the frost on
 thy forehead is molten: thy lips are aglow
As a lover's that kindle with kissing, and earth, with her
 raiment and tresses yet wasted and torn,
Takes breath as she smiles in the grasp of thy passion to
 feel through her spirit the sense of thee flow.

Fain, fain would we see but again for an hour what the wind
 and the sun have dispelled and consumed,
Those full deep swan-soft feathers of snow with whose
 luminous burden the branches implumed
Hung heavily, curved as a half-bent bow, and fledged not as
 birds are, but petalled as flowers,
Each tree-top and branchlet a pinnacle jewelled and carved,
 or a fountain that shines as it showers,
But fixed as a fountain is fixed not, and wrought not to last till
 by time or by tempest entombed,

As a pinnacle carven and gilded of men: for the date of its
doom is no more than an hour's,
One hour of the sun's when the warm wind wakes him to wither
the snow-flowers that froze as they bloomed.

As the sunshine quenches the snowshine; as April subdues thee,
and yields up his kingdom to May;
So time overcomes the regret that is born of delight as it passes
in passion away,
And leaves but a dream for desire to rejoice in or mourn for
with tears or thanksgivings; but thou,
Bright god that art gone from us, maddest and gladdest of
months, to what goal hast thou gone from us now?
For somewhere surely the storm of thy laughter that lightens,
the beat of thy wings that play,
Must flame as a fire through the world, and the heavens that
we know not rejoice in thee: surely thy brow
Hath lost not its radiance of empire, thy spirit the joy that
impelled it on quest as for prey.

Are thy feet on the ways of the limitless waters, thy wings
on the winds of the waste north sea?
Are the fires of the false north dawn over heavens where
summer is stormful and strong like thee
Now bright in the sight of thine eyes? are the bastions of
icebergs assailed by the blast of thy breath?
Is it March with the wild north world when April is waning?
the word that the changed year saith
Is it echoed to northward with rapture of passion reiterate
from spirits triumphant as we
Whose hearts were uplift at the blast of thy clarions as men's
rearisen from a sleep that was death
And kindled to life that was one with the world's and with
thine? hast thou set not the whole world free?

For the breath of thy lips is freedom, and freedom's the
sense of thy spirit, the sound of thy song,
Glad god of the north-east wind, whose heart is as high as the
hands of thy kingdom are strong,
Thy kingdom whose empire is terror and joy, twin-featured
and fruitful of births divine,
Days lit with the flame of the lamps of the flowers, and nights
that are drunken with dew for wine,
And sleep not for joy of the stars that deepen and quicken,
a denser and fierier throng,

And the world that thy breath bade whiten and tremble rejoices
    at heart as they strengthen and shine,
And earth gives thanks for the glory bequeathed her, and knows
    of thy reign that it wrought not wrong.

Thy spirit is quenched not, albeit we behold not thy face in
    the crown of the steep sky's arch,
And the bold first buds of the whin° wax golden, and
    witness arise of the thorn and the larch:
Wild April, enkindled to laughter and storm by the kiss
    of the wildest of winds that blow,
Calls loud on his brother for witness; his hands that were
    laden with blossom are sprinkled with snow,
And his lips breathe winter, and laugh, and relent; and
    the live woods feel not the frost's flame parch;
For the flame of the spring that consumes not but quickens
    is felt at the heart of the forest aglow,
And the sparks that enkindled and fed it were strewn from
    the hands of the gods of the winds of March.

# To a Seamew

When I had wings, my brother,
  Such wings were mine as thine;
Such life my heart remembers
In all as wild Septembers[o]
As this when life seems other,
  Though sweet, than once was mine:
When I had wings, my brother,
  Such wings were mine as thine.

Such life as thrills and quickens
  The silence of thy flight,
Or fills thy note's elation
With lordlier exultation
Than man's, whose faint heart sickens
  With hopes and fears that blight
Such life as thrills and quickens
  The silence of thy flight.

Thy cry from windward clanging
  Makes all the cliffs rejoice;
Though storm clothe seas with sorrow,
Thy call salutes the morrow;
While shades of pain seem hanging
  Round earth's most rapturous voice,
Thy cry from windward clanging
  Makes all the cliffs rejoice.

We, sons and sires of seamen,[o]
  Whose home is all the sea,
What place man may, we claim it;
But thine—whose thought may name it?
Free birds live higher than freemen,
  And gladlier ye than we—
We, sons and sires of seamen,
  Whose home is all the sea.

For you the storm sounds only
  More notes of more delight
Than earth's in sunniest weather:
When heaven and sea together
Join strengths against the lonely

Lost bark borne down by night,
For you the storm sounds only
More notes of more delight.

With wider wing, and louder
Long clarion-call of joy,
Thy tribe salutes the terror
Of darkness, wild as error,
But sure as truth, and prouder
Than waves with man for toy;
With wider wing, and louder
Long clarion-call of joy.

The wave's wing spreads and flutters,
The wave's heart swells and breaks;
One moment's passion thrills it,
One pulse of power fulfils it
And ends the pride it utters
When, loud with life that quakes,
The wave's wing spreads and flutters,
The wave's heart swells and breaks.

But thine and thou, my brother,
Keep heart and wing more high
Than aught may scare or sunder;
The waves whose throats are thunder
Fall hurtling each on other,
And triumph as they die;
But thine and thou, my brother,
Keep heart and wing more high.

More high than wrath or anguish,
More strong than pride or fear,
The sense or soul half hidden
In thee, for us forbidden,
Bids thee nor change nor languish,
But live thy life as here,
More high than wrath or anguish,
More strong than pride or fear.

We are fallen, even we, whose passion
On earth is nearest thine;
Who sing, and cease from flying;
Who live, and dream of dying:
Grey time, in time's grey fashion,

Bids wingless creatures pine:
We are fallen, even we, whose passion
On earth is nearest thine.

The lark knows no such rapture,
Such joy no nightingale,
As sways the songless measure
Wherein thy wings take pleasure:
Thy love may no man capture,
Thy pride may no man quail;
The lark knows no such rapture,
Such joy no nightingale.

And we, whom dreams embolden,
We can but creep and sing
And watch through heaven's waste hollow
The flight no sight may follow
To the utter bourne beholden
Of none that lack thy wing:
And we, whom dreams embolden,
We can but creep and sing.

Our dreams have wings that falter,
Our hearts bear hopes that die;
For thee no dream could better
A life no fears may fetter,
A pride no care can alter,
That wots not whence or why
Our dreams have wings that falter,
Our hearts bear hopes that die.

With joy more fierce and sweeter
Than joys we deem divine
Their lives, by time untarnished,
Are girt about and garnished,
Who match the wave's full metre
And drink the wind's wild wine
With joy more fierce and sweeter
Than joys we deem divine.

Ah, well were I for ever,
Wouldst thou change lives with me,
And take my song's wild honey,
And give me back thy sunny

Wide eyes that weary never,
And wings that search the sea;
Ah, well were I for ever,
Wouldst thou change lives with me.

*Beachy Head, September, 1886.*

# Neap-Tide

Far off is the sea, and the land is afar:
  The low banks reach at the sky,
  Seen hence, and are heavenward high;
Though light for the leap of a boy they are,
  And the far sea late was nigh.

The fair wild fields and the circling downs,
  The bright sweet marshes and meads
  All glorious with flowerlike weeds,
The great grey churches, the sea-washed towns,
  Recede as a dream recedes.

The world draws back, and the world's light wanes,
  As a dream dies down and is dead;
  And the clouds and the gleams overhead
Change, and change; and the sea remains,
  A shadow of dreamlike dread.

Wild, and woful, and pale, and grey,
  A shadow of sleepless fear,
  A corpse with the night for bier,
The fairest thing that beholds the day
  Lies haggard and hopeless here.

And the wind's wings, broken and spent, subside;
  And the dumb waste world is hoar,
  And strange as the sea the shore;
And shadows of shapeless dreams abide
  Where life may abide no more.

A sail to seaward, a sound from shoreward,
  And the spell were broken that seems
  To reign in a world of dreams
Where vainly the dreamer's feet make forward
  And vainly the low sky gleams.

The sea-forsaken forlorn deep-wrinkled
  Salt slanting stretches of sand
  That slope to the seaward hand,
Were they fain of the ripples that flashed and twinkled
  And laughed as they struck the strand?

As bells on the reins of the fairies ring
  The ripples that kissed them rang,
  The light from the sundawn sprang,
And the sweetest of songs that the world may sing
  Was theirs when the full sea sang.

Now no light is in heaven; and now
  Not a note of the sea-wind's tune
  Rings hither: the bleak sky's boon
Grants hardly sight of a grey sun's brow—
  A sun more sad than the moon.

More sad than a moon that clouds beleaguer
  And storm is a scourge to smite,
  The sick sun's shadowlike light
Grows faint as the clouds and the waves wax eager,
  And withers away from sight.

The day's heart cowers, and the night's heart quickens:
  Full fain would the day be dead
  And the stark night reign in his stead:
The sea falls dumb as the sea-fog thickens
  And the sunset dies for dread.

Outside of the range of time, whose breath
  Is keen as the manslayer's knife
  And his peace but a truce for strife,
Who knows if haply the shadow of death
  May be not the light of life?

For the storm and the rain and the darkness borrow
  But an hour from the suns to be,
  But a strange swift passage, that we
May rejoice, who have mourned not to-day, to-morrow,
  In the sun and the wind and the sea.

# The Interpreters

## I

Days dawn on us that make amends for many
Sometimes,
When heaven and earth seem sweeter even than any
Man's rhymes.

Light had not all been quenched in France, or quelled
In Greece,
Had Homer sung not, or had Hugo held
His peace.

Had Sappho's self not left her word thus long
For token,
The sea round Lesbos yet in waves of song
Had spoken.

## II

And yet these days of subtler air and finer
Delight,
When lovelier looks the darkness, and diviner
The light—

The gift they give of all these golden hours,
Whose urn
Pours forth reverberate rays or shadowing showers
In turn—

Clouds, beams, and winds that make the live day's track
Seem living—
What were they did no spirit give them back
Thanksgiving?

## III

Dead air, dead fire, dead shapes and shadows, telling
Time nought;
Man gives them sense and soul by song, and dwelling
In thought.

In human thought their being endures, their power
Abides:

Else were their life a thing that each light hour
        Derides.

The years live, work, sigh, smile, and die, with all
        They cherish;
The soul endures, though dreams that fed it fall
        And perish.

IV

In human thought have all things habitation;
        Our days
Laugh, lower, and lighten past, and find no station
        That stays.

But thought and faith are mightier things than time
        Can wrong,
Made splendid once with speech, or made sublime
        By song.

Remembrance, though the tide of change that rolls
        Wax hoary,
Gives earth and heaven, for song's sake and the soul's,
        Their glory.

*July 16th, 1885.*

# In Time of Mourning

'Return', we dare not as we fain
  Would cry from hearts that yearn:
Love dares not bid our dead again
  Return.

  O hearts that strain and burn
As fires fast fettered burn and strain!
  Bow down, lie still, and learn.

The heart that healed all hearts of pain
  No funeral rites inurn:
Its echoes, while the stars remain,
  Return.

*May, 1885.*

## To Sir Richard F. Burton

### (On his Translation of the Arabian Nights)

Westward the sun sinks, grave and glad; but far
   Eastward, with laughter and tempestuous tears,
   Cloud, rain, and splendour as of orient spears,
Keen as the sea's thrill toward a kindling star,
The sundawn breaks the barren twilight's bar
   And fires the mist and slays it. Years on years
   Vanish, but he that hearkens eastward hears
Bright music from the world where shadows are.

Where shadows are not shadows. Hand in hand
A man's word bids them rise and smile and stand
   And triumph. All that glorious orient glows
Defiant of the dusk. Our twilight land
   Trembles; but all the heaven is all one rose,
   Whence laughing love dissolves her frosts and snows.

# A Reiver's Neck-Verse

Some die singing, and some die swinging,
  And weel mot a' they be:
Some die playing, and some die praying,
  And I wot sae winna we,° my dear,
  And I wot sae winna we.

Some die sailing, and some die wailing,
  And some die fair and free:
Some die flyting, and some die fighting,
  But I for a fause love's fee, my dear,
  But I for a fause love's fee.

Some die laughing, and some die quaffing,
  And some die high on tree:
Some die spinning, and some die sinning,
  But faggot and fire for ye, my dear,
  Faggot and fire for ye.

Some die weeping, and some die sleeping,
  And some die under sea:
Some die ganging, and some die hanging,
  And a twine of a tow° for me, my dear,
  A twine of a tow for me.

## The Tyneside Widow

There's mony a man loves land and life,
  Loves life and land and fee;
And mony a man loves fair women,
  But never a man loves me, my love,
  But never a man loves me.

O weel and weel for a' lovers,
  I wot weel may they be;
And weel and weel for a' fair maidens,
  But aye mair woe for me, my love,
  But aye mair woe for me.

O weel be wi' you, ye sma' flowers,
  Ye flowers and every tree;
And weel be wi' you, a' birdies,
  But teen and tears wi' me, my love,
  But teen and tears wi' me.

O weel be yours, my three brethren,
  And ever weel be ye;
Wi' deeds for doing and loves for wooing,
  But never a love for me, my love,
  But never a love for me.

And weel be yours, my seven sisters,
  And good love-days to see,
And long life-days and true lovers,
  But never a day for me, my love,
  But never a day for me.

Good times wi' you, ye bauld riders,
  By the hieland and the lee;
And by the leeland and by the hieland
  It's weary times wi' me, my love.
  It's weary times wi' me.

Good days wi' you, ye good sailors,
  Sail in and out the sea;
And by the beaches and by the reaches
  It's heavy days wi' me, my love,
  It's heavy days wi' me.

I had his kiss upon my mouth,
  His bairn upon my knee;

I would my soul and body were twain,
  And the bairn and the kiss wi' me, my love,
  And the bairn and the kiss wi' me.

The bairn down in the mools,° my dear,
  O saft and saft lies she;
I would the mools were ower my head,
  And the young bairn fast wi' me, my love,
  And the young bairn fast wi' me.

The father under the faem, my dear,
  O sound and sound sleeps he;
I would the faem were ower my face,
  And the father lay by me, my love,
  And the father lay by me.

I would the faem were ower my face,
  Or the mools on my ee-bree;°
And waking-time with a' lovers,
  But sleeping-time wi' me, my love,
  But sleeping-time wi' me.

I would the mools were meat in my mouth,
  The saut faem in my ee;
And the land-worm and the water-worm
  To feed fu' sweet on me, my love,
  To feed fu' sweet on me.

My life is sealed with a seal of love,
  And locked with love for a key;
And I lie wrang and I wake lang,
  But ye tak' nae thought for me, my love,
  But ye tak' nae thought for me.

We were weel fain of love, my dear,
  O fain and fain were we;
It was weel with a' the weary world,
  But O, sae weel wi' me, my love,
  But O, sae weel wi' me.

We were nane ower mony to sleep, my dear,
  I wot we were but three;
And never a bed in the weary world
  For my bairn and my dear and me, my love,
  For my bairn and my dear and me.

I would my son and [illegible] were again,
And the bairn at the breast wi' me, my love,
And the [illegible] and the [illegible] wi' me.

The [illegible] down [illegible] the [illegible], my dear,
[illegible]
I would the [illegible] were around my head,
And the young bairn fast [illegible] me, my love,
And the young bairn fast wi' me.

The father under the [illegible], my dear,
[illegible] and sound sleeps he,
I would the [illegible] were upon my face,
And the father [illegible] by me, my love,
And the father by me.

I would the bent were over my face,
Or the moods on my [illegible]
And [illegible] with a' flowers,
But sleeping [illegible] me, my love,
But sleeping [illegible] wi' me.

I would the moods were about my mouth,
[illegible]
And the [illegible] the [illegible]
[illegible] my love,
To feed my [illegible]

My [illegible] sealed with [illegible]
And locked with love [illegible]
And [illegible] and I wake [illegible]
But [illegible] thought for me [illegible]
But he [illegible] thought for me.

We were wed [illegible] my dear,
O [illegible]
[illegible] the [illegible] world,
But [illegible] my love,
But O [illegible] me.

We were [illegible] my dear,
[illegible] but three
And [illegible]
For my bairn and my dear and me, my love,
For my bairn and my dear and me.

# ‘RECOLLECTIONS OF PROFESSOR JOWETT’ (1893)

Among the tributes offered to the memory of an illustrious man there may possibly be found room for the modest reminiscences of one to whom the Master of Balliol was officially a stranger,° and Mr Jowett was an honoured and valued friend. Because the work of his life was mainly if not wholly devoted to Oxford it does not follow and it would be a mistake to assume—as certain of his official mourners or admirers might induce their hearers or readers to assume—that apart from Oxford he was not, and that his only claim to remembrance and reverence is the fact that he put new blood into the veins of an old university. He would have been a noticeable man if he had known no language but the English of which he was so pure and refined a master; and if he had never put pen to paper he would have left his mark upon the minds and the memories of younger men as certainly and as durably as he did. For my own part, I always think of him, by instinct and by preference, as he was wont to show himself in the open air during the course of a long walk and a long talk, intermittent and informal and discursive and irregular to the last and most desirable degree. The perfect freedom, the quaint and positive independence, of his views on character and his outlook on letters would have given interest to the conversation of a far less distinguished man. That he was an active believer and worker in the cause of spiritual progress and intellectual advance was not more evident than that on some points he was rather more in touch with the past than many men of immeasurably less insight and less faith in the future. He was perhaps the last of the old Whigs; the last man of such brilliant and dominant intelligence to find himself on so many points in such all but absolute sympathy with the view or the purview of such teachers as Sydney Smith and Macaulay.° But here as everywhere the candour, the freedom, the manliness and fairness of his ethical and judicial attitude or instinct stood out unimpaired by prepossession or partizanship. With the unconscious malevolence of self-righteousness which distorted the critical appreciations and discoloured the personal estimates of Lord Macaulay, the most ardent Tory could not have had less sympathy than had this far more loyal and large-minded Whig. I am not likely to forget the pleasure with which I found that his judgment on the characters of Dryden and Pope° was as charitable (and therefore, in my humble opinion, as equitable and as reasonable) as Macaulay's was perversely one-sided and squint-eyed. To Swift he was perhaps almost more than just; to Rabelais I thought him somewhat less. Of Sydney Smith, again, I found him inclined—if it be possible, as perhaps it may not be—to make too much; of Charles Lamb—I fear I must not hesitate, however reluctant, to say so—at least as much too little. But there was in his own composition so much of quiet appreciative humour that it was always well worth hearing what he had to say upon humourists. These he divided into three categories or classes: those who are not worth reading at all; those who are worth reading once, but once only; and those who are worth reading again and again and for ever. In the second class he placed the *Biglow Papers*;° which famous and admirable work of American humour was as it happened, the starting-point of our discussion; and for which, as I can hardly think it admissible into the third and crowning class, I would suggest that a fourth might be provided, to include such examples as are worth, let us say, two or three readings in a lifetime.

Dickens, I am happy to think, can hardly have had a more cordial and appreciative admirer than Mr Jowett. Tennyson, Browning, and Carlyle were all still among us when I once happened to ask him whom he thought the first of living English writers. He hesitated for a minute or so, and then replied, 'If Dickens were alive, I shouldn't hesitate.' As it was, he gave of course the first place to Tennyson, and admitted that he must reluctantly give the second to Carlyle. Of the perverse and sinister and splendid genius which culminated in *Latter-day Pamphlets* and the *Life of Frederick the Great* he was wont to speak with a distaste and a severity which I for one do not in the least believe to have been in the least inspired or intensified by any personal animosity or resentment. Though I must confess that my own belief in the prophet of Craigenputtock as an inspired guide and teacher did not long survive the expiration of my teens, I thought Mr Jowett's impeachment of his ethics and aesthetics so singularly austere that I one day asked him what it was that he so much disliked or disapproved—in northerly English, what ailed him at Carlyle: and he replied that his enmity was grounded on the belief that no writer had done or was doing so much harm to young men as the preacher of tyranny and the apologist of cruelty.[o] On another occasion we were talking of Voltaire, and he asked me what I thought the best work of a writer whom he apparently did not greatly relish or appreciate: of *Candide* he spoke with rather too dainty distaste. I might of course have quoted Victor Hugo's incomparably exact and accurate definition—'Voltaire, c'est le bon sens à jet continu:'[o] but I merely replied that, as far as I knew or was able to judge, Voltaire's great work was to have done more than any other man on record to make the instinct of cruelty not only detestable but ludicrous; and so to accomplish what the holiest and the wisest of saints and philosophers had failed to achieve: to attack that most hideous and pernicious of human vices with a more effective weapon than preaching or denunciation: to make tyrants and torturers look not merely horrible and hateful, but pitiful and ridiculous. 'Yes,' Mr Jowett said: 'and that is the work that Carlyle would undo.'

An amusing if somewhat extreme example of his own exceptional kindliness and tolerance was provoked or evoked on another occasion by the genius of Dickens. One evening while he was a guest at my father's it appeared that he had not the honour and happiness of an acquaintance with the immortal and ever delightful figure misintroduced by his creator or his painter as 'Our Bore.'[o] His delight on making that acquaintance it would need the pen of a Dickens to describe; and I only wish Mr Dickens could have witnessed it. (This, however, as Charles Lamb's typically Scottish acquaintances would have objected, was impossible, because he was dead.) But after repeated eruptions and subsidences of insuppressible and really boyish laughter he protested—and not entirely, I fancy, in fun—that bores ought not to be so pitilessly made fun of, for they were usually good men. And I do not think this was said in the sardonic sense or in the subacid spirit of a disciple of Thackeray.

To the great genius and the coequally great character of Sir Walter Scott I rejoice to remember that no Scotchman can ever have paid more loyal homage than Mr Jowett. Scott's noble disclaimer of potential equality or possible rivalry with Burns as a poet aroused such generous and sympathetic admiration in his own high-minded and clear-sighted spirit as cannot be recalled without cordial pleasure. Of poetry he used to say that he considered himself not so much a good critic as 'a good foolometer;' but however that may have been, I always found him an admirable critic of character. Always, I must add, except in one instance: he retained so much of the singular Byronic superstition as to persist—even after Mr Froude's unanswerable and final demonstration of the truth°—in closing the eyes of his judgment if not of his conscience to the universal evidence of irrefragable proof against the character and the honour of Childe Juan. Upon affectation and pretention he was only not too severe because no man can be too severe: upon self-indulgence and sensuality he may have been inclined to pass sentence in a tone or spirit so austere as to prove, had other evidence been wanting, how perfectly and how naturally Spartan was his own devotion to a purely and exclusively intellectual and moral line of life and scheme of thought. And yet he had for the most affected of sensualists and the most pretentious of profligates a sort of tender or admiring weakness which does not as usual admit of the obvious explanation that he was himself a writer of bad verses. The one point on which I can understand or imagine that he should ever have felt himself in touch with Byron was about the very last that might have been expected from a studious and philosophic man of books and cloisters. I never knew a man of better nerve: and I have known Richard Burton.° The physical energy with which he would press up a hill-side or mountain-side—Malvern or Schehallion—was very agreeable and admirable to witness: but twice at least during a week's winter excursion in Cornwall I knew, and had reason to know, what it was to feel nervous: for he would follow along the broken rampart of a ruined castle, and stand without any touch of support at the edge of a magnificent precipice, as though he had been a younger man bred up from boyhood to the scaling of cliffs and the breasting of breakers.°

His love of nature, I should say, was temperate but genuine; certainly genuine, but decidedly temperate. The unique and incomparable sublimity of loveliness which distinguishes the serpentine rocks and cliffs and slopes and platforms of Kynance Cove° from any other possible presentation of an earthly paradise could not and did not fail to excite his admiring notice: but I doubt if he recognized that there could be nothing like it in the world. At Tintagel, and again at St Michael's Mount,° I noticed that his energetic perseverance in the rough and steep ascent was more remarkable, and to himself apparently more pleasurable, than his enjoyment of the glorious outlook so sturdily and so hardily attained. In this more than in most things his real and natural kinship to his beloved Dr Johnson ('our great friend,' as he used to call him in our many talks on the subject) was not undelightfully manifest I need not quote evidence from Johnson or from Boswell to that effect. That 'he rode harder at a fox-chase than anybody,'° as Johnson affirmed of himself, it would certainly surprise me to be assured: but I think he would have ridden pretty straight if he had ridden at all. And he would never have drawn rein to look about him in forgetfulness of the serious matter in hand: not though the hounds had been running up the Vale of Tempe or across the Garden of Eden.

A very sufficient proof of this indisputable fact is that his chosen favourite among all Shakespeare's comedies was the *Merry Wives of Windsor*. But a still clearer proof, to my mind, was afforded by his selection and rejection of passages and chapters from the Bible for the reading of children. It can hardly be now, I should hope and presume, an indiscretion or a breach of confidence to mention that he had undertaken this task, as he told me, to assist a friend, and asked me to assist him in it: and it certainly cannot be necessary to add how glad I was to do so, or how much and how naturally gratified by the cordial compliment he paid, when we had been some days at work, I dare not say to my scriptural scholarship, but I will say to my thorough familiarity with sundry parts of the sacred text. I noticed almost at once that his notion of what would be attractive to children excluded much of what I should have thought would be most attractive to an intelligent and imaginative child; that his excerpts would have been almost wholly historical or mythical or moral; and that he evidently did not understand, remember, or take into account, the delight that a child may take in things beyond the grasp of his perfect comprehension, though not beyond the touch of his apprehensive or prehensile fancy, and the incalculable fruitfulness of benefit that may be gradually and unconsciously derived from that delight. But at the assistant's or sub-editor's instigation his draught or scheme of a 'Child's Bible' came gradually and regularly to include so much more and more than his own design would have included of the prophetic or poetic elements in the text, that he said to me one night, with a smile, 'I wanted you to help me to make this book smaller, and you have persuaded me to make it much larger.' To which I replied with a quotation of what Balak said unto Balaam.°

No man, I suppose, can enjoy the dignity and exercise the authority of a 'Master' over boys at school or youths at college, without catching some occasional infection of autocratic infirmity; without contracting some dictatorial or domineering habit of mind or tone of manner which affects his natural bearing and impairs his natural influence. Even of the excellent husband of Jeanie Deans it is recorded that 'the man was mortal, and had been a schoolmaster;'° and even in Mr Jowett the Master of Balliol would occasionally, though rarely, break out and rise to the surface 'when there was no need of such vanity.'[o] But these slips or descents from the natural man into the professional pedagogue were admirably rare: and even if it cannot be confidently affirmed that his bright and brave intelligence was always wholly unaffected by the foggy damp of Oxonian atmosphere, it is certainly undeniable that the affection was never so serious as to make it possible for the most malignant imbecile to compare or to confound him with such morally and spiritually typical and unmistakable apes of the Dead Sea as Mark Pattison, or such renascent blossoms of the Italian renascence as the Platonic amorist of blue-breeched gondoliers who is now in Aretino's bosom. The cult of the calamus, as expounded by Mr Addington Symonds to his fellow-calamites, would have found no acceptance or tolerance with the translator of Plato.[o]

There was no touch in Mr Jowett of the singularly mean and perverse kind of stupidity which makes or used to make the professional parasites of Tennyson and of Browning, of Dickens and of Thackeray, respectively ready to decry or to depreciate the supposed competitor or rival of their master; nor were his critical estimates, I should say, at all generally or unduly coloured or biased by personal associations. Had the names of Robert Browning and Matthew Arnold been to him simple signs denoting the existence and the character of the artist or the thinker, his judgment of his friend's work could scarcely in either case have been more independent, impartial, and detached. I do not even think that the effusive Oxonolatry of Mr Arnold can at all have heightened or deepened Mr Jowett's regard for what he most relished and valued in the author of *Thyrsis*. The appearance of *Literature and Dogma*,[o] he told me, so changed and raised his opinion of Arnold's powers—gave him, it should seem, such a shock and start of surprise as well as admiration—that he had evidently never appreciated at its full value the best of its author's early work in poetry. Not, of course, that the exquisite fancy, melody, and pathos of such a poem as *The Forsaken Merman* gave any promise of the luminous good sense and serenity of intelligence which supplied us with the definition of 'a magnified and non-natural man'[o]—and reminded, I may add, a younger reader of his own previous and private definition of the only 'personal deity' conceivable or apprehensible by man as simply and inevitably 'man with a difference.'

Towards the great writer whose productions reach from the date of *Pauline* to the date of *Asolando*[o] and of whom it would be less just than plausible to say that his masterpieces extend from the date of Paracelsus to the date of *The Ring and the Book*, the mental attitude of Mr Jowett was more than peculiar: it was something, at least in my experience, unique. The mutual admiration, if I may for once use a phrase so contemptible and detestable to backbiters and dunces, of these two eminent men was and is unquestionable: but it would be difficult, setting aside merely personal and casual occasions of respect and regard, to discover or conjecture the cause—to touch the spring or to strike the root of it. Never did I see Mr Jowett so keenly vexed, irritated, arid distressed as he was when the responsibility for Mr Browning's adventurous aberrations into Greece was attributed to the effect of his influence: nor, of course, could I feel surprised. That over venturesome Balaustion,° the record of whose first 'Adventure' was cruelly rechristened by Rossetti's ever happy and spontaneous wit as 'Exhaustion's Imposture,'° was not likely to find favour with the critic who once wrote to me, and rejoiced my very soul by writing, 'I have been reading Euripides lately, and still retain my old bad opinion of him—Sophist, sentimentalist, sensationalist—no Greek in the better sense of the term.' It was all I could do, on another occasion, to win from him an admission of the charm and grace and sweetness of some of the shorter and simpler lyrics which redeem in some measure the reputation of the dreariest of playwrights—if that term be not over complimentary for the clumsiest of botchers that ever floundered through his work as a dramatist.

But even when Mr Browning was not figuring on Hellenic soil as a belated barbarian, it hardly seemed to me that Mr Jowett was inclined to do anything like sympathetic justice to his friend's incomparable powers. Such general admiration of the man's genius and such comparative depreciation of the writer's works it was so hard to reconcile that I once asked him what it was, then, that he admired in Browning: and the first quality he could allege as admirable to him was Mr Browning's marvellous range of learning. But of course he was not and he could not have been insensible to the greatness of so colossal a masterpiece, the masterpiece of so gigantic a genius, as the whole world of English readers arose to acclaim on the appearance of *The Ring and the Book*: though the close was over tragic in its elaborate anatomy of moral horror for the endurance of his instinct or his judgment. 'The second Guido is too dreadful,'° he said to me—and talked no more on the grim subject.

Mr Jowett, I believe, has been accused of setting too much store by the casual attributes of position, celebrity, and success: and this weakness, supposing it to have existed, is exactly the kind of infirmity which even the most vigorous judgment might perhaps have been expected to contract from the lifelong habit of looking to class-lists and examinations as a serious test, if not as the final touchstone, of crowning ability as well as of disciplined docility—of inborn capacity no less than of ductile diligence. But he could do justice, and cordial justice, to good work utterly and unaccountably ignored, not merely by the run of readers, but by men of culture, intelligence, and intuition such as universities are supposed to supply to natures naturally deficient in perception and distinction of good and bad. I have seldom if ever known him more impressed than by the noble and pathetic tragedy of *The Earl of Brecon*:° the motive or mainspring of the action was at once so new, so true, and so touching as to arouse at once and unmistakably his interest, his admiration, and his surprise. And the very finest works of so rare a genius as Robert Landor's—a genius as thoroughly and nobly and characteristically English on its ethical or sympathetic side as Chaucer's or Shakespeare's, Milton's or

Wordsworth's—are still even less recognized and appreciated than even the works of his yet more splendidly gifted brother. But for the generous kindness of my friend Mr William Rossetti I should never have possessed or been able to lend a copy of his beautiful and neglected and unprocurable plays.°

In his views on art Mr Jowett was something more than a conservative: he would actually maintain that English poetry had not advanced more than English painting had fallen off since the days of Goldsmith and Reynolds. But it should be needless to add that in his maintenance of this untenable paradox there was nothing of the brassy braggardism and bullying self-confidence of the anonymous amateur or volunteer in criticism whose gaping admiration for the French or American or Japanese art or trick of painting by spots and splashes induces him in common consistency to deride the art of Turner and the art of David Cox. And for the finest work of the great and greatly beloved and lamented painter whose death followed so closely on his own he had such cordial and appreciative admiration that the magnificent portrait of Mr Madox Brown by himself—a work more than worthy of a place among its rivals in the Uffizi—can never receive the tribute of a fuller and sincerer homage than Mr Jowett's.°

And this, for one thing, may suffice to show how admirably far from the tenacity of arrogance was his habitual tone of mind. A less important but by no means a less significant example may perhaps be worth citing in refutation of the preposterous malignity which would tax him with the positive and obstinate self-conceit of the typical or proverbial pedagogue. He once, to my personal knowledge, requested an old pupil,° then staying under his temporary roof, to go over his first version of Plato's *Symposium*, collating it with the original text, and see if he had any suggestion to offer. The old pupil would naturally, I suppose, have felt flattered by the request, even had his Oxonian career culminated in tolerable or creditable success instead of total and scandalous failure: at all events, he fell to and read that remarkable work of philosophic literature from end to end—'suppressing,' as Carlyle expresses it, 'any little abhorrences.'° And in one passage it did certainly seem to him that the Professor of Greek in the University of Oxford had mistaken and misconstrued his Plato: a view which no one but an impudent booby would have been ready or willing to put forward: but after some hesitation, feeling that it would be a rather mean and servile and treacherous sort of deference or modesty which would preclude him from speaking, he took upon himself to say diffidently that if he had been called upon to construe the sentence in question he should have construed it otherwise. Mr Jowett turned and looked at him with surprised and widened eyes: and said after a minute or so, 'Of course that is the meaning. You would be a good scholar if you were to study.' But we all know that there is 'much virtue in If.'

It was a source of grave if not keen regret to Mr Jowett that he could not read Dante in the original: Dean Church's wonderfully learned and devoted study found in him a careful and an interested student.° I had myself been studying the text of Foscolo's and Mazzini's noble and laborious edition° while he was reading that incomparable manual or introduction to the subject on which we naturally fell into conversation: when I was not surprised to hear him remark with amused and smiling wonder on what I had noted already as matter for unutterable astonishment: the learned Dean's amazing assumption that Dante's God was not at least as dead as Homer's; that his scheme of the universe moral and material, could be split up into segments for selection and rejection; that his theology could be detached from his cosmogony, and that it was not as rational and as possible to believe in the Peak of Teneriffe being the Mountain of Purgatory, with Paradise atop of it and Hell just at bottom, as to believe in the loving Lord God of unrighteousness who damns Francesca and glorifies Cunizza, damns Brutus and spares Cato, damns Farinata and sanctifies Dominic.° Yet after all this is hardly more bewildering to human reason than that excellent and intelligent multitudes of articulate mortals should call themselves believers in the teaching of their holy writ, and maintain that 'the spirit killeth, but the letter giveth life.'°

But Dante, the poet of midnight and all its stars, to whom the sun° itself was but one of them, could never have appealed to the serene and radiant intelligence of Mr Jowett as did the poet of noonday, for whom past and present were one luminous harmony of life—even if, as some have questionably thought, his outlook on the possible future was doubtful and unhopeful.° No one can ever have been readier with a quotation from Shakespeare, or happier and apter in the application of it. When he first heard of Mr Lowell's hideous and Bœotian jest on Milton's blindness—no lover of American humour can fail to remember it—he instantly exclaimed, 'O for a stone-bow to hit him in the eye!'° But he frankly and modestly disclaimed the honour of being what he really sometimes seemed to be, a living concordance to Shakespeare: to Boswell alone would he admit, with a smile of satisfaction, that he was or that he might be. And year after year did he renew the promise to fulfil his project and redeem his engagement to undertake the vindication of Boswell as genius and as man. Carlyle and Macaulay, with all their antagonistic absurdities and ineptitudes of misconception and misrepresentation, would then have been refuted and exposed. It is grievous to think that the time spent on translation and commentary should have left him no leisure for so delightful and so serviceable an enterprise.

Even Mr Jowett could hardly have affirmed of Dr Johnson that he never slipped into an absolute platitude; and once at least I was surprised to hear Mr Jowett enunciate the astonishing remark that he could not understand how it was possible at once to like a man and to despise him. We had been talking of a common acquaintance whose instinctive time-serving and obsequious submissiveness to every gust of popular fashion or casual revolution in opinion or in prejudice were as proverbially notorious as his easy amiability; of whom Richard Burton once said to me that he felt certain some good luck must be coming his way, for •••••••• was so very civil (the exact word was not 'very,' but by no means a less emphatic one) that he must evidently have heard of some imminent promotion or impending prosperity about to befall the returning traveller: a reasoning which I could not but admit to be more than plausible: and we afterwards used always to speak of this worthy as The Barometer.° If ever there was a man whose friendships were more independent of such pitifully instinctive calculation—a man more incapable of social cowardice and worldly servility—than Mr Jowett, I can only say that I never met or heard and never expect to meet or hear of him: but when I happened to observe of the elder in question that he was a man whom I thought it equally impossible not to like and not to despise, this noble and loyal man of large experience and liberal intelligence replied almost in the tone of a pulpiteer that 'he could not understand how you could like a man whom you despised.' Ingenuous youth happened to be present in some force on the occasion, and I kept silence: not for want of an answer, but out of consideration for their Master and my host.

Few men, I should say, whose line of life lay so far apart from a naturalist's or a poet's can ever have loved nature and poetry better; after the temperate though very real and serious fashion which I have already tried to define or to indicate; but his perception or recollection of the influences of nature upon poetry in particular instances was hardly always accurate. We were returning from a walk across and above the magnificent valley of the Spey, when I remarked on the likeness or kinship of the scenery about us to the poetry of Wordsworth, and he rejoined that he could not associate Wordsworth's poetry with a country which had no lakes in it; forgetting how little of water and how much of mountain or hillside there is in that poet's habitual and representative landscape: so little of the lakes and so much of the hill-tops that but for a senseless nickname we might hardly remember that his life had been spent beside the waters on which some of his finest verses commemorate the perennially happy results of his skating as a boy.

Of the average academic or collegiate one is inclined to think that, in Rossetti's accurate phrase, 'he dies not—never having lived—but ceases':° of Mr Jowett it is almost impossible at first to think as dead. I, at any rate, never found it harder, if so hard, to realize the death of any one. There was about him a simple and spontaneous force of fresh and various vitality, of happy and natural and wellnigh sleepless energy, which seemed not so much to defy extinction as to deride it. 'He laboured, so must we,'° says Ben Jonson of Plato in a noble little book which I had the pleasure of introducing to Mr Jowett's appreciative acquaintance; and assuredly no man ever lived closer up to that standard of active and studious life than the translator of Plato. But this living energy, this natal force of will and action, was coloured and suffused and transfigured by so rare a quality of goodness, of kindness, of simple and noble amiability, that the intellectual side of his nature is neither the first nor the last side on which the loving and mourning memory of any one ever admitted to his friendship can feel inclined or will be expected to dwell.

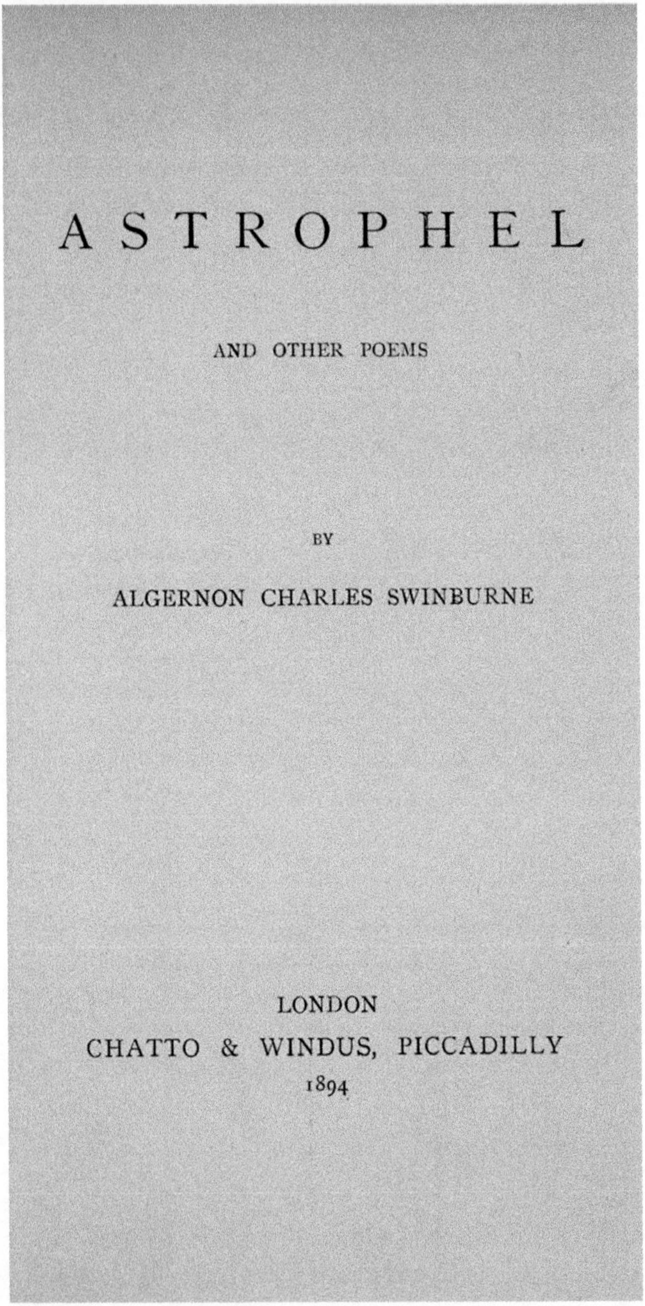

ASTROPHEL

AND OTHER POEMS

BY

ALGERNON CHARLES SWINBURNE

LONDON
CHATTO & WINDUS, PICCADILLY
1894

FIG. 9. Title page of *Astrophel and Other Poems* (London: Chatto & Windus, 1894), a copy from the Brotherton Library, Special Collections, University of Leeds, reproduced with permission.

# FROM *ASTROPHEL AND OTHER POEMS* (1894)

# A Nympholept

Summer, and noon, and a splendour of silence, felt,
  Seen, and heard of the spirit within the sense.
Soft through the frondage the shades of the sunbeams melt,
  Sharp through the foliage the shafts of them, keen and dense,
  Cleave, as discharged from the string of the God's bow, tense
As a war-steed's girth, and bright as a warrior's belt.
  Ah, why should an hour that is heaven for an hour pass hence?

I dare not sleep for delight of the perfect hour,
  Lest God be wroth that his gift should be scorned of man.
The face of the warm bright world is the face of a flower,
  The word of the wind and the leaves that the light winds fan
  As the word that quickened at first into flame, and ran,
Creative and subtle and fierce with invasive power,
  Through darkness and cloud, from the breath of the one
      God, Pan.

The perfume of earth possessed by the sun pervades
  The chaster air that he soothes but with sense of sleep.
Soft, imminent, strong as desire that prevails and fades,
  The passing noon that beholds not a cloudlet weep
  Imbues and impregnates life with delight more deep
Than dawn or sunset or moonrise on lawns or glades
  Can shed from the skies that receive it and may not keep.

The skies may hold not the splendour of sundown fast;
  It wanes into twilight as dawn dies down into day.
And the moon, triumphant when twilight is overpast,
  Takes pride but awhile in the hours of her stately sway.
  But the might of the noon, though the light of it pass away,
Leaves earth fulfilled of desires and of dreams that last;
  But if any there be that hath sense of them none can say[.]°

For if any there be that hath sight of them, sense, or trust
  Made strong by the might of a vision, the strength of
      a dream,
His lips shall straiten and close as a dead man's must,
  His heart shall be sealed as the voice of a frost-bound stream.
  For the deep mid mystery of light and of heat that seem
To clasp and pierce dark earth, and enkindle dust,
  Shall a man's faith say what it is? or a man's guess deem?

Sleep lies not heavier on eyes that have watched all night
　Than hangs the heat of the noon on the hills and trees.
Why now should the haze not open, and yield to sight
　A fairer secret than hope or than slumber sees?
　I seek not heaven with submission of lips and knees,
With worship and prayer for a sign till it leap to light:
　I gaze on the gods about me, and call on these.

I call on the gods hard by, the divine dim powers
　Whose likeness is here at hand, in the breathless air,
In the pulseless peace of the fervid and silent flowers,
　In the faint sweet speech of the waters that whisper there.
　Ah, what should darkness do in a world so fair?
The bent-grass heaves not, the couch-grass quails not or cowers;
　The wind's kiss frets not the rowan's or aspen's hair.

But the silence trembles with passion of sound suppressed,
　And the twilight quivers and yearns to the sunward, wrung
With love as with pain; and the wide wood's motionless breast
　Is thrilled with a dumb desire that would fain find tongue
　And palpitates, tongueless as she whom a man-snake stung,
Whose heart now heaves in the nightingale, never at rest
　Nor satiated ever with song till her last be sung.

Is it rapture or terror that circles me round, and invades
　Each vein of my life with hope—if it be not fear?
Each pulse that awakens my blood into rapture fades,
　Each pulse that subsides into dread of a strange thing near
　Requickens with sense of a terror less dread than dear.
Is peace not one with light in the deep green glades
　Where summer at noonday slumbers? Is peace not here?

The tall thin stems of the firs, and the roof sublime
　That screens from the sun the floor of the steep still wood,
Deep, silent, splendid, and perfect and calm as time,
　Stand fast as ever in sight of the night they stood,
　When night gave all that moonlight and dewfall could.
The dense ferns deepen, the moss glows warm as the thyme:
　The wild heath quivers about me: the world is good.°

Is it Pan's breath, fierce in the tremulous maidenhair,
　That bids fear creep as a snake through the woodlands, felt
In the leaves that it stirs not yet, in the mute bright air,
　In the stress of the sun? For here has the great God dwelt:
　For hence were the shafts of his love or his anger dealt.

For here has his wrath been fierce as his love was fair,
  When each was as fire to the darkness its breath bade melt.

Is it love, is it dread, that enkindles the trembling noon,
  That yearns, reluctant in rapture that fear has fed,
As man for woman, as woman for man? Full soon,
  If I live, and the life that may look on him drop not dead,
  Shall the ear that hears not a leaf quake hear his tread,°
The sense that knows not the sound of the deep day's tune
  Receive the God, be it love that he brings or dread.

The naked noon is upon me: the fierce dumb spell,
  The fearful charm of the strong sun's imminent might,
Unmerciful, steadfast, deeper than seas that swell,
  Pervades, invades, appals me with loveless light,
  With harsher awe than breathes in the breath of night.
Have mercy, God who art all! For I know thee well,
  How sharp is thine eye to lighten, thine hand to smite.

The whole wood feels thee, the whole air fears thee: but fear
  So deep, so dim, so sacred, is wellnigh sweet.
For the light that hangs and broods on the woodlands here,
  Intense, invasive, intolerant, imperious, and meet
  To lighten the works of thine hands and the ways of thy feet,
Is hot with the fire of the breath of thy life, and dear
  As hope that shrivels or shrinks not for frost or heat.

Thee, thee the supreme dim godhead, approved afar,
  Perceived of the soul and conceived of the sense of man,
We scarce dare love, and we dare not fear: the star
  We call the sun, that lit us when life began
  To brood on the world that is thine by his grace for a span,
Conceals and reveals in the semblance of things that are
  Thine immanent presence, the pulse of thy heart's life, Pan.

The fierce mid noon that wakens and warms the snake
  Conceals thy mercy, reveals thy wrath: and again
The dew-bright hour that assuages the twilight brake
  Conceals thy wrath and reveals thy mercy: then
Thou art fearful only for evil souls of men
  That feel with nightfall the serpent within them wake,
  And hate the holy darkness on glade and glen.

Yea, then we know not and dream not if ill things be,
  Or if aught of the work of the wrong of the world be thine.
We hear not the footfall of terror that treads the sea,

We hear not the moan of winds that assail the pine:
We see not if shipwreck reign in the storm's dim shrine;
If death do service and doom bear witness to thee
We see not,—know not if blood for thy lips be wine.

But in all things evil and fearful that fear may scan,
As in all things good, as in all things fair that fall,
We know thee present and latent, the lord of man;
In the murmuring of doves, in the clamouring of winds that call
And wolves that howl for their prey; in the midnight's pall,
In the naked and nymph-like feet of the dawn, O Pan,
And in each life living, O thou the God who art all.

Smiling and singing, wailing and wringing of hands,
Laughing and weeping, watching and sleeping, still
Proclaim but and prove but thee, as the shifted sands
Speak forth and show but the strength of the sea's wild will
That sifts and grinds them as grain in the storm-wind's mill.
In thee is the doom that falls and the doom that stands:
The tempests utter thy word, and the stars fulfil.

Where Etna shudders with passion and pain volcanic
That rend her heart as with anguish that rends a man's,
Where Typho labours, and finds not his thews Titanic,°
In breathless torment that ever the flame's breath fans,
Men felt and feared thee of old, whose pastoral clans
Were given to the charge of thy keeping; and soundless panic
Held fast the woodland whose depths and whose heights
were Pan's.

And here, though fear be less than delight, and awe
Be one with desire and with worship of earth and thee,
So mild seems now thy secret and speechless law,
So fair and fearless and faithful and godlike she,
So soft the spell of thy whisper on stream and sea,
Yet man should fear lest he see what of old men saw
And withered: yet shall I quail if thy breath smite me.

Lord God of life and of light and of all things fair,
Lord God of ravin and ruin and all things dim,
Death seals up life, and darkness the sunbright air,
And the stars that watch blind earth in the deep night swim
Laugh, saying, 'What God is your God, that ye call on him?°
What is man, that the God who is guide of our way should care
If day for a man be golden, or night be grim?'

But thou, dost thou hear? Stars too but abide for a span,
  Gods too but endure for a season; but thou, if thou be
God, more than shadows conceived and adored of man,
  Kind Gods and fierce, that bound him or made him free,
  The skies that scorn us are less in thy sight than we,
Whose souls have strength to conceive and perceive thee, Pan,
  With sense more subtle than senses that hear and see.

Yet may not it say, though it seek thee and think to find
  One soul of sense in the fire and the frost-bound clod,
What heart is this, what spirit alive or blind,
  That moves thee: only we know that the ways we trod
  We tread, with hands unguided, with feet unshod,
With eyes unlightened; and yet, if with steadfast mind,
  Perchance may we find thee and know thee at last for God.

Yet then should God be dark as the dawn is bright,
  And bright as the night is dark on the world—no more.
Light slays not darkness, and darkness absorbs not light;
  And the labour of evil and good from the years of yore
  Is even as the labour of waves on a sunless shore.
And he who is first and last,° who is depth and height,
  Keeps silence now, as the sun when the woods wax hoar.

The dark dumb godhead innate in the fair world's life
  Imbues the rapture of dawn and of noon with dread,
Infects the peace of the star-shod night with strife,
  Informs with terror the sorrow that guards the dead.
  No service of bended knee or of humbled head
May soothe or subdue the God who has change to wife:
  And life with death is as morning with evening wed.

And yet, if the light and the life in the light that here
  Seem soft and splendid and fervid as sleep may seem
Be more than the shine of a smile or the flash of a tear,
  Sleep, change, and death are less than a spell-struck dream,
  And fear than the fall of a leaf on a starlit stream.
And yet, if the hope that hath said it absorb not fear,
  What helps it man that the stars and the waters gleam?

What helps it man, that the noon be indeed intense,
  The night be indeed worth worship? Fear and pain
Were lords and masters yet of the secret sense,
  Which now dares deem not that light is as darkness, fain
  Though dark dreams be to declare it, crying in vain.

For whence, thou God of the light and the darkness, whence
  Dawns now this vision that bids not the sunbeams wane?

What light, what shadow, diviner than dawn or night,
  Draws near, makes pause, and again—or I dream—draws near?
More soft than shadow, more strong than the strong sun's light,
  More pure than moonbeams—yea, but the rays run sheer
  As fire from the sun through the dusk of the pinewood, clear
And constant; yea, but the shadow itself is bright
  That the light clothes round with love that is one with fear.

Above and behind it the noon and the woodland lie,
  Terrible, radiant with mystery, superb and subdued,
Triumphant in silence; and hardly the sacred sky
  Seems free from the tyrannous weight of the dumb fierce mood
  Which rules as with fire and invasion of beams that brood
The breathless rapture of earth till its hour pass by
  And leave her spirit released and her peace renewed.

I sleep not: never in sleep has a man beholden
  This. From the shadow that trembles and yearns with light
Suppressed and elate and reluctant—obscure and golden
  As water kindled with presage of dawn or night—
  A form, a face, a wonder to sense and sight,
Grows great as the moon through the month; and her eyes embolden
  Fear, till it change to desire, and desire to delight.

I sleep not: sleep would die of a dream so strange;
  A dream so sweet would die as a rainbow dies,
As a sunbow laughs and is lost on the waves that range
  And reck not of light that flickers or spray that flies.
  But the sun withdraws not, the woodland shrinks not or sighs,
No sweet thing sickens with sense or with fear of change;
  Light wounds not, darkness blinds not, my steadfast eyes.

Only the soul in my sense that receives the soul
  Whence now my spirit is kindled with breathless bliss
Knows well if the light that wounds it with love makes whole,
  If hopes that carol be louder than fears that hiss,
  If truth be spoken of flowers and of waves that kiss,
Of clouds and stars that contend for a sunbright goal.
  And yet may I dream that I dream not indeed of this?

An earth-born dreamer, constrained by the bonds of birth,
  Held fast by the flesh, compelled by his veins that beat

And kindle to rapture or wrath, to desire or to mirth,
  May hear not surely the fall of immortal feet,
  May feel not surely if heaven upon earth be sweet;
And here is my sense fulfilled of the joys of earth,
  Light, silence, bloom, shade, murmur of leaves that meet.

Bloom, fervour, and perfume of grasses and flowers aglow,
  Breathe and brighten about me: the darkness gleams,
The sweet light shivers and laughs on the slopes below,
  Made soft by leaves that lighten and change like dreams;
  The silence thrills with the whisper of secret streams
That well from the heart of the woodland: these I know:
  Earth bore them, heaven sustained them with showers and beams.

I lean my face to the heather, and drink the sun
  Whose flame-lit odour satiates the flowers: mine eyes
Close, and the goal of delight and of life is one:
  No more I crave of earth or her kindred skies.
  No more? But the joy that springs from them smiles and flies:
The sweet work wrought of them surely, the good work done,
  If the mind and the face of the season be loveless, dies.

Thee, therefore, thee would I come to, cleave to, cling,
  If haply thy heart be kind and thy gifts be good,
Unknown sweet spirit, whose vesture is soft in spring,
  In summer splendid, in autumn pale as the wood
  That shudders and wanes and shrinks as a shamed thing should,
In winter bright as the mail of a war-worn king
  Who stands where foes fled far from the face of him stood.

My spirit or thine is it, breath of thy life or of mine,
  Which fills my sense with a rapture that casts out fear?
Pan's dim frown wanes, and his wild eyes brighten as thine,
  Transformed as night or as day by the kindling year.
  Earth-born, or mine eye were withered that sees, mine ear
That hears were stricken to death by the sense divine,
  Earth-born I know thee: but heaven is about me here.

The terror that whispers in darkness and flames in light,
  The doubt that speaks in the silence of earth and sea,
The sense, more fearful at noon than in midmost night,
  Of wrath scarce hushed and of imminent ill to be,
  Where are they? Heaven is as earth, and as heaven to me
Earth: for the shadows that sundered them here take flight;
  And nought is all, as am I, but a dream of thee.

# Loch Torridon

To E.H.

The dawn of night more fair than morning rose,
Stars hurrying forth on stars, as snows on snows
Haste when the wind and winter bid them speed.
Vague miles of moorland road behind us lay
Scarce traversed ere the day
Sank, and the sun forsook us at our need,
Belated. Where we thought to have rested, rest
Was none; for soft Maree's dim quivering breast,
Bound round with gracious inland girth of green
And fearless of the wild wave-wandering West,
Shone shelterless for strangers; and unseen
The goal before us lay
Of all our blithe and strange and strenuous day.
For when the northering road faced westward—when
The dark sharp sudden gorge dropped seaward—then,
Beneath the stars, between the steeps, the track
We followed, lighted not of moon or sun,
And plunging whither none
Might guess, while heaven and earth were hoar and black,
Seemed even the dim still pass whence none turns back:
And through the twilight leftward of the way,
And down the dark, with many a laugh and leap,
The light blithe hill-streams shone from scaur to steep
In glittering pride of play;
And ever while the night grew great and deep
We felt but saw not what the hills would keep
Sacred awhile from sense of moon or star;
And full and far
Beneath us, sweet and strange as heaven may be,
The sea.

The very sea: no mountain-moulded lake
Whose fluctuant shapeliness is fain to take
  Shape from the steadfast shore that rules it round,
  And only from the storms a casual sound:
  The sea, that harbours in her heart sublime
  The supreme heart of music deep as time,
  And in her spirit strong
  The spirit of all imaginable song.

Not a whisper or lisp from the waters: the skies were not
silenter. Peace
Was between them; a passionless rapture of respite as soft as release.
Not a sound, but a sense that possessed and pervaded with
patient delight
The soul and the body, clothed round with the comfort of
limitless night.
Night infinite, living, adorable, loved of the land and the sea:
Night, mother of mercies, who saith to the spirits in prison,
Be free.
And softer than dewfall, and kindlier than starlight, and keener
than wine,
Came round us the fragrance of waters, the life of the breath
of the brine.
We saw not, we heard not, the face or the voice of the waters:
we knew
By the darkling delight of the wind as the sense of the sea in
it grew,
By the pulse of the darkness about us enkindled and quickened,
that here,
Unseen and unheard of us, surely the goal we had faith in
was near.
A silence diviner than music, a darkness diviner than light,
Fulfilled as from heaven with a measureless comfort the
measure of night.

But never a roof for shelter
And never a sign for guide
Rose doubtful or visible: only
And hardly and gladly we heard
The soft waves whisper and welter,
Subdued, and allured to subside,
By the mild night's magic: the lonely
Sweet silence was soothed, not stirred,
By the noiseless noise of the gleaming
Glad ripples, that played and sighed,
Kissed, laughed, recoiled, and relented,
Whispered, flickered, and fled.
No season was this for dreaming
How oft, with a stormier tide,
Had the wrath of the winds been vented
On sons of the tribes long dead:
The tribes whom time, and the changes
Of things, and the stress of doom,

Have erased and effaced; forgotten
As wrecks or weeds of the shore
In sight of the stern hill-ranges
That hardly may change their gloom
When the fruits of the years wax rotten
And the seed of them springs no more.
For the dim strait footway dividing
The waters that breathed below
Led safe to the kindliest of shelters
That ever awoke into light:
And still in remembrance abiding
Broods over the stars that glow
And the water that eddies and welters
The passionate peace of the night.

All night long, in the world of sleep,
Skies and waters were soft and deep:
Shadow clothed them, and silence made
Soundless music of dream and shade:
All above us, the livelong night,
Shadow, kindled with sense of light;
All around us, the brief night long,
Silence, laden with sense of song.
Stars and mountains without, we knew,
Watched and waited, the soft night through:
All unseen, but divined and dear,
Thrilled the touch of the sea's breath near:
All unheard, but alive like sound,
Throbbed the sense of the sea's life round:
Round us, near us, in depth and height,
Soft as darkness and keen as light.

And the dawn leapt in at my casement: and there, as I rose, at my feet
No waves of the landlocked waters, no lake submissive and sweet,
Soft slave of the lordly seasons, whose breath may loose it or freeze;
But to left and to right and ahead was the ripple whose pulse is the sea's.
From the gorge we had travelled by starlight the sunrise, winged and aflame,
Shone large on the live wide wavelets that shuddered with joy as it came;

As it came and caressed and possessed them, till panting and
laughing with light
From mountain to mountain the water was kindled and stung
to delight.
And the grey gaunt heights that embraced and constrained
and compelled it were glad,
And the rampart of rock, stark naked, that thwarted and
barred it, was clad
With a stern grey splendour of sunrise: and scarce had
I sprung to the sea
When the dawn and the water were wedded, the hills and
the sky set free.
The chain of the night was broken: the waves that embraced
me and smiled
And flickered and fawned in the sunlight, alive, unafraid,
undefiled,
Were sweeter to swim in than air, though fulfilled with the
mounting morn,
Could be for the birds whose triumph rejoiced that a day
was born.
And a day was arisen indeed[o] for us. Years and the
changes of years
Clothed round with their joys and their sorrows, and dead as
their hopes and their fears,
Lie noteless and nameless, unlit by remembrance or record
of days
Worth wonder or memory, or cursing or blessing, or passion
or praise,
Between us who live and forget not, but yearn with delight in
it yet,
And the day we forget not, and never may live and may think
to forget.
And the years that were kindlier and fairer, and kindled with
pleasures as keen,
Have eclipsed not with lights or with shadows the light on
the face of it seen.
For softly and surely, as nearer the boat that we gazed
from drew,
The face of the precipice opened and bade us as birds
pass through,
And the bark shot sheer to the sea through the strait of the
sharp steep cleft,
The portal that opens with imminent rampires[o] to right and
to left,

Sublime as the sky they darken and strange as a spell-struck dream,
On the world unconfined of the mountains, the reign of the sea supreme,
The kingdom of westward waters, wherein when we swam we knew
The waves that we clove were boundless, the wind on our brows that blew
Had swept no land and no lake, and had warred not on tower or on tree,
But came on us hard out of heaven, and alive with the soul of the sea.

# Elegy

## 1869–1891

Auvergne, Auvergne, O wild and woful land,
  O glorious land and gracious, white as gleam
The stairs of heaven, black as a nameless brand,
  Strange even as life, and stranger than a dream,

Could earth remember man, whose eyes made bright
  The splendour of her beauty, lit by day
Or soothed and softened and redeemed by night,
  Wouldst thou not know what light has passed away?

Wouldst thou not know whom England, whom the world,
  Mourns? For the world whose wildest ways he trod,
And smiled their dangers down that coiled and curled
  Against him, knows him now less man than god.

Our demigod of daring, keenest-eyed
  To read and deepest read in earth's dim things,
A spirit now whose body of death has died
  And left it mightier yet in eyes and wings,

The sovereign seeker of the world, who now
  Hath sought what world the light of death may show,
Hailed once with me the crowns that load thy brow,
  Crags dark as midnight, columns bright as snow.

Thy steep small Siena, splendid and content
  As shines the mightier city's Tuscan pride°
Which here its face reflects in radiance, pent
  By narrower bounds from towering side to side,

Set fast between the ridged and foamless waves
  Of earth more fierce and fluctuant than the sea,
The fearless town of towers that hails and braves
  The heights that gird, the sun that brands Le Puy;

The huddled churches clinging on the cliffs
  As birds alighting might for storm's sake cling,
Moored to the rocks as tempest-harried skiffs
  To perilous refuge from the loud wind's wing;

The stairs on stairs that wind and change and climb
  Even up to the utmost crag's edge curved and curled,

More bright than vision, more than faith sublime,
Strange as the light and darkness of the world;

Strange as are night and morning, stars and sun,
And washed from west and east by day's deep tide,
Shine yet less fair, when all their heights are won,
Than sundawn shows thy pillared mountain-side.

Even so the dawn of death, whose light makes dim
The starry fires that life sees rise and set,
Shows higher than here he shone before us him
Whom faith forgets not, nor shall fame forget.

Even so those else unfooted heights we clomb
Through scudding mist and eddying whirls of cloud,
Blind as a pilot beaten blind with foam,
And shrouded as a corpse with storm's grey shroud,

Foot following foot along the sheer straight ledge
Where space was none to bear the wild goat's feet
Till blind we sat on the outer footless edge
Where darkling death seemed fain to share the seat,

The abyss before us, viewless even as time's,
The abyss to left of us, the abyss to right,
Bid thought now dream how high the freed soul climbs
That death sets free from change of day and night.

The might of raging mist and wind whose wrath
Shut from our eyes the narrowing rock we trod,
The wondrous world it darkened, made our path
Like theirs who take the shadow of death for God.

Yet eastward, veiled in vapour white as snow,
The grim black herbless heights that scorn the sun
And mock the face of morning rose to show
The work of earth-born fire and earthquake done.

And half the world was haggard night, wherein
We strove our blind way through: but far above
Was light that watched the wild mists whirl and spin,
And far beneath a land worth light and love.

Deep down the Valley of the Curse, undaunted
By shadow and whisper of winds with sins for wings
And ghosts of crime wherethrough the heights live haunted
By present sense of past and monstrous things,

The glimmering water holds its gracious way
Full forth, and keeps one happier hand's-breadth green
Of all that storm-scathed world whereon the sway
Sits dark as death of deadlier things unseen.

But on the soundless and the viewless river
That bears through night perchance again to day
The dead whom death and twin-born fame deliver
From life that dies, and time's inveterate sway,

No shadow save of falsehood and of fear
That brands the future with the past, and bids
The spirit wither and the soul grow sere,
Hovers or hangs to cloud life's opening lids,

If life have eyes to lift again and see,
Beyond the bounds of sensual sight or breath,
What life incognisable of ours may be
That turns our light to darkness deep as death.

Priests and the soulless serfs of priests may swarm
With vulturous acclamation, loud in lies,
About his dust while yet his dust is warm
Who mocked as sunlight mocks their base blind eyes,

Their godless ghost of godhead, false and foul
As fear his dam or hell his throne: but we,
Scarce hearing, heed no carrion church-wolf's howl:
The corpse be theirs to mock; the soul is free.

Free as ere yet its earthly day was done
It lived above the coil about us curled:
A soul whose eyes were keener than the sun,
A soul whose wings were wider than the world.

We, sons of east and west, ringed round with dreams,
Bound fast with visions, girt about with fears,
Live, trust, and think by chance, while shadow seems
Light, and the wind that wrecks a hand that steers.

He, whose full soul held east and west in poise,°
Weighed man with man, and creed of man's with creed,
And age with age, their triumphs and their toys,
And found what faith may read not and may read.

Scorn deep and strong as death and life, that lit
With fire the smile at lies and dreams outworn

Wherewith he smote them, showed sublime in it
  The splendour and the steadfastness of scorn.

What loftier heaven, what lordlier air, what space
  Illimitable, insuperable, infinite,
Now to that strong-winged soul yields ampler place
  Than passing darkness yields to passing light,

No dream, no faith can tell us: hope and fear,
  Whose tongues were loud of old as children's, now
From babbling fall to silence: change is here,
  And death; dark furrows drawn by time's dark plough.

Still sunward here on earth its flight was bent,
  Even since the man within the child began
To yearn and kindle with superb intent
  And trust in time to magnify the man.

Still toward the old garden of the Sun, whose fruit
  The honey-heavy lips of Sophocles
Desired and sang,° wherein the unwithering root
  Sprang of all growths that thought brings forth and sees

Incarnate, bright with bloom or dense with leaf
  Far-shadowing, deep as depth of dawn or night:
And all were parcel of the garnered sheaf
  His strenuous spirit bound and stored aright.

And eastward now, and ever toward the dawn,
  If death's deep veil by life's bright hand be rent,
We see, as through the shadow of death withdrawn,
  The imperious soul's indomitable ascent.

But not the soul whose labour knew not end—
  But not the swordsman's hand, the crested head—
The royal heart we mourn, the faultless friend,
  Burton—a name that lives till fame be dead.

# Threnody

## October 6, 1892

### I

Life, sublime and serene when time had power upon it and ruled its breath,
Changed it, bade it be glad or sad, and hear what change in the world's ear saith,
Shines more fair in the starrier air whose glory lightens the dusk of death.

Suns that sink on the wan sea's brink, and moons that kindle and flame and fade,
Leave more clear for the darkness here the stars that set not and see not shade
Rise and rise on the lowlier skies by rule of sunlight and moonlight swayed.

So, when night for his eyes grew bright, his proud head pillowed on Shakespeare's breast,°
Hand in hand with him, soon to stand where shine the glories that death loves best,
Passed the light of his face from sight, and sank sublimely to radiant rest.

### II

Far above us and all our love, beyond all reach of its voiceless praise,
Shines for ever the name that never shall feel the shade of the changeful days
Fall and chill the delight that still sees winter's light on it shine like May's.

Strong as death° is the dark day's breath whose blast has withered the life we see
Here where light is the child of night, and less than visions or dreams are we:
Strong as death; but a word, a breath, a dream is stronger than death can be.

Strong as truth and superb in youth eternal, fair as the sundawn's flame

Seen when May on her first-born day bids earth exult
  in her radiant name,
Lives, clothed round with its praise and crowned with love
  that dies not, his love-lit fame.

## III

Fairer far than the morning star, and sweet for us as the
  songs that rang
Loud through heaven from the choral Seven° when all
  the stars of the morning sang,
Shines the song that we loved so long—since first such
  love in us flamed and sprang.

England glows as a sunlit rose from mead to mountain,
  from sea to sea,
Bright with love and with pride above all taint of sorrow
  that needs must be,
Needs must live for an hour, and give its rainbow's glory
  to lawn and lea.

Not through tears shall the new-born years behold him,
  crowned with applause of men,
Pass at last from a lustrous past to life that lightens
  beyond their ken,
Glad and dead, and from earthward led to sunward,
  guided of Imogen.°

## A Reminiscence

The rose to the wind has yielded: all its leaves
  Lie strewn on the graveyard grass, and all their light
  And colour and fragrance leave our sense and sight
Bereft as a man whom bitter time bereaves
Of blossom at once and hope of garnered sheaves,
  Of April at once and August. Day to night
  Calls wailing, and life to death, and depth to height,
And soul upon soul of man that hears and grieves.

Who knows, though he see the snow-cold blossom shed,
  If haply the heart that burned within the rose,
The spirit in sense, the life of life be dead?
  If haply the wind that slays with storming snows
Be one with the wind that quickens? Bow thine head,
  O Sorrow, and commune with thine heart: who knows?

## Hawthorn Dyke

All the golden air is full of balm and bloom
   Where the hawthorns line the shelving dyke with flowers.
   Joyous children born of April's happiest hours,
High and low they laugh and lighten, knowing their doom
Bright as brief—to bless and cheer they know not whom,
   Heed not how, but washed and warmed with suns and showers
   Smile, and bid the sweet soft gradual banks and bowers
Thrill with love of sunlit fire or starry gloom.

All our moors and lawns all round rejoice: but here
All the rapturous resurrection of the year
   Finds the radiant utterance perfect, sees the word
Spoken, hears the light that speaks it. Far and near,
   All the world is heaven: and man and flower and bird
   Here are one at heart with all things seen and heard.

# 'THE BALLADS OF THE ENGLISH BORDER'

The most famous Scotchman of the last generation was fond of quoting his master's inimitable and unanswerable query—'Can you teach me how to jump off my shadow?'° The most illustrious Scotchman of all time° bore evidence that he at all events could not perform that feat, when he gave to one of the most valuable books in our language the misleading & indeed mendacious title—'Minstrelsy of the Scottish Border'. Even Sir Walter Scott—a name not less beloved of Englishmen than of Scotchmen, & only less cherished than the name of Shakespeare—could not jump off the shadow of his birth; could not, however, unconscious & unsuspicious of any lurking touch in himself, his own noble nature of provincial vanity & insincerity, be fair & honest, according to the limited lights of English loyalty & veracity, when dealing with an apparently debatable question between Scotland & England. It needs no more acquaintance with the Borderland than may be gathered from print by an English Cockney or a Scotch Highlander, to verify the palpable & indisputable fact that, even if England can claim no greater share than Scotland in the glorious & incomparable ballad literature which is one of the crowning glories, historic or poetic, of either kingdom, Scotland assuredly can claim no greater share in it than England: & that the blatant Caledonian boobies whose ignorance is impudent enough to question the claims of the English ballad—nay, even to deny its existence, & consequently the existence of any ballads dealing with any such unheard of heroes as Robin Hood, Guy of Gisborne, Adam Bell, Clym o' the Cluigh, & William of Cloudesley°—maybe confuted & put to shame, if shame be possible for such thick-skinned audacity to feel or understand, by the veriest smatterer who has an honest & intelligent eye in his impartial head.

Quite as reasonably & quite as truthfully might Englishmen deny the existence of Scottish songs or Ballads, & claim for their own country the parentage of all that glorious & spontaneous poetry which is or should be at this time of day the common pride & delight of us all: but Englishmen do nothing of the kind, & never did, & never will.

No man, I hope & believe, would have regarded any false & mean & malignant assumptions or impertinences, which the baser sort among his scribbling countrymen might have been guilty, with more indignant & contemptuous disgust than Sir Walter Scott. But if—as seems only too certain—he did really cherish the envious provincial superstition that the Tweed rather than the

Tyne or the Jed divided the native land of ballads from the land in which they are not indigenous, the retribution which befell his vain conceit was as perfect as Northumbrian devotion could have desired or Northern briar humour could have devised. Surtees,° not Scott, is the name of the one modern poet who has written ballads fit to be named & able to hold their own with all but the best of our ballads: no Scotchman—Scott of 'Glenfinlas' or Leyden of 'The Mermaid', or Hogg or Jamieson or Motherwell° himself—has ever done that. And all the world knows how precious & unquestionable for antiquity were the ballads of Surtees in the eyes of Scott.

But this is of course a secondary though of course a significant Matter. What is not to be borne, & has been borne too long, is that English poems of immortal & incomparable beauty should be flaunted before the faces of Englishmen as evidence of the fact that England is incapable & Scotland is capable of producing such work by spontaneous inspiration of impulse. It is impossible to distinguish by difference of dialect—transcribed or transcriptible—a poem born a little to the north, or a little to the south of the Border. But if the evidence of locality is not to be accepted as sufficient, England might claim from Scotland that loveliest of all her numberless lovely songs, in which Arthur's Seat & St Suton's Well are glorified beyond the glory of Helicon & Ida.° It would be quite as fair & quite as reasonable to assume that this crowning flower of Scottish poetry belongs to England as to maintain that the finest of all ballads dealing with fairyland does not. At its opening, all maidens are forbidden, & for very sufficient reasons, 'to come or gang by Carterhaugh'.° Now, if Carterhaugh is in Scotland, I am a Scotchman: &, as Mr Peggotty expresses it, 'I can't say no fairer than that.'° *The Young Tamlane*,° then, is as certainly & evidently an English ballad as *Waly Waly*° is a Scottish song.

# FROM *A CHANNEL PASSAGE AND OTHER POEMS* (1904)

# The Lake of Gaube

The sun is lord and god,° sublime, serene,
   And sovereign on the mountains: earth and air
Lie prone in passion, blind with bliss unseen
   By force of sight and might of rapture, fair
   As dreams that die and know not what they were.
The lawns, the gorges, and the peaks, are one
Glad glory, thrilled with sense of unison
In strong compulsive silence of the sun.

Flowers dense and keen as midnight stars aflame
   And living things of light like flames in flower
That glance and flash as though no hand might tame
   Lightnings whose life outshone their stormlit hour
   And played and laughed on earth, with all their power
Gone, and with all their joy of life made long
And harmless as the lightning life of song,
Shine sweet like stars when darkness feels them strong.

The deep mild purple flaked with moonbright gold
   That makes the scales seem flowers of hardened light,
The flamelike tongue, the feet that noon leaves cold,
   The kindly trust in man, when once the sight
   Grew less than strange, and faith bade fear take flight,
Outlive the little harmless life that shone
And gladdened eyes that loved it, and was gone
Ere love might fear that fear had looked thereon.

Fear held the bright thing hateful, even as fear,
   Whose name is one with hate and horror, saith
That heaven, the dark deep heaven of water near,
   Is deadly deep as hell and dark as death.
   The rapturous plunge that quickens blood and breath
With pause more sweet than passion, ere they strive
To raise again the limbs that yet would dive
Deeper, should there have slain the soul alive.

As the bright salamander in fire of the noonshine exults and
         is glad of his day,
The spirit that quickens my body rejoices to pass from
         the sunlight away,
To pass from the glow of the mountainous flowerage, the
         high multitudinous bloom,

Far down through the fathomless night of the water,
the gladness of silence and gloom.
Death-dark and delicious as death in the dream of a lover
and dreamer may be,
It clasps and encompasses body and soul with delight to
be living and free:
Free utterly now, though the freedom endure but the space
of a perilous breath,
And living, though girdled about with the darkness and
coldness and strangeness of death:
Each limb and each pulse of the body rejoicing, each nerve
of the spirit at rest,
All sense of the soul's life rapture, a passionate peace in its
blindness blest,
So plunges the downward swimmer, embraced of the water
unfathomed of man,
The darkness unplummeted, icier than seas in midwinter,
for blessing or ban;
And swiftly and sweetly, when strength and breath fall short,
and the dive is done,
Shoots up as a shaft from the dark depth shot, sped straight
into sight of the sun;
And sheer through the snow-soft water, more dark than the
roof of the pines above,
Strikes forth, and is glad as a bird whose flight is impelled
and sustained of love,
As a sea-mew's love of the sea-wind breasted and ridden for
rapture's sake
Is the love of his body and soul for the darkling delight of
the soundless lake:
As the silent speed of a dream too living to live for a
thought's space more
Is the flight of his limbs through the still strong chill of
the darkness from shore to shore.
Might life be as this is and death be as life that casts off
time as a robe,
The likeness of infinite heaven were a symbol revealed of
the lake of Gaube.

Whose thought has fathomed and measured
The darkness of life and of death,
The secret within them treasured,
The spirit that is not breath?

Whose vision has yet beholden
  The splendour of death and of life?
Though sunset as dawn be golden,
  Is the word of them peace, not strife?
Deep silence answers: the glory
  We dream of may be but a dream,
And the sun of the soul wax hoary
  As ashes that show not a gleam.
But well shall it be with us ever
  Who drive through the darkness here
If the soul that we live by never,
  For aught that a lie saith, fear.

## In a Rosary

Through the low grey archway children's feet that pass
Quicken, glad to find the sweetest haunt of all.
Brightest wildflowers gleaming deep in lustiest grass,
Glorious weeds that glisten through the green sea's glass,
Match not now this marvel, born to fade and fall.

Roses like a rainbow wrought of roses rise
Right and left and forward, shining toward the sun.
Nay, the rainbow lit of sunshine droops and dies
Ere we dream it hallows earth and seas and skies;
Ere delight may dream it lives, its life is done.

Round the border hemmed with high deep hedges round
Go the children, peering over or between
Where the dense bright oval wall of box inwound,
Reared about the roses fast within it bound,
Gives them grace to glance at glories else unseen.

Flower outlightening flower and tree outflowering tree
Feed and fill the sense and spirit full with joy.
Nought awhile they know of outer earth and sea:
Here enough of joy it is to breathe and be:
Here the sense of life is one for girl and boy.

Heaven above them, bright as children's eyes or dreams,
Earth about them, sweet as glad soft sleep can show
Earth and sky and sea, a world that scarcely seems
Even in children's eyes less fair than life that gleams
Through the sleep that none but sinless eyes may know.

Near beneath, and near above, the terraced ways
Wind or stretch and bask or blink against the sun.
Hidden here from sight on soft or stormy days
Lies and laughs with love toward heaven, at silent gaze,
All the radiant rosary—all its flowers made one.

All the multitude of roses towering round
Dawn and noon and night behold as one full flower,
Fain of heaven and loved of heaven, curbed and crowned,
Raised and reared to make this plot of earthly ground
Heavenly, could but heaven endure on earth an hour.

Swept away, made nothing now for ever, dead,
Still the rosary lives and shines on memory, free
Now from fear of death or change as childhood, fled
Years on years before its last live leaves were shed:
None may mar it now, as none may stain the sea.

# Trafalgar Day

Sea, that art ours as we are thine, whose name
Is one with England's even as light with flame,
Dost thou as we, thy chosen of all men, know
This day of days when death gave life to fame?

Dost thou not kindle above and thrill below
With rapturous record, with memorial glow,
Remembering this thy festal day of fight,
And all the joy it gave, and all the woe?

Never since day broke flowerlike forth of night
Broke such a dawn of battle. Death in sight
Made of the man whose life was like the sun
A man more godlike than the lord of light.°

There is none like him, and there shall be none.
When England bears again as great a son,
He can but follow fame where Nelson led.
There is not and there cannot be but one.

As earth has but one England, crown and head
Of all her glories till the sun be dead,
Supreme in peace and war, supreme in song,
Supreme in freedom, since her rede° was read,

Since first the soul that gave her speech grew strong
To help the right and heal the wild world's wrong,
So she hath but one royal Nelson, born
To reign on time above the years that throng.

The music of his name puts fear to scorn,
And thrills our twilight through with sense of morn:
As England was, how should not England be?
No tempest yet has left her banner torn.

No year has yet put out the day when he
Who lived and died to keep our kingship free
Wherever seas by warring winds are worn
Died, and was one with England and the sea.

*October 21, 1895.*

## Cromwell's Statue[1]

What needs our Cromwell stone or bronze to say
His was the light that lit on England's way
  The sundawn of her time-compelling power,
The noontide of her most imperial day?

His hand won back the sea for England's dower;
His footfall bade the Moor change heart and cower;
  His word on Milton's tongue spake law to France
When Piedmont felt the she-wolf Rome devour.°

From Cromwell's eyes the light of England's glance
Flashed, and bowed down the kings by grace of chance,
  The priest-anointed princes; one alone
By grace of England held their hosts in trance.

The enthroned Republic from her kinglier throne
Spake, and her speech was Cromwell's. Earth has known
  No lordlier presence. How should Cromwell stand
With kinglets and with queenlings hewn in stone?

Incarnate England in his warrior hand
Smote, and as fire devours the blackening brand
  Made ashes of their strengths who wrought her wrong,
And turned the strongholds of her foes to sand.

His praise is in the sea's and Milton's song;
What praise could reach him from the weakling throng
  That rules by leave of tongues whose praise is shame—
Him, who made England out of weakness strong?

There needs no clarion's blast of broad-blown fame
To bid the world bear witness whence he came
  Who bade fierce Europe fawn at England's heel
And purged the plague of lineal rule with flame.

There needs no witness graven on stone or steel
For one whose work bids fame bow down and kneel;
  Our man of men, whose time-commanding name
Speaks England, and proclaims her Commonweal.

*June 20, 1895.*

[1] Refused by the party of reaction and disunion in the House of Commons on the 17th of June, 1895.

# Russia: An Ode

## 1890

### I

Out of hell a word comes hissing, dark as doom,
Fierce as fire, and foul as plague-polluted gloom;
Out of hell wherein the sinless damned endure
More than ever sin conceived of pains impure;
More than ever ground men's living souls to dust;
Worse than madness ever dreamed of murderous lust.
Since the world's wail first went up from lands and seas
Ears have heard not, tongues have told not things like these.°
Dante, led by love's and hate's accordant spell
Down the deepest and the loathliest ways of hell,
Where beyond the brook of blood the rain was fire,
Where the scalps were masked with dung more deep than mire,°
Saw not, where the filth was foulest, and the night
Darkest, depths whose fiends could match the Muscovite.
Set beside this truth, his deadliest vision seems
Pale and pure and painless as a virgin's dreams.
Maidens dead beneath the clasping lash, and wives
Rent with deadlier pangs than death—for shame survives,
Naked, mad, starved, scourged, spurned, frozen, fallen, deflowered,
Souls and bodies as by fangs of beasts devoured,
Sounds that hell would hear not, sights no thought could shape,
Limbs that feel as flame the ravenous grasp of rape,
Filth of raging crime and shame that crime enjoys,
Age made one with youth in torture, girls with boys,
These, and worse if aught be worse than these things are,
Prove thee regent, Russia—praise thy mercy, Czar.

### II

Sons of man, men born of women, may we dare
Say they sin who dare be slain and dare not spare?
They who take their lives in hand and smile on death,
Holding life as less than sleep's most fitful breath,
So their life perchance or death may serve and speed
Faith and hope, that die if dream become not deed?
Nought is death and nought is life and nought is fate

Save for souls that love has clothed with fire of hate.
These behold them, weigh them, prove them, find them nought,
Save by light of hope and fire of burning thought.
What though sun be less than storm where these aspire,
Dawn than lightning, song than thunder, light than fire?
Help is none in heaven: hope sees no gentler star:
Earth is hell, and hell bows down before the Czar.
All its monstrous, murderous, lecherous births acclaim
Him whose empire lives to match its fiery fame.
Nay, perchance at sight or sense of deeds here done,
Here where men may lift up eyes to greet the sun,
Hell recoils heart-stricken: horror worse than hell
Darkens earth and sickens heaven; life knows the spell,
Shudders, quails, and sinks—or, filled with fierier breath,
Rises red in arms devised of darkling death.
Pity mad with passion, anguish mad with shame,
Call aloud on justice by her darker name;
Love grows hate for love's sake; life takes death for guide.
Night hath none but one red star—Tyrannicide.°

## III

'God or man, be swift; hope sickens with delay:
Smite, and send him howling down his father's way!
Fall, O fire of heaven, and smite as fire from hell
Halls wherein men's torturers, crowned and cowering, dwell!
These that crouch and shrink and shudder, girt with power—
These that reign, and dare not trust one trembling hour—
These omnipotent, whom terror curbs and drives—
These whose life reflects in fear their victims' lives—
These whose breath sheds poison worse than plague's
thick breath—
These whose reign is ruin, these whose word is death,
These whose will turns heaven to hell, and day to night,
These, if God's hand smite not, how shall man's not smite?'
So from hearts by horror withered as by fire
Surge the strains of unappeasable desire;
Sounds that bid the darkness lighten, lit for death;
Bid the lips whose breath was doom yield up their breath;
Down the way of Czars, awhile in vain deferred,
Bid the Second Alexander light the Third.
How for shame shall men rebuke them? how may we

Blame, whose fathers died, and slew, to leave us free?
We, though all the world cry out upon them, know,
Were our strife as theirs, we could not strike but so;
Could not cower, and could not kiss the hands that smite;
Could not meet them armed in sunlit battle's light.
Dark as fear and red as hate though morning rise,
Life it is that conquers; death it is that dies.

# On the Death of Mrs Lynn Linton

Kind, wise, and true as truth's own heart,
  A soul that here
Chose and held fast the better part
  And cast out fear,

Has left us ere we dreamed of death
  For life so strong,
Clear as the sundawn's light and breath,
  And sweet as song.

We see no more what here awhile
  Shed light on men:
Has Landor seen that brave bright smile
  Alive again?

If death and life and love be one
  And hope no lie
And night no stronger than the sun,
  These cannot die.

The father-spirit whence her soul
  Took strength, and gave
Back love, is perfect yet and whole,
  As hope might crave.

His word is living light and fire:
  And hers shall live
By grace of all good gifts the sire
  Gave power to give.

The sire and daughter, twain and one
  In quest and goal,
Stand face to face beyond the sun,
  And soul to soul.

Not we, who loved them well, may dream
  What joy sublime
Is theirs, if dawn through darkness gleam,
  And life through time.

Time seems but here the mask of death,
  That falls and shows
A void where hope may draw not breath:
  Night only knows.

Love knows not: all that love may keep
  Glad memory gives:
The spirit of the days that sleep
  Still wakes and lives.

But not the spirit's self, though song
  Would lend it speech,
May touch the goal that hope might long
  In vain to reach.

How dear that high true heart, how sweet
  Those keen kind eyes,
Love knows, who knows how fiery fleet
  Is life that flies.

If life there be that flies not, fair
  The life must be
That thrills her sovereign spirit there
  And sets it free.

## Carnot

Death, winged with fire of hate from deathless hell
  Wherein the souls of anarchs hiss and die,
  With stroke as dire has cloven a heart as high
As twice beyond the wide sea's westward swell
The living lust of death had power to quell
  Through ministry of murderous hands whereby
  Dark fate bade Lincoln's head and Garfield's lie
Low even as his who bids his France farewell.

France, now no heart that would not weep with thee
  Loved ever faith or freedom. From thy hand
  The staff of state is broken: hope, unmanned
With anguish, doubts if freedom's self be free.
  The snake-souled anarch's fang strikes all the land
Cold, and all hearts unsundered by the sea.

*June 25, 1894.*

# The Transvaal

Patience, long sick to death, is dead. Too long
  Have sloth and doubt and treason bidden us be
  What Cromwell's England was not, when the sea
To him bore witness given of Blake how strong
She stood,° a commonweal that brooked no wrong
  From foes less vile than men like wolves set free
  Whose war is waged where none may fight or flee—
With women and with weanlings. Speech and song
Lack utterance now for loathing. Scarce we hear
  Foul tongues that blacken God's dishonoured name
  With prayers turned curses and with praise found shame
Defy the truth whose witness now draws near
  To scourge these dogs, agape with jaws afoam,
  Down out of life. Strike, England, and strike home.°

*October 9, 1899.*

# DEDICATION OF SWINBURNE'S *POEMS* (1904)

To Theodore Watts-Dunton

To my best and dearest friend I dedicate the first collected edition of my poems, and to him I address what I have to say on the occasion.°

You will agree with me that it is impossible for any man to undertake the task of commentary, however brief and succinct, on anything he has done or tried to do, without incurring the charge of egoism. But there are two kinds of egoism, the furtive and the frank: and the outspoken and open-hearted candour of Milton and Wordsworth, Corneille and Hugo, is not the least or the lightest of their claims to the regard as well as the respect or the reverence of their readers. Even if I were worthy to claim kinship with the lowest or with the highest of these deathless names, I would not seek to shelter myself under the shadow of its authority. The question would still remain open on all sides. Whether it is worth while for any man to offer any remarks or for any other man to read his remarks on his own work, his own ambition, or his own attempts, he cannot of course determine. If there are great examples of abstinence from such a doubtful enterprise, there are likewise great examples to the contrary. As long as the writer can succeed in evading the kindred charges and the cognate risks of vanity and humility, there can be no reason why he should not undertake it. And when he has nothing to regret and nothing to recant, when he finds nothing that he could wish to cancel, to alter, or to unsay, in any page he has ever laid before his reader,° he need not be seriously troubled by the inevitable consciousness that the work of his early youth is not and cannot be unnaturally unlike the work of a very young man. This would be no excuse for it, if it were in any sense bad work: if it be so, no apology would avail; and I certainly have none to offer.

It is now thirty-six° years since my first volume of miscellaneous verse, lyrical and dramatic and elegiac and generally heterogeneous, had as quaint a reception and as singular a fortune as I have ever heard or read of. I do not think you will differ from my opinion that what is best in it cannot be divided from what is not so good by any other line of division than that which marks off mature from immature execution—in other words, complete from incomplete conception. For its author the most amusing and satisfying result of the clatter aroused by it was the deep diversion of collating and comparing the variously inaccurate verdicts of the scornful or mournful censors who insisted on regarding all the studies of passion or sensation attempted or achieved in it as either confessions of positive fact or excursions of absolute fancy. There are photographs from life in the book; and there are sketches from imagination. Some which keen-sighted criticism has dismissed with a smile as ideal or imaginary were as real and actual as they well could be: others which have been taken for obvious transcripts from memory were utterly fantastic or dramatic. If the two kinds cannot be distinguished, it is surely rather a credit than a discredit to an artist whose medium or material has more in common with a musician's than with a sculptor's. Friendly and kindly critics, English and foreign, have detected ignorance of the subject in poems taken straight from the life, and have protested that they could not believe me were I to swear that poems entirely or mainly fanciful were not faithful expressions or transcriptions of the writer's actual experience and personal emotion. But I need not remind you that all I have to say about this book was said once for all in the year of its publication:° I have nothing to add to my notes then taken, and I have nothing to retract from them. To parade or to disclaim experience of passion or of sorrow, of pleasure or of pain, is the habit and the sign of a school which has never found a disciple among the better sort of English poets, and which I know to be no less pitifully contemptible in your opinion than in mine.

In my next work it should be superfluous to say that there is no touch of dramatic impersonation or imaginary emotion. The writer of 'Songs before Sunrise,' from the first line to the last, wrote simply in submissive obedience to Sir Philip Sidney's precept—'Look in thine heart, and write.'° The dedication of these poems,° and the fact that the dedication was accepted, must be sufficient evidence of this. They do not pretend and they were never intended to be merely the metrical echoes, or translations into lyric verse, of another man's doctrine. Mazzini was no more a Pope or a Dictator than I was a parasite or a papist. Dictation and inspiration are rather different things. These poems, and others which followed or preceded them in print, were inspired by such faith as is born of devotion and reverence: not by such faith, if faith it may be called, as is synonymous with servility or compatible with prostration of an abject or wavering spirit and a submissive or dethroned intelligence. You know that I never pretended to see eye to eye with my illustrious friends and masters, Victor Hugo and Giuseppe Mazzini, in regard to the positive and passionate confidence of their sublime and purified theology. Our betters ought to know better than we: they would be the last to wish that we should pretend to their knowledge, or assume a certitude which is theirs and is not ours. But on one point we surely cannot but be at one with them: that the spirit and the letter of all other than savage and barbarous religions are irreconcilably at variance, and that prayer or homage addressed to an image of our own or of other men's making, be that image avowedly material or conventionally spiritual, is the affirmation of idolatry with all its attendant atrocities, and the negation of all belief, all reverence, and all love, due to the noblest object of human worship that humanity can realise or conceive. Thus much the exercise of our common reason might naturally suffice to show us: but when its evidence is confirmed and fortified by the irrefragable and invariable evidence of history, there is no room for further dispute or fuller argument on a subject now visibly beyond reach and eternally beyond need of debate or demonstration. I know not whether it may or may not be worth while to add that every passing word I have since thought fit to utter on any national or political question has been as wholly consistent with the principles which I then did my best to proclaim and defend as any apostasy from the faith of all republicans in the fundamental and final principle of union, voluntary if possible and compulsory if not, would have been ludicrous in the impudence of its inconsistency with those simple and irreversible principles.° Monarchists and anarchists may be advocates of national dissolution and reactionary division: republicans cannot be. The first and last article of their creed is unity: the most grinding and crushing tyranny of a convention, a directory, or a despot, is less incompatible with republican faith than the fissiparous democracy of disunionists or communalists.°

If the fortunes of my lyrical work were amusingly eccentric and accidental, the varieties of opinion which have saluted the appearance of my plays have been, or have seemed to my humility, even more diverting and curious. I have been told by reviewers of note and position that a single one of them is worth all my lyric and otherwise undramatic achievements or attempts: and I have been told on equal or similar authority that, whatever I may be in any other field, as a dramatist I am demonstrably nothing. My first if not my strongest ambition was to do something worth doing, and not utterly unworthy of a young countryman of Marlowe the teacher and Webster the pupil of Shakespeare, in the line of work which those three poets had left as a possibly unattainable example for ambitious Englishmen. And my first book,° written while yet under academic or tutorial authority, bore evidence of that ambition in every line. I should be the last to deny that it also bore evidence of the fact that its writer had no more notion of dramatic or theatrical construction than the authors of 'Tamburlaine the Great,' 'King Henry VI.,' and 'Sir Thomas Wyatt.'° Not much more, you may possibly say, was discernible in 'Chastelard': a play also conceived and partly written by a youngster not yet emancipated from servitude to college rule. I fear that in the former volume there had been little if any promise of power to grapple with the realities and subtleties of character and of motive: that whatever may be in it of promise or of merit must be sought in the language and the style of such better passages as may perhaps be found in single and separable speeches of Catherine and of Rosamond.° But in 'Chastelard' there are two figures and a sketch in which I certainly seem to see something of real and evident life. The sketch of Darnley was afterwards filled out and finished in the subsequent tragedy of 'Bothwell.'

That ambitious, conscientious, and comprehensive piece of work is of course less properly definable as a tragedy than by the old Shakespearean term of a chronicle history. The radical difference between tragic history and tragedy of either the classic or the romantic order, and consequently between the laws which govern the one and the principles which guide the other, you have yourself made clear and familiar to all capable students.° This play of mine was not, I think, inaccurately defined as an epic drama in the French verses of dedication° which were acknowledged by the greatest of all French poets in a letter from which I dare only quote one line of Olympian judgment and god-like generosity. 'Occuper ces deux cimes, cela n'est donné qu'à vous.'° Nor will I refrain from the confession that I cannot think it an epic or a play in which any one part is sacrificed to any other, any subordinate figure mishandled or neglected or distorted or effaced for the sake of the predominant and central person. And, though this has nothing or less than nothing to do with any question of poetic merit or demerit, of dramatic success or unsuccess, I will add that I took as much care and pains as though I had been writing or compiling a history of the period to do loyal justice to all the historic figures which came within the scope of my dramatic or poetic design. There is not one which I have designedly altered or intentionally modified: it is of course for others to decide whether there is one which is not the living likeness of an actual or imaginable man.

The third part of this trilogy, as far as I know or remember, found favour only with the only man in England who could speak on the subject of historic drama with the authority of an expert and a master. The generally ungracious reception of 'Mary Stuart' gave me neither surprise nor disappointment: the cordial approbation or rather the generous applause of Sir Henry Taylor° gave me all and more than all the satisfaction I could ever have looked for in recompense of as much painstaking and conscientious though interesting and enjoyable work as can ever, I should imagine, have been devoted to the completion of any comparable design. Private and personal appreciation I have always thought and often found more valuable and delightful than all possible or imaginable clamour of public praise. This preference will perhaps be supposed to influence my opinion if I avow that I think I have never written anything worthier of such reward than the closing tragedy which may or may not have deserved but which certainly received it.

My first attempt to do something original in English which might in some degree reproduce for English readers the likeness of a Greek tragedy, with possibly something more of its true poetic life and charm than could have been expected from the authors of 'Caractacus' and 'Merope,'° was perhaps too exuberant and effusive in its dialogue, as it certainly was too irregular in the occasional license of its choral verse, to accomplish the design or achieve the success which its author should have aimed at. It may or may not be too long as a poem: it is, I fear, too long for a poem of the kind to which it belongs or aims at belonging. Poetical and mathematical truth are so different that I doubt, however unwilling I may naturally be to doubt, whether it can truthfully be said of 'Atalanta in Calydon' that the whole is greater than any part of it. I hope it may be, and I can honestly say no more. Of 'Erechtheus' I venture to believe with somewhat more confidence that it can. Either poem, by the natural necessity of its kind and structure, has its crowning passage or passages which cannot, however much they may lose by detachment from their context, lose as much as the crowning scene or scenes of an English or Shakespearean play, as opposed to an Æschylean or Sophoclean tragedy, must lose and ought to lose by a similar separation. The two best things in these two Greek plays, the antiphonal lamentation for the dying Meleager and the choral presentation of stormy battle between the forces of land and sea, lose less by such division from the main body of the poem than would those scenes in 'Bothwell' which deal with the turning-point in the life of Mary Stuart on the central and conclusive day of Carberry Hill.°

It might be thought pedantic or pretentious in a modern poet to divide his poems after the old Roman fashion into sections and classes; I must confess that I should like to see this method applied, were it but by way of experiment in a single edition, to the work of the leading poets of our own country and century: to see, for instance, their lyrical and elegiac works ranged and registered apart, each kind in a class of its own, such as is usually reserved, I know not why, for sonnets only. The apparent formality of such an arrangement as would give us, for instance, the odes of Coleridge and Shelley collected into a distinct reservation or division might possibly be more than compensated to the more capable among students by the gain in ethical or spiritual symmetry and æsthetic or intellectual harmony. The ode or hymn—I need remind no probable reader that the terms are synonymous in the speech of Pindar—asserts its primacy or pre-eminence over other forms of poetry in the very name which defines or proclaims it as essentially the song; as something above all less pure and absolute kinds of song by the very nature and law of its being. The Greek form, with its regular arrangement of turn, return, and aftersong, is not to be imitated because it is Greek, but to be adopted because it is best: the very best, as a rule, that could be imagined for lyrical expression of the thing conceived or lyrical aspiration towards the aim imagined. The rhythmic reason of its rigid but not arbitrary law lies simply and solely in the charm of its regular variations. This can be given in English as clearly and fully, if not so sweetly and subtly, as in Greek; and should, therefore, be expected and required in an English poem of the same nature and proportion. The Sapphic or Alcaic ode, a simple sequence of identical stanzas, could be imitated or revived in Latin by translators or disciples: the scheme of it is exquisitely adequate and sufficient for comparatively short flights of passion or emotion, ardent or contemplative and personal or patriotic; but what can be done in English could not be attempted in Latin. It seems strange to me, our language being what it is, that our literature should be no richer than it is in examples of the higher or at least the more capacious and ambitious kind of ode. Not that the full Pindaric form of threefold or triune structure need be or should be always adopted: but without an accurately corresponsive or antiphonal scheme of music even the master of masters, who is Coleridge, could not produce, even through the superb and enchanting melodies of such a poem as his 'Dejection,' a fit and complete companion, a full and perfect rival, to such a poem as his ode on France.°

The title of ode may more properly and fairly be so extended as to cover all lyrical poems in stanzas or couplets than so strained as to include a lawless lyric of such irregular and uneven build as Coleridge only and hardly could make acceptable or admissible among more natural and lawful forms of poetry. Law, not lawlessness, is the natural condition of poetic life; but the law must itself be poetic and not pedantic, natural and not conventional. It would be a trivial precision or restriction which would refuse the title of ode to the stanzas of Milton or the heptameters of Aristophanes; that glorious form of lyric verse which a critic of our own day, as you may not impossibly remember, has likened with such magnificent felicity of comparison to the gallop of the horses of the sun.° Nor, I presume, should this title be denied to a poem written in the more modest metre—more modest as being shorter by a foot—which was chosen for those twin poems of antiphonal correspondence in subject and in sound, the 'Hymn to Proserpine' and the 'Hymn of Man':° the deathsong of spiritual decadence and the birthsong of spiritual renascence. Perhaps, too, my first stanzas addressed to Victor Hugo may be ranked as no less of an ode than that on the insurrection in Candia:° a poem which attracted, whether or not it may have deserved, the notice and commendation of Mazzini: from whom I received, on the occasion of its appearance, a letter which was the beginning of my personal intercourse with the man whom I had always revered above all other men on earth. But for this happy accident I might not feel disposed to set much store by my first attempt at a regular ode of orthodox or legitimate construction; I doubt whether it quite succeeded in evading the criminal risk and the capital offence of formality; at least until the change of note in the closing epode gave fuller scope and freer play of wing to the musical expression. But in my later ode on Athens,° absolutely faithful as it is in form to the strictest type and the most stringent law of Pindaric hymnology, I venture to believe that there is no more sign of this infirmity than in the less classically regulated poem on the Armada;° which, though built on a new scheme, is nevertheless in its way, I think, a legitimate ode, by right of its regularity in general arrangement of corresponsive divisions. By the test of these two poems I am content that my claims should be decided and my station determined as a lyric poet in the higher sense of the term; a craftsman in the most ambitious line of his art that ever aroused or ever can arouse the emulous aspiration of his kind.

Even had I ever felt the same impulse to attempt and the same ambition to achieve the enterprise of epic or narrative that I had always felt with regard to lyric or dramatic work, I could never have proposed to myself the lowly and unambitious aim of competition with the work of so notable a contemporary workman in the humbler branch of that line as William Morris.° No conception could have been further from my mind when I undertook to rehandle the deathless legend of Tristram than that of so modest and preposterous a trial of rivalry. My aim was simply to present that story, not diluted and debased as it had been in our own time by other hands,° but undefaced by improvement and undeformed by transformation, as it was known to the age of Dante wherever the chronicles of romance found hearing, from Ercildoune° to Florence: and not in the epic or romantic form of sustained or continuous narrative, but mainly through a succession of dramatic scenes or pictures with descriptive settings or backgrounds: the scenes being of the simplest construction, duologue or monologue, without so much as the classically permissible intervention of a third or fourth person. It is only in our native northern form of narrative poetry, on the old and unrivalled model of the English ballad, that I can claim to have done any work of the kind worth reference: unless the story of Balen° should be considered as something other than a series or sequence of ballads. A more plausible objection was brought to bear against 'Tristram of Lyonesse' than that of failure in an enterprise which I never thought of undertaking: the objection of an irreconcilable incongruity between the incidents of the old legend and the meditations on man and nature, life and death, chance and destiny, assigned to a typical hero of chivalrous romance. And this objection might be unanswerable if the slightest attempt had been made to treat the legend as in any possible sense historical or capable of either rational or ideal association with history, such as would assimilate the name and fame of Arthur to the name and fame of any actual and indisputable Alfred or Albert of the future.° But the age when these romances actually lived and flourished side by side with the reviving legends of Thebes and Troy, not in the crude and bloodless forms of Celtic and archaic fancy but in the ampler and manlier developments of Teutonic and mediæval imagination, was the age of Dante and of Chaucer: an age in which men were only too prone to waste their time on the twin sciences of astrology and theology, to expend their energies in the jungle of pseudosophy or the morass of metaphysics. There is surely nothing more incongruous or anachronic in the soliloquy of Tristram after his separation from Iseult than in the lecture of Theseus after the obsequies of Arcite.° Both heroes belong to the same impossible age of an imaginary world: and each has an equal right, should it so please his chronicler, to reason in the pauses of action and philosophise in the intervals of adventure. After all, the active men of the actual age of chivalry were not all of them mere muscular machines for martial or pacific exercise of their physical functions or abilities.

You would agree, if the point were worth discussion, that it might savour somewhat of pretention, if not of affectation, to be over particular in arrangement of poems according to subject rather than form, spirit rather than method, or motive rather than execution: and yet there might be some excuse for the fancy or the pedantry of such a classification as should set apart, for example, poems inspired by the influence of places, whether seen but once or familiar for years or associated with the earliest memories within cognisance or record of the mind, and poems inspired by the emotions of regard or regret for the living or the dead; above all, by the rare and profound passion of reverence and love and faith which labours and rejoices to find utterance in some tributary sacrifice of song. Mere descriptive poetry of the prepense and formal kind is exceptionally if not proverbially liable to incur and to deserve the charge of dullness: it is unnecessary to emphasise or obtrude the personal note, the presence or the emotion of a spectator, but it is necessary to make it felt and keep it perceptible if the poem is to have life in it or even a right to live: felt as in Wordsworth's work it is always, perceptible as it is always in Shelley's. This note is more plain and positive than usual in the poem which attempts—at once a simple and an ambitious attempt—to render the contrast and the concord of night and day on Loch Torridon:° it is, I think, duly sensible though implicitly subdued in four poems of the West Undercliff,° born or begotten of sunset in the bay and moonlight on the cliffs, noon or morning in a living and shining garden, afternoon or twilight on one left flowerless and forsaken. Not to you or any other poet, nor indeed to the very humblest and simplest lover of poetry, will it seem incongruous or strange, suggestive of imperfect sympathy with life or deficient inspiration from nature, that the very words of Sappho should be heard and recognised in the notes of the nightingales, the glory of the presence of dead poets imagined in the presence of the glory of the sky, the lustre of their advent and their passage felt visible as in vision on the live and limpid floorwork of the cloudless and sunset-coloured sea. The half-brained creature to whom books are other than living things may see with the eyes of a bat and draw with the fingers of a mole his dullard's distinction between books and life: those who live the fuller life of a higher animal than he know that books are to poets as much part of that life as pictures are to painters or as music is to musicians, dead matter though they may be to the spiritually still-born children of dirt and dullness who find it possible and natural to live while dead in heart and brain. Marlowe and Shakespeare, Æschylus and Sappho, do not for us live only on the dusty shelves of libraries.

It is hardly probable that especial and familiar love of places should give any special value to verses written under the influence of their charm: no intimacy of years and no association with the past gave any colour of emotion to many other studies of English land and sea which certainly are no less faithful and possibly have no less spiritual or poetic life in them than the four to which I have just referred, whose localities lie all within the boundary of a mile or so. No contrast could be stronger than that between the majestic and exquisite glory of cliff and crag, lawn and woodland, garden and lea, to which I have done homage though assuredly I have not done justice in these four poems—'In the Bay,' 'On the Cliffs,' 'A Forsaken Garden,' the dedication of 'The Sisters'—and the dreary beauty, inhuman if not unearthly in its desolation, of the innumerable creeks and inlets, lined and paven with sea-flowers, which make of the salt marshes a fit and funereal setting, a fatal and appropriate foreground, for the supreme desolation of the relics of Dunwich;[o] the beautiful and awful solitude of a wilderness on which the sea has forbidden man to build or live, overtopped and bounded by the tragic and ghastly solitude of a headland on which the sea has forbidden the works of human charity and piety to survive: between the dense and sand-encumbered tides which are eating the desecrated wreck and ruin of them all away, and the matchless magic, the ineffable fascination of the sea whose beauties and delights, whose translucent depths of water and divers-coloured banks of submarine foliage and flowerage, but faintly reflected in the stanzas of the little ode 'Off Shore,'[o] complete the charm of the scenes as faintly sketched or shadowed forth in the poems just named, or the sterner and stranger magic of the seaboard to which tribute was paid in 'An Autumn Vision,' 'A Swimmer's Dream,' 'On the South Coast,' 'Neap-tide':[o] or, again, between the sterile stretches and sad limitless outlook of the shore which faces a hitherto undetermined and interminable sea, and the joyful and fateful beauty of the seas off Bamborough and the seas about Sark and Guernsey.[o] But if there is enough of the human or personal note to bring into touch the various poems which deal with these various impressions, there may perhaps be no less of it discernible in such as try to render the effect of inland or woodland solitude—the splendid oppression of nature at noon which found utterance of old in words of such singular and everlasting significance as panic and nympholepsy.

The retrospect across many years over the many eulogistic and elegiac poems which I have inscribed or devoted to the commemoration or the panegyric of the living or the dead has this in it of pride and pleasure, that I find little to recant and nothing to repent on reconsideration of them all. If ever a word of tributary thanksgiving for the delight and the benefit of loyal admiration evoked in the spirit of a boy or aroused in the intelligence of a man may seem to exceed the limit of demonstrable accuracy, I have no apology to offer for any such aberration from the safe path of tepid praise or conventional applause. I can truly say with Shelley that I have been fortunate in friendships:[o] I might add if I cared, as he if he had cared might have added, that I have been no less fortunate in my enemies than in my friends; and this, though by comparison a matter of ineffable insignificance, can hardly be to any rational and right-minded man a matter of positive indifference. Rather should it be always a subject for thankfulness and self-congratulation if a man can honestly and reasonably feel assured that his friends and foes alike have been always and at almost all points the very men he would have chosen, had choice and foresight been allowed him, at the very outset of his career in life. I should never, when a boy, have dared to dream that as a man I might possibly be admitted to the personal acquaintance of the three living gods, I do not say of my idolatry, for idolatry is a term inapplicable where the gods are real and true, but of my whole-souled and single-hearted worship: and yet, when writing of Landor, of Mazzini, and of Hugo, I write of men who have honoured me with the assurance and the evidence of their cordial and affectionate regard. However inadequate and unworthy may be my tribute to their glory when living and their memory when dead, it is that of one whose gratitude and devotion found unforgettable favour in their sight. And I must be allowed to add that the redeeming quality of entire and absolute sincerity may be claimed on behalf of every line I have written in honour of friends, acquaintances, or strangers. My tribute to Richard Burton° was not more genuine in its expression than my tribute to Christina Rossetti.° Two noble human creatures more utterly unlike each other it would be unspeakably impossible to conceive; but it was as simply natural for one who honoured them both to do honest homage, before and after they had left us, to the saintly and secluded poetess as to the adventurous and unsaintly hero. Wherever anything is worthy of honour and thanksgiving it is or it always should be as natural if not as delightful to give thanks and do honour to a stranger as to a friend, to a benefactor long since dead as to a benefactor still alive. To the kindred spirits of Philip Sidney and Aurelio Saffi° it was almost as equal a pleasure to offer what tribute I could bring as if Sidney also could have honoured me with his personal friendship. To Tennyson and Browning it was no less fit that I should give honour than that I should do homage to the memory of Bruno, the martyred friend of Sidney.° And I can hardly remember any task that I ever took more delight in discharging than I felt in the inadequate and partial payment of a lifelong debt to the marvellous and matchless succession of poets who made the glory of our country incomparable for ever by the work they did between the joyful date of the rout of the Armada and the woful date of the outbreak of civil war.

Charles Lamb, as I need not remind you, wrote for antiquity: nor need you be assured that when I write plays it is with a view to their being acted at the Globe, the Red Bull, or the Black Friars. And whatever may be the dramatic or other defects of 'Marino Faliero' or 'Locrine,' they do certainly bear the same relation to previous plays or attempts at plays on the same subjects as 'King Henry V.' to 'The Famous Victories'°—if not as 'King Lear,' a poem beyond comparison with all other works of man except possibly 'Prometheus' and 'Othello,'° to the primitive and infantile scrawl or drivel of 'King Leir and his three daughters.' The fifth act of 'Marino Faliero,' hopelessly impossible as it is from the point of view of modern stagecraft, could hardly have been found too untheatrical, too utterly given over to talk without action, by the audiences which endured and applauded the magnificent monotony of Chapman's eloquence—the fervent and inexhaustible declamation which was offered and accepted as a substitute for study of character and interest of action when his two finest plays, if plays they can be called, found favour with an incredibly intelligent and an inconceivably tolerant audience. The metrical or executive experiment attempted and carried through in 'Locrine'° would have been improper to any but a purely and wholly romantic play or poem: I do not think that the life of human character or the lifelikeness of dramatic dialogue has suffered from the bondage of rhyme or has been sacrificed to the exigence of metre. The tragedy of 'The Sisters,' however defective it may be in theatrical interest or progressive action, is the only modern English play I know in which realism in the reproduction of natural dialogue and accuracy in the representation of natural intercourse between men and women of gentle birth and breeding have been found or made compatible with expression in genuine if simple blank verse. It is not for me to decide whether anything in the figures which play their parts on my imaginary though realistic stage may be worthy of sympathy, attention, or interest: but I think they talk and act as they would have done in life without ever lapsing into platitude or breaking out of nature.

In 'Rosamund, Queen of the Lombards,'° I took up a subject long since mishandled by an English dramatist of all but the highest rank, and one which in later days Alfieri° had commemorated in a magnificent passage of a wholly unhistoric and somewhat unsatisfactory play. The comparatively slight deviation from historic records in the final catastrophe or consummation of mine is not, I think, to say the least, injurious to the tragic effect or the moral interest of the story.

A writer conscious of any natural command over the musical resources of his language can hardly fail to take such pleasure in the enjoyment of this gift or instinct as the greatest writer and the greatest versifier of our age must have felt at its highest possible degree when composing a musical exercise of such incomparable scope and fullness as 'Les Djinns.'° But if he be a poet after the order of Hugo or Coleridge or Shelley, the result will be something very much more than a musical exercise; though indeed, except to such ears as should always be kept closed against poetry, there is no music in verse which has not in it sufficient fullness and ripeness of meaning, sufficient adequacy of emotion or of thought, to abide the analysis of any other than the purblind scrutiny of prepossession or the squint-eyed inspection of malignity. There may perhaps be somewhat more depth and variety of feeling or reflection condensed into the narrow frame of the poems which compose 'A Century of Roundels' than would be needed to fulfil the epic vacuity of a Chœrilus or a Coluthus.° And the form chosen for my only narrative poem° was chosen as a test of the truth of my conviction that such work could be done better on the straitest and the strictest principles of verse than on the looser and more slippery lines of mediæval or modern improvisation. The impulsive and irregular verse which had been held sufficient for the stanza selected or accepted by Thornton and by Tennyson seemed capable of improvement and invigoration as a vehicle or a medium for poetic narrative. And I think it has not been found unfit to give something of dignity as well as facility to a narrative which recasts in modern English verse one of the noblest and loveliest old English legends. There is no episode in the cycle of Arthurian romance more genuinely Homeric in its sublime simplicity and its pathetic sublimity of submission to the masterdom of fate than that which I have rather reproduced than recast in 'The Tale of Balen': and impossible as it is to render the text or express the spirit of the *Iliad* in English prose or rhyme—above all, in English blank verse—it is possible, in such a metre as was chosen and refashioned for this poem, to give some sense of the rage and rapture of battle for which Homer himself could only find fit and full expression by similitudes drawn like mine from the revels and the terrors and the glories of the sea.

It is nothing to me that what I write should find immediate or general acceptance: it is much to know that on the whole it has won for me the right to address this dedication and inscribe this edition to you.

# FROM *THE AGE OF SHAKESPEARE* (1908)

# Christopher Marlowe

## (1883/1908)

The first great English poet was the father of English tragedy and the creator of English blank verse. Chaucer and Spenser were great writers and great men: they shared between them every gift which goes to the making of a poet except the one which alone can make a poet, in the proper sense of the word, great. Neither pathos nor humour nor fancy nor invention will suffice for that: no poet is great as a poet whom no one could ever pretend to recognize as sublime. Sublimity is the test of imagination as distinguished from invention or from fancy: and the first English poet whose powers can be called sublime was Christopher Marlowe.

The majestic and exquisite excellence of various lines and passages in Marlowe's first play must be admitted to relieve, if it cannot be allowed to redeem, the stormy monotony of Titanic truculence which blusters like a simoom through the noisy course of its ten fierce acts. With many and heavy faults, there is something of genuine greatness in 'Tamburlaine the Great'; and for two grave reasons it must always be remembered with distinction and mentioned with honour. It is the first poem ever written in English blank verse,° as distinguished from mere rhymeless decasyllabics; and it contains one of the noblest passages,° perhaps indeed the noblest in the literature of the world, ever written by one of the greatest masters of poetry in loving praise of the glorious delights and sublime submission to the everlasting limits of his art. In its highest and most distinctive qualities, in unfaltering and infallible command of the right note of music and the proper tone of colour for the finest touches of poetic execution, no poet of the most elaborate modern school, working at ease upon every consummate resource of luxurious learning and leisurely refinement, has ever excelled the best and most representative work of a man who had literally no models before him, and probably or evidently was often, if not always, compelled to write against time for his living.

The just and generous judgment passed by Goethe on the 'Faustus' of his English predecessor in tragic treatment of the same subject is somewhat more than sufficient to counterbalance the slighting or the sneering references to that magnificent poem which might have been expected from the ignorance of Byron or the incompetence of Hallam.° And the particular note of merit observed, the special point of the praise conferred, by the great German poet should be no less sufficient to dispose of the vulgar misconception yet lingering among sciolists and pretenders to criticism, which regards a writer than whom no man was ever born with a finer or a stronger instinct for perfection of excellence in execution as a mere noble savage of letters, a rough self-taught sketcher or scribbler of crude and rude genius, whose unhewn blocks of verse had in them some veins of rare enough metal to be quarried and polished by Shakespeare. What most impressed the author of 'Faust' in the work of Marlowe was a quality the want of which in the author of 'Manfred' is proof enough to consign his best work to the second or third class at most. 'How greatly it is all planned!' the first requisite of all great work, and one of which the highest genius possible to a greatly gifted barbarian could by no possibility understand the nature or conceive the existence. That Goethe 'had thought of translating it' is perhaps hardly less precious a tribute to its greatness than the fact that it has been actually and admirably translated by the matchless translator of Shakespeare—the son of Victor Hugo,° whose labour of love may thus be said to have made another point in common, and forged as it were another link of union, between Shakespeare and the young master of Shakespeare's youth. Of all great poems in dramatic form it is perhaps the most remarkable for absolute singleness of aim and simplicity of construction; yet is it wholly free from all possible imputation of monotony or aridity. 'Tamburlaine' is monotonous in the general roll and flow of its stately and sonorous verse through a noisy wilderness of perpetual bluster and slaughter; but the unity of tone and purpose in 'Doctor Faustus' is not unrelieved by change of manner and variety of incident. The comic scenes, written evidently with as little of labour as of relish, are for the most part scarcely more than transcripts, thrown into the form of dialogue, from a popular prose 'History of Doctor Faustus';° and therefore should be set down as little to the discredit as to the credit of the poet. Few masterpieces of any age in any language can stand beside this tragic poem—it has hardly the structure of a play—for the qualities of terror and splendour, for intensity of purpose and sublimity of note. In the vision of Helen,° for example, the intense perception of loveliness gives actual sublimity to the sweetness and radiance of mere beauty in the passionate and spontaneous selection of words the most choice and perfect; and in like manner the sublimity of simplicity in Marlowe's conception and expression of the agonies endured by Faustus under the immediate imminence of his doom° gives the highest note of beauty, the quality of absolute fitness and propriety, to the sheer straightforwardness of speech in which his agonizing horror finds vent ever more and more terrible from the first to the last equally beautiful and fearful verse of that tremendous monologue which has no parallel in all the range of tragedy.

It is now a commonplace of criticism to observe and regret the decline of power and interest after the opening acts of 'The Jew of Malta.' This decline is undeniable, though even the latter part of the play is not wanting in rough energy and a coarse kind of interest; but the first two acts would be sufficient foundation for the durable fame of a dramatic poet. In the blank verse of Milton alone, who perhaps was hardly less indebted than Shakespeare was before him to Marlowe as the first English master of word-music in its grander forms, has the glory or the melody of passages in the opening soliloquy of Barabas° been possibly surpassed. The figure of the hero before it degenerates into caricature is as finely touched as the poetic execution is excellent; and the rude and rapid sketches of the minor characters show at least some vigour and vivacity of touch.

In 'Edward the Second' the interest rises and the execution improves as visibly and as greatly with the course of the advancing story as they decline in 'The Jew of Malta.' The scene of the king's deposition at Kenilworth is almost as much finer in tragic effect and poetic quality as it is shorter and less elaborate than the corresponding scene in Shakespeare's 'King Richard II'.° The terror of the death-scene undoubtedly rises into horror; but this horror is with skilful simplicity of treatment preserved from passing into disgust. In pure poetry, in sublime and splendid imagination, this tragedy is excelled by 'Doctor Faustus'; in dramatic power and positive impression of natural effect it is as certainly the masterpiece of Marlowe. It was almost inevitable, in the hands of any poet but Shakespeare, that none of the characters represented should be capable of securing or even exciting any finer sympathy or more serious interest than attends on the mere evolution of successive events or the mere display of emotions (except always in the great scene of the deposition) rather animal than spiritual in their expression of rage or tenderness or suffering. The exact balance of mutual effect, the final note of scenic harmony between ideal conception and realistic execution, is not yet struck with perfect accuracy of touch and security of hand; but on this point also Marlowe has here come nearer by many degrees to Shakespeare than any of his other predecessors have ever come near to Marlowe.

Of 'The Massacre at Paris' it is impossible to judge fairly from the garbled fragment of its genuine text, which is all that has come down to us. To Mr Collier,° among numberless other obligations, we owe the discovery of a striking passage excised in the piratical edition which gives us the only version extant of this unlucky play; and which, it must be allowed, contains nothing of quite equal value. This is obviously an occasional and polemical work, and being as it is overcharged with the anti-Catholic passion of the time, has a typical quality which gives it some empirical significance and interest. That anti-papal ardour is indeed the only note of unity in a rough and ragged chronicle which shambles and stumbles onward from the death of Queen Jeanne of Navarre to the murder of the last Valois. It is possible to conjecture what it would be fruitless to affirm, that it gave a hint in the next century to Nathaniel Lee for his far superior and really admirable tragedy on the same subject, issued ninety-seven years after the death of Marlowe.°

The tragedy of 'Dido, Queen of Carthage,' was probably completed for the stage after that irreparable and incalculable loss to English letters by Thomas Nash,° the worthiest English precursor of Swift in vivid, pure, and passionate prose, embodying the most terrible and splendid qualities of a personal and social satirist; a man gifted also with some fair faculty of elegiac and even lyric verse, but in nowise qualified to put on the buskin left behind him by the 'famous gracer of tragedians,'° as Marlowe had already been designated by their common friend Greene from among the worthiest of his fellows. In this somewhat thin-spun and evidently hasty play a servile fidelity to the text of Virgil's narrative° has naturally resulted in the failure which might have been expected from an attempt at once to transcribe what is essentially inimitable and to reproduce it under the hopelessly alien conditions of dramatic adaptation. The one really noble passage in a generally feeble and incomposite piece of work is, however, uninspired by the unattainable model to which the dramatists have been only too obsequious in their subservience.

It is as nearly certain as anything can be which depends chiefly upon cumulative and collateral evidence that the better part of what is best in the serious scenes of 'King Henry VI' is mainly the work of Marlowe. That he is, at any rate, the principal author of the second and third plays passing under that name among the works of Shakespeare, but first and imperfectly printed as 'The Contention between the two Famous Houses of York and Lancaster,' can hardly be now a matter of debate among competent judges.° The crucial difficulty of criticism in this matter is to determine, if indeed we should not rather say to conjecture, the authorship of the humorous scenes in prose, showing as they generally do a power of comparatively high and pure comic realism to which nothing in the acknowledged works of any pre-Shakespearean dramatist is even remotely comparable. Yet, especially in the original text of these scenes as they stand unpurified by the ultimate revision of Shakespeare, there are tones and touches which recall rather the clownish horseplay and homely ribaldry of his predecessors than anything in the lighter interludes of his very earliest plays. We find the same sort of thing which we find in their writings, only better done than they usually do it, rather than such work as Shakespeare's a little worse done than usual. And even in the final text of the tragic or metrical scenes the highest note struck is always, with one magnificent and unquestionable exception, rather in the key of Marlowe at his best than of Shakespeare while yet in great measure his disciple.

It is another commonplace of criticism to affirm that Marlowe had not a touch of comic genius, not a gleam of wit in him or a twinkle of humour: but it is an indisputable fact that he had. In 'The Massacre at Paris,' the soliloquy of the soldier lying in wait for the minion of Henri III° has the same very rough but very real humour as a passage in the 'Contention' which was cancelled by the reviser. The same hand is unmistakable in both these broad and boyish outbreaks of unseemly but undeniable fun: and if we might wish it rather less indecorous, we must admit that the tradition which denies all sense of humour and all instinct of wit to the first great poet of England is no less unworthy of serious notice or elaborate refutation than the charges and calumnies of an informer who was duly hanged the year after Marlowe's death. For if the same note of humour is struck in an undoubted play of Marlowe's and in a play of disputed authorship, it is evident that the rest of the scene in the latter play must also be Marlowe's. And in that unquestionable case the superb and savage humour of the terribly comic scenes which represent with such rough magnificence of realism the riot of Jack Cade° and his ruffians through the ravaged streets of London must be recognizable as no other man's than his. It is a pity we have not before us for comparison the comic scenes or burlesque interludes of 'Tamburlaine' which the printer or publisher, as he had the impudence to avow in his prefatory note, purposely omitted and left out.°

The author of 'A Study of Shakespeare' was therefore wrong, and utterly wrong, when in a book issued some quarter of a century ago he followed the lead of Mr Dyce° in assuming that because the author of 'Doctor Faustus' and 'The Jew of Malta' 'was as certainly'—and certainly it is difficult to deny that whether as a mere transcriber or as an original dealer in pleasantry he sometimes was—'one of the least and worst among jesters as he was one of the best and greatest among poets,' he could not have had a hand in the admirable comic scenes of 'The Taming of the Shrew.'° For it is now, I should hope, unnecessary to insist that the able and conscientious editor to whom his fame and his readers owe so great a debt was over-hasty in assuming and asserting that he was a poet 'to whom, we have reason to believe, nature had denied even a moderate talent for the humorous.'° The serious or would-be poetical scenes of the play are as unmistakably the work of an imitator as are most of the better passages in 'Titus Andronicus' and 'King Edward III'.° Greene or Peele° may be responsible for the bad poetry, but there is no reason to suppose that the great poet whose mannerisms he imitated with so stupid a servility was incapable of the good fun.

Had every copy of Marlowe's boyish version or perversion of Ovid's 'Elegies' deservedly perished in the flames to which it was judicially condemned by the sentence of a brace of prelates,° it is possible that an occasional bookworm, it is certain that no poetical student, would have deplored its destruction, if its demerits—hardly relieved, as his first competent editor has happily remarked, by the occasional incidence of a fine and felicitous couplet°—could in that case have been imagined. His translation of the first book of Lucan alternately rises above the original and falls short of it; often inferior to the Latin in point and weight of expressive rhetoric, now and then brightened by a clearer note of poetry and lifted into a higher mood of verse. Its terseness, vigour, and purity of style would in any case have been praiseworthy, but are nothing less than admirable, if not wonderful, when we consider how close the translator has on the whole (in spite of occasional slips into inaccuracy) kept himself to the most rigid limit of literal representation, phrase by phrase and often line by line. The really startling force and felicity of occasional verses are worthier of remark than the inevitable stiffness and heaviness of others, when the technical difficulty of such a task is duly taken into account.

One of the most faultless lyrics and one of the loveliest fragments in the whole range of descriptive and fanciful poetry would have secured a place for Marlowe among the memorable men of his epoch, even if his plays had perished with himself. His 'Passionate Shepherd' remains ever since unrivalled in its way—a way of pure fancy and radiant melody without break or lapse. The untitled fragment,° on the other hand, has been very closely rivalled, perhaps very happily imitated, but only by the greatest lyric poet of England—by Shelley alone. Marlowe's poem of 'Hero and Leander,' closing with the sunrise which closes the night of the lovers' union, stands alone in its age, and far ahead of the work of any possible competitor between the death of Spenser and the dawn of Milton. In clear mastery of narrative and presentation, in melodious ease and simplicity of strength, it is not less pre-eminent than in the adorable beauty and impeccable perfection of separate lines or passages.

The place and the value of Christopher Marlowe as a leader among English poets it would be almost impossible for historical criticism to overestimate. To none of them all, perhaps, have so many of the greatest among them been so deeply and so directly indebted. Nor was ever any great writer's influence upon his fellows more utterly and unmixedly an influence for good. He first, and he alone, guided Shakespeare into the right way of work; his music, in which there is no echo of any man's before him, found its own echo in the more prolonged but hardly more exalted harmony of Milton's. He is the greatest discoverer, the most daring and inspired pioneer, in all our poetic literature. Before him there was neither genuine blank verse nor genuine tragedy in our language. After his arrival the way was prepared, the paths were made straight,° for Shakespeare.

# NOTES

## ODE TO MAZZINI

Not published in ACS's lifetime. The MS, with revisions, is now in the BL, Ashley MS 4424. A version of the 'Ode' was included in *Ode to Mazzini; The Saviour of Society; Liberty and Loyalty: Unpublished MSS Discovered Among the Author's Effects after his Death* (Boston: Bibliophile Society, 1913), in *PP*, 167–83, and Bonchurch, i.115–27. Initially part of strophe 4 and all of 5 were missing/omitted. The present text is directly from the MS, reproduced with the kind permission of the British Library. It is uncertain why ACS did not publish this poem. The argument that changing events rendered the poem quickly out-of-date does not fit with ACS's habit of printing or re-printing political poems after their immediate occasion had passed. Perhaps the theology of the poem ('We keep our faith—God liveth and is love', l.234) was, on second thoughts, unsupportable.

ACS matriculated at Balliol College Oxford on 24 January 1856 where he joined the 'Old Mortality' Society, formed in November 1856 as a liberal debating and essay club. At Balliol and in the Society he met John Nichol (1833–94), later Regius Professor of English Literature, Glasgow University. Nichol had first encountered Giuseppe Mazzini (1805–72) in London in 1850 and saw him again in 1858. Nichol's support for Mazzini as he 'struck at a monstrous evil—the Austrian rule' was shared by ACS: see W.A. Knight, *Memoir of John Nichol* (Glasgow: MacLehose, 1896), 97. Cf. Terry L. Meyers, 'On Drink and Faith: Swinburne and John Nichol at Oxford', *RES*, 55 (2004), 392–424.

Carlo Poerio (1803–67), a Risorgimento lawyer who had been incarcerated by Ferdinand II, king of the Two Sicilies, was not released until 1858 (the 'Ode' probably dates from early spring 1857). He was mentioned as a particularly bad case in many English reflections on Ferdinand including, crucially, in W.E. Gladstone's *Two Letters to the Earl of Aberdeen on the State Prosecutions of the Neapolitan Government* (London: Murray, 1851), an important political text for ACS. Gladstone said Poerio was held in 'a dungeon without light, and 24 feet or palms (I am not sure which) below the level of the sea. He is never allowed to quit it day or night, and no one is permitted to visit him there, except his wife—once a fortnight' (14). ACS's respect for, and expectations of, Gladstone as a liberal champion of human freedom began with these letters, which ultimately lie at the source of ACS's bitterness over Gladstone's subsequent 'betrayals' in relation to Russia, General Gordon, and Home Rule, and the final collapse of ACS's faith in Gladstonian liberalism during the Second Anglo-Boer War (1899–1902). Cf. ACS's observation in 1876 that 'History will perhaps account it the purest and most memorable right of [Gladstone] to aught of high or honourable remembrance, that he was once the champion of Poerio in his years of martyr's agony, and the scourge of Ferdinand II in his devil's hour of good fortune', *NER*, 18. ACS's poem, aside from its onslaught on Hapsburg/Bourbon rule, deplores the Papal States and the intimacy of the Catholic Church with monarchy.

ACS did not meet Mazzini until the evening of 30 March 1867 (see *SL*, i.236–7). He was introduced by the exiled German revolutionary Karl Blind (1826–1907). 'To be permitted', Swinburne told Blind probably the day afterwards, 'to meet face to face the man who from my boyhood has been to me the incarnate figure of all that is great and good, is in itself a privilege beyond price or thanks' (*SL*, i.238). Cf. 'After Nine Years: To Joseph Mazzini', 400–1; 'Lines on the Monument to Giuseppe Mazzini', 442–3; 'Memorial Verses on the Death of Karl Blind' (1907), *PP*, 162–6; and W.S. Landor, 'Garibaldi and Mazzini' in *Imaginary Conversations*, fifth series. Note also ACS's discussion of the ode form on 528–9.

The MS of the poem is heavily revised (the fourth section most extensively) and there are considerable errors in every published edition, corrected here. As noted (li) some discretion has been used in rendering ACS's calibrated indentations in a way that looks sensible in print. ACS uses 'and', '&', and what almost looks like '+' indiscriminately and I have chosen to render them all as 'and'.

*eagle-wings*: an eagle (often double-headed), emblem of Austria.

*railing*: this is often printed as 'vailing' (submitting, yielding, obeisance) but looks like 'railing' to me (fol.3).

*The Bourbons' murderous dotard*: Ferdinand II (1810–59), of the House of Bourbon, king of the Two Sicilies (a life-long representative tyrant for ACS).

*Naples*: there was discussion in the early months of 1857 that Ferdinand, fearful of assassination, wanted to moderate criticism of his rule by deporting political prisoners from Naples (e.g. *The Times*, 17 February 1857, 8).

*hound*: the Austrian Chargé d'Affaires left Italy following extreme criticism of Austrian rule in March 1857 from the Turin press.

*lie*: often printed as 'be', this looks like 'lie' to me.

*Her*: the MS says 'Her' but this is often given as 'That'.

*Savonarola*: Dominican friar and executed Florentine reformer (1452–98).

*Cromwell's England*: ACS is thinking of Gladstone's 1851 letters and of *The Times*' more general disapproval of Ferdinand's rule, especially the prisons (see headnote). Mazzini had lived in exile in London since 1837.

*meets*: the rhyme words 'greets' and 'meets' are often erroneously reversed in published versions of these two lines.

*Ischia*: Italian island to the west of Naples.

*Time's*: ACS's first thought was 'Truth's'.

*A dawn o'er sunless ages*: ACS first wrote: 'When the last chain is broken'.

## OF THE BIRTH OF SIR TRISTRAM, AND HOW HE VOYAGED INTO IRELAND

### Canto I

This poem was the only canto of a work, entitled *Queen Yseult*, published in ACS's lifetime. It appeared in the first instalment of *Undergraduate Papers*, December 1857,

41–50. The present copy-text is from *Queen Yseult: A Poem in Six Cantos*, ed. T.J. Wise with an introduction by Edmund Gosse (London: p.p., 1918).

*Undergraduate Papers* (now exceptionally scarce) was associated with the 'Old Mortality' Society at Balliol (see headnote to the 'Ode to Mazzini', 545–6) from December 1857 to April 1858. Writing on 13 December 1857, ACS told Nichol that 'reperusing my cantos I think they are too imperfect, feeble and unfinished to publish for a year or two. A thorough rewriting would be good for some of them, to prevent a monotony of tone which prevails as they now stand [...] Canto I stands well enough as a separate ballad, which the others would not do. I read it one evening to [William] Morris and the others, and they seemed to agree with me' (*SL*, i.12–13).

The poem draws on medieval precedent, particularly the Middle English romance *Sir Tristrem*: see *Sir Tristrem: A Metrical Romance of the 13th Century by Thomas of Erceldoune, called the Rhymer*, edited from the Auchinleck MS by Walter Scott (Edinburgh: Constable, 1804). ACS retells the history of Morholt (Moronde), a warrior slain by Tristram, and of Lady Blanchefleur, Tristram's mother. The tale involves events before Tristram's journey to collect the Irish princess, Yseult, as the bride of King Mark, which were developed in 'The Sailing of the Swallow', 313–31, and thus this poem is the starting point of *TL*. Elements of the story bear comparison with the history of the House of Atreus and *Hamlet*.

ACS's canto is influenced by Morris whom ACS met at Oxford ('their common enthusiasm for Malory and the Arthurian legend [at this point] drew them together', J.W. Mackail, *The Life of William Morris*, 2 vols ([1899] London: Longmans, Green, 1901), i.127). Note that TWD remembered ACS's later views: 'Swinburne had the utmost contempt for the narrowness of [Morris'] outlook. It was incredible! Outside his own domain he was unintelligent in his narrowness, and frequently bored and irritated his friends', 'Introduction' to TWD, *Old Familiar Faces* (New York: Dutton, 1916), 9.

Unbeknown to ACS, Richard Wagner was writing *Tristan und Isolde* as ACS published this poem: the music drama was first performed in June 1865. Many years later, on 15 February 1883, ACS observed (after hearing of Wagner's death) that 'I read today with delight that his "Tristan & Isolde" was his favourite work; for nothing in music ever did produce upon me the effect produced by first hearing—on the piano only, in private—[...] of the overture or prelude to that opera' (*UL*, ii.326). In August 1872, ACS said he was writing a poem in French on the effect of the overture on him (*SL*, ii.183), now lost, if ever begun.

*Ermonie*: in *Sir Tristrem*, the name of Tristrem's homeland (cf. Caroline D. Eck, 'The Meaning of "Ermonie" in "Sir Tristrem"', *Studies in Philology*, 93 (1996), 21–41).

## LETTER TO THE EDITOR OF *THE SPECTATOR*, 7 JUNE 1862 (pp. 632–3)

George Meredith published *Poems* in 1851 and *Modern Love, and Poems of the English Roadside, with Poems and Ballads* in 1862. He sent ACS a presentation copy of the latter (no. 503, *Library*). ACS's *PB* 1 echoes Meredith's title, as Meredith's repeats the unauthorized title of Keats' 'Modern Love', given to the short poem 'And what is love?' when published in 1848. Meredith was already known as a novelist, including for *The Ordeal of Richard Feverel: A History of Father and Son* (1859). *The Athenæum* said: 'In "Modern Love" we have disease, and nothing else', 31 May 1862, 719. More directly, ACS is responding to a review by R.H. Hutton in *The Spectator*, 35 (24 May 1862)—reproduced in *George Meredith: The Critical Heritage*, ed. Ioan Williams (London: Routledge, 1971), 92–6—which found the volume badly done. Its defects included 'grandiloquent ornament over modest meaning' (94), 'spasmodic ostentation of fast writing', and 'wretched jocularity' (95). *Modern Love*, Hutton said, meddles causelessly, 'and somewhat pruriently, with a deep and painful subject, on which [Meredith] has no convictions to express' and sometimes 'treats serius themes with a flippant levity that is exceedingly vulgar and unpleasant' (95). Responding, ACS drew attention to the aesthetic pleasures of *Modern Love* (as did *MP*, which discussed the 'powerful production' on 20 June 1862 (6)). Hutton was part proprietor and joint editor of *The Spectator* and ACS's viewpoint was published in the periodical, of course, with Hutton's consent. ACS's term 'sonnets' is misleading: each poem is sixteen lines in length.

*slings and arrows*: *Hamlet*, 3.1.60.

*Légende . . . King*: Victor Hugo's *La Légende des siècles*, 1re Série, 'Les petites épopées' ('the little epics'), was published in 1859 and intended to be part of a large cycle of poems on the evolution of humanity. Tennyson's *Idylls of the King* had begun with 'Enid', 'Vivien', 'Elaine', and 'Guinevere' in 1859.

*'deep . . . express'*: Hutton. See headnote.

*'We saw . . . skies'*: poem XLVII.

*'And in . . . bride'*: poem XLVII.

*sonnet . . . rose*: poem XLV.

*'I am . . . Heaven'*: poem XX.

*'All other . . . warm'*: poem IV.

*Pierre-Jean de Béranger*: (1780–1857), popular French nationalist poet, briefly imprisoned for his political writing against the restored Bourbon monarchy. English-speaking readers knew him from *One Hundred Songs of Pierre-Jean de Béranger with Translations by William Young* (London: Chapman and Hall, 1847).

## 'CHARLES BAUDELAIRE: *LES FLEURS DU MAL*'

This unsigned review appeared in *The Spectator*, 1784 (6 September 1862), 998–1000. EWG thought it 'written in a Turkish bath in Paris' (*LS*, 19), though on no clear evidence. Charles Baudelaire (1821–67) published the first edition of *Les Fleurs du mal* in

1857. Its fate lingered in ACS's mind after the first publication of *PB* 1. *Les Fleurs* was first issued at a moment that the French government was clamping down on offensive images and writing: 'turning [its] attention to the sale of pictures, which certainly never to have been allowed to see the light' and to 'flagitious poetry' (*The Standard*, 24 August 1857, 4). Baudelaire was found not guilty of writing material offensive to religion. But six poems for *Les Fleurs* fell foul of the prosecutor and were banned as an offence to public morality (*pièces condamnées*): Baudelaire was fined 300 francs and his printer and publisher 100. The *pièces condamnées* were the erotic and sado-masochistic 'Les Métamorphoses du vampire', 'Le Léthé', 'À celle qui est trop gaie', and 'Les Bijoux' together with two lesbian poems, 'Lesbos' and 'Femmes damnées' (cf. complaints about ACS's 'Anactoria', 144–51). *Les Fleurs du mal* was published in a second enlarged edition in 1861, 'augmentée de trente-cinq poëmes nouveaux'. Baudelaire's translations included Edgar Allan Poe's *Histoires extraordinaires*, published in 1856 and his critical writing included *Réflexions sur quelques-uns de mes contemporains* (1861). In this was discussion of, among others, Victor Hugo, Théodore Gautier (to whom *Les Fleurs du mal* was dedicated), and the poet Théodore Faullain de Banville (1823–91), whose *Odes funambulesques* had been issued in 1857 and admired by Hugo. In 1880, ACS called Banville the 'most honey-tongued of poets': 'Victor Hugo: *Religions et religion*', *FR*, 27 (1880), 761–8 (767). Note that Hotten, ACS's publisher for *PB* 1, issued *Translations from C. Baudelaire with a Few Original poems by Richard Herne Shepherd* in 1869.

Of other relevance is Baudelaire's 'Richard Wagner et *Tannhäuser* à Paris' in *La Revue européenne*, 1861, though the copy that Baudelaire sent to ACS did not reach him in time for 'Laus Veneris' (Wagner's *Tannhäuser* was first performed in October 1845 and first given in Paris on 13 March 1861). ACS planned to speak on the 'new *mutual* influence of contemporary French and English literature—e.g. the French studies of Arnold and the English of Baudelaire' in a Royal Literary Fund dinner on 2 May 1866 (*SL*, i.162–3). See Terry L. Meyers, 'Swinburne's Speech to the Royal Literary Fund, May 2, 1866', *Modern Philology*, 86 (1988), 195–201, for an argument that the speech was burlesque.

ACS sent Baudelaire a copy of this review. There followed some confusion and misdirection of mail (cf. Baudelaire's letter to Whistler, 10 October 1863, available from <http://www.whistler.arts.gla.ac.uk>). ACS did not republish his essay and it was greeted with some bafflement by the editor of *The Spectator*, R.H. Hutton, who asked: 'what is poetry & Art? Are they all "flowers"? Are they all to be judged by smell & sight? [...] Or what is your theory? I ask not in prejudice but because I really wish to get at the theory of a man who seems to me to have some narrow theory [...] imprisoning a very subtle & keen sense of the poetical within unnatural limits' (*UL*, i.16, letter probably early September 1862). On 16 September, Hutton added: 'your horror of "goodness" in connection with Art rather amazes [...] me. It seems to go over into a positive respect for Evil as the essence of all true Art [...] Surely it is not true that mere Beauty is the object of poetry. I should rather say "essential life" of all kinds is its object,—& as good is more at the root of the universe than Evil [...] didactic morality however mistaken [...] is more poetical than didactic immorality' (*UL*, i.17–18). See Introduction, xxiv–xxv.

*contemporary... France*: e.g. *Salon de 1845* and *Salon de 1846*, gathered in volume 2 of the *Œuvres Complètes* (Paris: Michel Lévy Frères, 1868) as 'Curiosités esthétiques'.

*dangerous... scents*: cf. Baudelaire's 'Une Martyre: Dessin d'un maître inconnu'.

*here*: 'Une Charogne' ('Carrion').

*Keats... ebb*: the sonnet 'To—', dated 4 February 1818; published in September 1844.

*Source of Ingres*: Ingres' *La Source*, completed in 1856; now in the Musée d'Orsay, Paris. Cf. DGR's '"Ruggiero and Angelica" by Ingres'.

*Fandrin... here*: Jean-Hippolyte Flandrin (1809–64) and his *Jeune Homme nu assis au bord de la mer, figure d'étude* (1835–36). It was exhibited in the International Exhibition, London, 1862 (and admired by *The Examiner*, 7 June 1862, 361).

*These verses*: from 'Chanson d'Après-Midi', italic added. This is the most extreme example of ACS's filleting of Baudelaire's poems for the review.

*'Sur... renoncule'*: the first line of stanza 5 of 'Une Martyre'.

*'mass... jewels'*: ACS translates 'La tête, avec l'amas de sa crinière sombre | Et de ses bijoux précieux', from stanza 4.

*'What hand... dared?'*: from Browning's 'Last Ride Together' (1855), stanza 6.

*'Ton époux... mort'*: the last stanza of 'Une Martyre'.

*design... master*: Baudelaire's subtitle.

*three... cats*: 'Le Chat' ('Dans ma cervelle'); 'Le Chat' ('Viens, mon beau chat'); 'Les Chats'.

*'Franciscæ meæ [laudes]'*: Baudelaire's 'In Praise of my Francisca'—and perhaps a further source text for ACS's 'Laus Veneris' (see 116–28).

*A une Madone*: subtitled 'Ex-voto dans le goût Espagnol' (cf. ACS's 'Dolores', 165–76 and 'Ex-Voto', *PB* 2).

## DEAD LOVE

This necrophilic short story in the manner of a medieval chronicle was first published *Once-A-Week*, 7 (October 1862), 432–4. The periodical had been launched by Bradbury and Evans in July 1859 and hoped to compete with Dickens' *All the Year Round* (1859–95). 'Dead Love' was submitted, according to ACS, at the invitation of Meredith (*SL*, i.46). ACS also published the poem 'The Fratricide' in *Once-A-Week*, later included in *PB* 1 as 'The Bloody Son'. The pamphlet *Dead Love*, dated 1864 and apparently published by the London publisher John W. Parker, is a Wise/Forman forgery from *c.*1890.

'Dead Love' was the only story published in ACS's lifetime from the projected sequence of short fictions, *The Triameron*. The obvious model is Boccaccio's *Decameron* but see also W.S. Landor's *The Pentameron* (1837), comprising five imaginary conversations between Petrarch and Boccaccio. 'Dead Love' was the Third Story of the First Day in ACS's scheme. Stories that were completed include 'The Marriage of Monna Lisa', 'The Portrait', and 'The Chronicle of Queen Fredegond'. For ACS's fiction, see Introduction, xxxix.

'Dead Love' is set during the Armagnac and Burgundian Civil War (1407–35) and begins with the death of a follower of the Burgundian lord, John the Fearless (1371–1419). The Civil War commenced after John had Louis I, Duke of Orléans, assassinated on rue Vieille du Temple, Paris, in November 1407 (see ACS's first sentence). ACS's interest in late Medieval and Early Modern French history had already been expressed in *The Queen Mother*, ACS's play about Catherine de' Medici and the St Bartholomew's Day Massacre in August 1572, which features another significant Yolande; see also the note to 'The Leper', 574. The play may be compared to J.E. Millais' *A Huguenot, on St Bartholomew's Day, Refusing to Shield Himself from Danger by Wearing the Roman Catholic Badge* (1852, private collection). *The Queen Mother* was first published with another drama, *Rosamond*, by Pickering in 1860 and re-issued by Hotten as a second edition in 1868. In relation to the use of necrophilia in 'Dead Love', cf. 'The Leper', 158–62; and 'Pope Celestin and Giordano', *PP*, 120–6.

'*Sus, sus!*': on, on top! (Old French).

## *ATALANTA IN CALYDON: A TRAGEDY* (LONDON: MOXON, 1865)

First published in March 1865, with financial support of 'considerably more than £100' from ACS's father (*SL*, ii.213). DGR designed gold decorations for the cover. *AiC*GL thinks there were 'little more than one hundred copies' printed of the first edition (xv); ACS said there were five hundred (*SL*, ii.213). From the first and second edition (which followed later in 1865), ACS noted on 20 December 1872 he received no income (*SL*, ii.213). Writing to ACS in January 1868 (*UL*, i.117), Hotten, who had taken over from Moxon, observed that royalties due on all the books bought from Moxon (including *AiC*) minus expenses came to £100 and an additional £75 had been obtained by the new Hotten edition of *AiC*. (The old sheets of *AiC* were acquired by Hotten in 1866 and re-issued with a new title page: two, possibly more, reprints followed.) *AiC*GL observes that *AiC* passed through at least twenty-eight editions and, before 1917, had sold *c.*14,000 copies—second only to *PB* 1, which sold 30,000 (xviii).

ACS first mentions the poetic drama ('poem') in a letter to Alice Swinburne on 31 December 1863 (*SL*, i.93). *AiC* was begun at Northcourt, Isle of Wight, with Mary Gordon and concluded at Tintagel with the painter J.W. Inchbold. The principal ancient sources are described in my notes: see also William R. Rutland, *Swinburne: A Nineteenth-Century Hellene, With Some Reflections on the Hellenism of Modern Poets* (Oxford: Blackwell, 1931), 93–189. A plot summary—i.e. the Classical Greek story—is best provided by ACS's 'Argument'.

ACS told Lady Trevelyan on 15 March 1865 that *AiC* was 'pure Greek, and the first poem of the sort in modern times, combining lyric and dramatic work on the old principle'. He noted that Shelley's *Prometheus Unbound* (1820) 'is magnificent and un-Hellenic, spoilt too, in my mind, by the infusion of philanthropic doctrinaire views and "progress of the species"' (*SL*, i.115). On its publication, *AiC* was generally popular (see Introduction, xix). It was, to be sure, thought insufficiently Greek by *PMG* (18 April 1865, 11) though a more satisfactory Greek experiment than Matthew Arnold's *Merope* (1858), an important text for ACS's endeavour in *AiC*. Of *Merope*, ACS remarked 'the clothes are well enough but where has the body gone?' (*SL*, i.115). Perhaps in 1904 or 1905, he added that *Merope* was 'Servile, spectral, bloodless, colourless, tuneless' (*NWS*, 78). John Nichol similarly observed that *Merope*, while impressively Greek, was lifeless: 'The poem is throughout orderly, and correct, and regular; only, by some unfortunate accident, Mr Arnold has omitted the poetry' ('Merope', *Fragments of Criticism*, 136). Arnold was Professor of Poetry at Oxford from 1857 and overlapped with ACS: Gosse remarks that ACS heard his lectures and found 'their moderation cold', *LACS*, 52. Peter Bayne compared ACS and Arnold as Greek-inspired writers in 'Mr Arnold and Mr Swinburne', *Contemporary Review*, 6 (November 1867), 337–56.

*AiC* was reviewed by Lord Houghton (who, the former Richard Monckton Milnes, assumed that title in 1863) in *The Edinburgh Review*, 122 (July 1865), 202–16: Houghton admired it though advised ACS to 'restrain the exuberance of language and imagery which has the double defect of often confusing or drowning the thought, and of inducing the poet to content himself with presenting the same image in varieties of words so accumulated as to convey the impression of poverty of ideas' (215). Following Classical Greek models, particularly Aeschylus, ACS offered narrated rather than represented action—and *MP*, 8 July 1865, thought this *too* Greek ('There is no action in the piece from the beginning to the end. The author has adhered throughout with undeviating exactitude to the Aristotelian law', 2). *SRev* on 6 May 1865, 540–2, took a middle course, observing that *AiC* had caught Greek practice well: the play 'is an attempt to reproduce a Greek tragedy in its ideas as well as its form, to some extent even in its metres—an attempt necessarily chargeable with faults and weaknesses, yet still one of the most brilliant that our literature contains' (540).

*AiC* draws on the form, moods, and lexis of Classical Greek tragedy as well as making an occasional attempt to render Greek metres in English (though see Introduction, xix). ACS became impatient with the success of the play and vexed by the irregularity and licence in the odes. He preferred *Erechtheus*. Structurally, *AiC* is divided into sections in accordance with Classical models, each marked in the notes as they begin: a prologue; a parados (the first choral song of a Greek drama); and then the poem alternates between episode (literally, 'coming in besides', the equivalent of 'Act'), and stasimon (in Aristotle's definition 'a Choric ode without anapaests or trochaic tetrameters', *Poetics*, trans. S.H. Butcher (London: Macmillan, 1902), 43). The final scene in ancient Greek theatre is an exodus, which in the case of *AiC* includes a long kommos (see note on 562).

Beside Greek material, *AiC* also draws on the Bible, Shakespeare, and other English poets including Shelley's *Prometheus Unbound*. The painting *Atalanta, Meleager, and the Calydonian Boar*, attributed to Rubens, had been exhibited at the Manchester Art-Treasures Exhibition in 1857 and sold at Christies on 9 April 1864. Another Rubens, *Meleager and Atalanta*, had been sold by Christie and Manson's on 16 June 1860. On the overall nature of *AiC*, compare ACS's statement in 'Emily Brontë' on 'high and pure tragedy', 421. Note Granville Bantock's *Atalanta in Calydon: A Choral Symphony for Unaccompanied Voices in Four Movements to Words by Swinburne* (1911). *AiC* was performed three times at the Lyceum 5–7 April 1911 in a production by (and starring) Elsie Fogerty. This was reviewed negatively as the poem, the reviewer said, was never intended for the stage (*The Times*, 5 April 1911, 11). Muriel Elliot composed the incidental music, published the following year (London: Elliot, 1912).

*Τοὺς . . . ῥέπει*: from a surviving fragment of Euripides' play, *Meleager* (*Μελέαγρος*). 'Do good to the living—once dead, every man is earth and shadow; what is nothing counts for nothing' (*Meleager*, 628–9).

*Landor*: cf. note to 'On the Death of Mrs Lynn Linton', 520–1.

*ᾤχεο . . . θεαῖς*: 'You have gone, turned away from the north, but the Nymphs with their sweet breath led you over the welcoming sea, filling your mouth with divine honey, lest Poseidon, hearing your melodious voice, harm you. So great a singer were you. We still mourn for you now that you are gone and long for you always. One of the Muses turning to another said, "Look, he has gone, the best loved of all men has gone. He gathered fresh-budding garlands with his old hands and he covered his grey head with laurel, to sing some sweet song upon Sicilian harps and strings. For he varied the tunes he played on his great lyre, and often Apollo found him seated in a glen and crowned him with flowers, and gave him delightful things to say: Pan never to be forgotten and Pitys, and unhappy Corythos, and the goddess Hamadryad whom a mortal loved. He lulled Cymodameia to sleep in the chambers of the sea; he restored Agamemnon's daughter to her father; and to sacred Delphi he sent Orestes, stricken by god, distressed here and there by the hateful goddesses' (Haynes, 384).

This poem remembers Landor's life (he travelled 'from the north' from England and Wales to Spain, France, and Italy, eventually settling in Florence) and some of his Hellenic verse. It was written before, and the remaining two poems after, Landor's death (cf. *SL*, i.104). The 'fresh-budding garlands' gathered 'with his old hands' are *Heroic Idyls, with Additional Poems* (London: Newby, 1863), published when Landor was, as he said in the 'Preface', 'within two paces of [his] ninetieth year' (n.p.). That volume included 'To Archdeacon Hare, with the Idyl of Pan and Pitys', relating to 'Pan and Pitys' in Landor's *Hellenics* (London: Moxon, 1847). *Hellenics* was a collection of new and previously published Greek-inspired material. ACS's poem alludes to: 'Corythos'; 'The Hamadryad'; 'Enallos and Cymodameia'; 'Iphigineia and Agamemnon'; 'The Shades of Agamemnon and of Iphigineia'; 'The Madness of Orestes'; and 'The Prayer of Orestes'. Houghton took issue with the accuracy of ACS's Greek in his review (202).

*ᾤχεο δὴ . . . φιλότητος ἄτερ*: 'You have gone away from friends and from song, to gather the flowers of gentle Persephone. You have gone, you will live no more, and never again will I sit next to you in awe, touching your hands with my devout hands. Bitter-sweet reverent awe has now again stolen over me, as I remember what I, such as I am, received from the man that you were. Never, old man, will my loving eyes take delight in your loved eyes, as I grasp, beloved old man, your right hand. Ah, dust crumbles, life crumbles: which of these passing things is less? Not dust but life. Yet you are far dearer to me than those who still live, for once you lived. I bring to you in death these things, few but from the heart; do not turn away. Take them, casting even nor a gentle look. I cannot, greatly though I wish it, give you what you deserve, since I am far from where you are buried, for it is not in my power. Nor can I provide a gleaning libation of milk and honey. O that it were possible to touch you with my hands and see you once again, to tend upon your dear head with tears and libations and your holy eyes and holy body. O that I could, for this would greatly relieve my sorrow. Now far away from your grave I make my lament, and do not keen the dirge over your tomb, but I am kept apart, with tears of sorrow. Farewell to you in death; know that you are honoured by men and gods, if any god is set over those below. Farewell, old man, farewell dear father, greatest of singers we have seen, greatest of singers to come. Farewell, may you have such happiness as dead men have, peace without hatred and without love' (Haynes, 384–5).

ACS's poem recalls that Landor lies buried in the Cimitero degli Inglesi, Florence.

*σήματος . . . ἄντι κακῆς*: 'When your tomb has vanished, there will be monuments to you; there will be loving memory of you when your monument has vanished. You the divine Graces mourn and Aphrodite mourns, she who took delight in the Muses' garlands and lovely dances. Never once has old age worn away holy singers. Your monument reveals this splendour. You were a mortal dear indeed to the blessed ones, and to you if to any the Nymphs gave their lovely, their final gifts, to possess. On them has brazen sleep come, and windless eternity; buried with you they share one fate. You too sleep, having come upon lovely and glorious sleep in the hollow earth, far away from your country, by the Etruscan wave of a golden stream, but still your mother land longs for you; but you keep apart, you renounced her of old, though you loved her. Sleep; blessed not wretched will you be to us. Brief is the time of mortals, and fate will master them. Gladness sometimes possesses them, grief sometimes. Many times the light harms them or the dark shrouds them when they weep, and sleep stings those who are awake. But when the eyes of the dead have fallen asleep in their graves, neither the dark nor the light of the sun will sting. No dream vision at night nor waking vision will ever be theirs when they rejoice or mourn. But all keep together one seat and abode forever, immortal instead of mortal, beautiful instead of evil' (Haynes, 385).

*The Argument*: ACS provides the background to the story of the Calydonian boar, explaining the link between Meleager and the burning branch on which the tragedy depends. The earliest account of Artemis sending the wild boar to punish King Oeneus for failing to honour her in sacrifices and of Meleager's hunt is the *Iliad*, Bk 9.529–99. ACS also drew details from Pseudo-Apollodorus, *Βιβλιοθήκη* (*Library*), 1.8.1–4. ACS invokes the practice of *ὑπόθεσις* (hypothesis) or plot summary of Classical tragedy. His archaic diction and syntax implies the play to follow was transcribed in the Middle Ages / Renaissance with the 'argument' translated or added.

*ἴστω … ἐς ἆμαρ*: Aeschylus, *The Libation Bearers*, ll.602–11: 'Let him be the witness, whose thought is not borne on light wings thro' the air, | But abideth with knowledge, what thing was wrought by Althea's despair; | For she marr'd the life-grace of her son, with ill counsel rekindled the flame | That was quenched as it glowed on the brand, what time from his mother he came, | With the cry of a new-born child; and the brand from the burning she won, | For the fates had foretold it coeval, in life and in death, with her son', *The House of Atreus, Being the Agamemnon, Libation-Bearers, and Furies of Æschylus*, translated into English verse by E.D.A. Morshead (London: Kegan Paul, 1881), 110.

*Maiden … divided deity*: the prologue. The huntsman addresses the triple goddess Selene-Artemis-Hecate, associated with the full moon, the waxing moon, and the waning moon respectively, or the heavens, the earth, and the underworld, respectively. ACS focuses on her triple nature not least to mirror the three Fates determining Meleager's future. There is an echo of the Warder's opening petition to the gods and stars at the beginning of Aeschylus', *Agamemnon*, ll.1–7 and Prometheus' opening speech in Shelley's *Prometheus Unbound*.

*hand … fierce*: remembering Artemis' role as huntress.

*Acheloüs*: a river in Epirus, ruled by a god of the same name. 'As one of the numerous suitors of Dejanira, daughter of Oeneus, he entered the lists against Hercules, and being inferior, changed himself into a serpent, and afterwards into an ox. Hercules broke off one of his horns, and Achelous, being defeated, retired in disgrace into this bed of waters' (Lemprière, 'Achelous'). 'Dejanira' or Deianira is Meleager's sister.

*Euenus*: the river Evenus that flows into the Ionian Sea through the Gulf of Patras.

*thou*: Apollo, twin brother of Artemis.

*Ladon … Mænalus*: Ladon is a river in the Peloponnese; Mænalus is the Latin name for a mountain range (the Mainalo) in northern Arcadia, favoured by Pan. It was well-wooded though many ancient trees were lost in fires at the beginning of the present century.

*Lelantian pasturage*: the fertile Lelantine plane is actually on the Greek island of Euboea.

*When the hounds*: the parados.

*mother of months*: Artemis. Cf. Shelley's 'mother of the months', *The Revolt of Islam*, l.1420.

*Itylus*: see headnote to 'Itylus', 568–9.

*Pan … Bacchus*: gods of the field and forest, and of wine and carousing respectively.

*Fleeter of foot … kid*: Haynes notes that this 'may be seen as a metrical equivalent to Aeschylus, *Seven Against Thebes*, l.229, *κρημναμενᾶν νεφελᾶν ὀρθοῖ* [when storm clouds hang over (his eyes)]. However, Swinburne is not attempting to imitate Greek [quantitative] metres but rather to bring into English poetry new rhythmical inventions inspired by Greek choral odes' (388). ACS may have the *Iliad*, Bk 6, ll.147–51 in mind as Hippolochus describes the coming of the spring and, in Latin, perhaps Catullus 46, a spring poem about 'eager feet'.

*Mænad and the Bassarid*: the maenads were female followers of Dionysius: *OED* defines a 'Bassarid' as 'A Thracian bacchanal; a bacchante', citing this usage as the first.

*What do ye singing?*: first episode.

*Yet one…gods*: ACS uses the single line exchanges—*stichomythia*—from Classical drama: e.g. *Agamemnon*, ll.1299–1306.

*Lo, where they heal…not*: cf. 'Althaea accepts the gods with Aeschylean faith and curses them with Euripidean audacity': Marion Clyde Wier, *The Influence of Aeschylus and Euripides on the Structure and Content of Swinburne's 'Atalanta in Calydon' and 'Erechtheus'* (Ann Arbor: Wahr, 1920), 30.

*Three weaving women*: the Moirai (*Μοῖραι*) or Fates, of whom the first (Clotho) was sometimes imagined to be a spinner.

*Eurythemis*: Althaea is the daughter of King Thestius and Eurythemis.

*Before…years*: first stasimon.

*Sows…reap*: cf. Galatians 6:7.

*O sweet new heaven*: second episode.

*Peleus the Larissæan*: Peleus was the son of Aeacus and Endeis and king of the Myrmidons at Phthia, Thessaly (cf. *Iliad*, Bk 24, ll.534–7) and in turn the father of Achilles. Achilles' mother was the Nereid (sea nymph) Thetis. Larissa is the largest city in Thessaly but ACS's presentation here differs from Pseudo-Apollodurus who describes 'Pirithous, son of Ixion, from Larissa; Peleus, son of Aeacus, from Phthia' among the hunters (*Library*, 1.8.2). In the episode as a whole, ACS loosely follows Bk 3, ll.151–244 of the *Iliad*, where a sorrowful Helen describes to Priam the Achaean warriors as they pass before Troy. The first warrior Helen sees—as Peleus is the first in Meleager's account of those who will join him in the hunt—is Agamemnon. Like ACS's scene, the Homeric episode is one of foreboding.

*Most swift*: ACS recalls the most frequent Homeric epithet for Achilles: *πόδας ὠκύς* (swift-footed).

*thy sister's sons*: Castor and Pollux, the twin sons of Leda. Castor was sometimes thought mortal as the son of Tyndareus; Pollux was immortal as the divine offspring of Zeus who raped Leda when in the form of a swan (cf. ACS's description of them as 'moulded like as gods'). Pseudo-Apollodorus simply describes them as 'Castor and Pollux, sons of Zeus and Leda, from Lacedaemon' (1.8.2). The sisters of Castor and Pollux were Helen and Clytemnestra and in turn the whole plot of *AiC* is part of the wider story of the House of Atreus. The subsequent history of Troy and the curse of the House renders Althaea's lines beginning 'Sweet days befall them' painfully ironic.

*Eurotas*: king of Laconia (the capital of which is Sparta). Pausanias says: 'This Eurotas having brought the stagnant water in the fields to the sea, by a channel, the water which was left, and which flowed like a river, was called after him, Eurotas', *The Description of Greece by Pausanias Translated from the Greek* (London: Faulder, 1794), 249.

*Telamon*: Peleus' brother, who accompanied Jason on the search for the Golden Fleece. He is the father of Ajax in the *Iliad* and became king of Salamis, the large island off Piraeus. ACS alludes to Euripides' *Meleager* fragments in presenting Telemon with a shield on which is 'a golden eagle to confront the boar—he had wreathed his head with grapes to honour his homeland of Salamis with its fine vines' (*Meleager*, 628/629). King Oeneus of Calydon is remembered for introducing wine-making to the region (*oinos*, *οἶνος* = wine). *OED* gives 1865, the year of *AiC*'s publication, as the first appearance of 'oenophile'.

*Ancaeus*... *Cepheus*: also Argonauts. Pseudo-Apollodorus notes: 'Ancaeus and Cepheus, sons of Lycurgus, from Arcadia' (1.8.2). The first is killed by the boar.

*Toxeus*... *Plexippus*: Althaea's brothers (and Meleager's uncles).

*twin-born fate*: 'twin-born' is a common ACS collocation. Here it refers to the fact that Meleager's future is in the hands of the Fates and his mother (cf. Althaea's 'Fate's are we, | Yet fate is ours a breathing-space; yea, mine, | Fate is made mine for ever', 94).

*old men honourable*: ACS told Lady Trevelyan on 15 March 1865 that these lines (up to 'look for such a death') alluded to Landor's 'life and death' (*SL*, i.115).

*wild wars*: I can find no source for this conception of a war in the house of Oeneus. ACS envisages it, with Ares and Artemis on opposite sides, as another reason for Artemis' curse on Calydon in addition to Oeneus' failure to honour her in sacrifice. Ares is sometimes regarded as the father of Meleager by Althaea (see *Meleager*, 618/619).

*undivided seas*: Althaea refers to Meleager's journey as one of the Argonauts.

*sail*: Meleager continues the account of Jason and the Argonauts as they sail towards Colchis (*Κολχίς*) to find the Golden Fleece. In the 'Argument' to William Morris' *The Life and Death of Jason* (London: Bell & Daldy, 1867), the story is told as follows: 'Jason, the son of Æson, king of Iolchos, having come to man's estate, demanded of Pelias his father's kingdom, which he held wrongfully. But Pelias answered, that if he would bring from Colchis the golden fleece of the ram that had carried Phryxus thither, he would yield him his right. Whereon Jason sailed to Colchis in the ship Argo, with other heroes, and by means of Medea, the king's daughter, won the fleece; and carried off also Medea; and so, after many troubles, came back to Iolchos again. There, by Medea's wiles, was Pelias slain; but Jason went to Corinth, and lived with Medea happily, till he was taken with the love of Glaucé, the king's daughter of Corinth, and must needs wed her;

whom also Medea destroyed and fled to Ægeus at Athens; and not long after Jason died strangely' (1).

*irremeable Symplegades*: Jason has to pass between the Συμπληγάδες (Symplegades), a pair of clashing rocks. Apollonius Rhodius' *Argonautica,* Bk 2, ll.561–71, narrates as follows: 'Euphemus sent forth the dove to dart forward on its wings, while all the crew together raised their heads to watch. She flew between them, and the two rocks came back together with a crash. A mass of seething spray shot up like a cloud, and the sea roared terrifyingly, and the vast sky rumbled all around. The hollow caverns at the base of the jagged rocks boomed as the sea surged within, while the white foam of the crashing wave spurted high above the cliff. Then the current began spinning the ship around. The rocks cut off the tips of the dove's tail feathers, but she flew away unharmed', *Argonautica*, trans. William H. Race, Loeb Classical Library, LCL 1 (Cambridge: Harvard University Press, 2008), 158 and 159. The Argonauts then pass between the rocks as they reel apart. 'Irremeable' means 'Admitting of no return; from, by, or through which there is no return': *OED* gives examples from 1569. Pope's translation of the *Iliad* uses the word at v.19.312. There is a fragment of an Aeschylus drama, *Phineus*, which narrates the Argonauts' journey just before they reach the Clashing Rocks and the navigation advice given to them by Phineus.

*Euxine*: Black Sea.

*gods... than fate*: one of the conceptual problems probed by Aeschylus' *Oresteia*.

*three suns old*: three days old.

*We have seen thee*: second stasimon.

*wings of a dove*: cf. Psalms 55:6 and 68:13.

*sea-foam*: cf. Ἀφροδίτη (Aphrodite) 'foam-born' (from the severed genitals of Uranus cast into the sea). This stasimon was reproduced in full in *Selections* as 'Anadyomene': that is Ἀφροδίτη ἀναδυομένη (Aphrodite Anadyomene): 'Aphrodite rising from the sea'. Cf. Ingres' *La Vénus anadyomène* (1848), now in the Musée Condé, Chantilly, and Botticelli's *Nascita di Venere* (*c.*1486), Uffizi.

*uttermost... sea*: cf. Psalm 139:9.

*Tyro*: Τυρώ, though married to Cretheus, loved the river-god Enipeus: she gave birth to the twin sons Pelias and Neleus by the god Poseidon disguised as Enipeus. They later killed Tyro's step-mother (not in Lemprière). Cf. George Grote's description of the lost Sophocles play on this topic: '[Tyro's] father had married a second wife, named Sidêrô, whose cruel counsels induced him to punish and torture his daughter on account of her intercourse with Poseidôn. She was shorn of her magnificent hair, beaten and ill-used in various ways, and confined in a loathsome dungeon [... Her sons] revenged her wrongs by putting to death the iron-hearted Sidêrô', *A History of Greece*, new edn, 8 vols (London: Murray, 1862), i.94.

*Sun, and clear light*: third episode.

*sun's white sister*: the moon (Artemis).

*Elis... horn*: Elis (*Ἦλις*) is a region in the Peloponnese; on the horn see the note to Acheloüs, above 555.

*Why... sit thou here*: cf. a speech possibly by Althaea in Euripides' *Meleager*: 'if men concerned themselves with the labour of weaving, and women were overcome by the joys of armed fighting; cast out from their proper sphere of knowledge, they would be good for nothing, and so would we', *Meleager*, 622–3.

*wise... endures*: cf. the epigraph from Euripides' *Meleager* (39).

*For spears... Tantalus*: Atalanta refers to the story of Niobe, 'a daughter of Tantalus, king of Lydia [...] The number of her children increased her pride, and she had the imprudence not only to prefer herself to Latona [the Greek Leto, mother of Apollo and Artemis] who had only two children, but she even insulted her, and ridiculed the worship which was paid to her. [...Latona] entreated her children punish the arrogant Niobe. Her prayers were heard, and immediately all the sons of Niobe expired by the darts of Apollo, and all the daughters, except Chloris, who had married Neleus king of Pylos, were equally destroyed by Diana [Artemis]' (Lemprière, 'Niobe'). The children were 'holy born' because Tantalus is the 'son of Jupiter [Zeus], by a nymph called Pluto' (Lemprière, 'Tantalus').

*I shall... love*: in *Meleager*, Atalanta only hopes that marriage will not happen (624–5).

*no man... more*: *All is True* (*King Henry VIII*), 3.2.228.

*Tegea*: Atalanta was associated with the worship of Athena in Tegea in Greece. See Ernest Gardner, 'The Atalanta of Tegea', *Journal of Hellenic Studies*, 26 (1906), 169–75.

*Who hath given*: third stasimon.

*weeping Seven*: the Pleiades, companions of Artemis, were not infrequently represented in mourning for their father Atlas. They were turned into a cluster of stars.

*well-head of lamentation*: recalling the transformation of the weeping Niobe (after the death of her children) into a fountain.

*wash... tribulation*: cf. Revelation 7:14.

*iron heaven*: ACS's translation of Homer's '*σιδήρεον οὐρανόν*', e.g. *Odyssey*, Bk 15, l.329.

*shake... root*: cf. Matthew 3:10.

*I heard within*: fourth episode.

*warder gods*: images of the protecting gods.

*Laertes... heart*: Laertes is king of Ithaca and step-father of Odysseus; Nestor is king of Pylos who was brought up in Gerenia in Messenia (cf. *Odyssey*, Bk 3, l.102); Panopeus was the son of Phocus; on Cepheus and Ancaeus, see note on 557; Iphicles was an Argonaut, the son of Thestius, and brother of Heracles; Theseus killed the Minotaur, ACS's 'biform bull', and is a leading figure in Ovid's account of the hunt (see below); Pirothous was king of the Lapiths; Eurytion was another Argonaut and king of Phthia who was accidentally killed by Peleus; Æacides is 'son of Aeacus', i.e. Peleus (see note on 556); on Telemon, see note to 557; Amphiaraus was a seer and king of Argos; 'Thy mother's sons' are Toxeus and Plexippus, Althaea's brothers; 'Thy sister's sons' are Castor and Pollux (see note on 556); Jason led the Argonauts in the search for the Golden Fleece; Dryas was murdered by his brother Tereus (for whose story, see headnote, 568–9); Idas and Lynceus were sons of Aphareus; Admetus was the husband of Alcestis whom Heracles rescued from the underworld allowing Admetus to be 'twice-espoused'; Hippasus and Hyleus were two other hunters, the latter killed by the boar. ACS draws for this account of the hunt on Pseudo-Apollodorius, *Library*, 1.8, and on Ovid's *Metamorphoses*, Bk 8, ll.246–450.

*Speed it... Goddess*: ACS departs from Ovid. In *Metamorphoses*, Bk 8, ll.350–4, Mopsus prays to Apollo/Phoebus: "'O Patron, help thy Priest!"' Artemis/Diana then intervenes: 'The God allow'd | His Pray'r, and, smiling, gave him what he cou'd: | He reach'd the Savage, but no Blood he drew; | *Dian* unarm'd the Javelin as it flew', Dryden, 'Meleager and Atalanta, Out of the Eighth Book of Ovid's *Metamorphoses*', ll.114–20.

*heavy strength, | Ancæus*: ACS departs from Ovid. Ancaeus in *Metamorphoses* makes a proud assertion that killing the boar should be his achievement and not a woman's. He is promptly killed by the boar, which pierces his groin with its tusks (ll.391–402).

*Laud ye the gods*: cf. 'Laud we the gods', *Cymbeline*, 5.6.478. *Cymbeline* was particularly admired by ACS: see 654–5.

*O that I now*: fourth stasimon.

*Iamus*: the son of Apollo (Artemis' 'brother's seed') and Evadne, who was left beneath violets ('duskier violet') on a mountain side, though survived to found a race of prophets. Iamus comes from ἴον, 'violet'.

*We beseech... night*: a summary of the roles of the triple goddess.

*Orion overthrown*: Artemis slays Orion for sleeping with Eod, the dawn (and thus blurring gods and men), in *Odyssey*, Bk. 5, ll.116–24. Between gods and men is one 'indissoluble zone'. But the Greek ζώνη (*zone*) means a girdle and can relate to preservation from sex before marriage (cf. Aeschylus, *Eumenides*, ll.607–8).

*Maidens*: fifth episode.

*it is here*: cf. *Hamlet*, 5.2.302.

*Meleager... grievous huntsman*: this is a pun present in the Euripides' *Meleager* fragments. In fragment 517, an unknown speaker puns on Μελέαγρε, μελέαν γάρ ποτ' ἀγρεύεις ('Meleager—malign indeed is the chase you've chosen': *Meleager*, 620–1) where the force depends on 'Meleager' read as 'mele' (μελέ, ill-fated) and 'agra' (ἄγρα, the chase).

*labouring... births*: cf. John 16:21.

*I would... sun*: Haynes (398) connects to Sophocles, *Oedipus the King*, ll.1425–31.

*shoot out lips*: cf. Psalm 22:7.

*Meleager...chafed*: in Ovid, *Metamorphoses*, Bk 8, ll.425–45, the scene involves more envious anger from Plexippus and Toxeus, and violence and cruelty from Meleager. Althaea's response is more extreme too, animated by outrage and vengeance. In Pseudo-Apollodorus, *Library*, 1.8.3, Althaea is motivated by grief.

*I would...these*: cf. 2 Samuel 18:33.

*Who shall get brothers*: Althaea's speech has something of Orestes' and Elektra's sentiments in mourning their murdered father in *The Libation Bearers*; Haynes (398) notes Antigone's speech about the irreplaceability of brothers (as distinct from husbands) in Sophocles' *Antigone*, ll.909–13.

*own hounds | Whine masterless*: note that the celebrated Greyfriars Bobby had already begun sitting—at least as the common story alleged—by his master's grave in Greyfriars' Kirkyard, Edinburgh (from 1858).

*shall hounds...at all?*: cf. *King Lear*, Quarto, Sc. 24, ll.300–2.

*nets and knives*: anticipation of Clytemnestra's mode of slaying Agamemnon in Aeschylus' conception.

*But never...more*: Edith, ACS's sister, had died on 25 September 1863.

*Eats thee...eats*: a parody of the Eucharist where Christians ritually share bread and wine as representative—in the Protestant tradition—of the body and blood of Jesus (thus confirming their part in the Body of Christ conceptually). Here the son eats a mother. More specifically, the words ironically recall of the minister's words at the Anglican consecration, including (at the consecration of the wine): 'Drink ye all of this; for this is my Blood of the New Testament, which is shed for you and for many for the remission of sins' (*BCP*).

*sect*: 'A cutting from a plant', perhaps from the 'Latin *sectum*, neuter past participle of *secāre* to cut' (*OED*).

*Lo how...sister*: cf. the opening of Sophocles' *Antigone* where Antigone defies command in order to retrieve the body of Polynices and provide him with an honourable burial.

*atone...same love*: a version of Orestes' conflict over slaying his mother for murdering Orestes' father in the *Agamemnon* (here it is the mother who is conflicted over killing her son).

*fire unquenchable*: see Luke 3.17.

*The house...stand*: cf. Mark 3:25.

*Not as with sundering*: fifth stasimon.

*heaven rang...came*: cf. Wordsworth, 'Ode: Intimations of Immortality', ll.65–6.

*Ho, ye that wail*: the exodus.

*doorway...lips*: cf. Psalm 141.3.

*name...healing*: ACS puns on ἄλθος (*althos*), healing.

*From...till I die*: cf. Jocasta's words in *Oedipus the King*, ll.1071–2): ἰοὺ, ἰού, δύστηνε· τοῦτο γάρ σ' ἔχω | μόνον προσειπεῖν, ἄλλο, δ' οὔποθ' ὕστερον ('woe, woe, wretched man—only that word can I say to you and never another again').

*She has filled*: the beginning of the kommos or lyrical lament in Athenian theatre ('a joint lamentation of Chorus and actors': Aristotle, *Poetics*, trans. S.H. Butcher, 43). ACS's kommos might be compared to, for instance, Oedipus' lament with the chorus after his blinding in *Oedipus the King*, ll.1297–1415, and to Orestes' and Elektra's dialogue with the chorus in *The Libation Bearers*, ll.306–478. The portion concerning Meleager (from 'Let your hands meet' to 'darken man's face before God' appeared in *Selections* as 'The Death of Meleager').

*Cry...at hand*: cf. *King Lear*, Quarto, Sc. 24: 259–60.

*Thou shouldst...spears*: cf. Orestes' 'Ah, would that 'neath Ilium's walls, my father, thou hadst been slain, gashed by some Lycian spear!', *The Libation Bearers*, ll.345–7, in *Aeschylus*, 2 vols, Loeb Classical Library, ed. and trans. H.W. Smyth (Cambridge, MA: Harvard University Press, 1926), ii.192–3.

*Acroceraunian*: the western chain of the Ceraunian Mountains ('thunder-split peaks') on the SW coast of Albania. Cf. 'From Tmolus to the Acroceraunian snow', Shelley, 'Prologue' to *Hellas*, l.174.

*Chersonese*: peninsula of the Dardanelles (Tauric Chersonese).

*sea-ride of Helle*: the Hellespont (the 'sea of Helle', now the Dardanelles) named after Helle, who died when she fell from into the waters from the back of a golden-fleeced ram.

*And...fruit*: cf. '*Ave Atque Vale*: In Memory of Charles Baudelaire': 'Are there flowers | At all, or any fruit?', 344.

*Who...song?*: Haynes (401) notes these lines might recall Blake's *Europe*, Plate 2, ll.28–9: 'And who shall bind the infinite with an eternal band, | To compass it with swaddling bands?' Certainly, these words are quoted (as prose) in ACS's *William Blake*, 245.

## FROM 'PREFACE' TO *A SELECTION FROM THE WORKS OF LORD BYRON* (1866)

ACS's *A Selection from the Works of Lord Byron* was published by Moxon in March 1866 with the poet's Preface dated 'Christmas, 1865' (the copytext here). ACS had once promised his mother, according to *LS*, 'not to read Byron, and in fact did not open that poet till he went to Oxford' (12). He noted that he was '*doing* Byron' for Moxon's series and was intending to 'do' Landor later in a letter to Lady Trevelyan, 10 December 1865 (*SL*, i.142). The Landor edition was not completed (note that Moxon had published a number of Landor volumes earlier including *The Works of Walter Savage Landor* (1846)). ACS reprinted this 'Preface' as 'Byron' in *ES*. The original volume was reviewed, mostly positively, in 'Mr Swinburne on Byron', *London Review*, 12 (24 March 1866), 342–3. For ACS's later views, see 'Wordsworth and Byron', *NC*, 15 (1884), 764–90. John Nichol published his *English Men of Letters* volume on *Byron* in 1880. He did not mention ACS though ACS declared Nichol's book 'the best thing ever written on the [ . . . ] subject by friend or foe' (*UL*, ii.229, letter of 8 September 1880).

*most delicate . . . critics*: 'Look at Byron, that Byron whom the present generation of Englishmen are forgetting': Matthew Arnold, 'Heinrich Heine', *Essays in Criticism* (London: Macmillan, 1865), 185. ACS later said rather peevishly, perhaps in 1904 or 1905, 'there can hardly have been worse critics than Matthew Arnold at his best' (*NWS*, 78).

*His sincerity . . . priceless*: cf. ACS's praise of sincerity in DGR's *The House of Life* (1870): 'A more bitter sweetness of sincerity was never pressed into verse than beats and burns here under the veil and girdle of glorious words', 'The Poems of Dante Rossetti', *FR*, 7 (1870), 551–79 (554).

*goddess . . . earth*: Claire Clairmont (1798–1879), mother of Byron's daughter Allegra.

*belly . . . life*: cf. Genesis 3:14.

*Haidée . . . English household*: Haidée falls in love with Don Juan in Canto 2; Dudù appears in Canto 6 ('a beauty that would drive you crazy', l.328); the shipwreck is in Canto 2 and siege in Canto 7; Canto 9 involves the court of Catherine II; the London mansion is in Canto 13.

*lake-water and sea-water*: terms from the 'Dedication' of *Don Juan*.

*the broad backs of the sea*: from *Iliad*, 2.159 (Ἀργεῖοι φεύξονται ἐπ' εὐρέα νῶτα θαλάσσης).

## FROM *POEMS AND BALLADS* (LONDON: MOXON then HOTTEN, 1866)

### Laus Veneris

First published *PB* 1 (the early 1866 pamphlet version seems most likely a forgery). EWG thought the poem in existence by 1862 (*LACS*, 145). 'Laus Veneris' ('In Praise of Venus') takes up a version of the German legend of the knight and poet, Tannhäuser. Tannhäuser discovers Venus has survived the destruction of paganism and continues, during the Christian Middle Ages, to inhabit the Venusberg (Hörselberg). Tannhäuser lives amorously with her for a year until, overcome by remorse, he seeks absolution from the Pope. The Pope refuses, saying that Tannhäuser will only be forgiven when the Pope's staff blooms. After Tannhäuser has left, the staff does indeed bloom. But Tannhäuser has returned to Venus.

Wagner's *Gesamtkunstwerk*, or synthesis of the arts, *Tannhäuser*, received its Dresden premiere in 1845 and a new version was premiered in Paris in 1861. Many versions of extracts and transcriptions were available in England. 'Hail! Hail to Thee! (Tannhäuser's Farewell to Venus)' with English words by A.F. Mullen was, for instance, published in London in 1866 as was William J. Chalmers' *Favourite Airs from Tannhäuser* and Robert Harold Thomas' *Fantasia on Themes from Wagner's Opera 'Tannhäuser'*, for piano. But if there was English cultural enthusiasm for Wagner's version of

Tannhäuser around the time of *PB* 1, the music drama does not appear to have been a source for ACS. On ACS's actual or possible sources, see Clyde Hyder, 'Swinburne's "Laus Veneris" and the Tannhäuser Legend', *PMLA*, 45 (1930), 1202–13; Robert Peters, 'The Tannhäuser Theme: Swinburne's "Laus Veneris"', *Pre-Raphaelite Review*, 3 (1979), 12–28; Kirsten Powell, 'Burne-Jones, Swinburne and *Laus Veneris*', in *Pre-Raphaelitism and Medievalism in the Arts*, ed. Liana de Girolami Cheney (Lampeter: Mellen, 1992), 221–40; and Haynes, 325–7.

Cf. also 'Un voyage à Cythère' in *Les Fleurs du mal* on voyaging to the Isle of Venus; Burne-Jones' now lost 1861 watercolour preparation for what became the painting *Laus Veneris* (1873–5), which is in the Laing Art Gallery, Newcastle-upon-Tyne; and WM's draft material on Venus in 1861 and 1862 eventually incorporated into 'The Hill of Venus' in *The Earthly Paradise*. Note also *Tannhäuser, or, The Battle of the Bards: A Poem* by Neville Temple [J.H.C. Fane] and Edward Trevor [E.R.B. Lytton] (London: Chapman and Hall, 1861).

*HEP* observes: 'Mr Swinburne, following [Edward Fitzgerald's *The Rubáiyát of Omar Khayyám* (1859)] has taken the principle of the terza, that of the single line unrhymed in the individual stanza; but though, again like his fore-runner, he has not attempted to make this the rhyme-staple of the next stanza, his third lines, unlike those of *Omar*, rhyme in pairs. By this means not merely is the [potential for monotony] of the individual stanza relieved, but each alternate stanza holds out a feeler to the next, making the arrangement almost an octave—a squadron charging in two troops. The poet has been wisely chary of enjambment between the quatrains, though using it when he wants it; while he has alternated enjambment and single-moulding, as regards contiguous lines in the stanza, with as careful a hand' (iii.339).

*NPR* said: 'Of the poem in which I have attempted once more to embody the legend of Venus and her knight, I need say only that my first aim was to rehandle the old story in a new fashion. To me it seemed that the tragedy began with the knight's return to Venus—began at the point where hitherto it had seemed to leave off. The immortal agony of a man lost after all repentance—cast down from fearful hope into fearless despair—believing in Christ and bound to Venus—desirous of penitential pain, and damned to joyless pleasure—this, in my eyes, was the kernel and nucleus of a myth comparable only to that of the foolish virgins and bearing the same burden. The tragic touch of the story is this: that the knight who has renounced Christ believes in him; the lover who has embraced Venus disbelieves in her. Vainly and in despair would he make the best of that which is the worst—vainly remonstrate with God, and argue on the side he would fain desert. Once accept or admit the least admixture of pagan worship, or of modern thought, and the whole story collapses into froth and smoke. It was not till my poem was completed that I received from the hands of its author the admirable pamphlet of Charles Baudelaire on Wagner's *Tannhäuser*. If any one desires to see, expressed in better words than I can command, the conception of the mediaeval Venus which it was my aim to put into verse, let him turn to the magnificent passage in which M. Baudelaire describes the fallen goddess, grown diabolic among ages that would not accept her as divine. In another point, as I then found, I concur with the great musician and his great panegyrist. I have made Venus the one love of her knight's whole life, as Mary Stuart of Chastelard's; I have sent him, poet and soldier, fresh to her fierce embrace. Thus only both legend and symbol appear to me noble and significant. Light loves and harmless errors must not touch the elect of heaven or of hell. The queen of evil, the lady of lust, will endure no rival but God; and when the vicar of God rejects him, to her only can he return to abide the day of his judgment in weariness and sorrow and fear' (16–17).

On Mary Stuart's poet lover, see ACS's *Chastelard* (London: Moxon, 1865), the first play of his Mary Queen of Scots trilogy, as well as his later *Bothwell* (1875), and W.S. Landor's 'Mary and Bothwell' in *Imaginary Conversations,* fourth series.

*Lors dit... 1530*: 'Then, weeping, he said, Alas, too miserable man and cursed sinner, never shall I see God's mercy and pity. I shall go now from here and hide myself in Mount Horsel, and request the blessing and loving mercy of my sweet Lady Venus, because for love I shall be damned to hell for ever. Here is the end of all my deeds of arms and all my beautiful songs. Alas, too beautiful was my lady's face and eyes, and a bad day when I saw them. Then away he went moaning, and to her returned, and lived there sadly, with great love, near his lady. Then afterwards, the Pope saw one day beautiful red and white flowers and many buds of leaves break from his staff, and also the renewal of all the bark. He was greatly afraid and moved, and took great pity on the knight who had left him without hope as a wretched and damned man. In turn he sent many messengers after him to bring him back, declaring that he would have the grace of God and a full absolution from his great sin of passion. But they never saw him, because this sorry knight remained always thereafter with Venus, the high and strong goddess, in the mountain of lovers.

The Book of Love's Marvels, written in Latin and French by Master Antoine Gaget. 1530.'

*asleep... is it*: cf. Keats, 'Ode to a Nightingale' (1819), l.80. ACS called the Nightingale ode 'one of the final masterpieces of human work in all time and for all ages' ('Keats', *Miscellanies*, 211).

*very soul... ache*: cf. 'Ode to a Nightingale', ll.1–2.

*Adonis*: in ancient Greek religion, a divinity associated with beauty and sexual desire, loved by Aphrodite (Venus in Roman religion).

*marvellous mouth*: of Helen of Troy. Cf. DGR's 'Helen of Troy' (1863), now in the Kunsthalle, Hamburg.

*the queen*: Cleopatra.

*Semiramis*: legendary Queen of Assyria, sometimes thought a harlot. Dante places her with the souls of the lustful in Canto 5 of Hell.

*slotwise*: 'The track or trail of an animal, esp. a deer, as shown by the marks of the foot; sometimes misapplied to the scent of an animal; hence generally, track, trace, or trail', *OED*.

*Dove*: the Holy Spirit.

*kissed mouth*: cf. DGR's *Bocca Baciata* (1859), now in the Museum of Fine Arts, Boston.

*Rise up*: cf. Song of Solomon 2:10.

*dove's beat... vain*: perhaps recalling DGR's *Beata Beatrix* (1864), now in Tate Britain.

*strange lands*: cf. Psalm 137:4.

*keys... loose*: the keys of St Peter, remembering the foundation of Papal authority in Matthew 18:18.

*Ethiop's stain*: cf. Jeremiah 13:23.

*naked sea... trod*: Venus / Aphrodite born from the foam of the sea (see note on 572).

*Strange spice... root*: cf. Baudelaire's 'Correspondances' from *Les Fleurs du mal*.

*Remembering love... space*: recalling Francesca's words in Canto 5.121–3 of Dante's Hell: 'Nessun maggior dolore | che ricordarsi del tempo felice | ne la miseria' ('There is no more greater sorrow than remembering happiness in misery').

*EXPLICIT LAUS VENERIS*: 'Here ends the praise of Venus'.

## The Triumph of Time

First published *PB* 1. Writing to WMR on 9 October 1866, ACS said: 'I should not like to bracket "Dolores" and the two following ["The Garden of Proserpine" and "Hesperia"] as you propose. I ought (if I did) to couple with them in front harness the "Triumph of Time" etc., as they express that state of feeling the reaction from which is expressed in "Dolores." Were I to rechristen these three as trilogy, I should have to rename many earlier poems as acts in the same play' (*SL*, i.197). 'The Triumph of Time' has often been interpreted as autobiographical in origin, connected to the emotions expressed in 'Dolores' (165–76) and, among others, 'A Leave-Taking' in *PB* 1. EWG declared that ACS had fallen in love with a relative of the physician, Dr John Simon (1816–1904) and his wife Jane (1816–1901), but the young woman had laughed at his hopes. EWG added that 'The Triumph of Time' was 'the most profound and the most touching of all his personal poems. Speaking to me of this incident [of rejection], in 1876, he assured me that the stanzas of this wonderful lyric represented with the exactest fidelity the emotions which passed through his mind when his anger had died down, and when nothing remained but the infinite pity and the pain' (*LACS*, 82–3).

Writing to EWG on the announcement of his (EWG's) marriage in 1875, ACS had said: 'I suppose it must be the best thing that can befall a man to win and keep the woman that he loves while yet young; at any rate I can congratulate my friend on his good hap without any too jealous afterthought of the reverse experience which left my own young manhood "a barren stock"—if I may cite that phrase without seeming to liken myself to a male Queen Elizabeth' (*SL*, iii.51). Giving more detail, W.H. Mallock remembered in 1920 a dinner party with Benjamin Jowett and Swinburne somewhere between late 1869 and 1872: 'There were three poems, [Swinburne] said, which beyond all the rest were biographical—"The Triumph of Time," "Dolores," and "The Garden of Proserpine." "The Triumph of Time" was a monument to the sole real love of his life—a love which had been the tragic destruction of all his faith in woman. "Dolores" expressed the passion with which he had sought relief, in the madnesses of the fleshly Venus, from his mined dreams of the heavenly. "The Garden of Proserpine" expressed his revolt against the flesh and its fevers, and his longing to find a refuge from them in a haven of undisturbed rest', *Memoirs of Life and Literature*, 2nd edn (London: Chapman and Hall, 1920), 57.

Who was the lady? EWG's suggestion has been both discounted and occasionally restored. At present, the most likely candidate remains ACS's cousin, Mary Charlotte Julia Gordon (d.21 February 1926). Cf. Francis O'Gorman, 'Swinburne and Mary Gordon', *N&Q*, 60 (2013), 263–5.

ACS's play *The Sisters* (1892) seems to make the link with Gordon clear (and is dedicated to her mother). Certainly, ACS's friendship with Mary Gordon had been close: 'we rode together constantly', she remembered, '[and we] would gallop along wildly, much absorbed in our conversation' (*BACS*, 18). They collaborated on a novel, *The Children of the Chapel* (London: Masters, 1864), in which Byrd, Morley, and Tallis feature, together with much flogging and mistreatment ('We had great amusement over the story', *BACS*, 20). As is clear from the letters included in *UL*, they shared an enthusiasm for flogging generally.

Mary Gordon married Robert William Disney Leith (1819–92, later General Disney Leith, CB) on 14 June 1865. It is not known when ACS learned of their engagement. Mrs Leith observes in *BACS* that 'I have been unable to trace the letter he wrote when I announced to him my engagement, and said that as he had always been to me like an elder brother, I should like to feel that I had his approval', 26. 'The Triumph of Time' can be read as a response to the engagement. Nevertheless, years later, Mrs Leith wrote: 'I am anxious to say once and for all that there was never, in all our years of friendship, an ounce of sentiment between us' (*BACS*, 4–5). ACS associated Mary with the music of G.F. Handel, which she played to him on the organ at Northcourt ('I can hardly *behave* for delight at some of the choruses', he said: *SL*, i.93). The title of 'The Triumph of Time' might allude to Handel's first oratorio, *Il trionfo del tempo e del disinganno* (1707, 'the triumph of time and disillusion'), later recast as *Il trionfo del tempo e della verità* (1737, 'the triumph of time and truth'). Cf. Shelley's 'The Triumph of Life'.

ACS's verse form is the same as the first chorus of *AiC* (see 46–7). For a memory of ACS reading this poem with apparently unforgettable personal intensity, see Edmund Gosse, 'Swinburne', *FR*, 85 (June 1909), 1019–39 (1034–5).

*We had stood ... world*: cf. Dante, *Paradiso*, 27.103–17; 34.145.

*great third wave*: Plato recognized the proverbial idea that the third of a group of three waves ('τρικυμία') was the greatest: Republic, 472a. The idea is used with metaphorical significance in *Erechtheus*.

*bread ... blood*: cf. 1 Corinthians 11:23–5.

*profit ... might*: cf. 1 Corinthians 13:3.

*fates are three*: the Greek fates (Μοῖραι): Clotho, Lachesis, Atropos.

*gate is strait*: cf. Matthew 7:13–14.

*balm... royal king's*: cf. Matthew 2:11.

*'What should... I do?'*: *Hamlet*, 3.1.129–31.

*worst after all*: cf. *King Lear*, Quarto, Scene 15.25–6.

*Should*: often incorrectly printed as 'Would'.

*mix her with me*: invoking the birth of Aphrodite (see note on 558).

*singer in France*: a summary of the legend of the twelfth-century troubadour, Jaufre Rudel (died *c.*1147). Cf. Robert Browning, 'Rudel and the Lady of Tripoli' (1842); William Motherwell, 'The Lay of Geoffrie Rudel' (1849); and ACS, 'The Death of Rudel' (from *Lancelot, the Death of Rudel, and Other Poems* (London: p.p., 1918)) and 'Rudel in Paradise' (mentioned in *SL*, i.16 for 17 February 1858).

## Les Noyades

First published *PB* 1. 'Les noyades' ('the drownings') was the name of notorious mass executions in the River Loire, ordered at Nantes by the anti-clerical revolutionary Jean-Baptiste Carrier (1756–94). He was alleged to have enforced 'republican marriages', the subject of ACS's poem, where a young man and woman were bound naked together before being drowned. See Carlyle's *The French Revolution* (1837): 'By degrees, daylight itself witnesses Noyades: women and men are tied together, feet and feet, hands and hands: and flung in: this they call Mariage Republicain, Republican Marriage. Cruel is the panther of the woods, the she-bear bereaved of her whelps: but there is in man a hatred crueller than that. Dumb, out of suffering now, as pale swoln corpses, the victims tumble confusedly seaward along the Loire stream; the tide rolling them back: clouds of ravens darken the River; wolves prowl on the shoal-places: Carrier writes, "Quel torrent revolutionnaire, What a torrent of Revolution!" For the man is rabid; and the Time is rabid. These are the Noyades of Carrier; twenty-five by the tale, for what is done in darkness comes to be investigated in sunlight: (*Procès de Carrier*, 4 tomes, Paris, 1795) not to be forgotten for centuries' (3.5.iii).

*Les noyades, or, The Maid of La Vendée, or, The Boat of Death* was a play, performed at the Pavilion Theatre (Whitechapel Road, London) in July 1861 while, earlier, *The Noyades, or, Love and Gratitude: A Drama in Two Acts*, by Richard Brinsley Peake (1792–1847), had been first performed at the Lyceum Theatre, 7 July 1828. 'Les noyades' were discussed at length in 'La Vendée and Brittany', reviewing George Lowth's *The Wanderer in Western France* (1863) in *MP*, 26 August 1863, 3.

ACS did not mention this poem in *NPR*, an admission *PMG* on 2 November 1866 thought indicated 'Les noyades', and 'one or two other atrocious trifles', were 'indefensible' (1). *HEP* admired the anapaestic quatrains (iii.241).

## Itylus

First published *PB* 1. Drawing on Ovid's *Metamorphoses*, Bk 6, 412–674, the poem is a monologue spoken by Philomela, the nightingale, to her sister Procne, the swallow.

Procne's husband Tereus, king of Thrace, has raped Philomela and cut off her tongue. She describes her rape, however, in a tapestry (the 'woven web') and the sisters take revenge by killing Tereus and Procne's son Itylus (Itys, Itylos) and serving him to Tereus to eat. When Tereus discovers what he has eaten, he pursues the sisters intending more violence but the gods transform them all into birds. Thucydides in *The History of the Peloponnesian War* observes that 'Tereus lived in Daulis, part of what is now called Phocis, but which at that time was inhabited by Thracians' (Bk 2, Ch. 6). It is not, however, on the coast.

Recent literature on the topic of Philomela's story included Matthew Arnold's 'Philomela' (1853) and Catulle Mendès' *Philoméla: livre lyrique* (1863). Itylus had appeared in the first stanza of the first chorus of *AiC* (46). ACS might also be remembering Elektra's sympathy for Itys in Sophocles' *Elektra*, ll.145–52. 'Itylus' the poem was reprinted admiringly in *The Leeds Mercury*, 14 August 1866 (1), ten days after the more critical reviews of *PB* 1 in the London press. WMR quoted the poem in full in *Poems and Ballads: A Criticism* (London: Hotten, 1866), 76–8, describing it as a 'classic in sympathy, [which] forms a perfect lyrical music of regretful beauty and reluctant desire'. WMR observed that the speaker reproaches Procne 'in memory of the horrible fate dealt by that sister's hand to her own son Itylus' (72), which is a debateable point. *Poems and Ballads: A Criticism* had additionally reprinted only 'A Leave-Taking' and 'A Ballad of Burdens' in full. 'Itylus' appears in *Selections*.

## Anactoria

First published *PB* 1. ACS's speaker is the Greek lyric poet Sappho (born sometime between 630–612 BC; died *c.*570 BC). She addresses Anactoria/Anaktoria, often described as one of her female lovers, together with Atthis. The female poet Erinna was sometimes thought Sappho's lover and was, for instance, depicted in an embrace with Sappho in Simeon Solomon's watercolour *Sappho and Erinna in a Garden at Mytilene* (1864), now in Tate Britain. Erotion, from 'Eros', is another (male) lover and also the title of a poem in *PB* 1 intended to accompany Solomon's *Damon and Aglae* (exhibited 1866). ACS's first acquaintance with Sappho was probably in the widely-used Eton text, *Poetae Graeci* (Eton: Pote, 1789), which included two pieces: firstly, the poem known as 'To a Beloved Girl' or 'The Peer of Gods' (*φαίνεταί μοι κῆνος ἴσος θέοισιν* (*Poetae Graeci*, 181–2; *GL* 31, 78–81), sometimes called the 'Ode to Anactoria'); and secondly the 'Ode to Aphrodite' (*Ποικιλόθρον' ἀθανάτ' Ἀφρόδιτα, Poetae Graeci*, 182–3, *GL* 1). Note that in *Poetae Graeci*, Sappho's poetry is followed by a single poem by 'Erinna the Lesbian' (185). *LS* observes that ACS 'devoured even that didactic anthology the "Poetæ Græci," a book which he long afterwards said "had played a large part in fostering the love of poetry in his mind"' (9). For more on ACS and Sappho, see the headnote to 'On the Cliffs'.

The poem may be influenced by the Marquis de Sade (1740–1814) or at least by an idea of the Marquis de Sade. ACS recorded his first reading of de Sade's *Justine ou les malheurs de la vertu* in its 1797 version on 18 August 1862 (*SL*, i.53). He first found the volume ridiculous ('I never laughed so much in my life'), then disappointing: '*is this all?* 'Weep with me', ACS told Monckton Milnes, 'over a shattered idol!' (*SL*, i.54). ACS's de Sade enthusiasms certainly pre-dated this reading: *NWS* includes a previously unpublished poem, 'Charenton en 1810', dated 27 October 1861, about the asylum where de Sade was incarcerated from 1803 to 1814.

'Anactoria' was among the poems that stirred controversy for the initial reviewers of *PB* 1. JM observed that the 'only comfort about the present volume is that such a piece as "Anactoria" will be unintelligible to a great many people, and so will the fevered folly of "Hermaphroditus," as well as much else that is nameless and abominable' (*CH*, 24: see Introduction, xxii–xxiii above). In *NPR*, ACS remarked that he had been:

> informed, and have not cared to verify the assertion, that this poem has excited, among the chaste and candid critics of the day or hour or minute, a more vehement reprobation, a more virtuous horror, a more passionate appeal, than any other of my writing. Proud and glad as I must be of this distinction, I must yet, however reluctantly, inquire what merit or demerit has incurred such unexpected honour. I was not ambitious of it; I am not ashamed of it; but I am overcome by it. I have never lusted after the praise of reviewers; I have never feared their abuse; but I would fain know why the vultures should gather here of all places; what congenial carrion they smell, who can discern such (it is alleged) in any rose-bed. [...] What certain reviewers have imagined [this poem] to imply, I am incompetent to explain, and unwilling to imagine. I am evidently not virtuous enough to understand them. [...]
>
> In this poem I have simply expressed, or tried to express, that violence of affection between one and another which hardens into rage and deepens into despair. (7–8)

*PMG*, responding in 'Mr Swinburne's Defence' on 2 November 1866, did not think this persuasive. The truth was that Sappho's ideas 'have inspired Mr Swinburne to write some very dirty verses'. Part of ACS's case was that 'Anactoria' was Classical in nature (see *NPR*, 9–10) and schoolboys had to learn Sappho by heart. Such writing belonged in a respectable tradition, ACS continued, including Catullus 51. *HEP* could not be 'unreservedly enthusiastic' about ACS's heroic couplets, observing: 'The stopped form is not quite in his way, and the enjambed encourages, rather too much, his tendency to be *Isaeo torrentior.*' This is a reference to Juvenal's *Satire* III, ll.71–2: 'Quick of wit and of unbounded impudence, they are as ready of speech as Isaeus [from Samuel Johnson's 'London'], and more torrential', *Juvenal and Persius*, trans. G.G. Ramsay, Loeb Classical Library No. 6 (Cambridge, MA: Harvard University Press, 1918), 36–7.

Not all writing about Sappho just before *PB* 1 had been serious. There was a burlesque, *Sappho, or, Look Before you Leap*, by F.C. Burnand performed on 18 June 1866 at the Standard Theatre, Shoreditch, London. That presumably drew on the heterosexual version of Sappho and her alleged love for the ferryman, Phaon, over whom she was sometimes supposed to have committed suicide by leaping into the sea. The last lines of 'Anactoria' recall this legend (cf. Lord Houghton's 'A Dream of Sappho'). On the rhymed decasyllabic couplets, ACS thought that 'my own scheme of movement and modulation in Anactoria, which I consider original in structure and combination', formed the basis for the rhythms and metre of *TL* (cf. 'The Sailing of the Swallow', 313–31), *SL*, ii.74. Cf. also DGR's 'One Girl'.

*τίνος... φιλότατα*: 'Whose love have you caught in vain by persuasion?' (Haynes' translation of an emended corrupt line in Sappho's Aphrodite ode, 333). Cf. Wharton, 47 (and ll.18–19 of the poem).

*Paphos*: on Cyprus, the location of Aphrodite's birth from the sea. One Sapphic fragment (*GL* 35, 82) mentions this (*ἤ σε Κύπρος καὶ Πάφος ἢ Πάνορμος*: 'Or Cyprus or Paphos or Panormos [holds] you').

*Whodoth... Sappho?*: ACS's translation of 'τίς σ', ὦ | Ψάπφ', ἀδικήει' from the 'Ode to Aphrodite'. Cf. *GL* 1, 54–5.

*weary Pleiads seven*: see note on 559.

*Pierian*: a spring, sacred to the Muses (Sappho herself was sometimes described as the tenth Muse). Sappho mentions the roses of the spring in *GL* 55, 98, which is the elegy ACS is loosely recalling here:

*κατθάνοισα δὲ κείσῃ οὐδέ ποτα μναμοσύνα σέθεν*
*ἔσσετ' οὐδὲ ποκ' ὔστερον· οὐ γὰρ πεδέχῃς βρόδων*
*τῶν ἐκ Πιερίας· ἀλλ' ἀφάνης κὴν Ἀίδα δόμῳ*
*φοιτάσεις πεδ' ἀμαύρων νεκύων ἐκπεποταμένα.*

'But thou shalt ever lie dead, nor shall there be any remembrance of thee then or thereafter, for thou hast not of the roses of Pieria; but thou shalt wander obscure even in the house of Hades, flitting among the shadowy dead.'

(Wharton, 109)

## Hymn to Proserpine

First published *PB* 1. In 'Dedicatory Epistle' (1904), ACS paired this poem with 'Hymn of Man (During the Session in Rome of the Œcumenical Council)' included in *SBS*: they were 'twin poems of antiphonal correspondence in subject and in sound [...] the deathsong of spiritual decadence and the birthsong of spiritual renascence' (see 529). 'Vicisti galilæe' ('You have conquered, Galilean') are words attributed to Flavius Claudius Julianus (*c.* AD 331–63, reigned AD 361–3), 'Julian the Apostate', the last pagan emperor of Rome. ACS might be ironically remembering their use in Robert Burton's *The Anatomy of Melancholy* (1621) in the aptly titled subsection: 'Causes of Melancholy. God a Cause' (1862 edn, i.238).

The context to the paired-rhyme poem is, firstly, the Edict of Milan (AD 313), which preceded Julian the Apostate's birth. This was the defining statement of the toleration of Christianity in the Roman Empire made by the co-emperors Constantine I (a Christian) and Licinius that ended the 'Great' or Diocletianic Persecution of Christians (AD 303–13) in the empire. Nearly seventy years after the Edict, the Emperor

Theodosius I (AD 379–95) established Nicene Christianity as the official religion of the empire in AD 380. The following year he effectively banned pagan worship. William Bright's influential *History of the Church from the Edict of Milan AD 313, to the Council of Chalcedon AD 451* had first been published in Oxford in 1860. Proserpina, daughter of Ceres, goddess of crops and agriculture, is the queen of the underworld who spends half the year on earth (spring and summer) and half in the underworld. She is associated with sleep, death, poppies, and Lethe, the river of forgetfulness.

In 1862, the Lincoln College undergraduate Arthur Compton Auchmuty won Oxford's Newdigate prize for poetry on that year's set theme, *Julian the Apostate*. The poem was recited in the Sheldonian Theatre, Oxford, on 11 July 1862 and published in Oxford by T. & G. Shrimpton at the same time. It draws on Edward Gibbon's *Decline and Fall of the Roman Empire*, vol. 1 (1776), Chs 22–4. Auchmuty admires Julian's mind and sees his death as a conquest by Christ: 'Time, Galilean, Thine the conqueror's fadeless crown!' (16). Aubrey de Vere's *'Julian the Apostate', and 'The Duke of Mercia': Historical Dramas*, originally published 1822–3, were reissued in London by Pickering in 1858: two years later, Pickering published ACS's *'The Queen Mother' and 'Rosamond'*. ACS's poem was discussed in an admiring article (though it was critical of his pessimism): 'The Paganism of Swinburne', *London Review*, 14 (1867), 447–8. For a later view of ACS's pessimism, see Robert Shindler, 'The Theology of Mr Swinburne's Poems', *The Gentleman's Magazine*, 271 (1891), 459–71 and Introduction, xix above.

*give us... breath*: cf. Matthew 6:11.

*New Gods*: the speaker does not understand Christianity is monotheistic and/or misunderstands the Trinitarian faith expounded in the Nicene Creed.

*I say... peace*: cf. John 14:27.

*Laurel... May*: *Laurus nobilis* is an evergreen.

*all knees bend*: cf. Romans 14:11.

*standing... the end*: cf. Tennyson, 'St Simeon Stylites', l.160.

*Cytherean*: the epithet for the Greek Aphrodite and her Roman equivalent, Venus, from her birthplace Cythera (*Κύθηρα*).

*maiden thy mother*: the Virgin Mary, mother of Jesus and Queen of Heaven (and the counterpart of Proserpina in the speaker's imagination).

*mother of Rome*: ACS refers to the birth of Aphrodite/Venus from the foam (*Ἀφροδίτη*, foam-born) of the sea; she is the 'mother' of Rome through her son, Aeneas, the city's founder.

*a slave... rejected*: the speaker refers to the Virgin Mary and, in part, to two narratives of Mary's 'rejection': the story of Jesus' birth in a stable rather than an inn (Luke 2:7) and the Flight to Egypt (Matthew 2:13). Mary is not, though, a 'slave among slaves'.

*ψυχάριον... νεκρόν*: a fragment of Epictetus ('you are a little soul, lifting up a corpse'); cf. Romans 8:10.

## Hermaphroditus

First published *PB* 1. ACS's sonnets respond to the marble *Hermaphroditus* in the Louvre, Paris. The most familiar narrative of Hermaphroditus is found in Ovid, *Metamorphoses*, Bk 4.274–388 where Hermaphroditus is the child of Hermes and Aphrodite and displays features, as the name suggests, of both father and mother. The Louvre statue is a Roman copy of a 2nd-century Hellenistic original. *NPR* declared that 'Hermaphroditus' was Classical in origin, addressing a Platonic idea, which had similarly interested Shelley. ACS added:

> Sculpture I knew was a dead art; buried centuries deep out of sight, with no angel keeping watch over the sepulchre; its very grave-clothes divided by wrangling and impotent sectaries, and no chance anywhere visible of a resurrection. I knew that belief in the body was the secret of sculpture, and that a past age of ascetics could no more attempt or attain it than the present age of hypocrites; I knew that modern moralities and recent religions were, if possible, more averse and alien to this purely physical and pagan art than to the others; but how far averse I did not know. There is nothing lovelier, as there is nothing more famous, in later Hellenic art, than the statue of Hermaphroditus. No one would compare it with the greatest works of Greek sculpture. No one would lift Keats on a level with Shak[e]speare. But the Fates have allowed us to possess at once Othello and Hyperion, Theseus and Hermaphroditus. At Paris, at Florence, at Naples, the delicate divinity of this work has always drawn towards it the eyes of artists and poets. A creature at once foul and dull enough to extract from a sight so lovely, from a thing so noble, the faintest, the most fleeting idea of impurity, must be, and must remain, below comprehension and below remark. It is incredible that the meanest of men should derive from it any other than the sense of high and grateful pleasure. Odour and colour and music are not more tender or more pure.
>
> (*NPR*, 17–18)

ACS visited Paris in March 1863 with James Abbott McNeill Whistler (1834–1903) whom he had first met in July 1862 (cf. 'Before the Mirror', 163–4). *PB* 1 included 'Fragoletta', on a hermaphrodite. ACS's essay on 'The Poems of Dante Gabriel Rossetti' began with a meditation on the hermaphrodite-like nature of great artists, alluding to Shelley's 'The Witch of Atlas' and Gautier. ACS's statement in 'Tennyson and Musset', *FR*, 29 (February 1881), 129–53, that 'great poets are bisexual; male and female at once' is often adduced in relation to 'Hermaphroditus' though it must be remembered that ACS meant 'bisexual' in that essay in terms of parenthood. The sentence continues: 'motherly not less than fatherly in their instincts towards little children; from the day when Homer put Astyanax into the arms of Hector to the day when Hugo found the sweetest of all cradle songs on the lips of the death-stricken Fantine' (130–1). On sonnets with only four rhymes, cf. DGR's *The House of Life*. Cf. also DGR's sonnets for pictures, 'A Venetian Pastoral by Giorgione' and 'An Allegorical Dance of Women by Andrea Mantegna', both on pictures in the Louvre. See also Catherine Maxwell, 'Swinburne, Gautier, and the Louvre Hermaphrodite', *N&Q*, 40 (1993), 49–50.

*Salmacis*: in Ovid, the nymph who loves Hermaphroditus. She dives into a pool to reach him, and is merged into him: the combined Hermaphroditus then speaks to his parents, but not in a man's voice and the pool thereafter is contaminated.

## The Leper

First published *PB* 1. This poem exists in an early 8-stanza draft as 'The Vigil', written on writing paper of the Oxford Union Society, watermarked '1857' and now in the BL, Ashley MS 1840. ACS invented the Old French source, which reads as follows:

> At this time, there was in this country a great number of lepers, which made the king greatly unhappy, seeing that God must be greatly vexed. Now it happened that a noble lady called Yolande de Sallières was infected and wholly wasted by this vile disease; all her friends and family, with the wrath of God before their eyes, ordered her from their houses and would neither welcome nor comfort one who was punished by God and to all men stinking and disgusting. This lady had been very beautiful and with a graceful figure; she had had a full form and a lascivious life. None of the lovers, however, who had often embraced and tenderly kissed her would give room to so ugly a woman and so wretched a sinner. Only one clerk who had first been her servant and then her go-between in matters of love received her, hiding her in a small cabin. There the great sinner died in terrible misery a bad death: and after her this clerk died who, from great love, had for six months attended, washed, dressed and undressed her with his own hands every day. They even say that this wicked man and cursed clerk, remembering the great beauty of this woman, now passed away and ravaged, delighted frequently to kiss her on her foul, leprous mouth and embrace her gently with a lover's hands. Thus, he died of the same dreadful sickness. This occurred near Fontainebellant in Gastinois. And when King Philip heard this tale, he marvelled greatly.
>
> *The Great Chronicles of France*, 1505

Leprosy was not only a medieval disease and ACS wrote this poem when it remained a threat in British colonies. A 244-page *Report on Leprosy by the Royal College of Physicians, Prepared for Her Majesty's Secretary of State for the Colonies* was published by Her Majesty's Stationery Office in 1867. T.S. Eliot, in 'Swinburne as Poet' (1921), observed that 'a volume of selections which should certainly contain *Atalanta in Calydon* entire', and '*The Leper, Laus Veneris* and *The Triumph of Time*' (*SW*, 144). Cf. 'Dead Love', 33–6.

*Will... right?*: cf. the end of Robert Browning's 'Porphyria's Lover' (1836/42), with which this poem might be compared, not least as a 'Madhouse cell'.

## Before the Mirror

First published *PB* 1 though the fourth and sixth stanzas had been published in the *Catalogue* of the Royal Academy Exhibition for 1865 in relation to Whistler's picture then called *The Little White Girl* (*Catalogue*, 28). Note the exhibition also included Frederick Sandys' 'Gentle Spring' (now in the Ashmolean), illustrating ACS's lines 'O virgin mother! of gentle days' (*Catalogue*, 20).

ACS wrote to Whistler on 2 April 1865 saying: 'Here are the verses, written the first thing after breakfast and brought off at once. I could not do anything prettier, but if you don't find any serviceable as an Academy-Catalogue motto and don't care to get all this printed under the picture, tell me *at once* that I may try my hand at it tomorrow again. Gabriel praises them highly, and I think myself the idea is pretty: I know it was entirely and only suggested to me by the picture, where I found at once the metaphor of the rose and the notion of sad and glad mystery in the face languidly contemplative of its own phantom and all other things seen by their phantoms. I wanted to work this out more fully and clearly, and insert the reflection of the picture and the room; but Gabriel says it is full long for its purpose already, and there is nothing I can supplant' (*SL*, i.118–20). ACS was, at least supposedly, responding to Whistler's oil-on-canvas, *The Little White Girl* (1864), now *Symphony in White, No. 2: The Little White Girl*, Tate Britain (No. 3418). Exhibited at the 97th Exhibition of the Royal Academy of Arts in 1865, the picture was analysed by *The Times* as an example of the 'strange painter's genius': both 'slovenly' and 'likely to impress itself deeply on minds finely attuned to the delicate harmonies of colour and the subtlest suggestions of form' (24 May 1865, 6). ACS's poem in fact drew partly on an earlier work, 'The Dreamer', which Wise claims was written in 1862 (*Bibliography*, ii.175). It comprises a version of the last three stanzas of 'Before the Mirror' with an additional penultimate stanza:

A painted dream, beholden
  Of no man's eye,
Framed in far memories, golden
  As hope when nigh
Holds fast her soul that hears
Faint waters flow like tears
By shores no sunbeam cheers
  From all the sky.
(Wise, *Bibliography*, ii.175)

Whistler is usually said to have had ACS's poem written on gold paper and attached to the frame (*The Times* does not mention this though it explains ACS's subtitle. DGR also used gold paper for poems appended to frames). ACS sent the poem in 1865 to John Ruskin (*UL*, iii.296) who would much later be taken to court over his views on Whistler. ACS, at the time of composition, was friends with Whistler, calling him 'Father' in correspondence (e.g. letter of 3 January 1866 available from <http://www.whistler.arts.gla.ac.uk>). The relationship deteriorated after ACS criticized the painter, in 'Mr Whistler's Lecture on Art', *FR*, 43 (June 1888), 745–51, for trivializing art, an exclusive concentration on Japanese designs, and an overall 'gospel of the grin' (751). Note ACS's 1888 poem in *PP*, 'To James McNeill Whistler': 'Fly away, butterfly, back to Japan' (150). Cf. DGR's two poems both called 'The Portrait'.

## Dolores

First published *PB* 1. On the likely personal background to this poem, see headnote to 'The Triumph of Time', 566–7. ACS mimics liturgical language and a hymn/prayer to the Blessed Virgin Mary in a poem that addresses a mysterious pain-bringing divinity associated with paganism and sado-masochism. 'Our Lady of Seven Sorrows' (Notre-Dame des sept douleurs) is an ancient name of the Virgin Mary in Catholic Christianity; the association between Mary and dolour is ancient too (*Mater dolorosa*). In DGR's painting *The Girlhood of Mary Virgin* (1849; reframed 1864), the palm leaves in the foreground are twined with a ribbon marked 'Tot dolores tot gaudia' ('so many sorrows; so many joys'). ACS noted this painting in 'The Poems of Dante Gabriel Rossetti'. See also DGR's 'Ave' (initially conceived in 1847) on the seven joys and sorrows, and eventually in seven stanzas. There is much biblical allusion in 'Dolores', to *BCP*, and Christian liturgy.

Writing to Charles Augustus Howell in May/June 1865, ACS sent some of 'Dolores' promising more in return for Howell's flogging writing. ACS wanted a 'little dialogue (imaginary) between schoolmaster and boy—from the first summons [...] to the last *cut* and painful buttoning up—a rebuke or threat at every lash (and *plenty* of them) and a shriek of agonized appeal from the boy in reply' (*SL*, i.123). ACS linked the poem with de Sade (*SL*, i.123). There is also a Baudelairean register: see ACS's admiration for 'Les litanies de Satan' and 'À une Madone: Ex-Voto dans le goût Espagnol' in *The Spectator* (26–32 above). *NPR* said: 'I have striven here to express that transient state of spirit through which a man may be supposed to pass, foiled in love and weary of loving, but not yet in sight of rest; seeking refuge in those "violent delights" which "have violent ends," in fierce and frank sensualities which at least profess to be no more than they are [...] It sports with sorrow, and jests against itself; cries out for freedom and confesses the chain; decorates with the name of goddess, crowns anew as the mystical Cotytto, some woman, real or ideal, in whom the pride of life with its companion lusts is incarnate [...] She is the darker Venus, fed with burnt-offering and blood-sacrifice' (12).

*HEP* thought the Praed-derived stanza of this poem (with ACS's innovation of a shorter final line), and its reusing for the 'Dedication' (180–2), the 'most striking triumph' of *PB* 1's prosody (iii.344). William Mackworth Praed (1802–39) employed a version of the octosyllabic stanza with ababcdcd rhyme schemes including, as a single example, 'Childhood and His Visitors'. 'Dolores' is a good instance of how daring ACS's rhymes could be ('no more is...Dolores'); rhymes that, in another context, might be comic.

*seventy times seven*: cf. Matthew 18:22.

*tower...ivory*: cf. Song of Solomon 7:4.

*Libitina...Greek*: Libitina is the Roman goddess of funerals, often associated with Venus; Priapus is the Greek god of gardens and fertility, associated with obscenity because of his outsized permanent erection.

*wine shed for me*: cf. Jesus' words at the Last Supper (e.g. Mark 14:23–5).

*corpses or wives*: ACS may be remembering that Mary Gordon had been turned into the wife of another (i.e. the line does not mean that marriage kills love in any general sense). Rikky Rooksby observes that the loved one turned into a corpse may be Edith Swinburne, ACS's sister, who died on 25 September 1863: 'A.C. Swinburne's *Lesbia Brandon* and the Death of Edith Swinburne', *N&Q*, 40 (1993), 487–90.

*Thalassian*: Venus/Aphrodite. ACS also wrote 'Pan and Thalassius: A Lyrical Idyl', *PB* 3, and 'Thalassius', 368–80.

*gardens... torches*: recollection of Nero's notorious use of human torches to light his gardens. See note below.

*harp-player... tyrant*: Nero (AD 37–68), Roman emperor associated with tyranny and excess, and popularly remembered for playing the fiddle while Roman burned.

*Vestal*: the chaste Vestal maidens maintained worship at the shrine of the goddess Vesta in Rome.

*Alciphron once or Arisbe*: lovers. The former is the name of a Classical Greek sophist, believed author of a set of fictional letters. See *Alciphron's Epistles in which are Described, the Domestic Manners, the Courtesans, and Parasites of Greece Now first Translated from the Greek* (London: Robinson *et al.*, 1791). Arisbe is noted in Pseudo-Apollodorus' *Library*, 3.12.5 as one of the wives of Priam, king of Troy.

*garden-god... fig-leaves*: cf. Genesis 3:7.

*Nam te... Carm. xviii*: ACS quotes from what at this point was believed to be one of Catullus' poems about Priapus. 'Thou, who in towns, that deck the shelly [oystery] coast | Of much-fam'd Hellespont, art worshipp'd most', Nott, ii.209.

*myrtles with Venus*: Plutarch, *Roman Questions*, 20, notes that myrtles were sacred to Venus (as Bacchus is regularly depicted crowned by vine leaves).

*Ipsithilla*: lover to whom Catullus 32 is addressed ('Amabo, mea dulcis Ipsitilla').

*Dindymus*: shrine of the Mother Goddess Cybele. Cf. Catullus 35.

*shaken*: some initial copies had 'skaken'.

*rod... hisses*: cf. Exodus 7:10.

*They shall... endure?*: cf. 1 Peter 1:24–5.

*Lampsacus... Aphaca*: the city of Lampsacus on the Hellespont was where Priapus was honoured, as described in Catullus 18 (cf. Pausanias, *Description of Greece*, 18.2–5, on the city's threat of destruction). 'The orgies of Aphaca, near Heliopolis in Phoenicia [were abolished by Constantine]', observed Algernon Herbert in *Nimrod: A Discourse on Certain Passages of History and Fable*, 4 vols (London: Priestley, 1828): 'Aphaca was not a city, but a paradise of pleasure consecrated to Venus and Adonis [...] the word aphaca signifies an embrace in Phoenician, the place being so called because Venus there embraced Adonis either for the first or for the last time' (ii.321).

*Cotytto... Ashtaroth*: Cotytto is an ancient Greek/Thracian goddess of lewdness, celebrated in nocturnal orgiastic rites. Astarte is an ancient Middle Eastern goddess of sexual love sometimes known as Astoreth (though this name may be a Hebrew repudiation of a corrupt divinity: cf. 1 Kings 11:33).

On 2 December 1868, ACS wrote to George Powell marking the '54th anniversary of the death [...] of that great and good man, the Marquis de Sade. I wish we were together and could devise some appropriate ceremony to celebrate the festival of that apostle and confessor of the faith as it is in Priapus. If I were even in London I would observe it by a partial reproduction (with female aid) of the rites of Artemis Orthia, mixed with those of the Europian [*sic*] Cotytto and the Asiatic Aphrodite of Aphaca' (*SL*, i.312). ACS fancied that de Sade was a descendent of Venus and Priapus (*SL*, i.75).

*tares...grain*: cf. Matthew 13:29.

## The Garden of Proserpine

First published *PB* 1. *NPR* remarked of this poem that it was 'expressive, as I meant they should be, of that brief total pause of passion and of thought, when the spirit, without fear or hope of good things or evil, hungers and thirsts only after the perfect sleep' (13). On the goddess Proserpine, see notes to 'Hymn to Proserpine'. Haynes (355) compares ACS's use of three consecutive rhymes (here, ababcccb) to Christina Rossetti's similar usage. The trimeters involve much hypercatalexis.

*earth her mother*: Proserpine is the daughter of Ceres, goddess of crops, harvest, and the earth's fertility.

## Dedication, 1865

First published *PB* 1, which was a volume with the initial inscription: 'To | My Friend | Edward Burne Jones | These poems | Are affectionately and Admiringly | Dedicated' (v). The painter, designer, and stained-glass maker EBJ had become friends with ACS in the early 1860s, presumably through DGR. They shared an interest in republicanism and Italy. Recent evidence suggests that in the early 1860s, with mutual friends including Simeon Solomon, George Powell, and Charles Augustus Howell, ACS and EBJ shared interests in smut. 'What a dreadful gift was yr last letter', EBJ wrote to ACS in the early 1860s in one of the few surviving letters: 'it lies before me now with its respectable edge of black and its wicked contents like...a sinful clergyman'. See John Christian, 'Speaking of Kisses in Paradise: Burne-Jones' Friendship with Swinburne', *JWMS*, 31 (1998), 14–24 (17). The stanza form is the same as for 'Dolores' (see 165–76). The 'Dedication, 1865' refers to female figures in *PB* 1. There were poems called 'Faustine', 'Fragoletta', 'Dolores', and 'Félise': Yolande appeared in the prose 'source' for 'The Leper' and Juliette is mentioned in 'Rococo'. 'Juliette' is also the name of de Sade's amoral heroine. *ACP* was dedicated to the memory of EBJ and WM.

*myrtles are sterile*: remembering myrtles as sacred to Venus.

## FROM 'MR ARNOLD'S *NEW POEMS*' (1867)

First published *FR*, 2 (October 1867), 414–45 as a review of Matthew Arnold's *New Poems* (London: Macmillan, 1867)—the copytext here. *New Poems* was advertised as 'New, except seven reprinted from *Empedocles on Etna* (London) 1852, viz.: "Empedocles on Etna", "Human Life", "Youth and Calm", "Youth's Agitations", "Lines Written in Kensington Gardens", "The Second Best", and "Progress"'. ACS reprinted the essay in *ES*, 123–83.

ACS may have heard Arnold lecture at Oxford after he was appointed Professor of Poetry in 1857 (see *SPP*, 36). He regarded *Merope* as a failure and *AiC* was intended to succeed where Arnold had failed: see headnote to *AiC*, 551–3. Nevertheless, ACS remained an admirer of some of Arnold's poetry, especially the early lyrics. His discussion of Arnold in 1867 allowed him to reflect again on the poetry of doubt and the legacy of Wordsworth. ACS's assertion that doubt was a weak basis for art may be compared with ACS's praise of Byron's sincerity (110–12). ACS also deplored, specifically in Byron, the 'hankering and restless habit of half fearful retrospect towards the unburied corpses of old creeds' in 'The Poems of Dante Gabriel Rossetti', *FR*, 41 (1871), 551–79 (583). Note that *New Poems* was the first volume to include Arnold's 'Dover Beach' (date of composition uncertain) with its account of the withdrawing Sea of Faith.

On 9 October 1867, ACS told Arnold that 'it gives me real & great pleasure to know that you have derived any satisfaction from my article; & especially that my choice of extracts accords with your own judgement, as I always have great regard to a man's own preferences in the matter of his work' (*UL*, i.110). He also noted that he had to sacrifice for space reasons a 'long passage on speculative English poetry, pitting for example your "Empedocles" as a spiritual study against Tennyson's "In Memoriam" on this hand & Browning's "Death in the Desert", "Easter Day" &c. on the other' (*UL*, i.111).

*perfection…workman*: cf. Yeats' 'The Choice' (*The Winding Stair and Other Poems*, 1933): 'The intellect of man is forced to choose | Perfection of the life, or of the work', ll.1–2.

*winning their suffrages*: cf. debates about electoral reform leading to the passing of the Second Reform Act in July 1867. ACS noted an advertisement for *New Poems c.*17 July 1867 (*SL*, i.253).

*not that…more*: cf. *Julius Caesar*, 3.2.21–2.

*tongues…angels*: cf. 1 Corinthians 13:1. On *FR*'s relationship with anonymous reviewing, see E.M. Everett, *The Party of Humanity: The 'Fortnightly Review' and its Contributors* (Chapel Hill: University of North Carolina Press, 1939).

*fifty copies…sold*: Arnold, *New Poems* (London: Macmillan, 1867), from the first note (to 'Empedocles'); unpaginated.

*'I hope…proofs'*: cf. Pompey's 'Why, very well; I hope here be truths', *Measure for Measure*, 2.1.122.

*former preface*: the 'Preface' to the first edition of *Poems* (1853).

*rock … land*: Isaiah 32:2.

*fortitude … grey*: from Arnold's 'Marcus Aurelius', *Essays in Criticism* (London: Macmillan, 1865), 272.

*'Ask … when known'*: 'Empedocles on Etna', l.111.

*Archbishop Trench*: 'Observe, for instance, how different is the word "self-sufficient" as used by us, and by the heathen nations of antiquity. The Greek word exactly corresponding to it is a word of honour, and applied to men in their praise. And indeed it was the glory of the heathen philosophy to teach a man to find his resources in his own bosom, to be thus sufficient for himself; and seeing that a true centre without him and above him, a centre in God, had not been revealed to him, it was no shame for him to seek it there; better this, such as it was, than no centre at all. But the gospel has taught us another lesson, to find our sufficiency in God: and thus "self-sufficient," which with the Greek was a word in honourable use, is not so with us. Self-sufficiency is not a quality which any man desires now to be attributed to him. We have a feeling about the word, which causes it to carry its own condemnation with it; and its different uses, for honour once, for reproach now, do in fact ground themselves on the central differences of heathenism and Christianity', Richard Chenevix Trench, *On the Study of Words*, 4th edn (London: Parker, 1853), 56. The NT Greek αὐτάρκεια ('autarkeia') means self-sufficiency, independence, a condition of perfection in which no support is required: see, for instance, 2 Corinthians 9:8.

*To tunes … chime'*: 'Empedocles on Etna', l.196.

*'we do … we do'*: 'Empedocles on Etna', ll.237–8.

*'the life … rain'*: 'Resignation', l.195.

*David Gray*: (1838–61), minor Scottish poet, friend of Robert Buchanan and Sydney Dobell, who had approached ACS's friend Richard Monkton Milnes for literary advice. Gray's *The Luggie: and Other Poems* with a memoir by James Hedderwick, and a prefatory notice by R.M. Milnes (Cambridge: Macmillan, 1862) was posthumous.

*Catacombs … Good Shepherd*: 'The Good Shepherd with the Kid'.

*'The leader … divine'*: 'Empedocles on Etna', ll.447–8.

*'The meed … tear'*: Milton, 'Lycidas', l.14.

*'land … off'*: Isaiah 13:17.

*'Year of the World'*: William Bell Scott's *The Year of the World: A Philosophical Poem on 'Redemption from the Fall'* (Edinburgh: Tait, Simpkin, and Marshall, 1846).

*Coleridge to Geneviève*: see Coleridge's 'Genevieve' published first in *The Morning Chronicle*, 15 July 1793, as 'Irregular Sonnet'.

*chorus of a Dejaneira*: Arnold's 'Fragment of Chorus of a "Dejaneira"' (1867): Deianira is the wife of Hercules who kills herself after inadvertently causing Hercules' death with the Shirt of Nessus.

*'immured … present'*: Arnold, 'Growing Old' (1867), ll.23–4.

'*the soul... hurt me*': Arnold, 'Joubert', *Essays in Criticism* (London: Macmillan, 1865), 240.

## FROM *WILLIAM BLAKE: A CRITICAL ESSAY, WITH ILLUSTRATIONS FROM BLAKE'S DESIGNS IN FACSIMILE* (LONDON: HOTTEN, 1868)

ACS shared his interest in the then little-known poet and artist William Blake (1757–1827) with significant friends including DGR and WMR as well as with Hotten, his publisher, who was the first to reprint a whole work by Blake after his death (*The Marriage of Heaven and Hell*, 1867). DGR had extensively contributed to the editing of the selected works of Blake that were included as the second volume of the posthumously published biography, *LWB*. WMR had also helped with that biography, as had Gilchrist's widow Anne, and WMR subsequently edited, with a prefatory memoir, *The Poetical Works of William Blake, Lyrical and Miscellaneous*, for Bell and Son, London, in 1874. ACS read that edition in draft, admiring not least the fact that it gave 'at once a fuller and a truer image of the real William Blake than either Gilchrist or I have succeeded in realizing or reproducing' (*SL*, ii.348, letter of 30 October 1874). ACS thought WMR good on Blake's sanity, which ACS also discussed in *William Blake: A Critical Essay*.

The *Essay* was (almost?) ready to be seen by WMR by 31 January 1864 (*SL*, i.93) and was probably sent to an unidentified publisher on 22 February 1864 (*SL*, i.95—though it is not certain this letter was posted). The essay did not appear until 1868 when, with a dedication to WMR, it was published by Hotten. The delay was caused in part by changing publishers during the *PB* 1 trouble. The *Essay*, initially conceived for a periodical, is a book-length review of *LWB*. In the portion reproduced here, ACS explains what he means by 'art for art's sake', not least by envisaging the opposing voices of those who supposedly require art to have moral purpose first and foremost (cf. 'Victor Hugo's *L'Année terrible*', 288–92 and Introduction, xxiv–xxv). ACS had researched Blake carefully, including reading what is now sometimes called the 'Rossetti manuscript' (*Notebook of William Blake*, BL Add MS 49460); he often uses slightly different texts from those reproduced in *LWB*, which may be a tactful way of avoiding notice of DGR's sometimes creative approach to Blake's originals.

'*poor Fine Arts... away*': unidentified.

*Savonarola... Boccaccio*: 'The terms fanatic, barbarian, destroyed of our ancient grandeur, were liberally bestowed on Savonarola. If an ancient manuscript had been lost, it was straightway declared to have been burned by Savonarola. If an edition of Boccaccio had become very scarce, it was certainly destroyed by the Friar', Pasquale Villari, *The History of Girolamo Savonarola and of his Times*, trans. Leonard Horner, 2 vols (London: Longman, Green, Longman, Roberts, & Green, 1863), ii.134.

*certain... leaders*: it is characteristic of ACS not to name whose argument, exactly, he is contending against or where he found it.

*Knox... 'Pléiade'*: John Knox (*c.*1514–72), Scottish Reformation leader and preacher; Pierre de Ronsard (1524–85), French poet who belonged to the poetic group, La Pléiade.

*Albigeois... Aucassin*: ACS refers to what were then thought to be heretics of southern France (mostly so-called 'Cathars') and the victims of La Croisade des Albigeois (1208–29), a violent campaign that attempted to exterminate them. The Albigeois are associated with the 12th/13th-century narrative *Aucassin et Nicolette* (see R. Griffin, '*Aucassin et Nicolette* and the Albigensian Crusade', *Modern Language Quarterly*, 26 (1965), 243–56). ACS mentioned to Edwin Hatch on 17 February 1858 that '*The Albigenses* are not yet organised; I must read more, and then dash at it in wrath' (*SL*, i.18). He might have been planning a long poem on this (*SL*, i.18n). Walter Pater's *Studies in the History of the Renaissance* (London: Macmillan, 1873) began with a chapter on 'Aucassin et Nicolette' (1–17), which subsequently became 'Two Early French Stories' in later editions ('Two Early French Stories' also discussed the story of Amis and Amile, which, like ACS's 'The Leper', represents compassion for a leper). Frederick II (1194–1250), the celebrated, scholarly Holy Roman Emperor, was particularly associated with the Sicilian School of poetry, founded in his own court. DGR included Frederick's 'Canzone: On his Lady in Bondage' in *The Early Italian Poets* (London: Smith, Elder, 1861), 19–21.

*appalling passage*: unknown (and unlike Chaucer's views). ACS must be thinking of a poem now not attributed to Chaucer.

*Hörsel legend*: see headnote to 'Laus Veneris', 563.

*famous speech*: 'Paradise? What have I to do there? I seek not to win Paradise, so I have Nicolette my sweet friend whom I love so well. For none go to Paradise but I'll tell you who. Your old priests and your old cripples, and the halt and maimed, who are down on their knees day and night, before altars and in old crypts; these also that wear mangy old cloaks, or go in rags and tatters, shivering and shoeless and showing their sores, and who die of hunger and want and cold and misery. Such are they who go to Paradise; and what have I to do with them? Hell is the place for me', Aucassin in *Aucassin and Nicolette*, trans. F.W. Bourdillon (London: Kegan Paul, Trench, Trübner, 1908), 23.

*'monkeys... brick'*: an image from Blake's *Marriage of Heaven and Hell*.

*'pantopragmatic'*: 'of or relating to "pantopragmatics" (*obs.*). Now more generally: interfering in or occupied with everything; incessantly meddling': *OED* gives the first usage as 1861.

*'Art the handmaid of Religion'*: a commonplace often associated with post-Enlightenment conceptions of the place of religion in the Middle Ages and Renaissance.

*all... to her*: cf. Luke 12:31.

*taken away... has*: cf. Matthew 25:29.

*comment... passage*: on the false rumour of the death of Baudelaire, see the note to '*Ave Atque Vale*', first published in January 1868, 621, and my 'Note on the Texts', xlix.

*'Ergo... vale'*: 'Therefore forever brother, hail and farewell' (see headnote to '*Ave Atque Vale*', 621).

*l'hérésie de l'enseignement*: Baudelaire speaking of Gautier; see Baudelaire's *L'Art romantique* (Paris: Conard, 1925), 157.

*pluck... mills*: the story of Samson in Judges 13–16.

*Victor Hugo... moral*: cf. 'Victor Hugo's *L'Année terrible*', 288–92 and Introduction, xxiv-xxv.

*Cave canem*: Lat. 'beware of the dog'.

*honey-cake*: in the *Aeneid*, Bk VI, Cerberus, the many-headed dog guarding the entrance to the underworld, is drugged with honey-cake so that Aeneas may pass ('cui vates, horrere videns iam colla colubris, | melle soporatam et medicatis frugibus offam | obicit', ll.419–21.)

*fourfold... vision*: cf. Blake's *Milton*, Bk 1, Plate 20, ll.38–9 ('Gates open behind Satans Seat to the City of Golgonooza | Which is the spiritual fourfold London, in the loins of Albion').

*the Poetic Genius... derivative*: all from *LWB*, ii.82 and, in turn, from *The Marriage of Heaven and Hell*.

*'antinomian mysticism'*: Antinomianism is a term in Christian doctrinal history for the view that, as God's gift of faith is held to be sufficient for a believer's salvation, adherence to a moral code is irrelevant. It is an extreme (heretical) form of the belief that justification is through faith alone.

*contraries*: remembering Blake's 'Without Contraries is no progression', Plate 3, *The Marriage of Heaven and Hell*.

*'Après?'*: 'After' with the sense of 'And so?'

*French essayist*: unidentified.

*Balzac... researches*: on Balzac and Swedenborg, cf. Balzac's novel *Louis Lambert* (1832). ACS was from early on an admirer of *La Comédie humaine* (e.g. ACS's letter of 16 December 1859, noting DGR's enthusiasm for Balzac and encouraging William Bell Scott to read him, *SL*, i.28).

*prose Shakespeare*: Charles Lamb called Thomas Heywood (*c.*1570–1641) 'a sort of *prose* Shakespeare', *The Works of Charles Lamb*, ed. T.N. Talfourd, 2 vols, *Essays of Elia* (New York: Harper, 1838), ii.369.

*all Balzac's... reject*: see Robert Browning, 'Bishop Blougram's Apology' (1864):

> We mortals cross the ocean of this world
> Each in his average cabin of a life;
> The best's not big, the worst yields elbow-room.
> Now for our six months' voyage—how prepare?
> You come on shipboard with a landsman's list
> Of things he calls convenient: so they are!
> An India screen is pretty furniture,

A piano-forte is a fine resource,
All Balzac's novels occupy one shelf,
The new edition fifty volumes long;
(ll.100–9)

*The pure... asserts*: cf. ACS's criticism of Hugo in his essay 'Victor Hugo: *L'Homme qui rit*' (*FR*, vi, July 1869, 73–81): 'It may be there is perceptible in Victor Hugo something too much of positive intention' (81).

*straight... crooked*: cf. Isaiah 40:4.

*untimely death... writer*: Alexander Gilchrist (b.1828) died of scarlet fever on 30 November 1861.

*end... ball*: from 'To the Christians' at the head of Plate 77 of Blake's *Jerusalem* (*c.*1804–20).

*easier... pipe*: *Hamlet*, 3.2.357–8.

*Blair, of Hayley, or of Young*: Blake's work with Robert Blair was principally *The Grave: A Poem Illustrated by Twelve Etchings Executed by Louis Schiavonetti, from the Original Inventions of William Blake* (London: Bensley, 1808): see *LWB*, Ch. 24, 'Designs for Blair'. His work with William Hayley included illustrations to Hayley's *Designs to a Series of Ballads* (Chichester: Seagrave, 1802); and with Edward Young, *The Complaint, and the Consolation, or, Night Thoughts, with 43 Engravings by William Blake* (London: Noble, 1797).

*Chap. xxxv*: 'Mad or Not Mad'.

*The good work... over-estimate*: praise of DGR, who principally edited the selection of Blake's work in *LWB*.

*'dieu ganache des bourgeois'*: 'the elephant-headed god of the bourgeoisie'.

*ἐντὶ... κάθηται*: Theocritus, *Idylls*, 1.17–18 '[I durst not, Shepherd, O I durst not pipe | At noontide; fearing Pan, who at that hour | Rests from the toils of hunting.] Harsh is he; | Wrath at his nostrils aye sits sentinel', *Theocritus: Translated into English Verse* by C.S. Calverley (London: Bell, 1892), 2.

*Ideas of Good and Evil*: this is the title DGR uses from Blake's *Notebook* for the selection of Blake's poems after *Songs* in volume II of *LWB*.

*dignity of a reprint*: ACS may refer to James J.G. Wilkinson's edition (London, 1839) or the more recent *Songs of Innocence and Experience: With Other Poems* with a Preface by R.H. Shepherd and wood-engraved vignettes throughout (London: Pickering, 1866).

*text... lamb*: Isaiah 11:6 and 65:25.

*'And there... weep'*: Blake, 'Night', cf. *LWB*, ii.39.

*'And we... grove'*: Blake, 'The Little Black Boy', cf. *LWB*, ii.30.

*last... Innocence*: in DGR's version, 'The Voice of the Ancient Bard'.

*first... second series*: 'Introduction', beginning, as below: 'Hear the voice of the bard!'

*'Hear...renew!'*: Blake, 'Introduction' to *Songs of Experience*, cf. *LWB*, first two stanzas, ii.47.

*Word...children*: 'Word' the language of the opening of John's gospel; 'dwellers... earth' can be compared to Isaiah 18:3; 'made...children' to Matthew 18:3.

*blind...hear*: cf. Luke 7:22.

*'O Earthy...day'*: the second two stanzas (cf. *LWB*, ii.47).

*'Prisoned...ancient men'*: Blake, 'Earth's Answer', cf. *LWB*, ii.48.

*'Can...plough?'*: Blake, 'Earth's Answer'.

*refluent wave*: cf. 'then the refluent sea, | May at God's pleasure work amendment here', H.F. Cary's translation of Dante, *Paradiso*, 21:92–3.

*MS....pains*: for discussion of Blake's revisions in the *Notebook*, see Martin K. Nurmi, 'Blake's Revisions of the Tyger', *PMLA*, 71 (1956), 669–85 and *The Note-Book of William Blake, called The Rossetti Manuscript*, ed. Geoffrey Keynes (London: Nonesuch, 1935).

*'Did he . . . make thee?'*: 'The Tyger', ll.19–20.

*'rock of offence'*: 1 Peter 2:8.

*'Burnt...fire'*: cf. the version of this stanza from 'The Tiger' in *LWB*, ii.59: 'In what distant deeps or skies | Burned that fire within thine eyes? | On what wings dared he aspire? | What the hand dared seize the fire?'

*'Soon spreads...shade'*: Blake, 'The Human Abstract', cf. *LWB*, ii.64.

*'the priests...dawn'*: Blake, 'A Song of Liberty'.

*'miscreative brain'*: cf. Shelley, *Prometheus Unbound*, I.448.

*'Gods...sea'*: 'The Human Abstract'.

*once fairly afloat...prophecy*: the subject of Ch. 3 of ACS's study ('The Prophet Books').

*'to work...sleep'*: Blake, 'To Tirzah'.

*transcriber and editor*: DGR.

## FROM 'NOTES ON DESIGNS OF THE OLD MASTERS AT FLORENCE' (1868)

First published *FR*, 4 (July, 1868), 16–40 and subsequently reprinted in *ES* (copytext is *FR* here). ACS visited Florence in spring 1864, writing to Lord Houghton on 31 March about his two visits to Landor on via della Chiesa (*SL*, i.96–8). In the essay, ACS drew on Gautier's practices as a critic (cf. Michael Clifford Spencer, *The Art Criticism of Théophile Gautier* (Genève: Librairie Droz, 1969)) and in turn might have inspired Walter Pater, including *Studies in the History of the Renaissance* (1873) though early Pater biographers, including those who knew him, did not make this link. ACS told JM on 11 April 1873 that Pater had once told him at Oxford, that he, Pater, considered the essays in *FR* that were eventually included in *The Renaissance* as 'owing their inspiration entirely to the example of my own work in the same line' (*SL*, ii.241). JM doubted this, thinking the principal inspiration for Pater was ACS's poetry (*UL*, i.283). 'Notes' provides ACS's descriptions of Italian masters (including Carpaccio, Gentile and Giovanni Bellini, Titian, and Giorgione): the section reproduced here is the opening. ACS defended both his claims as a poet to write about the visual arts, and the legitimacy of praising the work of friends, in the 'Preface' to *ES*, vii–xii.

A letter from ACS to WMR on 18 May 1868 indicates that there had been some disruption in ACS's relationship with *FR* over money. Its editor, JM, hoped that ACS would 'yet allow [*FR*] to print my notes on Florentine drawings, *if* I will reconsider the demand of a pound per page' (*SL*, i.298). ACS observed to Matthew Arnold on 3 July that year that he had 'a paper of mine on some unclassed drawings at Florence by the old Masters, which cost me some time and care to draw up. If you care for such things, the article may interest you—I can only answer for its cautious and literal accuracy' (*SL*, i.301). Cf. the discussion of pictures in the Palazzo Pitti at the end of DGR's 'Hand and Soul' (1850).

*Uffizj*: the Galleria degli Uffizi, designed by Giorgio Vasari (1511–74) for Cosimo I de' Medici (1560–81). Painter and designer, Vasari was best known for his biographical studies, *Le Vite de' più eccellenti pittori, scultori, ed architettori* (1550). The most familiar English version at this point was *Lives of Seventy of the Most Eminent Painters, Sculptors and Architects*, trans. Mrs Jonathan Foster, 5 vols (London: Bohn, 1850–52), and its successive editions. ACS was looking through the Gabinetto Desegni e Stampe.

*change of rule*: unknown.

*Andrea del Sarto*: (1486–1530), Florentine painter.

*Leonardo*: Leonardo da Vinci (1452–1519), inventor, painter, man of polymathic skill, was born near Florence. For evidence of which pictures ACS was considering, see C. Pedretti and G. Dalli Regoli, *I disegni di Leonardo da Vinci e della sua cerchia: Galleria degli Uffizi, Firenze* (Florence: Giunti Editore, 1985).

*own palace*: Casa Buonarroti, Florence.

*Michel Angelo*: (1475–1564), painter, sculptor, and man of polymathic skill, he was born of a Florentine family near Arezzo. For evidence of which pictures ACS was considering, see Frank Zollner, Christof Thoenes, and Thomas Popper, *Michelangelo 1475–1564: Complete Works* (Cologne: Taschen, 2007).

*πολλὴ . . . θεά*: Aphrodite's words at the beginning of Euripides' *Hippolytus*, ll.1–2 ('Great among men, and not without name I am, | The goddess').

*Persian Amestris*: wife of Xerxes I of Persia (*c.*519–465 BC). Cf. Aeschylus' *Persians* in which Xerxes' Queen, the mother of Darius, is a principal figure.

*Cleopatra*: ACS published his poem 'Cleopatra' in *The Cornhill*, 14 (September 1866), 331–3. It is reproduced in *MPSP*, 415–18.

*Ahab's . . . Jezebel*: The story of Ahab, ancient king of Israel, and his wife Jezebel is described in 1 and 2 Kings. Both had a reputation for ill-doing: 'But there was none like unto Ahab, which did sell himself to work wickedness in the sight of the LORD, whom Jezebel his wife stirred up', 1 Kings 21:25.

*Cleopatra... Nile*: cf. *Antony and Cleopatra*, 1.5.25.

*Salammbô*: Gustave Flaubert's historical novel, published in 1862. ACS is describing Salammbô as she appears in Ch. 10, 'Le serpent'.

*'ghost of a flea'*: Blake's miniature 'The Ghost of a Flea' (1819–20), now in Tate Britain (No. 5889). In *UTM*, ACS noted that 'A critic is, at worst, but what Blake painted—the ghost of a flea; and the man must be very tough of skin or very tender of spirit who would not rather have to do with the shadow than the substance' (*SR*, 37).

*hell... Luca Signorelli*: (*c.*1445–1523), Italian Renaissance painter, particularly of frescoes. His design of Hell is 'Demoni e dannati', Uffizi catalogue n.1246E.

*Filippo Lippi*: (*c.*1406–69), Italian painter (and subject of Browning's 1855 monologue 'Fra Lippo Lippi'). Lucrezia Buti was formerly a nun, and later the wife of Lippi and the mother of Lippi's son, the painter Filippino Lippi (*c.*1457–1504).

*Angelico*: Fra Angelico (*c.*1395–1455), Italian Dominican Friar and painter.

*Benozzo*: Benozzo Gozzoli (*c.*1421–97), Florentine painter. ACS noted he intended to see Gozzoli's frescoes in 'some chapel or other' (*SL*, i.98) on 1 April 1864. He presumably meant the frescoes of the procession of the Magi (1459–61) in the Capella Medici, Palazzo Medici Riccardi.

## FROM *NOTES ON THE ROYAL ACADEMY EXHIBITION, 1868* (1868)

Published in *ES* in a revised form as 'Notes on Some Pictures of 1868', this essay first appeared as *Notes on the Royal Academy Exhibition, 1868* (London: Hotten, 1868), with Part 1 by WMR, and Part 2 by ACS. The final portion of ACS's essay (the copy-text is the original version, 45–51), reproduced here, discussed DGR, whose poetry ACS would praise two years later in 'The Poems of Dante Gabriel Rossetti' (see 231–5). In part DGR's work is itself the model for this essay as ACS might be recalling his friend's reviews of, for instance, the Old Water Colour Gallery (1850), 'The Modern Pictures of all Countries, at Lichfield House' (1851), 'Exhibition of Sketches and Drawings in the Pall Mall East, 1851', and others eventually gathered by WMR in volume 2 of *The Collected Works of Dante Gabriel Rossetti*, 2 vols (London: Ellis and Scrutton, 1886).

The pictures analysed in this portion are as follows. ACS considers firstly the original version of *Lady Lilith*, begun *c.*1864, and finished *c.*1868, using the face of Fanny Cornforth [Sarah Cox] (1836–*c.*1906) as a model. DGR repainted the picture, exchanging Cornforth's face for that of Alexa Wilding (*c.*1845–8 to 1884) in 1872–3 (now in the Delaware Art Museum). ACS's description and DGR's watercolour replica are among the important surviving evidence of how the original picture looked. The image ACS pairs with this is *Sibylla Palmifera*, 'Sibyl with palm', begun in 1866 using Alexa Wilding as a model: now hanging in the Lady Lever Art Gallery, Port Sunlight. *Beata Beatrix* (begun perhaps as early as 1851) is in Tate Britain (No. 1279): its model was DGR's wife, Elizabeth Siddal (1829–62) though WMR noted it was 'a reminiscence' of Siddal not a portrait (*DGRFL*, i.239). *Venus Verticordia* (1864–8), using Alexa Wilding as a model, is now in the Russell-Cotes Art Gallery, Bournemouth (see Figure 8). The oil painting *La Pia de' Tolomei* (1868–80), with Jane Morris (1839–1914) as the model, is in the Spencer Museum of Art, University of Kansas, Lawrence, Kansas.

ACS mentions other pictures at the close: the first is now known as *Dante's Dream at the Time of the Death of Beatrice* (1856), in Tate Britain; and the second is the sketch, *Aspecta Medusa* (1865–8), (Birmingham City Museum and Art Gallery). The painting that should have followed the sketch was not completed. Rossetti's paintings that ACS described in *Notes* were not exhibited in the 1868 RA exhibition. Indeed, DGR never exhibited there or very often anywhere else. ACS creates in prose a 'virtual' gallery, implicitly pointing to the fact that the Academy had generally not welcomed Pre-Raphaelitism or Pre-Raphaelitism the Royal Academy. DGR's own discussion of the limits of the Academy can be found in his 'Exhibition of Modern British Art at the Old Water-Colour Gallery, 1850'. DGR invited ACS to see pictures in his studio on 18 May 1868, emphasizing those that ACS writes about in the *Notes* and in effect ACS's essay was written to order. 'I just heard from [WMR]', DGR wrote to ACS, with rather broken syntax and grammar: 'that you are describing in your pamphlet my *Lilith* & *Palmifera*. It is jolly beyond measure to be included in what you write if still possible at this date to give reference to my work [of] leading importance in respect of other unexihibited things described [...] There is also the Beata Beatrix (which you have seen) the La Pia (which I have not yet shown you but which I trust to make my best single figure picture on hand) and the design of "Aspecta Medusa" which I shall shortly commence painting. It would be important to me at this moment that the above 3 should not be left without some mention if possible': *The Correspondence of Dante Gabriel Rossetti*, ed. William A. Fredeman, 9 vols (Cambridge: Brewer, 2002–9), iv.68–9 (letter 68.92).

Hotten hoped for more from ACS on painting but noted on 14 June 1869 that he had been told by an intermediary that 'the task of writing any more "Notes" was a distasteful one to you' (*SL*, ii.16). Richard Herne Shepherd (1842–95), editor of Blake and Shelley, and translator of Baudelaire, wrote them thereafter. Looking back on 5 June 1873, as he prepared *ES*, ACS observed that he did not want the whole of the original essay reproduced: 'Some of that half pamphlet', he said, 'I should like to preserve, as I remember Rossetti expressed himself pleased with the criticism of himself, and I think there is some good writing in it' (*SL*, ii.252). The *ES* version omits reproductions of DGR's verses. On the title and manner, cf. Ruskin's *Academy Notes* (1855–9).

*painter . . . time*: note ACS's friendship with EBJ, to whom *PB* 1 had been dedicated.

*'She excels . . . again'*: lines about Lilith from Goethe's *Faust* in Shelley's translation, Sc. 2, ll.318–19. They were appended to *Lady Lilith* and are found in DGR's *Notebook* (1866), Duke University Library collection.

*'Je trouve... la vertu'*: 'I find the earth as beautiful as the sky, and I think correctness of form is virtue', Théophile Gautier, *Mademoiselle de Maupin*, 2 vols (Paris: Crès, 1922), ii.32. Cf. ACS's 'Sonnet (with a copy of *Mademoiselle de Maupin*)', 353.

*'Ma mia suora... giorno'*: with the missing first line, 'Per piacermi a lo specchio, qui m'addorno', these are the words of Lia (Leah), the first wife of Jacob, in Dante's *Purgatorio*, Canto 27.103–4: '[To find pleasure in this mirror, I adorn myself,] but my sister Rachel never leaves her mirror, sitting there all day'. Cf. DGR's 'Dante's Vision of Leah and Rachel' (1855), now in Tate Britain (which also used Elizabeth Siddal as the model for Rachel).

*So, rapt... light*: cf. Pater's description of *La Giaconda* in 'Notes on Leonardo Da Vinci', *FR*, 6 (November 1869), 494–508 (506–7).

*maiden meditation*: *A Midsummer Night's Dream*, 2.1.164.

*Beata Beatrix... Nuova*: cf. DGR's *Beata Beatrix*. Dante's *La Vita Nuova* concerns his love for 'la gentilissima Beatrice'.

*'sitting alone... widow'*: cf. 'How doth the city sit solitary, that was full of people! how is she become a widow!', *Dante's Vita Nuova Together with the Version of Dante Gabriel Rossetti*, ed. Herman Oelsner (London: Chatto & Windus, 1908), 143.

*deadly marriage-ring*: Pia de' Tolomei was a Sienese noblewoman, allegedly murdered by her husband. In *Purgatorio*, Canto 5, ll.134–6, she speaks to Dante and Virgil: 'Siena mi fé, disfecemi Maremma: | salsi colui che 'nnanellata pria | disposando m'avea con la sua gemma' ('Siena made me; Maremma unmade me: he knows it who gave me as a wedding ring his jewel when we married'). La Pia was allegedly killed in a castle in the Maremma, which at the time consisted of a sequence of malarial marshes in SW Tuscany.

*two... artists*: ACS had, immediately prior to discussing DGR, considered Whistler.

*Rien... beau*: 'Nothing is true but beauty'.

*La beauté... demi*: 'Beauty is perfect; beauty can do anything; beauty is the only thing in the world that cannot exist by halves', Victor Hugo, *Notre-Dame de Paris* (Paris: L'Imprimerie Nationale/Librairie Ollendorff, 1904), 320. Cf. the views of Pater's 'Conclusion' to *The Renaissance* of 1873.

## FROM 'THE POEMS OF DANTE GABRIEL ROSSETTI' (1870)

These are the final paragraphs (574–9) from an essay first published *FR*, 7 (May 1870), 551–79, and reprinted in *ES*. 'The Poems of Dante Gabriel Rossetti' grew out of a long friendship, begun in 1857 when ACS and DGR met in Oxford. That friendship was now entering its final period of close contact before a permanent remoteness consequent on DGR's declining health. The remoteness was physical rather than intellectual or in terms of emotional bond: note that *Library* no. 671 is a copy of DGR's *Poems* with the autograph inscription: 'To Algernon Swinburne, with all affection, D.G. Rossetti, 1879'. ACS's *Notes on the Royal Academy Exhibition* admired DGR's work as a painter not least in terms of his inter-relation of images and words (see 225–30). After the death on 10 February 1862 of Elizabeth Siddal, DGR's wife, ACS was able to say that he was 'almost always' with his friend (*SL*, i.50). They had shared Tudor House, Cheyne Walk, from *c.*24 October 1862 at which, WMR remembered, ACS wrote *Atalanta*, *PB* 1, *William Blake*, and finished *Chastelard* (*DGRFL*, i.236). ACS's essay is a review of DGR's *Poems* published in London by Ellis in 1870 (Ellis published *SBS*). DGR corresponded with ACS extensively over the former's poems in the first three months of 1870—a constructive dialogue over work-in-progress (cf. my observations on ACS and literary circles, liii–liv).

*Poems* included material recovered from Siddal's grave in the exhumation at Highgate (West) Cemetery in October 1869. In turn, ACS's essay attempted to reassure ACS's friend that the exhumation—which DGR told him about on 26 October 1869 (*SL*, ii.42–3)—had been appropriate. On its publication, DGR observed on 4 May that he had 'been duly thunderstruck at Swinburne's miraculous article': *DGRFL*, ii.227.

*'swagger . . . own eyes'*: *Troilus and Cressida*, 5.2.139.

*'it was all Horace . . . Claudian now'*: cf. *The Letters and Journals of Lord Byron*, ed. Thomas Moore ([1830] London: Murray, 1873), 367; letter of 15 September 1817.

*'the bosom-beats of Raffael'*: Robert Browning, 'One Word More', *Men and Women* (1855), l.20. Browning asserts that Raphael 'made a century of sonnets' (l.5) though the volume is now lost ('Suddenly, as rare things will, it vanish'd', l.31).

*giant-god his rival*: Michelangelo. ACS's point is that both Raphael (in Browning's conception) and Michelangelo are painters and poets, like DGR.

*cradle-song . . . revolution*: ACS presently clarifies what texts he means (and see the next note but one).

*Gretchen . . . 'Cenci'*: Margaret's song 'Es war ein König in Thule' in Goethe's *Faust*, Part 1; Beatrice's song 'False friend, wilt thou smile or weep' from Act 5 Sc. 3 of Shelley's *The Cenci*.

*Fantine's song . . . Noir*: ACS refers to 'Nous achèterons de bien belles choses', sung by Fantine in Bk 7, Ch. 6 of Hugo's *Les Misérables*; Hugo's poems 'Guitare' from *Les Rayon et les ombres* (1837), 'Le Chant de ceux qui s'en vont sur mer' and 'Le Chasseur noir'.

*'New-Year's Eve . . . Book'*: 'New-Year's Eve' is uncertain (unless ACS means Tennyson's *In Memoriam*, lyric 106); 'The Grandmother' (1864), 'Œnone' (1833), 'Boadicea' (1864), and *Maud* (1855) by Tennyson, and *The Ring and the Book* (1868–9) by Robert Browning.

*'the soul . . . man'*: untraced as a quotation.

*Pan . . . river*: see Elizabeth Barrett Browning, 'A Musical Instrument' (1862).

*'Thyrsis . . . Harp-player'*: Matthew Arnold's 'Thyrsis' (1866) and 'The Harp-Player on Etna' (1855), comprising Callicles' songs from 'Empedocles on Etna' (1852) except 'Cadmus and Harmonia'.

*'Earthly Paradise'*: WM, *The Earthly Paradise*, 7 vols (London: Ellis, 1868–70).

*'as one... air'*: 1 Corinthians 9:26.

*born... men*: terms suggestive of Apollo.

*last birth... death*: unknown.

## FROM *SONGS BEFORE SUNRISE* (LONDON: F.S. ELLIS, 1871)

### Super Flumina Babylonis

First published *FR*, 6 (October 1869), 386–9. Its title, 'Upon/By the Rivers of Babylon', is from Psalm 137:1. The complete portion in *KJV* reads: 'By the rivers of Babylon, there we sat down, yea, we wept, when we remembered Zion. We hanged our harps upon the willows in the midst thereof. For there they that carried us away captive required of us a song' (vv.1–3). The poem draws widely on Biblical sources, most plainly the crucifixion and resurrection narrative (e.g. John 18–20) and the exile context of Psalm 137. TWD and ACS were disappointed that this poem was omitted from *Atalanta in Calydon, and Lyrical Poems*, edited by William Sharp (1855–1905) / 'Fiona Macleod' (Leipzig: Tauchnitz, 1901). ACS said Sharp included 'so much that might well be spared—nay, would be better away' (*SL*, vi.153, letter of 6 October 1901). On 24 August 1882, ACS observed to F.W.H. Myers (1843–1901) that this poem 'has always been rather a favourite of my own' (*UL*, ii.306). On the title, compare the opponent of the Second Empire, Eugène Pellatan's *La Nouvelle Babylone: Lettres d'un provincial en tournée à Paris* (Paris: Pagnerre, 1862).

*they knew... forefathers*: ACS might have noticed that this alleged Italian forgetfulness of the past was beginning to change after reunification when, a few months before this poem was published, there was a celebration in Florence of the 400th anniversary of Machiavelli's birth, reported at length in *MP*, 15 May 1869, 6.

*Eridanus*: Latin name for the Po River in northern Italy. Cf. Robert Lytton's paraphrase of Virgil's fourth Georgic: 'with double horn, | Golden bull-brow'd Eridanus', in *Orval, or The Fool of Time and Other Imitations and Paraphrases* (London: Chapman and Hall, 1869), 301.

*Aceldama*: Aramaic name ('field of blood') for the area of Jerusalem associated with Judas Iscariot, betrayer of Jesus (it is the 'Potter's Field', with its dark red clay).

*angel's... stone*: cf. Matthew 28:1–7.

*gravecloths... gloom*: cf. John 20:6–7.

*risen indeed*: Luke 24:34.

*no trust... kings*: cf. Psalm 146:3.

*life... known*: Psalm 143:15–16.

*pavement... snow*: cf. Esther 1:6.

## Mentana: First Anniversary

First published *SBS*. The first anniversary of the Battle of Mentana was 3 November 1868. The battle was the final stage of the Risorgimento's military operation to capture Rome—one of the last remaining areas of Italy in 1867 remaining outside Italian control—from Franco-Papal regiments. Rome had been declared the official capital of the newly re-unified Italy in 1861 but occupying forces remained to defend Pope Pius IX (1846–78) and the Papal States. The battle, with Italian forces led by Giuseppe Garibaldi (1807–82), resulted in heavy defeat. *The Times* reported that this was because the Risorgimento force was '[i]mperfectly disciplined, poorly armed, and with scarcely any artillery', facing highly trained and well-equipped soldiers. Like Tennyson refashioning calamity into valour in 'The Charge of the Light Brigade' (1854), ACS endeavours to turn 'news of Garibaldi's disaster' (*The Times*, 9 November 1867, 10) into heroism. Rome was finally captured on 20 September 1870. When published in 1871, 'Mentana: First Anniversary' had a feeling of both prophecy and belatedness. It was immediately preceded in *SBS* with 'The Halt Before Rome, September, 1867'.

'Mentana: Second Anniversary' and 'Mentana: Third Anniversary' were included in 'Diræ' of *STN*, previously published in *The Examiner* in the early summer of 1873 (the schedule was discussed with TWD on 8 April 1873, *SL*, ii.237–8; the second anniversary poem was included in ACS's letter to WMR on 8 January 1870, *SL*, ii.79–81). Cf. Emma M. Pearson, *From Rome to Mentana* (London: Saunders, Otley, 1868) and Sydney Dobell's optimistic 'Mentana' (1874?), printed in *Poetical Works*, ii. 419–21. Cf. also Hugo's *La Voix de Guernesey (Mentana)* (1867).

*high-priest*: Pius IX.

*Lycoris*: the Roman courtesan Lycoris attended a famously louche banquet with Cicero in 46 BC, here emblematizing the decadence of Italy's past. Cf. W.A. Becker, *Gallus: or, Roman Scenes of the Time of Augustus* (1844), which had appeared in a third edition (London: Longmans, Green) in 1866.

## The Litany of Nations

First published *SBS*. Liberty for ACS meant government free from tyranny where a nation, in the Mazzinian sense of the term, was free to express its own distinctive and long-determined nature (see Introduction, xxvi–xxvii). Here, Greece is hailed as the founder of republican and democratic principles; Italy is Greece's inheritor but suffering under tyranny; Spain ponders the Spanish Americas; France remembers the Revolution; Russia languishes under Tsarist rule; Switzerland recalls her resistance to Austria; Germany remembers her dreams of freedom; and England speaks of a divided condition partly free but also subject to monarchical and aristocratic government. The form is derived, in the Anglican tradition, from the Litany of *BCP*, with its repeated petition: 'good Lord, deliver us'.

*μᾶ Γᾶ... ἀπότρεπε*: Aeschylus, *The Suppliant Women*, ll.890–1: 'Mother Earth, Mother Earth, turn away his fearful eyes!'

*divers-coloured days*: from the opening of Sappho's 'Ode to Aphrodite'; see headnote on 569; *GL* 1, 52.

*Isis*: mother goddess in ancient Egypt.

*dead times near us*: Napoleon III, Emperor of the French from 2 December 1852, had been defeated by Prussian forces at the Battle of Sedan on 1 September 1870. The Third Republic had then been proclaimed in France. Cf. Victor Hugo's *L'Année terrible* (1872) and ACS's review of it, 288–92.

## Hertha

First published *SBS*. The poem existed in part by 26 October 1869 when ACS sent DGR a portion of it. He described it as 'another mystic atheistic democratic anthropologic poem' in which the 'earth spirit of vital principle of matter [speaks]' (*SL*, ii. 45). At this stage, ACS was already planning a collection of poems called *Songs of the Republic* (see *SL*, ii.45) though he announced (probably) to the future publisher on 28 January 1870 that 'I have taken your advice & altered the title "Songs of the Republic" for "Songs before Sunrise", a title which Mr Rossetti approves of as best, & I prefer myself' (*UL*, i.180: to F.S. Ellis?). The final title relates to Hugo's *Les Chants du crépuscule* [Songs of Twilight] (Paris: Hetzel & Cie, 1835).

Hertha is the god-like soul of man, compounded of truth, liberty, and love. *SEML*, which thought 'Hertha' 'perhaps the best organised of all Swinburne's compositions', observed: 'The supremacy of this, the human over-soul, is based upon no precedence and no domination; it is coeval with man; it is at once objective and subjective; it is at once the master and the servant' (137). Writing to WMR on 15 January 1870, ACS said that he 'had completed and copied out my Hertha—the poem I think which if I were to die tonight I should choose to be represented and judged by, if one single and separate poem were perforce to be picked out of my lot (though but 140 lines long). It has the most in it of my deliberate thought and personal feeling or faith, and I think is as good in execution and impulse of expression as the best of my others' (*SL*, ii.85). ACS had already summed up the poem, and a philosophical problem, to WMR on 8 January 1870. After remarking that the 'best stanzas [...] of "Hertha" strike such a blow at the very root of Theism', he observed:

> [...] I have broken the back (not only of God, but) of the poem in question by this time, having perfected the verses necessary to bring out the root or master-thought, and to combine and harmonize all connecting links of the idea: which needed to be done with all distinctness and delicacy at once, as it was not at first evident *why* the principle of growth, whence and by which all evil not less than all good proceeds and acts, should *prefer* liberty to bondage, Mazzini to Buonaparte, Peabody to Troppmann, Christ to de Sade—'ce mauvais babeleur' [the bad babbler] to 'ce bon marquis' [the good marquis]—as I have represented the goddess emphatically as

doing. There of course *is* the problem in all our speculation, and here *was* the problem to solve in expression, the difficulty to reconcile in words. But while expatiating on her universality and the immeasurable equanimity of time and matter and their forces, I have made the All-Mother a good republican—as thus:

> I bid you but be:
>  I have need not of prayer;
> I have need of you free
>  As your mouths of mine air:
> That my heart may grow greater within me, beholding the fruits of me fair.

This much I think may be reasonably supposed and said, without incurring the (to me) most hateful charge of optimism, a creed which I despite as much as ever did Voltaire.

(*SL*, ii.79–80)

George Peabody (1795–1869) was a rich American banker and philanthropist and founder of the Peabody Trust and Peabody Institute; the story of the impoverished French counterfeiter, Jean Baptiste Troppmann (1848–70), was a recent sensation: seeking wealth, Troppmann had become a multiple killer and was executed in Paris for eight murders on 19 January 1870.

On 12 February 1870, ACS wrote to DGR with a comic further stanza to 'Hertha':

> By the spirit forecasting
>  That builds me a house,
> The Lord God Everlasting
>  Is cracked like a louse,
> And his Son becomes visibly less than a highly diminutive mouse.

(*SL*, ii.90)

'Hertha' takes its name from the German fertility goddess Nerthus who had Old Norse origins; the poem also alludes to the Old Norse conception of the 'twilight of the gods' applied here as a term for the destruction of mistaken religious faith (note that Wagner's *Götterdämmerung* was not performed till August 1876). The poem maintains only two rhymes per stanza and repeats the stanza form of the dialogue between the Chorus and Meleager at the end of *AiC*. Cf. 'Quia Multum Amavit' in *SBS*. 'Hertha' was included in *Selections*.

*before God was, I am*: ACS told DGR on 26 October 1869 that that he was 'thinking of making [Hertha] say—as being that womb of nature whence came forth all spirits upper and under of life stronger of weaker—"Before God was, I am"; a parody on the claims of a deceased Hebrew notoriety which will I trust find favour with the religious world' (*SL*, ii, 46). ACS refers to John 8:58 ('Jesus said unto them, Verily, verily, I say unto you, Before Abraham was, I am'), where Jesus draws on Exodus 3:14.

*I the mark... is*: *MPSP* compares Baudelaire's 'L'Héautontimorouménos' ('The Man who Tortures Himself'). On the kissed mouth, cf. DGR's *Bocca Baciata*.

*fashioned thee*: *MPSP* compares the next four stanzas with Job 38–9.

*tripod*: from which oracles were delivered in ancient Greece.

*Born, and not made*: cf. 'very God of very God, begotten, not made' (Nicene Creed).

*Green... death*: red, white, and green had been colours included in many Italian flags prior to the adoption in 1861 of a tricolour as the new flag of the united Kingdom of Italy with these colours in vertical stripes (initially with the arms of Savoy in the centre). Red, white, and green continue implicitly or explicitly in the poem. Note that the same colours were associated with other nineteenth-century revolutions: the flag of Hungary in the 1848 revolution, led by Lajos Kossuth whom ACS admired, deployed them.

*tree many-rooted*: cf. Yggdrasil, the giant world-tree with three huge roots in Norse mythology.

*In the buds... die*: cf. Genesis 2:17.

## Before a Crucifix

First published *SBS*. ACS told WMR on 25 November 1869 that he had 'begun a democratic poem—"Before a Crucifix"—addressed to the Galilean (Ben Joseph) in a tone of mild and modified hostility which I fear and hope will exasperate his sectaries more than any abuse'. ACS had recently been reading in the history of religion, adding: 'Have you read—do read thoroughly as I have—Deutsch's splendid article on Islam in the Quarterly? It is of intense interest as well as illumination' (*SL*, ii.56–7). ACS refers to an article by the Semitic scholar, Emanuel Oscar Menahem Deutsch (1829–73), 'The Koran', *Quarterly Review*, 127 (1869), 293–353, with its sympathetic discussion of the rise and nature of Islam and its views on tolerance, which might have attracted ACS: 'If there be any true gauge of an age or a nation, it is the manner in which such age or nation deals with religious phases beyond the pale' (296). WMR told ACS that 'Before a Crucifix' was '"very soothing"—*very* soothing: I enjoy it hugely, and reckon it indeed as also among your finest things. Its comparative simplicity of rhythm and structure are as delightful as in some other cases the contrary qualities' (19 April 1870, *SLWMR*, 253). On one feature of the poem's reception, see Introduction, xxxiii.

*wrought... race*: cf. 1 Corinthians 15:49.

*hast thou... earth?*: cf. Luke 12:51.

*forsaken thee*: cf. Matthew 27:46.

*blinding... crown*: cf. Mark 15:17–20.

*blood-bought field*: see note on 591.

*stripes unhealed*: cf. Isaiah 53:5.

*With iron... stone*: details from the crucifixion and entombment narratives, including Mark 16:1–6.

*rich man's grave*: Jesus' tomb belongs to 'a rich man of Arimathaea, named Joseph, who also himself was Jesus' disciple', Matthew 27:57.

*have... head*: cf. Luke 9:58.

*sponge... poison*: cf. Matthew 27:48.

*longing... come!*: cf. Matthew 6:10.

*soldiers... whole*: cf. John 19:23–4.

*Lazarus... republican*: cf. John 11:43.

*save thyself... us*: cf. Luke 23:39.

*shalt... away*: cf. 1 John 1:9.

*ingraffed*: engrafted. *OED* dates to *c.*1420.

*Too foul... bride*: cf. Revelation 21:2.

*Thou bad'st... thee*: cf. Matthew 19:14.

## Tenebræ

First published *SBS*. Lang suggests that it was this poem to which ACS referred in a letter to WMR on 21 April 1870: 'Can you give me a better title than "Sublustri Luce"? I debated the thing with Topsy [WM] the other day—and he couldn't. You must have heard the poem before, but it has not been printed'. This was in reply to WMR's letter of 19 April, asking whether this 'very fine' poem was in print (*SLWMR*, 253). WMR replied on 1 May that he thought the title 'Sublustri Luce' is 'euphonious' but 'the phrase is not exactly a familiar one, unmistakeable in meaning. If it *entirely* corresponds to our "Twilight" [...] I *don't* particularly see why the English word should not be substituted' (*SLWMR*, 254). 'Tenebræ'—'darkness', 'shadows'—ironically recalls the Holy Week liturgy of the same name.

*unsloken*: unslaked (this is the only example *OED* gives).

*desire... eyes*: cf. Ezekiel 24:16 or 25.

*Brutus*: Marcus Junius Brutus (85–42 BC), Roman Senator and leading assassin of Julius Caesar.

## Cor Cordium

First published *SBS*. The poem takes its title ('heart of hearts') from Shelley's gravestone, Cimitero degli Inglesi, Rome. ACS told WMR on 2 December 1869 that he 'wrote the other day a sonnet to the Cor Cordium from another point than your admirable one—a sort of "Ora pro nobis et re publicâ" [pray for us and the republic]' (*SL*, ii.62). ACS was responding to WMR's poem that would eventually be published as 'Shelley's Heart: To Edward John Trelawny' in *The Dark Blue*, 1 (1 March 1871), 35.

That poem, with allusion to 'To a Skylark', was particularly admired by DGR. Including an epigraph, it read as follows:

'What surprised us all was that the heart remained entire. In snatching this relic from the fiery furnace, my hand was severely burnt.'—Trelawny's 'Recollections of Shelley'

Trelawny's hand, which held'st the sacred heart,
The heart of Shelley, and has felt the fire
Wherein the drossier framework of that lyre
Of heaven and earth was molten—but its part
Immortal echoes always, and shall dart
Pangs of keen love to human souls, and dire
Ecstatic sorrow of joy, as higher and higher
They mount to know thee, Shelley, what thou art—
Trelawny's hand, did then the outward burn
As once the inward? O cor cordium,
Which *wast* a spirit of love, and now a clot,
What other other flame was wont to come
Lambent from thee to fainter hearts, and turn—
Red like thy death-pyre's heat—their lukewarmth hot!

Writing again to WMR on 16 December, ACS reproduced the sonnet as it then was and added some questions (bold added to indicate differences):

O heart of hearts, the chalice of love's fire,
Hid round with flowers and all the bounty of **bloom.**
O wonderful and perfect heart, for whom
The lyrist **Liberty** made life a **lyre.**
O heavenly heart, at whose most dear desire
Dead love, living and singing, **clove** his tomb,
And with him **risen, in glow of things and gloom,**
All day thy choral pulses rang full **choir.**
**Love of loves, holy of holies, light of lights,**
**And** sole thing sweeter than thine own songs were,
Help us for thy free love's sake to be free,
True for thy truth's sake, **righteous for thy rights,**
Till very liberty make clean and fair
The nursing earth as the sepulchral sea.

Please tell me whether any of these would be better readings in your mind. *Truth's* fire, or *time's* for *God's*; *through* glow of *life*, for *in* glow of *things*—or either word altered only. And for the last line

Thy nursing earth as thy sepulchral sea.
In either case, I rather like the last allusion.
(*SL*, ii.70–1)

The poem continued to give ACS some cause for concern. On 28 August 1870, he wrote to WMR to say:

> You objected to the use of Galilean imagery in my sonnet to the *Cor Cordium*; so in deference to your opinion I have altered the line (I presume the only one) liable to that grievous charge, and instead of the verse
>
> 'Love of loves, holy of holies, light of lights'
> substituted this
> 'O heart whose beating blood was running song,'
> and changed the verse corresponding into
> 'True for thy truth's sake, for thy strength's sake strong.'
> I thought also of this reading,
> 'O singing heart that our turn trembling to,'
> (the other line being simply inverted for the rhyme).
>
> Do you like the change, and think it wholly removes any tainting trace of the slimy trail of the Galilean serpent? I see and smell none left; and as you otherwise approved the sonnet, I have taken some pains to perfect it.
>
> (*SL*, ii.121)

Note that *SS* was dedicated to Trelawney. On this textual history, see 'Note on the Texts', liv. Cf. Alfred Austin's 'At Shelley's Grave' (1872) and DGR's 'Percy Bysshe Shelley: Inscription for the Couch, Still Preserved, on which he Passed the Last Night of his Life'.

*sepulchral sea*: Shelley drowned while sailing back to Lerici from Livorno on 8 July 1822.

## In San Lorenzo

This sonnet, first published *SBS*, is a political meditation on Michelangelo's allegorical marble figure *La Notte* ('Night', 1526–31) in the Sagrestia Nuova, chiesa di San Lorenzo, Florence. The last line contains a pun. 'In San Lorenzo' was included in *Selections*. ACS included translations from Michelangelo and Giovanni Strozzi of 'Night' in *PB* 3.

*Let... light*: Genesis 1:3.

## On the Downs

First published *SBS*. 'On the Downs' combines ideas about world spirits from 'Hertha', the anti-theistic poetry of *PB* 1, with a political sense of a new beginning.

*iron-zoned*: see note on 560.

*truth makes free*: cf. John 8:32.

*furled flag . . . delight*: colours of the new flag of the united Kingdom of Italy (and see note on 589).

## An Appeal

With the title 'An Appeal to England Against the Execution of the Condemned Fenians', this poem, with a number of small differences, was first published *MS*, 22 November 1867 and as a broadside (reproduced Collins, plate 25). The separate pamphlet apparently published in Manchester in 1867 (reproduced Collins, plate 26), is a Wise/Forman forgery. It was then included in *SBS* with the present title, intensifying the focus on (English) judicial cruelty (see Introduction, xxix–xxx).

Three members of the Irish Republican Brotherhood (Fenians)—William Philip Allen, Michael Larkin, and Michael O'Brien (Michael Gould)—were accused of killing a police officer on 18 September 1867 while rescuing other members of the Brotherhood from a waggon in Hyde Road, Manchester. Initial reports suggested upwards of fifty people were involved in the rescue. Twenty-six were eventually brought to trial that began on 28 October and lasted five days. Five Irishmen were sentenced to death but one had the sentence commuted and another was pardoned. A deputation of working men presented the Home Secretary with an appeal for clemency for the remaining condemned men on 18 November (*The Times*, 19 November 1867, 10) because of grave doubts about their involvement and a certainty that the death was accidental. But the Westminster Government maintained 'large and imposing military demonstrations' in Manchester throughout the week (*The Times*, 20 November 1867, 12) and refused to commute the sentences after much national debate. The Fenians (the 'Manchester Martyrs') were hanged outside the Manchester (Salford) New Bailey Prison on 23 November, the first Fenians executed for murder in England (*The Times*, 25 November 1867, 9). ACS noted to WMR on 28 November 1867 that the poem had 'drawn down on my head (pass for public abuse, but—what I *do* mind—) the devil's own correspondence. O Justine! tu voulais faire une bonne action—tu devais souffrir [O Justine! you wanted to do a good deed—you had to suffer]' *SL*, i.274.

'An Appeal' has for many years confused understanding of ACS's relationship with Ireland. It caused ACS difficulties in subsequent decades (and even now) as many readers have taken it to signify he once fully supported Irish nationalism: see, for instance, Standish O'Grady's enthusiastic letter to him about the Fenian cause of 19 January (1868?), *UL*, i.119–20; or the Irish student who admired *SBS* and, when accompanying Alfred Noyes past The Pines, always took his hat off (Alfred Noyes, *Two Worlds for Memory* (New York: Lippincott, 1953), 43–4). 'An Appeal', in comparison with the later explicitly Unionist poetry, has regularly seemed to provide evidence that ACS had changed his mind. But the poem provides no proof of support for Fenianism only of ACS's characteristic dislike of a state's cruel and unjustice imprisonment and execution (intensified in ACS's change to the original title). ACS's topic is England behaving poorly. On 28 April 1870, ACS declared he was not ashamed of these verses (*SL*, vi.267) and later maintained the same point that they represented an unchanging perspective. He wrote to *The Times* on 3 May 1887, for instance, in the midst of his annoyance over Parnell, declaring that he had not altered his mind since 1867 and that he had objected to the treatment of the Fenians only because they were not to be classed with criminals for 'they did not kill [...] basely or treacherously' (*SL*, v.189). In fact, there was no certain evidence that the men were involved in the killing at all. ACS maintained his consistency as a champion of liberty against state cruelty in the 'Dedication' to the 1904 edition of his poems (see 524–35).

For a reaction of ACS's general views on capital punishment, see 'Mr Swinburne and Gibbeting', *London Review*, 15 (1867), 591–2. ACS strongly disagreed with Hugo's disapproval of state executions (see *SVH*, 11–13) and, for instance, thought in 1886 that someone who starved children to death 'might very properly be subjected to vivisection without anaesthetics' (*SVH*, 12). But the Manchester Martyrs were not in such a category. Terry Meyers observes that Sir Algernon Edward West's *Private Diaries*, ed. Horace G. Hutchinson (New York: Dutton, 1922), contains the assertion from Gladstone's private secretary, George Murray, that ACS was deprived the laureateship because he never repudiated *PB* 1, *NPR*, or 'An Appeal' (SM, 11 May 2014). That suggests the personal significance of a persistent misreading (though it is only one of several accounts about ACS and the laureateship: see Francis O'Gorman, 'Swinburne and Tennyson's Peerage', *English Studies*, 96 (2015), 277–92).

*Strangers... Exiles*: ACS probably had, for instance, Karl Blind, Giuseppe Mazzini, Gabriele Pasquale Giuseppe Rossetti (DGR's father), and Aurelio Saffi (1819–90, republican politician and ally of Mazzini who was teaching Italian in Oxford while ACS was at Balliol) in mind as political exiles who sought the safety of England.

*Let slaughter... not*: possibly thinking of 'While yet we live, scarce one short hour perhaps, | Between us two let there be peace', *Paradise Lost*, X.923–4. But cf. Milton's 'On the Late Massacre at Piedmont' (1655).

*Now... France*: a reference presumably to the government of Napoleon III's France but untraced.

*daughter... war*: the 'daughter' is the United States of America. The celebrated marching hymn of the American Civil War (1861–65), 'The Battle Hymn of the Republic', included the line: 'He is trampling out the vintage where the grapes of wrath are stored', drawing on Revelation 19:15.

*Stretch... save*: cf. Psalm 138:7.

*ghost... grave*: cf. Shelley's 'England in 1819'.

## FROM 'SIMEON SOLOMON: NOTES ON HIS "VISION OF LOVE" AND OTHER STUDIES' (1871)

Published *The Dark Blue*, 1 (July 1871), 568–77 and not reissued. Simeon Solomon (1840–1905) was a painter and poet, born into a Jewish family (cf. the comparison with Heine below) who knew ACS through DGR and EBJ. He exhibited widely in the

1860s, including in the Dudley Gallery. *ODNB* observes: 'In 1873 Solomon was arrested in a public lavatory and charged with committing buggery. Although the incident was not reported in the newspapers his public career was effectively at an end; he did not exhibit at either the Dudley or Royal Academy exhibitions that year nor thereafter. Most of his former friends disowned him and he began an obscure and precarious existence which led him to the workhouse and financial dependence upon institutional and family charity.' ACS was among the friends to reject Solomon: see Introduction, xlii. Solomon's prose poem *A Vision of Love Revealed in Sleep* was published privately 'for the author' in London in 1871, comprising a small volume of thirty-seven pages and one leaf of plates. Chris White provides the complete text in her *Nineteenth-Century Writings on Homosexuality: A Sourcebook* (London: Routledge, 1999), abbreviated here as 'White'. *Dark Blue* was established by the Oxford undergraduate John Christian Freund in 1871 and produced at extravagant quality with an exceptional list of contributors. It collapsed in debt in 1873. ACS corresponded with Solomon over this essay in May 1871: 'You may be sure that the longer and fuller what you write', Solomon said ungrammatically, 'will be the more satisfaction it will give me' (late May 1871, *UL*, i.213). Later, on reading the essay, Solomon declared it 'splendid' (*UL*, i.214).

*terror or the pity*: cf. Aristotle, *Poetics* 13 and 14, with its discussion of the fearful and pitiable (φοβερὸν καὶ ἐλεεινόν) as constitutent of tragedy.

*great... critic*: Gautier.

*glad... mouth*: unidentified.

*Not... tone*: Keats, 'Ode on a Grecian Urn', ll.13–14.

*celebrity*: in *OED*'s third sense: 'The condition of being much extolled or talked about; famousness'.

*Heine*: Heinrich Heine (1797–1856), German poet and critic. He was born Jewish and converted to Catholicism.

*'o'er inform its tenement'*: cf. Dryden, 'Absalom and Achitophel', l.158: 'And o'er-informed the tenement of clay.'

*wings... cherubim*: cf. Ezekiel 11:22.

*rocks of offence*: cf. 1 Peter 2:8.

*'And she... child'*: White, 300.

*The depth*: editorial paragraph break.

*'unburied... dried'*: White, 290–1.

*'as a tune... tune'*: DGR, 'The Card-Dealer', l.4.

*'as subtle... woof'*: *Troilus and Cressida*, 5.2.154–5.

*'wounded... friends'*: cf. Zachariah 13:6.

*stations of the cross*: in (principally Catholic) Christian commemoration and liturgy, representations of stages on the Via Dolorosa, the journey of Jesus to Golgotha.

*Daedalian maze*: Daedalus built the labyrinth at Crete to contain the Minotaur.

*One of these... Payne*: see 'Sleepers and One that Watches (A Sketch by Simeon Solomon)' in John Payne's *Intaglios: Sonnets* (London: Pickering, 1871). Solomon's painting *The Sleepers and One that Watcheth* was exhibited Dudley Gallery 1870 and is now in Leamington Spa Museum and Art Gallery; a preliminary sketch, to which ACS refers, has not survived though there is a photograph of it in Birmingham City Art Gallery (1931P329.2).

*cloud-compeller*: cf. 'cloud-gatherer' (*Νεφεληγερέτα*), a term for Zeus.

*Roman ladies... imagination*: ACS refers to Solomon's *Habet!* (exhibited at the Royal Academy 1865; and now part of a private collection on loan to Bradford Art Gallery).

*Alphonse Karr*: Jean-Baptiste Alphonse Karr (1808–90), French journalist and novelist. The most keenly absorbed of the women watching a gladiator fight in Solomon's picture is blonde. Karr's views were well-known, e.g. Theodore de Banville, *Dames et demoiselles* (Paris: Charpentier, 1886), 100.

## TRISTRAM AND ISEULT: PRELUDE OF AN UNFINISHED POEM

First published *Pleasure: A Holiday Book of Prose and Verse* (London: King, 1871), 45–52. This book was edited (anonymously) by the novelist, journalist, and writer James Hain Friswell (1825–78). ACS knew Friswell enough to receive an invitation from him—declined—to a dinner for Disraeli probably on 2 March 1868 (*SL*, i.292)—though Friswell clearly did not know ACS well enough *not* to invite him to meet a Conservative Prime Minister. Hain included a chapter on ACS in his *Modern Men of Letters Honestly Criticised* (London: Hodder and Stoughton, 1870) though there were errors (e.g. ACS's date of birth is given as 1843 and his upbringing is claimed to have been in France). Hain is generally negative, summing up ACS's achievement to date (principally *PB* 1): 'His chief and most high works are but mocking songs of the atheist that erst might have been sung in Sodom, and lascivious hymns to Adonis that might fitly have been howled in Gomorrah' (310). Later, ACS was apparently pleased that George Augustus Sala successfully sued Friswell over the same book in 1871: see *UL*, i.211 (Sala sued him for defamation and was awarded £500 damages; the book thereafter was suppressed). Nevertheless, ACS sent Friswell, and Friswell accepted and published, the 'Prelude'. Money worries—ACS wanted £50 for the poem (*SL*, ii.172)—might well have led to the publication of the 'Prelude' in *Pleasure* and ACS overcoming his scruples about Friswell's views. ACS noted that the poem was finished on 12 February 1870 (*SL*, ii.90) and *Pleasure* as a whole was reviewed approvingly (and ACS's poem quoted) in *The Examiner*, 3337 (13 January 1872), 42.

ACS's poem was later used with some revision—as intended—as 'Prelude: *Tristram and Iseult*' at the commencement of *TL*, included in *TLOP*. Rikky Rooksby gives the collation as evidence that ACS 'was more sensitive to the selection of his words and concerned with the precision of his texts than is commonly thought' in 'Swinburne's

Revision of the "Prelude" to *Tristram of Lyonesse*', *N&Q*, 42 (1995), 200–1 (201). The 'Prelude of an Unfinished Poem' is first mentioned in ACS's correspondence on 22 December 1869 when ACS wrote to DGR about the longer poem that became *TL*. ACS observed he had written the 'Prelude' 'all yesterday' (*SL*, ii.73) and that although 'the British buffer may say I am following Topsy [WM] in the choice of metre for romantic narrative', it was actually modelled 'not after the Chaucerian cadence of [WM's *The Life and Death of Jason* (1867)] but after my own scheme of movement and modulation in Anactoria, which I consider original in structure and combination' (*SL*, ii.74). See also the headnote to 'The Sailing of the Swallow', 615–18 and ACS's qualified praise of WM in 'Morris' *The Life and Death of Jason*', *FR*, 2 (July 1867), 19–28. See also headnote on 546–7.

*relume*: cf. 'These indeed let him breathe on and relume!', Browning, *The Ring and the Book*, Bk 1, l.738.

*Helen*: the daughter of Zeus and Leda; her abduction by Paris precipitates the Trojan War.

*Hero* . . . *Marlowe*: Marlowe's *Hero and Leander* (1598) retells the first portion of the tragic story of two lovers divided by the Hellespont. Hero lights a lamp in her tower to guide Leander as he swims.

*Alcyone*: 'or Halcyone, daughter of Aeolus, married Ceyx, who was drowned as he was going to Claros to consult the oracle. The gods apprised Alycone, in a dream, of her husband's fate; and on the morrow she threw herself into the sea, and was with her husband changed into birds of the same name' (Lemprière, 'Alcyone').

*birth-month*: ACS was born on 5 April 1837.

*Rosamond*: Rosamund Clifford, the 'Fair Rosamund' (*c.*1149–*c.*1176), mistress of Henry II.

*Carthaginian* . . . *fire*: Dido, founding Queen of Carthage, who, in *Aeneid*, Bk 4, kills herself on a pyre for love of Aeneas: he has left her to continue his journey to Rome.

*Veronese*: Shakespeare's *Romeo and Juliet* is set in Verona though ACS might also be thinking of the richness of the paintings of Paolo Veronese (1528–88).

*Cleopatra*: died 12 August 30 BC.

*Phaethon*: who loses control of the chariot of the sun (a figure of autumn here).

*Francesca*: the history of the adulterous love of Francesca and Paolo is given in Dante's *Inferno*, Canto 5.

*Thisbe*: in Roman legend, she is the secret lover of Pyramus in Babylon, who slays herself on finding Pyramus dead: he has killed himself, mistakenly believing Thisbe to have been slain by a lion. Pyramus' blood darkens mulberry fruit ever afterwards.

*Angelica*: the beautiful princess of Cathay in Matteo Maria Boiardo's *Orlando Innamorato* (1495) who has differently disastrous relationships with Orlando and his cousin Rinaldo.

*hers*: Beatrice's, of Dante's (the 'Florentine') *Divina Commedia* and *Vita Nuova*.

*Eyes heavenly... wonderfully lit*: ACS subsequently repented of the '"damnable iteration" of heavenly, heaven, & heavenly (*bis*)' and changed these lines in *TLOP* to 'Wherein the godhead thence transfigured lit | All time for all men with the shadow of it', to the disappointment of F.W.H. Myers who liked the original (*UL*, ii.306–7).

*Saw Dante*: Virgil shows Dante the lovers Helen, Achilles, Paris, and Tristan in Canto 5 of the *Inferno*, 'e più di mille | ombre mostrommi e nominommi a ditto, | ch'amor di nostra vita dipartille' ('and he indicated and named more than a thousand shades who left our life because of love').

*Out of my life... death?*: cf. Robert Browning discussing his 'resurrectionary' method in *The Ring and the Book*, Bk 1, ll.760–72:

> Was not Elisha once?—
> Who bade them lay his staff on a corpse-face.
> There was no voice, no hearing: he went in
> Therefore, and shut the door upon them twain,
> And prayed unto the Lord: and he went up
> And lay upon the corpse, dead on the couch,
> And put his mouth upon its mouth, his eyes
> Upon its eyes, his hands upon its hands,
> And stretched him on the flesh; the flesh waxed warm:
> And he returned, walked to and fro the house,
> And went up, stretched him on the flesh again,
> And the eyes opened. 'Tis a credible feat
> With the right man and way.

See also the Introduction, xxxviii.

## FROM 'VICTOR HUGO'S *L'ANNÉE TERRIBLE*' (1872)

First published *FR*, 12 (September 1872), 243–67 and then included with some minor corrections in *ES* (copytext is *FR*). Hugo's *L'Année terrible* (Paris: Michel Lévy Frères, 1872) is a collection of poems gathered into sections by month, dedicated 'to Paris', which recounts chronologically recent French history, beginning with August 1870 and the build-up to the Battle of Sedan (1 September 1870) and the surrender of Napoleon III. The volume concludes with July 1871. *L'Année terrible* was many times re-issued. ACS asked JM if he could review it in a letter of 25 April 1872 (*SL*, ii.176): he later said that the whole 'elaborate article' took 'three weeks' work' (*SL*, ii.184). *L'Année terrible*'s account of France's trials should be read alongside Hugo's denunciation of Napoleon III, *Les Châtiments* (1853, reissued in an expanded version in 1870). ACS's statement on Hugo's political poetry in 1872 underlined his—variously expressed—views on *l'art pour l'art* in relation to content: see Introduction, xxiv–xxv.

*SVH* observed that Hugo, 'Poet, dramatist, novelist, historian, philosopher, and patriot, the spiritual sovereign of the nineteenth century was before all things and above all things a poet' (3). As a Frenchman, a rebel, republican, critic, dramatist, novelist, and historian, but above all a poet, Hugo was a natural hero for ACS. Hugo wrote back to ACS on 22 September 1872, praising *SBS* and declaring that ACS's article on *L'Année terrible* 'a excité et tenu en éveil l'attention de Paris [...] Vous êtes un admirable esprit et un grand cœur' ['has excited and held the attention of Paris [...] You have a fine spirit and a great heart'] (*SL*, ii.186).

*credited... authorship*: Théophile Gautier.

*shall be... her*: Matthew 6:33. ACS is loosely referring to part of the chapter on 'Lyric Poetry' from *William Blake: A Critical Essay*. See 197–218 in the present edition.

*Goethe... Tyrtæus*: Christian Gottfried Körner (1756–1831), German writer, lawyer, patron of the arts, correspondent with Goethe, and friend of Schiller. Tyrtæus (Τυρταῖος) was, probably, an ancient Greek elegiac poet writing from Sparta. He is included in *Poetae Graeci*, 175–80 (where he is immediately followed by Sappho: ACS was remembering a contrast from his reading at Eton: see headnote on 569).

*Lesbian music*: Sappho's.

*Bævius or a Shadwell*: Bavius, in Lemprière, was, with Mævius, one of 'two stupid and malevolent poets in the age of Augustus, who attacked the superior talents of the contemporary writers' (under 'Bavius'). Thomas Shadwell (*c.*1642–92) was Poet Laureate after Dryden and had been much mocked by him. ACS changed this reference to 'Settle' for *ES*: Elkanah Settle (1648–1724) is one of the dunces in Pope's *Dunciad*, e.g. Bk 1. In the 'Remarks' to Bk 3, Settle is compared to Bavius: *The Dunciad* (London: Gilliver, 1729), 136. Settle is also an emblematically poor writer in *UTM* (*SR*, 50). Dryden said of both Shadwell and Settle: 'Two fools that crutch their feeble sense on verse' (*Absalom and Achitophel*, l.409).

*'handmaid'*: cf. note on 582.

*Persæ... Vita Nuova*: Aeschylus' play *Persai* (*The Persians*) is the only major surviving dramatic work from ancient Greece on a contemporary event (the Battle of Salamis, 480 BC). ACS ironically described Robert Buchanan's belief in the 'marked pre-eminence' of the *Persai* among the 'imperfect and obsolete productions of the Greek stage' in *UTM* (*SR*, 84). The laments of the defeated Xerxes in Aeschylus' drama share something of the emotional territory of both *AiC* and *Erechtheus*. Referring to the *Vita Nuova*, Dante's quasi-autobiographical spiritual diary, ACS means a text, as he sees it, without (apparently) the sustained theological and moral purposes of the *Divina Commedia*.

*Auguste Vacquerie*: (1819–95), writer and journalist; admirer of Hugo; friend of ACS. Cf. ACS, *Auguste Vacquerie* (Paris: Michel Lévy Frères, 1875), taken from ACS's article on Vaquerie's *Aujourd'hui et demain* in *The Examiner*, 6 November 1875, 1247–50. See also *Miscellanies*, 303–22.

*renounce... works*: cf. the question to godparents in the order of baptism in *BCP*: 'Dost thou, in the name of this Child, renounce the devil and all his work[?]'.

*dead…dead*: Luke 9:60.

*live…being*: cf. Acts 17:28.

*poetess…America*: Elizabeth Barrett Browning and Walt Whitman. Cf. 'To Walt Whitman in America', *SBS*. For ACS's later criticism of Whitman in 1887, see 'Whitmania', *FR*, 42 (August 1887), 170–6, which complains of Whitman's formal (in)competence. Hotten published *Poems by Walt Whitman*, edited by WMR in 1868; Chatto & Windus brought out a new edition in 1886.

*principle of life*: cf. Hutton's questions and comments to ACS after the Baudelaire essay, noted on 549–50.

*Greek drama*: ACS published his second long Greek dramatic poem (after *AiC*), *Erechtheus: A Tragedy*, in 1876.

*bone to his bone*: cf. Ezekiel 3:1–14 (Ezekiel's narrative of re-animated bones lies behind ACS's paragraph).

*Talleyrand*: (1754–1838), French diplomat of the *ancien régime*, revolutionary France, the Bourbon restoration, and the July Monarchy.

*Trimalchio…dead*: Trimalchio is a character in Petronius' *The Satyricon*; François-Auguste Romieu (1800–55) was a minor French writer and administrator and a supporter of Napoleon III. ACS refers to a line in Victor Hugo's *William Shakespeare* (Paris: Librairie Internationale, 1864), 299.

*'mistrust…heroic bones'*: ACS slightly misquotes Elizabeth Barrett Browning's *Aurora Leigh*, Bk 5, ll.189–98.

*'migrate…wanderings'*: Whitman's 'Song of the Exposition' ('SE'), ll.15–17. For ACS on Whitman, see note above ('*poetess . . . America*).

*'closed for ever'*: misremembering 'SE', l.41.

*'dissolved…exhalation'*: 'SE', l.47.

*'She has…is here'*: cf. 'SE', l.32.

*'by thud…stay'*: 'SE', ll.56 and 58.

*'servile…influences'*: *Measure for Measure*, 3.1.9.

*light…countenance*: Psalm 4:6.

*Whether or not…Europe*: cf. ACS's distancing himself from Hugo's Christianity on 525.

## FROM *BOTHWELL: A TRAGEDY* (LONDON: CHATTO & WINDUS, 1874)

ACS's 5-act verse drama was dedicated to Hugo with ACS's sonnet 'Comme un fleuve'. It is the second part of the Mary Stuart trilogy that began with *Chastelard: A Tragedy* (London: Moxon, 1865) and ended with *Mary Stuart: A Tragedy* (London: Chatto & Windus, 1881). James Hepburn, 1st Duke of Orkney and 4th Duke of

Bothwell (1534–78), was Mary's third husband, widely suspected of involvement in the death of Darnley, Mary's second husband, though formally acquitted. The third marriage met with resistance from Mary's opponents, who eventually imprisoned the Queen in Lochleven Castle and forced her abdication on 24 July 1567. She escaped from Lochleven on 2 May 1568 but her forces were quickly scattered outside Glasgow at the Battle of Langside (13 May 1568). After staying for a few nights with her ally Lord Herries, Mary escaped to England on 16 May hoping for assistance from Queen Elizabeth I. In the final scene of ACS's play, reproduced here, Mary, having spent a last night in Dundrennan Abbey, leaves Scotland for England where she will land at Workington and be taken into custody. The departure to England, with which ACS ends, is ultimately a catastrophe and the last words of *Bothwell* portend Mary's execution in England in 1587 (Bothwell himself died insane, imprisoned in exile).

*Bothwell* includes reference to Swinburne's own family whom he believed had been supporters of Mary. The writing of the play had taken some six years. Having 'made a careful analysis of historical events from the day of Rizzio's murder', ACS told JM on 16 December 1872, 'to that of Mary's flight into England, I find that to cast into dramatic mould the events of those eighteen months it is necessary to omit no detail, drop no link in the chain, if the work is to be either dramatically coherent or historically intelligible' (*SL*, ii.211–12). Later, ACS remarked to JM on 28 March 1874, shortly after finishing the play, that Mary Stuart 'might, I think, have been content with ruining my ancestors by the simple process of making them give land and life for her, and not have exacted the best work of my brains as well as the last sacrifice of their heads' (*SL*, ii.293). ACS's expertise as a scholar of Mary Queen of Scots led to an invitation to write the essay on her for the ninth edition of *Encyclopædia Britannica*. ACS's piece was published in volume 15 in 1883, 594–602.

The play was admired. *The Standard* observed: 'It is not improbable that many persons, on opening Mr Swinburne's "Bothwell," will stand aghast before 532 pages of close-printed blank verse, containing in all some 16,000 lines, and their alarm will, perhaps, be heightened when they discover that these compose one 5-Act tragedy. We can only advise them not to be deterred by the apparent magnitude of the task of reading so huge a work. They will find it easy, and ever easier as they proceed. Mr Swinburne, whatever may be his incidental defects, has given the world assurance of a poet—a poet original, impassioned, musical, highly trained, and occasionally muscular. They will here find him at his very best if manliness, dignity, and [fullness] of style are superior to mere pleasant singing and alliterative lyrics' (25 May 1874, 5). ACS in July 1874 tolerated consideration of 'stagification' but left all the details to TWD: 'I stipulate only that nothing is to be added or substituted; I give the fullest license of selection and excision' (*SL*, ii.312–13). No performance, however, was, to my knowledge, attempted. This, to some, seemed a wiser course of action than that of Tennyson whose *Queen Mary* (London: King, 1875) was unsatisfactorily produced at London's Lyceum in 1876. Performing *Queen Mary* certainly appeared an error to *The Era* in comparison to Swinburne who 'wrote *Bothwell*, but has never dared to produce it' (23 April 1876, 12).

This extract was included in *Selections*. See Introduction, xliv–xlv.

*five-years' child*: Mary was five years old when she was taken to France to be betrothed to the Dauphin, later François II (1544–60) in August 1548.

*come back*: François II, by then Mary's husband, died on 5 December 1560, and she presently returned to Scotland in search of clarity about her future role.

*to bruise... heel*: cf. Genesis 3:15.

## FROM *SONGS OF TWO NATIONS* (LONDON: CHATTO & WINDUS, 1875)

### *From* Diræ

'Diræ' comprised sonnets initially published in *The Examiner* between 22 March and 14 June 1873 (and in the New York *Independent*, 22 May–10 July). They drew inspiration from Hugo's political writing and, in England, from Landor and Shelley. The Diræ were 'the daughters of Acheron and Nox, who persecuted the souls of the guilty. They are the same as the Furies, and some suppose that they are called Furies in hell, Harpies on earth, and Diræ in heaven' (Lemprière, 'Diræ'). The press announced that ACS's 'Diræ' was to be a 'series of political sonnets by Mr Swinburne', which 'deal chiefly with incidents in the history of the Papacy and the French Empire during the past twelve or fourteen years, eight of the numbers having reference to the late Emperor Napoleon III' (*Glasgow Herald*, 5 April 1873, 1). Napoleon III died on 9 January 1873. Celæno was one of the harpies; 'Mastai' is Giovanni Maria Mastai Ferretti (1792–1878), Pope Pius IX (1846–78), who in 1869 remained head of the Papal States (they fell to the Italian nationalists in 1870). Cf. 'The Litany of Nations' and 'Mentana: First Anniversary', 245–9 and 242–4, respectively.

*triple-headed... God*: ACS wrote to WMR on 16 December 1869: 'What should you say to a sonnet on the Most Holy Trinity, entitled "Cerberus"?' (*SL*, ii.71). The line recalls Milton's 'triple tyrant' as a name for the Pope in 'On the Late Massacre in Piedmont', l.12.

*chief priest's*: Pius IX.

*As on the night... Heartless*: cf. 'They [the augurs] would not have you [Julius Caesar] stir forth today. | Plucking the entrails of an offering forth, | They could not find a heart within the beast', *Julius Caesar*, 2.2.37–40.

*The snake... deeds*: cf. Genesis 3:15.

## FROM 'REPORT OF THE FIRST ANNIVERSARY MEETING OF THE NEWEST SHAKESPEARE SOCIETY, 1 APRIL 1876' (1876/1880)

This was first published *The Examiner*, 3557 (1 April 1876), 381–3 (see also ACS's 'The Newest Shakespeare Society: Additions and Corrections' in *The Examiner*, 1 April 1876, 440–1). It was subsequently re-cast as an appendix to *A Study of Shakespeare*

(London: Chatto & Windus, 1880) and entitled 'Report of the Proceedings on the First Anniversary Session of the Newest Shakespeare Society'. Because the second version of this piece is fuller, it is the copytext here.

ACS first noted the essay, as a 'burlesque', in a letter to JM on 13 February 1876 (*SL*, iii.139). ACS's letter to TWD on 24 March 1876 (*SL*, iii.158) described the 'Report' as initially focusing on *Othello*, though it clearly grew to cover a wider range of issues related to alleged joint authorship of Shakespeare's plays. Reading *A Study of Shakespeare*, John Nichol observed 'Your "report of the proceedings" of Fartiwell & Co & all about his Shitspeare Society is inimitable' (letter of 3 February 1880, *UL*, ii.201).

The general context is the scrutiny of questions of Renaissance and Jacobean authorship by newly professional textual editors and critics: cf., for instance, F.G. Fleay, 'Who wrote our old plays?', *Macmillan's Magazine*, 30 (1874), 408–17. But ACS's principal target is F(rederick) J(ames) Furnivall (1825–1910) and his New Shakspere Society, founded in 1873, which included Fleay. ACS referred to the Society as the 'most pestilent swarm of parasites that ever settled [on Shakespeare]' (*SL*, iii.160–1). The New Shakspere Society followed from John Payne Collier's Shakespeare Society, founded in 1840, which was supported by, among others, James Orchard Halliwell-Phillipps (1820–89), ACS's friend. Furnivall founded many societies including the Early English Text Society in 1864, the Chaucer Society (1868), and the Ballad Society (1868). Like Fleay, he had studied mathematics at Cambridge and proposed to bring 'scientific' principles to the study of Shakespeare, particularly to questions of authorship. A minor part of the contention was about the spelling of Shakespeare's name: Halliwell-Phillipps' *Which Shall It Be? New Lamps or Old? Shaxpere or Shakespeare* (Brighton: Fleet and Bishop, 1879) wryly considered the evidence. ACS thought historical data pointed clearly to the traditional spelling (cf. letter to WMR, 6 January 1880, *UL*, ii.189–90). Furnivall's 'Shakspere' publications included *The Succession of Shakspere's Works and the Use of Metrical Tests in Settling it, &c.: Being the Introduction to Professor Gervinus's 'Commentaries on Shakspere'* (London: Smith, Elder, 1874). He introduced an edition of the complete works (the 'Leopold' edition) in 1877 and oversaw the publication in facsimiles of the quartos in forty-four volumes. Furnivall also issued *Mr Swinburne's 'Flat Burglary' on Shakspere: Two Letters from the 'Spectator' of September 6th & 13th, 1879* (London: p.p., 1879). The row, during the 1880s, was vocal and vicious, and sometimes bitterly scholarly: e.g. Furnivall's etymological inquiry 'Swinburne—Swine's Brook' in *The Antiquary*, 1 (1880), 47.

ACS maintained friendly but formal contact with Halliwell-Phillipps, receiving from him material on Shakespeare's life and work in February 1876 (*SL*, iii.139–40). This helped Furnivall turn against Halliwell-Phillipps. ACS, who dedicated *A Study of Shakespeare* to Halliwell-Phillipps, was hurt in early 1881 by Furnivall's description of ACS 'in so many words—[as] a "person of damaged character"' (*SL*, iv.196) and endeavoured to enlist the support of Robert Browning, President of the New Shakspere Society. Halliwell-Phillipps tried to do the same, issuing a pamphlet entitled *Copy of Correspondence between J.O. Halliwell-Phillipps and Robert Browning, Concerning Expressions Respecting Halliwell-Phillipps, used by F.J. Furnivall in the Preface to a*

*Facsimile of the Second Edition of 'Hamlet', published in 1880* (Brighton: p.p., 1881). Furnivall replied with *The 'Co.' of Pigsbrook & Co.* (London: p.p., 1881), an open letter from 8 February 1881 about Halliwell-Phillipps ('Hell.-P.') playing on the Old English origins of 'Swinburne' again. Furnivall's 'insolence to me', Halliwell-Phillipps said to ACS after reading this, 'is but subsidiary to a violent and disgraceful personal attack on you, for which latter he deserves to be heartily trounced in the Law Courts' (*UL*, ii.252). At times, ACS could not bring himself to write Furnivall's name (*SL*, iv.191). For ACS's early fury over the integrity of Robert Browning, see the unpublished 'The Chaotic School' (sometime between May 1863 and May 1864), reproduced in *NWS*, 40–60. For more on ACS and Fleay, see note on 668.

*Cyril Tourneur... Tragedy*: this play is now usually ascribed to Thomas Middleton. For ACS's conception of Tourneur, see 'Cyril Tourneur', 356.

*Bussy d'Ambois*: by George Chapman.

*full... Webster*: in Webster's 'Address to the Reader' at the beginning of *The White Devil*.

*when[:]*: editorial addition.

*Anthony Munday*: (baptized 1560–1633), playwright.

*Lord Burghley*: William Cecil, 1st Baron Burghley (1520–98), chief advisor to Elizabeth I.

*'that kind... alone'*: *Romeo and Juliet*, 2.1.35–6.

*Anjou marriage*: that is, Lord Burghley's involvement in the proposed marriage between Elizabeth I and Henri, Duke of Anjou, third son of Catherine de' Medici, in 1571.

*George Peele... bounty*: the playwright George Peele (baptized 1556, d.1596) dedicated *The Tale of Troy* to Lord Burghley in the hope of patronage in the last year of his life.

*Christopher Sly*: in *The Taming of the Shrew*, this minor figure is seen drunk at the opening of Act 1.1 outside an alehouse as his hostess endeavours to make him to pay for his drinks.

*'loose and humorous'*: cf. *Loose and Humorous Songs* [from Bishop Percy's manuscript] edited by J.W. Hales and F.J. Furnivall, assisted by W. Chappell (London: Trübner, 1867).

*William Haughton... Money*: Haughton's comedy *Englishmen for My Money, or A Woman Will Have Her Will* (1598). Haughton collaborated extensively with other playwrights including Thomas Dekker.

*'Night's... out'*: *Romeo and Juliet*, 3.5.9.

*'Night's... obscure'*: Haughton, *Englishmen for My Money*, 3.1.3.

*Sir John Harrington*: ACS is thinking of Sir John Harington (1561–1612) and his *A New Discourse of a Stale Subject, Called the Metamorphosis of Ajax* (1596) where 'Ajax' is a newly-invented flush toilet.

*Sir Thomas Lucy*: the young Shakespeare was traditionally thought either to have poached from Sir Thomas' estate (cf. Thomas Brooks' painting, *Shakespeare Before Thomas Lucy* (1857), now in the Royal Shakespeare Company Collection) or to have written a ballad against him that punned on Lucy/lousy. Such puns on luces [pikes]/louses are made in Act 1.1 of *The Merry Wives of Windsor* and it might be that Justice Shallow is a version of Lucy who had three luces on his coat of arms.

*135th, 136th, and 143rd sonnets*: 'Whoever hath her wish, thou hast thy Will'; 'Swear to thy blind soul that I was thy Will'; 'So will I pray that thou mayst have thy "Will" '.

*[Shakespeare]*: ACS's square brackets.

*Black Will and Shakebag*: murderers in the anonymous play *Arden of Feversham* (1592) with which Shakespeare has sometimes been linked.

*coloured bust... Stratford*: that is, in the memorial above Shakespeare's grave. The bust, dated some time before the First Folio of 1623, has been repainted on a number of occasions.

*Spanish Tragedy*: revenge tragedy by Thomas Kyd, *c.*1590.

*adycions to Jeronymo*: Ben Jonson was lent money for writing additions to the *Spanish Tragedy, or Hieronimo is Mad Again*, as noted in *The Works of Ben Jonson*, ed. W. Gifford, 9 vols (London: Bulmer, 1816), i.34n.

*lameness*: a question derived from l.3 of Sonnet 89: 'Speak of my lameness, and I straight will halt'.

*'This shoe... sole'*: *Two Gentlemen of Verona*, 2.3.14–17.

*novel*: the Spanish romance, *Diana Enamorada* (1564), available in an English translation in 1598.

*'made lame... spite'*: Sonnet 37, l.3.

## FROM *NOTE OF AN ENGLISH REPUBLICAN ON THE MUSCOVITE CRUSADE* (LONDON: CHATTO & WINDUS, 1876)

First published December 1876. On 28 November 1876, a long letter from Thomas Carlyle, written on 24 November, was published in *The Times*, headed 'Mr Carlyle on the Eastern Question'. In it, Carlyle praised Russia as a force for good in Europe and urged Turkey out of Bulgaria:

> In the first place, then, for 50 years back my clear belief about the Russians has been that they are a good and even noble element in Europe. Conspicuously they possess the talent of obedience, of silently following orders given, which in the universal celebration of ballot-box, divine freedom, &c, will be found an invaluable and peculiar gift. Ever since Peter the Great's appearance among them, they have been in steady progress of development. In our own time they have done signal service to God and man in drilling into order and peace anarchic populations all

over their side of the world. The present Czar of Russia I judge to be a strictly honest and just man, and, in short, my belief is that the Russians are called to do great things in the world, and to be a conspicuous benefit, directly and indirectly, to their fellow men.

[...] It seems to me that something very different from war on his behalf is what the Turk now pressingly needs from England and from all the world—namely, to be peremptorily informed that we can stand no more of his attempts to govern in Europe, and that he must *quam primum* [as soon as possible] turn his face to the eastward, for ever quit this side of the Hellespont, and give up his arrogant ideas of governing anybody but himself. [...] The only clear advice I have to give is, as I have stated, that the unspeakable Turk should be immediately struck out of the question, and the country left to honest European guidance; delaying which can be profitable or agreeable only to gamblers on the Stock Exchange, but distressing and unprofitable to all other men.

(*The Times*, 28 November 1876, 6)

Carlyle was notorious among liberals not least as the supporter of Governor Eyre (1815–1901) in his repression of the Morant Bay rebellion in Jamaica in October 1865, including the execution of George William Gordon, whom Eyre believed to be the ringleader of the uprising, and reports of the flogging of pregnant women. ACS refers to this rebellion. British liberals had formed the Jamaica Committee to denounce Eyre and bring him to trial over Gordon's death and were supported by John Stuart Mill. But Eyre's return to England in August 1866 prompted the formation of the Eyre Defence Committee to protect him from prosecution. Members of this included Charles Kingsley, J.A. Froude, John Ruskin, and Carlyle. The role of Ruskin in this Committee is considered in David R. Sorensen, 'Ruskin and Carlyle' in *The Cambridge Companion to John Ruskin*, ed. Francis O'Gorman (Cambridge: Cambridge University Press, 2015), 189–201.

The *Note* draws on Carlyle's reputation among liberals as an anti-democrat and an opponent of liberty (cf. Carlyle's *Macmillan Magazine* article, 'Shooting Niagara: And After?' in August 1867 on the Second Reform Bill), as well as a defender of cruelty, authoritarian rule, and the slave system (cf. Carlyle's 'Occasional Discourse on the Negro Question', in *Fraser's Magazine*, February 1849). ACS observed to WMR on 22 January 1880 that 'In common with such reactionary royalists or objectionably "moderate Liberals" as Louis Kossuth & Karl Blind, I take the attitude of a man's mind towards Russia as the test of the worth & the sincerity of his [...] faith in freedom' (*UL*, ii.196).

The context for ACS's *Note* is the recent events in the on-going problem of the Eastern Question: the fall-out from the slow disintegration of the Ottoman Empire during the course of the 19th century. The conflict was economic, cultural, ethnic, and religious, with tension between Christians and Muslims at a particularly low point in April 1876 when an uprising by Bulgarians, aimed at the liberation of Bulgaria and its establishment as an independent nation-state, was repressed by Ottoman forces. Events included the Batak Massacre from 30 April 1876 into early May. During this, the Ottoman commander Ahmet Aga and an army of irregular and often disorderly troops known as Bashi-bazouks ('leaderless') massacred civilian Christian Bulgarians in the town of Batak on the northern slopes of the Rhodope Mountains. International outcry was considerable though the British Prime Minister, Benjamin Disraeli, was cautious and suspicious, much to the disapproval of liberals.

As in the Crimean War, part of the problem was the role of Russia in any pan-Slavic reform. The more access Russia had to Eastern Europe, the greater the potential for radical changes to the balance of European power. The notion of a pan-Slavic alliance led by Tsarist Russia appalled ACS. But he was also bothered by why British liberals were so concerned by Batak but not by many similar acts of violent repression elsewhere. On 8 December 1876, ACS sent TWD an announcement of a 'philo-Bulgarian conference to be held in St James' Hall', and observed that 'this outbreak of English sympathy with suffering Bulgars, especially in quarters where I had never been able to find or awaken a spark on behalf of Italy, Hungary, or Poland, reminded me irresistibly of the query addressed so persistently to her Lord by the chaste Mrs Jonathan Wild, *née* Letitia Snap—"But methinks, Mr Wild, I would fain know, Why Bitch?" In like manner, I said, I could not but feel tempted to put on this occasion as modest and pertinent a query—Why Bulgar?' (*SL*, iii.228). See also ACS's 'The Ballad of Bulgarie', *NWS*, 17–19.

ACS initially planned his *Note* as a long newspaper letter (*SL*, iii.221). He was supported in his views, as on the Anglo-Irish Union, by Karl Blind (*UL*, ii.91). He was also supported by John Nichol who, while thinking the essay would have been more powerful if shorter, also thought—in a peculiarly out-of-control letter on 29 December 1876 written presumably while drunk—that Carlyle's impotence was the problem: 'It is not the murders & massacres [Carlyle] objects to: those he rather likes *wherever found*: it is the ravishing, which he never affected & the power of which he has outlived' (*UL*, ii.95). Nichol had expressed qualified admiration for Carlyle in 'Might and Right', an essay suggested by Carlyle's *The History of Friedrich II* and reproduced in Nichol's *Fragments of Criticism* (Edinburgh: Nichol, 1860), 77–88. Criticism of ACS came, for instance, from George Augustus Sala, who found the term 'crusade' puzzling and asked 'why Mr Swinburne, who, to my mind, is from head to heel an Aristocrat, should call himself (and not for the first time, I grant) a Republican. He has about the same claim to the title as M. le Vicomte Victor Hugo', 'The Grand Turk at Home', *The Gentleman's Magazine*, 240 (May 1877), 584–604 (584). Cf. 'After Looking into Carlyle's Reminiscences' included in *TLOP*.

*Francia*: Carlyle had reviewed a variety of books in the *Foreign Quarterly Review*, 31 (July 1843), 544–89, on the despotism of José Gaspar Rodriguez de Francia (1766–1840), lawyer and leader of Paraguay, in which he expressed qualified support ('O Francia, though thou hadst to execute forty persons, I am not without some pity for thee!', 589).

*Mouravieff*: Count Michael Nikolayevich Muraviev (1845–1900), who suppressed the January Uprising in 1863 in the Polish-Lithuanian Commonwealth. ACS called him a 'hellish miscreant' in 1889 (*SL*, iv.203).

*greatest English writer*: Carlyle (Scottish writer in English).

*one Englishman*: Landor?

*Mr Gladstone... political philanthropy?*: Gladstone's *Bulgarian Horrors and the Question of the East* (London: Murray, 1876) had been a diagnosis of the Bulgarian uprising and a criticism of Disraeli's handling of it, which concluded: 'Let the Turks now carry away their abuses in the only possible manner, namely by carrying off themselves [from Bulgaria]. Their Zaptiehs and their Mudirs, their Bimbashis and their Yuzbachis, their Kaimakams and their Pashas, one and all, bag and baggage, shall, I hope, clear out from the province they have desolated and profaned' (38). 'Bag and baggage' became a popular phrase in relation to British policy in the Ottoman Empire.

*'divine freedom, &c.'*: see Carlyle's letter in headnote.

*Hungary, of Poland*: ACS is thinking of Tsar Nicholas I (1796–1855) and both his conquest of Poland in the Polish-Russian War (1830–1) and his assistance in the repression of the Hungarian revolution of 1848–9 (cf. Carlyle's *Latter-Day Pamphlet*, No. 4, 'The New Downing Street', 15 April 1850, and ACS's 'Preface' to *Miscellanies*).

*satrap*: 'A subordinate ruler; often suggesting an imputation of tyranny or ostentatious splendour', *OED*.

*small group... gutter*: 'Truly one knows not whether less to venerate the Majesty's Ministers, who, instead of rewarding their Governor Eyre, throw him out of window to a small loud group, small as now appears, and nothing but a group or knot of rabid Nigger-Philanthropists, barking furiously in the gutter, and threatening one's Reform Bill with loss of certain friends and votes', Carlyle, 'Shooting Niagara: And After?', *The Works of Thomas Carlyle*, ed. H.D. Traill, 30 vols (London: Chapman and Hall, 1896–9), xxx.12.

*[forgoes]*: 'foregoes' in the copytext.

*hoc habeat... sepulchro*: 'may he possess it still, and retain it in his grave', Virgil, *Aeneid*, Bk 4, l.29: *The Works of Virgil Translated into English Prose*, translated by John Davidson, 2 vols, new edn (London: Longman, Law, etc., 1794), i.5.

*Tiberius*: Jesus was executed during the reign of the Emperor Tiberius (cf. Luke 3:1).

*Latter-day... Nazarene Question*: parodying two of Carlyle's publication titles.

*'the unspeakable... question'*: from the last paragraph of Carlyle's letter to *The Times* (see headnote).

*very shame*: *Taming of the Shrew*, 3.3.53.

*English philosophers*: J.S. Mill and the committee to prosecute Governor Eyre.

*soft quality... accursed*: in Vol. 3, Bk 8, Ch. 4 of Carlyle's *The History of Friedrich II of Prussia, called Frederick the Great*, published between 1858 and 1865.

*biographer of Frederic William*: *The History of Friedrich II*.

*poor old*: ACS is referring to a portion of Vol. 3, Bk 8, Ch. 4 of Carlyle's *The History of Friedrich II* that recounts summary executions ordered by Friedrich including of a 'poor old soul' named Hesse who could not find some money when it was asked for: after his hanging, the money was discovered in his rooms. Carlyle concludes: 'it is on the hard quality of justice, first of all, that Empires are built up, and beneficent and lasting things become achievable to mankind, in this world'.

*'rhythmic drill'*: a term often associated with Carlyle (cf. 'Mr Carlyle on Reform', *Littell's Living Age*, 6 (1867), 614).

*honest... Othello*: referring to the discussion of 'honest' in Act 3 Sc. 3.

*seventy... times*: cf. Matthew 18:22.

*'in our... world'*: see the passage from Carlyle's letter in the headnote.

*Moloch*: a god who required child sacrifice from parents (cf. 2 Kings 23:10).

*'the Czar... wrongs'*: all from Carlyle's *Times* letter.

## THE SAILING OF THE SWALLOW (1877)

First published in *The Gentleman's Magazine*, 240 (March 1877), 287–308 (the copy text here) and subsequently included, with revisions, as the first canto of *TL* published in *TLOP* (note that additional alterations were included in later Chatto & Windus editions, presumably with ACS's authority). *The Gentleman's Magazine* was by now published by Chatto & Windus (previously John Henry and James Parker). Together with 'Tristram and Iseult: Prelude of an Unfinished Poem', 281–7, 'The Sailing of the Swallow' was the only other portion of *TL* published separately. The poem was prematurely announced as 'finished' in *The Orchestra*, 17 (19 January 1872), 248, but nothing appeared in print for another five years. ACS had corrected proofs by 2 December 1876. The title recalls WM's 'The Sailing of the Sword' from *The Defence of Guenevere, and Other Poems*. It is matched in *TL* by the final canto, 'The Sailing of the Swan' (which opens with a similarly long incantatory sentence with 'Love' replaced by 'Fate').

ACS's principal sources for *TL* as a whole are Malory's *Le Morte Darthur* (1485) and *Sir Tristrem: A Metrical Romance of the Thirteenth Century*, ed. Sir Walter Scott, 3rd edn (Edinburgh: Constable, 1811). Some important material comes from the Prose *Lancelot*, as indicated in notes below. ACS asked, when writing to EBJ, for Malory, 'Scott's chaos', and Francisque Michel's *Tristan: Recueil de ce qui reste des poëmes relatifs à ses aventures, composés en françois, en anglo-normand, et en grec dans les XII. et XIII. siècles*, 3 vols (London: Pickering, 1835–9) while preparing the poem on 4 November ?1869 (*SL*, ii.50).

Writing to EBJ in the same letter, ACS observed: 'I want my version to be based on notorious facts [cf. Browning's 'How it Strikes a Contemporary', l.35], and to be acceptable for its orthodoxy and fidelity to the dear old story: so that Tristram may not be mistaken for his late Royal Highness the Duke of Kent, or Iseult for Queen Charlotte, or Palomydes for Mr Gladstone [...] I want to have in everything *pretty* that is of any importance, and is in keeping with the tone and spirit of the story—not burlesque or dissonant or inconsistent. The thought of your painting and Wagner's music ought to abash but does stimulate me: but my only chance I am aware will be to adhere strongly to Fact and Reality—to shun Fiction as perilously akin to lying, and make this piece of sung or spoken History a genuine bit of earnest work in these dim times.

Ahem' (*SL*, ii.51). The reference to EBJ's painting might be to *The Madness of Sir Tristram* (*c.*1862) or, just possibly, to the early stages of a painting called *Tristram and Iseult* that was abandoned in 1872 (now in a private collection). This *Tristram and Iseult* was first exhibited in 2012 (*sic*). EBJ had contributed four stained glass panels for Morris & Co's *Tristram and Iseult* for Harden Grange in 1862.

Similarly, in dispute with Tennyson's Arthurian poems and *Idylls of the King*, ACS said of *TL* to DGR on 22 December 1869: 'My first sustained attempt at a poetic narrative may not be as good as Gudrun [part of 'November' from WM's *Earthly Paradise*: 'The Lovers of Gudrun']—but if it doesn't lick the Morte d' [Tennyson's 'Morte d'Arthur'] I hope I may not die without extreme unction' (*SL*, ii.73). ACS continued:

> On board ship I mean to make the innocent Iseult ask Tristram about the knights and ladies, and him tell her of Queen Morgause of Orkney and her incest with the 'blameless king,' [a common formulation in Tennyson's *Idylls*] and other larks illustrative of the Alberto-Victorian purity of the Court: but delicately, sparing respectfully the innocence of her who was to make the first and greatest scandal there of all in time—as in days past at Oxford, when we first met, you fellows might have respected my spotless adolescence.
>
> (*SL*, ii.74–5)

Having required £50 for the 'Prelude' (see 602), ACS said on 10 November 1876 he would be glad to receive the same amount for 'The Sailing of the Swallow', 'though it *is* worth at least twice as much as the Prelude (mine, not Wordsworth's!) in size and importance' (*SL*, iii.218).

'The Sailing of the Swallow' covers the journey of Tristram from Ireland to Cornwall, accompanying Iseult of Ireland to her future husband, King Mark. Iseult has previously helped heal wounds Tristram received in defeating Morholt, who had been demanding tribute from Mark. Tristram and Iseult are accompanied by Iseult's maid, Brangwain, who has been given a love potion made by Iseult's mother to ensure that King Mark and Iseult fall in love with each other. By accident, the potion is drunk by Tristram and Iseult at the end of this canto, leading to the tragic events that the remaining nine books of the complete poem relate. Prior to drinking the potion, Tristram tells stories about the knights of King Arthur, many of which involve accidents and the fall-out of King Arthur's unintended incest with his half-sister. Cf. ACS's comments on *TL* in the 1904 'Dedication', 530.

*mother*: Lady Blancheflour's story is told in ACS's 'Of the birth of Sir Tristram', 12–22.

*bitter name*: Tristram, recalling 'triste' (sad).

*The second . . . fame*: the second most famous of Arthur's knights.

*sad queen*: Lady Blancheflour.

*mother's magic*: Iseult's mother—Queen Iseult—is a magician. The young Iseult is here imagined helping heal Tristram's wounds that he received in defeating Morholt, Iseult's uncle. He had been demanding tribute payments from King Mark.

*Galahault*: this detail, as ACS noted (*SL*, ii.75), comes from the Prose *Lancelot*, where Galahault (Galehot/Galehaut/Galeotto), after making war against Arthur, surrenders to gain Lancelot's friendship. He later arranges the meeting at which Lancelot and Guenevere first declare their love.

*Arthur's sister*: Morgan Le Fay, mistress of the Isle of Avalon. In ACS's version, she is unhappily married, adulterous, and doomed to know the fate of the Round Table and the sin of Lancelot and Guenevere.

*third... Launcelot*: i.e. the knight ACS calls Lamoracke. Cf. Malory, 'betwixt three knights is departed clearly knighthood, that is Launcelot du Lake, Sir Tristram de Liones, and Sir Lamorak de Galis' (139).

*No herb... drink*: Morgan le Fay is associated with magic drinks. Cf. Malory: 'So he departed from him with Sir Driant, and by the way they met with a knight that was sent from Morgan le Fay unto King Arthur; and this knight had a fair horn harnessed with gold, and the horn had such a virtue that there might no lady nor gentlewoman drink of that horn but if she were true to her husband, and if she were false she should spill all the drink, and if she were true to her lord she might drink peaceable. And because of the Queen Guenever, and in the despite of Sir Launcelot, this horn was sent unto King Arthur; and by force Sir Lamorak made that knight to tell all the cause why he bare that horn. Now shalt thou bear this horn, said Lamorak, unto King Mark, or else choose thou to die for it; for I tell thee plainly, in despite and reproof of Sir Tristram thou shalt bear that horn unto King Mark, his uncle, and say thou to him that I sent it him for to assay his lady, and if she be true to him he shall prove her. So the knight went his way unto King Mark, and brought him that rich horn, and said that Sir Lamorak sent it him, and thereto he told him the virtue of that horn. Then the king made Queen Isoud to drink thereof, and an hundred ladies, and there were but four ladies of all those that drank clean' (189).

*wittingly he sinned*: Arthur sleeps with Morgause of Orkney, unaware she is his half-sister.

*Morgause of Orkney*: in Malory, Gawaine is the son of King Lot of Orkney and his wife Margause (37). As the half-sister of Arthur, she is, as explained, the mother of Mordred.

*Twain... mother*: the mother of both is Igraine. Arthur's father is Uther Pendragon; Morgause's is the Duke of Cornwall.

*April yet*: cf. Thomas Morley's madrigal, 'April is in my mistress' face'.

*son... loins*: Merlin was born the son of a queen and a supernatural incubus.

*Nimue*: the Lady of the Lake, or in other versions one of the Ladies of the Lake, who gives the sword Excalibur to Arthur and later marries Sir Pelleas. In some versions, she raises Lancelot after the death of his father, King Ban. Nimue accompanies Arthur's body to Avalon. Mary Byrd Davis notes this passage summarizes the early part of the Prose *Lancelot* which ACS 'seems to have read': 'Swinburne's Use of His Sources in "Tristram of Lyonesse"', *Philological Quarterly*, 55 (1976), 96–112 (98).

*Ettarde*: the story of Ettare's deceptive flattery of Pelleas, who has fallen in love with her beauty, is included in Tennyson's 'Pelleas and Ettare' (1869), *Idylls of the King*. ACS observed to DGR on 22 December 1869: 'As for Tennyson's Pelleas, you flatter him by calling him a school-boy who misses the birch', continuing: 'the very birch could hardly have drawn human blood [...] from that biped' (*SL*, ii.75).

*King Claudas and King Ban*: King Claudas fights and eventually kills King Ban and his brother King Bors, champions of King Arthur. Nimue at this point takes the orphaned Lancelot (her 'mighty nursling') to her lake.

*Balen*: the story of Balen and Balin, virtuous but cursed knights, is told in Malory, Bk 2, and 'Balin and Balan' (1885), *Idylls of the King*. Cf. ACS, *The Tale of Balen* (1896).

*Mordred*: the treacherous knight who eventually wounds Arthur fatally. He is 'misborn' as he is Arthur's son fathered through accidental incest with Morgause. Mordred and his half-brother Agravaine expose Lancelot's adultery with Guenevere (see Malory, Bk 19).

*Gawain*: a noble knight, son of King Lot of Orkney and his wife Margause and thus brother of Gareth, Mordred, and Agravaine.

*Gareth*: a noble knight, the youngest son of Lot and Margause.

*The breath... and die*: cf. the close of the 'Prelude', 287.

*Other lords... fare so well*: cf. John 2:10.

*Galahault was the cup*: see note on 617.

## FROM *POEMS AND BALLADS, SECOND SERIES* (LONDON: CHATTO & WINDUS, 1878)

### The Last Oracle

First published *Belgravia*, 29 (May 1876), 329–32. On 1 February 1876, ACS wrote to JM saying that he had just finished 'The Last Oracle' and was offering it to *FR*. ACS noted that he never received less than '£10 down' for 'a little thing, sonnet or song of but a dozen lines', but wanted more for a 'poem nine or ten times the length of such a piece'. He continued:

> So much for the Grub Street side of the matter; and I will not press my wares by any further advertisement than a mention of the subject, which starts from the message sent back (to the effect that there was none) from Delphi to Julian when he sent to consult the oracle the year of his accession, and passes into an invocation of the healing and destroying God of song and of the sun, taken as the type of the 'light of thought' [Shelley, 'To a Skylark', l.37] and spirit of speech which makes and unmakes gods within the soul that it makes vocal and articulate from age to age: not really therefore son of Zeus the son of Chronos [conventional Classical

formulation], but older than all time we take count of, and father of all possible gods fashioned by the human spirit out of itself for types of worship.

This sounds rather metaphysical, but I don't think the verse is obscure or turbid—the form of a hymn or choral chant, and the alternate metre of twelve long trochaic lines and twelve shorter anapaestic, carry the thought on and carry off the symbolic or allegoric ambiguity; at least so I flatter myself. But I must not be recommending this superior article now in stock by putting my own price on it in the style of the poets of *The Dunciad*. I need hardly warn you that it is *not* exactly qualified by its tone to conciliate a Christian public; tho' I have somewhat softened the anti-Galilean fervour of my first conceptions.

(*SL*, iii.129–30)

ACS glossed the poem further in a letter to TWD on 8 February 1876:

My newly finished poem—'The Last Oracle'—is 144 lines long, burden counted. I have written to Morley that he may have it for the Fortnightly if he likes or can afford to bid fair. Starting from the answer brought back from Delphi to Julian by his envoy (AD 361), I go on to reinvoke Apollo to reappear in these days when the Galilean too is conquered and Christ has followed Pan to death, not as they called him in Greece, merely son of Zeus the son of Chronos, but older than Time or any God born of Time, the Light and Word incarnate in man, of whom comes the inner sunlight of human thought or imagination and the gift of speech and song whence all Gods or ideas of Gods possible to man take form and fashion—conceived of thought or imagination and born of speech or song. Of this I take the sun-god and the singing-god of the Greeks to be the most perfect type attained, or attainable; and as such I call on him to return and re-appear over the graves of intervening Gods.—This is the subject-matter; metre—twelve long trochaics followed by twelve shorter anapaestic lines, alternating through six stanzas of 24 verses.

(*SL*, iii.137)

ACS discussed this epigraph concerning the Oracle's announcement that 'it was all up with Phoebus' (*SL*, iii.141) with Edwin Harrison on 13 and 17 February 1876 (*SL*, iii.140–5; see also 652). He was still discussing how much he wanted to be paid after failing to agree with *FR* in March (*SL*, iii.156–7). ACS again advised TWD he wanted £50 on 4 April (*SL*, iii.173). Eventually, the poem went to *Belgravia*, a journal that Chatto & Windus took over as proprietors in March as the novelist Mary Elizabeth Braddon stepped down as editor. ACS did not like the name. '"Belgravia" *stinks*', he told TWD (*SL*, iii.163, letter of 31 March 1876); he was not wholly happy with his poem appearing there either (*SL*, iii.176) though Chatto & Windus wanted to use his work to help increase the quality of the journal (*UL*, ii.69). ACS wrote to Mallarmé on 1 June 1876 thanking him for a presentation copy of *L'Après-midi d'un faune* (Paris: Darenne, 1876) and claimed that London was screaming against his own poem that was both pagan and disgusting ('ils ne hurlent à Londres contre le "poëme paiën [*sic*] et dégoûtant"', *SL*, iii.193). I have not found evidence to support this. When the poem was included in *PB* 2, it was picked out by *SRev* for (qualified) admiration: 'In "The Last Oracle" there are some fine stanzas in Mr Swinburne's philosophic, or rather gnomic, strain', *SRev*, 46 (20 July 1878), 86. TWD reviewed the volume anonymously for *The Athenæum*, 6 July 1878, 7–9.

'The Last Oracle' may be compared with 'Delphic Hymn to Apollo (B.C.280) Done into English by Algernon Charles Swinburne', *NC*, 36 (1894), 315–16. The rhyme schemes make this a peculiarly virtuosic poem.

*Εἴπατε τῷ… ὕδωρ*: ACS thought this one of the last Delphic oracles, delivered to Oribasios as an envoy of Emperor Julian the Apostate (see headnote on 571–2): 'Tell the emperor that my hall has fallen to the ground. Phoibos no longer has his house nor his mantic bay nor his prophetic spring; the water has dried up': see Joseph Fontenrose, *The Delphic Oracle: Its Responses and Operations with a Catalogue of Responses* (Berkeley: University of California Press, 1978), 353. Cf. stanza 29 of Milton's 'On the Morning of Christ's Nativity' and the translation ACS provides, ll.7–10.

*mid shrine*: it is half way up the ceremonial pathway of the Delphi temple complex.

*bowed… head*: cf. John 19:30.

*Thou hast conquered… Galilean*: see headnote on 571.

*Paian*: *παιάν*, 'healer', one of the terms of address for Apollo (see next note).

*paeans*: also *παιάν*, paean, a hymn usually addressed to Apollo (see previous note).

*Son of God*: Apollo is the son of Zeus and Leto.

*Thou… life*: gathering various attributes of Christ to address Apollo.

*Day by day*: though a commonplace, this collocation might ironically allude to 'Per singulos dies benedicimus te' from the *Te Deum* ('Day by day we magnify thee').

## A Forsaken Garden

First published *The Athenæum*, 22 July 1876, 112. ACS first mentioned this poem on 30 August 1875, along with 'A Song in Season' (*PB* 2). 'A Forsaken Garden', ACS told TWD, was 'the more important of the two and written in the higher key and graver metre, one more of my own devising' (*SL*, iii.62). Note the stress patterns of the three syllable lines. He discussed the name ('A forsaken—or deserted—or ruined Garden' will do; let them choose which participle they please') with TWD when arranging terms with *The Athenæum* (*SL*, iii.125–6). By 31 March 1876, ACS was still wondering what TWD had agreed about publication: 'When am I to hear the last word about the appearance of the old-garden poem?' (*SL*, iii.162). The garden is presumably based on West Undercliff, near East Dene, Isle of Wight. Note that ACS had stayed on the Isle in the summer of 1874 (John Churton Collins referred to it as 'a little poem you wrote about a garden in the Isle of Wight' on 24 March 1876 (*UL*, ii.71)). East Dene, Bonchurch, had been ACS's childhood home; it was purchased by the Tory MP John Snowdon Henry (1824–96) in 1865 (cf. 'By the North Sea', 407–20). The garden, then, had not only been forsaken by the Swinburnes but also, in ACS's conception of things, by anyone liberal. 'A Forsaken Garden' was included in *Selections*.

*We shall sleep*: cf. 1 Corinthians 15:51.

## Relics

First published as 'North and South', *FR*, xiii (May 1873), 564–6. 'Relics', originally conceived as 'Two Flowers', gained its present title when reissued in *PB* 2. ACS asked JM what title the poem should have on 11 April 1873, observing that the '*names* of the flowers would make far too ponderous and polysyllabic a title for anything under a South Sea Idyl or epic' (*SL*, ii.240). The 'south' portion of the poem is the hill-top Tuscan town of San Gimignano, linked here with Santa Fina (1238–53), a young woman of faith who is still venerated there (though not formally canonized a saint).

*laurustine*: *Viburnum tinus* (Laurustinus, or Laurestine) is a white flowered ever-green shrub, particularly growing in southern Europe.

## *Ave Atque Vale:*
In Memory of Charles Baudelaire

First published *FR*, 3 (January 1868), 71–6. On 19 April 1866, ACS noted that he had seen 'in the papers a notice of the death of a man whom I deeply admired and believed in—Charles Baudelaire [. . .] It is a great loss to all men, and great to me personally, who have had the honour to be coupled with Baudelaire as a fellow labourer, and have exchanged with him messages and courtesies' (*SL*, i.164). Later, on 22 May, he told George Powell that he was 'writing a little sort of lyric dirge for my poor Baudelaire' (*SL*, i.246). Certainly, a variety of papers carried the story of the French poet's death, often misspelling Baudelaire as 'Bandelaire'. *The Newcastle Courant* on 20 April 1866, for instance, observed that the poet 'Charles Bandelaire has died in a mad-house. He was a most eccentric man, lived on opium, and was an admirer of De Quincey's works, and adopted his system of exciting his brain, the result of which is proved by his early death' (6). *PMG* noticed on 16 April that 'M. Charles Bandelaire, the well-known realist French poet, author of the "Fleurs du Mal," has just died at Brussels' (6). This was all false. Baudelaire died on 31 August 1867 in Paris after a stroke. See 'Note on the Texts', xlix.

Writing many years later about William Sharp's edition of ACS (see headnote to 'Super flumina Babylonis', 591), ACS said: 'I should have preferred on all accounts that *In the Bay* had filled the place you have allotted to *Ave Atque Vale*, a poem to which you are altogether too kind in my opinion, as others have been before you. I never had really much in common with Baudelaire, though I retain all my early admiration for his genius at its best' (*SL*, vi. 153). ACS draws on poems from *Les Fleurs du mal* and many individual words and phrases recall Baudelaire. Most substantially, the poem refers to 'Lesbos' in stanza 2 (one of the *pièces condamnées*) and the giantess in stanza 6 draws on 'La géante'. ACS's title is derived from Catullus' celebrated line 'atque in perpetuum frater ave atque vale' (Catullus 101) on the death of his brother ('and forever brother hail and farewell'). Cf. ACS's use in *William Blake*, above, 200.

*[Certes]*: 'Certe' in copy-text.

*Nous devrions . . . ingrats*: 'We must take him some flowers; | The dead, the poor dead have great suffering, | And when October blows, the pruner of old trees, | His melancholy winds around their tombs, | Certainly, they must perceive the living ungrateful', adapted from 'La servante au grand cœur', composed before the end of 1843, and included in the 1857 and 1861 edition of *Les Fleurs*.

*Leucadian grave*: on Sappho and her 'Leucadian leap' as a result of her love for Phaon, see headnote to 'Anactoria', 569–70.

*Seeing . . . reap*: cf. Job 4:8.

*It is enough*: cf. 1 Kings 19:4, 'But he himself went a day's journey into the wilderness, and came and sat down under a juniper tree: and he requested for himself that he might die; and said, It is enough; now, O Lord, take away my life; for I am not better than my fathers.'

*Orestes-like . . . hair*: ACS images himself like exiled Orestes who leaves two locks of his hair on his father Agamemnon's grave in the first speech of Aeschylus' play, *Libation Bearers* (*Χοηφόροι*), the second play of the *Oresteia*. His sister, Elektra, mourning her father too, makes clear that the lock is a peculiarly solemn offering (l.173) and also that the House of Atreus is cursed: ACS, linking himself with Orestes, suggests a bond with Baudelaire as a writer who had been persecuted.

*no hand . . . stricken*: Agamemnon in Aeschylus' version is slain by his wife Clytemnestra.

*lord of light*: Apollo, god of light, music, and poetry.

*Therefore . . . crown*: Apollo mixes his laurel wreath with the cypress, long associated with mourning.

*That obscure . . . hill*: see the Tannhäuser legend described in the headnote on 564–5.

*Cytherean . . . Erycine*: both local names for Aphrodite.

*break in blossom*: from the Tannhäuser legend.

*Niobean womb*: Niobe (*Νιόβη*) in ancient Greek religion is an ancestor of Orestes and Elektra who loses all (or nearly all) her daughters and sons in an act of divine punishment; she turns into a rock, and her tears become a stream.

## Memorial Verses on the Death of Théophile Gautier

First published *FR*, 13 (January 1873), 68–73. ACS had to write to JM chasing up payment on 20 July 1874 (*SL*, ii.315). 'Memorial Verses' was also included in *Le Tombeau de Théophile Gautier* (Paris: Alphonse Lemerre, 1873), commemorating Gautier's death on 23 October 1872. *Le Tombeau* contained poems by Théodore de Banville, Emile Bergerat, François Coppée, Anatole France, Victor Hugo, and ACS, among others.

ACS noted his planned contributions for *Le Tombeau*—'in French English Greek or Latin'—in a letter to Nichol, 19 November 1872 (*SL*, ii.198). ACS eventually contributed in each of those languages and all poems except the Greek 'epigrams' were included in *PB 2*. Gautier's death prompted obituaries from the English press (e.g. the notice in *MP*, 25 October 1872, 5, and in *PMG*, 26 October 1872, 11, which hailed Gautier as a 'brilliant writer'). On 21 November 1872, just before ACS planned to complete the poem, he wrote to JM:

> My poem on Gautier is in a metre which I may call 'quarta rima'; in corresponsive quatrains like those of my *Laus Veneris*, except that there the 3rd line of the 1st quatrain rhymes with the 3rd of the 2nd, and so on to the end, whereas here the musical scheme is at once more connected and more complicated; for the 3rd line of every quatrain rhymes with the 1st, 2nd, and 4th lines of the next. The metrical effect is, I think, not bad, but the danger of such metres is diffuseness and flaccidity. I perceive this one to have a tendency to the dulcet and luscious form of verbosity which has to be guarded against, lest the poem lose its foothold and be swept off its legs, sense and all, down a flood of effeminate and monotonous music, or lost and split in a maze of what I call draggle-tailed melody.
>
> (*SL*, ii.198–9)

*La Morte amoureuse* is Gautier's short story published in the *Chronique de Paris*, 23–26 June 1836, about a priest who falls in love with a beautiful woman who proves to be a vampire. Her eyes initially captivate him: 'Quels yeux! avec un éclair ils décidaient de la destinée d'un homme; ils avaient une vie, une limpidité, une ardeur, une humidité brillante que je n'ai jamais vues à un œil humain' ('What eyes! with a flash they could determine a man's destiny; they had a life, a limpidity, an ardour, a brilliant mistiness that I had never seen in a human eye'). The short novel, *Une Nuit de Cléopâtre*, was serialized in *La Presse* during November and December 1838. It tells the story of Cleopatra, Meïamoun, and a single night's orgy that ends as dawn breaks with Meïamoun's poisoning.

*House of Fame*: name borrowed from Chaucer's poem.

*brand consume*: an ironic recollection of *AiC*.

*chryselephantine*: from the Greek χρῡσελεφάντινος ('of gold and ivory'); 'applied to statues overlaid with gold and ivory, such as the Olympian Zeus and Athene Parthenos of Phidias' (here figurative), *OED*.

*ninefold light Pierian*: the Pierian spring, sacred to the nine Muses.

*Couldst thou . . . blossoms?*: Gautier was only sixty-one when he died. Cf. 'Epicede (James Lorimer Graham died at Florence, April 30, 1876)' in *PB* 2.

*Mademoiselle de Maupin*: ACS is thinking of a passage at the end of Ch. 3 of Gautier's novel in which the narrator imagines erotic relationships with female figures in old German paintings, stained-glass windows, and missals ('Femmes, quand vous voyez votre amant devenir plus tendre que de coutume, vous étreindre dans ses bras avec une émotion extraordinaire' ['Women, when your lover becomes more tender than usual, he embraces you in his arms with extraordinary emotion . . . ']. For the other allusions, see headnote.

## Sonnet

(with a copy of *Mademoiselle de Maupin*)

First published *Le Tombeau de Théophile Gautier* (1873). The 'Preface' to Gautier's novel *Mademoiselle de Maupin*, 2 vols (Paris: Poussin pour Eugène Renduel, 1835–36), is a significant early statement of *l'art pour l'art*.

## In Memory of Barry Cornwall
(October 4, 1874)

First published *FR*, 16 (November 1874), 659–60. This poem commemorates the death of the poet and writer Bryan Waller Procter (1787–1874). To his mother, ACS wrote on 22 October 1874 saying that she would have noticed the death announcement of 'poor old Mr Procter ('Barry Cornwall'), the last left of the poets of the beginning of the century' (*SL*, ii.346). ACS noted that he had written some lines (which became 'Age and Song: To Barry Cornwall' in *PB* 2) in 1868 (see *SL*, i.308). He added that he was now 'writing a little "epicede" or funeral song for the deceased' (*SL*, ii.346–7). ACS's association of 'Barry Cornwall' with a previous poetic age was continued in his friendship with his widow, Ann Benson Skepper (1799–1888): 'Mrs P. is a link with such far-off famous men and times', ACS told his mother, 'that she has got a letter from Burns addressed to her mother, and (what is even more interesting to me—and that is saying a *great* deal) remembers a Mr Sharpe the engraver bringing to the house, when she was yet a young unmarried lady, *the* man of all others who were alive in any part of this century (except, perhaps, Shelley) that I should most have liked to see and speak to in person—Blake' (*SL*, ii.350, letter of 2 November 1874). Note that Mrs Procter told ACS she had often copied ACS's 'Age and Song', a 'touching & graceful tribute, from the young and successful Poet, to the old & forgotten one' (*UL*, i.313, letter of 23 May 1874). 'In Memory of Barry Cornwall' challenged the idea that Procter was or would be forgotten.

*one goes... another*: Sydney Dobell (1824–74), 'Spasmodic' poet, critic, and literary writer. ACS wrote to TWD on 29 August 1874, a week after Dobell's death on 22 August: 'I am most truly sorry, though I never met him personally, for the death of Sydney Dobell. I had never ceased to hope that I might some day be able to express my admiration of his genius on the appearance of some work which might at length do it justice' (*SL*, ii.334). This is a polite way of criticizing Dobell's poetic achievement. ACS was sent *The Poetical Works of Sydney Dobell with an Introductory Notice and Memoir by John Nichol* (London: Smith, Elder, 1875) by Nichol himself (a friend of Dobell) in early April 1875 (see *SL*, iii.28). Dobell was committed to Italian liberation and helped form what was afterwards known as the 'Friends of Italy'. It was Dobell's politics, and enthusiasm for Mazzini, which ACS principally admired. ACS had once made a good deal of fun of 'Spasmodic' poetry, implicitly including Dobell, in his first surviving hoax, 'The Monomaniac's Tragedy' (1858): *NWS*, 81–7. Kirstie Blair endeavours to locate *PB* 1 among the 'Spasmodics' in 'Swinburne's Spasms: *Poems and Ballads* and the "Spasmodic School"', *The Yearbook of English Studies*, 36 (2006), 180–96.

## Inferiae

First published *PB* 2. ACS said that he wrote this poem on the day after the death of his father, Admiral Charles Henry Swinburne (b.1797), who died on 4 March 1877.

ACS did not express his feelings at any length in letters, writing on 6 March to Nichol to say:

> I write just a line to let my oldest and best friend know that on the day before yesterday my father died. Among many points of feeling and character that I like to think we have in common, I doubt if there is any stronger on either side than our *northerly* disinclination for many or effusive words on matters of this kind.
>
> So I add nothing beyond a word to say how confidently, and in no conventional sense, I may reckon on the sincerity of your sympathy—and that to know this is some genuine relief and satisfaction.
>
> (*SL*, iii.295–6)

On 2 April, ACS told Norman MacColl that he would like 'Inferiae' to appear in *The Athenæum*, 'which has contained so many worthy tributes of prose and verse to the newly dead from friends or strangers' (*SL*, iii.313). This, however, did not occur. The title refers to the ancient Roman sacrifices offered to the souls of dead friends and heroes. Shortly after writing, ACS discussed pathos in literature with MacColl. 'I for one', he said 'was never moved to tears (like many of my betters) by Dickens' "Little Nell," over which (or whom) Landor wept like a lion-headed fountain; whereas some of Landor's own writing (Latin and English), and some of Miss Brontë's, completely knock me up and break me down (almost) even to think of. E.g. his epitaph on the Spanish patriots ['For a Gravestone in Spain']—and her whole portrait of Paul Emanuel [in *Villette* (1853)]' (*SL*, iii.315, letter of 4 April 1877). It is indicative of ACS's sense of pathos in poetry, then, that Landor's poem reads simply:

> Say thou who liest here beneath,
> To fall in battle is not death.
> You, tho' no pall on you was cast,
> Heard the first trump nor fear'd the last.
>
> Walter Savage Landor, *Heroic Idyls, with Additional Poems* (London: Cautley Newby, 1863), 273

Note the distinctive aaab rhyme with the inter-relations of the last line rhymes (last—past—last—sea—we—sea). ACS had dedicated *ES* to his father in 1875. Cf. 'Ex-Voto', *PB* 2.

## Cyril Tourneur

First published *PB* 2. ACS wrote to EWG on 21 September 1877, thanking him for his review of John Churton Collins' edition of *The Plays and Poems of Cyril Tourneur* (London: Chatto & Windus, 1878), published in *The Academy* on 22 September. ACS called Cyril Tourneur (1575–1626) 'Unsaint Cyril' (*SL*, iv.19) and was still writing to EWG about him on 5 December 1892: 'I am glad to find you orthodox about Tourneur—but surely you were once a blasphemer? Of course no mortal thinks of him as existing outside the range of tragic drama—but there he holds his own high narrow little fortress (like one of our Border "peels," if you know what they are) apart from all others and inexpugnable by any' (*SL*, vi.46). Since it is an apt term, it is worth knowing that a 'peel' is a 'small fortified (or sometimes moated) tower or dwelling [...] a private defence against raiders' (*OED*, n.2). ACS assumes Tourneur to be the author of *The Revenger's Tragedy* (1608), which provides him with the topic for this sonnet. Thomas Middleton is now usually thought responsible. Cf. ACS, 'Cyril Tourneur', *NC*, 121 (1887), 415–27.

*Chastity*: cf. 'All thriues but Chastity, she lyes a cold', *The Revenger's Tragedy*, l.899.

## A Ballad of François Villon
### Prince of All Ballad-Makers

First published *The Athenæum*, 15 September 1877, 337 and in the *Aberdeen Weekly Journal*, 17 September 1877, 1. ACS's regard for the French vagabond/thief-poet François Villon (*c.*1431–?1464) was shared with, among others, Gautier and DGR: on 8 February 1876, ACS told Mallarmé that, with DGR, he had once hoped to translate the whole of Villon and Dante, who, with Chaucer, comprised 'la trinité poétique du moyen âge' (*SL*, iii.132). DGR had included 'Three Translations from François Villon, 1450' in *Poems* (1870): 'The Ballad of Dead Ladies', 'To Death, of his Lady', and 'His Mother's Service to Our Lady' (cf. ACS's unpublished 'The Ballad of Villon and Fat Madge' and 'Villon' ('To my good mother') included in *NWS*, 13–16). ACS told Nichol on 2 April 1876 that Villon was 'the third great poet of the Middle Ages: date of birth (presumably in the gutter) 1431, of death (presumably on the gallows) unknown to man'. ACS thought Villon representative not only of his nation but also of a medieval class and nation: the 'commons of France' (as distinct from Dante who was representative of Italy and the aristocratic class, and Chaucer of England who belonged to the educated, professional class): *SL*, iii.164.

A new edition of Villon had been published as *Œuvres complètes de François Villon, suivies d'un choix des poésies de ses disciples*, ed. Pierre Jannet after Bernard de La Monnoye (Paris: E. Flammarion, 1867). Chapter 5 of Walter Besant's *Studies in Early French Poetry* (London: Macmillan, 1868) was an analysis of Villon: it was reviewed in *PMG* on 24 October 1868 and the reviewer perhaps implicitly connected ACS with 'the Parnassian jail-bird', remarking that 'in the middle of the fifteenth century [Villon] invented the literature of Bohemianism, which has been so much developed in the nineteenth' (12). Auguste Longnon's *Étude Biographique sur François Villon après les documents inédits conservés aux archives nationales* (Paris: H. Menu, 1877) was also reviewed by *PMG*, 27 February 1877, 12. ACS was still waiting for his copy of Longnon to be delivered on 4 March 1877 (*UL*, ii.110). *The Cornhill* published Robert Louis Stevenson's 'François Villon: Student, Poet, and Housebreaker' in Vol. 36 (August 1877), 215–34. Cf. also John Payne, *The Poems of Master Francis Villon of Paris, Now First Done into English Verse in the Original Form* (London: private distribution for the Villon Society, 1878), and reviewed in *SRev*, 46 (2 November 1878), 560–2.

## A Vision of Spring in Winter

First published *FR*, 17 (April 1875), 505–7. ACS offered it to JM on 9 March for publication in the following month: 'I think myself April and not autumn or winter would be the time of the year for its birth—especially as it begins and ends with a reference to the "birth-month"' (*SL*, iii.23), i.e. the month of Shakespeare's birth. ACS was working at this time on the essays published as 'The Three Stages of Shakespeare' in *FR* in May 1875 and January 1876 ('I am well on with the first division of my essay on Shakespeare', he told JM in the same letter that offered him 'A Vision'). These essays were later extended to form part of *A Study of Shakespeare*: see 362–7. The poem may be thought addressed to Proserpine; *MPSP* thinks it might be 'usefully read as if spoken [...] by Demeter' (484).

*greenwood*: cf. *As You Like It*, 2.5.1.

*Chill... spring*: cf. Keats, 'Ode on a Grecian Urn', 1.2.

## The Epitaph in Form of a Ballad, Which Villon Made for Himself and His Comrades, Expecting to Be Hanged along with Them

First published in *PB* 2 and translated from Villon's 'La ballade des pendus' ('Frères humains qui après nous vivez'). Cf. 'A Reiver's Neck-Verse', 469. Subsequent printings, including the 'second impression' of *PB* 2, followed ACS's usual practice of indenting to follow the rhyme scheme for some reason omitted in the copytext.

## FROM *A STUDY OF SHAKESPEARE* (LONDON: CHATTO & WINDUS, 1880)

The book was first published in January 1880, dedicated to J.O. Halliwell-Phillipps (see headnote to 'Report of the First Anniversary Meeting', 608–10). It drew together material published first in *FR* for May 1875 and January 1876 and in *The Gentleman's Magazine*, August and September 1879. Halliwell-Phillipps wrote to ACS on 1 January 1880 to acknowledge 'your truly important book on Shakespeare, in which greater powers of genius are displayed than in any other work on the subject. I do not know that I can pay a higher compliment, yet it is not one in the shape of flattery, it being an honest opinion that may have some value as emanating from one who has read so many works of the same class' (*UL*, ii.188–9). EWG remembered ACS's letter to him of 31 January 1875 observing:

> I am now at work on my long-designed essay or study on the metrical progress or development of Shakespeare, as traceable by ear and *not* by finger, and the general changes of tone and stages of mind expressed or involved in this change or progress of style.
>
> Bonchurch, xix.207

*A Study* was divided into three parts that covered what ACS agreed were Shakespeare's three periods (Lyric and Fantastic; Comic and Historic; Tragic and Romantic): the extract here is from the opening of the 'Third Period' concerning *King Lear* and *Othello*. Some of the old quarrel with Furnivall was revived in a letter about the book, 'Mr Swinburne and Fletcher's Share in "Henry VIII"', published in *The Academy*, 425 (26 June 1880), 476: 'A more crude and contradictory theory of the structure of *Henry VIII* that that which Mr Swinburne has put forth I never saw'. *PMG* remarked in its review on 17 January 1880 that ACS 'had become abominable in the eyes of the new sect who have discovered that the heart of the great masters of verse can be unlocked by minute verbal comparisons, and the secret of their numbers cast up in tables. He is reprobate, however, in passably good company; and for ourselves we make bold to think that his "Study of Shakespeare" is like to survive a considerable part of the works of the New Shakspere Society' (11). Cf. Victor Hugo's *William Shakespeare* (1864).

*With dreadful... arms*: as Adam and Eve leave Paradise in the last lines of Milton's *Paradise Lost*, these dreadful faces cluster around the gates.

*Æschylean of his works*: ACS always admired Aeschylus (though he was sometimes doubtful about *The Persians*). When he provided *PMG* with a list of his 'one hundred best books' a few years later on 26 January 1886, first was Shakespeare; second was Aeschylus (2).

*Prometheus... Orestes*: ACS thinks of *Prometheus Bound*, which he believed to be by Aeschylus, and Aeschylus' *Oresteia*.

*'As flies... to the gods'*: *The Tragedy of King Lear*, 4.1.37–8.

*Eumenides*: the final play of the *Oresteia* (after *Agamemnon* and *The Libation Bearers*).

*The veil... twain*: cf. Mark 15:38.

*chaos... again*: cf. *Othello*, 3.3.93.

*fire-flaught*: 'flaught' is 'A spreading out, as of wings for flight; a fluttering or agitated movement; a commotion', *OED*.

*Even Goneril... slayer*: Goneril's rebuke of Albany in (Folio text) 4.2 (specifically ll.30–7).

*musty... proverb*: cf. *Hamlet*, 3.2.330–1.

*Calchas... Iphigenia*: in Euripides' play *Iphigenia in Aulis* (Ἰφιγένεια ἐν Αὐλίδι), Calchus is the seer who announces to Agamemnon that he must sacrifice his daughter Iphigenia.

*more sinned... sinning*: *King Lear* (Folio) 3.2.59–60.

*Struck... God*: Shelley, 'Adonais', 1.42 (with lower case 'god').

*'the motive-hunting... malignity'*: see *Coleridge's Shakespearean Criticism*, ed. Thomas Middleton Raysor, 2 vols (London: Constable, 1930), i.49.

*inarticulate poet*: unidentified.

*'the very... machine'*: Wordsworth, 'She was a Phantom of Delight', l.22.

*Circe de la Mothe-Valois*: ACS refers to the thief and trickster Jeanne de Saint-Rémy de Valois, 'Comtesse de la Motte' (1756–91), who was involved in the Affair of the Diamond Necklace. This episode helped destabilize the position of the French queen Marie-Antoinette in the mid-1780s, prior to the French Revolution. Thomas Carlyle's *The Diamond Necklace* (London: Fraser, 1837) described her as a 'Female Dramatist' (17) playing out a remarkable role in a fraud (she is more frequently 'Dramaturgic').

*constructive... Hamlet*: Carlyle observes 'Could Madame de Lamotte, then, have written a *Hamlet*? I conjecture, not. More goes to the writing of a *Hamlet* than completest "imitation" of all characters and things in this Earth; there goes, before and beyond all, the rarest *understanding* of these, insight into their hidden essences and harmonies' (*The Diamond Necklace,* 17).

*a fair Vittoria Colonna... Frederic-William*: Vittoria Colonna (1490–1547), the aristocrat with whom Michelangelo had an intense friendship and to whom he wrote some of his sonnets; Megaera is one of the Eumenides, peculiarly associated with jealousy; Friedrich Wilhelm I (1688–1740) was King in Prussia and Elector of Brandenburg, and the harsh father of Frederick the Great, the subject of Carlyle's *The History of Friedrich II of Prussia*.

*His stanza... polished*: cf. 'This Lifeguard Regiment of foot, for instance, in which the Crown-Prince now is,—Friedrich Wilhelm got it in his Father's time, no doubt a regiment then of fair qualities; and he has kept drilling it, improving it, as poets polish stanzas, unweariedly ever since', Carlyle, *Friedrich II*, Bk 5 ('Of the Potsdam Giants, As a Fact').

*'to fust in him unused'*: cf. *Hamlet*, Additional Passages: 4.4.30.

*torments... lips*: cf. *Othello*, 5.2.312.

*Farinata degli Uberti*: (1212–64), Italian nobleman believed to be a heretic who appears in Canto 10 of Dante's *Inferno* (see headnote to 'Recollections of Professor Jowett', 648).

*Malebolge*: the eighth circle of Hell in the *Inferno* ('evil ditches').

*'marriage... hell'*: cf. Blake's *The Marriage of Heaven and Hell* (1790–3).

*Vidocq... Vautrin*: Eugène François Vidocq (1775–1857), a former criminal, established the first private detective agency in France: Balzac used him as a model for Vautrin in the *Comédie humaine.*

*Lepidus*: Marcus Aemilius Lepidus (*c.*30 BC–AD 33), celebrated Roman general and senator.

*'a tried and valiant soldier'*: '[Octavius]: But he's a tried and valiant soldier. [Antony]: So is my horse, Octavius', *Julius Caesar*, 4.1.28–9.

*'which . . . most'*: 'As the curtain drops, which do we pity the most?' from some MS notes and marginalia on *Othello*, though this line is now often regarded as an addition made by Coleridge's nephew Henry Nelson Coleridge (1798–1843): see *Coleridge on Shakespeare*, ed. Terence Hawkes (Harmondsworth: Penguin, 1969), 195 and n.

*'most blessed conditions'*: cf. *Othello*, 2.1.249–50.

*'gentle Desdemona'*: cf. *Othello*, 1.2.25.

## FROM *SONGS OF THE SPRINGTIDES* (LONDON: CHATTO & WINDUS, 1880)

### Thalassius

First published *SS*, May 1880. ACS said on 10 October 1879 that he once thought of writing 'a symbolical quasi-autobiographical poem after the fashion of Shelley or of Hugo, concerning the generation, birth and rearing of a by-blow of Amphitrite's [. . .] reared like Ion in the temple-service of Apollo. It would be a pretty subject, but when should I hear the last of my implied arrogance and self-conceit?' (*SL*, iv.106; Amphitrite is the wife of Poseidon). The plan developed into 'Thalassius', a poem reflecting on ACS's recent transference to The Pines and his escape from death through the care of TWD, as well as confirming his credentials both as a poet and a political writer. Cf. 'Pan and Thalassius: A Lyrical Idyl', *The Athenæum*, 3122 (27 August 1887), 278. The poem formally invokes Milton's 'Lycidas'. Cf. also Shelley's 'Epipsychidion' and Introduction, xxxi, above.

*Cymothoe*: 'one of the Nereides' (Lemprière).

*hyaline*: 'poetic term for the smooth sea, the clear sky, or any transparent substance', *OED*. It derives from the translation of θάλασσα ὑαλίνη [*thalassa hualine*] (Revelations 4:6), 'A sea of glass like unto crystal', and so gives ACS his title Thalassius, 'of the sea'.

*ineluctable*: 'neluctable' in the first edition: clearly an error.

*Bassarides*: see note on 556.

*Erigone*: daughter of Icarius who 'gave wine to some peasants who drank it with the greatest avidity, ignorant of its intoxicating nature. They were soon deprived of their reason, and the fury and resentment of their friends and neighbours were immediately turned upon Icarius, who perished by their hands' (Lemprière). Erigone is often said to have hanged herself over her father's grave.

*wild mares in Thessaly*: referring to the Cextauri, a 'people of Thessaly, half men and half horses. They were the offspring of Centaurus, son of Apollo' (Lemprière).

*levin*: lightning flash.

## On the Cliffs

First published *SS*. ACS told TWD about what he later called 'my nightingale Sapphics' (*SL*, iv.82) on 30 July 1879:

> I have a new poem to read you, longer (I will not say better, whether I think so or not) than any (except the ever edifying 'Dolores') in either of my collections. 'Anactoria' which is next longest is ninety-four lines short of this new-born one—which however was long since conceived though but now brought forth. You will regret to hear that in subject-matter and treatment it is not akin to either of the above-named. I fear there is not overmuch hope of a fresh scandal and consequent 'succès de scandale' from a mere rhapsody just four lines short of four hundred (oddly enough) on the song of a nightingale by the sea-side. I don't think I ever told you, did I? my anti-Ovidian theory as to the real personality of that much misrepresented bird—the truth concerning whom dawned upon me one day in my midsummer school holidays, when it flashed on me listening quite suddenly 1) that this was *not* Philomela—2) in the same instant, *who* this was. It is no theory, but a fact, as I can prove by the science of notation.
>
> (*SL*, iv.77–8)

ACS's theory is that the song is Sappho's. To EWG on 17 October, ACS added that 'On the Cliffs' is 'in the irregular Italian metre of Lycidas. Watts—as I possibly may have told you—says (what a man generally likes to hear of his latest work) that it is *the* best poem I ever wrote' (*SL*, iv.109–10). The poem draws on the Classical Greek story of the cursed House of Atreus in the version used by Aeschylus for the *Oresteia*. ACS incorporates a number of lines from Sappho's surviving *œuvre*. Writing to John Addington Symonds about Wharton's proposed translation on 9 January 1883, ACS observed that he would be 'delighted to help, in any smallest degree, an enterprise in honour of the supreme lyric poet—but I have never ventured on any attempt at making a version of any of her fragments. In two of my poems—"Anactoria," & "On the Cliffs"—I have given here & there a rendering of some single line or a paraphrase of some particular passage. These of course are at anybody's service who might think them worthy the honour of quotation. Anything further in the way of translation I have never dreamed of daring to attempt' (*UL*, ii.320). Wharton, quoting ACS, repeated much of this view in the Preface to the first edition: Wharton, ix–x. Cf. Keats, 'Ode to a Nightingale'.

*ἰμερόφωνος ἀήδων*: see note below to 'sweet-voiced nightingale' with an editorial correction to the standard form of 'ἀήδων'.

*tortive*: twisting; cf. *Troilus and Cressida*, 1.3.8.

*'sweet-voiced nightingale'*: from Sappho (*GL* 136, p. 152: ἦρος ἄγγελος ἰμερόφωνος ἀήδων ['Messenger of spring, sweet-voiced nightingale']).

*O mother ... children*: ACS draws on Aeschylus' *Eumenides* (*Εὐμενίδες*), remembering Orestes' pursuit by the furies, the daughters of Night who avenge the slaying of parents, because Orestes has slain Clytemnestra who, previously, had slain Agamemnon.

*Hear us... night*: cf. *Eumenides*, ll.321–3.

*Ah, ah, the doom*: ACS translates Cassandra's words from Aeschylus' *Agamemnon* (*Ἀγαμέμνων*), ll.1146–9, after the chorus compares her to the sorrowing nightingale ('Alas, for the fate of the clear-voiced nightingale! The gods invested *her* with a winged body, and a pleasant life with nothing to bewail; but for *me* there is in store a cleaving blow with a two-edged axe', F.A. Paley, *Aeschylus Translated into English Prose*, 2nd edn (Cambridge: Deighton, Bell, 1871), 164. Cassandra foresees that she will be killed but her gift of prophecy, given by Apollo, is joined with the curse that no one will believe her.

*bodeful bondslave*: Cassandra is the slave or concubine of Agamemnon, seized after the fall of Troy with which *Agamemnon* begins (cf. ll.1440–1).

*dragnet*: Agamemnon in Aeschylus' version is killed after a blanket or net is cast over him to restrict movement (cf. ll.1114–16 ('ἒ ἔ, παπαῖ παπαῖ...'): '*Cas.* Ah! ah! O me! What is this that presents itself to view? A net of Hades? 'Tis the wife of his bed who is the stake-net—who is the accomplice with another in the murder', Paley, *Aeschylus*, 163). In Sophocles' *Elektra*, Agamemnon is killed with an axe.

*But thou*: Sappho.

*strange-tongued slave*: Cassandra.

*houndlike*: cf. the Chorus, listening to Cassandra's prophecies of slaughter in *Agamemnon*, ll.1093–4: 'The stranger seems to be keen-scented as a hound, and to be seeking whose murders she shall discover', Paley, *Aeschylus*, 163.

*Even hers*: presumably Aphrodite's.

*Priam's seed*: Cassandra was the daughter of Priam, king of Troy (cf. *GL* 44, p. 88).

*of him*: Apollo.

*Name... names*: cf. Philippians 2:9–10.

*Since first... me*: cf. the note on *Poetae Graeci* in the headnote to 'Anactoria', 569.

*Majano*: it has been suggested that this is ACS's recollection of his visit to Maiano, Italy, in 1863 where he apparently declared poetry to the nightingales (Maxwell, 108).

*Daulian dream of Itylus*: Daulis is the home town of Tereus. See note to 'Itylus'.

*O thou... souled*: ACS translates the opening of Sappho's 'Ode to Aphrodite' (*ποικιλόθρον' ἀθανάτ' Ἀφρόδιτα, | παῖ Δίος δολόπλοκε, λίσσομαί σε*, *GL* 1, p. 52).

*boskage*: 'A mass of growing trees or shrubs; a thicket, grove; woody undergrowth; sylvan scenery', *OED*.

*Leucadian*: see note on 622.

*I loved thee*: ACS translates Sappho's fragment to Atthis (*GL* 49, 94: *ἠράμαν μὲν ἔγω σέθεν, Ἄτθι, πάλαι ποτά* ['I loved you, Atthis, once, long ago']).

*Child of God*: another version of the opening of the 'Ode to Aphrodite'.

*Æolian*: Lesbos is in the Aegean.

*sevenfold shields*: cf. 'The seven-fold shield of Ajax cannot keep | The battery from my heart', *Antony and Cleopatra*, 4.15.38–9.

## FROM *SPECIMENS OF MODERN POETS: THE HEPTALOGIA OR THE SEVEN AGAINST SENSE: A CAP WITH SEVEN BELLS* (LONDON: CHATTO & WINDUS, 1880)

### The Higher Pantheism in a Nutshell

First published as the opening poem of seven in *The Heptalogia*, the title of which is a play on Aeschylus' *Seven against Thebes* (Ἑπτὰ ἐπὶ Θήβας) and picks up Landor's *Pentalogia*, appended to *The Pentameron* (London: Saunders & Otley, 1837). On 15 January 1870, ACS told DGR that after he had finished writing 'Hertha':

> I looked at Tennyson's 'Higher Pantheism' again—not bad verse altogether, but what gabble and babble of half-hatched thoughts in half-based words!—and wrote at the tail of it this summary of this theology:
>
> 'God, whom we see not, is; and God, who is not, we see:
> Fiddle, we know, is diddle: and diddle is possibly dee.'
>
> I think it a terse and accurate as a Tennysonian compendium.
>
> (*SL*, ii.86)

Tennyson's poem appeared in *The Holy Grail, and Other Poems* (London: Strachan, 1870), 201–3:

> The sun, the moon, the stars, the seas, the hills and the plains—
> Are not these, O Soul, the Vision of Him who reigns?
>
> Is not the Vision He, tho' He be not that which He seems?
> Dreams are true while they last, and do we not live in dreams?
>
> Earth, these solid stars, this weight of body and limb,
> Are they not sign and symbol of thy division from Him?
>
> Dark is the world to thee; thyself art the reason why,
> For is He not all but thou, that hast power to feel 'I am I'?
>
> Glory about thee, without thee; and thou fulfillest thy doom,
> Making Him broken gleams and a stifled splendour and gloom.
>
> Speak to Him, thou, for He hears, and Spirit with Spirit can meet—
> Closer is He than breathing, and nearer than hands and feet.
>
> God is law, say the wise; O soul, and let us rejoice,
> For if He thunder by law the thunder is yet His voice.

Law is God, say some; no God at all, says the fool;
For all we have power to see is a straight staff bent in a pool;

And the ear of man cannot hear, and the eye of man cannot see;
But if we could see and hear, this Vision—were it not He?

ACS wanted *The Heptalogia* to be issued anonymously on the same day as *Studies in Song* (*SL*, iv.180). Reviewers were quick to identify the author (e.g. *The Graphic*, 9 April 1881, 358). ACS thought appreciation of this volume of parodies 'sweeter to my foolish soul than praise of *Bothwell* and *Erechtheus*' (*SL*, iv.211). Although ACS needed no model for a volume of parodies, he might have remembered James and Horace Smith's successful *Rejected Addresses: Or, The New Theatrum Poetarum* (1812), parodying major Romantics or, perhaps, the so-called *'Bon Gaultier' Ballads* by William Edmonstoune Aytoun and Theodore Martin, published in book form in 1845. For another Tennyson parody, see ACS's 'Disgust: A Dramatic Monologue', *PP*, 189–92.

*ditch*: later printings added a further stanza at this point: 'More is the whole than a part: but half is more than the whole: | Clearly, the soul is the body: but is not the body the soul?'

## Nephelidia

First published *The Heptalogia*. The title is derived from the Greek *nephos* (*νέφος*), clouds, with the sense of 'cloudlets'. The poem is an example of ACS's self-parody (cf. 'Poeta Loquitur', 396–7).

*grimness of God*: subsequent versions ended with a further four lines:

Blank is the book of his bounty beholden of old, and its binding is blacker than bluer:
Out of blue into black is the scheme of the skies, and their dews are the wine of the bloodshed of things;
Till the darkling desire of delight shall be free as a fawn that is freed from the fangs that pursue her,
Till the heart-beats of hell shall be hushed by a hymn from the hunt that has harried the kennel of kings.

## Poeta Loquitur (c.1880?)

Not published in ACS's lifetime (first printed Bonchurch, v.295–7) and another example of ACS's self-parody (cf. 'Nephelidia', 395). Its date of composition is unknown though linked here with *The Heptalogia* for the obvious reason. 'Poeta Loquitur'—'the poet speaks'—was not unheard-of as a title for satirical or comical poetry. Cf. 'The Knight and the Poet', with 'Poeta Loquitur' as its first part, by 'SK' in *Liverpool Mercury*, 17 January 1812, 231, or 'Out at Last, or, The Fallen Minister' (1816) by Peter Pindar (John Wolcot), which includes a comic section under a 'Poeta Loquitur'.

## FROM *STUDIES IN SONG* (LONDON: CHATTO & WINDUS, 1880)

### After Nine Years. To Joseph Mazzini

First published *SS*. ACS, recalling both his own early 'Ode to Mazzini' (1–11) and *SBS* nine years previously, looks back also to Mazzini's death on 10 March 1872 with a verse form rhyming aabbccc, and an often iambic 4-syllable fourth line.

*Primâ dicte... Camenâ*: Horace, *Epistle* 1, Bk 1: 'Theme of my earliest Muse in days long past' (Conington).

### Evening on the Broads

First published *SS*. The date of composition is uncertain but the poem relates to 'A Forsaken Garden' (338–9), 'On the Cliffs' (381–91), and 'By the North Sea' (407–20). The Broads (often 'the Norfolk Broads') is an area of fens, lakes, rivers, and canals in Suffolk and Norfolk. Shakespeare's *The Winter's Tale* is relevant and the recovery of Perdita in Act 3.3.

*rampire*: archaic term for rampart.

*face... deep*: cf. Genesis 1:2.

### By the North Sea

First published *SS*. ACS first mentioned this poem to EWG on 5 July 1880 in preparing *SS*: 'There is one poem in seven parts, just a little longer than *Thalassius*, which Watts likes better than anything I ever did (and in metrical and antiphonal effect I prefer it myself to all my others): so I shall inscribe it to him' (*SL*, iv.158). ACS described the Dunwich setting, 'its six great churches and cathedral now not more than a little village that will hardly last to the end of the century', in a letter in French to Benjamin Buisson (*SL*, iv.175–6, letter sometime in December 1880). To Lord Houghton on the 18th of the same month, he said: 'Do you know the "dead cathedral city" which I have tried to describe in the last poem in this book—Dunwich, in Suffolk? The whole picture is from life—salt marshes, ruins, and bones protruding seawards through the soil of the crumbling sandbanks' (*SL*, iv.179). ACS had first been to Dunwich in the autumn of 1875 (*SL*, iii.111–12). The text of 'By the North Sea' was abbreviated and broken into three separate poems in *Selections*: 'By the North

Sea' (I); 'In the Salt Marshes' (III–IV); and 'Dunwich' (VI–VII). Cf. 'A Solitude', 453; 'To a Seamew', 459–62; 'On the South Coast' in *AOP*; and Philip Bourke Marston's 'The Old Churchyard at Bonchurch'. Cf. also DGR's 'The Sea-Limits'. See also Andrew Fippinger, 'Intimations and Imitations of Immortality: Swinburne's "By the North Sea" and "Poeta Loquitur"', *Victorian Poetry*, 47 (2009), 675–90. For the MS of stanza six, see Figure 7.

*'We are . . . us'*: from verses included in Landor's 'Prince Maurocordato and General Colocotroni' in *Imaginary Conversations*, 2 vols (London: Colburn, 1826), ii.389.

*In the . . . set*: cf. Joel 3:14: 'Multitudes, multitudes in the valley of decision: for the day of the Lord is near in the valley of decision.'

*Saw darkness . . . god*: cf. Joel 3:15–16.

*Anticleia*: the mother of Odysseus, whose spirit he encounters in the *Odyssey*, Bk 11, when visiting the underworld.

*Love . . . death*: cf. Song of Solomon 8:6.

*Here . . . vain hands*: Odysseus tries three times to embrace his mother but, she being incorporeal, his arms pass through her, *Odyssey*, Bk 11:204–10.

*Clasp . . . implore*: Odysseus is left to plead with his mother that they may lament together: *Odyssey*, Bk 11:210–15.

*Self-begotten . . . not made*: ACS borrows language about the Incarnation from the Nicene Creed.

## EMILY BRONTË (1883)

First published *The Athenæum*, 16 June 1883, 762–3; reprinted in *Miscellanies*. An early critical work from the Putney period, it followed ACS's *A Note on Charlotte Brontë* (London: Chatto & Windus, 1877). The essay is a review of A. Mary F. Robinson's *Emily Brontë*, 'Eminent Women Series' (London: Allen, 1883). Robinson wrote to thank him for 'your beautiful notice' on 15 June 1883 (*UL*, ii.344).

ACS notes the inevitability of Emily's imagination, the convincing way in which her characters act, and how her story unfolds as if there can be no alternative to it. This is a development of ACS's praise of Charlotte in 1877 who, he said, possessed a 'power to make us feel in every nerve, at every step forward which our imagination is compelled to take under the guidance of another's, that thus and not otherwise, but in all things altogether even as we are told and shown, it was and it must have been with the human figures set before us in their action and their suffering; that thus and not otherwise they absolutely must and would have felt and thought and spoken under the proposed conditions' (*A Note on Charlotte Brontë*, 13–14). In the *Note*, Charlotte is compared favourably with George Eliot whose *The Mill on the Floss* (1860), ACS thinks, was flawed by the improbability of the relationship between Stephen and Maggie.

A review of Robinson by James Ashcroft Noble in *The Academy*, 576 (19 May 1883), 340, asserted that ACS 'was the first to remove Emily Brontë from out the shadow of her great sister's fame'. But this was disputed in G. Barnett Smith's 'Emily Brontë', *The Academy*, 577 (26 May 1885), 368, who pointed to his own 'The Brontës', *Cornhill Magazine*, 28 (July 1873), 54–71. Cf. the discussion of the 'inevitable' plot in ACS's essay in relation to *AiC*.

*Mehalah*: ACS compares *Wuthering Heights* to the recent sensation of Sabine Baring-Gould's *Mehalah: A Story of the Salt Marshes* (London: Smith, Elder, 1880), a novel about a fisher-girl named Mehalah who is pursued by a Heathcliff-like villain, Elijah Rebow. The story ends with Rebow's brutal drowning of the newly-married girl. *PMG* said of Baring-Gould's novel: 'The fibre of the story is as rough and coarse as that of "Wuthering Heights". Even the genius of Emily Brontë was heavily handicapped by the unvarying ferocity of her savages, men and women who bit, scratched, and kicked like Liverpool corner-men' ('Mehalah', 13 November 1880, 12). ACS observed to Nichol on 21 June 1883 that 'I did not mean—Heaven forbid!—to set *Mehalah*, on the whole, beside or near *Wuthering Heights*: but it is the only book I know which shows anything of the same power' (*SL*, v.27).

*the sweet... problem*: Gaskell offers little evidence of Emily's nature in *The Life of Charlotte Brontë* (1857) observing, for instance, that: 'The first impression made on the visitor by the sisters of her school-friend was, that Emily was a tall, long-armed girl, more fully grown than her elder sister; extremely reserved in manner. I distinguish reserve from shyness, because I imagine shyness would please, if it knew how; whereas, reserve is indifferent whether it pleases or not. Anne, like her eldest sister, was shy; Emily was reserved' (Book 1, Ch. 7).

*it is inconceivable... public*: the letter from Branwell disclosing his affair with Mrs Robinson and his subsequent breakdown (Robinson, 120–2). Mary Robinson later told ACS: 'though I am perhaps wrong in printing that letter, I did not do it without a great deal of thought' (*UL*, ii.344, 15 June 1883).

*'it was... numbness'*: Robinson, 125.

*die standing*: Branwell determined 'he would die as he thought no one had ever died before, standing', Robinson, 221.

*a senseless piece... law*: untraced (could it be TWD?).

*dreamland and delirium*: Catherine's dream of dying and wanting to be taken back to the moors (Ch. 9); and her death (see the next note).

*'masterly pathos... appealing'*: Robinson refers to the death of the first Catherine in *Wuthering Heights*: 'A fit she had had alone and untended during those three days of isolated starvation had unsettled Catherine's reason. The gradual coming-on of her delirium is given with a masterly pathos that Webster need not have made more strong, nor Fletcher more lovely and appealing', 190.

*Webster's Cornelia*: in *The White Devil*.

*Madge Wildfire*: in Scott's *The Heart of Midlothian* (1818).

*divine… legend*: *Prometheus Bound* (*Προμηθεὺς Δεσμώτης*), which ACS believes written by Aeschylus (now sometimes disputed).

*dauntless… read*: Robinson asserted that the last lines Emily wrote were the poem, 'No coward soul is mine' (232).

*'unutterable' vanity of creeds*: 'Vain are the thousand creeds | That move men's hearts: unutterably vain' ('No coward soul is mine', Robinson, 232).

*Hymn to God of Cleanthes*: ACS is thinking of the 'Hymn to Zeus' by the 3rd-century BC Stoic philosopher-poet Cleanthes.

*Porch*: the Painted Porch (*ἡ ποικίλη στοά*) in the Agora of Classical Athens from where Stoicism was first taught.

*'some… prompting'*: 'by some shy ostrich prompting, Emily chose to call [this poem] "The Old Stoic"', Robinson, 136.

*Wilkie Collins*: cf. ACS's 'Wilkie Collins', *FR*, 46 (1889), 589–99.

*Pendennis… Firmins*: both Thackeray's *The Newcomes: Memoirs of a Most Respectable Family* (1855) and *The Adventures of Philip on his Way Through the World: Shewing Who Robbed Him, Who Helped Him, and Who Passed Him By* (1861–2), which contains the story of the Firmins, are narrated by Arthur Pendennis, the leading character of Thackeray's *The History of Pendennis* (1848–50).

*'assume the virtue'*: cf. *Hamlet*, 3.4.151.

*French 'naturalist'*: ACS is thinking principally of Émile Zola. Zola's *L'Assommoir* (1877) made a reader 'literally and actually sick', ACS said, 'with pure physical horror and loathing [more] than I could have believed it possible for any mere literary bestiality and brutality to do' (*SL*, iii.268). ACS's 'Note on a Question of the Hour', *The Athenæum*, 16 June 1877, 768, protested about *L'Assommoir*'s publication.

*'vivid and fearful scenes'*: Charlotte's words, complaining that passages from *Wuthering Heights* kept the reader awake, from her 'Preface' to the 1850 reissue of the novel, and often repeated. See, for instance, Gaskell's *The Life of Charlotte Brontë* (London: Smith, Elder, 1857), 264.

## FROM *A CENTURY OF ROUNDELS* (LONDON: CHATTO & WINDUS, 1883)

ACS told EWG that this collection—a 'little book of songs'—was 'nearly ready for publication' (*SL*, v.11) on 28 March 1883, a fresh product of his move with TWD to Putney. It was out by 7 June when ACS sent the first copy to the dedicatee, Christina Rossetti (*SL*, v.22). There was later some confusion over whether Christina had actually given permission for this dedication (*SL*, v.88). ACS on 22 June said that he had started with a roundel that was an elegy for a child ('A Baby's Death') and then taken 'a fancy to the form and went on scribbling in it till in two months' time I had a hundred of these samples ready for publication. It is really a much simpler and easier form of verse than the Italian type of sonnet which, since Milton, has driven out our own old English or Shakespearean kind' (*SL*, v.27). *The Athenæum,* reviewing the volume, observed that: 'The experiment commenced by the latest French Pléiade, and continued by its English disciples and admirers, of reproducing the forms in which French poets from the fourteenth century in to the seventeenth loved to fetter the muse, has at length won the adhesion of a writer of genius' (16 June 1883, 755).

The effects ACS sought with the form might be described in 'The Roundel', 433. The structure relates to the medieval/Renaissance French *rondeau* with its *rentrement* or refrain. ACS's version has eleven lines, two interlocking rhymes (sometimes alternating masculine and feminine) and is noticeable for the variations of line length from poem to poem, from the twenty-syllable lines of the third roundel of 'The Death of Richard Wagner' to the six or seven-syllable lines of 'Wasted Love'. The *rentrement* also varies in length from, for instance, 'A roundel is wrought' ('The Roundel') to 'Sark' ('"Insularum Ocelle"').

*A Century of Roundels* was, as indicated, well received. 'Mr Swinburne's new volume is one the most delightful he has ever published', said *The Derby Mercury*, thinking that the 'turn of the verse [form]' was rarely anything 'other than perfect'. There was admiration for the distance between this new collection and earlier ACS, too: 'In matter it is strong, human, virile—wholly devoid of the elements which rendered the first series of "Poems and Ballads" so unfit *virginibus puerisque* ["for girls and boys"]. Here, in fact, is nothing whatever of the supersensuousness which, more or less, marked all Mr Swinburne's earlier utterances' ('Mr Swinburne's New Volume', *The Derby Mercury*, 13 June 1883, 6). In a substantial article in *The Times*, 6 June 1883, the reviewer noted that 'Mr Swinburne is losing much of his early efflorescence, and is giving us more of the poetic fruit' (4):

> In his recent volumes there was a notable development in this respect, and it is continued in the present work. In none of its predecessors has there been manifested a deeper sense of the responsibility of the poet's office. Although case in a mould usually associated with the lighter forms of French verse, it deals with some of the vital questions affecting humanity with suggestiveness and solemnity. Occasionally we find a pathos and a dignity which are almost without parallel in the author's previous works, and when the difficulty of the setting is remembered, this will be recognized as a very high merit. There are many lines and thoughts in this volume which would do honour to any living poet.

W.E. Henley published 'Roundel (From the French of Charles of Orleans)' in *Belgravia*, 50 (March 1883), 128.

*In Harbour*: cf. Tennyson's 'The Lotos-Eaters' (1832).

*Plus Ultra*: 'further beyond'. Cf. Coleridge's 'Ne Plus Ultra' (1834).

*Richard Wagner*: died 13 April 1883. On 11 September 1876, George Powell had written to ACS to tell him that he had 'just had a long conversation (over tea at the Wagner's [*sic*] house) with Madame Cosima Wagner, about your works, w$^{h}$. has resulted in my offer to send her all your writings' (*UL*, ii.86). If this no doubt polite interest resulted in anything, I do not know.

*Plus Intra*: 'further within'.

*Fantin*: ACS met the French painter Henri Fantin-Latour (1836–1904) on his visit to Paris with Whistler in March 1863 and referred to him as 'my friend' in 1866 (*SL*, i.164). Fantin-Latour painted many still-life flower pictures.

*To Catullus*: ACS addresses Catullus as a brother, celebrated for mourning his own brother with the line: 'atque in perpetuum frater ave atque vale' (Catullus 101). On 18 August 1894, ACS told F.W.H. Myers that 'the first if not the only Latin poet I ever thoroughly loved is Catullus' (*UL*, iii.72).

*To thee... dread*: cf. Catullus 93, with its indifference to Caesar.

*'Insularum Ocelle'*: from Catullus 31: 'Paene insularum, Sirmio, insularumque ocelle' ('Sirmio, thou precious little eye of all peninsulas and islands', *The Poems of Catullus and Tibullus*, ed. and translated into prose by Walter Kelly (London: Bohn, 1864), 29). Sark is a small island among the Channel Islands. ACS visited in May 1876 and September 1882. He had hoped to see Hugo—who lived on the Islands while in exile from France—on the second visit but was disappointed (*SL*, iv.294). Cf. 'The Garden of Cymodoce', *SS*.

*Propontis... Pontic bark*: alluding to Catullus 4 ('The Praise of the Pinnace', *The Poems of Catullus and Tibullus*, 11). Propontis is the Sea of Azov, off the Black Sea ('Pontic Bay').

## FROM *A MIDSUMMER HOLIDAY AND OTHER POEMS* (LONDON: CHATTO & WINDUS, 1884)

### IX. On the Verge

First published *MHOP*, the last of nine poems comprising 'A Midsummer Holiday'. These were dedicated to TWD in memory of vacations together. Land's End is the furthest south western tip of Cornwall and thus the 'end' of Great Britain in a diagonal from John O'Groats on the north eastern tip of Scotland. As a poem of theological speculation 'On the Verge' can be compared to ACS's views of Arnold and the poetry of doubt (see 'Matthew Arnold's *New Poems*', 183–95). The visual appearance on this poem in the first edition is a striking example of the issue of line spacing discussed on li as each line is broken so that the text appears to have a one- to five-syllable line alternating with a longer one. Note that Chatto's printers (Spottiswoode & Co.) break the first sentence at 'Where we stand,' so that the capitalization further decoys the reader into uncertainty about the formal disposition of the verse. There was unusually no indentation that follows the rhyme scheme.

*fire... brand*: cf. the death of Meleager in *AiC*.

### Lines on the Monument of Giuseppe Mazzini

First published *MHOP*. The poem concerns the monument in Mazzini's home town of Genoa. *The Times* noted this column topped with Mazzini's statue as 'very lately inaugurated' on 4 October 1880, observing that Genoa 'still keeps alive the agitation of which Mazzini was the first mover' (9). *The Leeds Mercury* recorded the forthcoming unveiling on 21 June 1882 (29 May 1882, 2). ACS appears to have been invited: there is a letter drafted for him by Emilie Venturi, giving his apologies (*UL*, ii.300). *MHOP*, indicative of ACS's Italian political sympathies, contained no equivalent on the death of Garibaldi (d.2 June 1882). Emilie Ventura no doubt expressed ACS's view when calling Garibaldi a 'vain old monarchist' (*UL*, ii.300). ACS published 'The Statue of Victor Hugo' in *The Gentleman's Magazine*, 252 (September 1881), 284–90, included in *TLOP*. Thomas Purnell had sent ACS 'relics' from the tomb of Mazzini in February 1884 (*UL*, 2.361). Cf. Hugo's 'Le rétablissement de la statue de Henri IV' and George Barlow's 'To Mazzini Triumphant' (1878). Note that a 19th-century photograph of Mazzini's tomb has been pasted by an unknown hand into the front end-papers of the MS of 'Ode to Mazzini' (1–11), BL Ashley MS 4424.

*Alighieri... Angelo*: Dante and Michelangelo. The latter knew Dante's work and alludes to *La Divina Commedia* in *The Last Judgement* in the Sistine Chapel.

*Since man... son*: the Incarnation.

*And bade... again*: cf. John 11:43–4. ACS alludes to the Risorgimento ('revival'/ 'resurrection').

*City superb*: la Superba, the nickname for Genoa, birthplace of Christopher Columbus (1451–1506) and Mazzini. The latter is buried in Genoa's Cimitero monumentale di Staglieno.

## Les Casquets

First published as 'Les Casquettes', Macmillan's *English Illustrated Magazine*, 1 (October 1883), 16–21. ACS asked TWD on 8 October 1882 whether the following stanza from a new poem would 'pass muster?':

> Peace for her was the dower as a guerdon
> Given of the storm to their cradle-child:
> Peace the note of the sea's chant's burden
> For leagues of triumph that flamed and smiled
> From dawn through morn to the sunset season,
> A watchword whispered of dawn to noon
> For all the dark deep's trouble and treason,
> And sealed by night of the moon.
>
> (*SL*, iv.305)

These lines did not appear in the published version and were replaced by those beginning 'Peace rose crowned with the dawn'. ACS told TWD either on 19 or 26 October that he had 'finished my "Casquettes" poem this very hour of writing' (*SL*, iv.309), observing to his friend on 31 October that 'My last poem is just the length to which I usually (as in Hertha and the Hymn of Man) confine myself—200 lines (25 stanzas of eight)' (*SL*, iv, 310). The final published version actually comprises two hundred and eight lines, and twenty-six stanzas, mostly of ten-syllables with a final three-feet line. Les Casquets are a group of partially submerged rocks seven miles west of Alderney, the northern-most Channel Island. The capital of Alderney is St Anne's. Many ships have fallen victim to Les Casquets, leading to the establishment of an effective lighthouse in the 18th century.

*basnets*: a basnet is 'A small, light, steel headpiece, in shape somewhat globular, terminating in a point raised slightly above the head, and closed in front with a ventail or visor; when used in action without the ventail, as was frequently the case in England, the great "helm", resting on the shoulders, was worn over it', *OED*.

*Nor eye . . . reckon*: Biblical syntax (cf. 1 Corinthians 9).

*past[.]*: full stop omitted from first edition.

*girl's lone life*: ACS alludes to a well-known story retold in Edith F. Carey's *The Channel Islands* (London: Black, 1904):

> In 1779 [a primitive lighthouse] was superseded by an oil light in a copper lantern, and in 1790 three lighthouses named St Peter, St Thomas, and Donjon respectively were built and lit by a number of Argand lights. These were looked after by a single Alderney family named Houguez, of which the man, his wife, and his six children took turns at watching and relighting the lamps so often broken and extinguished by the sea that—
>
> Mounting to the welkin's cheek,
> Dashes the fire out. [*The Tempest*, 1.2.4–5]
>
> To these exiles Alderney constituted both mainland and metropolis, and the details are still recalled of a visit the eldest girl was induced to pay to her relations at St Anne's. After a short sojourn in what—to her—was a giddy whirl of society, 'aweary of this great world' she joyfully returned to her rock.
>
> (289)

In relation to this story of longing and isolation at sea, cf. Arnold's 'Forsaken Merman' (1849) (and ACS in 'Matthew Arnold's *New Poems*', 193 and 'Recollections of Benjamin Jowett', 478) as well as Philip Bourke Marston's 'Caught in the Nets' and ACS's 'Grace Darling' in *AOP*.

## In Sepulcretis

First published as 'Post Mortem (Four Sonnets)', *FR*, 35 (January 1884), 65–6. ACS was anxious about the privacy of his own life but the occasion for this poem was the publication of Harry Buxton Forman's edition of *Letters of John Keats to Fanny Brawne Written in the Years MDCCCXIX and MDCCCXX and now given from the Original Manuscripts* (London: Reeves and Turner, 1878) and the more recently issued *Poetical Works and Other Writings of John Keats: Now First Brought Together, Including*

*Poems and Numerous Letters not before Published*, 4 vols (London: Reeves and Turner, 1883). ACS's 'foreman of the flock' is a pun. ACS's friend Lord Houghton had tactfully avoided significant mention of Keats' romantic relationships in *The Life and Letters of John Keats* (1848; 2nd edn, 1867), including no more 'intrusive record of them than is absolutely necessary for the comprehension of the real man' (204). ACS's shared that perspective. The Brawne letters were controversial. *The Athenæum* thought their publication 'the greatest impeachment of a woman's sense of womanly delicacy to be found in the history of literature' and that

> Mr Forman's extraordinary preface is no less notable as a sign of the degradation to which the bookmaker has sunk [...] To publish the love-letters of a dead man who, if he were living, would cry out from the depths of his soul against it, seems to the common understanding of those to whom the affections are more than fame a heinous offence.
>
> 'Our Library Table', *The Athenæum*, 16 February 1878, 218.

Forman (1842–1917) made his name as a bibliographer, collector, and editor. In the 20th century, he was revealed also to be a forger and, with his forger-acquaintance T.J. Wise (co-editor of Bonchurch), was responsible for distorting the publishing history of major English writers, including ACS's. Cf. the story of 'The Devil's Due' in Collins, 125–32 and Nicholas Barker and John Collins, *Sequel to An Enquiry: The Forgeries of H. Buxton Forman and T.J. Wise Re-Examined* (London: Scolar, 1983).

'In Sepulcretis' disguised the fact that ACS had received the *Letters of John Keats to Fanny Brawne* from Forman himself with whom ACS maintained a correspondence. ACS wrote to thank him on 22 February 1878 (*SL*, iv.44) and again on 15 March, observing that he could 'hardly, though overwhelmed with pressure of immediate personal business, keep from devouring [them] at once' (*SL*, iv.46). Although ACS privately referred to Forman as 'Mr Fuxton Bor(e)man' (*SL*, iii.191), the correspondence continued, surprisingly, after 'In Sepulcretis' with its description of Forman as an ass: ACS, signing himself 'Yours very truly', wrote to Forman in response to questions about the novelist 'Rosa Matilda' (Charlotte Dacre (1771/2–1825) on 22 November 1886 (*SL*, v.174–5). Cf. 'After Looking into Carlyle's "Reminiscences"' in *TLOP*.

*Vidistis ipso... cœnam*: 'who from funeral flames as collecting her meat', Nott, i.157 (Nott comments: 'The indigent, such as half-starved women of pleasure, would attend funerals, to pick up parts of the *silecernium*, or funeral supper [...] laid on the pile, and burnt with the body', i.156n).

*To publish... of felony*: a well-known statement. There is a version in *The Memoirs of Heinrich Heine and Some Newly-Discovered Fragments of His Writings* (London: Bell, 1884), 138.

*foreman... flock*: see headnote.

*Not Shakespeare's... rhymes*: Shakespeare's grave in Holy Trinity, Stratford-upon-Avon, includes a curse: 'Good frend for Iesvs sake forbeare, | To digg the dvst encloased heare. | Blese be ye man yt spares thes stones, | And cvrst be he yt moves my bones'.

## On the Death of Richard Doyle

First published *The Athenæum*, 29 December 1883, 865. Richard Doyle (1824–11 December 1883) was an illustrator for seven years at *Punch* (to 1850) and a prolific artist, illustrating for Dickens on *The Chimes* and *The Cricket on the Hearth* and providing images for John Ruskin's *The King of the Golden River* (London: Smith, Elder, 1851). ACS alludes to this in l.9. Doyle was a friend of many artists and writers and his best-known achievement, to which ACS alludes, was *In Fairyland: A Series of Pictures from the Elf-World with a Poem, by William Allingham* (London: Longmans, Green, Reader, & Dyer, 1870).

*Hyblæan*: of honey.

## A Solitude

First published *MHOP*. Cf. 'By the North Sea', 407–20.

## Clear the Way!

First published *PMG*, 19 August 1884, 4 (an instalment that included, on p. 6, '"The Peers and the People": A Reply by Lord Carnarvon', detailing a speech by the Earl of Carnarvon at the Newbury Working Men's Conservative Club, defending the House of Lords). The poem principally refers to discussions around the Third Reform Bill (which became the Representation of the People Act [Third Reform Act], 1884). The Act extended the enfranchising property qualifications from the boroughs (as established by the 1867 Second Reform Act) to all counties of the kingdom. It was passed on 6 December 1884, coming into force on the first day of 1885. The Act's passage prompted ACS to consider the non-representative nature of the unreformed House of Lords. *MHOP* contained poems expressing ACS's disapproval of aristocrats, including 'The Twilight of the Lords' and the three sonnets 'Vos Deos Laudamus ['we praise you gods']: The Tory Journalist's Anthem'. The first of these sonnets was aimed at Tennyson who had accepted a barony in September 1883. See Francis O'Gorman, 'Swinburne and Tennyson's Peerage', *English Studies*, 96 (2015), 277–92. ACS was invited to become a Vice-President of the Lords Abolition League partly in response to 'Clear the Way!' (*UL*, ii.371). He declined. There was a withering response to ACS (called 'Reply') in *The National Review*, 4 (September 1884), 137–8, proposing that poets should be cleared away.

*house*: this was the more appropriate 'House' in the *PMG* printing.

## FROM *POEMS AND BALLADS, THIRD SERIES* (LONDON: CHATTO & WINDUS, 1889)

### March: An Ode, 1887

First published as 'March: An Ode', *NC*, 23 (March 1888), 317–20.

*whin*: 'The common furze or gorse, *Ulex europæus*. Often *collect. pl.* and *sing.* for a clump or mass of the shrub', *OED*.

### To a Seamew

First published *PB* 3. '[In] my boyhood', he told Mary Molesworth on 7 November 1886, 'I was always regarded at home as belonging naturally to that tribe [of sea birds]. I met one the other day at Beachy Head and made him a song on the spot' (*SL*, v.169). ACS had visited Beachy Head, near Eastbourne in East Sussex, at the end of September 1886. The poem, celebrating the sea, also obliquely remembers the blind poet Philip Bourke Marston (1850–87), drawing on marine and light imagery ACS shared with him. But what began as a sympathetic tribute at the point of composition became a memorial when it was published, for Marston died on 14 February 1887. Note that TWD always associated Marston with a blinded gull (see Thomas Hake and Arthur Compton-Rickett, *The Life and Letters of Theodore Watts-Dunton*, 2 vols (London: Jack, 1916), i.149–50). When ACS wrote his last surviving letter to Marston (15 November 1886), inviting him to visit, he observed that 'I will read you a lyric made near Beachy Head while returning from a long walk thither' (*SL*, v.174). ACS wrote a sonnet on Marston included in TWD's obituary in *The Athenæum*, 19 February 1887 (257) and other memorial poems including 'Light: An Epicede: To Philip Bourke Marston' in *AOP*. Cf. also Charlotte Smith, 'Beachy Head' and DGR, 'To Philip Bourke Marston, inciting me to do poetic work' (October 1878) and 'To Philip Bourke Marston (in answer)' (October 1878). Note that Beachy Head's association with suicide was long-standing. See Francis O'Gorman, 'Swinburne and the "unutterable sadness" of Philip Bourke Marston', *Literary Imagination*, 15 (2013), 165–80.

*wild Septembers*: cf. Emily Brontë's 'wild Decembers' in 'Cold in the earth' ('Remembrance'), l.9.

*sons... seamen*: ACS remembers himself as the son of an admiral.

### Neap-Tide

First published *PB* 3. 'Neap' refers to 'a tide occurring just after the first or third quarters of the moon, when the high-water level is lowest and there is least difference between high- and low-water levels', *OED*. ACS observed to his mother on 7 March 1889 that 'I think you may perhaps recognize the locality of the little poem. The last walk I took last year from Lancing to Shoreham was by the sands, and the sea was so far out and the shore slopes so much that even the tops of the downs were out of sight behind the low sea-bank which shut out everything on shore. It was wonderfully lonely and striking' (*SL*, v.261–2). Writing to WMR on 17 October 1889, ACS added that the poem was 'the exact picture of one particularly grim & dreary day last year, which I enjoyed in its way, tho' hopeful of a change to brighter & fresher weather on the morrow' (*UL*, ii.482). Cf. Edward Thomas' observation in *Algernon Charles Swinburne: A Study* (London: Secker, 1912), 192: 'The third series of *Poems and Ballads* gave an unsurpassable exhibition of metrical experiments. They can only be judged when rendered by an excellent voice.'

## The Interpreters

First published *English Illustrated Magazine*, 3 (October 1885), 3–4. ACS told the editor J.W. Comyns Carr (1849–1916) on 21 July 1885 that the poem should be included in a summer edition 'if you can find a place for it. It was born out of doors on a hot day, and ought to be read by midsummer sunlight if the mood it was made in is to be appreciated' (*SL*, v.120).

## In Time of Mourning

First published *The Athenæum* (as 'May 1885'), 3138 (17 December 1887), 825. Victor Hugo died on 22 May 1885 after a short illness. W.E. Henley published an obituary in *The Athenæum* on 30 May (695–8), hailing him in Swinburnean terms as belonging 'to the race of Aeschylus and Shakspeare' (695) while ACS wrote on 21 May to his mother: 'we have never had anybody who was like Shakespeare and Milton and like Wilberforce or Howard all at once [. . .] When I think of his greatness as a poet and his goodness as a man combined, I really think sometimes that there never was or will be anybody like Victor Hugo' (*SL*, v.108). The poem is a roundel (cf. *A Century of Roundels*, 427–38).

## To Sir Richard F. Burton
(On his Translation of the Arabian Nights)

First published *The Athenæum*, 6 February 1886, 199. Richard Francis Burton (1821–90), celebrated and fearless traveller and author, first met ACS on 6 June 1861 at a breakfast given by Richard Monckton Milnes. Unconventional, brave, sexually daring, a man of learning and a dazzling linguist, Burton had many qualities ACS admired. Burton, the dedicatee of *PB* 2, dedicated his translation of *The Lyricks [of] Camoëns: Sonnets, Canzons, Odes and Sextines*, 2 vols (London: Quaritch, 1884) to ACS. The following year Burton began the publication of his major work, *The Book of the Thousand Nights and a Night: A Plain and Literal Translation of the Arabian Nights*

*Entertainments*, 16 vols (p.p., 1885–8). Both ACS and TWD offered subscriptions. Cf. 'Elegy 1869–1891', 498–501 and notes, 652–4.

## A Reiver's Neck-Verse

First published *PB* 3. Without the second stanza, this was originally included in ACS's unpublished novel, *Lesbia Brandon*. It is called 'Willie's Neck-Song' and introduced with the words:

> 'I like much better that song of a border thief whom his wife or some other woman betrayed into the hands of justice—you know?'
>
> 'Oh, I know,' said Cecil, with eyes now dry and bright; 'Willie's neck-song: Bulmer used to pitch into the maid for singing it. Oh, I say, do sing that.'
>
> She bowed to the boy, smiling, and played some loud rapid music as she sang: turning first towards the youngest with a word or two.
>
> 'You see, Ethel, this woman—his wife—he had come back out of hiding to see her. He was a reiver, you know that that is, and had lifted ever so many heads of kye; a thief, and they wanted to hang him. He was safe I suppose where he was, but he must needs have a look of her, poor man. Well, when she had him safe at home, she gave him up. And they made this song for him at the gallows. They say he made and sang it, but I doubt that.'
>
> *NACS*, 338

A reiver is 'A robber, a plunderer; a marauder, a raider. Also *fig.* Freq. with reference to the groups of marauders that raided the border between Scotland and England from 13th–16th centuries' (*OED*). Cf. ACS's Villon poems. On ACS and Northumbrian ballads, see the headnote for 'The Ballads of the English Border', 655–6. Cf. Percy Grainger, *A Reiver's Neck-Verse: Song for a Man's Voice and Piano* (London: Schott, 1911).

*I wot sae winna we*: I know so will we.

*tow*: 'A hangman's rope, a halter', *OED*.

## The Tyneside Widow

First published *FR*, 43 (April 1888), 477–9 and originally included in the unpublished *Lesbia Brandon*, *NACS*, 335–8.

*mools*: soil used to fill a grave (Northern England, Scottish, Irish).

*on my ee-bree*: on my eye brow.

## RECOLLECTIONS OF PROFESSOR JOWETT (1893)

First published *NC*, 34 (December 1893), 912–21; reprinted in *Studies in Prose and Poetry* (London: Chatto & Windus, 1894), 26–43 (the copytext for this version). Benjamin Jowett (1817–93) was one of the best-known dons of 19th-century Oxford: contributor ('On the Interpretation of Scripture') to *Essays and Reviews* (1860); editor of Aristotle, Plato, and Thucydides; from 1855, Regius Professor of Greek; from 1870, Master of Balliol. Jowett made influential friends among Balliol men including ACS (ACS's self-described failure at Oxford obviously did not affect their relationship). Jowett died after a prolonged illness on 1 October 1893. ACS told his mother on 2 November that this essay was 'the first time I ever attempted anything of the sort', i.e. a prose recollection or memorial tribute: '[...] I thought I wouldn't try to versify my feelings, but would just write down some records of our intercourse—especially as all the accounts and estimates and reminiscences of Mr Jowett (which are probably numerous and voluminous enough already) deal only with his relations to Oxford, and I could tell—and have told—what sort of a man he was away from Oxford. I think you will say it is done with the right sort of taste and feeling, and I hope you will be interested by my tribute to the memory of so good and true and tried a friend' (*SL*, vi.61–2). TWD composed three sonnets on Jowett's death, 'The Last Walk from Boar's Hill (for A.C.S.)', published in *The Athenæum*, 3445 (4 November 1893), 627. Cf. Tennyson's 'To the Master of Balliol' in *The Death of Œnone, and Other Poems* (London: Macmillan, 1892).

*Master... stranger*: allusion to what ACS will presently exaggeratedly call own his 'total and scandalous failure' at Balliol.

*Sydney Smith and Macaulay*: wit and writer Sydney Smith (1771–1845) was a well-known Whig as a young man; the historian, politician, and poet Thomas Babington Macaulay (1800–59) was, as a mature man, a Whig figurehead and architect of its intellectual identity.

*characters... Pope*: of Dryden, Macaulay said: 'His life was commensurate with the period during which a great revolution in the public taste was effected; and in that revolution he played the part of Cromwell. By unscrupulously taking the lead in its wildest excesses, he obtained the absolute guidance of it. By trampling on laws, he acquired the authority of a legislator. By signalizing himself as the most daring and irreverent of rebels, he raised himself to the dignity of a recognised prince. He commenced his career by the most frantic outrages. He terminated it in the repose of established sovereignty,—the author of a new code, the root of a new dynasty', '[Review of] *The Poetical Works of John Dryden*', *Edinburgh Review*, 47 (1828), 1–36 (1). On Pope, Macaulay wrote that: 'His own life was one long series of tricks, as mean and as malicious as that of which he suspected Addison and Tickell. He was all stiletto and mask. To injure, to insult, and to save himself from the consequences of injury and insult by lying and equivocating, was the habit of his life', *The Life and Writings of Addison* (London: Longman, Brown, Green, and Longmans, 1852), 78.

*Biglow Papers*: satirical poems by James Russell Lowell (1819–91), issued in two series, in periodicals then in two volumes in 1847 and 1867 respectively. They were reprinted many times in Great Britain including by Hotten.

*tyranny… cruelty*: cf. *Note of an English Republican* (1876), 308–12.

*'Voltaire… continu'*: 'Voltaire, it's commonsense in a continuous stream'.

*'Our Bore'*: Dickens' short story 'Our Bore' (1852).

*Mr Froude… truth*: cf. J.A. Froude's account of Byron view of Shelley and his conviction that 'Byron as little believed that Jane Clermont had sent a second child to the Foundling Hospital as he believed that Shelley had been the child's father', 'A Leaf from the Real Life of Lord Byron', *NC*, 14 (August 1883), 228–42 (242).

*Richard Burton*: see headnote on 652–3.

*boyhood… breakers*: ACS is speaking of himself as a masculine ideal, referring to his (alleged) climb of Culver Cliff (see xxiii n) and his love of sea-swimming.

*Kynance Cove*: a popular visiting place in the 19th century on the south-west tip of Cornwall. ACS wrote to George Powell on 21 January 1874 that he had 'just returned from a prosperous ten days' tour to the Land's End with the Master of Balliol which has left me in love for life with Kynance Cove where (to use an original expression) I could live and die' (*SL*, ii.266).

*Tintagel… St Michael's Mount*: Tintagel is on the northern coast of Cornwall, its castle long associated with King Arthur. St Michael's Mount is a small tidal island off the south-western tip of Cornwall.

*'he rode… anybody'*: a breakfast boast of Dr Johnson that Boswell records in the *Life* for 24 September 1778.

*Balak said unto Balaam*: 'And Balaam answered and said unto the servants of Balak, If Balak would give me his house full of silver and gold, I cannot go beyond the word of the LORD my God, to do less or more', Numbers 22:18. Jowett had spent the Long Vacation 1872 in the Scottish Highlands helping prepare *The School and Children's Bible* (London: Longman, Green, 1873). ACS visited in August.

*the man… schoolmaster*: from Ch. 46 of Scott's *The Heart of Midlothian*.

*'when there… vanity'*: from *The Heart of Midlothian*, Ch. 8: 'Butler had not escaped the tinge of pedantry which naturally flowed from his education, and was apt, on many occasions, to make parade of his knowledge, when there was no need of such vanity'.

*Pattison… Plato*: ACS refers to: Mark Pattison (1813–84), Rector of Lincoln College, a significant force in the development of research at the University of Oxford; Walter Pater (1839–94), aesthete, Fellow of Brasenose, author of *Studies in the History of the Renaissance* (1873); John Addington Symonds (1840–93), scholar, Italianist, author of *Studies of the Greek Poets* (London: Smith, Elder, 1873), writer on homosexuality. Symonds was a Balliol man and in fact a life-long friend of Jowett whose tolerance was considerable—and of which ACS was a beneficiary.

ACS makes a half-veiled allusion to Symonds' sexuality: Whitman's *Calamus* poems from *Leaves of Grass* (1860 edn) deal with same-sex love and ACS fuses the term with catamites: boys kept for homosexual purposes. ACS criticism of Symonds' homosexuality is noted in Introduction, note 119 on xlii and in *UL*, i.253–4n.

*Literature and Dogma*: Arnold's *Literature and Dogma: An Essay Towards a Better Appreciation of the Bible* (1873).

*'magnified and non-natural man'*: cf. 'What we in general do is to take the best thinking and loving of the best man, to better this best, to call it *perfect*, and to say that this is God. So we construct a magnified and non-natural man, by dropping out all that in man seems a source of weakness, and by heightening to the very utmost all that in man seems a source of strength, such as his thought and his love', Matthew Arnold, *God and the Bible* ([1875] London: Smith, Elder, 1897), 15.

*Pauline...Asolando*: Browning's *Pauline: A Fragment of a Confession* appeared in March 1833; *Asolando: Fancies and Facts* on the day of his death on 12 December 1889.

*Balaustion*: Browning's *Balaustion's Adventure: Including a Transcript from Euripides* (1871) was partly a version of Euripides' *Alcestis.*

*'Exhaustion's Imposture'*: DGR gave *Balaustion's Adventure* this name in a letter of 13 August 1871 to William Bell Scott (*The Correspondence of Dante Gabriel Rossetti*, v.113 (letter 71/123): 'it is so absolutely everything that Greek ideas are not').

*'The second Guido...dreadful'*: referring to Book 11 of *The Ring and the Book*, the second of Guido Franceschini's monologues, which is spoken before his execution for murder.

*The Earl of Brecon*: 5-Act tragedy by Robert Eyres Landor (1781–1869), the brother of W.S. Landor.

*copy...plays*: Landor's *'The Early of Brecon'; 'Faith's Fraud', and 'The Ferryman'* (London: Saunders and Otley, 1841).

*magnificent...Jowett's*: does this refer to Brown's *Self-Portrait* (1850), now in Manchester City Art Gallery? Madox, born on 16 April 1821, had died on 6 October 1893.

*old pupil*: ACS's story about himself.

*'any little abhorrences'*: presumably the *Symposium*'s discussion of homosexuality (cf. note 119 on xlii). The phrase comes from Bk XVI, Ch. X of Carlyle's *The History of Friedrich II.*

*Dean Church...student*: Richard William Church's popular essay originally from 1850, reprinted, for instance, as *Dante: An Essay* (London: Macmillan, 1878).

*I had...edition*: *La Commedia di Dante Allighieri illustrata da Ugo Foscolo* [collected and edited by Mazzini], 4 vols (London: Rolandi, 1842–3).

*Francesca...Dominic*: Dante places the 'treacherous' lover Francesca da Rimini in Hell in Canto 5 of the *Inferno*; Cunizza da Romano eloped with the poet Sordello but Dante places her in Paradise (Canto 9); Brutus is damned to Hell as a traitor to

Julius Caesar in Canto 34 while the conflict of Cato the Younger with Julius Caesar does not exclude him from being one of only a handful of pagans saved in *La Divina Commedia*: he is the guardian of Purgatory. Farinata degli Uberti is damned to Hell in Canto 10 for his posthumously alleged heresy (see below) while St Dominic, founder of the Dominicans, is placed in Paradise in Canto 12. ACS is remembering the Saint's (disputed) association with the Inquisition. For Church's discussion, see *Dante: An Essay*, 71 and 129.

*'the spirit . . . life'*: 'the letter killeth, but the spirit giveth life', 2 Corinthians 3:6.

*poet of midnight . . . sun*: cf. the last lines of *Paradiso*.

*doubtful and unhopeful*: part of Farinata degli Uberti's alleged heresy was that he was thought to deny eternal life. Dante places him with Epicurus and 'tutti suoi seguaci, | che l'anima col corpo morta fanno' ('all his followers, who say the soul dies with the body').

*'Mr Lowell . . . eye!'*: 'If [Milton] is blind, it is with excess of light, it is a divine partiality, an overshadowing with angels' wings', James Lowell, *The English Poets* (London: Scott, 1888), 191.

*The Barometer*: identity uncertain.

*sense nickname*: a 'Lake Poet'.

*skating as a boy*: in Book I of Wordsworth's *The Prelude* (1850).

*'he dies . . . but ceases'*: adapted from DGR's sonnet 'The Choice', l.13, in *The House of Life*.

*'He laboured, so must we'*: from 'Timber; or Discoveries Made upon Men and Matter' in *The Works of Ben Jonson*, with an essay by Barry Cornwall (London: Moxon, 1838), 757.

## FROM *ASTROPHEL AND OTHER POEMS* (LONDON: CHATTO & WINDUS, 1894)

### A Nympholept

First published *Black and White*, 23 May 1891, 513–15 with illustrations by Charles Ricketts (1866–1931): the opening two stanzas were in *PMG*, 22 May 1891, 2. Writing to William Sharp on 6 October 1901 about Sharp's selection of ACS (see headnote to 'Super Flumina Babylonis', 591), ACS observed that he was 'pleased to find the *Nympholept* in a leading place, as I think it one of the best and most representative things I ever did' (*SL*, vi.153). *The Standard* said that in 'A Nympholept' 'there breathes the noblest spirit of a refined Paganism' (26 April 1894, 2); *The Bookman* added that this was 'one of the finest subtlest [poems] he has ever written [. . . ] The vision of the waking poet at noon admits of no paraphrase, and a few lines will hardly suggest it. The sense of the presence his being was aware of, not Pan's but another's, and how fear vanished into rapture, are thrilled into you rather than spoken to your ear': 'Mr Swinburne's "Astrophel"', *The Bookman*, 6 (June 1894), 74–6 (76). A nympholept (from νυμφόληπτος: caught by nymphs, raptured, frenzied) is one suffering from nympholepsy, a 'Passion supposedly inspired in men by nymphs; an ecstasy or yearning, esp. that caused by desire for something unattainable', *OED*. ACS may have known Horace Smith's *Amarynthus, the Nympholept: A Pastoral Drama, With Other Poems* (London: Longman, 1821). Cf. Robert Browning's 'Numpholeptos' (1876). ACS's text inspired Bax's tone poem, *Nympholept* (1912 but not performed till 1961).

*say[.]*: full stop omitted from first edition.

*world... good*: cf. Genesis 1:10, 12, 18, 31.

*Shall... tread*: cf. Genesis 3:8.

*Typho labours... Titanic*: Typhon was the 'father of all monsters' in ancient Greek mythology: Zeus buried him beneath Mount Etna.

*What God... him?*: cf. Psalm 8:4.

*first and last*: cf. Revelation 22:13.

## Loch Torridon

First published Cassell and Co's *Magazine of Art*, January 1890, 70–7, with engravings by John MacWhirter ARA of 'Loch Maree', 'Loch Torridon', and 'Looking out to Sea from Loch Torridon'. The poem was dedicated to ACS's friend Edwin Harrison (1844–99) who had matriculated at Balliol in 1867. Harrison was permanently weak, sometimes, he told ACS on 7 February 1890, finding it 'almost impossible to read except by brief snatches' (*UL*, iii.5). His potential remained unfulfilled. Like ACS, Harrison was a friend of Jowett (see 473–82). Harrison shared ACS's love of sea-swimming and much of their correspondence concerned Classical Greek (cf. the note to 'The Last Oracle', 619). Harrison read 'Loch Torridon' with 'pleasure & pride': 'What a glorious swim we had that day, to be sure!', he told ACS: 'I hear you now chaunting snatches of [Arnold's] "Forsaken Merman" as we cleave to the clear waters side by side, & gaze into the many-coloured depths' (*UL*, iii.4). The poem records a visit in the summer of 1871 with Jowett, Harrison, and other Balliol men to Scotland and in particular to Loch Torridon, a sea loch in the North West Highlands that ACS reached via the famously beautiful freshwater Loch Maree. ACS rarely provides himself with the opportunity to use such a variety of forms in a single poem (note in particular the freedom of the first portion, with its unequal line lengths and changing rhyme schemes: cf. 'Thalassius', 368–80). Cf. 'The Lake of Gaube', 510–12.

*rampires*: ramparts (archaic).

*arisen indeed*: cf. Luke 23:34.

## Elegy
## 1869–1891

First published *FR*, 52 (July 1892), 1–5. ACS's elegy on the death of Richard Burton (see headnote to 'To Sir Richard F. Burton (On his Translation of the Arabian

Nights)') recalled a holiday ACS had taken with Burton, including a tour of Auvergne from 24 August 1869. The scenery was described in a letter to ACS's mother on 31 August: '*I* never saw anything of the sort so grand [...] There is between Le Puy and Polignac one great cliff front of towering columns which faces the valley of the Borne river—columns broken off at a great height, and as regular as if designed for a cathedral' (*SL*, ii.26–7).

There is vexation in this poem with Lady (Isabel) Burton (née Arundel, 1831–96) though she too had been ACS's friend. She came from an Old Catholic family and, while assisting her husband, also disapproved of his attitude to religion. ACS noted to TWD on 23 July 1891 that 'I have added a few stanzas to my Auvergne elegy. I think the landscape is good: the sentiments will hardly be grateful to Lady B[urton] or her fellow conspirators against a deathbed on behalf of the Oly Cartholic Church' (*SL*, vi.10). Lady Burton had had her husband buried in accordance with Catholic rites and announced in *MP* ('Sir Richard Burton's Manuscripts', 19 June 1891, 3) that she had destroyed the MS of his translation from the Arabic of the erotic *Scented Garden*. She said that 'what a gentleman, a scholar, a man of the world may write when living, he would see very differently to what the poor soul would see standing naked before its God, with its good or evil deeds along to answer for, and their consequences visible to it for the first moment, rolling on to the end of time'. *PMG* reprinted the letter (19 June 1891, 6) under the title 'How Lady Burton Sacrificed 6,000 Guineas'. ACS did not welcome Lady Burton either though felt constrained in what he could say in public. 'It is not my part to strip and whip the popish mendacities of that poor liar Lady Burton', he told Eliza Lynn Linton on 24 November 1892: 'Only one whom we knew and loved [i.e. Landor] could have done it adequately—and been subjected to legal penalties for telling the bitter truth in duly bitter words. Of course she has befouled Richard Burton's memory like a harpy—and of course it might have been expected. But I can't hit her harder or straighter than I did in my Elegy' (*SL*, vi.45). Linton had already expressed a mildly critical view of Lady Burton in 'Partisans of Wild Women', *NC*, 31 (1892), 455–64: 'he was no sooner dead than his widow surrounded him with the emblems and rites of her own faith—which was not his' (461).

*Thy steep...pride*: ACS noted to his mother on 31 August 1869: 'Don't believe one word that the wretch Murray says about the cathedral of Le Puy; it is one of the grandest as well as one of the strangest churches ever built, and adapted with almost a miraculous instinct of art to the tone of the landscape and character of the country about, where, except the deep fields and lawns of grass that spread about and slope up from the narrow valleys made by the two streams Borne and Loire, there is nothing but alternately brown and grey mountain-land ending in a long and beautifully undulating circle of various heights and ranges. These mountain colours are most delicately repeated in the alternate stripes of the cathedral front; the effect, like that of the whole town, reminded me as well as Burton (who spent 18 months there as a boy) of my beloved Siena. Indeed Le Puy is a smaller Siena—the highest praise *I* can give' (*SL*, ii.27). ACS was presumably using Murray's *A Hand-Book for Travellers in France*, 11th edn (London: Murray, 1869), which described Notre-Dame du Puy as a 'heavy ungainly building, in the Romanesque style, very venerable, rather singular than beautiful; its interior not improved by the repairs and stucco applied at the expense of Louis XVIII' (446). Cf. ACS's 'An Evening at Vichy, September 1869: Written on the News of the Death of Lord Leighton' in *ACP*.

*whose full... poise*: cf. Wordsworth, 'On the Extinction of the Venetian Republic', ll.1–2.

*Sun... sang*: a fragment of one of Sophocles' lost plays concerns the judgment of Paris (and thus an apple from the Garden of Hesperides). See *Sophocles, Fragments*, ed. Hugh Lloyd-Jones, Loeb Classical Library (Cambridge, MA: Harvard University Press, 2003 edn), 193 and 194.

## Threnody
October 6, 1892

First published, as 'Threnody, Alfred Lord Tennyson, October 6th, 1892', *NC*, 33 (January 1893), 1–3. Tennyson (b.1809) had died at Aldworth on 6 October 1892. ACS told his mother on 13 November 1892 that he had 'written some verses on Tennyson's beautiful and enviable death in the arms of Shakespeare, as one may say, reading *my* favourite poem of all [*Cymbeline*] just before the end [...] They are in the same metre as those I wrote last year on his birthday, with which he was (as he wrote) so much pleased—and the two poems are just of the same length' (*SL*, vi.42—ellipsis here is Mrs Leith's). ACS refers to 'Birthday Ode, August 6, 1891', which preceded 'Threnody' in *AOP*. Lady Tennyson wrote to ACS on 19 December 1892, thanking him for a copy of the poem: 'To us who cannot think of death and of *him* together, your splendid tribute so full of life cannot but be especially welcome' (*UL*, iii.45).

On 12 October 1892, in Westminster Abbey, Tennyson was buried next to Browning (b.1812) who had died on 12 December 1889. ACS commemorated Browning with 'A Sequence of Sonnets on the Death of Robert Browning', *FR* (January 1890), 1–4, included in *AOP*.

*Shakespeare's breast*: on 14 October, Hallam Tennyson had written a letter about his father's death to the Chairman of the Executive Committee, Shakespeare's Birthplace, which was printed in *Blackwood's*, 152 (November 1892), 767. This letter was expanded (to include the passage in square brackets) on 21 October 1892 in a version published in *The Dundee Courier & Argus* (5):

> My father was reading King Lear, Troilus and Cressida, and Cymbeline through the last days of his life. On Wednesday he asked for his Shakespeare. I gave him the book, but said—'You must not try and read.' He answered—'I have opened the book.' I looked at the book at midnight on Thursday when I was sitting by him lying dead, and found he had opened it at one of the passages which he called the tenderest in Shakespeare. [He could not part with this volume, but we buried the Shakespeare with him. We had the book enclosed in a metal box, and laid by his side.]

Sir Theodore Martin's sonnet, 'Tennyson and "Cymbeline"', on his last request, appeared in the same edition of *Blackwood's*, 767. Note that Martin's wife, the actress Helena Faucit (1817–98), had been particularly celebrated for her portrayal of Rosalind and Imogen. I do not know where, exactly, ACS had read the story of Tennyson's last hours.

*Strong as death*: cf. Song of Solomon 8:6.

*choral Seven*: cf. Sydney Dobell, 'On the Death of Mrs Browning': 'Which of the Angels sang so well in Heaven | That the approving Archon of the quire | Cried, "Come up hither!" and he, going higher, | Carried a note out of the choral seven' (*Poetical Works*, ii.351).

*Imogen*: cf. ACS's statement in *A Study of Shakespeare* (1880): 'above them all, and all others of [Shakespeare's] divine and human children, the crowning and final and ineffable figure of Imogen' (170). The name is now sometimes given as 'Innogen'.

## Reminiscence

First published *AOP*. The four-rhyme sonnet form is that used by DGR in *The House of Life* (see note on 573).

## Hawthorn Dyke

First published *The Athenæum*, 24 June 1893, 798. Cf. 'The Promise of the Hawthorn', 'Hawthorn Tide', and 'The Passing of the Hawthorn' in *ACP*. Note *HLS*: '[ACS's] prime favourites were the Hawthorns. When the May was in full blossom the poet's enthusiasm was wonderful to witness. He never tired of talking about the beauty of these sweet-smelling bushes' (77).

# THE BALLADS OF THE ENGLISH BORDER

The date of composition *c.*1895? ACS planned an anthology of ballads at the end of the 1850s and T.J. Wise thought this was meant to be the Preface. The MS, BL Ashley 5070, is bound with the ballad collection. Wise's dating is an odd mistake given that the hand-writing of the supposed 'preface' is clearly from late in ACS's life (and the piece is obviously a working draft not a fair-copy). Anne Henry Ehrenpreis in 'Swinburne's Edition of Popular Ballads', *PMLA*, 78 (1963), 559–71, argues convincingly for a date in the late 1890s. The essay responds to Andrew Lang's introduction to *Border Ballads* (London: Longmans, Green, 1895), which doubted the quality of English balladry in comparison to Scottish. Some of ACS's ballads were gathered in *Border Ballads by Algernon Charles Swinburne*, ed. T.J. Wise (Boston: Bibliophile

Society, 1912) while William A. MacInnes published *Ballads of the English Border by Algernon Charles Swinburne* (London: Heinemann, 1925) with many inaccuracies. For further discussion of ACS's work on ballads, see Lakshmi Krishnan, 'Editing Swinburne's Border Ballads', *Modern Language Review*, 104 (2009), 333–52, which includes an exact transcription of the original of this essay (344–6). I have checked this against the original and have omitted ACS's first thoughts. ACS's comments can be read in relation to Scott's essays included in the 1849 edition (Cadell) of the *Minstrelsy of the Scottish Border*: 'Remarks on Popular Poetry' and 'Imitations of the Ancient Ballad'.

*most famous... shadow*: See 'What shall I teach thee, the foremost thing? | Couldst teach me off my Shadow to spring!', 'Goethe's Works' in *The Works of Thomas Carlyle*, ed. H.D. Traill, 30 vols (London: Chapman and Hall, 1896–9), xxvii.432.

*illustrious... all time*: the novelist, poet, and writer Sir Walter Scott (1771–1832). ACS refers to Scott's ballad collection, *Minstrelsy of the Scottish Border: Consisting of Historical and Romantic Ballads, Collected in the Southern Counties of Scotland with a few of Modern Date founded upon Local Tradition*, 3 vols (Edinburgh: Ballantyne, 1802–3).

*Robin Hood... William of Cloudesley*: all subjects of ballads. Guy of Gisborne belongs in the Robin Hood cycle: Gisborne attempts to apprehend Robin on behalf of the sheriff of Nottingham. Adam Bell, Clym o'the Cleugh, and William of Cloudeslie are other outlaws like Robin Hood but primarily associated with Cumbrian folk legend. Cf. Egan Pierce (1814–80), *Adam Bell, Clym o'the Cleugh, and William of Cloudeslie* (London: Hextall, 1842).

*Surtees*: Robert Surtees (1779–1834), historian of County Durham, antiquarian, and author of many ballads. A friend of Scott, Surtees managed to persuade him that his own ballad 'The Death of Featherstonhaugh' was an original old Northumberland text: Scott included it in *Minstrelsy*. Other Surtees' ballads included 'The Reever's Penance' (cf. ACS's 'A Reiver's Neck Verse', 469).

*Scott of 'Glenfinlas' ... Motherwell*: Scott included 'Glenfinlas: or, Lord Ronald's Coronach' in *Minstrelsy*, iv.167–82 and John Leyden's 'The Mermaid', *Minstrelsy*, iv.285–91. The novelist and poet James Hogg (1770–1835) collected Scottish ballads, publishing *The Mountain Bard: Consisting of Ballads and Songs founded on Facts and Legendary Tales* (Edinburgh: Ballantyne, 1807); the northern ballad collector Robert Jamieson (1780?–1844) published *Popular Ballads and Songs, from Tradition, Manuscripts, and Scarce Editions with Translations of Similar Pieces from the Ancient Danish language, and a few Originals by the Editor* (Edinburgh: Murray, 1806); William Motherwell (1797–1835) published significant editions from his collections of local ballads, including *The Harp of Renfrewshire* (Paisley: Lawrence, 1819) and *Minstrelsy, Ancient and Modern* (Glasgow: Wylie, 1827). ACS's collection, Ashley MS 5070, draws on Motherwell significantly.

*Arthur's Seat... Ida*: an odd mistake. ACS refers to his own version of 'Waly Waly', one of the ballads from the projected ballad collection of the 1850s bound with this essay in Ashley MS 5070. ACS's stanza reads: 'Now Arthur's Seat shall be my bed,

| The sheets shall ne'er be filled by me; | Saint Anton's well shall be my drink | Since my true love's forsaken me' (fol.30). Helikon is a Greek mountain celebrated in ancient Greece for possessing two springs sacred to the Muses; Mount Ida is a sacred mountain of Classical Greek and Roman culture.

*'to come... Carterhaugh'*: 'The Young Tamlane' is a ballad included by ACS in the Ashley MS 5070 collection (fols.28–29b) and it includes the lines: 'I forbid ye maidens a' | That wear gowd on your hair, | To come as gang by Carterhaugh, | For young Tamlane is there' (fol.28).

*'I can't say... that'*: Mr Peggotty in Dickens' *David Copperfield* (1849–50), Ch. 63.

*Young Tamlane*: see two notes above.

## FROM *A CHANNEL PASSAGE AND OTHER POEMS* (LONDON: CHATTO & WINDUS, 1904)

### The Lake of Gaube

First published *The Bookman*, 17 (October 1899), 4–5. ACS wrote on 27 October 1904 to WMR, who had been reading *ACP*: 'I hasten to return with thanks the list of the poems honoured by your preference, which I have marked as such in my copy of the book. I myself like The Lake of Gaube as well as any. But perhaps the reviewer [unidentified] was right who said that only swimmers could properly appreciate and relish that poem' (*SL*, vi.188). The Lac de Gaube is in the French Pyrenees, near Cauterets and so ACS's poem invites comparison with Tennyson's 'In the Valley of Cauteretz' (1861). ACS had told Mary Gordon in autumn 1864 that he thought Tennyson's poem on the death of Hallam 'very musical and perfect' (*SL*, i.109).

ACS thought himself a keen swimmer (though whether this was a masculinity myth is hard to say): cf. 'A Swimmer's Dream' in *AOP*. He says of the Lake in his essay version of 'Victor Hugo's Notes of Travel', *ESS*: 'Of all great poets that ever lived, with the one possible and doubtful exception of Dante, Victor Hugo is the one who would have seemed most fit to describe and most capable of describing the lake of Gaube; and he, of all men and all tourists, was the one to turn back down the half-ascended valley, and leave it unvisited' (222). ACS also describes swimming in the 'effable and breathless purity of the clasping water' in the same essay (ibid.). The poem consists of 8-line decasyllabic lines, rhyming ababbccc; then couplets, often anapaestic in feel; and finally a sequence of 8-syllable lines, rhyming ababcdcd, etc.

ACS observed that the lake is among those 'said to be bottomless' (*UL*, iii.201). In 'Song for the Centenary of Walter Savage Landor' (included in *SS*), he described 'The steel-cold Lake of Gaube, | Deep as dark death and keen as death to smite'. He would have known the melancholy history of the Lake for English visitors: William and Sarah Pattison had drowned there on honeymoon on 20 September 1832. The event was commemorated in Richard Monckton Milnes' narrative poem, 'The Tragedy of the Lac de Gaube in the Pyrenees'. ACS might have remembered their death not least because it recalled the accidental drowning of Victor Hugo's much-loved daughter Léopoldine and her husband, Charles Vacquerie, in the Seine on 4 September 1843 when their boat capsized shortly after they had married.

*the sun...god*: 'the sun is god' have long been thought among J.M.W. Turner's last words.

## In a Rosary

First published *ACP*. 'Rosary' is used here in the sense of a rose garden. ACS may be playing on the reader's surprise in not finding this text about a Catholic rosary (which, like the poem, is divided into sections of five). Maxwell observes that 'in the alchemical lexicon ['rosary'] also represents an area of esoteric knowledge' (109). Cf. *OED*, 'rosary', 2: 'With capital initial. (The name of) a treatise on alchemy, the *Rosarium philosophorum* ("Rosary of the philosophers")'.

## Trafalgar Day

First published *NC*, 38 (November 1895), 713–14. One of several late poems on the British military (cf. 'The Centenary of the Battle of the Nile' and 'A Word for the Navy' in *ACP*, and 'The Armada 1588:1888' in *PB* 3). ACS marked the 90th anniversary of the Battle of Trafalgar, 21 October 1805, which saw the British Admiral Viscount Nelson (b.1758) defeat a combined Spanish and French fleet. Nelson was killed during the Battle after being struck by a French musket ball. ACS's poem joins several retrospections (e.g. 'After Ninety Years', *The Speaker*, 12 (1895), 433–4) but is also part of a life-long dislike of Napoleon (Bonaparte as well as III). He shared an interest in the Napoleonic wars with Thomas Hardy. ACS claimed, in his letter to Hardy on 23 January 1904 about *The Dynasts* (1904), that ACS had a direct link with Nelson. ACS's father, he said, had served as a midshipman under Cuthbert Collingwood (1748–1810), Nelson's admiral (*SL*, vi.175). ACS may have known of Hardy's family link with Nelson's flag captain, Thomas Masterman Hardy (1769–1839), who was walking with Nelson when he was fatally shot. ACS made the same claim about Admiral Swinburne to Sir John Frederick Maurice on 2 June 1890 (*UL*, iii.11). It was untrue as the dates of Admiral Swinburne's career (which commenced after Collingwood's death in 1810) make clear. Cf. 'To a Seamew', 459–62.

*lord of light*: Apollo.

*rede*: perhaps 'principle or course of action; mode of procedure' as well as 'Fate, lot', and 'story', *OED*.

## Cromwell's Statue

First published *NC*, 38 (July 1895), 1–2. An enduring supporter of the English republic, ACS had long recognized what he thought Cromwell's strengths as well as his limitations. Composing a letter to his mother (to whom, it is true, he generally presented a less radical version of himself in politics and religion) on 18 June 1880, ACS observed that while writing on Milton he had 'pitched into Puritanism and the selfish ambition and stupid shortsightedness of Cromwell in a way of which you, I think, will not disapprove, though a good many others will, as if goes heavily against the present fashion of blind and parrot-like Cromwell-worship, set first on foot by that hoary villain Carlyle' (*SL*, iv.152). He begrudgingly recognized—at least to his mother—the 'tyranny' of Cromwell in Ireland (*SL*, v.14–15). ACS admired Victor Hugo's play *Cromwell* (1827), which presented, he said, a figure 'as far from the faultless monster of Carlyle's creation and adoration as from the all but unredeemed villain of royalist and Hibernian tradition: he is a great and terrible poetic figure, imbued throughout with active life and harmonized throughout by imaginative intuition: a patriot and a tyrant, a dissembler and a believer, a practical humourist and a national hero' (*SVH*, 9).

'Cromwell's Statue' masks these reservations behind hero-worship for a specific context: a bitter argument about the proposed statue to Oliver Cromwell, to be situated on Whitehall, discussed in Parliament and the press through the summer of 1895. For obviously conflicting reasons, there was strong Tory and Irish disapproval (see, for instance, 'The Proposed Statue to Cromwell: Tory and Irish Opposition', *North-Eastern Daily Gazette*, 15 June 1895, and 'The Cromwell Statue Debate', *Freeman's Journal*, 17 June 1895, 6). William Redmond, MP for Wexford (scene of the notorious Cromwellian massacre of October 1649) told the Chancellor of the Exchequer on 17 June, that 'every newspaper in Ireland, of all shades of opinion, had condemned this proposal' (Hansard, HC 17 June 1895, vol. 34 *c.*1271). ACS's poem is anti-Tory, anti–Irish nationalist, anti-monarchist, anti–the non-Unionist Liberals (and implicitly anti–House of Lords). It is, obviously, pro-Republican.

ACS's anger at Gladstonian Liberals for supporting Parnell's Home Rule ambitions in the previous decade is relevant because he objects implicitly to Irish nationalist complaints about the statue (note ACS's description of the Liberals as the party of 'disunion': see Introduction, xxix). Eventually private rather than state funding was found (in fact, though I do not know if ACS could have realized this, the money came from Lord Rosebery, Liberal Prime Minister 1894–5). Hamo Thornycroft's statue of Cromwell was duly unveiled outside the Palace of Westminster in 1899. It is still there and still a matter of controversy. Cf. W.S. Landor, 'Oliver Cromwell and Walter Noble' in *Imaginary Conversations*, second series.

*His word...devour*: ACS refers to the Catholic massacre of the Waldensians in Piedmont by forces of Charles Emmanuel II, Duke of Savoy (1634–75), an event that troubled Cromwell for the rest of his life. Milton had been Latin Secretary for the Commonwealth.

## Russia: An Ode, 1890

First published *FR*, 47 (August 1890), 165–7, with the subtitle '(Written after reading the account of "Russian Prisons," in the *Fortnightly Review* for July, 1890)'. ACS's support for tyrannicide in pre-revolutionary Russia resonates with events nine years earlier when Tsar Alexander II (1818–81) was assassinated in a bomb plot organized by the radical freedom group *Narodnaia volia* ('the people's will'). Alexander II had been succeeded by his son, Alexander III (1845–94), who repealed significant portions of his father's liberal reforms. ACS's poem was prompted by new revelations, some from Russian refugees arriving in France, about prison conditions in Siberia, particularly from E.B. Lanin's 'Russian Prisons: The Simple Truth', *FR*, 48 (July 1890), 20–43. This essay countered recent apologists for the Russian prison system, e.g. "'Siberian Horrors": Madame Novikoff's Tribute to Truth', *Review of Reviews*, 1 (May 1890), 406.

ACS's 'Ode' caused a commotion and a threat of prosecution early in August for inciting murder from Patrick O'Brien (*c.*1847–1917), MP for Monaghan North. O'Brien used ACS's poem to remind the House of Commons of the treatment of Irish prisoners in English gaols and to expose the inconsistency of the government's attitude to written incitements to crime during the Special Commission (1888–9) into the forged 'Parnell letters' where Parnell's supposed links with physical force nationalism were keenly scrutinized. Coulson Kernahan in *Swinburne as I Knew Him* (London: Bodley Head, 1919) suggested that the reason ACS was not offered the Laureateship on the death of Tennyson 'was not unconnected with what Swinburne had once written about the Czar' (56) though there is no certain evidence for this. For the legal context of this poem (Offences Against the Person Act 1861) under which ACS could, perhaps have been tried, and the relevance of the *Freiheit* prosecution, see Francis O'Gorman, 'Swinburne and Cowardice', forthcoming.

Cf. Landor's 'Tyrannicide' and Sydney Dobell's Crimean sonnet 'Czar Nicholas' (1855), which also encourages the slaying of a Tsar. Note ACS's admiration in his 1882 *Encyclopaedia Britannica* essay on W.S. Landor for Landor's 'bitter and burning pity for all wrongs endured in all the world [that] found only their natural and inevitable outlet in his life-long defence or advocacy of tyrannicide as the last resource of baffled justice' (*Miscellanies*, 207). Lord Houghton strongly disagreed with his friend Landor on this: see *Monographs: Personal and Social* (London: Murray, 1873), 121–2.

On ACS's views of Russia more generally, see *Note of an English Republican*, 308–12; poems including 'Litany of Nations', 245–9; 'The White Czar' in *PB* 2, and 'Russian Persecution of the Jews', *The Musical World*, 60 (28 January 1882), 53, which was gathered into *TLOP*; and ACS's letter of 30 January 1905 in *The Morning Leader* (31 January, 4), jointly signed with others including Thomas Hardy, George Meredith, and Bernard Shaw, protesting against the imprisonment of the anti-Tsarist writer Maxim Gorky (*UL*, iii.261). On Tsar Alexander II, see 'The Launch of the *Livadia*' in *SS*.

*Ears . . . like these*: cf. 1 Corinthians 2:9.

*Where beyond . . . mire*: ACS refers to Phlegethon, the river of boiling blood and fire in the seventh circle of Dante's hell, and to the fate of flatterers, covered in human dung, in the eighth.

*Tyrannicide*: *OED* dates this to 1652. The line caused particular consternation as an outright encouragement to politically motivated murder (see headnote).

## On the Death of Mrs Lynn Linton

First published *ACP*. Elizabeth (Eliza) Lynn Linton (1822–98) had been a friend of ACS for many years: *SL* gives their first letter as 4 June 1874. Eliza married the republican W.J. Linton (1812–97) in March 1858 but they parted and did not see each other after 1867. Eliza presented a version of her life from the perspective of a man in *The Autobiography of Christopher Kirkland* (London: Bentley, 1885).

Important to ACS was Linton's connection with Landor. ACS had first met Landor in Florence in March 1864 and dedicated *AiC* to him (see headnote on 553). ACS admired Landor's support for the 1848 revolutions and Italian unification, and was sympathetic to Landor's unconventional, migratory, and sometimes stormy life, and his faith in the high value of poetry. Landor regarded Eliza, whom he first met in 1847, as an honorary daughter. In *A Note on Charlotte Brontë*, ACS thought Brontë, Elizabeth Barrett Browning, and Linton a trinity of exceptional female writers. He observed that Brontë could be compared with 'no living English authoress one half so strongly or so clearly marked' as with 'the illustrious and honoured lady—honoured scarcely more by admiration from some quarters than by obloquy from others—to whom we owe the over-true story of "Joshua Davidson", and the worthiest tribute ever yet paid to the memory of Walter Savage Landor' (4). ACS refers to Linton's popular return-of-Jesus novel, *The True History of Joshua Davidson, Christian and Communist* (London: Strachan, 1872). Eliza left ACS a framed photograph of Landor in her will (*UL*, iii.136). Cf. W.J. Linton's 'A Spanish Lady's Love: Wordsworth with Swinburne' from *Heliconundrums* (Hamden: Appledore, 1892).

## Carnot

First published *NC*, 36 (July 1894), 1. In contrast to the incitement to assassinate the head of an absolute monarchy in 'Russia: An Ode, 1890' (517–19), *ACP* contained this Hugo-inspired sonnet mourning an assassinated leader of a republic. ACS commemorates Marie François Sadi Carnot (b.1837), fourth President of the Third French Republic from 1887, stabbed to death by Sante Geronimo Caserio (1874–94), an Italian anarchist, on 24 June 1894. ACS associates Carnot's death with the assassination of the 16th President of the United States, Abraham Lincoln (b.1809) on 15 April 1865 and of the 20th President, James Abram Garfield (b.1831) on 2 July 1881, though neither was killed by anarchists. The point is that they were all leaders of republics. ACS early on admired Whitman's lament for Lincoln, 'When Lilacs Last in the Dooryard Bloom'd' (*UL*, i.80, letter of 3 November 1866)). Cf. TWD's sonnet 'To Madame Carnot', *The Athenæum*, 3479 (30 June 1894), 837 and 'To Mrs Garfield (On the Death of the President)', in *The Coming of Love, Rhona Boswell's Story and Other Poems* (London: Bodley Head, 1899), 267–8.

The sonnet carefully avoids recognition of the fact that one of Carnot's most significant political roles was in the Franco-Russian Alliance (1892–1917) in which France obtained the support of Russia against any attack. The Alliance was a significant re-configuration of European power. Carnot had been welcomed by the Tsar's family at Kronstadt when the French navy was reviewed by the Russians in the summer of 1891. And in October 1893, just a few months before the president was knifed to death, Russian representatives of the Tsar were fêted in Paris and Russian warships together with army and navy personnel were welcomed at Toulon by the President. Given the sentiments of *Note of an English Republican* and 'Russia: An Ode', Swinburne must have struggled in writing this poem with his belief in the natural purity of a republic, producing a sonnet that mourned an assassinated republican who had made friends with the very head of state Swinburne wanted blown to pieces. See Francis O'Gorman, 'Swinburne in Difficulty', in *SEL: Studies in English Literature 1500–1900*, Vol. 57:4 (Fall 2017).

## The Transvaal

First published *The Times*, 11 October 1899, 7, marked 'This poem is not copyright'. Cf. 'The non-copyright patriotic poem is becoming a fashion. To Mr Kipling, who has set many fashions in his time, belongs the praise—or, should we say, the blame?', 'Literary Gossip', *The Outlook*, 4 (14 October 1899), 344.

ACS's sonnet concerns the last few hours of the build-up to the Second Anglo-Boer War (1899–1902), fought between soldiers of the British Empire and the Boers (Afrikaans-speaking Dutch settlers) of the Transvaal Republic and the Orange Free State. There were many events leading to war including the failed Jameson Raid between 29 December 1895 and 2 January 1896 (which may well lie behind Rudyard Kipling's 'If' (1910)). War itself was somewhat reluctantly declared on 11 October 1899, two days after this poem is dated (the reluctance was partly to do with the uncertain readiness of the British army). The conflict, as ACS understood it, was justified in terms of his life-long commitment to liberty because it was, he believed, intended to defend British South Africans (*uitlanders*) in the two republics and to protest against the treatment of black South Africans by the Boers (ACS was not interested in any economic dimension: see Introduction, xxix–xxx). As ACS wrote, major signs of preparation were clear. Parliament had been recalled on 9 October and the President of the Orange Free State, F.W. Reitz (1844–1934) had sent an ultimatum to the British Government that arrived on 10 October and expired on 11 October. This demanded the removal of British troops from state borders and a negotiated peace. *The Times* and many politicians perceived the ultimatum as a pretext for war.

The sonnet marks the beginning of the final stage in ACS's break with the non-Unionist remains of the Liberal party as the Liberal leader Sir Henry Campbell-Bannerman (1836–1908) denounced a war that ACS thought a moral necessary (Campbell-Bannerman would later be an even more prominent critic of British methods in South Africa, especially Kitchener's concentration camps). For ACS, Campbell-Bannerman was the last 'traitor' to the rather naive ideal of freedom ACS had once perceived in (or rather projected onto) Gladstone and his sympathy for Poerio (see xxviii and 545). During the War, the Liberal Unionists entered a formal coalition with Lord Salisbury's Conservatives (the two parties finally merged in May 1912), clinching ACS's predicament as a man without a party (insofar as he was a party man).

ACS perceived the Anglo-Boer War as a point when his own country (despite Campbell-Bannerman) was able to act on the side of forces of freedom, fighting against what he believed, not least from reports in *The Times*, as the cruel Boers. It cannot have helped ACS's attitudes that Irish nationalists were generally, though not exclusively, pro-Boer.

There were plenty who disagreed with the nature of ACS's rhetoric. *The Outlook* observed sceptically on 14 October 1899 that 'one wonders how many Englishmen really consider the people of the Transvaal in the light of "dogs agape with jaws afoam"' (344). ACS's sonnet is noticeable as an encouragement of war against a republic (two, in fact) rather than an encouragement of republican forces against opponents (see Introduction, xxvi–xxvii), a conceptual problem he avoids addressing. On the overall topic, cf. 'Mr Swinburne on Boer Tyranny', *SR*, 92 (16 November 1901), 621–2 and the succession of Anglo-Boer War poems reproduced in *ACP*.

*Cromwell... stood*: ACS refers to the sea supremacy of the British navy during Cromwell's period as Lord Protector, established by Cromwell's General-at-Sea, Robert Blake (1598?–1657), regarded with Drake and Nelson as Great Britain's best naval leaders. Cf. W.S. Landor, 'Admiral Blake and Humphrey Blake' in *Imaginary Conversations*, second series.

*Strike... home*: cf. Tennyson's *Maud* (1855), ll.51–2: 'That the smooth-faced snubnosed rogue would leap from his counter and till, | And strike, if he could, were it but with his cheating yardwand, home'.

## DEDICATION OF SWINBURNE'S *POEMS* (LONDON: CHATTO & WINDUS 1904)

First published in volume I of *The Poems of Algernon Charles Swinburne*, 6 vols (London: Chatto & Windus, 1904). ACS's essay includes discussion of his dramas, which were also re-issued in five volumes between 1905 and 1906. He wrote to TWD on 27 July 1896 to observe that he was writing this introduction (*SL*, vi.105). On 7 September, he said he wanted 'to finish my introductory essay [...] I do not in the least care when the collected edition is to appear [...] but I must get the business off my hands once for all as soon as may be' (*SL*, vi.113). It was eight more years before the edition was issued.

*To... occasion*: see the discussion of literary circles in the Introduction, xli-xlii, and Note on the Texts, liii-liv.

*nothing... reader*: cf. the discussion of ACS's consistency in the Introduction, xxix–xxx.

*thirty-six*: ACS means *PB* 1; a number presumably added in 1902 (see headnote).

*There are... book*: see, for instance, the headnote to 'The Triumph of Time', 566–7.

*this book... publication*: *NPR*.

*'Look... write'*: Sonnet 1, l.14 from *Astrophel and Stella* (1591).

*dedication ... poems*: *SBS* was dedicated to Mazzini.

*I know ... principles*: cf. the Introduction, xxix.

*The first and last ... communalists*: see the discussions of Ireland in the Introduction (xxix) and in the headnote to 'An Appeal', 599–600.

*first book*: *'The Queen Mother' and 'Rosamond'* (1860).

*'Tamburlaine ... Wyatt'*: plays by Marlowe (1587/8?), Shakespeare (1591?), and Dekker and Webster (printed 1607) respectively.

*Catherine ... Rosamond*: in *The Queen Mother* and *Rosamond* respectively.

*you have ... students*: a generous gesture to TWD's 'Introductory Essay' to Edmund Gosse's *King Erik: A Tragedy* (London: Chatto & Windus, 1876).

*epic ... dedication*: *Bothwell* was dedicated to Victor Hugo in a sonnet that described a 'drame épique' (l.3).

*'Occuper ... vous'*: 'The conquest of these two peaks [poetry and drama] has been given only to you'.

*Sir Henry Taylor*: (1800–86), dramatist, author of the popular *Philip van Artevelde* (1834), set in medieval Ghent and Bruges, which ACS admired. See 'On the Death of Sir Henry Taylor', *PB* 3.

*'Caractacus' and 'Merope'*: William Mason's *Caractacus: A Dramatic Poem: Written on the Model of the Ancient Greek Tragedy* (London: Knapton, 1759) and the poem by Arnold (see headnote on 546).

*Carberry Hill*: the battle of 15 June 1567 between the forces of Mary Queen of Scots and the opponents to her marriage to Bothwell, after which Mary abdicated. See xliii-xlv.

*Dejection ... ode on France*: Coleridge's 'Dejection: An Ode' (4 October 1802) and 'France: An Ode' (16 April 1798).

*a critic ... sun*: this may be ACS inexactly remembering his own comparison. In *SS*, 68, in the prose introduction to 'Grand Chorus of Birds from Aristophanes', he said:

> And my main intention, or at least my main desire, in the undertaking of this brief adventure, was to renew as far as possible for English ears the music of this resonant and triumphant metre, which goes ringing at full gallop as of horses who
>
> 'dance as 'twere to the music
> Their own hoofs make.'
>
> I would not seem over curious in search of an apt or inapt quotation: but nothing can be fitter than a verse of Shakespeare's to praise at once and to describe the most typical verse of Aristophanes.

ACS is misquoting 'dancing, as 'twere, to th' music | His own hooves made', *The Two Noble Kinsmen*, 5.6.59–60.

*'Hymn of Man'*: 'Hymn of Man (During the Session in Rome of the Ecumenical Council)' in *SBS*.

*first verses... Candia*: 'To Victor Hugo' from *PB* 1; 'Ode on the Insurrection in Candia' appeared in *FR* for March 1867 then in *SBS*.

*ode on Athens*: in *TLOP*.

*Armada*: 'The Armada', published in *FR*, August 1888, then in *PB* 3.

*Even had... Morris*: see headnote to 'Tristram and Iseult: Prelude of an Unfinished Poem', 602–3.

*diluted... other hands*: ACS means principally Tennyson and Arnold.

*Ercildoune*: Earlston, reputed birthplace of Thomas the Rhymer / Thomas of Erceldoune, often described as the author of the prose *Sir Tristrem* (see headnote on 547).

*Balen*: see *The Tale of Balen* (London: Chatto & Windus, 1896).

*Alfred... future*: see the headnote to 'The Sailing of the Swallow', 615–16.

*Theseus... Arcite*: Theseus' speech 'The firste mover of the cause above' in Chaucer's *The Knight's Tale*.

*Loch Torridon*: see 493–7.

*four poems... Undercliff*: as presently to be described. 'In the Bay' was included in *PB* 2; for 'On the Cliffs', see 381–91; 'A Forsaken Garden', see 338–9; 'The Dedication to a Forthcoming Play' initially appeared in *The Athenæum*, 23 April 1892, then included, as 'Dedication', in the published version of *The Sisters: A Tragedy*.

*Dunwich*: see xxxvii.

*'Off Shore'*: in *SS*.

*'An Autumn' ... 'Neap-Tide'*: the first three in *AOP*; for the last, see 463.

*Bambrough... Guernsey*: Bambrough is the location, for ACS, of Joyous Gard (see Canto 6 of *TL*); for Channel Island poems, see, for instance, ' "Insularum Ocelle" ' (438) and 'Les Casquets' (444–9).

*Shelley... friendships*: see Shelley's dedication of 29 May 1819 to Leigh Hunt of *The Cenci* ('I had already been fortunate in friendships when your name was added to the list') and l.575 of 'Julian and Maddalo'.

*Richard Burton*: see headnote on 652–3.

*Christina Rossetti*: ACS's 'A New Year's Eve: Christina Rossetti died December 29, 1894', first published in *NC*, 37 (February 1895), 367–8, was included in *ACP*.

*Philip... Saffi*: 'Astrophel: After Reading Sir Philip Sidney's *Arcadia* in the Garden of an Old English Manor-House' first appeared in *The Pall Mall Magazine* [*sic*], 1 (May 1893), 1–7; 'In Memory of Aurelio Saffi' was first published in *The Athenæum*, 3262 (3 May 1890), 566 ('Beloved above all nations, land adored'). A second poem with the same name appeared in the same periodical, 3581 (13 June 1896), 779, dated 1890 ('The wider world of men that is not ours').

*Tennyson... Sidney*: ACS's 'Threnody' for Tennyson appeared in *NC*, 33 (January 1893), 1–3; later included in *AOP*. 'A Sequence of Sonnets on the Death of Robert

Browning' was printed in *AOP*; 'Giordano Bruno' was published in *The Athenæum*, 3216 (15 June 1889), 758, then included in *AOP*.

*'Marino Faliero' or 'Locrine'*: for the former, see xxxvii; ACS published *Locrine: A Tragedy* in 1887.

*'Famous Victories'*: *The Famous Victories of Henry V* (1598 in the earliest printed edition) is often regarded as a source text for Shakespeare's play, as the early drama *King Leir* is for *King Lear*.

*'Prometheus' and 'Othello'*: cf. the discussion of these plays, and of Shakespeare in comparison with Aeschylus, in *A Study of Shakespeare* (above, 362–7).

*The metrical... 'Locrine'*: in the words of Arthur Symons, *Locrine* 'is written throughout in rhyme, and the dialogue twists and twines, without effort, through rhyme arrangements which change in every scene, beginning and ending with couplets, and passing through the sonnet, Petrarchan and Shakespearean, ottava rima, terza rima, the six-line stanza of crossed rhymes and couplet, the seven-line stanza used by Shakespeare in the *Rape of Lucrece*, a nine-line stanza of two rhymes, and a scene composed of seven stanzas of chained octaves in which a third rhyme comes forward in the last line but one (after the manner of terza rima) and starts a new octave, which closes at the end in a stanza of two rhymes only, the last line but one turning back instead of forward to lock the chain's circle. No other English poet who ever lived could have written dialogue under such conditions', *Figures of Several Centuries* (London: Constable, 1916), 184.

*'Rosamund... Lombards'*: ACS's *Rosamund, Queen of the Lombards: A Tragedy* was published in 1899.

*Alfieri*: Vittorio Alfieri's *Rosmunda* (1783).

*'Les Djinns'*: by Victor Hugo from *Les Orientales* (1829).

*Chœrilus... Coluthus*: the former, Choerilus of Samos, was a Greek epic writer at the end of the 5th century BC; the latter an epic poet writing in Greek at the end of the 5th and beginning of the 6th century AD.

*only narrative poem*: *The Tale of Balen*. The poem is in 8-line stanzas in iambic tetrameters with the demanding rhyme scheme: aaaabcccb.

## FROM *THE AGE OF SHAKESPEARE* (LONDON: CHATTO & WINDUS, 1908)

### Christopher Marlowe (1883/1908)

The first version of this essay was included in *Encyclopaedia Britannica*, 9th edn (Edinburgh: 1883), xv.556–8. It was revised for its inclusion in *The Age of Shakespeare*. The second, revised, version is the copytext here. The book was dedicated 'To the Memory of Charles Lamb'. ACS admired Lamb, especially his Shakespeare and related publications that included *Specimens of English Dramatic Poets who Lived about the Time of Shakespeare* (London: Longman, Hurst, Rees, and Orm, 1808) and 'Essays on the Tragedies of Shakespeare' in Volume I of *The Prose Works of Charles Lamb*, 3 vols (London: Moxon, 1836–8). Cf. ACS, 'Charles Lamb and George Wither', *NC*, 17 (1885), 66–91; 'On Lamb's Specimens of Dramatic Poets' in *TLOP*; and William Archer, 'Webster, Lamb, and Swinburne', *The New Review*, 8 (1893), 96–106.

ACS published twenty-one 'Sonnets on English Dramatic Poets (1590–1650)', including one on Marlowe, in *TLOP*. See also 'Inscriptions for the Four Sides of a Pedestal', *FR*, 49 (March 1891), 345–6, included in *AOP* and 'In the Bay', *PB* 2. A.D. Wraight's assertion in her *In Search of Christopher Marlowe* (London: Macdonald, 1965) might be remembered: 'It is perhaps fitting that the most appreciative of the early critics of Marlowe should have been a poet, Algernon Charles Swinburne, with whom the 20th-century reassessment of Marlowe may be said to begin, in conjunction with the editing of his works and the publication of his biography by C.F. Tucker Brooke and J.H. Ingram' (332). Note that Rupert Brooke, a keen reader of ACS, was one of the founding player-members of the Marlowe Society of the University of Cambridge, the first performance of which in November 1907 was *Dr Faustus*.

*first... verse*: cf. 'If Marlowe did not re-establish blank verse, which is difficult to prove, he gave it at least a variety of cadence, and an easy adaptation of the rhythm to the sense, by which it instantly became in his hands the finest instrument that the tragic poet has ever employed for his purpose', Henry Hallam, *Introduction to the Literature of Europe*, 3 vols (Paris: Baudry, 1839), ii.232.

*one... passages*: Tamburlaine's apostrophe to Zenocrate beginning 'What is Beauty? saith my sufferings then'.

*Goethe... Hallam*: Goethe allegedly announced after reading *Doctor Faustus*: 'How greatly it is all planned!' He is also remembered for adding that 'He had thought of translating it. He was fully aware that Shakespeare did not stand alone.' See *Marlowe's Doctor Faustus: A Casebook*, ed. John Jump (London: Macmillan, 1969), 29. Hallam observed of *Doctor Faustus*: 'It is full of poetical beauties; but an intermixture of buffoonery weakens the effect, and leaves it on the whole rather a sketch by a great genius than a finished performance. There is an awful melancholy about Marlowe's Mephistopheles, perhaps more impressive than the malignant mirth of that fiend in the renowned work of Goethe', *Introduction to the Literature of Europe*, ii.233.

*Hugo*: see *Le Faust de Christopher Marlowe, traduit par François-Victor Hugo* (Paris: Michel Lévy Frères, 1858).

*'History of Doctor Faustus'*: *The Historye of the Damnable Life and Deserued Death of Doctor Iohn Faustus* (1592).

*vision of Helen*: Mephistopheles brings Helen to Faustus and the three scholars and again after Faustus is rebuked by the Old Man. On the second occasion ('Was this the face that launch'd a thousand ships | And burnt the topless towers of Ilium?'), Faustus kisses her.

*immediate... doom*: the speech beginning 'O Faustus | Now hast thou but one bare hour to live'.

*opening*... *Barabas*: the speech beginning 'So that of thus much that return was made'.

*corresponding*... *Richard II*: Act 5 Sc. 1.

*Mr Collier*: ACS refers to the 'Collier leaf', claimed to have been found by the scholar, bibliographer, and forger John Payne Collier (1789–1883) and transcribed in his *History of English Dramatic Poetry to the Time of Shakespeare*, 3 vols (London: Murray, 1831), iii.134–5. The leaf records the first part of Scene XIX of *The Massacre at Paris*, written in an Elizabethan secretary hand. After Collier, it was passed to ACS's friend Halliwell-Phillipps (see 609–10) and is now in the Folger Library.

*Nathaniel Lee*... *Marlowe*: Lee's *The Massacre of Paris: A Tragedy* was published in London in 1690. Like Marlowe's, it concerned the St Bartholomew's Day Massacre, the subject of ACS's own play *The Queen Mother* (1860).

*Thomas Nash*: Nash(e) (*c.*1567–*c.*1601), wit, dramatist, and collaborator died of unknown causes; he was a friend of the wit and dramatist Robert Greene (*c.*1558–92). The title page of the 1594 Quarto of *Dido, Queen of Carthage* declared it 'written by Christopher Marlowe, and Thomas Nash. Gent.' The extent of Nashe's involvement has been disputed and the play is usually thought to have been posthumously revised by Nashe. Nevertheless, F.G. Fleay in his *Biographical Chronicle of the English Drama, 1559–1642*, 2 vols (London: Reeves and Turner, 1891) had, as ACS wrote, recently changed his mind on the authorship of *Dido*, asserting that it was a joint composition of Marlowe and Nashe (ii.147–8). For more on ACS and Fleay, see 609–10.

*'famous gracer of tragedians'*: from Greene's *Groats-Worth of Witte, Bought with a Million of Repentance: The Repentance of Robert Greene* (1592, London: Bodley Head, 1923), 43. It is not certain that Greene refers to Marlowe.

*Virgil's narrative*: that is, the history of Dido and Aeneas in Bks 1, 2, and 4 of the *Aeneid*.

*nearly certain*... *judges*: The Marlowe Society currently recognizes Marlowe's possible but unproven involvement in *The First Part of the Contention betwixt the Two Famous Houses of York and Lancaster*, *The True Tragedy of Richard, Duke of York*, and *Henry VI*, which formed the basis for the plays usually ascribed to Shakespeare ('and others'), *2 Henry VI*, *3 Henry VI*, and *1 Henry VI* respectively.

*soldier*... *Henri III*: Sc. 19 of *The Massacre at Paris* (beginning 'Now, sir, to you that dares make a Duke a cuck- | Cold').

*realism*... *Cade*: *The First Part of the Contention* concerns in part the 1450 rebellion of Jack Cade against Henry VI. The comedy of the riots, while London Bridge is on fire, derives partly from Cade's wit.

*printer*... *left out*: 'I have purposely omitted and left out some fond and frivolous gestures, digressing, and, in my poor opinion, far unmeet for the matter, which I thought might seem more tedious unto the wise than any way else to be regarded', from the printer's prefatory note to the 1590 edn.

*Mr Dyce*: literary scholar Alexander Dyce (1798–1869), editor of *The Works of Christopher Marlowe with Notes and Some Account of his Life and Writings*, 3 vols (London: Pickering, 1850).

*The author... Shrew*: ACS, *A Study in Shakespeare*, 125.

'*to whom... humorous*': Dyce, *Works*, i.lxvii.

*King Edward III*: cf. ACS, 'Note on the Historical Play of King Edward III', *The Gentleman's Magazine*, 245 (1879), 170–81.

*Peele*: George Peele (*c.*1556–96), poet and playwright.

*judicially... prelates*: Marlowe's translation of Ovid's *Amores* was condemned by the Archbishop of Canterbury and the Bishop of London on 1 June 1599 to be publicly burned.

*fine... couplet*: cf. 'I doubt if more can be said in praise of this version than that it is occasionally spirited and flowing', from the introduction to Dyce's *Works*, i.lxvii.

*untitled fragment*: Marlowe's 'I walked along a stream for pureness rare' (1600).

*make straight*: cf. Matthew 3.3.

# INDEX OF FIRST LINES OF POEMS


A faint sea without wind or sun 268
A light of blameless laughter 452
All the golden air is full of balm and bloom 505
A roundel is wrought as a ring 433
Art thou indeed among these 273
A sea that heaves with horror of the night 356
Asleep or waking is it? 116
At the chill high tide of the night 262
At the time when the stars are grey 242
Auvergne, Auvergne, O wild and woful land, 498
A voice comes from the far unsleeping years 1

Before our lives divide for ever 129
Between the moondawn and the sundown 381
Bird of the bitter bright grey golden morn 357
By the waters of Babylon we sat down and wept 238

Clear the way, my lords and lackeys! 454
Cold eyelids that hide like a jewel 165

Days dawn on us that make amends 465
Death, what hast thou to do with me? 347
Death, winged with fire of hate 522

Ere frost-flower and snow-blossom faded and fell 456

Faith is the spirit that makes man's body and blood 300
Far beyond the sunrise and the sunset rises 429
Far off is the sea, and the land is afar 463
From the depth of the dreamy decline 395
From the depths of the waters that lighten and darken 444

Goodnight and goodbye to the life whose signs denote us 428

Heart's ease or pansy, pleasure or thought 436
Here begins the sea that ends not till the world's end 440
Here, down between the dusty trees 256
Here, where the world is quiet 177

I am that which began 250
If a person conceives an opinion 396
If with voice of words or prayers thy sons may reach thee 245
I have lived long enough 152
In a coign of the cliff 338
In the garden of death 354
In the noble days were shown 12
It is not then enough that men who give 450
Is thine hour come to wake, O slumbering Night? 267
Italia, mother of the souls of men 442

Kind, wise, and true as truth's own heart 520

Lay the corpse out on the altar 300
Life, sublime and serene when time had power 502
Lift up thy lips, turn round, look back for love 156
Love, that is first and last of all things made 282
Love's twilight wanes in heaven above 435

Men, brother men, that after us yet live 361
Mourning on earth, as when dark hours descend 430
My brother, my Valerius 437
My life is bitter with thy love 144

Nothing is better, I well think 158

O heart of hearts, the chalice of love's fire 266

One, who is not, we see 394
O strong Republic of the nobler years 301
O tender time that love thinks long to see 358
Out of hell a word comes hissing 517
Over two shadowless waters 402

Patience, long sick to death, is dead 523

'Return,' we dare not as we fain 467

Sark, fairer than aught in the world that the lit skies cover 438
Sea beyond sea, sand after sweep of sand 453
Sea, that art ours as we are thine, 515
*Sea, wind, and sun, with light and sound and breath* 407
Shall I strew on thee rose or rue or laurel 342
Some die singing, and some die swinging 469
Soul within sense, immeasurable, obscure 432
Spring, and the light and sound of things on earth 355
Summer, and noon, and a splendour of silence 486
Swallow, my sister, O sister swallow 142
The blind king hides his weeping eyeless head 300
The dawn of night more fair than morning rose 493
There's mony a man loves land and life 470
The rose to the wind has yielded 504
The sea gives her shells to the shingle 180
The shadows fallen of years are nine 400
The sun is lord and god, sublime, serene 510
This is the golden book of spirit and sense 353
This flower that smells of honey and the sea 340
Through the low grey archway 513

Upon the flowery forefront of the year 368

Westward the sun sinks 468
What needs our Cromwell stone or bronze 516
Whatever a man of the sons of men 139
What shall be done for sorrow 434
When I had wings, my brother 459
White rose in red rose-garden 163

Years have risen and fallen in darkness 334

# INDEX OF ALL TITLES


'A Ballad of François Villon, Prince of All Ballad-Makers' 357
'A Choice' 300
'A Counsel' 301
'A Flower-piece by Fantin' 436
'A Forsaken Garden' 338
'After Nine Years' 400
'Anactoria' 144
'An Appeal' 273
'A Nympholept' 486
'A Reiver's Neck-Verse' 469
'A Reminiscence' 504
'A Solitude' 453
*A Study of Shakespeare* 362
*Atalanta in Calydon* 39
'*Ave Atque Vale*: In Memory of Charles Baudelaire' 342
'A Vision of Spring in Winter' 358

'Before a Crucifix' 256
'Before Sunset' 435
'Before the Mirror' 163
*Bothwell* 293
'By the North Sea' 407

'Carnot' 522
'Celæno' 300
'Charles Baudelaire, *Les Fleurs du mal*' 26
'Christopher Marlowe' 538
'Cor Cordium' 266
'Clear the Way!' 454
'Cromwell's Statue' 516
'Cyril Tourneur' 356

'Dead Love' 33
'Dedication, 1865' 180
'Dedication' (1904) 524
'Diræ' 300
'Dolores' 165

'Elegy 1869–1891' 498
'Emily Brontë' 421
'Evening on the Broads' 402

'Hawthorn Dyke' 505
'Hermaphroditus' 156
'Hertha' 250
'Hymn to Proserpine' 152

'In a Rosary' 513
'Inferiae' 355
'In Harbour' 428
'In Memory of Barry Cornwall' 354
'In San Lorenzo' 267
'In Sepulcretis' 450
'"Insularum Ocelle"' 438
'In Time of Mourning' 467
'Itylus' 142

'Laus Veneris' 116
'Les Casquets' 444
'Les Noyades' 139
Letter to the Editor of *The Spectator*, 7 June 1862 23
'Lines of the Monument of Giuseppe Mazzini' 442
'Loch Torridon: To E.H.' 493

'March: An Ode' 456
'Memorial Verses on the Death of Théophile Gautier' 347
'Mentana: First Anniversary' 242
'Mr Arnold's *New Poems*' 183

'Neap-Tide' 463
'Nephelidia' 395
*Note of an English Republican on the Muscovite Crusade* 308
'Notes on Designs of the Old Masters at Florence' 219
*Notes on the Royal Academy Exhibition, 1868* 225

'Ode to Mazzini' 1
'Of the birth of Sir Tristram, and how he voyaged into Ireland' (*Queen Yseult*) 12
'On the Cliffs' 381
'On the Death of Mrs Lynn Linton' 520

'On the Death of Richard Doyle' 452
'On the Downs' 268
'On the Verge' 440

'Plus Intra' 432
'Plus Ultra' 429
'Poeta Loquitur' 396
'Preface' to *A Selection from the Works of Lord Byron* (1866) 110

'Recollections of Professor Jowett' 473
'Relics' 340
'Report of the First Anniversary Meeting of the Newest Shakespeare Society' 302
'Russia: An Ode' 517

'Simeon Solomon: Notes on his "Vision of Love and Other Studies"' 276
'Sonnet (With a Copy of *Madamemoiselle de Maupin*)' 353
'Super flumina Babylonis' 238

'Tenebræ' 262
'Thallasius' 368
'The Augurs' 300
'The Ballads of the English Border' 506
'The Death of Richard Wagner' 430
'The Epitaph in Form of a Ballad, which Villon made for Himself and his Comrades, Expecting to be Hanged along with them' 361
'The Garden of Proserpine' 177
'The Higher Pantheism in a Nutshell' 394
'The Interpreters' 465
'The Lake of Gaube' 510
'The Last Oracle' 334
'The Leper' 158
'The Litany of Nations' 245
'The Poems of Dante Gabriel Rossetti' 231
'The Roundel' 433
'The Sailing of the Swallow' 313
'The Transvaal' 523
'The Triumph of Time' 129
'The Tyneside Widow' 470
'Threnody October 6, 1892' 502
'Trafalgar Day' 515
'To a Seamew' 459
'To Catullus' 437
'To Sir Richard F. Burton (On his Translation of the Arabian Nights)' 468
'Tristram and Iseult: Prelude of an Unfinished Poem' 281

'Victor Hugo's *L'Année terrible*' (1872) 288

'Wasted Love' 434
*William Blake: A Critical Essay* 197